Violence and Disability

An Annotated Bibliography

by

Dick Sobsey, R.N., Ed.D., FAAMR
Don Wells
Richard Lucardie
and Sheila Mansell

University of Alberta
Developmental Disabilities Centre
Abuse & Disability Project
Edmonton, Alberta
Canada

·P A U L·H·
BROOKES
PUBLISHING CO.

Baltimore • London • Toronto • Sydney

Paul H. Brookes Publishing Co.
Post Office Box 10624
Baltimore, Maryland 21285-0624

Manufactured in the United States of America by
BookCrafters, Chelsea, Michigan.

This bibliography was prepared with support from the Social Sciences and Humanities Research
Council of Canada (Project Number 410 91665). Portions of this bibliography were also supported
under a grant from The Joseph P. Kennedy, Jr. Foundation. The opinions expressed in this work
represent the authors and not necessarily those of the funding organizations. All royalties from this
book provide support for the International Coalition on Abuse & Disability.

Library of Congress Cataloguing-in-Publication Data

Violence and Disability :   an annotated bibliography   /   edited by Dick Sobsey . . . [et al.]
      p.   cm.
  Includes indexes.
  ISBN 1-55766-172-3
  1. Handicapped—Crimes against—Bibliography.   2. Handicapped—Abuse of—Bibliography.
3. Handicapped children——Crimes against—Bibliography. 4. Handicapped Children —Abuse of—
Bibliography. —Institutional care—Abstracts
I. Sobsey, Richard.
Z5703.4H36V56   1995
[HV6626.7]
016.36288'087—dc20
                                             94–30747
                                                CIP

British Library Cataloguing-in-Publication data are available from the British Library.

Contents

Censorship Defied

•

Foreword

In his essay *Bibliographies: Their Aims and Methods,* Krummel (1984) claims that "the compiling of bibliographies implies an active opposition to censorship, related to our faith in the importance of human diversity." If Krummel's claim is correct, *Violence and Disability: An Annotated Bibliography* could be seen as a cultural force, which helps to establish the boundaries between the obvious and the camouflaged, and what is distinctive and what is considered anarchic by society when portraying violence in the lives of people with disabilities.

Censorship is usually an act committed or supported by the state, which prevents the public from knowing something that is believed to upset the status quo. In the case of violence against disabled people,[1] society's policies and practices have normalized and standardized so much of the culture's maltreatment of disabled people that labeling various medical and social treatments as violence will implicate the very institutions and individuals that perpetuate those same policies and practices.

Camouflaging and perpetuating the concealment of violence protects the status quo, and enables violence to continue in too many ways. The government devalues the seriousness of violence in the lives of those of us with disabilities when the courts give reduced sentences to criminals who rape disabled women; when federal, state, and local policy resist the inclusion of disabled people as a protected class in hate crimes legislation; or when the criminal justice system does not provide the means to do background checks on people hired to provide personal assistant services to us in our homes or even in institutions, where so much violence occurs. In the words of one disabled women, "providers are being paid to abuse us."

The culture has masked many forms of violence by calling them medical treatments—when poisoning is called chemical restraint or the murder is called physician-assisted suicide. In addition, by supporting policies of segregation, the government allows the violence to be committed in covert forms. Consequently, perpetrators of violence continue to commit their acts against disabled adults and children in the isolation of the nuclear family and in institutions.

Dick Sobsey defies these acts of censorship by bringing together under one volume a collection of references, broad in scope, which he calls violence against disabled people. By establishing a broad conceptualization of violence, Sobsey reflects the depth of the political oppression that disabled people face, and as a consequence speaks to the distinctly unique nature of violence in disabled people's lives. While similarities in violent acts directed at us and at other oppressed groups exist, many acts of violence toward those of us with disabilities are different from those other groups due to: the conditions within which we live, the ways in which people are involved in our lives, the public and private ways disability-based prejudice is played out, and the significant force that medicine plays in defining our life problems and futures.

However, not all scholars and policy makers agree with this broad conceptualization of violence. At a recent government-sponsored meeting to determine an agency's research agenda on disabled women's lives, there was resistance to the more far-reaching understanding of violence because of a fear that such a broad definition would water-down the conventional definition of violence and be considered anarchy to the research establishment, therefore delegitimizing the research. The more conventional understanding of violence was advocated.

Similarly, in 1991 I had an opportunity to meet with a Congressional staff member who worked on the federal Hate Crimes Statistic Act. During our discussion of how to amend the law to include disabled people as a protected class, I pointed out that at times the way violence looks when directed at disabled people can be different. The staff member retorted, "Well, if it doesn't look the same as we defined in the legislation, then disabled people won't make it in the legislation."

But when disabled people's lives are understood through a disability perspective, the scenarios of violence include and diverge from the customary understanding of violence against disabled children and adults. At one end of the spectrum of violence are more subtle forms that have defied identification until now: Deaf activists accuse hearing parents who do not learn sign language to communicate with deaf children to be committing intentional neglect. A nondisabled husband who prevents his wife from using a wheelchair as she experiences an increasing inability to walk from the effects of postpolio syndrome, is committing a degree of spousal abuse. Disabled children who are repeatedly paraded, naked, in front of a team of doctors are experiencing a form of child sexual assault known as public stripping.

---

[1]Person-first language is not used in this foreword at the request of the author in order to express the concept of disability as a social identity.

At the other end of the spectrum of violent crime is the category of hate crimes, a formerly unacknowledged dimension in violence against disabled people. Hate crime includes murder, non-negligent manslaughter, forcible rape, aggravated assault, simple assault, intimidation, arson, and destruction, damage, or vandalism of property. Each crime occurs within the disability community more than we know: the vandalism and fire bombings by bigoted neighbors of community-integrated group homes inhabited by cognitively disabled adults; German skinheads directing physical violence toward disabled Germans in public places, and the murder by parents of disabled children who do not respond to rehabilitative treatment designed to "cure" them.

This broad understanding of disability-biased crimes that Sobsey has presented will, one hopes, in time, counteract those studies that conclude that disabled people share responsibility for their own maltreatment because of their behavior and impairments, and that the violence is an outcome of stress resulting from dependency. While these studies are included in this current edition of *Violence and Disability* as well, future editions should make them outdated.

The first annotated bibliography, *Disability, Sexuality, and Abuse,* prepared by Dick Sobsey, Sharmaine Gray, Don Wells, Diane Pyper, and Beth Reimer-Heck, broke new ground. As a physical object, it confirmed that disability-related violence is a distinct and critical area of study. It brought together the universe of research that existed up to that time.

That another bibliography was compiled and published speaks at the same time to a progressive and pessimistic change in disability-related violence; an increased interest by researchers, policy makers, educators, and activities to studying and preventing violence; and an increase in the incidence and types of violent acts toward disabled children and adults. Because of these changes, the need to organize the expanding world of recorded knowledge about this problem becomes all the greater.

Organizing a bibliography is similar to organizing a community. In this instance the community is one of interest, with close ties based on shared academic, social, and political interests in seeing an end to violence in the lives of people with disabilities. Indeed, by Sobsey organizing *Violence and Disability* he created a network of individuals who can influence a change in the way public policy treats disability-biased crimes.

As this community grows, its members have a two-fold commitment to the disability community, beyond the research it will continue to generate. First, facts about disability-based violence, including the facts that lead to it, must be communicated to the grassroots of disabled people. It must not stop at teaching us prevention strategies.

The disability rights movement must have the facts on violence, and include those facts in our activism around independent living policy: personal assistant services, housing, health and welfare reform. It must also be included in the movement's efforts around civil rights and economic justice, especially with regard to the continuing efforts to implement the Americans with Disabilities Act. Indeed, as members of the disability community become more integrated socially and begin to advance economically and politically, we may become targets for more overt acts of hate-violence.

The second commitment by researchers of violence must be to redress the power inequities in scholarship and services. If violence itself is predicated on power inequities, self-determination is the antidote. In other words, disabled researchers must be brought into studies as principal investigators, not only to bring a disability perspective into the research, but also to direct the course of research and services for violence in the lives of people with disabilities.

Barbara Faye Waxman
Project Director
Americans with Disabilities Act
Training and Technical Assistance
Los Angeles Regional Family Planning Council

REFERENCES

Krummel, D.W. (1984). *Bibliographies: Their aims and methods.* London: Mansell.

Sobsey, D., Gray, S., Wells, D., Pyper, D., & Reimer-Heck, B. (1991). *Disability, sexuality, and abuse: An annotated bibliography.* Baltimore: Paul H. Brookes Publishing Co.

Enough Is Enough

There Is No Excuse for a Hundred Years of Violence Against People with Disabilities

•

An Introduction

Abuse of people with disabilities has been a well-recognized problem for at least 100 years. At the close of the nineteenth century, participants at the National Conference on Charities and Corrections were warned that "imbecile girls and women everywhere are an easy prey to the wiles and lust of brutal men" (Carson, 1898, p. 296). Dorthea Dix had already described women with mental retardation as "the helpless prey of profligate men and idle boys" (Deutsch, 1949, p. 167). Almost a hundred years later, as the millennium winds to a close and a new one waits on the horizon, it seems fitting to examine what has changed in the twentieth century.

The solutions proposed for this problem at the end of the nineteenth century were to confine, segregate, and sterilize the victims. It was the victims who were seen as the threat to society, and it was the victims who paid a heavy price. As suggested by Walter Fernald, there was "a widespread and insistent demand that these women be put under control" (Fernald, 1904, p. 383). On the other hand, the perpetrators of these sexual assaults were portrayed sympathetically as blameless victims of the women they sexually assaulted. These women were responsible for the "unspeakable and debauchery and licentiousness which pollutes the whole life of young boys and youth in the community" (Fernald, 1904, p. 383). It is interesting that Fernald chose to portray the perpetrators as impressionable boys and youth who could not be expected to bear responsibility for their own actions. The clear and implicit message was "boys will be boys."

The deadly mixture of moral chauvinism, pseudoscience, and class politics developed into the eugenic fervor. Sexually segregated institutions and sterilization became the chosen methods of eliminating people with disabilities.

The twentieth century has been a time of great change in contemporary society. Three major social changes had enormous implications for people with disabilities.

First, society made a major shift from local to national and international economies. This was an extension of the impact of the industrial revolution. While this trend had many positive effects, it also resulted in the deterioration of community ties and kinship systems. This trend began in the last half of the previous century but accelerated and spread after the turn of the century. The effect of this deterioration of communities on people with disabilities was largely increasing institutionalization. This trend becomes clear when comparing rates of institutionalization in industrial versus nonindustrial states. In fact, it appears clear that institutionalization was closely associated with industrialization (Sobsey & McDonald, 1988). Prior to this era, families and local communities were primarily responsible for the welfare of individuals with disabilities. When violence and abuse occurred, it was often at the individual level. In many cases, families and communities provided safety for people with disabilities.

Second, society moved more from a philosophy of religion to a philosophy of science. This does not necessarily imply that society or its individual members became more rational; it simply means that actions were justified in rationale or empirical rather than spiritual or religious terms. This also may have been driven, in part, by the shift to national and international industry. The shift to national and international industry required a uniform belief system in order to function across communities and countries. For example, the eugenics movement has been widely criticized for its misinformation, due both to deliberate misrepresentations and bad science (Gould, 1981). However, eugenics was characterized by the mantle of science that provided "rational" arguments for eliminating people with disabilities. Its underlying motives and outcomes may not have been substantially different from Martin Luther's sixteenth-century exhortations to drown children with disabilities because they were devils or fairytales about changelings left in place of real children by leprechauns, but it appeared more rational (Sobsey, 1994).

Violence against people with disabilities in the twentieth century has been shaped by the effects of industrialization and the reign of science. This violence is often uniquely interwoven with the human services industry that has replaced natural community supports for people with disabilities, and it is often rationalized "scientifically," making it particularly difficult to prevent or eliminate.

At the opening of the twentieth century, the treatment of people with disabilities was already a topic for serious discussion. Sterilization laws were first proposed in Michigan in 1897 and Pennsylvania in 1905, but both of these laws were defeated. Indiana passed the first sterilization bill in 1907, and by 1910, three other states had enacted their own sterilization laws (Burgdorf & Burgdorf, 1977). It was the Eugenics Section of the American (Cattle) Breeders Society who mapped out the fate of people with mental retardation in the early part of the twentieth century. Their report, in 1912, concludes that sterilization and sexually segregated institutionalization were the only acceptable means for eliminating these individuals from society (Burgdorf & Burgdorf, 1977).

Assisted suicide and mercy killing were also under discussion in the early years of the twentieth century. In 1920, Karl Binding, a German lawyer, and Alfred Hoche, a German psychiatrist published *Die Freigabe der Vernichtung Lebensunwerten Lebens* (The permission to end lives not worth living). This book suggests that people with severe disabilities have worthless lives and that assisting them to die is in their best interest (Lifton & Hackett, 1990; Meyer, 1988). This book supplied the intellectual arguments that were put into practice two decades later during the Third Reich. With the publication of this book, the intellectual foundation for the elimination of people with disabilities was now complete, and it only required the necessary political will to carry it out.

In 1927, the United States Supreme Court supported the laws requiring involuntary sterilization of people with mental retardation. Justice Oliver Wendell Holmes, one of America's best known jurists, spoke for the court affirming the Virginia sterilization statute of 1924 in the landmark *Buck v. Bell* decision, saying, "three generations of imbeciles are enough" (274 US 200, p. 207). It did not matter that Carrie Buck, who was sterilized as a result of this decision, showed no evidence of mental retardation. It did not matter that she was only diagnosed as "defective," institutionalized, and sterilized after she became pregnant as the result of a rape by her foster-parents' nephew (Lombardo, 1985).

Perhaps it was also unimportant that Carrie Buck was poorly represented at the trial. Her lawyer did not call a single witness on her behalf; his cross-examinations of the witnesses who testified on behalf of sterilization were extremely weak; and he submitted only a short brief on her behalf (Lombardo, 1985). The lawyer who "represented" Carrie Buck was Irving Whitehead, a former director of the Central Virginia Training Center where Carrie Buck was incarcerated and lifelong friend of the lawyer for the opposition. Whitehead continued as member of the Board of the institution and, as such, continued to authorize the sterilizations that he was supposed to be fighting in court. A building at the institution was named in his honor about two months before Carrie Buck was admitted. He appeared before the board of the institution with Aubrey Strode, the opposing lawyer, before the trial detailing how the case would be lost. In

simple terms, "Whitehead failed as Carrie's attorney not because he was incompetent, underpaid, or merely ineffectual. He failed because he intended to fail" (Lombardo, 1985). This Supreme Court decision not only permitted the sterilization of Carrie Buck, but her sister Doris was sterilized the next year (Gould, 1981). This decision also resulted in the sterilization of approximately 60,000 other Americans with mental retardation over the next 50 years (Smith & Polloway, 1993), and it supported a model that was adopted by many other countries, who developed their own sterilization laws. The collusion of these lawyers to fix the Supreme Court decision had far reaching effects, but those things happen.

In 1933, the Nazi party took control of Germany, and the mass killing of people with disabilities began shortly thereafter (Wilhelm, 1990). The political will was now available to actualize the philosophical and intellectual foundations already in place. The exact number of people with disabilities killed under the Nazi T4 euthanasia program will never be known because death records were commonly forged, but the number of people with disabilities who were murdered is estimated at about 275,000.

Germany's sterilization and euthanasia programs had considerable support in the international community. Only a few months before Germany declared war on the United States, an official editorial in *The American Journal of Psychiatry* (Euthanasia, 1942) urged that children with severe disabilities be killed on their fourth birthdays.

At the end of World War II, euthanasia and sterilization of people with disabilities were declared crimes against humanity at the Nuremberg trials. Nevertheless, many of these procedures continued for decades as routine practices in the United States, Canada, and other allied nations who took part in condemning them (Sengstock, Magerhans-Hurley, & Sprotte, 1990).

During the 1940s, 1950s, and 1960s, people with disabilities were used as subjects in a variety of clandestine experiments. Institutionalized children and adolescents with mental retardation were fed radio-active oatmeal in one set of experiments sponsored by the U.S. Atomic Energy Commission and the Quaker Oats Company. Parental consent was gained through deception (*"U.S. Experiments,"*1993). Other children with mental retardation were deliberately injected with hepatitis viruses. In the 1960s, patients in mental hospitals were subjected to CIA brainwashing experiments that involved massive electroconvulsive shock. While the account in scientific journals of the times reported no ill-effects and remarkable recovery (Cotter, 1967), an independent account of the same experiment suggests that all of the subjects died

(Thomas, 1988). During the 1950s and 1960s, residents of psychiatric hospitals were also used in a variety of other brainwashing experiments that used sensory deprivation, drugs, restraint, and a variety of other tools to break their wills (Thomas, 1988).

In 1972, Rivera's classic report on institutional abuse and neglect at Willowbrook State School in New York made national headlines. After three years of court battles, the institution finally signed a consent decree to improve conditions. Seven years later, the court found the institution had failed to adequately improve conditions and began the process that would close Willowbrook down (Sobsey, 1994), but the horror had not ended. Jennifer Schweiger was a twelve-year-old girl with Down syndrome who lived happily with her family. In 1987, her body was found in a shallow grave in a previously closed area of the Willowbrook institution (Neuffer, 1987). She had been abducted and taken there to be raped and murdered by former Willowbrook attendant, Andre Rand.

Rand was one of many caregivers who tortured, raped, or murdered the people with disabilities whom he was entrusted to protect. Gary Heidnik, licensed practical nurse and self-proclaimed minister of a church that catered to people with mental and physical disabilities, tortured, raped, and murdered women with mental retardation in the Philadelphia area (Gruson, 1987). Daniel Lee Siebert wanted a job teaching art at the Alabama Institute for the Deaf and Blind so much that he offered to teach for free. Then he killed at least two of his students (Newton, 1990). Michael Fox was a psychiatric nurse in England. He was sentenced in 1994 to nine life sentences for a series of sexual assaults of women with developmental disabilities, and he is suspected of murdering others (Frost, 1994). Such caregivers as Rand, Heidnik, Siebert, and Fox represent only a tiny minority, yet the service delivery system has shown remarkable resistance to doing anything to eliminate such people from the ranks of service providers (Sobsey, 1994).

In October of 1992, the trial of four high school athletes accused of raping a young woman with a mental disability began in Glen Ridge, New Jersey. Two other young men had already been allowed to plead guilty to a reduced charge, endangering the welfare of a mentally incompetent person, and sentenced to 60 days community service (Laufer, 1994). The four defense lawyers at the trial did not deny the facts that their clients had been among the group of 13 who took this young woman to a basement on false pretenses. They did not deny that their clients had penetrated her vagina with a dowel, a broomstick, and a baseball bat. They simply dismissed these acts as trivial infractions and suggested that the young woman had consented, and she wanted the boys to perform these acts. After all, "boys will be boys. Pranksters. Fool-

arounds. Do crazy things. Experiment with life, and disregard their parents. Boys will be boys," said defense lawyer Michael Querques (Laufer, 1994, p. 69). Two of these young men had previously been among a group that tricked the same young woman into eating dog feces (Hanley, 1992). Perhaps they thought she wanted that, too. Oh, well, boys will be boys.

After conviction, these four young men were given indefinite sentences and allowed to remain free pending appeal on only $2,500 bail. They remained on bail even after another young woman submitted an affidavit to the court claiming that one of the four felons sexually assaulted her while on bail. One juror, seeing the convicted rapists freed by the judge, expressed his frustration and said, "it's like the judge was telling us that the time we were out in deliberation didn't matter" (Laufer, 1994, p. 151).

While some felt that the indefinite sentence and low bail set for these convicted rapists trivialized this crime, it did not seem out of place when compared to the sentence given to four other young men convicted in a fatal beating of Paul Devareaux, a coworker with a developmental disability. One of these men was sentenced to a few years in prison, while three youthful offenders received only probation and community service sentences (Engman, 1992). The judge indicated that this sentence was appropriate because it was not a serious assault (Engman & Crockatt, 1992).

Two teenagers admitted breaking into the home of another man with a developmental disability and beating him to death in a small Oklahoma town (Retarded man killed, 1994). The assailants were reported to snicker in court as the medical examiner described the chunks of plastic from an electronic "talk-back" device that were embedded in Robert Ballard's skull by the force of the beating. The community bristled when the teenagers were reported to joke about poking a finger through Mr. Ballard's eye-socket, which was left vacant from the beating.

Such violent acts against people with disabilities are only a small tip of a much larger iceberg submerged in our contemporary society. In Edmonton, Alberta, the local community was shocked and enraged when firefighters found a woman burning in the snow. Even the experienced firefighters who extinguished the fire by packing snow around the victim, were aghast to find that the woman had been soaked in gasoline and set ablaze. A man was seen running from the scene, and evidence indicated that the woman had been beaten and was probably already unconscious when she was set on fire. Joyce Cardinal clung to life for many days after the barbaric attack before finally succumbing to her injuries. Community interest in this case appeared to decline rapidly, however, after Joyce Cardinal was identified as a Native woman with severely impaired speech and limited communication. Only a few weeks after the brutal attack had been front-page headlines, police indicated that the investigation was faltering because of a lack of community interest or support.

In the same city, Michelle Kshyk, a young woman with a mild to moderate developmental disability wanted to meet people and make new friends. She met a man through a radio station's call-in dating show and left to meet him after telling others she was going on a date. Michelle was missing for three years before her skull was found in a remote location at the edge of town.

Some people's disabilities result from violence. In the same city, Jason Carpenter was less than two years old when he was taken from his mother by social services in order to protect him from the the seemingly obvious risks of the crack house where he lived with his mother. Protective foster care seemed like a reasonable option that might give him a chance for a better life. Unfortunately, only six weeks later, Jason was rushed to the hospital with a severe head injury, covered with bruises, cigarette burns, and pinholes. Jason's "protective fosterparents" were convicted of the assaults that left him in a coma, permanently disabled for the rest of his life (Engman & Tanner, 1993).

Individual accounts of experiences like Jason's, Joyce's, and Michelle's are disturbing, but they are not very uncommon. How many people are disabled by violence like Jason? How many people with existing disabilities become victims of violence like Joyce or Michelle? Perhaps the true numbers will never be known, but the emerging picture suggests some staggering figures. Here are a few examples.

One large-scale prospective study of a nationally representative sample of abused children in the United States found that children with disabilities were 70% more likely to be abused than children without disabilities (Crosse, Kaye, & Ratnofsky, 1993). The incidence of physical abuse was more than twice as high and the incidence of sexual abuse was 80% higher than the corresponding risk for children without disabilities. Projecting these figures along with census information suggests that more than 200,000 substantiated cases of abused children with disabilities will be reported each year in the United States. Since the majority of abuse cases go unreported and unsubstantiated, the total number probably exceeds 500,000 each year.

Equally disturbing information from this report concerns children who are disabled as a result of abuse (Crosse et al., 1993). According to this report, 32.8% of these children sustain injuries as a result of abuse, and 36.8% of those injuries result in long-term or permanent disabilities. This suggests that about 150,000 children are disabled as a result of child abuse each year and that over 1,000,000 children currently living in the United States have disabilities because they have been subjected to violence. This may also be a very conservative estimate since it does not include children born with disabilities as result of assaults on their mother's during pregnancy, which a growing body of evidence suggests that this may be a frequent cause of disability.

Other studies of adults with disabilities provide equally disturbing data. One study of women with disabilities, for example, found that 73% had been victims of violence; another study found that 10% of people with physical disabilities have been physically assaulted by their personal care attendants (Stimpson & Best, 1991). A study of criminal offenses against adults in South Australia found that people with mental retardation were 2.9 times as likely to be victims of physical assaults and 10.7 times as likely to be victims of sexual assault as other adults (Wilson & Brewer, 1992).

Fundamental issues of access to equal justice compound these problems. There is growing reason to believe that crimes committed against people with disabilities are sometimes given lower priorities for investigation and prosecution than crimes against other members of society. In some cases, even after conviction occurs, lighter sentences appear to be given to offenders who commit crimes against people with disabilities (Sobsey, 1994).

Abuse survivors with disabilities often are denied access to treatment services (Mansell, Sobsey, & Calder, 1992). When they can access services, the services often fail to accommodate their individual needs.

Most of the twentieth century has been characterized by widespread violence and abuse against people with disabilities. This violence continues in many forms.

HAS THERE BEEN ANY PROGRESS?
While the events and situations that have been previously described are tragic, this should not be a time of hopelessness. While progress has been painfully slow, it would be a shame to believe that no progress has been made in protecting the rights of people with disabilities.

For example, while it is incredible that the "boys will be boys" defense could be used in the 1990s to defend the Glen Ridge rapists, it is equally important to recognize that this case went to court and led to a conviction. In previous times, this would have been extremely unlikely. The "boys will be boys" defense may have alienated the jury rather than gaining its sympathy. In fact, the defense's inexplicable lack of insight into the psychological dimensions of their own case may have ensured their own loss. The spectacle of four male defense lawyers taking turns at manipulating the vulnerable witness while their clients sat and watched provided a mental parallel to the original assault. Were they unaware of the imagery that they were creating? Did they believe that showing how easily they could coerce her would encourage jurors to believe that she was to blame, or were they simply unable to resist the urge to exercise this form of control over her? Perhaps their strategy might have even been successful if they had not given the jury the impression that they too were being manipulated (Laufer, 1994).

Perhaps the saddest fact about the Glen Ridge case is the price required to get this conviction. While the defense portrayed the victim as a sex-crazed menace whose "genitals' signals are greater than normal" (Defense Attorney Michael Querques quoted in Laufer, 1994, p. 51), the prosecution portrayed her as a "helpless creature" and "a mentally defective girl [who] was pathetically eager to please people" (Prosecuting Attorney Glenn Goldberg quoted in Laufer, 1994, p. 149). It is difficult to say which of these two images is less flattering or which of these images preserves less human dignity. It would be interesting to know what Betty Harris thinks about this trial or how she feels about her day in court. It would be interesting to know how these images may have influenced the five Iredell County, North Carolina, teenagers arrested during the Glen Ridge trial and charged with an apparent copycat offense, using a broomstick to rape a woman with mental retardation (Laufer, 1994).

Repatriation and Inclusion

One of the most hopeful areas of progress in the last half of this century has been the return of many people with disabilities to the community. Even more hopeful has been the fact that many people who might have been institutionalized in previous decades are now remaining in their communities.

This return to the community provides both direct and indirect benefits. First, incarceration in institutions is in itself a form of infringement on the rights of people with disabilities. Second, since we know that institutional living is associated with about twice the rate of abuse found in community settings, people with disabilities as a whole will be safer in the community (Levine Powers, Mooney, & Nunno, 1990).

Nevertheless, many challenges remain. While the risk may be reduced in the community, it is by no means eliminated. Furthermore, when many abuse problems were isolated in institutions, communities did not have to deal with them. Therefore, more community-based prevention and treatment programs

will be required. In addition, many people with disabilities remain in institutional care, and it remains doubtful that society will ever see total closure of institutions. Unless and until that happens, people living in institutions need protection. We cannot abandon efforts to ensure they are protected as long as people remain in institutional care. Even the definition of institutional care needs careful consideration. While many people are being served in smaller buildings with fewer residents at each site, which are geographically located in local communities, these people are often still isolated from interaction with all but paid caregivers. These people sometimes lead lives that are not very different from those of others living in bigger, more isolated institutions. Such changes would be better called decentralization than deinstitutionalization.

Perhaps the greatest challenge that exists in community repatriation and inclusion is that communities and kinship networks are changing. Some might argue that in some senses they are disappearing. There is little doubt that closely woven local communities and extended families provide excellent environments that deter violence; however, with increased transience of the population and smaller families, community and family ties are eroding. People often work, shop, and involve themselves in leisure activities at various locations far from where they live. There is little reason for people to know their neighbors. This makes all of us more vulnerable. People with disabilities are particularly likely to suffer the consequences because they are particularly dependent on natural support networks, but their dependence differs only in degree. We all need community and family ties. Community-based crime prevention and other attempts at overcoming modern alienation have attempted to counteract the trend, but it is too soon to judge the long-term success of such efforts (Sobsey, 1994).

Empowerment

The growing self-advocacy movement among people with disabilities also has contributed to changes. People with disabilities have been vulnerable to abuse because of power inequities. While some of the power inequities experienced by people with disabilities are the direct effects of impairments (e.g., a person who is quadriplegic is less likely to be able to carry out effective self-defense or to escape a violent confrontation), most of these inequities result from disempowerment. The liberties and rights of people with disabilities have often been severely restricted, leaving them vulnerable to violence and exploitation. As people with disabilities empower themselves individually and collectively, some of these power imbalances are restored (Sobsey, 1994). As people with disabilities gain more power over their own lives, they become less vulnerable to abuse (Westcott, 1992).

Violence Prevention

Society's growing response to child abuse and other forms of violence has had some benefits for people with disabilities. The child welfare movement was already growing at the opening of the twentieth century (Radbill, 1987). The second half of the century brought a growing understanding of child abuse. In the 1940s, Caffey's (1946) description of head injuries and fractures opened the door to recognition of physically abused children. The medical profession was slow to accept the implications of Caffey's work. Many of these professionals were unwilling to believe that such severe harm was frequently the result of deliberate maltreatment. This debate continued in academic and professional circles throughout the 1950s. In 1961, however, when Henry Kempe chaired the American Academy of Pediatrics and convened a conference on the "Battered Child Syndrome," public and media attention forced physicians and the public to face the problem (Radbill, 1987).

As soon as child abuse began to receive attention as a medical phenomenon, the relationship between abuse and disability began receiving attention. By the late 1960s, unexpectedly high proportions of children with disabilities were apparent among abused children (Elmer & Gregg, 1967), but at first, it was unclear whether these disabilities may have all resulted from abuse. Shortly thereafter, it became apparent that abuse was more frequent, even among children with congenital disorders, suggesting that in at least some cases the disability was present before the abuse.

Unfortunately, this finding was used as a basis for the assumption that there was something about children with disabilities that provoked abuse. As a result, the theory that excess stress associated with parenting a child with a disability was the principle factor connecting disability with abuse; and because of this assumption, studies tended to focus too heavily on the characteristics of abuse victims while largely ignoring the social realities that left them vulnerable (see Rusch, Hall, & Griffin, 1986).

VIOLENCE AND DISABILITY

Fortunately, the scientific investigation of the relationship between violence and disability is entering a new era. There no longer can be any doubt about the fact that violence is, for many, what Waxman (1992, p. 66) calls "the hidden truth about disabled people's lives." Only a few years ago in 1991, the unique relationship between violence and disability was still largely ignored and often denied or challenged by those who pointed toward the lack of large, representative samples and well-controlled studies.

A large-scale, methodologically rigorous, prospective study of a nationally representative American sample released in 1993 (Crosse et al., 1993) has left little doubt about the extent of increased risk of abuse for people with disabilities. As previously described, this study suggests that children with disabilities are almost twice as likely to be reported as abused as other children. Many other studies are helping to fill in the details of how abuse occurs (Sobsey & Doe 1991; Sullivan, Brookhouser, Scanlan, Knutson, & Schulte, 1991; Turk & Brown, 1993).

Information from these and many other studies is fueling the development and refinement of a model of violence and disability. An emerging model draws heavily on ecological perspectives, suggesting that social response to disability may be more important than disability itself in increasing vulnerability (see Doe, 1990; Sobsey, 1994; Westcott, 1993). This emerging model also includes elements from the behavioral counter-control model, the attachment theory, the social learning theory, the social labeling theory, the ambivalence theory, and a number of other conceptual sources (Sobsey, 1994). The data and the model are providing guidance for the development of prevention and intervention programs.

AVAILABLE ORGANIZATIONS

While research is a vital part of the change that is taking place, it is only one part of a growing movement. Change is also being generated from disability advocacy groups, service providers, and other sources. Several organizations have been started to help coordinate these efforts.

In the United States, the National Coalition on Abuse and Disability (NCAD, P.O. Box T, Culver City, CA 90230-0090 USA) is a network of researchers, advocates, and service providers concerned with abuse problems. In Britain, the National Association for the Protection from Sexual Abuse of Adults and Children with Learning Disabilities (NAPSAC, Department of Learning Disabilities, Floor E, South Block, University of Nottingham Medical School, Queens Medical Centre, Nottingham NG7 2UH England) serves a similar function. The International Coalition on Abuse & Disability (ICAD, E-Mail address: editors@psych.educ.ualberta.ca) is a computer network that addresses violence and disability issues and connects researchers and other interested parties in countries around the world.

ABOUT THIS BIBLIOGRAPHY

In 1991, the University of Alberta Abuse & Disability Project produced a previous annotated bibliography. *Disability, Sexuality, and Abuse* (Sobsey, Gray, Wells, Pyper, & Reimer-Heck, 1991) summarized the literature on sexual and physical abuse of children and adults with disabilities.

Since that time, there has been a tremendous increase in new information on violence and disability.

While we have retained about 200 of the citations from the first bibliography because of their continued relevance, most of this bibliography is new, and much of it represents information that was not yet available when the previous bibliography was produced.

There has also been a shift in focus in this bibliography. The 1991 bibliography included substantial amounts of information on healthy sexuality and sex education for people with disabilities. This information was included because we felt that it was important to emphasize the need for healthy sexuality in order to understand the sexual abuse of people with disabilities. The denial of normal sexual opportunities was one factor that predisposed many people with disabilities to sexual abuse and exploitation. We still believe that is true. Nevertheless, this bibliography does not attempt to cover that vast amount of related information on sexuality and disability. The focus of this volume is violence against people with disabilities.

This bibliography does include considerable amounts of information on eugenics, euthanasia, and assisted suicide. This information has been included partly because the integrated-ecological model of violence and disability (Sobsey, 1994) suggests that such phenomenon are more closely related to other forms of violence against people with disabilities than was previously thought. In addition, this information is included partly because of the growing discussion in Canada and the United States of new legislative mandates for assisted suicide.

This bibliography is intended primarily as resource for other researchers, clinicians, and advocates who want to do work related to violence and disability. The authors hope that readers will find it useful in developing their own work. The researchers, clinicians, and advocates currently working on violence and disability issues will help determine the attitudes about disability, violence, community gender relationships, and a variety of other vital topics for the twenty-first century. Some people believe that boys will be boys. They always have been, and they always will be. The authors of this bibliography believe this attitude has to change, and we believe that you, the reader, will bring about this change.

ABOUT TERMINOLOGY
Whenever possible, the terms used in this bibliography reflect the terms used by the original authors. For example, such terms as *severe* or *profound* mental retardation have been retained even though they are no longer consistent with commonly used definitions and classifications. Person-first (e.g., "person with a disability") language is generally used to be consistent with the publisher's style. In some cases, authors' use of disability-first language (e.g.," disabled person") is used to retain emphasis on disability as identity.

The term *victim* is used frequently throughout this bibliography, although the term has sometimes been avoided as stigmatizing or implying blame. The authors' deliberate choice to retain this word is based partially on the origin and definition of the word, which do not support such interpretations. It is based even more firmly, however, in the belief that people have a right and sometimes a need to be recognized as a victim of oppression or abuse without attribution of blame. We recognize and support that right asserted by such groups as "Victims of Violence." While alternatives such as "survivors of abuse" have been proposed, we consider the use of euphemisms to avoid the use of the word "victim" to be disrespectful. Unfortunately, it is also inaccurate since many victims of abuse are not survivors. Therefore, we use the word survivor only to refer specifically to individuals who have successfully withstood the effects of violence and retain the word *victim* to refer to all individuals who have been targets of abuse.

This bibliography uses the word *violence* in its broadest sense, as an abuse of power. It includes both more obvious criminal offenses such as assault, homicide, child abuse, and rape, but it also considers legitimized violence such as intrusive treatments, unjustifiable restraint, dehumanizing programs, and denial of life-saving medical care. It is expected that each reader will develop a personal definition of violence and a sense of what he or she considers to fall within that definition. Our broad view of violence is inherent in our ecological view of the nature of abuse of people with disabilities. This ecological view (Sobsey, 1994) suggests that none of the individual forms of violence can be understood in isolation but all must be considered in an interactive psychosocial framework. This framework includes the ambivalence theory (Söder, 1990), which suggests that society's general attitudes about people with disabilities include both empathetic and rejecting responses. In an extreme form, these rejecting responses can be viewed as hatred (Waxman, 1991) that drives many forms of violent behavior. These empathetic and rejecting responses interact according to the situation in which people encounter people with disabilities and have the potential to disinhibit aggression against people with disabilities.

Dick Sobsey, R.N., Ed.D, FAAMR
Abuse & Disability Project
University of Alberta
6-123 Education North
University of Alberta
Edmonton, AB T6G 2G5
CANADA

REFERENCES

Buck v. Bell. (1927). Supreme Court of the United States, 274 U.S. 200.

Burgdorf, R., & Burgdorf, M. (1977). The wicked witch is almost dead: Buck v. Bell and the sterilization of handicapped persons. *Temple Law Quarterly, 50,* 995–1000.

Caffey, J. (1946). Multiple fractures in the long-bones of infants suffering from chronic subdural hematoma. *American Journal of Roentgenology, 56,* 163–173.

Carson, J. C. (1898). Prevention of feeble-mindedness from a moral and legal standpoint. *Proceedings of the National Conference on Charities & Correction* (pp. 294–303). Albany, NY: National Conference on Charities & Correction.

Cotter, L. H. (1967). Operant conditioning in a Vietnamese mental hospital. *American Journal of Psychiatry, 124,* 23–28.

Crosse, S. B., Kaye, E., & Ratnofsky, A. C. (1993). *A report on the maltreatment of children with disabilities* (Contract No: 105-89-1630). Washington, DC: National Center on Child Abuse and Neglect.

Doe, T. (1990). Towards an understanding: An ecological model of abuse [Special Issue: Sexual abuse]. *Developmental Disabilities Bulletin, 18*(2), 13–20.

Deutsch, A. (1949) *The mentally ill in America: A history of their care and treatment from colonial times* (2nd ed.). New York: Columbia University Press.

Elmer, E., & Gregg, G. S. (1967). Developmental characteristics of abused children. *Pediatrics, 40*(4, Part I.), 596–602.

Engman, K. (1992, June 17). Teens get probation for torture of handicapped man. *The Edmonton Journal,* p. A1.

Engman, K., & Crockatt, J. (1992, June 18). Anger rises over youths' probation in fatal beating of handicapped man, *The Edmonton Journal,* p. B1.

Engman, K., & Tanner, A. (1993, June 11). Jason's own mother isn't a saint, but was never cruel—relative. *The Edmonton Journal,* pp. A1, A9.

Euthanasia. (1942). *The American Journal of Psychiatry, 99,* 141–143.

Fernald, W. E. (1904) Care of the feeble-minded. *Proceedings of the National Conference on Charities & Correction* (pp. 380–390). Albany, NY: National Conference on Charities & Correction.

Frost, B. (1994, February 11). Ex-nurse given nine life sentences for string of sex attacks. *Times* (London), p. 3.

Gould, S. J. (1981). *The mismeasure of man.* New York, NY: W.W. Norton & Company

Gruson, L. (1987, March 27). Prosecutors to ask death penalty in torture case. *The New York Times,* p. A12.

Hanley, R. (1992, November 11) Sister calls woman in assault case pliable. *The New York Times,* p. B6.

Laufer, P. (1994). *A question of consent: Innocence and complicity in the Glen Ridge rape case.* San Francisco, CA: Mercury House.

Levine Powers, J., Mooney, A., & Nunno, M. (1990). Institutional abuse: A review of the literature. *Journal of Child and Youth Care, 4*(6), 81–95.

Lifton, R. J., & Hackett, A. (1990). Physicians, Nazi. In I. Gutman (Ed.), *Encyclopedia of the Holocaust* (Vol. 3, L–R, pp. 1127–1132). New York: Macmillan.

Lombardo, P. A. (1985). Three generations, no imbeciles: New light on Buck v. Bell. *New York University Law Review, 60*(1), 30–62.

Mansell, S., Sobsey, D., & Calder, P. (1992). Sexual abuse treatment for persons with developmental disability. *Professional Psychology: Research and Practice. 23,* 404–409.

Meyer, J. E. (1988). "Die Freigabe der Vernichtung Lebensunwerten Lebens" von Binding und Hoche im Spiegel der deutschen Psychiatric vor 1933 ("The release for extermination of those unworthy of living" by Binding and Hoche:The response of German psychiatry prior to 1933). *Nervenzart, 59,* 85–91.

Neuffer, E. (1987, August 14). Body unearthed on S.I. is that of missing girl. *The New York Times*, p. B3.

Newton, M. (1990). *Hunting humans: An encyclopedia of modern serial killers.* Port Townsend, WA: Loompanics Unlimited.

Radbill, S. X. (1987). Children in a world of violence. In R. E. Helfer & R. S. Kempe (Eds.), *The battered child* (4th ed., pp. 3–22). Chicago, IL: University of Chicago Press.

Retarded man killed. (1994, 12 June). *Associated Press wirestory.*

Rivera, G. (1972). *Willowbrook: A report on how it is and why it doesn't have to be that way.* New York, NY: Vintage Books.

Rusch, R. G., Hall, J. C., & Griffin, H. C. (1986). Abuse-provoking characteristics of institutionalized mentally retarded individuals. *American Journal of Mental Deficiency, 90*(6) 618–624.

Sengstock, W. L., Magerhans-Hurley, H., & Sprotte, A. (1990). The role of special education in the Third Reich. *Education and Training in Mental Retardation, 25,* 225–236.

Smith, J. D., & Polloway, E. A. (1993). Institutionalization, involuntary sterilization, and mental retardation: Profiles from the history of the practice. *Mental Retardation, 31*(4), 208–214.

Sobsey, D. (1994). *Violence and abuse in the lives of people with disabilities: The end of silent acceptance?* Baltimore, MD: Paul H. Brookes Publishing Co.

Sobsey, D., & Doe, T. (1991). Patterns of sexual abuse and assault. *Sexuality and Disability, 9*(3), 243–259.

Sobsey, D., Gray, S., Wells, D., Pyper, D., & Reimer-Heck, B. (1991). *Disability, sexuality, and abuse: An annotated bibliography.* Baltimore, MD: Paul H. Brookes Publishing Co.

Sobsey, D., & McDonald, L. (1988). Special education: Coming of age. In B. Ludlow, A. P. Turnbull, & R. Luckasson (Eds.), *Transitions to adult life for people with mental retardation—Principles and practices* (pp. 21–43). Baltimore, MD: Paul H. Brookes Publishing Co.

Söder, M. (1990). Prejudice or ambivalence? Attitudes toward people with disabilities. *Disability, Handicap & Society, 5,* 227-241.

Stimpson, L., & Best, M. C. (1991). *Courage above all: Sexual assault against women with disabilities.* Toronto: DisAbled Women's Network.

Sullivan, P. M., Brookhouser, P. E., Scanlan, J. M., Knutson, J. F., & Schulte, L. E. (1991). Patterns of physical and sexual abuse of communicatively handicapped children. *Annals of Otology, Rhinology, Laryngology, 100,* 188–194.

Thomas, G. (1988). *Journey into madness: Medical torture and the mind controllers.* London: Gorgi Books. .

Turk, V., & Brown, H. (1993). The sexual abuse of adults with learning disabilities: Results of a two year incidence survey. *Mental Handicap research, 6*(3), 193–216

U. S. experiments on people compared to Nazi atrocities. (1993, December 29). *The Edmonton Journal,* p. B8.

Waxman, B. F. (1991). Hatred: The unacknowledged dimension in violence against disabled people [Special Issue: Sexual exploitation of people with disabilities}. *Sexuality and Disability, 9*(3), 185-199.

Waxman, B. F. (1992, Winter). Review of *Disability, sexuality, and abuse: An annotated bibliography. Disabilities Studies Quarterly,* 65–67.

Westcott, H. (1992). Vulnerability and the need for protection. In J. Gibbons (Ed.), *The Children Act of 1989 and Family Support: Principles into practice* (pp. 89–100). London: Her Majesty's Stationery Office.

Westcott, H. L. (1993). *Abuse of children and adults with disabilities.* London: National Society for the Prevention of Cruelty to Children.

Wilhelm, H. H. (1990). Euthanasia Program. In I. Gutman (Ed.), *Encyclopedia of the Holocaust* (Vol. 2, E–K, pp. 451–454). New York: Macmillan.

Wilson, C., & Brewer, N. (1992). The incidence of criminal victimization of individuals with an intellectual disability. *Australian Psychologist, 27*(2), 114–117.

Acknowledgments

Abstracts were written by Tansel Erdem, Sharmaine Gray, Richard Lucardie, Marya Owen, Sheila Mansell, Lorraine McPherson, Diane Pyper, Beth Reimer-Heck, Gill Rutherford, Dick Sobsey, Madhavan Thuppal, Don Well, and Andre Zawallich.

Sheila White and Jan Coulter of the University of Alberta Herbert T. Coutts Education Library provided valuable assistance in locating many of the documents that are abstracted in this bibliography.

Sarah Cheney, Acquisitions Editor, Paul H. Brookes Publishing Co., deserves special thanks for her recognition of the need for this work, her confidence in our ability to carry it out, and her development of an innovative editing and production process. Kristine DeRuchie, Production Editor, also deserves special thanks for her diligence, patience, and flexibility.

We are also indebted to all of the authors whose work is cited and abstracted in this bibliography. It is through their work that our understanding of violence and disability is growing. We have attempted to reflect their work as accurately as possible.

To
Joyce Cardinal
Jason Carpenter
and
Michelle Kshyk

To all people with disabilities
who become victims of violence

and

To all victims of abuse
who are disabled by violence

Violence and Disability

•A•

1. **Abel, E. L., & Sokol, R. J. (1987). Incidence of fetal alcohol syndrome and economic impact of FAS-related anomalies.** *Drug and Alcohol Dependence, 19,* 51–70.
This article discusses the incidence of fetal alcohol syndrome (FAS) (estimated to be 1.9 per 1,000 live births) and its associated anomalies and the financial cost of support programs and medical coverage in the United States. It states that FAS is the leading cause of mental retardation and that it costs approximately $321 million a year to finance support programs and medical treatment. It claims that approximately 11% of support cost associated with mental retardation (estimated to cost $11.7 billion a year) is attributed to individuals with FAS. Also, this article includes a further breakdown of the incidence of FAS and the costs of supporting and treating individuals with fetal alcohol syndrome.

2. **Abel, E. L., & Sokol, R. J. (1991). A revised conservative estimate of the incidence of FAS and its economic impact.** *Alcoholism: Clinical and Experimental Research, 15*(3), 514–524.
This article presents a re-estimate of the incidence and costs related to fetal alcohol syndrome (FAS), a topic first discussed in a 1987 article by the same authors. In this article, the authors estimate the incidence rate of FAS for the Western world at a more conservative rate of 0.33 cases per 1,000 and suggest that the annual treatment cost for individuals with FAS is $74.6 million a year, an estimate that does not include specific alcohol-related birth defects.

3. **Abrahams, N., Casey, K., & Daro, D. (1992). Teachers' knowledge, attitudes, and beliefs about child abuse and its prevention.** *Child Abuse & Neglect, 16,* 229–238.
This article discusses a nation-wide questionnaire survey that was conducted with teachers from 40 school districts in 29 counties about their knowledge, attitudes, and beliefs concerning child abuse and child abuse prevention. This survey was conducted by the National Committee for Prevention of Child Abuse. Five hundred sixty-eight elementary or middle school teachers (501 females, 47 males, 20 no gender identification) responded to the survey. The mean age of respondents was 40, and the respondents represented grades 1 through 6, with 20% teaching first grade, and 9%, 22%, 17%, 12%, and 16% of respondents teaching each consecutive grade. One percent of teachers taught special education. The mean average of teaching experience was 13 years. The results of this survey indicate the following: the majority of teachers felt teacher education was insufficient with regard to the identification, reporting, and intervention of child abuse; 74% of teachers had encountered child abuse and neglect, with 90% reporting it; barriers to the reporting of child maltreatment cases consisted of a lack of information on the detection and reporting of child maltreatment, legal ramifications concerning false allegations, and relationship ramifications with regard to the parent-teacher relationships and teacher-child relationships; and 97% of the respondents felt child assault prevention programs were valuable.

4. **Abrams, H., Nuehring, E., & Zuckerman, M. (1984).** *Preventing abuse and neglect: A staff training curriculum for facilities serving developmentally disabled persons* **(Vol. 1). Miami Shores, FL: Barry University, Abuse and Neglect Prevention Project.**
This four-part training program for direct care staff who work with persons with developmental disabilities presents instructions for identifying and reporting abuse and neglect. It explains normalization and presents a bill of rights for persons with developmental disabilities. It also discusses behavior management and aggression control techniques (ACT). Trainer tips include advice on preparation, delivery techniques, and learning theory. The first three modules provide instructions for presenting this training program and include the following: planning notes, objectives, preparation checklists, outlines, lesson plans, handouts, visual aids, posttests, and evaluation forms. The last module, on ACT, contains an implementation plan, including the following: a system of certification, retraining, and monitoring; seven references; four appendices concerning the ACT test; and approximately 50 illustrations.

5. **Abrams, R. C. (1988). Dementia research in the nursing home.** *Hospital and Community Psychiatry, 39*(3), 257–259.
This article addresses the ethics of geriatric psychiatric research with nursing home residents with dementia. It pays special attention to the patient's competence, autonomy, and protection because the patient's diminished cognitive abilities might affect his or her ability to give an informed consent. The author suggests the monitoring of consent by proxy and by consent auditors.

6. **Abuse: How to respond. (1992, February/March).** *Transition,* pp. 9–10.
This article is excerpted from the booklet entitled *Responding to the Abuse of People with Disabilities,* published by the Advocacy Resource Centre for the Handicapped (ARCH). This article provides information on the handling of abusive situations and deals with the following issues: suspicion of abuse, confidentiality, legal and ethical responsibilities, being made aware of an abusive situation, reporting abuse, and assisting the victim. (Editors' note: To order the booklet, please contact ARCH at 40 Orchard View Blvd., Suite 255, Toronto, Ontario, M4H 1B9, [416] 482-8255, Fax [416] 482-2981.)

7. **Adams, N. H. S., & Hafner, R. J. (1991). Attitudes of psychiatric patients and their relatives to involuntary treatment.** *Australia and New Zealand Journal of Psychiatry,* **25, 231–237.**
The authors of this article state that the province of South Australia enacted a new Mental Health Act in 1979 that established the Guardianship Board to help people with developmental disabilities meet their needs. This article describes a study that was conducted to determine the attitudes of psychiatric patients and their relatives to involuntary treatment. The sample for this study included 79 patients and 47 of their relatives. The patients in this study were asked to complete the Brief Symptom Inventory and a specially designed questionnaire that examined their views on their psychiatric disorder and the Guardianship Board. The relatives in this study completed the Hostility and Direction of Hostility Questionnaire and a specially designed questionnaire that examined their views about the Guardianship Board. The results of this study indicate that patients generally object to the board (70%) but favorably view the board's ability to supply psychiatric treatment and medication and that the patient's relatives were in favor of the board.

8. **Adams Hillard, P. J. (1985). Physical abuse in pregnancy.** *Obstetrics and Gynecology,* **66(2), 185–190.**
This article discusses a study that was conducted to assess the extent to which pregnant women are physically abused. This study obtained information from 742 women who were treated at the University of Virginia obstetric clinics. From this sample of 742 women, 81 of them had a history of abuse, and 29 of them reported present abuses. Twenty-one percent of the women who were presently abused reported an increase in abuse during pregnancy. The results of this study reveal that abused women were more often older, single women of greater parity than controls.

9. **Adelstein, A. M., Goldblatt, P. O., Stracey, S. C., & Weatherall, F. A. C. (1982). Nonaccidental injury. In Office of Population Censuses and Surveys/ London School of Hygiene and Tropical Medicine (Ed.),** *Studies in sudden infant deaths* **(pp. 51–56). London: Hobbs the Printers of Southampton.**
This report discusses the problems associated with estimating the number of deaths resulting from the nonaccidental injury of children in England and Wales. It examines the difficulty in recognizing nonaccidental injury deaths using evidence available from the Registrar General's statistics. The authors conclude that nonaccidental injury deaths are not overlooked by the Registrar General.

10. **Aguilar, S. (1984). Prosecuting cases of physical and sexual assault of the mentally retarded. In** *Prosecutor's notebook:* *Volume III.* **Sacramento: California District Attorneys Association.**
This chapter is written for people working in the criminal justice system, and it focuses on people with intellectual disabilities who have been sexually abused. It describes different kinds of abuse and neglect and discusses certain U.S. Penal Code sections that deal with sexual/physical abuse and neglect of people with developmental disabilities. Also, this chapter examines the competency of people with intellectual disabilities to consent to sexual activities and their ability to testify in court. This chapter includes detailed information on court preparation activities.

11. **Aiello, D. (1984–1986). Issues and concerns confronting disabled assault victims: Strategies for treatment and prevention.** *Sexuality and Disability,* **7(3/4), 96–101.**
This article discusses the unavailability of specific services for assault victims with developmental disabilities. It points out that many rape crisis centers and abuse shelters are inaccessible to those with mobility impairments and that transportation is a big problem for most persons with disabilities. This article presents an overview of relevant issues in developing and providing services for people with disabilities. This article also includes suggestions for counseling victims with disabilities, and it focuses on education and prevention services.

12. **Aiello, D., Capkin, L., & Catania, H. (1983). Strategies and techniques for serving the disabled assault victim: A pilot training program for providers and consumers.** *Sexuality and Disability,* **6(3/4), 135–144.**
This article describes a training program on sexual assault and disability that was conducted by Moss Rehabilitation Hospital of Philadelphia. The purpose of the program was to provide information on medical, psychological, social, and criminal justice issues surrounding the assault of persons with disabilities. This program addressed four areas: myths and attitudes concerning rape victims with disabilities, emergency crisis services for assault victims, the criminal justice process in relation to assault, and strategies for prevention.

13. **Aikenhead, S. (1993, January 29). Disabled removed as abuse alleged: Cardinal won't renew group home licences.** *The Edmonton Journal,* **p. A7.**
This newspaper article reports that two Delvee ranch homes in Granum and Claresholm, Alberta, will not have their group home licenses renewed due to allegations of abuse and neglect. The Delvee homes are owned and operated by Lori Williams-Morgan, a psychologist, and these homes offer services to adults with autism. The Delvee facilities came under investigation by Social Service Minister Mike Cardinal and by the Royal Canadian Mounted Police after the CBC aired an inter-

view with Delvee employees who admitted that they physically assaulted residents. Social Services had been contacted several years prior to the CBC news item about concerns of physical, psychological, and sexual abuse, in addition to neglect and safety violations at the group homes. The government currently has a $1 million contract with Delvee.

14. Aikenhead, S. (1993, January 30). Province had planned to shut group home. *The Edmonton Journal*, p. A8.

This newspaper article reports that alleged abuses against people with autism at the DelVee Ranch in Claresholm, Alberta, had led to the planned closing of the government-funded group home 3 years prior to new allegations of abuse. Social Service Minister John Oldring backed away from the decision to close down the home in 1990 due to legal concerns about being sued for the closure. New Social Service Minister Mike Cardinal has decided not to renew the licenses of two Delvee homes. This move came a day after a CBC-TV broadcast reported alleged abuses and neglect of residents at the homes.

15. Albin, J. B. (1992). Sexual abuse in young children with developmental disabilities: Assessment and treatment issues. *Journal on Developmental Disabilities, 1*(1), 29–40.

This article discusses assessment and treatment of sexually abused children with developmental disabilities. It presents two case studies to help illustrate some of the difficulties encountered during assessment, and it suggests recommendations for problem solving during assessment and treatment.

16. Alexander, P. C. (1992). Application of attachment theory to the study of sexual abuse. *Journal of Consulting and Clinical Psychology, 60*(2), 185–195.

This article examines attachment theory and its use in understanding the predictors and consequences of sexual abuse. According to the author, attachment theory claims that a biological bond exists between a child and his or her primary caregiver. Also, in those child–caregiver relationships with an insecure attachment, the author feels that the relationship will have incidences of abuse. The results of this examination suggest that childhood attachment formation is carried into adulthood, and it found the following themes in sexually abusive families: rejection, role reversal/parentification, and fear/unresolved trauma. Also, this examination found the following consequences of sexual abuse as it relates to attachment theory: interpersonal problems, affect regulation, and disturbance of self. The author discusses the clinical and research implications of this examination of attachment theory.

17. Alfaro, J. D. (1988). What can we learn from child abuse fatalities? A synthesis of nine studies. In D. J. Besharov (Ed.), *Protecting children from abuse and ne-*

glect: Policy and practice (pp. 219–264). Springfield, IL: Charles C Thomas.

This chapter examines the data from nine studies that deal with child abuse fatalities. It provides a description of the methods and a thematic summary of the findings from these nine studies. It describes in greater detail the planning, implementation, and outcomes of four studies. This chapter discusses the overall implications and trends and includes suggestions for future research.

18. Allegations of death, abuse to be probed. (1992, April 2). *The Calgary Herald*, p. A14.

This newspaper article reports that a police investigation has been initiated into several deaths that occurred at the Oak Ridge Division of the Penetanguishene Mental Health Centre. The center houses psychiatric patients who are held indefinitely on lieutenant governer's warrants. The investigation concerns 10 deaths and 27 allegations of physical and sexual abuses at the center and covers a 20-year period.

19. Allen, C., & Savvides, N. (1992, November 22). "Child" adults suffer sexual abuse. *The Observer*, p. 10.

This newspaper article examines the conspiracy of silence surrounding the sexual abuse of adults with developmental disabilities in hospitals and residences in England. While no national survey has been conducted, it is estimated that approximately 1,000 cases of sexual abuse against people with developmental disabilities have been reported. Perpetrators are usually not convicted because victims are considered unreliable witnesses. This article provides case examples.

20. Allen, G. (1990, November 28). Auditor censures deaths of disabled: Monitoring called inadequate. *The Globe and Mail*, pp. A1, A4.

This newspaper article discusses an auditor's report that suggests the deaths of 15 residents at the Brantwood Residential Development Centre for people with disabilities resulted from severe malnutrition, dehydration, and neglect by staff. The report notes that the Brantwood Centre had also failed to report the deaths of four residents prior to a random investigation of the provincially supported institution. Additional provincially financed institutions were also investigated at random. The investigators conclude that suspicions of abuse of residents are allowed to go unreported, deaths or other serious incidents are unreported, nutritional needs of residents are not assessed, and prosecutions of homes that violate provincial standards are in decline.

21. Allington, C. L. J. (1992). Sexual abuse within services for people with learning disabilities: Staff's perceptions, understandings of, and contact with the problem of sexual abuse. *Mental Handicap, 20*(2), 59–63.

This article describes a survey of 107 staff members in day care and residential services for people with developmental disabilities. The results indicate the following: although all respondents felt that people with developmental disabilities were at risk for sexual abuse, 32% never discuss the topic; more than two thirds (68%) believed that the risk was greater for people with disabilities than for people without disabilities; and 88% felt more information should be provided to caregivers.

22. Alternatives to Fear. (no date). *Self-defense for visually impaired women.* Seattle, WA: Author.

This paper describes a self-defense course for women with visual disabilities. It examines problems encountered by women with visual disabilities and discusses teaching methods and self-defense techniques. This course is designed for women who use white canes and guide dogs and women who are legally blind or have enough vision to function without aids. According to this paper, Alternatives to Fear plans to institute regionwide or nationwide instruction for the trainers program.

23. Aman, M. G. (1985). Drugs in mental retardation: Treatment or tragedy? *Australia and New Zealand Journal of Developmental Disabilities, 10*(4), 215–226.

According to this article, treatment with psychotropic and anticonvulsant drugs is common for people with mental retardation, ranging from about 20% in noninstitutionalized children to about 50% to 60% in institutionalized populations. This article describes the major types of drugs used to treat people with mental retardation, and it singles out four groups for further discussion: neuroleptics, anticonvulsants, anti-anxiety drugs, and cerebral stimulants. The question of rationale is raised, and the author suggests that the main objective of pharmacotherapy is the suppression of a wide variety of acting-out behaviors. The author discusses the extreme attitudes sometimes expressed by workers in the field regarding the propriety of drug treatment and presents a brief summary concerning some of the clinical research findings on neuroleptic, anticonvulsant, enxiolytic, and stimulant medication. Also, this article discusses, in considerable detail, the work of a very influential research group in Coldwater, Michigan. The author notes that this group has produced a number of controversial reports that suggest that the most commonly used medications may actually impede the treatment or development of patients with mental retardation. The author identifies certain difficulties with this group's work as well as a lack of independent research support from other centers and suggests that judgment regarding the role of pharmacotherapy in this field should not be overly influenced by these reports. Finally, the author identifies a number of factors that may hinder drug research with subjects with mental retardation.

24. Aman, M. G., Field, C. J., & Bridgman, G. D. (1985). City-wide survey of drug patterns among non-institutionalized mentally retarded persons. *Applied Research in Mental Retardation, 6*(2), 159–171.

This article describes a survey of 1,012 noninstitutionalized persons with mental retardation living in a medium-size metropolitan area. The sample in this study was drawn from special schools and two service agencies in Auckland, New Zealand, that serve preschoolers and adults with mental retardation. These special schools and service agencies are the main organizations serving people with mental retardation in Auckland, and collectively, they include a large proportion of noninstitutionalized individuals with mental retardation. A comprehensive summary of current medication was obtained for each subject. This study collected a variety of demographic, medical, social, and sleep data, and where appropriate, information was gathered regarding time elapsed since the last seizure. This study found that 2% of the preschoolers, 3% of the special school students, and 14% of the adults were receiving psychotropic drugs. It found that anticonvulsant drugs were prescribed for 31% of the preschoolers, 17% of the special school cases, and 18% of the adults. Also, it found that a large proportion of the demographic, medical, and social/sleep variables was associated with drug prescription patterns. This article discusses these factors with respect to other surveys and offers possible explanations to account for their relationship to pharmacotherapy.

25. Aman, M. G., & Singh, N. N. (1986). A critical appraisal of recent drug research in mental retardation: The Coldwater studies. *Journal of Mental Deficiency Research, 30*(2), 121–130.

This article attempts to assess public and professional attitudes toward drug treatment for people with mental retardation and concludes that considerable sentiment has developed in recent years against the use of pharmacotherapy. It identifies and discusses a number of factors contributing to this prevailing attitude. In particular, it summarizes a series of investigations carried out by researchers at the Coldwater Regional Center for developmental disabilities (Michigan), studies that have had negative implications for the use of drug treatment for people with mental retardation. These studies have suggested that psychotropic drugs, especially the antipsychotics, may adversely affect the clinical management of people with mental retardation, depress learning performance, and interfere with the efficacy of reinforcement contingencies. However, the authors note that certain features of these studies, such as the procedures for selecting these subjects, the doses used, and the overall funding philosophy, appear to limit their relevance. The authors compare these investigations to a number of other studies that show circumscribed positive clinical effects, a lack of interference with learning, and little or no disruption of reinforcement contingencies. The authors conclude that all-encompassing judgments about the value of pharmacotherapy for people with mental retardation are premature at this time. They suggest that clinical drug research should look for the enhancement of adaptive functioning by discovering appropriate subject–treatment combinations while remaining vigilant for adverse effects.

26. Aman, M. G., Singh, N. N., & White, A. J. (1987). Caregiver perceptions of psychotropic medication in residential facilities. *Research in Developmental Disabilities,* **8, 449–465.**

This article discusses a survey of psychopediatric nurses at two residential hospitals for persons with developmental disabilities in New Zealand in order to determine their perceptions, opinions, and knowledge of psychotropic drugs. The survey addressed the following areas: the dynamics of drug administration, most commonly used and preferred methods for assessing drug effects, perception of the likelihood for different types of behavior problems leading to the use of medication, endorsement of behavior modification as an alternative to drug therapy, adequacy of training in psychotropic drugs, and any changes the respondents would like to see the way psychotropic drugs are used in their facilities. The results of this survey indicate the following: the decision to use the psychotropic medications was predominantly made by the unit doctors and the unit supervisors; the interdisciplinary team had little impact on the decision-making process; acting out behavior was considered the most important reason for starting or continuing drug treatment; global impressions and informal diaries were used for assessing medication effects, and global impressions and behavior observations were ranked as the most appropriate method for selecting medications; 61% to 72% of the respondents felt behavior modification was usually but not always an alternative form of treatment; the respondents wanted more information about side-effects and clinical indications for various drugs; and the respondents suggested more frequent drug reviews and greater use of a team approach as the best method for administrating psychotropic medications. The authors conclude that there is a need for more education on a variety of social, pharmacological, and behavioral issues as they relate to medication use.

27. Amaro, H., Fried, L. E., Cabral, H., & Zuckerman, B. (1990). Violence during pregnancy and substance use. *American Journal of Public Health,* **80(5), 575–579.**

This article discusses a study that was conducted to assess the incidence of violence toward pregnant women from mostly inner-city neighborhoods. The results of this study reveal that 92 women (7% of the 1,243 women who participated in the study) reported being physically or sexually abused while pregnant. This study found that these women were substance abusers and had partners who abused substances and that abused women appeared to have a greater incidence of past depressive episodes.

28. American Academy of Pediatrics. (1985). Prolonged infantile apnea: 1985. *Pediatrics,* **76(1), 129–131.**

This article, prepared by a task force on prolonged apnea, examines prolonged apnea and its relation to sudden infant death syndrome (SIDS). It reports that there are many causes for prolonged apnoeic episodes in children and that one of them is abuse. It suggests that the relation of prolonged apnea to SIDS is minimal, with no evidence of prolonged apnea observed in the majority of SIDS cases. This article discusses the use of monitors for monitoring apnoeic episodes and the resources needed for evaluation and management of these cases.

29. American Association on Mental Retardation. (1989). Supreme Court hears death penalty case. *News & Notes (quarterly newsletter of the American Association on Mental Retardation),* **2 (1), 1.**

This article discusses the Supreme Court of the United States' review of the death penalty case of *Penry v. Lynaugh,* which involves a man with mental retardation who killed a Texas housewife. It examines the violation of the Eighth Amendment banning cruel and unusual punishment. The American Association on Mental Retardation and other sister organizations have filed an *amici cuiae* brief concerning this case. They argue that mental retardation should be considered a mitigating circumstance in sentencing selection and should never result in the death penalty.

30. Ammerman, R. T. (1992). Sexually abused children with multiple disabilities: Each is unique, as are their needs. *NRCCSA (National Resource Center on Child Sexual Abuse) News,* **1(4), 13–14.**

This article discusses the risk, treatment, and prevention of sexual abuse of people with multiple disabilities. It suggests that language and physical restrictions as well as the problem with the physical indicators of sexual abuse are some of the issues that must be considered when dealing with this population. This article recommends individual treatment, with the use of toys, dolls, and puppets as a way to communicate with people with multiple disabilities, and stresses prevention through education.

31. Ammerman, R. T., & Baladerian, N. J. (1993). *Maltreatment of children with disabilities* **(Working Paper 860). Chicago: National Committee to Prevent Child Abuse.**

This working paper provides a general overview of issues related to abuse of people with disabilities. It includes information on definitions, epidemiology, identification, factors that cause abuse, effects of maltreatment, prevention of abuse, treatment of abused children, and the responsibilities of care providers and professionals. This paper also includes a list of names and addresses of organizations that do work related to abuse and disability.

32. Ammerman, R. T., Cassisi, J. E., Hersen, M., & Van Hasselt, V. B. (1986). Con-

sequences of physical abuse and neglect in children. *Clinical Psychology Review, 6*, 291–310.

This review of the literature focuses on the negative consequences of physical abuse and neglect during childhood. While some of the studies examined have limitations because of their research methods, some consensus has been reached concerning the consequences of physical abuse and neglect during childhood. This article points out that academic and cognitive impairment has been noted in maltreated children and that behavioral disorders, psychopathology, and impaired social competence are exhibited by these children. The authors offer recommendations for future research.

33. **Ammerman, R. T., Hersen, M., & Lubetsky, M. J. (1988). Assessment and treatment of abuse and neglect in multihandicapped children and adolescents. *International Journal of Rehabilitation, 11*(3), 313–314.**

This article briefly describes the objectives of a proposed study that intends to investigate factors associated with the abuse and neglect of children with disabilities who live at home. The objectives of the study include the following: the development of an assessment strategy for examining the incidence and characteristics of abuse and neglect in psychiatrically referred children with multiple disabilities and their families, and the implementation and evaluation of a comprehensive behavioral treatment plan for remediation in these families. This article describes the proposed methodology. This study expects the following outcomes: measures of the incidence of abuse and neglect in psychiatrically hospitalized children and adolescents with disabilities and multiple disabilities, the description of the psychosocial characteristics of abusing parent(s), and the description of the behavioral and psychiatric characteristics of abused children and adolescents as compared to unabused children and adolescents. The remedial program planned as part of this study is a 12-week skills-based intervention that emphasizes child management skills, stress reduction, anger control training, and problem-solving training.

34. **Ammerman, R. T., Lubetsky, M. J., Hersen, M., & Hasselt, V. B. V. (1988). Maltreatment of children and adolescents with multiple handicaps: Five case examples. *Journal of the Multihandicapped Person, 1*(2), 129–139.**

This article describes five cases of abused children with multiple disabilities and discusses issues regarding abuse of children with multiple disabilities. The authors identify several factors that they link to greater risk of abuse for children with multiple disabilities: for example, disruption of bonding between parents and their children, increased stress for families, and decreased counter-control due to decreased communication. The authors also discuss the difficulty associated with recognizing abuse and neglect of children with multiple disabilities and the need for multidisciplinary intervention with families.

35. **Ammerman, R. T., Van Hasselt, V., & Hersen, M. (1987). The handicapped adolescent. In V. B. Van Hasselt & M. Hersen (Eds.), *Handbook of adolescent psychology* (pp. 413–423). Toronto: Pergamon Press.**

This chapter addresses the psychological adjustment of adolescents with disabilities. A variety of studies have found that many children and adolescents with disabilities are at increased risk for increased psychological maladjustment. The authors discuss the nature and characteristics of problems encountered by these adolescents and discuss methodological problems that have made studies in this area difficult to interpret. This article discusses the following topics: personality characteristics, psychopathology and behavioral disorders, social adjustment, and treatment. Abuse is not discussed in the article.

36. **Ammerman, R. T., Van Hasselt, V. B., & Hersen, M. (1988). Maltreatment of handicapped children: A critical review. *Journal of Family Violence, 3*(1), 53–72.**

This review focuses on risk factors associated with the abuse of children with disabilities. It addresses investigations of abuse and neglect with specific populations of children with disabilities, and it discusses methodology and research recommendations.

37. **Ammerman, R. T., Van Hasselt, V., Hersen, M., McGonigle, J. J., & Lubetsky, M. J. (1989). Abuse and neglect in psychiatrically hospitalized multihandicapped children. *Child Abuse & Neglect, 13*, 335–343.**

The medical histories of 150 consecutive admissions of children with multiple disabilities to an American psychiatric hospital were examined, and this examination reveals the following: 39% of these children had experienced abuse or neglect or showed signs of likely abuse or neglect; physical abuse was most common (69%), followed by neglect (45%), and then sexual abuse (36%); clients with less severe impairments were more likely to have a history of abuse; the child's abuse or neglect was rarely a focus of treatment during hospitalization; and a high percentage of sexually abused children also experienced other forms of abuse.

38. **Anderson, C. (1982). *Teaching people with mental retardation about sex abuse prevention: An illusion theatre guide.* Santa Cruz, CA: Network Publications.**

This document describes how puppets may be used to teach children with mental retardation about sexual abuse. (Editors' note: Puppets may offer a viable alternative to role playing.)

39. **Anderson, C., & McGehee, S. (1991). *Bodies of evidence.* New York: St. Martin's Press.**

This "true-crime" book tells the story of Judias Buenoano, who was convicted on May 13, 1980, of murdering her 19-year-old son, Michael Buenoano Goodyear, by drowning near Milton, Florida, with the apparent help of his younger brother. It describes how Michael's minor childhood disabilities (he had learning difficulties, awkward movements, and hyperactivity) were entirely unacceptable to his mother, who managed to isolate him in residential schools for most of his childhood. It discusses his mother's attempt to poison him with arsenic after insuring him for over $100,000. It states that this attempt to kill Michael proved unsuccessful but left him more severely disabled with peripheral nerve damage and almost no use of his arms or legs. After this unsuccessful attempt on his life, Michael's mother and brother took him for a canoe ride and "accidentally" tipped the canoe in the middle of Florida's East River. Because he was paralyzed and wore heavy metal leg braces and grasping prosthesis, Michael sank quickly. His death was ruled accidental, as were those of two previous victims who were murdered by Judias Buenoano; but when two unsuccessful attempts on the life of a fourth heavily insured victim became apparent, the earlier deaths were thoroughly investigated. Judias Buenoano was convicted and sentenced to death. Her murders of her husband and boyfriend indicated that her son's disabilities were not her only motivation for committing murder, but her selection of this son for rejection and "sacrifice" while continuing an apparently close relationship with her daughter and second son suggests that his disabilities were a factor in her decision to kill her son.

40. **Anderson, F. E. (1992).** *Art for all the children: Approaches to art therapy for children with disabilities.* **Springfield, IL: Charles C Thomas.**
This book discusses and illustrates the uses of art therapy for children with physical and/or developmental disabilities. It provides an overview of generalized artistic development in children and different approaches to art therapy, and it illustrates the psychoanalytic, developmental, adaptive, and cognitive-behavioral approaches with case examples. It examines art and the individualized education program and art therapy in public schools, and it discusses the adaptation of art therapy in terms of physical environment, art tools and media, instructional sequence, and technological adaptions for children with disabilities. This book also addresses the development of a sense of self through art.

41. **Anderson, J. G., & Caddell, D. P. (1993). Attitudes of medical professionals toward euthanasia.** *Social Science and Medicine,* *37*(1), 105–114.
This article discusses a study that examined the attitudes of 63 oncology health care professionals, including nurses, pharmacists, and social service workers, toward euthanasia and how those attitudes are affected by religion, previous experience in withdrawing care, and years in the health care profession. The 41 Protestants, 14 Catholics, and 8 others who participated in this study completed a self-administered questionnaire. The findings of this study suggest the following: Protestants tend to support euthanasia more than Catholics, those with high religious commitments tend to disagree with euthanasia based on professional norms, agreement with euthanasia is inversely related to years in the profession, and those with previous experience with withdrawing care tend to disagree with euthanasia based on legal/self-interest reasons.

42. **Anderson, R. J., & Antonak, R. F. (1992). The influence of attitudes and contact on reactions to persons with physical and speech disabilities.** *Rehabilitation Counseling Bulletin, 35*(4), 240–247.
The study discussed in this article examined the relationship between attitudes and prior contact on the reaction of people without disabilities to people with physical and speech disabilities. Forty-one undergraduate students from the University of North Carolina participated in the study. Their experience with people with disability varied with regard to type, duration, and intimacy. The participants were assigned to either a high or low favorable attitude group, depending on their score on the Attitude Toward Disabled Persons Scale, Form A. Then, the participants were randomly assigned to view either a videotape of an actor with a speech disability or a videotape of an actor with a physical disability. After viewing the videotape, the participants completed the Adjective Check List and were interviewed to determine their reaction to the videotape. The results of this study indicate the following: the actor with the speech disability was rated as less socially acceptable than the actor with a physical disability, regardless of participants' attitudes toward people with disabilities; and no difference was found between subjects in the high versus low favorable attitude groups on reaction measures following the experiment.

43. **Anderson, S. (Speaker). (1985).** *Sexual abuse of the developmentally disabled* **(Cassette Recording No. L-172-14). Seattle, WA: Seattle Rape Relief Crisis Center.**
This 104-minute cassette is a workshop presentation given by Shirley Anderson, a pediatrician working with the Seattle Rape Relief Crisis Center. Much of the information presented is an account of the Seattle Rape Relief Crisis Center's experience serving clients with a wide range of disabilities. This presentation cites incidence and prevalence figures, discusses service delivery issues, and presents principles for accommodating special populations. The figures cited in this presentation suggest that the sexual abuse of people with disabilities is as common or more common than among with people without disabilities. This presentation concludes there is a tendency for under-reporting cases in this population that exceeds under-reporting with other populations and that generic services require some specialization to meet the needs of this group.

44. Andersson, L., Mullins, L. C., & Johnson, D. P. (1987). Parental intrusion versus social isolation: A dichotomous view of the sources of loneliness [Special issue: Loneliness: Theory, research, and applications]. *Journal of Social Behavior and Personality, 2*(2, Pt. 2), 125–134.

This article examines Weiss's (1987) assertion that emotional isolation is better understood than social isolation (see Reflections on the present state of loneliness research. *Journal of Social Behavior & Personality, 2*[2, Pt. 2], 1–16). The authors suggest that this may be due in part to the influence of attachment theory, which claims that neglect in early childhood might lead to relationship problems later in life. They believe that this emphasis on neglect may be too restrictive and that too much parental intrusion in childhood socialization might limit the child's potential for self-development and lead to narcissistic difficulties and loneliness. This article presents retrospective data from 207 elderly women (mean age 77) in order to examine the relationship between loneliness and narcissistic intrusion. The results of this study indicate that loneliness is greater among the narcissistic group when compared to those whose parental influence was not intrusive. This article concludes that too much or too little parental control may result in narcissistic difficulties and loneliness.

45. Andre, C. E. (1985). Child maltreatment and handicapped children: An examination of family characteristics and service provision. *Dissertation Abstracts International, 46*(3), 792A.

This abstract describes a study conducted to estimate the prevalence of children with disabilities served by public social service agencies, to identify family characteristic differences between groups of maltreated and nonmaltreated children with disabilities and groups of maltreated and nonmaltreated children without disabilities, and to examine the nature of services provided to maltreated children with and without disabilities. This study examined 308 maltreated children with disabilities, 301 nonmaltreated children with disabilities, 295 maltreated children without disabilities, and 319 nonmaltreated children without disabilities who were randomly selected from children receiving public social services in 1977. The data from this study were analyzed in the following ways: bivariate correlation analysis, two-way analysis of variance, discriminant analysis of variance, and discriminant analysis. The findings of this study reveal the following: a higher prevalence of children with disabilities among maltreated children (23%) than among all children served by public social service agencies (16%); maltreated children with disabilities had more caregivers with substance abuse and emotional problems and had a greater likelihood of not being under parental custody; these children were more likely to be in out-of-home placements; except for the provision of protective services, there was little difference in the services provided to maltreated children, with and without disabilities, and nonmaltreated children; there was a notable lack of child-oriented services to maltreated children with and without disabilities, such as counseling or mental health services; and maltreated children with and without disabilities may be subject to professional neglect. The author believes that the relative lack of child-oriented services for maltreated children must be addressed by service planners. Also, the author suggests that the large proportion of maltreated children with disabilities in long-term placement points out a need for services designed to facilitate a child's return to the natural family or for arrangements for permanent placement through adoption.

46. Andrew, A. K. (1989). Meeting the needs of young deaf-blind children and their parents: I. *Child Care, Health and Development, 15*(3), 195–206.

In this article, the author describes the special considerations required in order to manage, diagnose, and assess children who are deaf and blind. These considerations include: the frequency and causes of deaf-blindness, special problems of the child who is deaf and blind (e.g., poor mother–child bonding, parental overprotection), and learning difficulties (e.g., acquisition of language). This article suggests that early accurate diagnosis of the child who is deaf and blind is essential so that appropriate aids and treatment are made available at the earliest opportunity to enable optimal use of residual vision and hearing. It points out that problems assessing the child who is deaf and blind result from a lack of data on the patterns of development and on the norms of the people who are deaf and blind. The author concludes that caution is required in selecting instruments for assessment and in using assessments as predictors of development or indicators of IQ for people who are deaf and blind.

47. Andrews, A. B., & Veronen, L. J. (1993). Sexual assault and people with disabilities [Special issue: Sexuality and disabilities: A guide for human service practitioners]. *Journal of Social Work and Human Sexuality, 8*(2), 137–159.

This article provides a general review of why people with disabilities experience greater risk for sexual victimization. It concludes that increased risk is an unfortunate but well-documented reality for this group but that risk-reduction programs can help. It also discusses the need for accommodation of people with disabilities in treatment programs.

48. Annas, G. J., & Glantz, L. H. (1986). Rules for research in nursing homes. *New England Journal of Medicine, 315*(18), 1157–1158.

The authors of this article feel that the rights and welfare of nursing home patients, particularly those who have mental impairments, need to be protected when conducting research with this population. They discuss the issue of informed consent or consent by proxy, especially in cases of incompetence or future incompetence resulting from degenerative diseases such as AIDS or Alzheimer's disease. The authors suggest that patients who are mentally impaired should be used only if it is not possible to use patients who are mentally competent.

49. Anonymous. (1993). Sexual abuse of a disabled woman. *Tok Blong Pasifik, 45,* **19.**
This article is a personal account of the sexual abuse of a woman from the Pacific Islands with physical disabilities who was chronically sexually assaulted and abused by her brother-in-law. She was unable to tell others about her abuse because she was afraid of being blamed and because she had no other place to live than her sister's house. The abuse was disclosed, however, when she became pregnant. Then, as she predicted, she was blamed and punished for allowing the abuse to occur. Three days after her baby girl was born, the infant was taken from her, and she has never seen it again because she was considered an unfit mother due to her disability. Her life improved greatly when she left the hospital and went to live with other women with disabilities in a safe house. There, she has made friends, has improved her education, and feels that she has begun a new life.

50. Anthony, E. J. (1986). Terrorizing attacks on children by psychotic parents. *Journal of the American Academy of Child Psychiatry, 25*(3), 326–335.
This article discusses a study conducted to examine the long-term individual developmental effects of terrorizing psychotic attacks on children by their parents. This study conducted baseline assessments of all members of the family before the attacks, tabulated the immediate reactions to these attacks, and preformed follow-ups at 5, 10, and 15 years. The findings of this study are examined with regard to the degree of resilience exhibited by the children subjected to these attacks. The families were selected for the study if one of the parents suffered from schizophrenia or manic depression. In total, 12 children were involved in the study. Also, this article presents two case examples: One case highlights paranoid terrorism, the other case examines manic terrorism.

51. Anti-Slavery Society for the Protection of Human Rights. (1985). Sexual exploitation of children. 10th Session of the United Nations Economic and Social Council, Commission on Human Rights (1984, Geneva, Switzerland). *Response to the Victimization of Women and Children, 8*(2), 13–14.
This article discusses the sexual exploitation of children, child prostitution, child pornography, and sex tourism. It concentrates on the situations in Thailand, the Philippines, and Peru and examines how sexual exploitation affects children. This article emphasizes the relation between poverty and exploitation and between sexual attitudes and cultural practices. This article concludes that poverty may be a factor that links abuse and disability in many parts of the world.

52. Antonak, R. F., Fielder, C. R., & Mulick, J. A. (1993). A scale of attitudes toward the application of eugenics to the treatment of people with mental retardation. *Journal of Intellectual Disability Research, 37,* 75–83.
This article describes the 32-item Scale of Attitudes Toward Mental Retardation and Eugenics (AMRE). It discusses data collection, analysis, and application of this assessment tool. Also, this article defines eugenics as the science of improved genetic breeding of healthy human offspring.

53. Anzia, D. J., & la Puma, J. (1991). An annotated bibliography of psychiatric medical ethics. *Academic Psychiatry, 15*(1), 1–17.
This bibliography consists of 102 annotations from journals published between 1981 and 1990. The bibliography deals with the empirical and conceptual analysis of ethical problems encountered in psychiatry, and it is categorized according to four main headings: the psychiatrist as professional, the psychiatrist and patient, the psychiatrist's practice, and the psychiatrist and society. This bibliography also includes notes on medical ethics.

54. Appathurai, C., Lowery, G., & Sullivan, T. (1986). Achieving the vision of deinstitutionalization: A role for foster care. *Child and Adolescent Social Work, 3*(1), 50–67.
This article discusses deinstitutionalization and the move toward specialized foster care for children and adolescents with developmental disabilities. It examines the successful recruitment of foster families and placement stability. The authors conclude that empirically based program planning and development are necessary in order to ensure the success of specialized foster care for children with developmental disabilities.

55. Appelbaum, A. S. (1980). Developmental retardation in infants as a concomitant of physical child abuse. In G. J. Williams & J. Money (Eds.), *Traumatic abuse and neglect of children at home* (pp. 304–310). Baltimore: John Hopkins University Press.
This chapter describes a study that compared 30 abused children with 30 nonabused children in order to determine the effects of child abuse on developmental retardation. The average age of the children was 14.66 months. This study used the Bayley Scales of Infant Development and the Revised Denver Developmental Screening Test; the results indicate that both cognitive and gross motor development were delayed for the abused group.

56. Armstrong, H. (1993, March). Building bridges: Training for response to child abuse. *National Association for the Pro-*

tection from Sexual Abuse of Adults and Children with Learning Disabilities, 3, 10–13.
This article discusses a 3-day training program for responding to child abuse of children with disabilities. It describes the Hackney Youth Project from the Huddleston Centre in Hackney, East London, provided for staff members. The program deals with the following issues: power in abuse, responding to abuse, communication between staff and patrons, communication between other professionals and agencies, self-mutilation, safety concerns regarding patrons, and supervision. The Huddleston Centre also supports a variety of other services: for example, a play group; a family support group; and an employment liaison with the Hackney Youth Project, which organizes activities for children and youths with severe and multiple disabilities.

57. **Armstrong, J. G., & Roth, D. M. (1989). Attachment and separation difficulties in eating disorders: A preliminary investigation.** *International Journal of Eating Disorders, 8*(2), 141–155.
This article discusses a study that used the Separation Anxiety Test (SAT) to examine the implications of Bowlby's attachment theory and eating disorders. This study hypothesized that patients with eating disorders would exhibit anxious attachment and separation-based depression on the SAT. Twenty-seven people were tested in this study: 11 of them had anorexia nervosa, 12 suffered from bulimia nervosa, and 4 had atypical eating disorders. The average age of the participants was 20 (range 17–43), and the mean duration of eating disorder was 5.8 years. These data were compared to two groups in order to examine the relationship between separation distress and internal aspects of separation and attachment. The first group, a mature identity group, consisted of 89 females between the ages of 18 and 25 who had similar social/economic levels and marital status. The second group, a mature intimacy group, consisted of 60 male New Zealand University students between 18 and 19 years of age. The results of this study indicate that there was no significant difference between the way anorexic or bulimic students responded to the test. The results also support the hypothesis that the anxious attachment of the eating disorder sample differs significantly in frequency and intensity from the comparison groups.

58. **Asch, A., & Fine, M. (1988). Introduction: Beyond pedestals. In M. Fine & A. Asch (Eds.),** *Women with disabilities: Essays in psychology, culture, and politics* **(pp. 1–37). Philadelphia: Temple University Press.**
This introduction to *Women with Disabilities: Essays in Psychology, Culture, and Politics* raises a number of issues that confront women with disabilities. It also provides information on the methodological perspective (primarily qualitative) that characterizes the chapters in this book. It discusses issues of sexuality: involuntary sterilization, parenthood, sexual violence, and sexual

isolation. It also examines the physical abuse of girls and the battering of women with disabilities. This introduction suggests that the enforced dependency of women with disabilities makes reporting difficult and may force some to choose to stay in abusive situations rather than face even more devastating alternatives. It points out that caregivers are often the abusers, and although abuse occurs frequently in institutional settings, abuse is also frequent in community settings.

59. **Asen, K., George, E., Piper, R., & Stevens, A. (1989). A systems approach to child abuse: Management and treatment issues.** *Child Abuse & Neglect, 13*, 45–57.
This article discusses a family systems approach for managing and treating child abuse. It describes the numerous systems and subsystems that need to be addressed when using a family systems model: the family–professional system, the family within the extended family/friendship system, and the nuclear family. It describes the Marlborough Family Service treatment program, which uses a multifamily group approach. The authors conclude that the systemic model, which uses observable patterns of interaction within families and professional networks, is useful for the treatment and prevention of child abuse.

60. **Ashman, A. F. (1990). Sterilization and training for normal sexual development: Human rights and obligations.** *Australia and New Zealand Journal of Developmental Disabilities, 16*(3), 359–368.
This article examines the issues of human sexuality and sterilization of people with intellectual disabilities in an attempt to address the general neglect of these subjects in the literature and in service delivery. The author points out that the importance of such scrutiny is clear given the recent Family Court decisions to approve the sterilization of five young women with severe intellectual disabilities. The author discusses critical issues regarding informed consent and the "best interests" of the individual concerned in relation to the community's obligation to provide appropriate education and training for children and adult caregivers in order to enable them to deal effectively with issues of human sexuality. The author contends that failure to provide these resources in order to ensure the protection of an individual's rights leads to the trauma of sterilization, which is discussed in terms of implicit genetic engineering. The author questions the ethical and legal decision-making processes currently employed and favors the recognition of our social responsibility to ensure the effective protection of the human rights of those who are not able to make their voices heard.

61. **Association for Residential Care, National Association for the Protection from Sexual Abuse of Adults and Children with Learning Disabilities. (1993).** *It could never happen here! The prevention* *and treatment of sexual abuse of adults with learning disabilities in residential settings.* **Chesterfield and Nottingham, England: Authors.**

This book presents guidelines for residential services for sexual abuse prevention, detection, reporting, investigation, and treatment. The guidelines are based substantially on a 2-day workshop held early in 1993, when about 30 participants identified basic content. Following the workshop, an editorial committee of four developed a draft that was circulated to workshop participants and other knowledgeable individuals for refinement. This book includes an introduction to the topic, a discussion of legal issues, guidelines for interagency cooperation, risk-reduction strategies, staff hiring and training principles, guidelines for administrative responsibilities, standards for support of victims and others who may be adversely affected, and much more.

62. Augoustinos, M. (1987). Developmental effects of child abuse: Recent findings. *Child Abuse & Neglect, 11,* **15–27.**

This literature review focuses on the developmental effects of child abuse. It examines recent studies and summarizes pre-1982 study findings. It highlights mediating variables in childhood development and distinguishes the consequences of diverse forms of child maltreatment. This literature review notes that there is a consensus on the adverse effects of child abuse, but it concludes that the interrelationship between abuse and future dysfunctional manifestations is diverse and complex.

63. Augusto, C. R., & McGraw, J. M. (1990). Humanizing blindness through public education. *Journal of Visual Impairment and Blindness, 84,* **397–400.**

The authors of this article suggest that society's perception of people with visual impairments is founded on brief social contacts with them and by the media's portrayal of people with visual impairments. Given this limited exposure, they claim that biased and sometimes inaccurate perceptions are formed about people with visual impairments. The authors conclude that a more accurate perception of people with visual impairments would be obtained by accessing special interest and consumer groups working with people with visual impairments, perusing literature in this area, and working with related professionals in the field.

64. Averill, S. C., Beale, D., Benfer, B., Collins, D. T., Kennedy, L., Myers, J., Pope, D., Rosen, I., & Zoble, E. (1989). Preventing staff-patient sexual relationships. *Bulletin of the Menninger Clinic, 53*(5), **384–393.**

This article summarizes the report of a study group that investigated reports of staff-patient sexual contact in a hospital setting. The authors found many instances of inappropriate sexual contact, but they felt that the ambiguity of the rules contributed to the problem. They conclude that there is a great need for staff training about acceptable and unacceptable interactions, and they feel that training would significantly reduce the incidence of inappropriate contact. The authors also feel that training would make violations clearer and make the response to violations easier.

65. Ayers, J. W. T., Moinipanah, R., Bennett, C. J., Randolph, J. F., & Peterson, E. P. (1988). Successful combination therapy with electroejaculation and in vitro fertilization–embryo transfer in the treatment of a paraplegic male with severe oligoasthenospermia. *Fertility and Sterility, 49*(6), **1089–1090.**

This article provides some details about electroejaculation and in vitro fertilization–embryo transfer involving a male with a spinal cord injury and severe oligoasthenospermia (infertility). This article uses technical and medical terminology.

66. Azar, S. T., Barnes, K. T., & Twentyman, C. T. (1988). Developmental outcomes in physically abused children: Consequences of parental abuse or the effects of a more general breakdown in caregiving behaviors? *The Behavior Therapist, 11*(2), **27–32.**

This article reviews the developmental consequences of physical child abuse, especially cognitive and behavioral impairment. The authors suggest that a broader perspective is needed when addressing the impact of physical child abuse. According to the authors, it is necessary to look at the abusive family environment and parental practices of childrearing rather than only focusing on the impact of physical abuse on the child. The authors examine the characteristics, assessment, and treatment approaches for the abused child and offer suggestions for future research.

•B•

67. Bach, J. R., & Campagnolo, D. I. (1992, October). Psychosocial adjustment of post-poliomyelitis ventilator assisted individuals. *Archives of Physical Medicine and Rehabilitation, 73,* **934–939.**

This article discusses a study that was conducted to determine the quality of life for individuals with severe disabilities with tracheostomies who require post-poliomyelitis ventilator assistance. Three hundred eighty people with disabilities and 273 health care professionals (controls) responded to a questionnaire survey. The survey consisted of the Campbell's Scale of Life Domain Satisfaction Measures and Semantic Differential Scale of General Affect. The social and vocational impact of ventilator assistance for those who required it was also assessed. The results of this study indicate that 14.7% of ventilator-assisted respondents and 8.5% of controls expressed dissatisfaction with their lives. It found that controls significantly underestimated the responses of ventilator users with regard to life satisfaction and significantly overestimated their hardships. The study notes that 42% of the ventilator users were gainfully employed.

68. Bach, J. R., Campagnolo, D. I., & Hoeman, S. (1991). Life satisfaction of individuals with Duchenne muscular dystrophy using long-term mechanical ventilatory support. *American Journal of Physical Medicine & Rehabilitation, 70*(3), 129–135.

This article discusses a study that assessed the quality of life of 83 ventilator-assisted people with Duchenne muscular dystrophy (DMD) and a control group consisting of 273 health care professionals. This study used a mail-out survey that consisted of three assessment tools, including the Campbell's Life Domain Satisfaction Measures and Semantic Differential Scale of General Affect. It also used an assessment instrument that looked at the degree of desirability of mechanical ventilation. The results of this study indicate that 12.5% of the DMD group and 9% of the controls expressed dissatisfaction with their lives. The study discovered a discrepancy between the control group's perceived dissatisfaction of quality of life for the DMD group and the DMD group's actual response. It also appears that the controls overestimated the perceived hardships for the DMD group.

69. Baer, D. M. (1990). Good rules, bad rules, the rulers, and the ruled. *Mental Retardation, 28*(2), 101–103.

This article describes a symposium on the nature of rules in facilities that care for people with developmental disabilities. The author claims that rules are powerful because they attempt to ensure a particular outcome. As a result, rules can possess both strengths and weaknesses in their application and can be problematic and ineffective in excess. This article suggests guidelines for what constitute acceptable and unacceptable rules for facilities that serve people with developmental disabilities.

70. Bajt, T. R., & Pope, K. S. (1989). Therapist-patient sexual intimacy involving children and adolescents [Special issue: Children and their development: Knowledge base, research agenda, and social policy application]. *American Psychologist, 44*(2), 455.

This article discusses the results of a survey of 90 psychologists, 22 of whom reported having been sexually intimate with clients 3 to 17 years of age.

71. Baladerian, N. J. (1976, January, 29). *How to approach sexuality.* **Paper pre-** sented at the Southern California Regional American Association on Mental Deficiency Conference, Newport Beach, CA.

This paper discusses a number of key issues in human sexuality education and highlights the need to overcome our inhibitive socialization in order to communicate effectively about sexuality with individuals who have disabilities. It suggests that coming to terms with one's own sexuality is essential for open and honest communication; being "askable" is advocated as a preferred alternative to the conspiracy of silence often associated with human sexuality. A number of human rights regarding sexuality are outlined as they apply to all people; the author believes that it is necessary to perceive and treat all human beings with respect. Specific considerations for teaching individuals with disabilities about physical, social, and moral aspects of sexuality are provided, as are a number of basic issues to be considered in any education effort. The roles of parents in particular and the community in general are discussed in terms of raising awareness and developing effective methods for facilitating relevant sexuality education. The importance of the development of personal responsibility through informed decision making and dealing with consequences is emphasized and discussed in relation to issues of parenthood by people with disabilities. In conclusion, the author stresses the importance of creating an atmosphere conducive to ongoing communication and learning in what is a lifetime education process for everyone.

72. Baladerian, N. J. (1983). *Sexuality information/comprehension evaluation.* Culver City, CA: Author.

This book uses a case study format to evaluate the comprehension abilities of Susan, a woman with intellectual disabilities. Susan's lover was accused of rape by the residence staff, and this book discusses her ability to consent to sexual activity. It questions the misconceptions related to the sexual maturity of people with disabilities and argues that their overprotected lifestyle may lead to a lack of expression of sexuality as an adult.

73. Baladerian, N. J. (1985). *Response to: "Prosecuting cases of physical and sexual assault of the mentally retarded" issued by the California District Attorney's Association.* Culver City, CA: Author.

The author of this paper criticizes several aspects of S. Aguilar's "Prosecuting cases of physical and sexual assault of the mentally retarded" ([1984]. In *Prosecutor's notebook—Volume III*. Sacramento: California District Attorneys Association): for example, Aguilar's choice of language, how the author measures the abilities of people with developmental disabilities to comprehend sexual relationships, and the standard by which he determines their competency. Baladerian notes the importance of the psychologist's skills and experience in assessing sexuality and developmental disabilities.

74. Baladerian, N. J. (1987). How to address sexual victimization of the mentally retarded. *Sexuality Today, 10,* 25.

This article is written for health care providers and focuses on the significance of asking people with developmental disabilities if they have been sexually victimized. This article discusses the importance of education for people with developmental disabilities that helps them differentiate good (nonabusive) and bad (abusive) touches. This article emphasizes the necessity of questioning because of underreporting of sexual abuse cases.

75. Baladerian, N. J. (1990). *Sexual and physical abuse of developmentally disabled people.* **Culver City, CA: Mental Health Consultants.**

This report provides important basic information about abuse of children and adults with disabilities. It includes information about increased risk, prevention, and treatment services.

76. Baladerian, N. J. (1991). Sexual abuse of people with developmental disabilities. *Sexuality and Disability, 9*(4), 323–335.

This article summarizes some statistical information on people with developmental disabilities, includes definitions of different types of abuse, and examines the relation between abuse and disabilities. This article discusses identifying perpetrators and the incidence and prevalence of physical and sexual abuse of people with disabilities, and it emphasizes the strong need for prevention and treatment programs.

77. Baladerian, N. J. (1992). *Interviewing skills to use with abuse victims who have developmental disabilities.* **Washington, DC: National Aging Resource Center on Elder Abuse.**

This report discusses interviewing skills that can be used when interviewing people with developmental disabilities who have been abused. It examines the myths and stereotypes surrounding disability and defines developmental disability. It concentrates on specific strategies and approaches that deal with communication and signs of abuse. This report discusses preinterview and postinterview suggestions for the preparation of the interviewer's conduct.

78. Baladerian, N. J. (1992). RAPPORT model aids victims with developmental disabilities. *NRCCSA (National Resource Center on Child Sexual Abuse) News, 1*(4), 8–9.

This article presents a treatment model for people with developmental disabilities who have been abused, the RAPPORT model. It points out that treatment for this group is essentially the same as treatment for other abuse victims. It describes and addresses the seven aspects of the model: **R**eferral, **A**ttitude, **P**rovider qualifications, Pretreatment considerations, One-on-one treatment, **R**esources, and **T**ermination.

79. Baladerian, N. J. (no date). *Abuse causes disability: A report from Spectrum Institute.* **Culver City, CA: Spectrum Institute.**

This paper examines the legislation concerning abuse and disability in 13 states. It suggests factors that the author feels should be included in future legislation. It includes a literature review dealing with violence-induced disability and disability caused by neglect. The findings from this literature review are summarized in a table according to their related topics and discussed in relation to the fiscal impact of people with disabilities on society and its resources. The author feels that the next important step for government agencies in the areas of child protection and disability is the creation of a national program on abuse prevention.

80. Baladerian, N. J., & Waxman, B. F. (1985). *Rape treatment recommendations for disabled people.* **Culver, CA: Authors.**

This book examines several factors associated with the rape treatment of people with disabilities: the risk factors, perceptions of people with disabilities about service providers, and terminology. It examines the following procedural issues: medical examination, legal problems, and access to community services for all groups of disabilities. This book also discusses myths about sexual assault and people with disabilities.

81. Baldwin, J. A., & Oliver, J. E. (1975). Epidemiology and family characteristics of severely abused children. *British Journal of Preventive and Social Medicine, 29,* 205–221.

This article describes a study that examined severe child abuse, which was defined in the following ways: assault resulting in death, skull or facial fractures, injury to the brain resulting in cognitive impairment, two or more instances of mutilation requiring medical services, three or more instances of fractures or bruising requiring medical services, and multiple fractures or internal injuries. This study collected retrospective (from 1965 to 1971) and prospective data (from January 1972 to June 1973) from reported cases of abuse that met the study's definition of severe child abuse in Northeast Wiltshire, United Kingdom. This study identified 38 retrospective cases (16 girls, 22 boys) and 22 prospective cases (14 girls, 8 boys) of severe child abuse. The majority of these abused children were under 1 year of age. The children in the retrospective study suffered a total of 225 separate incidents of abuse that resulted in one or more injuries. The incidence of severe abuse for children less than 4 years of age was calculated at 1 child per 1,000. The death rate for this group was 0.1 per 1,000 children. This study obtained detailed family information for the participants of the retrospective study, and this information revealed the following: These families were large in size; young; had unstable employment, residence, and household situations; and the parents were noted for their high frequency of psychiatric, medical, and social pathologies.

82. Baldwin, L. C. (1990). Child abuse as an antecedent of multiple personality disorder. *American Journal of Occupational Therapy, 44*(11), 978–983.
This article addresses the need for occupational therapists to recognize and become more proficient in the treatment of childhood multiple personality disorders (MPD). It presents a short review of the literature as well as the symptoms, characteristics, etiology, and family dynamics of individuals with multiple personality disorder. This article discusses the differences between childhood and adult MPD, credibility problems with children, and failure to diagnose MPD as well as the treatment and recognition of this disorder in the clinical setting.

83. Bamford, J. (1992). Response to "Cautions and considerations for providing sex education for people with developmental disabilities who live within group homes." *Journal of Developmental Disabilities, 1*(1), 48–50.
Bamford responds to Hingsburger's article ([1992]. *Journal of Developmental Disabilities, 1*[1], 42–47) concerning the provision of sex education for people with developmental disabilities who are living in residential care. Bamford's positive experiences with a community agency in Toronto are discussed in order to demonstrate what can be achieved through the development of in-agency expertise in implementing appropriate and effective sexuality education programs. The advantages of such an "in-home" approach, as distinct from the provision of programs by an "outside expert," are examined in terms of equipping staff to better meet the specific needs of their clients.

84. Baradon, T. (1991). Some thoughts on eccentricity and victimization: A report on the treatment of a latency boy [Special issue: Work with children with an illness or disability]. *Journal of Child Psychotherapy, 17*(1), 79–93.
This article provides a case study of an 11-year-old boy who had become a target of bullying after developing very bizarre behavior. This boy's treatment began by attempting to develop a new self-image and went on to teach separation of rational thinking and fantasy.

85. Barahal, R. M., Waterman, J., & Martin, H. P. (1981). The social cognitive development of abused children. *Journal of Consulting and Clinical Psychology, 49*(4), 508–516.
This article addresses the psychological consequences of child abuse by comparing the social cognitive develop-

ment of 17 abused children (12 boys, 5 girls) with 16 controls (12 boys, 4 girls). The abused children in this study were referred by the Department of Social Services in Adams County, Colorado. The controls were chosen from a summer camp enrollment list. All of the children were matched for similar family backgrounds, gender, and ethnicity, and they were between the ages of 6 and 8. The children were assessed for locus of control, social sensitivity, cognitive perspective taking, understanding of social roles, moral judgment, and intelligence. The results of this study indicate the following: controls obtained significantly higher scores in intelligence, abused children assumed less personal responsibility for negative outcomes than controls, and the abused children had less comprehension of complex social roles than controls.

86. Barbaree, H. E., & Marshall, W. L. (1988). *Treatment of the adult male child molester: Methodological issues in evaluating treatment outcome.* Ottawa, ON: Family Violence Prevention Division, National Clearinghouse on Family Violence. (National Health Research and Development Programs, Health and Welfare Canada, Project No. 6606-3638)
This report reviews outcome studies in order to determine the efficacy of the treatment of adult male child molesters. It provides a comprehensive description of cognitive-behavioral treatments for child molesters and examines research methodology issues that pertain to evaluating outcome studies. Using the outcome data from several treatment programs, this report suggests that the rate of reoffense may be reduced by 60% among child molesters who receive treatment.

87. Barmann, B. C., & Murray, W. J. (1981). Suppression of inappropriate sexual behavior by facial screening. *Behavior Therapy, 12*, 730–735.
This article describes a treatment program that was designed to help reduce the public genital stimulation of a 14-year-old boy with severe mental retardation. This treatment involved facial screening and the placement of a terrycloth bib on the face. This intervention was administered at school, on the school bus, and at home by teachers and parents using baseline periods of 5, 9, and 15 days, respectively. Three 30-minute sessions per day were used while the child was in school and at home. Two 30-minute sessions were used while the child was on the bus. The results of this treatment indicate that the inappropriate sexual behavior was suppressed at school (98%), on the bus (88%), and at home (92%) in comparison to pretreatment baseline conditions. Post-intervention measures performed after 6 months indicated little regression.

88. Barron, D. (Assisted by E. Banks). (1981). *A price to be born. Twenty years in a mental institution.* Leeds, England: Leeds University Printing.

This monograph provides a firsthand account of life in a mental institution. The story describes exploitation and significant physical abuse. The most devastating element, however, appears to be the total disempowerment and dehumanization of residents.

89. Barry, G. (1994). How the police help. In S. Hollins (Ed.), *Proceedings: It did happen here: Sexual abuse and learning disability: Recognition and action* (pp. 43–46). London: St. George's Hospital Medical School, Division of the Psychiatry of Disability.

This chapter provides an English police perspective on sexual abuse of people with mental retardation. The author, Detective Inspector Greg Barry of the Kent County Constabulary, is one of the few police officers with specific expertise regarding vulnerable victims. He cites figures for sex crime in 1992 in Kent. Of the 1,070 sexual offenses, 104 (9.7%) involved victims with mental retardation. Of those, 70 were children, and 34 were adults.

90. Barry, R. (1992). The paradoxes of "rational death." *Society, 29*(5), 25–28.

This article presents arguments against assisted suicide. In discussing the social consequences of permitting assisted suicide, Barry points out that people with few real options are often those who choose suicide. In this model, the individual who is killed is seen as consenting to his or her killing rather than the individual who carries out the killing being seen as an assistant to a suicide.

91. Bass, M., Kravath, R. E., & Glass, L. (1986). Death-scene investigation in sudden infant death. *New England Journal of Medicine, 315*(2), 100–105.

This article describes the investigation of 26 diagnosed sudden infant death syndrome (SIDS) cases that occurred between October 1983 and January 1985. All of the cases involved infants age 1 year or less, and all of the infants were brought to the Kings County Hospital Center emergency room. The death-scene investigations, which involved the evaluation of the residence, temperature readings in the room where the infant slept, and interviews with the family, supported an alternative diagnosis to SIDS. The most common diagnoses were asphyxiation by household objects, smothering by overlying, hyperthermia, and Shaking Baby Syndrome.

92. Bates, W. J., Smeltzer, D. J., & Arnoczky, S. M. (1986). Appropriate and inappropriate use of psychotherapeutic medications for institutionalized mentally retarded persons. *American Journal of Mental Deficiency, 90*(4), 363–370.

This article examines the appropriate and inappropriate use of psychotherapeutic medications for institutionalized persons with mental retardation. The authors claim that evaluations of psychiatric treatment in institutions must be based not only on the numbers and types of drugs prescribed, but also on diagnoses and other characteristics of the patients. They cross-tabulated psychotherapeutic medication regimens against diagnoses for 242 institutionalized adolescents and adults with mental retardation selected for psychiatric treatment. The drugs had generally been prescribed by nonpsychiatrists but diagnoses were determined by consensus of evaluation teams that included fully trained psychiatrists. According to widely accepted standards for psychopharmacologic treatment, 45.4% to 60.9% of the regimens were rated as appropriate, and 39.1% to 54.6% were rated as inappropriate for the diagnosed conditions.

93. Battin, M. P. (1991). Euthanasia: The way we do it, the way they do it [Special issue: Medical ethics: Physician-assisted suicide and euthanasia]. *Journal of Pain and Symptom Management, 6*(5), 298–305.

This article discusses how assisted suicide is treated in Germany, Holland, and the United States. According to this article, assisted suicide occurs in each of these three countries in different forms. Only the United States makes a strong distinction between active and passive euthanasia. This article discusses concerns and objections in relation to the practices of all three countries, and it explores cultural differences in regard to attitudes toward assisted suicide.

94. Baudouin, J. L. (1990). Biomedical experimentation on the mentally handicapped: Ethical and legal dilemmas. *Medicine and Law, 9,* 1052–1061.

This article discusses the ethical and legal concerns regarding biomedical experimentation on people with mental disabilities. The main issues concern the client's inability to give an informed consent and international attitudes toward biomedical experimentation on people with mental disabilities.

95. Baum, D., & Wells, C. (1985, Summer). Promoting handicap awareness in preschool children. *Teaching Exceptional Children, 17,* 282–287.

This article discusses the promotion of disability awareness for preschool children. It suggests activities that could be incorporated and integrated during the established school curricula: story time, art, science, dramatic play, language, and snack time.

96. Baumeister, A. A., & Sevin, J. A. (1990). Pharmacologic control of aberrant behaviour in the mentally retarded: Toward a more rational approach. *Neuroscience and Biobehavioural Reviews, 14*(3), 253–262.

The authors of this article advocate a rational approach to the pharmacologic control of aberrant behavior of people with mental retardation. They note that drugs are frequently used to control the aberrant behavior of people with mental retardation; however, despite decades of research, this approach to behavioral management has had very limited success. They feel that the slow progress in this area can be attributed, in part, to the lack of a theoretical framework to guide research. They suggest that clinical research in this area should be integrated with evidence concerning the neurochemical mechanisms that mediate aberrant behaviors. The authors conclude that a theoretical framework that takes into account the biological mechanisms that underlie disordered behavior and the actions of drugs provides the basis for a more rational approach to the development of pharmacologic therapies for people with mental retardation.

97. Baumhardt, L. A., & Lawrence, S. (1983). Transforming negatively labeled student groups into support groups. *Social Work in Education, 5*(4), 229–240.
The authors of this article point out that students who are classified as educably mentally disabled are often thought to be ineligible for participation in the group process. This article provides a description of a school group psychotherapy program that improved self-esteem, competence, and mutual support in a class of adolescents with mental retardation. The process required to develop the group included the following: a thorough understanding of the group's composition, the development of operational goals, careful planning, the use of metaphor, the presence of two cotherapists, and considerable patience.

98. Bavolek, S. J. (1989). Assessing and treating high-risk parenting attitudes. In J. T. Pardeck (Ed.), *Child abuse and neglect: Theory, research, and practice* (pp. 97–110). New York: Gordon and Breach Science Publishers.
This chapter examines the assessment and treatment of high-risk parenting attitudes of parent and preparent populations. It describes high-risk parenting attitudes as those that might lead to abusive or neglectful parenting. This chapter provides four constructs thought to represent abusive and neglectful parenting practices: inappropriate parental expectations of the child, lack of empathy toward the child's needs, parental value of physical punishment, and parent-child role reversal. This chapter describes the Adult-Adolescent Parent Inventory (AAPI), a psychometric tool that assesses current parenting attitudes, and discusses studies using this tool.

99. Baxter, C. (1989). Investigating stigma as stress in social interactions of parents. *Journal of Mental Deficiency Research, 33*, 455–466.
This article describes a study that examined stigma as a stress factor in the social interactions of parents who have children with mental impairments. This study investigated two stress-induced and stigmatizing variables: the child's characteristics that are the result of mental retardation and the attitudes of other people. This study used a 5-point Likert-type scale to determine the stress

associated with social attitudes for 130 parents of children with mental retardation. The parents in this study were divided into three cohorts based on the age of their child: ages 3 to 5, 10 to 12, and 17 to 19. This study found that parental stress was most commonly associated with the child's speech and behavior management and how noticeable it was to others. It found that parents felt stress due to certain reactions of others: for example, staring, discomfort, inappropriately ignoring, and drawing attention to the child. This article suggests that stigma as a stress inducer is a promising area for future research.

100. Beating ruling sparks anger. (1992, June 19). *The Calgary Herald*, p. C17.
This newspaper article reports the outrage at the lenient sentences of two teenagers involved in the beating of Paul Devereaux, an Edmontonian with mental disabilities, voiced by advocates for people with disabilities. The two teens were given probation and community service for their part in the beating, which eventually resulted in the death of Mr. Devereaux.

101. Beaton, J. (1993). Sexuality. *Bridges, 2*(1), 16–17.
This article addresses the need for AIDS awareness education for people with developmental disabilities. The author examines some of the barriers that confront rehabilitation agencies when they try to provide sex education, which include both parent and staff attitudes.

102. Beck, M., & Miller, S. (1992, October 19). The flames of a crusader: The gadfly of nursing homes vows to fight on. *Newsweek*, p. 58.
This magazine article reports that a fire at the home of Sue and Jack Harang has motivated the FBI and federal prosecutors in Boston to launch an investigation of New Medico Healthcare System. The Harangs are advocates for nursing home patients and their families. Sue investigates abuse or neglect in nursing homes, while Jack represents clients as a personal injury lawyer. They have helped file lawsuits against Beverly Enterprises, the largest nursing home chain in the United States, and are currently looking into New Medico for neglect of a patient. The fire damaged case records, court documents, and computer files. New Medico is based in Massachusetts and specializes in neurologic rehabilitation.

103. Belkin, L. (1991, January 3). Retarded woman at center of furor has baby. *The New York Times*, p. A13.
This newspaper article discusses the case of Debra Lynn Thomas, a 33-year-old woman with severe mental retardation who is a resident at the Lubbock State School for the Mentally Retarded in Houston. Her pregnancy and the subsequent birth of a son has prompted an investigation into who fathered the child. Possible suspects are the immediate family, with whom this woman resides on weekends, or employees of the school. It states that the possible subjects have had DNA testing. The investigation

allows for the perusal of school records, which seem to indicate that 29 prior cases of alleged abuse have occurred involving residents of the school. In addition, this article notes that five cases of pregnancy involving school residents have been reported, with one resident giving birth on two occasions.

104. Belkin, L. (1991, January 18). Texas woman's kin is accused in rape that led to inquiry. *The New York Times*, p. A22.

This newspaper article is a follow-up to the article that described the case involving Debra Lynn Thomas, a 33-year-old resident of the Lubbock State School for the Mentally Retarded in Houston. The investigation trying to determine who fathered her child has resulted in the arrest of her brother-in-law on the charge of rape. The investigation into the rape of Ms. Thomas, who has since given birth to a son, led to the use of DNA testing of family and employees of the school. Using the baby's DNA, a positive match was made with Jim Wooten's DNA. An abortion was authorized for Ms. Thomas, but it was never performed. The quest for authorization for the abortion led to the investigation.

105. Bell, C. C., & Jenkins, E. J. (1993). Community violence and children on Chicago's South Side [Special issue: Children and violence]. *Psychiatry, Interpersonal and Biological Processes, 56*(1), 46–54.

This article reports the results of a study that examined the effects of violence on children in an inner-city community. It also includes an analysis of victimization histories of 84 children who were psychiatric outpatients and 107 children who were medical outpatients. The children who were psychiatric outpatients had suffered more physical and sexual violence.

106. Beloff, J. (1986). Killing or letting die? Is there a valid moral distinction? *Euthanasia Review, 1*(4), 208–212.

This article provides arguments that passive killing is no more ethically acceptable than active killing. "Allowing someone to die" in some cases is as certain and intentional as active killing, but it increases and prolongs suffering while helping the medical profession avoid personal responsibility for committing the act.

107. Benedict, M., White, R. B., Wulff, L. M., & Hall, B. J. (1990). Reported maltreatment in children with multiple disabilities. *Child Abuse & Neglect, 14*, 207–217.

In this article, the authors examine abuse cases among 500 children with multiple disabilities assessed by the Kennedy Institute in Baltimore. They found 53 cases of confirmed abuse. (Editors' note: Although the authors do not mention the following statistic, this rate appears to

be 4.43 times the expected rate.) The authors analyze their data in order to determine if the severity of disability is a predictor of abuse within their sample and find that severity does not predict abuse status.

108. Benedict, M. I., Wulff, L. M., & White, R. B. (1992). Current parental stress in maltreating and nonmaltreating families of children with multiple disabilities. *Child Abuse & Neglect, 16*, 155–163.

This article describes a questionnaire survey that was conducted with abusive and nonabusive families of children with multiple disabilities in order to determine any differences between the two groups concerning parental stress and the perception of burden of care. In this study, 257 parents from 25 abusive and 232 nonabusive families completed the Friedrich Short Form of the Holroyd's Questionnaire on Resources and Stress. This 52-item questionnaire was used to assess stress in four areas: parental and family problems, pessimism about the future, child characteristics, and the child's physical impairments. The ages of the children in this study ranged from 2 to 21, with most of the children less than 10 years of age. The authors note that more than 90% of the surveys were completed by the mother or maternal caregiver. The results of this study indicate that perceived stress levels were similar for both abusive and nonabusive families of children with multiple disabilities.

109. Berenson, A. B., San-Miguel, V. V., & Wilkinson, G. S. (1992). Prevalence of physical and sexual assault in pregnant adolescents. *Journal of Adolescent Health, 13*(6), 466–469.

This article discusses a study that interviewed 342 pregnant teenagers (17 years old or younger) about any history of assault. These interviews reveal the following: 1) 9% of the teenagers had experienced physical assault, 8% sexual assault, and 8% both physical and sexual assault; 2) White non-Latino teenagers were more likely to report sexual abuse or a combination of physical and sexual abuse than African-American or Latino teenagers; 3) Latinos were less likely to report combined abuse compared to other groups; 4) 40% of the physically abused teenagers experienced abuse during pregnancy; 5) the most frequent perpetrator of physical assault was a member of their family (46%) compared to a mate (33%), although during pregnancy, a boyfriend or spouse was the attacker in 80% of cases; and 6) while the face or neck was the most common target, 14% of the teenagers reported being hit in the abdomen, 33% of them being assaulted during pregnancy. This article concludes that a significant proportion of pregnant teenagers have experienced violence and should be screened routinely for a history of abuse.

110. Berenson, A. B., San-Miguel, V. V., & Wilkinson, G. S. (1992). Violence and its relationship to substance use in ado-

lescent pregnancy. *Journal of Adolescent Health, 13*(6), 470–474.
This article discusses a survey of 153 White, 115 African-American, 73 Latino, and 1 Asian pregnant adolescents (17 years old or younger) with a history of physical or sexual assault and substance use. This survey found that substance abuse was reported seven times more often for teenagers with a history of combined physical and sexual assault, five times more frequently by those who had been sexually assaulted, and three times more often for those who had been physically assaulted than teenagers without a history of assault. Although the relationship between violence and substance abuse was different among ethnic groups, violence appeared to be associated with substance use in all ethnic groups. Among Latinos, there appeared to be an association between physical assault and tobacco use; among African Americans, sexual and combined physical and sexual assault were strongly associated with the use of alcohol. This survey reveals that drug use appears most strongly related to assault by a mate and that tobacco and/or alcohol use appear more often associated with assault by a member of the victim's family.

111. Berger, C. (1986). *Preventing the sexual abuse of individuals with developmental disabilities: A resource guide*. Madison: Wisconsin Council on Developmental Disabilities and Developmental Disabilities Office, Department of Health and Social Services.
These proceedings from two leadership conferences cosponsored by the Wisconsin Council on Developmental Disabilities Team for Preventing the Sexual Abuse of Individuals with Disabilities (a team developed to investigate the sexual abuse of individuals with developmental disabilities) discuss training, technical assistance, and educating the public about prevention. These proceedings also include recommendations developed by the Wisconsin Council on Developmental Disabilities Team for Preventing the Sexual Abuse of Individuals with Disabilities.

112. Berger, D. (1979). Child abuse simulating "near-miss" sudden infant death syndrome. *Journal of Pediatrics, 95*(4), 554–556.
This article presents two case histories of child abuse that involved near-miss sudden infant death syndrome (SIDS). One case history concerns a 5-month-old girl, and the other case history deals with a 6-week-old girl, both of whom were admitted to a hospital with apnoeic and cyanotic episodes. The child in the first case had two siblings who had previously died unexpectedly at the age of 6 weeks and 4.5 months with the diagnosis of SIDS. The mothers in both cases abused their children by using suffocation. Both children are now asymptomatic and in the care of relatives.

113. Berkman, A. (1984–1986). Professional responsibility: Confronting sexual abuse
of people with disabilities. *Sexuality and Disability, 7*(3/4), 89–95.
This article examines the health professional's obligations to clients with disabilities and to colleagues regarding sexual abuse. It notes that most sexual abuse is committed by caregivers, and fear of retribution is a barrier to reporting abuse. This article examines three areas of professional responsibility: clinical, management, and personal. The author claims that prevention of sexual assault is a primary professional obligation, and an outline is offered for developing a systematic approach to deal with the problems of sexual abuse within an institutional setting.

114. Berliner, L. (1984). Some issues for prevention of child sexual assault. *Journal of Preventive Psychiatry, 2*(3/4), 427–431.
This article suggests that the growing body of data surrounding child sexual assault provides important information for the creation of prevention programs. It pays special attention to offender behavior, which slowly grooms a child for abuse. Initially, this behavior may not be overtly sexual, and intervention at this point may be problematic. This article concludes that intervention programs should be direct and honest in descriptions about molestation and that it is important not to place responsibility for preventing abuse on children.

115. Bernheim, K. F. (1990). Promoting family involvement in community residences for chronic mentally ill persons. *Hospital and Community Psychiatry, 41*(6), 668–670.
This article examines promoting a family's involvement in the rehabilitation of family members with chronic mental illness. The East House Corporation in Rochester, New York, provides a mental health program for mentally ill residential care patients. Staff members were trained to help run a family support program that focused on orientation, family consultation, group activities, and ongoing communication between administration, staff, and concerned family members. Training for staff members placed emphasis on promoting empathy toward relatives of residents. This article points out that staff anxiety stemmed mainly from the involvement of the family in the traditional roles of rehabilitation.

116. Berry, J. O., & Jones, W. H. (1991). Situational and dispositional components of reactions toward persons with disabilities. *Journal of Social Psychology, 13*(5), 673–668.
This article reports the results of study of attitudes of people without disabilities toward people with disabilities. The results of this study indicate the following: both dispositional (related to basic attitudes of respondents) factors and situational (related to the degree of intimacy or threat of the situation) factors contributed to the degree of anxiety and reactions of the respondents.

117. **Besharov, D. J. (1987, November/December). Policy guidelines for decision making in child abuse and neglect.** *Children Today,* pp. 7–10.

This article notes that considerable legal progress has been made in the protection of neglected and abused children. It states that these legal changes have resulted in an enormous increase in reported cases of child abuse and neglect. In spite of this increase in reports, child protection services still are inadequate as many professionals fail to report the abuse of children. This article points out that many reports of abuse are unsubstantiated, and there is a definite need for clear guidelines regarding what should or should not be reported. This article provides some guidelines that may be helpful in the decision-making process regarding what constitutes neglect and abuse.

118. **Besharov, D. J. (1987). Reporting out-of-home maltreatment: Penalties and protections.** *Child Welfare, 66*(5), 399–408.

This article points out that amendments to many child abuse laws mandate that real or suspected incidences of child abuse or neglect occurring in out-of-home settings must be reported by staff. This article discusses penalties for failure to report as well as protective measures for staff members who do report.

119. **Beyer, H. A. (1988). Litigation and the use of psychoactive drugs in developmental disabilities. In M. G. Aman & N. N. Singh (Eds.),** *Psychopharmacology of the developmental disabilities* (pp. 29–57). **New York: Springer-Verlag.**

This chapter claims that litigation, particularly in the United States, has resulted in the establishment of a number of legal rights regarding the administration of psychoactive medication to individuals with developmental disabilities. According to this article, during the last 15 years, courts have fashioned rules and standards for regulating psychoactive drug use, particularly in institutional settings. It states that there is general agreement among numerous jurisdictions that high professional standards should be mandated for drug use, but substantial differences remain concerning the circumstances under which such medication may be administered to refusing individuals or to persons incapable of giving an informed, competent consent. The author reviews these legal developments and suggests four general principles for regulating the administration of psychoactive drugs to people with questionable competence.

120. **Bigras, J., Leichner, P., Perreault, M., & Lavoie, R. (1991). Severe paternal sexual abuse in early childhood and systematic aggression against the family and the institution.** *Canadian Journal of Psychiatry, 36*(7), 527–529.

The authors of this article present two case studies written by an attending nurse at a psychiatric hospital. This nurse presents her opinion that a significantly high number of patients identified with a psychiatric disorder have been the victims of incest. This article suggests that these sexually abusive experiences may give rise to aggression and animosity toward the generalized family unit.

121. **Biklen, D. (1988). The myth of clinical judgment.** *Journal of Social Issues, 44*(1), 127–140.

This article presents a powerful position on the relationship between people with disabilities (especially developmental disabilities) and the professional service industry. The author suggests that service professionals legitimize the disempowerment of people with disabilities by emphasizing their need for treatment rather than their human rights. Biklen argues that this is particularly unfortunate since the "treatment" provided for people with disabilities has produced few positive and many negative outcomes for the people it is intended to help. Clinical judgment is discussed as a tool by which professionals force unwanted and intrusive intervention into the lives of people with disabilities.

122. **Biller, H. B., & Solomon, R. S. (1986). Theoretical models of child maltreatment. In H. B. Biller & R. S. Solomon (Eds.),** *Child maltreatment and paternal deprivation: A manifesto for research, prevention and treatment* (pp. 33–49). **Lexington, MA: D. C. Heath and Co.**

This chapter proposes several theoretical models to explain why parents maltreat and abuse children: the psychiatric model, the social systems model, and the transactional model. The psychiatric model views psychopathological behavior as behavior that reflects underlying dysfunctional psychological processes. This model prescribes intensive psychotherapy and/or medication as a treatment for these dysfunctional psychological processes. The social systems model comprises two perspectives, sociocultural and social-situational, both of which deal with the social environment. The sociocultural perspective emphasizes cultural values and mores of appropriate and expected adult-child interaction. The social-situational perspective examines neighborhood characteristics and family structure, in other words, an ecological approach to maltreatment of children by adults. The transactional model or interactionist perspective uses a multivariable approach and explains maltreatment and abuse as the interaction of numerous causal variables. This chapter includes a critique of each model.

123. **Billmire, M. E., & Myers, P. A. (1985). Serious head injury in infants: Accident or abuse?** *Pediatrics, 75*(2), 340–342.

This article describes a reassessment of 84 infants admitted to the hospital for serious head injury using medical records and computed tomography scans. This reassessment reveals that 95% of intracranial injury and 64% of all head injuries, excluding those with skull fractures, were associated with child abuse. The authors conclude that intracranial injury is most often directly related to physical child abuse and not accidental trauma.

124. Bindman, S. (1993, November 5). Most sexually-assaulted kids hide abuse for a year—Study. *The Edmonton Journal*, p. A11.
This newspaper article reports that the findings from the Child Witness Project in London, Ontario, suggest that disclosure by children who have been sexually assaulted is delayed by approximately 1 year. This project found that delayed disclosure is usually seen in cases where the offender is a family member as opposed to a nonfamily member and that girls were more likely to disclose abuse than boys, although they were also more likely to receive hostile or ambivalent reactions from their parents when compared to boys. The project found that disclosure usually occurs after another victim discloses or when the child is questioned after the suspicion of sexual assault.

125. Birenbaum, A. (1992). Courtesy stigma revisited. *Mental Retardation, 30*(5), 265–268.
This article reviews Goffman's concept of courtesy stigma as related to children with mental retardation. Courtesy stigma is a devaluation of family members or others closely associated with a devalued person (e.g., an individual labeled with mental retardation). While some studies support the existence of courtesy stigma, the author suggests that its effects may be variable and depend on the situation: For example, parents may be valued for their commitment to their child but devalued for asking for more services.

126. Bissland, T. (1984). *Death shift: The digoxin murders at "Sick Kids."* Toronto: Methuen.
This book tells the bizarre story of the deaths of about 25 infants at Toronto's Hospital for Sick Children. While strong evidence appears to point toward a particular nurse, she remains on paid leave years after the deaths and has never been charged. This book provides a good account of the difficulties of conducting a police investigation in a hospital setting.

127. Blacher, J., & Bromley, B. (1987). Attachment and responsivity in children with severe handicaps: Mother and teacher comparison. *Child Study Journal, 17*(2), 121–132.
In this article, the authors discuss a study that examined attachment and sensitivity between four children with severe disabilities (ages 28 to 40 months) and their parents and teachers. The purpose of this study was to determine the relative degrees to which these children demonstrated attachment behaviors toward their mothers and teachers and if differences in maternal sensitivity and child responsivity existed between mother-child and teacher-child dyads. An adaptation of the Ainsworth Strange Situation was used separately to measure attachment of the children to their mothers and to their teachers. The following areas were measured using a 5-point sensitivity scale: three areas of adult-child interaction gratification, affect and sensitivity, and responsivity. This article provides a descriptive comparison of each mother-child and teacher-child interaction. The results of this study indicate the following: these children demonstrated a wider range of attachment behaviors in the presence of their mothers than their teachers, no child demonstrated stronger attachment for his or her teacher than for his or her mother, all mothers scored relatively high on maternal sensitivity, and teachers had low sensitivity scores when the child's responsivity scores were low and high when the child's scores were high. The authors provide recommendations for future research.

128. Black, D. (1981). The extended Munchausen syndrome: A family case. *British Journal of Psychiatry, 138*, 466–469.
In this article, the author describes the case history of three siblings who were all victims of Munchausen syndrome by proxy. In this case, the mother had fabricated physical illness in her children and distorted their medical history. Frequent hospital admissions for accidental injury and diverse symptoms were noted for all the children, and Munchausen syndrome by proxy was recognized in the mother.

129. Blatt, E. (1990). Staff supervision and the prevention of institutional child abuse and neglect. *Journal of Child and Youth Care, 4*(6), 73–80.
This article explores the relationship between staff supervision and child abuse in residential or institutional facilities. It outlines the issues related to the prevalence of institutional child abuse: for example, environmental factors, values held by the supervisor, and training and emotional needs of the staff. The author acknowledges the correlation between stressful working conditions and subsequent abuse patterns and suggests methods for arranging the conditions of the residence in order to reduce the causes of or opportunity for child abuse.

130. Blatt, E. R., & Brown, S. W. (1986). Environmental influences on incidents of alleged child abuse and neglect in New York State psychiatric facilities: Toward an etiology of institutional child maltreatment. *Child Abuse and Neglect, 10*(2), 171–180.
The authors of this article investigated child abuse cases in institutions in the state of New York to determine whether environmental stresses on staff precipitated incidents of child abuse in the same way that parental stress can contribute to incidents of familial abuse. A statistical analysis of the results show that sexual abuse constituted 11% of the total number of abuse cases in institutions and only 3% of the total abuse cases outside of institutions.

131. Blistein, S. (1992). Life with the H-team: From narcissism to team spirit: Social group treatment for the dually diagnosed in group homes. *Social Work with Groups, 15*(2/3), 37–51.

The author of this article presents a dramatic account of the process of empowering adults with developmental disabilities in an intermediate care group residence. The author documents the evolution of self-absorbed, dependent, adult "kids" who were challenged through group encounters to develop, in phases, into grown-up, responsible group members at Hull House.

132. Blomberg, P. S. (no date). *The sexually assaulted developmentally delayed person...the victim no one believes...: Fact sheet on informed consent assessment and evaluation procedures for persons with a developmental disability.* Sacramento, CA: Author.

The author of this paper states that the overprotective environments in which people with developmental disabilities live prevent them from being exposed to a variety of learning opportunities. The author suggests that these environments may not allow for the healthy development of decision-making skills. Consequently, before including a person with developmental disabilities in a study, the author states that the comfort level of people with developmental disabilities for making decisions needs to be assessed for the following reasons: voluntary consent, capability of giving consent, and having all the necessary information to make the decision are the elements in a legally valid consent; and a consent requires the full understanding of the nature and consequences of the situation. The author provides interview strategies and suggestions for assessing the validity of informed consent.

133. Blomberg, P. S. (no date). *Vulnerability issues of children with developmental disabilities.* Sacramento, CA: Author.

This paper discusses the vulnerability of children with developmental disabilities to sexual abuse, and it describes risk factors that contribute to the vulnerability of children with developmental disabilities: their lack of access to basic information about human sexuality and sexual abuse, their difficulties in recognizing the consequences of actions, and their lack of critical judgment. This paper also examines parental concerns about providing sexuality education to their children with developmental disabilities.

134. Blomberg, P. S., & Steward, M. (1987). *The use of anatomically correct dolls in determining sexual abuse in a girl with athotid cerebral palsy.* Sacramento, CA: Authors.

The authors of this report discuss the results of a study that used anatomically correct dolls in a structured interview setting with a girl who has athotid cerebral palsy. This study included sample projective questions, such as correct identification of specific points on the illustrations and genital recognition. This study focused on issues such as sexual molestation by a known person, a caregiver, or a stranger and date rape.

135. Bloom, R. B. (1992). When staff members sexually abuse children in residential care. *Child Welfare, 71*(2), 131–145.

This article examines the practical considerations of handling charges of child sexual abuse brought against a caregiver employed by a residential care agency. The author describes the responsibility of the agency to the child victim and its other charges, the indicted staff member and the other staff, and the continued integrity and management of the agency.

136. Blumler, J., Keyte, M., & Wiles, A. (1987). Training foster parents about sexual abuse. *Adoption & Fostering, 11*(2), 33–35.

This article describes a training course on child sexual abuse for foster parents living in the London Borough of Merton. The following themes are presented at four training sessions: abuse and prevention, facts and feelings, breaking the silence, and fostering a sexually abused child. This article provides a brief description of each training session.

137. Blyth, E., & Milner, J. (1989). Compliance and abuse. *Special Children, 33*(1), 8–9.

This article discusses current special education practices that can contribute to abuse and suggests prevention education as means of reducing the risk for abuse. The authors stress that too much stress on teaching compliance makes students more vulnerable to being abused.

138. Bogdan, R., Biklen, D., Shapiro, A., & Spelkoman, D. (1990). The disabled: Media's monster. In M. Nagler (Ed.), *Perspectives on disability* **(pp. 138–142). Palo Alto, CA: Health Markets Research.**

In this chapter on attitudes toward people with disabilities, the authors examine the media's portrayal of people with disabilities in films, television, comics, and newspapers. They note that a common theme in mass communication is the association of disability with ugliness, violence, revenge, criminal behavior, fear, and evil. The authors suggest that these social constructs stereotype people with disabilities unfairly and do nothing to educate the public and promote acceptance of people with disabilities.

139. Bogdan, R., Brown, M. A., & Bannerman Foster, S. (1992). Be honest but not cruel: Staff/parent communication on a neonatal unit. In P. M. Ferguson & S. J. Taylor (Eds.), *Interpreting disability: A qual-*

itative reader (pp. 19–37). New York: Teachers College Press.

This chapter discusses a study that examined staff-parent communication on a neonatal unit. Using participant observation, interviews with staff and parents, and file reviews during a 1-year period, this study examined staff perspectives on patients, parents, other staff members, and talking to parents about their premature infants. It describes an informal classification of patients and parents by staff members, and it addresses the parents' perspective concerning the neonatal unit and communication with staff.

140. Bogdan, R., Taylor, S., deGrandpre, B., & Haynes, S. (1974, June). Let them eat programs: Attendants' perspectives and programming on wards in state schools. *Journal of Health & Social Behavior, 15*, 142–151.

This article discusses a study that used participant observation to examine attendants' perspectives of their supervisors, their work, and residents in state schools serving children and young adults with mental retardation. This study examined the attendants' perspectives and the resulting effects on the implementation of new programs designed by supervisors and professional staff to assist residents. The study concentrated on an infant/children's ward, an adolescent girls' ward, and a young adults' ward for males with severe mental retardation from three institutions ranging in size from 400 to 3,000 residents. Generally, it was found that attendants thought their supervisors and the professional staff were out of touch with the needs and capabilities of the residents. In part, the attendants question the capabilities and integrity of supervisors and professional staff. Attendants' perspectives on the residents were equally discouraging because they had little regard for their potential to learn or change. This study found that attendants viewed innovative programming for residents with skepticism and fatalism, which resulted in the discontinuation of most programs.

141. Bolte, B. (1989, December 11). It's been a dismal decade for the disabled. *Los Angeles Times*, p. B5.

In this newspaper article, Bill Bolte, a writer and activist for the civil rights of people with disabilities, examines government cutbacks and how they affect the poor, elderly, and, especially, people with disabilities.

142. Boniface, J. (1994). Can justice be done? In S. Hollins (Ed.), *Proceedings: It did happen here: Sexual abuse and learning disability: Recognition and action* (pp. 52–55). London: St. George's Hospital Medical School, Division of the Psychiatry of Disability.

This chapter provides the unique perspective of a mother of a daughter with mental retardation who was sexually abused. This mother became very involved in the successful prosecution of her daughter's case and went on to form VOICE, an organization of parents and some professionals that works to prevent sexual abuse and support victims with mental retardation and their families.

143. Boniface, J., & Boniface, I. (1992, September). VOICE. *Mental Handicap Bulletin, 86*, 1–4.

This article describes the founding of VOICE, an advocacy group in the United Kingdom. The major goals of VOICE are to help people with disabilities take cases of abuse to court and to ensure that staff in services to people with disabilities are properly screened with police checks. This organization attempts to meet these objectives through advocacy and public education.

144. Bopp, J., Jr. (1985). Protection of disabled newborn. *Issues in Law & Medicine, 1*(3), 173–200.

This article examines the protection of newborns with disabilities. The author points out that the decision to administer life-preserving medical treatment for these infants is usually left to the parents in consultation with the attending physician and that the decision-making process is guided by the government, which has a vested interest in protecting the rights of the infant in relation to public safety, health, morals, and welfare. This article uses legal case examples to examine constitutional standards and limitations.

145. Borko, N. (1992). Education is key to successful prosecution. *NRCCSA (National Resource Center on Child Sexual Abuse) News, 1*(4), 6, 12.

This article discusses issues regarding the prosecution of cases of abuse of children with disabilities. It is written from a prosecutor's perspective and suggests that prosecutors can overcome many obstacles to prosecution if they are motivated and have the necessary skills. This article addresses the importance of educating abuse victims with disabilities about the legal process because the credibility of victims with disabilities as reliable witnesses is crucial in having these cases go to trial. The author states that educating the victim with disabilities about the legal process empowers him or her with the competence to testify in court. The author also suggests that using expert testimony to present facts versus misconceptions about disabilities to the judge and jury is an important step in reinforcing the victim's credibility.

146. Bosmann, H. B., Kay, J., & Conter, E. A. (1987). Geriatric euthanasia: Attitudes and experiences of health professionals. *Social Psychiatry, 22*(1), 1–4.

This article reports the result of a survey of 190 health care professionals that examined attitudes toward geriatric euthanasia. The results of this survey indicate the following: Most of the respondents in this study had experience with passive euthanasia, 83% indicated they knew of cases of passive euthanasia, 56% had participated in passive euthanasia, a significant minority had experience with active euthanasia, 44% indicated that they knew of cases of active euthanasia, and 21% had participated in active euthanasia. The authors conclude that there is a need for clear guidelines for euthanasia, with input from individuals providing care.

147. Bosnian hospital convoy stopped by heavy snow. (1993, November 18). *The Edmonton Journal*, p. A20.

This newspaper article reports on the plight of patients at two psychiatric hospitals in the towns of Fojnica and Bakovici, Bosnia-Herzegovina. As a result of heavy fighting between the warring factions, the staff at both hospitals have fled, leaving approximately 560 patients, both children and adults, to fend for themselves. A shortage of staff, a lack of medication, a lack of heat, and a shortage of running water are some of the problems faced by these patients. A United Nations relief force trying to get to the area has been delayed due to heavy snow and ice.

148. Bowlby, J. (1953). Some pathological processes set in train by early mother-child separation. *Journal of Mental Science, 2*, 265–272.

This article examines the effect of a mother-infant separation on a child's ability to make continuous cooperative relationships. It discusses an 11-year-old boy who experienced several separations from mother figures during the first 5 years of his life and 49 cases of children separated from mother figures between the ages of 12 and 48 months. The findings of this examination reveal that these children were thrown into states of acute stress, which generated very powerful emotions, such as fretting, denial of need for love, and hating the loved object. In some cases, these reactions persisted throughout life. The author claims that these reactions are influenced by the following: the age of the child, length of separation, quality of the mother-child relationship before and after separation, quality of substitute mothering, and heredity. Also, this article suggests that the immaturity of the cerebral structure, the stage at which the child is developing love relationships, and learning responses under stress may account for the relative indelibility of neurotic or psychopathic behaviors.

149. Bowlby, J. (1958). The nature of a child's tie to his mother. *International Journal of Psycho-Analysis, 39*, 350–373.

In this article, the author discusses the four theories dealing with the positive aspects of a child's bond with his or her mother: 1) The child has a number of physiological needs which must be met, particularly for food and warmth, but no social needs, a theory the author calls Secondary Drive; 2) infants have a built-in need to relate to the human breast and eventually to the mother, also called the theory of Primary Object Sucking; 3) infants have a built-in need to cling to a human being, called the Primary Object Clinging; and 4) infants resent being taken from the womb and attempt to return to it, also called Primary Return-to-Womb Craving. The author

proposes a fifth theory to explain the positive aspects of mother-infant ties, which he calls Component Instinctual Responses. He believes that infant attachment behavior is made up of a number of component instinctual responses that are at first relatively independent of each other. He identifies three responses in which the infant is the active participant (sucking, clinging, and following) and two responses that are used by infants to stimulate maternal behaviors (crying and smiling). The author also describes the theories of Instinct and Instinctual Response, stating that he favors the ethological instinct theory. The author concludes that his theory is no more than tentative but that it is the best explanation of the facts as he sees them and that his theory should act as a stimulus for future research.

150. Bowlby, J. (1983). Attachment and loss: Retrospect and prospect. *Annual Progress in Child Psychiatry and Child Development, 29*–47. (Reprinted from *American Journal of Orthopsychiatry*, 1982, *52*[4], 664–678)

This article presents a historical sketch showing the ill-effects of separation, loss, and maternal deprivation during the early years. Using this historical perspective, the author shows how attachment theory has been developed for understanding personality development and psychopathology.

151. Boyd, J. (1989). Problems and concerns with a diverse population. *Music Therapy Perspective, 6*, 34–36.

This article examines the use of music therapy with children and adolescents who have been abused or neglected and addresses problems and concerns brought about by this program. This therapy program is offered at Olive Crest Treatment Centres for Abused Children in Garden Grove, California, and serves children between the ages of 2 and 18. Group and individual sessions are included in this program, with the groups containing no more than 6 children. Group sessions usually last 1 hour, with individual sessions lasting half an hour. Individual sessions are designed to facilitate positive self-concept, self-expression, and self-awareness and improved self-esteem. Group sessions work to improve social interaction, develop trust, and improve self-esteem. This article examines the age appropriateness of the therapy, meeting the needs of participants, appropriate assessment, and alternative intervention within the confines of music therapy.

152. Boylan, E. (1991). *Women and disability*. London: Zed Books.

Originally presented as a kit for the 1981 International Year of Disabled Persons, this book was subsequently prepared as part of a Women and World Development Series, developed by United Nations agencies and nongovernmental organizations. Contributions from women with disabilities, professionals, nongovernmental organizations, and United Nations organizations are included to provide information concerning the particular challenges faced by women with disabilities everywhere in terms of both sheer survival and belonging to their community. Several topics are discussed: for example, the stigma of disability, which subjects women to a double discrimination because of their gender and their particular disability. This book discusses the human rights of women with disabilities, and it emphasizes "the most human of rights," the right to form relationships. This book addresses the violation of these rights, as in the case of violence and sexual abuse, and considers issues of prevention, rehabilitation, education, employment, caregiving, aging, and taking control of one's life. The book also provides guidelines (in the form of seminar outlines and lists of useful organizations, readings, and audiovisual resources) for improving the quality of life for all women who happen to have a disability.

153. Bradley, R. H., Caldwell, B. M., Fitzgerald, J. A., Morgan, A. G., & Rock, S. L. (1986). Experiences in day care and social competence among maltreated children. *Child Abuse & Neglect, 10,* **181–189.**
This article discusses an analysis of behavior and quality of care for 39 maltreated children in three types of child-care facilities. No comparison group of nonmaltreated children was included in the study. This analysis found the following: the effects of quality child care may not reverse the effects of a disadvantaged home life; child-care facilities that are specifically designed to meet the needs of maltreated children appear to be of a higher quality than average centers; and there was a wide variability in social behavior presented by each child; however, for the most part, maltreated children reacted positively to caregivers and peers. This article suggests that the organization of the child-care center, expectations and traits of the caregivers, and physical layout of the center were all related to the social behavior of the children.

154. Bradshaw, J., & Lawton, D. (1978). Tracing the causes of stress in families with handicapped children. *British Journal of Social Work, 8*(2), **181–192.**
This article describes a study that examined stress in mothers of children with severe disabilities. This study used the Malaise Inventory to assess the mental well-being of 303 mothers of children with disabilities and found the following: 1) these mothers had higher levels of emotional disturbances (about twice as high) than the general population, 2) they had emotional disturbances similar to those of mothers of children with spina bifida, 3) there were no significant differences between mothers of children who had different disabilities or mothers of children with different degrees of disability, and 4) there was no significant relationship between the age of the mother and the child and the social and economic factors of the family and the mother's malaise score. This article also discusses a second study that pretested and posttested 190 mothers of children with severe disabilities using the Malaise Inventory following social assistance. This second study found no significant difference in malaise scores after intervention.

155. Brahams, B. (1987). Court of Appeal agrees to sterilisation of 17-year-old mentally handicapped girl under wardship jurisdiction. *Lancet, 1,* **757–758.**
This article discusses a court case that involves the sterilization of a 17-year-old girl with developmental disabilities. The official solicitor (guardian) and the girl's mother both initiated proceedings to have her made a ward of the court, which would allow for her sterilization, because of her limited cognitive ability and her increased sexual awareness. Although this authority has been granted and has been upheld by the Court of Appeal, a further appeal could be brought before the House of Lords. The author addresses some of the legal issues concerning wardship and the jurisdiction of the court.

156. Bramley, J., & Elkins, J. (1988). Some issues in the development of self-advocacy among persons with intellectual disabilities. *Australia and New Zealand Journal of Developmental Disabilities, 14*(2), **147–157.**
This article discusses the history and emergence of self-advocacy among people with intellectual disabilities in the United States and Australia. The authors point out that self-advocacy of people with intellectual disabilities is a relatively recent phenomenon in Australia, stemming largely from changing government and agency policies in such areas as deinstitutionalization. Although there is a paucity of literature on this subject, the authors attempt to provide an overview of current developments. They outline the common ground shared by these groups in terms of the gradual process of establishing a self-advocacy group and the general purposes and structures of and the difficulties experienced by self-advocacy groups. These difficulties include the following: the achievement of an optimal level of support by advisors, which requires a fine balance between guidance and empowerment; community antipathy to the idea of self-advocacy; and vulnerability in terms of dependence on key members for group survival. The authors recognize the need for considerable growth in this field, both in terms of the power of self-advocates and in the willingness of those in power to listen and act upon the self-advocacy groups' recommendations; consequently, they strongly recommend further research in this area.

157. Brannan, C., Jones, J. R., & Murch, J. D. (1992). *Castle Hill report: Practice guide.* **Ludlow, England: Shropshire County Council.**
This report discusses the inquiry into the sexual abuse of boys at the Castle Hill Independent Special School in Ludlow. Ralph Morris, principal and joint owner of the school, was convicted of physically and sexually abusing students between 11 and 16 years of age between 1984 and 1989 and sentenced to 12 years in prison. The 30–60 (at various times) boys at the school were classified as

moderately mentally retarded and maladjusted. The inquiry revealed a number of problems with the reporting and investigation of the abuse.

158. Brassard, M. R., Hart, S. N., & Hardy, D. B. (1991). Psychological and emotional abuse of children. In R. T. Ammerman & M. Hersen (Eds.), *Case studies in family violence* **(pp. 255–270). New York: Plenum.**

This chapter examines the psychological and emotional abuse of children. It uses a case example of a dysfunctional family in order to define some of the problems encountered when working in this area. The authors examine the assessment of the family, family characteristics, and psychological maltreatment within the family, and they discuss medical, legal, social, and family issues. They also suggest treatment options.

159. Brassard, M. R., Tyler, A., & Kehle, T. J. (1983). Sexually abused children: Identification and suggestions for intervention. *School Psychology Review, 12*(1), 93–97.

This article describes how school staff can identify children who have been sexually abused and offers suggestions for intervention. It suggests that, in a school setting, referral of a child to the school psychologist concerning issues of sexual abuse might be initiated as a result of inappropriate sexual conduct in class or after the disclosure of sexual abuse to a teacher. Also, this article examines additional physical and behavioral indicators of sexual abuse as well as interviewing techniques for use with the child and his or her parents.

160. Braungart, S. (1990, March 2). Burns lead to probe of ranch. *The Calgary Herald,* **pp. A1, A2.**

This newspaper article reports that an 18-year-old autistic male who resided at the Delvee Ranch in Claresholm, Alberta, is currently being treated for burns to his feet that might have resulted from abuse. The government-sponsored treatment center and director Lori Williams-Morgan have previously been under investigation by the Department of Social Services, which resulted in the removal of four adults with autism. Psychologist Williams-Morgan explained that the youth's feet were burned as a result of the hot water being turned on by the youth when left unattended in the bathtub. Additional bruises and other injuries were said to have been self-inflicted, although some of the injuries sustained by the youth appear to resemble cigarette burns. Williams-Morgan, who owns two other centers, explained that her workers at the ranch are not employed by her but by a holding company owned by Williams-Morgan's son. Both the Royal Canadian Mounted Police and the Department of Social Services are currently investigating allegations of abuse.

161. Braungart, S. (1990, March 3). Officials thwarted in burn probe bid. *The Calgary Herald,* **pp. A1, A2.**

This newspaper article reports that an investigation by Alberta Social Services into the physical abuse of an autistic youth who suffered burns and other injuries while residing at the Delvee Ranch in Claresholm, Alberta, has come up against a contract that forbids unannounced visits to the ranch. The Delvee Ranch is a government-sponsored treatment center for autistic adults. Former employees at the ranch claim that clients work without pay at the Delvee Deli, which is associated with Delvee Ranch owner Lori Williams-Morgan. It has also been claimed that clients are fed spoiled leftovers from the deli, sleep on the ground without mattresses, are not provided toilet paper, and are verbally and physically abused by other employees.

162. Brayden, R. M., Altemeier, W. A., Tucker, D. D., Dietrich, M. S., & Vietze, P. (1992). Antecedents of child neglect in the first two years of life. *Journal of Pediatrics, 120*(3), 426–429.

This article describes a prospective study that was conducted to identify prenatal characteristics that might predict child neglect by low income women. Between September 1975 and December 1976, this study obtained demographic information on and administered the Maternal History Interview to 1,400 women who were registered for prenatal care at an urban hospital. On the basis of established criteria, 273 women were categorized as being at high risk for child maltreatment. Complete information was gathered on 255 of these women, with those women (1,121) who were not considered at high risk for child maltreatment constituting the comparison group. The 255 infants from the high-risk mothers were compared with 225 randomly selected infants from the comparison group of mothers. Apgar scores, birth weight, and the presence of congenital anomalies were noted for the infants, and the infants were assessed using the Brazelton Neonatal Behavioral Assessment Scale, the Carey Infant Temperament Questionnaire, and the Bayley Scales of Infant Development. The results of this study indicate that those women who were identified as being at high risk for child maltreatment prenatally were more likely to be identified as being neglectful within 2 years of the initial assessment. Their profile suggests less than a high school education, a greater number of children under the age of 6, poorer scores on the Parenting subscale of the Maternal History Interview, and poorer support systems. The authors note that neglected children were significantly lower in birth weight, were rated by their mothers as more temperamental, and had lower developmental scores on the Bayley Scales of Infant Development.

163. Brent, S. B., Speece, M. W., Gates, M. F., & Kaul, M. (1993). The contribution of death-related experiences to health care providers' attitudes toward dying patients: II. Medical and nursing students

with no professional experience. *Omega Journal of Death and Dying, 26*(3), 181–205.
This article discusses a study that investigated the attitudes of 276 first-year medical and nursing students without prior professional death-related experiences with terminally ill patients. The study attempted to determine any preconceived attitudes these students might bring into their profession. The results of this study indicate the following: 1) nursing students held more positive attitudes on five of the six attitude measures than medical students of either gender, 2) there was little difference between the attitudes of male and female medical students, 3) it appears that experience with and coursework in death and dying significantly influenced the students' attitudes toward discussing the subject of death with terminally ill patients, and 4) other attitude measures were not significantly changed.

164. **Briggs, S. E. (1991). Medical issues with child victims of family violence. In R. T. Ammerman & M. Hersen (Eds.),** *Case studies in family violence* **(pp. 87–96). New York: Plenum.**
This chapter focuses on child victims of family violence. It discusses the use of clinical examinations and behavioral changes in children for identifying child victims of family violence. It features anatomical differences in children and their response to injury and includes characteristics of specific child abuse injuries.

165. **Brock, D. W. (1992). Voluntary active euthanasia.** *Hastings Center Report, 22*(2), 10–22.
This article identifies common arguments against euthanasia and offers counter-arguments defending the practice. The author argues that the good would outweigh the bad. Even in defending euthanasia, however, the author presents some worrisome views of its potential for moving from voluntary to involuntary deaths. He suggests "that legalization of voluntary active euthanasia might soon be followed by strong pressure to legalize some involuntary euthanasia of incompetent patients unable to express their own wishes" (p. 20). He cites evidence from the Dutch experience that suggests that voluntary euthanasia has led to the involuntary killing of incompetent patients; nevertheless, he suggests that procedural safeguards might be developed to minimize this problem, and since at least some of the people killed involuntarily would probably want to die anyway, if they could make their own choice, the author concludes that this is not as big a problem as it first appears.

166. **Broekgaarden, R., Schenk, L., deVries, T., Wagenborg, P., & Scholten, U. (1985, September, 12–14).** *Playtherapy with the mentally retarded.* **Paper presented at the Netherlands Organization for Post Graduate Education in Social Sciences (PAOS) International Sym-**posium on Play—Play Therapy—Play Research, Amsterdam, the Netherlands.
This paper examines the use of play therapy with children and adults who have mental retardation. It notes the inadequate state of research on play therapy, provides a review of the psychoanalytically oriented play therapy approaches, and explores the use of play therapy with people who have mental retardation. It describes some of the therapeutic benefits of play therapy: For example, play therapy provides opportunities for behavior change and encourages positive outcomes from the relationship with the therapist. This paper discusses specific challenges to the therapist working with people with mental retardation and emphasizes the individual's previous experience with rejection.

167. **Brolley, D. Y., & Anderson, S. C. (1986, Fall). Advertising and attitudes.** *Rehabilitation Digest, 17,* 15–17.
The effects of mass media advertising and information sharing on attitudes with regard to people with disabilities is discussed in this article. It describes methods for the effective and ineffective formation of attitudes concerning people with disabilities.

168. **Brolley, D. Y., & Anderson, S. C. (1990). Advertising and attitudes. In M. Nagler (Ed.),** *Perspectives on disability* **(pp. 147–150). Palo Alto, CA: Health Markets Research.**
This chapter discusses media advertising, people with disabilities, and the public attitudes fostered by advertising. It describes a study that was conducted to examine whether positive advertising of people with disabilities would have a positive influence on public opinion as opposed to a negative portrayal of people with disabilities in the media. Two groups were chosen for this study: 91 in the positive advertising group and 73 in the negative advertising group. Both groups were exposed to the ads and then completed an Attitude Toward Disabled Persons Scale and a Media Feedback Form. The results of this study indicate that no significant difference was exhibited between the attitudes of the two groups toward people with disabilities.

169. **Brookhouser, P. E. (1987). Ensuring the safety of deaf children in residential schools.** *Otolaryngology Head and Neck Surgery, 97*(4), 361–368.
This article notes that more than 25% of all children with hearing impairments live in residential schools, and it claims that these children are at increased risk for maltreatment by surrogate caregivers. It discusses barriers to administrative response: for example, disbelief and fear of public reaction. It stresses that health providers must assume a special responsibility in the prevention and detection of abuse and neglect of their child patients with disabilities. This article discusses the relevant aspects of the American health delivery system as well as specific strategies for the detection, documentation, and preven-

tion of maltreatment of this particularly vulnerable group of children.

170. Brown, C. (1992). Dealing with the sexual behaviour of dually diagnosed adolescents. In *Crossing new borders* **(pp. 165–168). Kingston, NY: National Association for the Dually Diagnosed.**
This chapter discusses sexually inappropriate and sexually abusive behavior as well as healthy sexual behavior in dually diagnosed adolescents. Sexually inappropriate behavior is defined as sexual behavior that is socially unacceptable (e.g., masturbation in a public place) but does not exploit or harm another individual. Abusive sexual behavior is defined as sexual activity involving an unwilling other who is exploited, demeaned, or harmed. The author estimates that 25% of dually diagnosed adolescents referred for treatment have committed abusive sexual behavior and concludes that staff attitudes and education supporting healthy sexuality are essential for restoring normal behavior.

171. Brown, D. E. (1988). Factors affecting psychosexual development of adults with congenital physical disabilities. *Physical & Occupational Therapy in Pediatrics, 8*(2/3), 43–58.
The author of this article interviewed 26 adults with congenital physical disabilities in order to explore the following areas: self-concept; the roles family, peers, and educators play in the development of sexual identity; sources of sexual information; and the prevalence of sexual abuse. The results of these interviews indicate that significantly lower scores in self-concept could be detected in areas concerned with acceptability of body image, degree of dependency on family members, and the nature of familial relationships. This study reveals that the development of sexual identity could be influenced considerably by parents' failure to accept the child and provide support and information in this area. This article notes that denying persons with disabilities access to information about sexuality increases their risk for problems in the development of a sexual identity; and because there is a lack of access to sexual information for people with disabilities, peers appear to be a prevalent source of sexual information. This article proposes intervention strategies to help promote growth at each stage of the sexual development of a person with disabilities.

172. Brown, G. W. (1990). Rule-making and justice: A cautionary tale. *Mental Retardation, 28*(2), 83–87.
This article describes the suicide of a group home resident with mental retardation and the inquiry into this death. It examines the issue of well-intentioned rules and the potential abuse that can result from these rules.

173. Brown, H. (1991). Mental handicapped nursing: Sexual abuse: Facing facts. *Nursing Times, 87*(6), 65–66.

This article examines some of the characteristics of sexual abuse of people with developmental disabilities, in particular, female victims. This article discusses incidence rates and prevention approaches such as sex education and changes in legislation.

174. Brown, H. (1992). Abuse of adults with learning difficulties. *Mental Handicap Bulletin, 86*(4), 18–19.
This article presents the preliminary results from a survey of 120 cases of reported sexual abuse (more than 70% confirmed) of adults with mental retardation. These results indicate the following: perpetrators were other service users (41.7%), family members (17.8%), other known adults (16.7%), staff or volunteers (14.3%), strangers (8.3%), and others (1.2%). The vast majority (97%) of perpetrators were male, while most (73%) of victims were female.

175. Brown, H. (1992). Abuse of children with learning difficulties. *Nursing Standard, 6*(26), 18–19.
This article discusses a 3-year study conducted at the University of Kent in order to discover patterns of sexual abuse and assault committed against adults with mental retardation. This study reports many cases involving perpetrators who have mental retardation, but it also includes cases of abuse committed by family members, paid caregivers, and others.

176. Brown, H., & Craft, A. (1989). *Thinking the unthinkable: Papers on sexual abuse and people with learning difficulties.* **London: FPA Education Unit.**
This book contains five papers, an introduction, and a postscript on sexual abuse as it affects people with learning difficulties. The papers include the following: "The need for safeguards" (Walmsley); "Child sexual abuse and mental handicap: A child psychiatrist's perspective" (Vizard); "Keeping safe: Sex education and assertiveness skills" (Craft & Hitching); "Uncovering and responding to sexual abuse in psychotherapeutic settings" (Sinason); and "Sexual abuse and adults with mental handicap: Can the law help?" (Gunn).

177. Brown, H., & Craft, A. (1992). *Working with the "unthinkable": A trainers' manual on the sexual abuse of adults with learning difficulties.* **London: Family Planning Association.**
This training manual is intended for professionals and other staff working with adults with developmental disabilities who have been sexually abused. It contains a number of exercises and fact sheets to raise awareness of the abuse issue, to assist in recognizing signs of abusive or high-risk situations, and to encourage participants to discuss concerns and potential solutions.

178. Brown, H., & Turk, V. (1992, June). Defining sexual abuse as it affects a-

dults with learning disabilities. *Mental Handicap, 20,* 44–55.
In this article, the authors attempt to define sexual abuse as it applies to people with learning disabilities. They examine sexual activity involving adults with learning disabilities that might be construed as being abusive, and they discuss the issue of meaningful consent. The authors also examine possible indicators of sexual abuse.

179. Brown, H., & Turk, V. (1994). Sexual abuse in adulthood: Ongoing risks for people with learning disabilities. *Child Abuse Review, 3*(1), 26–35.
This article discusses a survey of 119 cases of sexual abuse of people with mental retardation. The results indicate the following: 73% of the victims were women and 27% were men; physical contact was present in 95% of the cases, and penetration or attempted penetration occurred in 67% of cases; no action was taken against the perpetrators in almost half the cases; and prosecution or disciplinary action took place in only 18.5% of cases.

180. Brown, L. L. (1991). Sexual abuse and persons with mental handicaps: Four myths of invulnerability. *Research Review of the Vocational and Rehabilitation Research Institute, 1*(1).
This article discusses the myths of invulnerability associated with the sexual abuse of people with developmental disabilities. According to this article, the public either denies the existence of sexual abuse of people with developmental disabilities or believes that people with disabilities are not hurt by sexual abuse. This article examines the societal devaluation of people with developmental disabilities and how this devaluation leads to sexual offenses against people with developmental disabilities.

181. Browne, K., & Saqi, S. (1988). Mother-infant interaction and attachment in physically abusing families [Special issue: Early child maltreatment]. *Journal of Reproductive and Infant Psychology, 6*(3), 163–182.
This article examines the differences in behaviors and interaction between 46 mother-infant pairs from abusing and nonabusing two-parent families. The infants in this study ranged in age from 7 to 24 months, and this study used a strange situation procedure, consisting of four episodes: 1) videotaping mother and infant alone, 2) preseparation, 3) separation, and 4) reunion. The results of this study reveal that abused infants demonstrate less visual exploratory behavior, present higher levels of distress, and initiate fewer interactions with the stranger than nonabused infants. This article concludes that abused infants are more likely to have an insecure attachment with their mothers, which enhances stranger anxiety and inhibits exploratory behavior.

182. Bruno, A. L. (1988). Child neglect and abuse: A family case study. *Journal of Child Care, 3*(5), 41–45.
This article describes an intervention treatment program for a single-parent family with two children, ages 2 and 6. The mother and children all have a history of physical abuse. A family support worker coordinated the treatment program, which consisted of the following: child management modeling, enrollment in a parenting course and an anger and discipline course, and individual counseling. The author states that the goal of effective parenting was achieved for this mother.

183. Bryan, T., Pearl, R., & Herzog, A. (1989). Learning disabled adolescents' vulnerability to crime: Attitudes, anxieties, experiences. *Learning Disabilities Research, 5*(1), 51–60.
This article reported the results of a study that compared 95 high school students with learning disabilities with 102 high school students without disabilities. This study found that students with learning disabilities were more likely to have been victims of crime, but vulnerability appeared to interact with race and ethnicity.

184. Buchanan, A., & Oliver, J. E. (1977). Abuse and neglect as a cause of mental retardation: A study of 140 children admitted to subnormality hospitals in Wiltshire. *British Journal of Psychiatry, 131,* 458–467.
This article discusses a survey of 140 children under 16 years of age in two subnormality hospitals to determine the prevalence of mental retardation as the result of abuse. This survey found the following: 3% of the children had definitely been rendered mentally disabled as a consequence of violent abuse, and this number might possibly reach a maximum total of 11%; and neglect was considered to be a contributory factor in reducing intellectual potential for 24% of these children. The authors conclude that impairment of intellect from abuse and neglect, especially in those with "vulnerable" brains due to preexisting abnormality, may be much more common than is generally realized.

185. Buchanan, A., & Wilkins, R. (1991). Sexual abuse of the mentally handicapped: Difficulties in establishing prevalence. *Psychiatric Bulletin, 15,* 601–605.
This article presents the results of a survey of 37 residential and field workers from 24 agencies and discusses the lack of statistical information regarding the incidence of sexual abuse and other crimes against people with developmental disabilities. The 37 workers identified a total of 52 cases where sexual abuse or exploitation was known or was strongly suspected.

186. Buckley, J. A. (1992). Major legal issues in child sexual abuse cases. In W. O'Donohue & J. H. Geer (Eds.), *The* *sexual abuse of children: Theory and research* (Vol. 1, pp. 139–167). Hillsdale, NJ: Lawrence Erlbaum Associates.

This chapter presents legal issues surrounding child sexual abuse cases in court. It examines children as witnesses and focuses on their competency, credibility, and vulnerability when it comes to testifying in court. It discusses the use of psychological expert testimony and how it is used in the courts by both defendants and the prosecution. This chapter also examines allegations of child sexual abuse in cases involving custody and visitation rights.

187. Bugental, D. B., Mantyla, S. M., & Lewis, J. (1989). Parental attributions as moderators of affective communication to children at risk for physical abuse. In D. Cicchetti & V. Carlson (Eds.), *Child maltreatment theory and research on the causes and consequences of child abuse and neglect* **(pp. 254–279). Cambridge, England: Cambridge University Press.**

In this chapter, the authors propose a transactional model of physical abuse that takes into account the effects of reciprocal behavior and the potential moderating role of attributions. They focus on the communication of affect as a mediating variable in the family transactional system and predict that difficult child behavior elicits negative and inconsistent messages from caregivers. The authors claim that this is more pronounced with caregivers who take little responsibility or credit for their caregiving successes and who attribute higher blame to the child for caregiving failures. The authors conclude that high-blame women who attributed high responsibility to children for unsuccessful interactions were found to be more likely to show negative affect and tension in voice and that difficult children have a more negative impact on low-power caregivers than on high-power caregivers.

188. Bullard, D. G., & Knight, S. E. (Eds.). (1981). *Sexuality and physical disability: Personal perspectives.* **St. Louis: C. V. Mosby.**

This collection of articles addresses many aspects of sexuality and physical disability. The contributors to this volume, many of whom have a disability, share personal and professional perspectives on the following: specific disabilities and medical conditions, individual and family concerns, education, therapy and counseling, and specific issues relating to women. The book includes an article outlining the work of the Seattle Rape Relief Developmental Disabilities Project, which addresses the issue of sexual abuse of people with disabilities and offers prevention alternatives through an education and training program. This training program emphasizes counteracting vulnerability with realistic self-protection skill training in order to reduce the incidence and devastating effects of sexual abuse. References are made throughout this book to the specific concerns about the negative aspects of sexuality faced by women with disabilities.

Also, the book includes a bibliography and resource list of agencies dealing with sexuality and disability.

189. Bullock, L. F., & McFarlane, J. (1989). The birth-weight/battering connection. *American Journal of Nursing,* **89, 1153–1155.**

This article discusses a study that assessed 300 pregnant women from private hospitals and 289 pregnant women from a public hospital for physical battery. In total, 120 women (20.4%) reported being battered while pregnant. This study also found that battered women had a two to four times greater incidence of infants with low birth weight.

190. Bunder, L. (1989, September 16). Police cleared in suffocation of a retarded Brooklyn man. *The New York Times,* **p. A31.**

This newspaper article discusses the suffocation death of Kevin Thorpe, a 31-year-old Brooklyn man with mental retardation. This article states that a Brooklyn grand jury decided against indicting the involved police officers. The court concluded that no criminal conduct was involved during the arrest and restraint of Mr. Thorpe.

191. Burke, F. (1989). A two-lesson program for the prevention of sexual abuse. *Perspectives for Teachers of the Hearing Impaired,* **8(1), 14–17.**

This article discusses adapting a sexual abuse prevention program, "The Children's Self-Help Project," to meet the needs of children who are deaf and hard of hearing. This program aims to reduce the power imbalance between adults and children or children of different ages, and the curriculum targets children from kindergarten to grade 12. This program presents some basic concepts: saying "no," awareness of what they like and do not like, and asking for help or telling someone about abuse.

192. Burningham, S. (1989). The deaf child as a double victim. *Social Work Today,* **21(4), 18–19.**

This article is an interview with Margaret Kennedy, founder of Keep Deaf Children Safe, an organization affiliated with Britain's National Deaf Children's Society. This organization works to prevent abuse of deaf children and provides access to appropriate services for deaf children who have been abused.

193. Byard, R. W., & Beal, S. M. (1993). Munchausen syndrome by proxy: Repetitive infantile apnoea and homicide. *Journal of Paediatric Child Health,* **29, 77–79.**

This article discusses Munchausen syndrome by proxy (MSBP) and induced recurrent apnoea in infants. It examines the characteristics of cases involving infantile apnoea and the association of sudden infant death syndrome in siblings of indexed cases. The syndrome itself is reviewed, and the authors suggest procedural action to be taken when there is a suspicion of MSBP.

194. Byrd, K. E., & Elliott, T. R. (1985). Feature films and disability: A descriptive study. *Rehabilitation Psychology, 30*(1), 47–51.
This article discusses a study that reviewed volumes 43 through 50 of the *Monthly Film Bulletin* in order to determine the frequency and nature of disability in feature films. This study reviewed 1,051 films and found the following: 11.4% of these films depicted a disability; the most frequent disability depicted was psychiatric disorders; men were depicted with a disability more often than women; and based on the critics' reviews, the majority of the films depicted disability in a negative light.

•C•

195. Cahill, B. (1992). *Butter box babies*. Toronto: Seal Books.
This book describes the Ideal Maternity Home in East Chester, Nova Scotia, where orphaned children who were born to unwed mothers were sold for profit. The owners, Lilla and William Young, kept this practice of baby farming from the natural parents. Those infants who were not adopted contributed to the high infant mortality rate at the home. The makeshift coffins that were used to bury the dead infants were butter boxes used for delivering groceries.

196. Call, J. D. (1984). Child abuse and neglect in infancy: Sources of hostility within the parent-infant dyad and disorders of attachment in infancy. *Child Abuse & Neglect, 8*, 185–202.
This article addresses child abuse and neglect resulting from attachment disorders within the parent-infant dyad. It identifies sources of aggression within the mother-infant dyad such as infant development, crying, and other infant distresses. It provides a historical perspective that focuses on child maltreatment as it relates to attachment disorders. Normal attachment behavior is categorically described according to the age of the infant. This article defines "Reactive Attachment Disorder of Infancy" and suggests that this disorder is a common variable in infants diagnosed with failure to thrive without organic cause.

197. Callahan, D. (1992). Self-determination runs amok. *Hastings Center Report, 22*(2), 52–55.
This article suggests that the central argument for the contemporary case for euthanasia is the self-determination argument: That is, people have a right to choose whether or not they want to continue their lives. However,

Callahan suggests that the self-determination argument is counterfeit. He makes two major counter-arguments. First, proposed legislation puts decision making in the hands of the physician and relatives rather than the patient. Second, consent does not absolve all immoral acts: For example, murder and slavery remain illegal and consent does not alter their status.

198. Calling client a monster, nurse's lawyer asks lesser charge. (1989, December 7). *The New York Times*, p. B6.
The article reports on the closing arguments in the Richard Angelo hospital murder trial. The former nurse of the Good Samaritan Hospital was indicted for the murder of four patients and three assaults by means of lethal injection. According to the prosecution, Mr. Angelo wanted to appear to be a hero by being the first person on the scene of an emergency that he created by injecting patients with muscle relaxation drugs. The defense asked for a finding of criminal negligence, which carries a maximum jail sentence of 4 years, while the prosecution asked for a murder finding, with a jail sentence from 25 years to life.

199. Cameron, S. J., Dobson, L. A., & Day, D. M. (1991). Stress in parents of developmentally delayed and non delayed preschool children. *Canada's Mental Health, 39*(1), 13–17.
This article reports the results of a comparison of the scores of 39 mothers of children with developmental disabilities and 40 children without disabilities on the the Parenting Stress Index (PSI). No significant differences were found on total stress scores or the parent domain of the index; in fact, the scores of the two groups on the parent domain were almost identical, with the parents of children with disabilities reporting slightly less stress. However, the stress scores on the child domain of the test were higher for the parents of children with disabilities. While the authors appear to interpret the findings as indicating that parents of children with disabilities are more stressed and less accepting of their children, they fail to consider that the child domain of the PSI confounds measures of stress and measures of disability.

200. Campbell, J. (1990). *Review of safeguards in children's residential programs: A report to the Ministers of Community and Social Services and Correctional Services*. Toronto: Ministry of Community and Social Services and Ministry of Correctional Services.
This report reviews safeguards designed to protect children and adolescents against different types of abuse in residential settings. This report focuses on the following areas: how residential services are currently provided, how to respond to allegations of abuse, and how to protect children and adolescents in residential settings from abuse. This report also discusses the

following legal issues: legal basis for the children's residential services system, legal safeguards against abuse, risk and safety issues in residential facilities, and foster parenting operated under the Child and Family Services Act of 1984.

201. Campling, J. (1981). *Images of ourselves: Women with disabilities talking.* **London: Routledge & Kegan Paul.**
This volume consists of a selection of writings by and about women with disabilities. It addresses their experiences of education, employment, personal relationships, sexuality, and motherhood as well as practical daily life concerns. Also, it discusses the attitudes of (British) society toward women with disabilities. The women represent considerable diversity, yet the similarity of some of their experiences and strength in meeting challenges are recognized and well documented.

202. Canadian Association for Community Living. (1991). *The economic costs of segregating people with a mental handicap.* **Toronto: Author.**
This report discusses the Canadian Association for Community Living's preliminary estimates of the economic costs involved in segregating people with mental disabilities from society. It includes some basic assumptions regarding segregation used to estimate these costs.

203. Canadian Conference of Catholic Bishops. (1992). *Breach of trust, breach of faith: Child sexual abuse in the church and society: Materials for discussion groups.* **Ottawa, ON: Author.**
This trainer's manual includes five outlines for discussion group sessions on abuse: 1) sexual abuse of children in the church, 2) the dynamics of sexual abuse, 3) factors in society and the church that may contribute to child sexual abuse, 4) personal and community responsibility in child sexual abuse, and 5) preventing child sexual abuse. Although these materials are clearly specific to abuse within the Catholic Church, much of the outline could be used by anyone exploring issues of sexual abuse within human services systems.

204. Canadian Conference of Catholic Bishops. (1992). *From pain to hope: Report from the ad hoc committee on child sexual abuse.* **Ottawa, ON: Author.**
This report on sexual abuse of children by priests includes a wealth of recommendations that might be adapted to a variety of other settings where sexual abuse is a problem. These recommendations emphasize the need for open discussion of the issue and direct investigation of allegations. They emphasize the need to allow and encourage civil authorities to investigate and prosecute when appropriate. They also address selection and training of men who wish to become priests.

205. Caparulo, F. (1987). *A comprehensive evaluation of a victim/offender of sex-* *ual abuse who is intellectually disabled.* **Orange, CT: Centre for Sexual Health and Education.**
This paper discusses an evaluation that was conducted by a sex therapist working with special populations. The purpose of this evaluation was to determine the extent of the client's offending behaviors, to measure the level of risk he or she presents, to evaluate his or her suitability as a candidate for outpatient treatment, and to determine the nature of treatment to be undertaken. The components of this evaluation procedure include the following: a 3-hour interview and the administration and interpretation of the Socio-Sexual Knowledge and Attitude Assessment Instrument. This paper offers some recommendations for therapists, and it discusses the use of Depo-Provera as a suppressant of libido in male sex offenders.

206. Caparulo, F. (1991). Identifying the developmentally disabled sex offenders. *Sexuality and Disability, 9*(4), 311–322.
This article examines a framework for the treatment of sex offenders with developmental disabilities. It discusses the major elements of the framework: the sex history of the offender, level of sexual knowledge, moral development, level of deviance from socially accepted norms, potential risk level, chronology of sexual behaviors, and suggestions for treatment. This article includes a short literature review on the following topics: identification of sex offenders with developmental disabilities, assessment of sex offenders with developmental disabilities, and treatment of sex offenders with developmental disabilities.

207. Caparulo, F., & Gafgen, J. (no date). *A case study: The assessment, diagnosis and treatment of a mentally retarded sex offender presenting with paraphilias.* **Unpublished manuscript.**
This manuscript discusses a case study that describes the assessment, diagnosis, and treatment of a sex offender with mental retardation. It provides the following: the results of interviews; the results of the Sexual Knowledge and Attitude Assessment instrument; estimations of the offender's levels of moral development, social deviance, and risk predictors; and a classification of the offender's abnormal sexual behaviors. Also, this manuscript suggests some treatment programs.

208. Caplan, P. J., & Dinardo, L. (1986). Is there a relationship between child abuse and learning disability? [Special issue: Family violence: Child abuse and wife assault]. *Canadian Journal of Behavioural Science, 18*(4), 367–380.
This article reviews seven studies that attempt to test the association between learning disability and child abuse. The studies that they review are criticized for: using small, nonrandom samples; failure to discriminate children who exhibited learning disabilities before being abused from children who exhibited learning difficulties

after abuse; and other methodological problems. The authors conclude that there is no compelling evidence that children with learning disabilities are more likely than other children to be abused.

209. Capuzzi, C. (1989). Maternal attachment to handicapped infants and the relationship to social support. *Research in Nursing and Health, 12*(3), 161–167.
This article describes a study that compared the parent-infant attachment of 36 mothers; 15 of the mothers had infants with physical, visual, or mental disabilities that varied in severity and chronicity. Both groups of women were not statistically different, except the mothers of infants with disabilities felt they received less social support. This study used the Social Support Questionnaire and the Nursing Child Assessment Feeding Scale to measure mother and infant behaviors at 1, 6, and 12 months. The study found the following: there were significant differences in attachment at 1 month, with mothers of infants with disabilities exhibiting fewer attachment behaviors; there were no differences in attachment behaviors among the mothers at 6 or 12 months; and when the effects of the subjects' prenatal social support were taken into account, there were no longer significant differences between the two groups. The author concludes that social support appears to decrease the effects of having an infant with disabilities on attachment and stresses the need for evaluation of programs that attempt to enhance or increase social support.

210. Carbino, R. (1991). Child abuse and neglect reports in foster care: The issue for foster families of "false" allegations. *Child and Youth Services, 15*(2), 233–247.
This article discusses the problem of false allegations of child maltreatment in foster care. The author points out many reasons why such false allegations might occur: For example, because many children entering foster care already have a history of abuse, they may be more likely to allege abuse if upset or angry. The author suggests that fear of false allegations of abuse may deter some potentially good foster parents from providing foster care. Recommendations to reduce and manage problems associated with false allegations without ignoring actual abuse are provided in four areas. First, agencies must remember that allegations are sometimes false and must be aware of the traumatic effects that their responses to allegations may have on foster families. Second, it is essential that agencies have clear policies and procedures for dealing with allegations of abuse in foster care. Third, information about abuse and how reports are handled should be provided to all foster care providers, and more information should be provided if abuse has been alleged. Fourth, agencies should respond to allegations of abuse carefully in order to ensure that false or unsubstantiated allegations do not cause further harm to the family.

211. Carlson, B. E. (1991). Emotionally disturbed children's beliefs about punish-
ment. *Child Abuse & Neglect, 15,* 19–28.
This article discusses a study that examined 58 emotionally disturbed children (ages 7 to 12) in order to assess their views on the use of punishment. Most of the children (10 girls, 48 boys) in this study were suspected of being victims of either physical or sexual abuse by a parent. Most of these children were from White lower or working class families in New England. In Part 1 of the study, the children were shown four vignettes involving misbehaving children: Two of the vignettes involved losing a pen or taking money; the other two vignettes involved aggressive physical behavior toward a sibling or peer. After hearing each story, the child was asked to assume the role of parent and rate the degree of misbehavior. Part 2 of the study used two vignettes that presented problem situations likely to be encountered by children. The results of this study indicate that most of the children did not endorse the use of physical punishment; but when compared to a previous study using emotionally stable children not suspected of having been abused, the children in this study did endorse more physical punishment for misbehavior than the emotionally stable children.

212. Carmody, M. (1990). *Sexual assault of people with intellectual disability: Final report.* Sydney, Australia: New South Wales Women's Co-Ordination Unit.
This report reviews the issue of sexual assault of people with mental retardation and makes recommendations in nine areas: principles, department and agency responsibilities, sexuality policies, police procedures, legislative reforms, court reforms, community education, training, and monitoring. The report also briefly discusses the prevalence of intellectual disabilities among a group of adults referred to Sexual Assault Services in New South Wales. Of 855 adults who were referred, 55 had intellectual disabilities, about twice the number that would be randomly expected. The report also found that 12 of 14 adults entering a sex education program in New South Wales reported previous sexual abuse or sexual assault experiences.

213. Carmody, M. (1991). Invisible victims: Sexual assault of people with an intellectual disability. *Australia and New Zealand Journal of Developmental Disabilities, 17*(2), 229–236.
This article describes how helping professionals, police, and government social support and legal systems in New South Wales, Australia, fail to recognize sexual abuse of people with developmental disabilities. The author addresses the incidence of assault and vulnerability to sexual assault of people with developmental disabilities, examines the procedural guidelines and provisions of the police, legislation, and the court system in matters involving victims with disabilities who have been assaulted, and discusses the inadequacies of these systems.

214. Carson, R. (1992). Washington's I-119. *Hastings Center Report, 22*(2), 7–9.
This article traces the history of Washington State's Initiative 119 that would have allowed physician-assisted suicide. The initiative appeared to have great support, easily collecting the required signatures and raising huge amounts of money for support; yet when the final votes were counted, the initiative failed decisively. Polls of physicians were also negative, with 75% saying that they would not take part in assisted suicide.

215. Carter, G., & Jancar, J. (1984). Sudden deaths in the mentally handicapped. *Psychological Medicine, 14*, 691–695.
This article describes a retrospective survey that investigated the sudden deaths of patients with developmental disabilities at the Stoke Park Group of Hospitals during a 50-year period. This study examined the incidence and causes of death of these patients and divided the deaths into two categories: deaths that occurred in the first 25 years and deaths that occurred in the last 25 years. The sudden deaths were categorized as the following: arterial degenerative disease, status epilepticus, asphyxia, pulmonary embolism, and gastrointestinal causes. The results of this study show that 70 patients died between 1930 and 1955, and 134 patients died between 1956 and 1980. This study found a decrease in deaths resulting from epilepticus in the 1956 to 1980 group and that this group had an increase in deaths resulting from arterial degenerative disease and asphyxia.

216. Casanova, G. M., Domanic, J., McCanne, T. R., & Milner, J. S. (1992). Physiological responses to non-child-related stressors in mothers at risk for child abuse. *Child Abuse & Neglect, 16*, 31–44.
The authors of this article state that it is not clear if the physiological reactivity of physical child abusers and at-risk parents are child specific, but in relation to comparison subjects, they suggest that physical child abusers and adults at risk for child abuse appear to be more physiologically reactive to child-related stressors. The authors examined changes in heart rate and skin conductance in response to four nonchild-related stressors in at-risk and low-risk mothers: a cold pressor, a stressful film depicting industrial accidents, unsolvable anagrams, and an annoying car horn. The results of this study indicate that at-risk mothers had greater and more prolonged sympathetic activation during the presentation of the cold pressor and the stressful film than the low-risk mothers. The authors conclude that these data, combined with previous data, support the idea that generalized sympathetic activation to both child and nonchild-related stressors may act as a mediator of physical child abuse.

217. Cash, T., & Valentine, D. (1987). A decade of adult protective services: Case characteristics. *Journal of Gerontological Social Work, 10*(3/4), 47–60.
This article discusses a descriptive analysis of 17,355 reports submitted to the South Carolina Department of Social Services, Adult Protective Service Division from 1974 to 1984. It includes the characteristics of case types, victim types, and the resource and service systems for 17,273 of these cases. This analysis found the following: 85.1% or 11,302 cases reported neglect as the form of maltreatment, 57% of victims were age 65 or older, 63% of the maltreated population were female, and maltreatment was almost evenly distributed between African Americans and Whites. Forty-one percent of the reports were submitted by social agencies.

218. Casner, M., & Marks, S. F. (1984, April 23–27). *Playing with autistic children.* **Paper presented at the 62nd Annual Convention of the Council for Exceptional Children, Washington, DC.**
This article discusses the development of a play group for children with autism. It presents the program's philosophy, the play group model, and actual lessons. The children in the group were between 5 and 9 years old and often chose self-stimulating and/or repetitive activities for play. This program provided mainstreaming opportunities through daily motor, lunch, and recess periods and academics. It provided therapy and speech-language services on an individual or small group basis. The play group was designed to facilitate positive social interactions, verbal and/or nonverbal. The design of the play group allowed the clinician to structure activities to accommodate the child's level of functioning. The toys used for a play group lesson were selected for their realism, structure, responsiveness, and functional complexity. The authors provide a sample lesson plan for three therapy sessions. At the end of the program year, the children in this program could demonstrate many modeled interactions that were not seen in the earlier stages of the play group.

219. Cassell, J. L. (1990). Disabled humor: Origin and impact. In M. Nagler (Ed.), *Perspectives on disability* **(pp. 151–157). Palo Alto, CA: Health Markets Research.**
This chapter examines the history and significance of disabled humor in everyday social interactions. It defines disabled humor as humor in which the context of the joke is a disabling condition or disability. This chapter examines disabled humor's early beginnings and its place in the modern period and in the 20th century. It presents different theoretical positions to help define the significance of disabled humor in relation to such concepts as rehabilitation, deviance, and degradation. Also, this chapter focuses on possible ways to recondition society to respond more positively to people with disabilities.

220. Caton, D. J., Grossnickle, W. F., Cope, J. G., Long, T. E., & Mitchell, C. C. (1988). Burnout and stress among employees at a state institution for men-

tally retarded persons. *American Journal of Mental Retardation, 93*(3), 300–304.
This article describes a study that used the Maslach Burnout Inventory and the Ivancevich Job Stress Scale to measure stress and burnout among 192 employees of a state institution. The following employees participated in this study: developmental technicians, professional staff (e.g., social workers, psychologists, occupational therapists, teachers, and nurses), educational development assistants, and environmental personnel (e.g., housekeepers, secretaries, and food service personnel). The results of this study indicate that, in general, stress and burnout are best considered as separate constructs.

221. Cauffiel, L. (1992). *Forever and five days.* **New York: Zebra Books.**
This "true-crime" book details the murders of elderly patients at the Alpine Manor nursing home in Grand Rapids, Michigan. Nurse's aides Catherine May Wood and Gwendolyn Gail Graham were convicted of five murders. Although the suffocation deaths were sometimes portrayed as mercy killings, testimony revealed other motivations. The two nurse's aides, who were also lovers, used the murders to bind each other to a love pact and played a game of selecting victims trying to spell out "Murder" with their first initials. Wood is quoted as saying, "We did it because it was fun" (p. 254).

222. Cavara, M., & Ogren, C. (1983). Protocol to investigate child abuse in foster care. *Child Abuse & Neglect, 7,* 287–295.
This article focuses on the investigation of child abuse that occurs in foster care. It describes the Protocol for the Investigation of Institutional Abuse and Neglect of Children, developed by the Hennepin County Community Services Department in Minneapolis. It discusses the investigation of 125 foster care child abuse and neglect cases (all 125 cases occurred between May 1980 and November 1981), and the results of these investigations indicate that the victims were generally 4-year-old to 12-year-old males. These results also indicate the following: foster mothers who were abusive were usually single, abusive foster families had a long-term commitment to foster care, and abusive foster families were less likely to have biological children. This article provides suggestions for the criteria and implementation of investigations of child abuse or neglect and the prevention of foster care abuse.

223. Chandler, L. K., & Lubeck, R. C. (1989). The appropriateness and utility of a child focused view of jeopardy: A family focused alternative. *Topics in Early Childhood Special Education, 9*(2), 101–116.
This article questions the appropriateness of characterizing children with disabilities as being at greater risk for abuse or maltreatment than the general population. The authors' examination of studies of incidence of child maltreatment with this population leads them to

conclude that some of these studies are methodologically flawed. They propose shifting the focus toward a family perspective that takes into consideration the child, the family, and environmental variables in determining risk. The authors feel that the available resources could then be used to meet the needs of the child and the family.

224. Charles, G. P., & Matheson, J. E. (1990). Children in foster care: Issues of separation and attachment. *Community Alternatives International Journal of Family Care, 2*(2), 37–49.
This article discusses prolonged exposure to unpredictable or nonsupportive environments and the effects of this exposure on attachment. It also examines the negative consequences of unresolved separation that may occur when a young person is removed from the care of his or her family and placed in the care of the state. These consequences are examined in relation to the theories of attachment, separation, and loss. The authors offer suggestions aimed at assisting foster parents in choosing appropriate interventions for the young person in care. Also, this article discusses functional admissions and discharges and suggest ways to ease these procedures.

225. Chasnoff, I. J. (1989). Cocaine, pregnancy, and the neonate. *Women and Health, 15*(3), 23–35.
This article discusses a study that compared women who used cocaine during pregnancy and their neonates with a control group who did not exhibit any substance abuse. This study found that a greater number of women from the substance abuse group had complications during labor and delivery. It also noted that premature labor, impaired intrauterine growth, and perinatal morbidity were more frequent for the substance abuse group.

226. Chasnoff, I. J., Burns, W. J., Schnoll, S. H., Burns, K., Chisum, G., & Kyle-Spore, L. (1986). Maternal-neonatal incest. *American Journal of Orthopsychiatry, 56*(4), 577–580.
Three case studies of mother-infant incest are presented in this article. All three infants were male, and the mothers were enrolled at a perinatal center for chemical dependency. The authors describe several characteristics common to these mothers: social isolation, substance abuse prior to pregnancy, estrangement from sexual partner, and sexual identity confusion.

227. Chasnoff, I. J., & Griffith, D. R. (1989). Cocaine: Clinical studies of pregnancy and the newborn. *Annals of the New York Academy of Sciences, 562,* 260–266.
This article describes a study that examined cocaine abuse during pregnancy and how substance abuse affects the neonate. This study compared 23 pregnant women who used cocaine up to the first trimester with 52 women who used cocaine throughout their pregnancy. The neonates born to these women were medically examined. The

study found a significantly greater number of infants with low birth weight, small head circumference, and short length born to those women who had continued to use cocaine during their pregnancy. The authors note that both groups of infants displayed neurodevelopmental impairment.

228. Chasnoff, I. J., Lewis, D. E., & Squires, L. (1987). Cocaine intoxication in a breast-fed infant. *Pediatrics, 80(6),* **836–838.**
This article examines the detrimental effects of cocaine intoxication on infants by using a case history of a 2-week-old girl who ingested cocaine through breast milk. It includes the results from medical examinations.

229. Chenoweth, L. (1993). Invisible acts: Violence against women with disabilities. *Australian Disability Review, 2,* **22–28.**
This article discusses violence against women with disabilities and provides arguments that they are marginalized or made powerless by their gender in addition to their disability. The author suggests that this marginalization has made abused women with disabilities "invisible" to society and prevented any acknowledgment of the crimes against them.

230. Chesnay, M. D., Stephens, D., & West, L. (1990). Child sexual abuse: A review of research. In R. L. Goldman & R. M. Gargiuloj (Eds.), *Children at risk* **(pp. 203–243). Austin, TX: PRO-ED.**
This chapter reviews the literature on child sexual abuse. Although many of the articles deal with offenders and families, the majority of them examine how sexual abuse affects the victims and its prevalence. The authors discuss the literature covering the following areas: psychological problems, sexual issues, medical diseases, mental and psychogenic pain, and self-destructive effects. They discuss articles that examine familial characteristics as factors in incest: for example, maternal distance, systems theory, disorganized and organized families, alcohol consumption, and marital power. They examine articles that describe male, adolescent, and female offenders' behavior, traits, and characteristics. They also cover the following: attribution of blame, prevention, and suggestions for resolving methodological issues. The authors conclude that variations in research design, method, lack of random samples, definitional differences, retrospective reviews, and the population sampled make it difficult to compare and generalize the results.

231. Chess, S., & Thomas, A. (Eds.). (1987). *Annual Progress in Child Psychiatry and Child Development.* **New York: Brunner/Mazel.**
This annual review of child psychiatry and child development consists of a collection of 38 selected articles published during 1986. The pieces in this collection are either original works or review articles, and they are categorized under 10 topic areas: 1) studies of infancy (consistency of imitation of mothers' behavior toward infant siblings), 2) developmental issues (resilience and risk in early mental development), 3) gender identity (early sex role development, gender identity in childhood, and sexual orientation), 4) sociocultural issues (child survivors, cross-cultural comparison of patterns of family interaction), 5) studies of temperament (rudiments of infant temperament, ratings of temperament in families of young twins), 6) children of divorce (long-term effects of divorce and remarriage on the child adjustment), 7) depression in childhood and adolescence (developmental considerations, suicidal behavior), 8) autism (neurophysiology of infantile autism, outcomes in adulthood), 9) clinical issues (child sexual abuse, siblings of chronically ill children, assessment and therapeutic intervention with African-American children), and 10) intervention programs (assessing the Head Start program; the efficacy of early intervention; the clinician as advocate).

232. Christoffel, K. K., & Liu, K. (1983). Homicide death rates in childhood in 23 developed countries: U.S. rates atypically high. *Child Abuse & Neglect, 7,* **339–345.**
This article uses statistical data gathered by the World Health Organization to compare the homicide rate of the United States to 23 other developed countries. The findings of this comparison indicate that the United States ranks second only to Northern Ireland in its high homicide rate for the general population. Finland, which came in third, had a homicide rate one fourth that of the United States. The U.S. homicide rate ranked in the top five for children less than 1 year of age and between 1 and 4 years of age. This comparison suggests that male children less than 1 year of age and female children between the ages of 1 and 4 were at particular risk. This article discusses possible explanations for these rates.

233. Christoffel, K. K., Liu, K., & Stamler, J. (1981). Epidemiology of fatal child abuse: International mortality data. *Journal of Chronic Disease, 34,* **57–64.**
This article discusses data on fatal child abuse and neglect obtained by the World Health Organization. The authors obtained death rate information for 1974 from 52 countries and categorized these data into three age groups (all ages, under the age of 1, between 1 to 4) and three categories of death (homicide and injury purposely inflicted, injury undetermined whether accidentally or purposely inflicted, and all causes). The countries were categorized according to their degree of economic development, with 23 developing, 24 developed, and 5 centrally planned countries. The results of this analysis indicate the following: For children under 1 year of age, death rates due to definite inflicted injury (DII) are independent of death rates due to DII for all ages; DII death rates in children under 1 year of age are the same in developing and developed countries; DII death rates for children between the ages of 1 and 4 in developing coun-

tries are independent of death rates for all ages, although these rates in developed countries almost correlate with those for all ages; and DII death rates for children between the ages of 1 and 4 are greater in developed countries than in developing countries.

234. Clarizio, H. F., & McCoy, G. F. (1983). *Behavior disorders in children* **(3rd ed.). New York: Harper & Row.**

This book provides an introduction to the field of behavior disorders in children and adolescents. The text presents information using a developmental framework. Part 1 explores developmental and diagnostic considerations: notions of normality; social and personality development; emphasizing subjects such as attachment, dependency, moral development, anxiety, and aggression; the incidence and diagnosis of various forms of maladjustment; and the impact of labelling. Part 2 addresses five specific disorders in children: compulsive, obsessive, and phobic reactions; learning disabilities; mental subnormality or mental retardation; childhood psychoses; and juvenile delinquency. It presents incidence, identifications, and treatment approaches for each of the five disorders. Intervention and prevention strategies constitute the final section of the text. This book also discusses selected treatment approaches: for example, psychotherapy and play therapy, community resources, behavioral and other approaches used to address classroom discipline difficulties, and the prevention of behavior disorders. The authors use case material throughout the book.

235. Clark, A. K., Reed, J., & Sturmey, P. (1991). Staff perceptions of sadness among people with mental handicaps. *Journal of Mental Deficiency Research,* **35, 147–153.**

This article describes a study that used a behavior checklist to examine caregivers' perceptions of sadness in a hospital population of people with mental disabilities. The authors report that only three checklist items had acceptable levels of interrater agreement (physical aggression, crying, and verbal abuse) and that there was no significant difference in behavior, regardless of the severity of the mental disability. The authors suggest that future research should examine the caregivers' concept of sadness and their ability to identify it.

236. Clark, J. (1991). Where you live can make you vulnerable. *Entourage,* **6(4), 11.**

The author of this article, an advocate for people with mental disabilities who presented at the 1991 National Conference of the Canadian Association for Community Living, discusses the importance of community integration and independent decision making for people with disabilities.

237. Clarke, D. J. (1989). Antilibidinal drugs and mental retardation: A review. *Medicine, Science and the Law,* **29(2), 136–146.**

According to this article, the increased sexual drive of some people with mental retardation frequently leads them into conflict with law. It suggests that the administration of progestogens such as medroxyprogesterone or specific drugs with antilibidinal action such as cyproterone acetate (CPA) and benperidol might be considered, in addition to psychotherapy and sexual counseling procedures, in the management of these people's sexual drives. It points out that ethical and legal issues have to be carefully considered before initiating such treatment. This article provides, in detail, the description, contraindications for use, and the efficacy of a steroid analogue cyproterone acetate and other drugs. The evidence concerning the efficacy of antilibidinal drugs is based on clinical observation rather than controlled study. The conditions treated are heterogeneous, and the outcome measures employed in most of the studies are varied; hence, this article suggests that there is a need for controlled studies in this area. An antilibidinal is likely to reduce the intensity of sexual drive, but it will not alter its direction; consequently, this article concludes that concurrent psychotherapy and sexual counseling are needed for these people.

238. Clarke, D. J., Kelly, S., Thinn, K., & Corbett, J. A. (1990). Psychotropic drugs and mental retardation: 1. Disabilities and the prescription of drugs for behaviour and for epilepsy in three residential settings. *Journal of Mental Deficiency Research,* **34(5), 385–395.**

This article describes a study that used the Birmingham Special Needs Register, a computerized database, to examine the use of psychoactive (psychotropic and antiepileptic) drugs among 1,825 people over the age of 20 with mental retardation. This study compared people living in three different types of residential settings: hospitals, community residential facilities, and family homes. It found that the incidence of physical disability, impaired communication, and incontinence was highest among residents in hospitals, followed by those living with their families, and lowest for people who lived in community residential facilities. It discovered that the use of psychotropic drugs prescribed to alter behavior was highest in hospitals (prescribed for 40.2% of these people), followed by community residential facilities (19.3%), and lowest in family homes (10.1%). The study also found that most hospital residents who received medication to alter behavior did not have a diagnosed psychiatric disorder; in fact, although drugs for epilepsy were prescribed for 26.2% of hospital residents, 9.3% of people in community residential facilities, and 18.5% of people living with their families, the reported prevalence of behavior disorders among the three populations was not significantly different.

239. Clearinghouse on Child Abuse and Neglect Information. (1993). *Developmental disabilities.* **Washington, DC: U.S. Department of Health and Human Services.**

This bibliography contains references and annotations dealing with developmental disabilities. Citations date from 1986 to 1992.

240. Cleckler, K. (1991). Making a good girl bad: Art therapy with the overly-compliant child. *Pratt Institute Creative Arts Therapy Review, 12,* **30–35.**
This article presents a case example that demonstrates the use of art therapy in helping an overly compliant girl deal with her history of abuse and neglect. The therapy was used to help the girl express her repressed negative emotions and to build the child's sense of security and self-esteem. The author notes that art therapy can be conducted individually or in groups.

241. Cockram, J., Jackson, R., & Underwood, R. (1992). Perceptions of the judiciary and intellectual disability. *Australia and New Zealand Journal of Developmental Disabilities, 18,* **189–200.**
This article presents results from an ongoing study in western Australia concerning the criminal justice system and people with developmental disabilities. Judges and magistrates were interviewed to examine their perceptions, beliefs, and procedures concerning people with developmental disabilities and their overrepresentation in the criminal justice system. Nineteen judiciary members (18 male, 1 female) with diverse years of experience were interviewed for this study. The structured interview touched upon such areas as sentencing options, characteristics of offenders with developmental disabilities, and general issues of concern pertaining to offenders with developmental disabilities. A questionnaire followed that consisted of 55 questions related to the topics discussed in the interview. The questions allowed for one of five responses, ranging from strongly agree to strongly disagree. Respondents were also asked to prioritize 10 possible solutions concerning the issue of contact between people with developmental disabilities and the criminal justice system. The findings indicate that both the structured interview and the questionnaire supported each other. Concerning the characteristics of people with developmental disabilities, the majority of respondents agreed that people with developmental disabilities were at a greater disadvantage once they were in the criminal justice system. Respondents agreed on more training for police in the area of people with developmental disabilities and that more sentencing options were needed. Service agencies should be involved in developing sentencing options and special training for lawyers with regard to interviewing skills with people with developmental disabilities and having the person with developmental disabilities present in any legal discussions with guardians was strongly supported by respondents. The area of protection for people with developmental disabilities was given the highest ranking by the respondents.

242. Coelho, R. J., & Dillon, N. F. (1990). A survey of elderly persons with de- velopmental disabilities. *Journal of Applied Rehabilitation Counseling, 21*(1), **9–15.**
This article discusses a survey of 67 older adults receiving services from a comprehensive mental health service in three Michigan counties. The results of this study reveal the following: There is a clear need for greater monitoring of health and sensory functioning, diagnosis should be improved, and there should be greater service planning for service differentiation. Also, the authors recommend that service options be expanded to increase social interaction.

243. Cohen, M. E., Anday, E. K., & Leitner, D. S. (1989). Effects of in-utero cocaine exposure on sensorineural reactivity. *Annals of the New York Academy of Sciences, 562,* **344–346.**
This article discusses a study that compared 19 in utero cocaine-exposed infants with 19 nondrug-exposed infants on variables of behavioral reactivity using a reflex augmentation procedure. The results of this study indicate that cocaine-exposed infants are more behaviorally reactive than drug-free infants.

244. Cohen, R. M. (1992). Re-establishing trust, communication goals for deaf and hearing impaired children. *NRCCSA (National Resource Center on Child Sexual Abuse) News, 1*(4), **13.**
This article deals with treatment therapy for sexually abused children who are deaf or have a hearing impairment. It focuses on the reestablishment of trust and self-esteem as a means of treating these abused children. The author suggests that one strategy for dealing with this issue is play therapy.

245. Cohen, S., & Warren, R. D. (1987). Preliminary survey of family abuse of children served by United Cerebral Palsy centers. *Developmental Medicine and Child Neurology, 29,* **12–18.**
This article discusses a survey questionnaire that was administered at 42 preschool and 14 respite care programs affiliated with United Cerebral Palsy. This study assessed the incidence of violence-induced disability and abuse of children with disabilities and collected data for 2,771 children from 42 preschool programs and 435 children from 14 respite care programs. This study found that 227 children had acquired disabilities, of which 11.9% of them were known to have been abused and an additional 12.3% of them were suspected of being abused (abuse in these programs was reported for 303 children [10.8%]); and there appears to be a higher incidence of abuse of children with disabilities in preschool programs than in respite care programs. The authors recommend that staff should be more aware of and report abuse in programs for young children with disabilities.

246. Cohen, S., & Warren, R. D. (1990). The intersection of disability and child abuse

in England and the United States. *Child Welfare, 71,* 253–262.

This article discusses the findings of a World Rehabilitation Fund Fellowship study on the intersection of child abuse, family support, and disability in England. The authors compare these findings with American information about the intersection of child abuse, family support, and disability and discuss implications for future research.

247. **Cohen, T. B., Galenson, E., van Leeuwen, K., Steele, B. F., Sherkow, S. P., & Etezady, M. H. (1987). Sexual abuse in vulnerable and high risk children.** *Child Abuse & Neglect, 11,* 461–474.

This article presents a discussion by professionals about sexual abuse and children. It covers the following topics: sexual development arrest versus intrapsychic conflict in preoedipal females, sexual abuse of children, resistance to analysis, and some sequelae of sexual maltreatment of children. It includes case studies for the first two topics, and Freudian psychoanalysis predominates the discussion of these cases.

248. **Cole, A. (1985). 27 babies left to starve and die.** *Just Cause, 3*(3), 14–16.

This article discusses the ethical considerations of parental decisions to refuse medical treatment for infants born with disabilities. This article uses the cases of 27 infants born with Down syndrome who were refused medical treatment by their parents between January 1952 and December 1971, and were left to die at the Hospital for Sick Children in Toronto in order to examine the ethics of refusing medical treatment for children with disabilities.

249. **Cole, L. (1972).** *Our children's keepers: Inside America's kid prisons.* **New York: Grossman.**

This book provides a classic expose of institutional abuse of children in New York, Colorado, Louisiana, California, and several other states. The book's primary focus is on neglect, physical punishment, and sexual abuse of children in residential reformatories. As a final chapter, the book also includes a Walt Kelly comic strip, "the Town on the edge of the End," a parable, based on the Pied Piper, on how society often blames children for its misfortunes. This book suggests that widespread abuse is inevitable in isolated institutions and that public recognition of the problem is the first step to meaningful reform.

250. **Cole, S. S. (1984–1986). Facing the challenges of sexual abuse in persons with disabilities.** *Sexuality and Disability, 7*(3/4), 71–88.

According to the author of this article, the presence of developmental or physical disabilities adds another dimension to sexual exploitation. The person who is dependent on relatives and care providers for personal care may be unable to distinguish appropriate affectionate behavior and touch from exploitative touch. The author states that the first step toward prevention is the acknowledgment that sexual abuse is common; and once the prevalence of sexual abuse is recognized, it is necessary to provide programs that inform individuals of their rights to their own bodies. The author discusses the indicators of sexual abuse and the steps to recovery.

251. **Cole, S. S. (1988). Women, sexuality, and disabilities.** *Women and Therapy, 7*(2/3), 277–294.

This article discusses how women with disabilities experience social expectations and misperceptions regarding their sexuality. It discusses guidelines for therapists.

252. **Cole, S. (1992). Sex education: Our school's responsibility.** *Journal on Developmental Disabilities, 1*(1), 51–54.

This article supports sex education for students with mental disabilities who are integrated into the regular school system. The author feels that it is the school's responsibility to provide sex education for students with mental disabilities.

253. **Coles, C. D., Platzman, K. A., Smith, I., James, M. E., & Falek, A. (1992). Effects of cocaine and alcohol use in pregnancy on neonatal growth and neurobehavioral status.** *Neurotoxicology and Teratology, 14,* 23–33.

This article describes a study that examined substance abuse during pregnancy by predominantly low-income African-American women and the affect this abuse had on neonatal outcome. The study focused on fetal growth and neonatal behavior. It assessed 107 full-term infants on three separate occasions using the Brazelton Neonatal Behavioral Assessment Scale and measured birth weight, length, and head circumference. The findings of this study indicate that neonatal growth was adversely affected by cocaine and/or alcohol use during pregnancy, but neonatal behavior was within clinical normality.

254. **Coles, W. (1990). Sexual abuse of persons with disabilities: A law enforcement perspective.** *Developmental Disabilities Bulletin, 18*(2), 35–43.

The author of this article, a Royal Canadian Mounted Police officer, discusses the investigation of cases involving the sexual abuse of people with disabilities. He details several techniques and compares sexual abuse investigations involving children and people with disabilities. The author suggests amendments to Canada's Criminal Code in order to help protect people with disabilities.

255. **Collins, B. C., Schuster, J. W., & Nelson, C. M. (1992). Teaching a generalized response to the lures of strangers to adults with severe handicaps.** *Exceptionality, 3,* 67–80.

This article describes an instructional program that was conducted with three adults with severe mental retardation who were trained to resist the lures of strangers. This program used in vivo instruction using such settings as shopping malls, parks, public libraries, and apartment complexes. A constant time delay instructional procedure was employed, and the program used a pool of university students, staff, and faculty and friends and families of the authors to act as strangers who interacted with the three subjects. Correct responses to the lures of strangers consisted of saying "no" and moving away from the stranger. This program used both probe trials, which employed the strangers, and training trials, which gave immediate feedback to these adults following their performance on the probe trials. The lures varied in context from general questions to authoritative statements and incentives. The results of this instructional program indicate that target responses were learned by these adults in controlled role playing, but these responses did not generalize consistently to realistic probe trials.

256. Collins, B. C., Wolery, M., & Gast, D. L. (1992). A national survey of safety concerns for students with special needs. *Journal of Developmental and Physical Disabilities, 4*(3), 263–276.

This article describes a national survey of special education teachers that was conducted to assess their views on which safety skills they thought were most important to teach children at various ages. One hundred thirty-five Survey of Safety Concerns were returned by special education teachers in preschool (*n*=30), elementary school (*n*=39), junior high school (*n*=31), and senior high school (*n*=35). The respondents were predominantly female, between the ages of 30 and 40. The results of this survey indicate the following: teachers felt that some safety skills were more critical than other skills to learn, instructions in specified safety skills depended on the child's age, longitudinal safety instruction was suggested because of the overlap of safety skills across age groups, and safety skills training for children with disabilities was seen as a legitimate area of instruction by teachers.

257. Colorado Department of Social Services (Interagency Project for Prevention of Abuses in Out-of-Home Child Care Settings). (1987). *Selection and screening of personnel: An effort toward the prevention of maltreatment of children and youth in out-of-home care settings in Colorado.* Denver: Author.

These proceedings include several papers presented in a conference sponsored by The Interagency Project for the Prevention of Abuses in Out-of-Home Child Care Settings. These papers focus on the selection and screening of child-care personnel and examine the following areas: the history and dynamics of child abuse, the responsibilities of child-care staff, and relevant statutes.

258. Condon, J. T. (1986). The spectrum of fetal abuse in pregnant women. *Journal of Nervous and Mental Disease, 174*(9), 509–516.

This article presents case studies of fetal abuse through assault and substance abuse. It discusses the relationship of fetal and child abuse and reviews the familial triad.

259. Condon, J. T. (1987). "The battered fetus syndrome": Preliminary data on the incidence of the urge to physically abuse the unborn child. *Journal of Nervous and Mental Disease, 175*(12), 722–725.

This article discusses a survey that questioned 150 pregnant couples who attended an antenatal clinic about the urge to assault the fetus. The survey was completed by 112 couples. The survey found the following: 8% of the women and 4% of the men stated that at times they felt the urge to hurt or punish the fetus, 21% of the women and 8% of the men had felt irritation toward the developing fetus during the 2 weeks prior to the completion of the survey, and 9% of the male partners believed that their female partners had the urge to hurt the fetus on occasion.

260. Conley, R. W., Luckasson, R., & Bouthilet, G. N. (Eds.). (1992). *The criminal justice system and mental retardation: Defendants and victims.* Baltimore: Paul H. Brookes Publishing Co.

This book provides many important perspectives on the participation of people with mental retardation in the criminal justice system. Most of the chapters deal with issues primarily relevant to people with disabilities who have been accused of crimes; nevertheless, since these chapters often discuss issues of competency, attitudes, and accessibility, they also have implications for crime victims with disabilities. Chapter 11, "People with mental retardation as victims of crime," provides a more specific discussion of people with disabilities who have been victims.

261. Conte, J. R. (1988). The effects of sexual abuse on children: Results of a research project. In R. A. Prentky & V. L. Quinsey (Eds.), *Human sexual aggression: Current perspectives* (pp. 310–326). New York: New York Academy of Sciences.

This chapter describes a study that examined how sexual abuse affects children in order to identify the factors that are associated with different effects. This study used the Child Behavior Profile, a 38-item symptom checklist and a clinical assessment form, and a follow-up assessment on the children. The study indicates that children who are sexually abused are perceived by their parents to behave differently from nonabused children. Also, abuse appears to affect several different clusters of behaviors. The author suggests that broad band multi-item, multifactor measures of child behavior and functioning are not that useful clinically as they tend to be too abstract, may not be behaviorally specific enough, and may be limited to observable behavior and ignore the more severe consequences of sexual abuse. Broad measures of functioning may also lack theoretical foundation. The author concludes that it is necessary to identify the mediators between abuse and abuse-related experiences and problems and that it is also important to design abuse-sensitive interventions that deal directly with the problems associated with abuse.

262. Cooke, T., & Cowan, M. R. (1991 September). Confronting sexual abuse in the deaf community. *Vibrations*, pp. 9–11.

The authors of this article assert that sexual abuse is not related to the hearing impairments of the victims. They claim that people who are deaf are included in the risk group as a result of the way society has treated them, and they discuss the following factors that contribute to the vulnerability of children who are deaf: the denial of language, issues of power, self-governing schools, education, institutions, and access to information. The authors stress that these risk factors need to be addressed in the deaf community.

263. Cooper, S. (1987). The fetal alcohol syndrome. *Journal of Child Psychology and Psychiatry*, 28(2), 223–227.

This article discusses fetal alcohol syndrome (FAS) and its characteristics. The areas examined include the following: criteria for diagnosis, toxology of alcohol, incidence, and effects of alcohol during pregnancy. The author concludes that more research is necessary to address the effects of prenatal exposure to alcohol.

264. Corin, L. (1984–1986). Sexual assault of the disabled: A survey of human service providers. *Sexuality and Disability*, 7(3/4), 110–116.

This article describes an informal survey of human services providers in order to uncover the depth of the problem of sexual abuse of adults and children with disabilities. The results of this study reveal a great deal of concern but few statistics to record the incidence of abuse. Following the survey, a petition was organized for legislation to establish a commission for protection of persons with disabilities in Massachusetts.

265. Cornell, W. F., & Olio, K. A. (1991). Integrating affect in treatment with adult survivors of physical and sexual abuse. *American Journal of Orthopsychiatry*, 61(1), 59–69.

This article presents a theoretical and technical model for the treatment of adult survivors of physical and sexual abuse. It concentrates on the use of affective and body-centered techniques. The authors suggest that the symptoms displayed by victims of abuse indicate post-traumatic stress disorder. They discuss the roles that dissociation and denial play within therapy, and they highlight treatment strategies and some treatment precautions.

266. Corrigan, J. P., Terpstra, J., Rurrow, A. A., & Thomas, G. (1981). Protecting the rights of institutionalized individuals. In *Proceedings of the Fifth National Conference on Child Abuse and Neglect* (pp. 181–194). Milwaukee: University of Wisconsin, Region V Child Abuse and Neglect Resource Center.

This chapter is included in a collection of papers from a workshop on protecting the rights of children who are institutionalized that reviewed child abuse and neglect. This chapter describes the prevention activities of the Administration of Children, Youth, and Families and examines the following topics: development of a definition of institutional abuse and neglect, principles for the reduction of abuse, the impact of the U.S. Civil Rights of Institutionalized Persons Act, changes in parents' and children's rights, and the erosion of the state's authority in child management.

267. Costner, W., & Crichetti, D. (1993). Research on the communicative development of maltreated children: Clinical implications. *Topics in Language Disorders*, 13(4), 25–38.

This article reviews the literature on the effects of child abuse on language development. Maltreated children have consistently been reported to have difficulties with a variety of language and communication skills. They have also been shown to have difficulty developing self-esteem and secure attachment, which may underlie some of their communication impairment. The authors suggest that many interacting factors may be responsible for these communication deficits and suggest that there is a critical need for more research to clarify these relationships.

268. Cotter, L. H. (1967). Operant conditioning in a Vietnamese mental hospital. *American Journal of Psychiatry*, 124(1), 61–66.

Dr. Lloyd Cotter describes his use of operant conditioning on Vietnamese adults with chronic mental illness (most of the patients are described as schizophrenic) at the Bien Hoa Mental Hospital in South Viet Nam during the Viet Nam war. Cotter attempted to get these patients to participate in a work force in order to speed their recovery and allow them to be discharged from the hospital. As an incentive, Cotter gave unmodified electroconvulsive treatments (ECT) to those patients unwilling to work clearing fields for crops. Eventually, all of the male patients started working. In the women's ward of 130 patients, 20 of the women were given treatments, and 15 women went to work. Cotter also used additional reinforcement, for example, withholding meals. In Cotter's own words, "after three days without food, all the remaining patients volunteered for work." Cotter goes on to explain how his volunteer patients were contracted out to work for the American Special Forces. (Editors' note: G. Thomas's book, *Journey into madness: Medical torture and the mind controllers*, claims that Cotter's alleged work with schizophrenic patients was actually medical treatment or torture on Vietcong prisoners of war. Thomas goes on to explain that one soldier received six shocks, a 12-hour reprieve, and then additional shocks. After a week of treatment, a total of 60 shocks, the soldier died. Thomas contends that thousands of shock treatments were carried out during the treatment program, and all of the patients died at the end of the treatment program.)

269. Coulborn Faller, K. (1991). What happens to sexually abused children identified by Child Protective Services? *Children and Youth Services Review,* *13,* **101–111.**
This article examines Child Protective Services intervention in cases of child sexual abuse and the effects of this intervention. The author gathered follow-up information for 58 sexually abused children (88% girls, 12% boys) who were identified as having been abused approximately 3 years earlier. The average age of the abused children was 7.9 years, with a range in age from 2 years to 16, and 36 children were placed outside the home. At follow-up, the author found the following: the family structure had changed for 32 cases; rereferrals for other forms of maltreatment were made for 13 (22%) cases, with 10 children residing in the same residence where they were abused; and sexual abuse and physical abuse were the most prominent reasons for rereferrals. The author notes that 30 cases were still open at follow-up.

270. Coulter, D. (1990, November 23). Simple, insecure man's friends dealt him torture and death. *The Edmonton Journal,* **pp. B1, B3.**
This newspaper article reports that Paul Devereaux, a 24-year-old man with developmental disabilities, died as a result of kidney failure caused by injuries endured during several days of beatings. One adult and three youths are currently on trial for aggravated assault against Mr. Devereaux. One of the accused, Jose Antonio Cobo, had worked with Mr. Devereaux as a wheelchair porter at an extended care facility as a result of having to complete community service hours for a previous crime. The beatings lasted several days and included acts of degradation and torture.

271. Coulter, D. (1991). The failure of prevention. *Mental Retardation, 29*(5), iii–iv.
This editorial addresses the failure of prevention programs to prevent mental retardation. The author suggests that this failure is in part due to the narrow conceptual framework of mental retardation and limited knowledge about etiological factors.

272. Coulter, D. (1991). Medical treatment. In L. H. Meyer, C. A. Peck, & L. Brown (Eds.), *Critical issues in the lives of people with severe disabilities* (pp. 553–558). Baltimore: Paul H. Brookes Publishing Co.
This chapter introduces three guidelines dealing with the provision of medical treatment for people with severe disabilities: The individual should always receive the best possible medical treatment, the individual should be the first person to make decisions concerning medical treatment, and medical treatment should be provided for people with severe disabilities. A framework for the decision-making process is suggested, and application of this process is examined using several medical disorders found in infancy: Down syndrome, anencephaly, and other disabilities. The author discusses treatments such as nutrition and hydration and hormone therapy. The rights of people with severe disabilities, regardless of their disability, to appropriate medical treatment is strongly supported by the author.

273. Couwenhoven, T. (1992). *Beginnings: A parent/child sexuality program for families with children who have developmental disabilities.* **Madison: Wisconsin Council on Developmental Disabilities.**
This guide consists of a series of lessons on sexuality and sexual abuse prevention. It is designed for use by community facilitators, parents, and children with developmental disabilities. This guide is designed to be used with a Waisman Center program that promotes positive sexuality and prevention of sexual abuse for people with developmental disabilities. The author also provides a comprehensive annotated bibliography of resources to teach sexual and social education.

274. Craft, A. (1991). The living your life program. *British Journal of Education,* *18*(4), **157–160.**
This article describes a curriculum development project for sex education of students with developmental disabilities. The author discusses the lack of currently available materials. Materials being developed by the project are intended to extend existing materials in order to eliminate gaps and make them more suitable for students with severe disabilities.

275. Craft, A. (1992, December). The sexual abuse of people with learning difficulties: Implications for services and for staff. *National Association for the Protection from Sexual Abuse of Adults and Children with Learning Disabilities,* *2,* **3–6.**
This article examines sexual abuse and its implications for services and employees who serve people with learning disabilities. It claims that recognizing the problem and responding to abusive incidents are the first two steps that need to be taken when dealing with sexual abuse. It states that recognition involves awareness and the establishment of both policy and guidelines on sexual abuse.

It points out that responding consists of proper staffing procedures such as recruitment and training. This article concludes that protection is necessary for both the victim and perpetrator in any care system and that it is important to consider the issue of adequate support and treatment after abuse.

276. Craft, A. (Ed.). (1993). *Practice issue in sexuality and learning disabilities.* **London: Routledge.**

This book addresses a wide range of issues and practices related to sexuality and developmental disabilities. The majority of the book addresses sexual health and education issues, but three chapters are particularly relevant to sexual abuse: "Sexual abuse of individuals with intellectual disability," "Between ourselves: Experiences of a women's group on sexuality and sexual abuse," and "Working with sexually abused individuals who have a learning disability."

277. Craft, A., & Hitching, M. (1989). Keeping safe: Sex education and assertiveness skills. In H. Brown & A. Craft (Eds.), *Thinking the unthinkable: Papers on sexual abuse and people with learning difficulties* **(pp. 29–38). London: FPA Education Unit.**

This chapter discusses the need for sex education and assertiveness training for individuals with learning difficulties to help reduce the chance of sexual abuse or exploitation. The authors include some general and specific suggestions for curriculum and instructional strategies.

278. Crane, D. (1975). *The sanctity of social life.* **New York: Russel Sage Foundation.**

This monograph provides critical evidence of discrimination in medical decisions. The author sent simulated case histories of patients to surgeons and asked whether heart surgery should be performed. When the patient was described as having a physical disability, 90% of the surgeons indicated they would want to operate, but when the patient was described as having a mental disability, less than 60% of the surgeons indicated that they would want to operate. This number dropped to less than 20% when the family's attitude was described as unfavorable. When the author checked actual hospital records of children with and without Down syndrome, she found that 100% of children without Down syndrome with atrial-ventricular canal defect received surgery, but only 29% of children with the same defect who had Down syndrome had the surgery. The study compares factors considered by physicians in making a variety of life and death decisions and found that the physician's judgment regarding the potential "usefulness" of the patient and the perceived impact on the family were ranked among the most influential factors in making life or death decisions. Based on her findings, the author concludes that "social variables play a more important role than medical variables in determining whether or not such operations are performed" (p. 100).

279. Cranford, R. E. (1992). The contemporary euthanasia movement and the Nazi program. In A. L. Kaplan (Ed.), *When medicine went mad: Bioethics and the holocaust* **(pp. 201–210). Totawa, NJ: Humana Press.**

This chapter argues that the contemporary Dutch euthanasia program is significantly different from the Nazi program because of internal safeguards, specifically that the patient must be competent and the choice must be voluntary.

280. Creighton, S. J. (1979). An epidemiological study of child abuse. *Child Abuse & Neglect, 3,* **601–605.**

This article provides an analysis of 905 cases of suspected nonaccidental injury in the United Kingdom. The injured children were divided into five categories according to severity and type of injury. This article includes epidemiological data on the children, their parents, the families, and the environment in which they lived. The data reveal that children of the youngest age groups, boys, and low birth weight infants were all overrepresented among the injured children; parents were characterized by early parenthood, large families, abnormal family structures, low social class, mobility, and high unemployment.

281. Creighton, S. J. (1987). Quantitative assessment of child abuse. In P. Maher (Ed.), *Child abuse: The educational perspective* **(pp. 23–34). Oxford: Basil Blackwell.**

This chapter focuses on the role that a teacher can play in the recognition and prevention of child abuse. The author examines the different manifestations of child abuse, and using information obtained from the National Society for the Prevention of Cruelty to Children, the author describes the prevalence of maltreatment and the demographics of abuse cases. This chapter examines the factors involved in child abuse, and it discusses the teacher's role in the management of child abuse.

282. Crittenden, P. M. (1985). Maltreated infants: Vulnerability and resilience. *Journal of Child Psychology and Psychiatry and Allied Disciplines, 26(1),* **85–96.**

This article discusses two studies that investigated the following areas: to determine if differences existed at birth between maltreated and adequately reared infants, to test if behavioral differences were irreversible, and to determine if there were any differences between the behavior patterns of abused infants and neglected infants. The first study examined 38 low socioeconomic mother-infant dyads. In this study, the infants ranged in age from 1 to 19 months (mean 7.2 months); the mothers, 8 of whom were abusing, 10 neglecting, 10 problematic, and 10 adequate, ranged in age from 15 to 49 (mean 22). The procedures used in this study involved videotaping play sessions and administration of the Bayley Scales of Infant Development. The second study examined 73 mother-infant dyads of similar characteristics to the first study: infants ranged in age from 2 to 24 months (mean 13.7 months); mothers ranged in age from 13 to 35 (mean 22). This study used procedures similar to those in the first study, with the addition of assessing the infants' attachment to their mothers using the Ainsworth Strange Situation. The results of these studies support a model of bidirectional effects where the mother initiates the maltreatment but both mother and infant behaviors maintain the situation. Neither study found any congenital differences between the maltreated and adequately raised infants; however, maltreated infants displayed patterns of behavior that were harder to manage and more disagreeable to mothers. The studies reveal that the exact pattern of abnormal behavior depended on the type of maltreatment received (e.g., when stressed, abused infants were difficult, mildly delayed, and angry; neglected infants were passive, significantly delayed, and helpless). After intervention with the mother, the author states that the maltreated infants made developmental gains and behaved more cooperatively during interaction, supporting the suggestion that maltreated infants favorably respond to improvements in the environment.

283. Crittenden, P. M., & Craig, S. E. (1990). Developmental trends in the nature of child homicide. *Journal of Interpersonal Violence,* **5**(2), 202–216.

This article examines child homicide in infancy, early childhood, and late childhood in order to determine if there are any trends associated with the different age groups. It uses data on 171 children under the age of 12 who were murdered in Dade County, Florida. It found that neonatal risk of homicide was characterized by death during the first day of life, and infanticide was closely related to maternal isolation. The results of the analysis show that homicide in early childhood, which includes infants, toddlers, and preschoolers, was most often characterized by parental control of child behavior through the use of punishment. It shows that homicide in late childhood was associated with minimal parental supervision and the availability of firearms. The authors note that the perpetrators were most often family members.

284. Cross, M. (1992). Abusive practices and disempowerment of children with physical impairment. *Child Abuse Review,* **1**, 194–197.

This article describes various practices commonly used with children who have physical disabilities in health care settings and discusses how these practices are disempowering and sometimes abusive: For example, these children are often depersonalized by talking about them rather than to them and requiring them to undress in public view. These practices may be abusive in themselves, but they also increase vulnerability to other abuse. The author provides a list of recommendations for reforming current practices.

285. Cross, M., Gordon, R., Kennedy, M., & Marchant, R. (1993). *The ABCD pack: Abuse and children who are disabled.* **Leicester, England: ABCD Consortium.**

This large training package includes a monograph and a training manual. It is intended for training child protection workers to work with children with disabilities. It includes basic information about disability, specific information about abuse of children with disabilities, and implications for investigation and intervention.

286. Crosse, S. B., Kaye, E., & Ratnofsky, A. C. (1993). *A report on the maltreatment of children with disabilities* **(Contract No. 105-89-1630). Washington, DC: National Center on Child Abuse and Neglect.**

This report discusses a study that investigated the maltreatment of children with disabilities. This study gathered information on the maltreatment of children with disabilities (MCD) from 35 Child Protective Services agencies in the United States. These agencies were asked to report incidences of substantiated child maltreatment for a period of 4 to 6 weeks. These agencies reported 1,249 cases of maltreatment that involved 1,834 children. The study found the following: The incidence of maltreatment and emotional neglect among children with disabilities was 1.7 times and 2.8 times higher, respectively, than among children without disabilities; in 47% of MCD cases, the child's disability contributed to the maltreatment; the rate of physical and sexual abuse among children with disabilities was 1.8 and 1.6 times higher, respectively, than among children without disabilities; 37% of children in this study became disabled as a result of their maltreatment; 42% of the families in this study were know to Child Protective Services prior to the recorded case of maltreatment; and the maltreated children with disabilities in this study were most often White males who were over the age of 4 and came from single-child families. This study found that 21% of the male victims of abuse were disabled compared to only 7.7% of the female victims. While this difference could be partially explained by the fact that 55% of children with disabilities are boys and 45% are girls, it also lends support for the findings of other researchers that males are overrepresented among abuse victims with disabilities when compared to abuse victims without disabilities. The study also reports that White children were overrepresented in the group with disabilities. Maltreated White children were significantly more likely to be classified as having disabilities. While this difference was too large to ignore, it is difficult to interpret without further research. It is possible that White children were more likely to be identified as disabled. The effect also could be related to cultural differences in the values placed on children with disabilities or to the related concept of cultural devaluation. This would predict that since nonWhites are already stigmatized and devalued in contemporary American society disability makes less difference. This report provides a well-controlled, large-scale comparison of the relative risks for children with disabilities and other children. The authors point out several limitations that generally seem to suggest that the study is likely to underestimate risk for children with disabilities, although the extent of underestimation is difficult to assess. First of all, the study is based on identified disabilities; the authors' post hoc models suggest that some children with disabilities were not reported as having disabilities. Second, the figures are based only on reported cases, and other studies suggest that abuse of children with disabilities may be less likely to be reported. Third, children in institutional settings were excluded from the study.

287. Crossmaker, M. (1986). *Empowerment: A systems approach to preventing assaults against people with mental retardation and/or developmental disabilities.* **Columbus, OH: The National Assault Prevention Centre.**

This book includes a wide range of information about institutional abuse and specific information on prevention. It describes APT (Assault Prevention Training), which is a systems approach to risk management. It emphasizes training to reduce personal risk for victimization, but it also recognizes the need for reforming institutional practices that encourage abuse.

288. Crossmaker, M. (1989). *Increasing safety for people receiving mental health services.* **Columbus, OH: National Assault Centre.**

This handbook describes the Assault Prevention Training (APT) program. It includes detailed explanations, role plays, evaluations, and lists the effects of sexual assault and myths of crisis intervention. The main theme of this handbook is understanding and addressing the risk factors in the socialization of people with disabilities. The author concludes that understanding the risk factors will lead to the individual's empowerment and self-esteem.

289. Crossmaker, M. (1991). Behind locked doors: Institutional sexual abuse [Special issue: Sexual exploitation of people with disabilities]. *Sexuality and Disability, 9*(3), 201–219.

This article examines institutional abuse of people with developmental disabilities. It discusses the variables that contribute to victimization: for example, personal attitudes, the dynamics of institutionalization, and the dynamics of institutions. It describes the imbalance of power between residents and caregivers and discusses reporting and investigating instances of sexual abuse and the need for advocacy for institutionalized people with disabilities. This article offers suggestions for increasing safety for residents of institutions.

290. Crossmaker, M. (no date). *Abuse and neglect: Awareness and reporting for individuals labeled as mentally ill.* **Columbus: Ohio Legal Rights Service.**

This booklet is written for individuals receiving mental health services or their advocates living in Ohio who require information about physical, sexual, or emotional abuse issues. It examines the following issues: personal rights, definitions of abuse, reporting abuse, reasons for not reporting abuse, resources and services available, and a Bill of Rights for People Receiving Mental Health Services.

291. Cruz, V. K., Price-Williams, D., & Andron, L. (1988). Developmentally disabled women who were molested as children. *Social Casework: The Journal of Contemporary Social Work, 69*(7), 411–419.

This article addresses the need for expanded treatment programs for women with developmental disabilities who were molested as children. It discusses treatment issues and the parental relationships of this group of women.

292. Csapo, M. (1988). Sexual abuse of children. *BC Journal of Special Education, 2,* 121–145.

This article reviews Canadian reports and legislation that emphasize the importance of school in the prevention and reporting of sexual abuse. The author lists the risk factors that lead to the vulnerability of children with disabilities: the dependency of children with disabilities on the abusive caregiver, the need for attention and friendship, inability to disclose or understand the nature of the abusive situation, lack of information about sexuality and abuse prevention, lack of credibility, and ease of manipulation with threats and tricks.

293. Culhane, C. (1987). Prisoners and disabilities. *Just Cause, 4*(4), 8–12.

This article looks at offenders with disabilities in the Canadian prison system. It notes that prison systems are disabling for every prisoner because they are physically and psychologically abusive. The author hopes to bring about an attitudinal change in the reader by showing that these offenders, regardless of their crimes, still have basic rights.

294. Cummer, D. (1982). The problem of the mentally handicapped offender. *Liaison, 8*(4), 7–10.

This article addresses the issue of offenders with mental disabilities and the criminal justice system. It concludes that the justice system is ill-equipped to handle these types of offenders, and it suggests that changes should be made to the system.

295. Cunningham, D. (1991, October 3–9). Sex case terror of children in care. *International Express*, pp. 1–3.

This newspaper article reports that a 13-year undetected physical and sexual child abuse spree is over at the Ratcliffe Road, The Beeches, and the Poplars children's homes in Leicester, Great Britain. Frank Beck, chairman of The Ratcliffe, George Lincoln, a social worker, and Peter Jaynes, former deputy head for two children's homes, are charged with 29 criminal counts, including buggery (anal intercourse), rape, attempted buggery, sexual assault, and assault causing bodily harm. These men are accused of abusing 13 boys, 1 girl, and 4 staff members.

296. Cutsforth, T. D. (1990). Personality crippling through physical disability. In M. Nagler (Ed.), *Perspectives on disability* **(pp. 57–60). Palo Alto, CA: Health Markets Research.**

The author of this chapter suggests that societal attitudes toward people who are visually impaired disables individuals to a greater degree than the impairment itself and causes insecurity, social inadequacy, and lack of self-assurance. The author notes that the manifestation of these inadequacies in the personality is characteristic of neurosis. While the measures taken to make up for these perceived inadequacies lead, at times, to success, the author feels that they seldom help resolve personality conflicts.

•D•

297. Dalley, T. (Ed.). (1984). *Art as therapy: An introduction to the use of art as a therapeutic technique.* **London: Tavistock Publications.**

Using a wide variety of clinical perspectives, this book examines the development and current practice of art therapy in Great Britain. It contains thirteen chapters that describe different aspects of art therapy and how art therapy may be used with different populations: "A consideration of the similarities and differences between art teaching and art therapy" (Waller); "Art, psychotherapy, and symbol systems" (Henzell); "Art therapy as a form of psychotherapy" (Birtchnell); "Alternative models for describing the development of children's graphic work: Some implications for art therapy" (Dubkowski); "The child and art therapy: A psychodynamic viewpoint" (Wood); "A Jungian approach to art therapy based in a residential setting" (Robinson); "The use of art therapy in the treatment of anorexia nervosa" (Murphy); "Art therapy for people who are mentally handicapped" (Stott & Males); "Art therapy with the elderly and the terminally ill" (Miller); "Art therapy in prisons" (Laing); "Art games and group structures" (Liebmann); "Art therapy with long-stay residents of psychiatric hospitals" (Charlton); and "Training in art therapy" (Waller & James).

298. Dattilo, J., & Smith, R. W. (1990). Communicating positive attitudes toward people with disabilities through sensitive terminology. *Therapeutic Recreation Journal, 24*(1st Quarter), 8–17.

The authors of this article suggest that the communication of positive attitudes toward people with disabilities is facilitated by terminology that accurately describes the individual's abilities. They claim that positive attitudes could be shaped by conveying respect, focusing on the individual, and being consistent when addressing people with disabilities. They discuss the most recent preferred terminology and the ensuing controversy. The authors conclude that professionals should become the frontrunners in changing society's attitudes toward people with disabilities.

299. Davies, R. K. (1979). Incest and vulnerable children. *Science News, 116,* 244–245.

The author of this article found that 77% of a sample of 22 incest victims had abnormal electroencephalograph readings, and 27% of the sample had overt seizure activity. These rates were three to four times higher than those present in a control group of other hospital admissions.

300. Davis, D. (1986). *Working with children from violent homes: Ideas and techniques.* **Santa Cruz, CA: Network Publications.**

This book suggests ways to help children from violent families cope with their ordeals. The introduction gives background information on abusers, spouses' reasons for staying in an abusive situation, and symptoms of child abuse. It discusses techniques that help children who have been abused focus on self-esteem building and communication of feelings. This book includes some case examples to illustrate these techniques.

301. Davis, E., Fennoy, I., Laraque, D., Kanem, N., Brown, G., & Mitchell, J. (1992). Autism and developmental abnormalities in children with perinatal cocaine exposure. *Journal of the National Medical Association, 84*(4), 315–319.

This article describes the assessment for behavioral and developmental impairment of 70 children who had been exposed to cocaine in utero. It found that poly-drug use during pregnancy was present for approximately 50% of these cases. The mean age of the infants tested in this assessment was 19.2 months. The assessment shows that these infants had growth retardation and neurodevelopmental delays, and 11.4% of them were autistic.

302. Davis, H., & Rushton, R. (1991). Counselling and supporting parents of children with developmental delay: A research evaluation. *Journal of Mental Deficiency Research, 35,* 89–112.

This article describes a study that evaluated the use of generalized family counseling to provide support for English-speaking and Bangladeshi families with children who have developmental or multiple disabilities. The intervention groups in this study consisted of 16 Bangladeshi and 31 English-speaking families, and the controls consisted of 12 Bangladeshi and 21 English-speaking families. The majority of families had low socioeconomic status, and many of the members of these families were unemployed. The children most often had cerebral palsy, Down syndrome, or an unspecified diagnosis. Preassessments and postassessments were done with the mother and child using the following assessment tools: a support questionnaire, a child repertory grid, a parent repertory grid, a relationship repertory grid, Malaise Inventory, Griffiths Mental Development Scales, and the Behaviour Screening Questionnaire. The results of this study indicate the following: the greatest benefits from intervention were achieved by the Bangladeshi families, who were generally more deprived and less well supported; mothers who participated in counseling showed improvement in ratings of themselves and their family and in perceived support; and children in the treatment group showed developmental and behavioral improvements.

303. Davis, K. R., & Shapiro, L. J. (1979). Exploring group process as a means of reaching the mentally retarded. *Social Casework, 60*(6), 330–337.
The article describes the use of group process skills with nine women with mental disabilities (ages 22 to 55). The group process skills were used to help these women develop verbal and social skills and increase self-concept, appearance, and mutual support. These women participated in 2-hour weekly meetings that were lead by male and female coleaders. The primary purpose of the group was to discuss and share feelings and thoughts. The authors conclude that the group process is a powerful strategy for the treatment and education of people with mental retardation.

304. Dawson, R. (1985). *The abuse of children in foster care: A study of incidence characteristics and precipitating characters.* **Toronto: Ontario Association of Children's Aid Societies.**
This report discusses a survey that investigated reports of abuse in Ontario foster care settings between 1979 and 1981. The results of this survey reveal the following: the nature of abuse, the characteristics of the abused foster child and the offending foster family, and the outcomes for the child and foster family following an investigation of abuse.

305. Dawson, R. (1989). Improving the quality and status of treatment foster care: The concept of certification for providers. *Community Alternatives: International Journal of Family Care, 1*(1), 11–21.
This article examines a certification program for foster care providers who provide residential treatment services to children. It addresses this program's certification and academic requirements and discusses the program's

financial compensation system that based compensation on the level of education and experience attained by the provider. Using informal results, the author concludes that this certification program increased the competence of providers and improved the quality of care.

306. Day, K. (1988). Services for psychiatrically disordered mentally handicapped adults—A U.K. perspective. *Australia and New Zealand Journal of Development Disabilities, 14*(1), 19–25.
This article examines the move in the United Kingdom away from institutionalization to community care for adults with developmental disabilities who have psychiatric disorders. This article discusses some of the areas of community services that are currently being debated: specialized or generic services, organization of services, and services for people with behavior disorders. It suggests future considerations for psychiatric services and includes an appendix that lists the services available for people with developmental disabilities in the United Kingdom.

307. Day, N. L., Robles, N., Richardson, G., Geva, D., Taylor, P., Scher, M., Stoffer, D., Cornelius, M., & Goldschmidt, L. (1991). The effects of prenatal alcohol use on the growth of children at three years of age. *Alcoholism: Clinical and Experimental Research, 15*(1), 67–71.
This article describes a study that examined prenatal exposure to alcohol and its long-term effects on the growth of 519 children. This study assessed the children in this study at age 24 hours, 8 months, 18 months, and 36 months. The mothers in this study were interviewed during their pregnancy at the 4th and 7th prenatal months. At 3 years of age, weight, length, and head circumference impairments were measured in the children. A greater number of physical anomalies were also present in this study group. The results of this study were statistically significant after controlling for such variables as nutrition, present environmental conditions, and substance exposure during lactation.

308. Dead girl's parents hope for new clues. (1994, February 11). *The Times*, p. 3.
This newspaper article reports that the abduction and murder of Jo Ramsden, a 21-year-old woman with Down syndrome from Dorset, England, has led police to question a former psychiatric nurse who was sentenced for the kidnapping and sexual assault of several women with mental retardation. Michael Fox, sentenced to nine concurrent life terms, will be questioned again about the murder of Ms. Ramsden. Fox was formerly arrested with her kidnap, but charges were dropped due to insufficient evidence. Jo Ramsden's body was found in a shallow grave in the woods in March 1992, 11 months after her disappearance. Fox's sexual assault victims were all abandoned in isolated areas following the assaults.

309. DeAngelis, T. (1993). Trivializing disabilities gives immunity to fears. *A P A Monitor, 24*(8), 47–48.

This article discusses the findings of a generalized survey conducted by the American Psychological Association that collected general biographical information to be included in an update of the APA's biographical membership directory. This survey included a question that asked the participant to "indicate any disabilities below": for example, sensory disability, physical disability, mental/emotional disability, and/or other disability. In the "other" category, many respondents answered lightheartedly. This trivialization of disabilities is explained as a fear response to issues with which we feel uncomfortable or we do not understand. Trivialization of disabilities can generalize across professions and educational levels. The author addresses additional findings of negative attitudes toward people with disabilities.

310. Death of L. I. nurse's patient ruled homicide, aide says. (1988, January 6). *The New York Times*, p. B2.

This newspaper article reports that the death of a former patient of nurse Richard Angelo from the Good Samaritan Hospital in West Islip has been ruled a homicide. Death resulted from a lethal injection of the muscle paralyzing drug, Pavulon. In total, 20 bodies have been exhumed for the presence of the drugs Pavulon or Anectine. Motive for the injections stems from Angelo's desire to appear the hero in assisting these patients during their emergencies. The charges of assault result from Mr. Angelo's attempt on another patient's life.

311. Degener, T. (1992). The right to be different: Implications for child protection. *Child Abuse Review, 1,* 1–5.

This article searches for the historical roots of labeling a child with a disability as "abnormal." It examines the attitudes related to disability and their relation to depriving a child with a disability of child protection services. It points out that women with disabilities receive environmental messages of "disablism," and these messages affect their children. The author concludes that "disablist" beliefs and attitudes constitute a source of emotional abuse for children with disabilities.

312. Degkwitz, R. (1985). Medizinisches Denken und Handeln im Nationalsozialismus [Medical thinking and way of acting in the national socialist era]. *Fortschritte der Neurologie, Psychiatrie, 53*(6), 212–225.

This article describes some of the events of the Nazi euthanasia program and raises questions about whether such principles of mercy killing and eugenics are exclusively a Nazi phenomenon. While this article provides examples from the Nazi experience, it also includes examples from other societies.

313. Denkowski, G. C., Denkowski, K. M., & Mabli, J. (1984). A residential treat-
ment model for MR adolescent offenders. *Hospital and Community Psychiatry, 35*(3), 279–281.

The authors of this article describe a 3-stage community inpatient model that was designed to rehabilitate adolescent offenders who have mental retardation. In this model, responsible social behavior is encouraged, and traditional services such as skills training, group counseling, and basic academics are provided to the adolescents. These activities enable the residents to learn and practice appropriate behaviors in contexts that are similar to their educational or training environments. The treatment begins in an entry unit composed of two self-contained living-training wings: One wing is locked, and the other is set up as a conventional group home. The resident's performance is used to determine if the adolescent can advance into a conventional group home or should be considered for long-term treatment in the program's other secure facility, a 15-bed intensive unit. The program uses a point-based token economy system to induce and maintain behavioral change in the residents. Points are earned by demonstrating habilitative behaviors, such as attending class. The authors conclude that this program is suitable for rehabilitating young offenders within the community while protecting society.

314. Dent, H. R. (1986). An experimental study of the effectiveness of different techniques of questioning mentally handicapped child witnesses. *The British Psychological Society, 25,* 13–17.

This article examines different interviewing techniques used to obtain information from abused children with mild intellectual disabilities. It points out that research concerning intellectual disabilities suggests the following: children's recall is the poorest when unprompted or when heavily prompted, an intermediate form of cuing recall is most functional, and general questions lead to optimal recall in terms of completeness and accuracy.

315. Department of Justice. (1993). *Amendments to the Criminal Code and the Canada Evidence Act with respect to persons with disabilities* (Cat. No. J2-122/1993 ISBN: 0-662-59774-5). Ottawa, ON: Author.

This consultation paper examines 11 separate issues concerning the Criminal Code and the Canada Evidence Act, which require a review to determine if the criminal justice system is accessible to people with disabilities. These issues include the following: the oath and promise to tell the truth, communication assistance for witnesses, hearsay evidence, identification of the accused, videotaped evidence, sodomy, qualification of jurors, remands, sexual exploitation, sexual assault, and aggravated offenses.

316. DesNoyers Hurley, A. (1989). Behavior therapy for psychiatric disorders in mentally retarded individuals. In R. Fletcher & F. J. Menolascino (Eds.), *Mental re-*

tardation and mental illness (pp. 127–140). Lexington, MA: Lexington Books.
This chapter addresses the use of behavior therapy with people with developmental disabilities. It uses case studies of patients with mild mental retardation who were diagnosed with phobias, depression, and anorexia. It describes counterconditioning, desensitization, and a cognitive behavioral approach and provides case examples for each therapeutic approach.

317. DesNoyers Hurley, A. (1989). Individual psychotherapy with mentally retarded individuals: A review and call for research. *Research in Developmental Disabilities, 10,* 261–275.
This article discusses the use of individual psychotherapy with people with developmental disabilities. It provides a review of the literature that supports psychotherapy for people with developmental disabilities. It includes six recommendations for success in therapy: the appropriate matching of therapeutic techniques to the cognitive and developmental level of the client, a directive therapy approach, the need for flexibility in therapy, involvement of family and staff, careful management of transference/countertransference issues, and addressing the client's disability. This article suggests additional research to study the benefits of therapy for people with developmental disabilities.

318. Deutsch, H. (1983, May 29–June 2). *Linking residential and vocational services to enhance client programming.* **Paper presented at the 107th annual meeting of the American Association on Mental Deficiency, Dallas.**
The author of this paper claims that individuals with mental retardation may have chronic emotional responses to stress and conflict situations such as attending separate classes, moving to new living situations, or being separated from their family. This article discusses a survey administered to 51 service providers in mental retardation and mental health settings, and the findings suggest the following: service networks for people with mental retardation frequently fail to consider their needs for emotional assistance, about 78% of the respondents indicated that they experienced discomfort when dealing with the emotional needs of people with mental retardation, the respondents indicated that they preferred a psychotherapeutic approach (58%) to behavior modification (36%), and these service providers considered the two orientations mutually exclusive. The findings of this survey suggest that there is a need for desensitization to precede professional training programs so that service providers will have an adequate comfort level when addressing the emotional needs of people who have mental retardation.

319. Deutsch, H., & Placona, M. (1983). *The concept of home and family to mentally retarded individuals placed in*

residential facilities: Implications for counseling. Scranton, PA: Authors.
This paper discusses a study that examined the notions of home and family in children and adults with mental retardation who live in community living arrangements. This study administered questionnaires to 151 direct care staff and addressed the following items: residents' age, sex, length and type of institutionalization, behavioral characteristics, and methods used to express ideas of home and/or family. The results of this study suggest the following: 1) at least occasionally, 85% of the residents expressed ideas of home and family; 2) there were no significant differences in the frequency of expression of ideas of family and home related to level of functioning, sex, or type of residence; 3) there appeared to be some connection between increasing lengths of separation from home and decreased expression of ideas of home and family and between frequent contact and increased expression; 4) over 19% of the residents used fantasy as a way to express ideas of home; 5) 14% who spoke frequently of home acted out; 6) the staff identified behavior patterns that were considered to be affected by the home situation but not related to the resident's expression of the notions of home and family; and 7) heightened staff reaction was noted when residents' discussions about home contained strong emotional content. The authors conclude that these findings point out the importance of knowing when to refer a resident for professional assistance and understanding that an individual's emotional growth can be hindered by separation from home.

320. Deutsch, H., & Placona, M. (1983). *Psychotherapeutic approaches to dealing with mentally retarded adolescents and adults in community settings.* Scranton, PA: Authors.
This paper presents the results of a questionnaire intended to examine therapeutic approaches used with emotionally disturbed people with mental retardation. The questionnaire was administered to 51 professionals from education, psychology, nursing, counseling, social work, and direct care. The questionnaires were accompanied by three different case studies concerning young men with mild retardation. The results of this study reveal the following: 1) the most frequently chosen treatments were individual and family therapy, behavior modification, and group therapy; 2) the choices of behavior modification and psychotherapy were selected 194 times out of a possible 306 treatment options; 3) selection of either treatment approach depended on the type of case presented (this finding suggests that these decisions may reflect social values and norms about the needs of certain types of clients); 4) level of education did not appear to affect the treatment that was chosen; and 5) psychotherapy was chosen more frequently than behavior modification. The authors conclude that these two treatment approaches are mutually exclusive, a view that may be an outgrowth of behavior modification.

321. Diamond, L. J., & Jaudes, P. K. (1983). Child abuse in a cerebral-palsied popula-

tion. *Developmental Medicine and Child Neurology,* 25, 169–174.

This article discusses a study that examined the abuse of children with cerebral palsy. The results of this study indicate the following: of children with cerebral palsy seen in one care center over a 12-month period, 17 had been subject to child abuse, and 8 of these children's cerebral palsy was a result of abuse. These findings suggest that there is a high incidence of child abuse among children with cerebral palsy. The authors conclude that there is a "double indication" for abuse, both as a cause and a result of cerebral palsy.

322. Dicks, H. V. (1972). *Licensed mass murder: A socio psychological study of some SS killers.* **London: Sussex University Press.**

This book is one of a series that came from a multidisciplinary, international research project undertaken to investigate how persecutions and mass exterminations can happen. This book uses a social/psychology and a human adaptation model to explain Nazi mass murder during World War II. It points out how the mass murder of citizens with disabilities under the euphemistic guise of mercy killing, euthanasia, and "assisted death" made other forms of mass murder more acceptable. Chapter 7, "Two medical humanitarians," provides very interesting insight. Interviews were conducted with a physician and a practical nurse who received life sentences for euthanasia-related crimes. In each case, personality traits combined with social pressure, social reinforcement for brutality and murder, and absolute power of death over victims led to increasingly brutal and deadly behavior.

323. Dietrich, D., Berkowitz, L., Kadushin, A., & McGloin, J. (1990). Some factors influencing abusers' justification of their child abuse. *Child Abuse & Neglect,* 14, 337–345.

This article discusses a study that conducted statistical analysis of data obtained from 73 interviews with caregivers who abuse children. The study sample included 21 men (3 stepfathers, 18 biological fathers) and 52 women (50 biological mothers, 1 foster mother, 1 stepmother), with an average age of 30.6 years. The abused children (42 females, 31 males) had a mean age of 8.3 years. The interview was coded according to the following variables: justification for abuse, history of abuse, child defiance, abuser depressed, abuser irritable, abuser stress, changes in obedience, and abuser loss of temper. The results of this analysis indicate the following: Most (58.9%) abusive caregivers indicated feeling remorse for their actions, but 41.1% indicated feeling no regrets; more than half of the abusive caregivers (50.7%) felt the abuse was the fault of the child, and 62.5% felt that their abuse was justified in some way; abuse was also rationalized by many caregivers (30.1%), who indicated that the child's behavior had improved as a result of the abusive punishment, while (58.9%) reported no such improvement; and the remaining 11% could not be characterized on per-

ceived changes in obedience "for various reasons, such as the death of the victim due to the abuse" (p. 342). This study provides clear evidence that many abusive caregivers rationalize their actions and blame the victims of their abuse, and this article discusses the implications of this study for protective service practice.

324. Dietrich-MacLean, G., & Walden, T. (1988). Distinguishing teaching interactions of physically abusive from nonabusive parent-child dyads. *Child Abuse & Neglect,* 12, 469–479.

This article describes a study that attempted to determine if child protective service workers can reliably discriminate between physically abusive and nonabusive parent-child dyads by observing behaviors in parent-child interaction. In this study, 52 participants watched four 3-minute videotapes of parent-child interactions (2 abusive, 2 nonabusive dyads). This study found the following: The participants were able to identify the abusive dyads 76% of the time, 40% of the participants identified abusive dyads 100% of the time, there appeared to be no relationship between increased protective service experience and increased accuracy, and the lack of prior experience was associated with chance performance. The authors suggest using clinical observations of parent-child interactions as part of the assessment conducted to discover physical child abuse in suspected families.

325. Dilalla, D. L., & Crittenden, P. M. (1990). Dimensions of maltreated children's home behavior: A factor analytic approach. *Infant Behavior and Development,* 13, 439–460.

This article describes a study that used factor analysis and home observation to identify the home behavior of abusing parents and their abused children. One hundred twenty children (51% male, 49% female) and their primary caregivers were assessed in this study. Children ranged in age from 2 months to 48 months; caregivers had a mean age of 24. Families were classified according to their childrearing practices: 21 abuse, 30 abuse and neglect, 19 neglect, 22 marginally maltreating, and 28 adequately reared (controls). Three composite groups were then formed: primary abused (n=51), primary neglected (n=41), and adequately reared children (n=28). A 1-hour in-home observation was made of the child and the primary caregiver in order to observe common day activity in the household. A transcript was made of the observed behavior, and the factors identified for the children include the following: self-directed behavior, affiliative behavior, negativity, positive social interaction, and questioning. The factors identified for the parents include the following: positive social interaction, caregiving, discipline, refusal, and hostility. The results of this study indicate the following: When compared to controls, abused and neglected children and their abusing parents participated in fewer positive social interactions; abusive parents were the most hostile toward their children; neglecting parents exhibited the least positive social interactions; abusive parents displayed less hostility to older children; and parents in general displayed less caregiver behavior toward older children.

326. DiMaio, V. J. M., & Bernstein, J. D. (1974). A case of infanticide. *Journal of Forensic Sciences, 19,* 744–754.
This account of multiple infanticide details the story of Martha Woods, an army wife who smothered to death her three biological children, a niece, a nephew, a neighbor's child in her care, and her adopted child. In addition to two other children in her care who survived, all of these children had cyanotic episodes. The repeated cyanotic episodes requiring hospitalization suggests Munchausen syndrome by proxy. This is a legal precedence-setting case because evidence of prior acts of infanticide was allowed as evidence.

327. Disabled person removed from concert. (1992, February 17). *The Press (Christchurch),* p. 8.
This article reports on the removal of Ying Chueng, a young woman with cerebral palsy, from a concert. During a live broadcast of the BBC Philharmonic Orchestra to promote arts for people with disabilities, guest conductor Guenther Herbig requested that Ying Chueng be removed from the auditorium before continuing with the concert. The conductor objected to the involuntary noises made by Ms. Chueng, which were picked up by the microphones.

328. Disabled woman dies after being set afire. (1993, December 22). *The Globe and Mail,* p. A5.
This newspaper article reports the homicide death of an Edmonton, Alberta, woman with mental retardation. At this time, the assailant and the motive are unknown. Joyce Cardinal, 36, died in the hospital after receiving third-degree burns over most of her body. She had been doused with gasoline and set on fire. She was found by firefighters in a city park, who were responding to what they believed was a rubbish fire. The authorities believe she was attacked around midnight while walking home from a house party. A man was seen fleeing the scene.

329. Dixon, R. (1988, June). Silent victims find a voice. *Interaction,* pp. 5–8.
This article examines some case examples of abuse and neglect of the elderly and people with developmental disabilities investigated by the Office of the Public Advocate in Victoria, Australia. This office was set up to protect individuals unable to protect themselves. The office investigates 20 new cases of maltreatment a week.

330. Docherty, J. (1989). *Indicators of abusive residential care facilities.* **Toronto: James Docherty & Associates.**
The author suggests guidelines for reducing abuse in residential care facilities: 1) all clients and their advocates must be fully informed of their rights and how to report alleged abuse, 2) clients must not be restricted from their families and friends, 3) clients must not be restricted

from open communication with the outside world, 4) clients should attend school and other community facilities that are independent of their residential institution, and 5) institutions and other agencies should provide complete cooperation and support for investigations by law enforcement officials and child welfare agencies.

331. Docherty, J., & McGee, R. (1990). A study of child abuse allegations in residential care facilities. *Newsbrief: The Institute for the Prevention of Child Abuse, 5,* 1–7.
This newsletter article discusses a study that examined the investigations conducted by Children's Aid Societies into allegations of abuse in residential care settings in Ontario. This study found the following: only 10% of the 177 abuse allegation cases carried out over a 3-year period lead to convictions; adolescents were the most likely to be abused in residential care facilities; females were most commonly subjected to sexual abuse, whereas males were found to be more physically abused; and physical abuse allegations were almost 50% less likely to be verified than sexual abuse allegations.

332. Dodge Reyome, N. (1990). Executive directors' perceptions of the prevention of child abuse and maltreatment in residential facilities. *Journal of Child and Youth Care, 4*(6), 45–60.
This article discusses a study that surveyed executive directors of institutional child-care agencies and facilities who provide services for the New York State Department of Social Services and the New York State Division for Youth in order to determine which factors they believe are necessary to prevent child abuse and maltreatment. The survey assessed executive characteristics, agency characteristics, and factors pertaining to institutional maltreatment. The results of this study indicate that staff supervision, staff professionalism in child-care, organizational issues such as policies and procedures, and staff recruitment are considered the most important issues in the prevention of child abuse and maltreatment. This article elaborates on these findings.

333. Doe, J. (1982). "Enlightened" treatment: A staff infection. *Issues in Radical Therapy, 10*(2), 19–22.
The author of this expose has written under a pseudonym in order to protect himself and his family. John Doe relates his experience as an employee at the Jacksonville State Hospital for the Mentally Retarded. He describes the abuses and brutality perpetrated against patients of the hospital by the hospital's employees. The author discusses his induction into this system during the 1970s and his acceptance of these coercive methods as a means of social control. Doe provides a telling participant observation account of the culture of institutions. He quotes institutional staff as indoctrinating new members with statements such as "I'd knock the fucking shit out of them" (p. 20) and "Hitler had the right idea. He killed

these worthless motherfuckers" (p. 20). He indicates that the "rite of passage" that all new employees must undergo before being accepted was the witnessing of an act of gross brutality. If they failed to report, they would be accepted. If they reported to their supervisors, they would be disbelieved. He describes how staff taught new members proper punching and kicking techniques and methods for concealing evidence. Doe makes reference to a number of murders of patients and readily admits that he also committed abuse.

334. Doe, T. (1990). Towards an understanding: An ecological model of abuse [Special issue: Sexual abuse]. *Developmental Disabilities Bulletin, 18*(2), 13–20.
This article discusses the issue of sexual abuse of people with disabilities using an ecological model. This ecological model has four levels: a microsystem, which involves the relationship between abuser and victim; a macrosystem, the setting in which the abuse takes place; an exosystem of cultural and social beliefs, which allows the abuse to occur and continue; and a mesosystem, which describes the dynamics among the other three systems. There is a discussion of the caregiver-victim phenomenon that can occur as a result of segregated school and residential placement. The author recommends a systematic comprehensive program at each level to ensure the safety of persons who are at risk for abuse.

335. Doe, T. (1993). Institutionalized abuse of people with disabilities. *A R C H • Type, 10*(6), 4–6.
This article defines institutionalized abuse as abuse that occurs in "situations that are controlled and funded by governments." The author focuses on residential treatment programs for people with mental health diagnoses, residential schools for Aboriginal children, and residential schools for people who are deaf. She provides a personal perspective and an interesting analysis of institutional care.

336. Donaldson, J. (1980). Changing attitudes toward handicapped persons: A review and analysis of research. *Exceptional Children, 46*, 504–514.
This article reviews various approaches used to change attitudes toward people with disabilities. It suggests theoretical models for those approaches that appear successful in changing attitudes and discusses future research possibilities and applications.

337. Donnellan, A. M. (1984). The criterion of the least dangerous assumption. *Behavioral Disorders, 9*(2), 141–150.
This article articulates the principle of the criterion of the least dangerous assumption. This principle states that when information is incomplete or unavailable to guide educational decision making, then educational decisions should be made based on the assumption that will be least harmful if incorrect. Donnellan exemplifies the

principle in relation to instructional issues, but the same principle can be easily applied to abuse prevention issues.

338. Dossa, P. A. (1989). Quality of life: Individualism or holism? A critical review of the literature. *International Journal of Rehabilitation Research, 12*(2), 121–136.
This article suggests that a holistic approach is necessary when examining the quality of life of people with developmental disabilities. It discusses both the subjective and the objective approaches, which use measures of satisfaction versus measures of social indicators.

339. Dossa, P. A. (1990). Women and disability: The myth of the autonomous individual. *Journal of Practical Approaches to Developmental Handicap, 14*(2), 37–42.
This article examines the characterization of women with disabilities as autonomous individuals. The author suggests that these women are viewed more as victims of society than as autonomous individuals. The issue of victimization is viewed from a feminist perspective, with gender considered a construct of culture and social relations. The myth of the autonomous individual is illustrated with a case example.

340. Doucette, J. (1986). *Violent acts against disabled women*. Toronto: DAWN (DisAbled Women's Network) Canada.
This report includes information on sexual and physical violence against women with disabilities based on a study of 30 women with disabilities and 32 women without disabilities. In the group with disabilities, 67% had experienced physical abuse in childhood, compared to 34% in the group without disabilities. Women with disabilities were also more likely to have experienced sexual abuse in childhood. In the group with disabilities, 47% had experienced sexual abuse, compared to 34% in the group without disabilities. Thus, the rate for physical abuse of women with disabilities was 1.97 times higher than for women without disabilities, and the rate for sexual abuse of women with disabilities was 1.38 times higher than for women without disabilities.

341. Doucette, J. (1988). Disabled women and violence. In A. D'Aubin (Ed.), *Breaking the silence* (pp. 35–40). Edmonton, AB: Coalition of Provincial Organizations of the Handicapped (COPOH).
This chapter is actually an interview with Joanne Doucette, a Canadian authority on women with disabilities and violence issues. She discusses her work with the DisAbled Women's Network (DAWN). She found that 67% of the women with disabilities that she interviewed had been abused as children, twice as many as she found among women without disabilities. She identifies

violence prevention and violence intervention services as high priorities for women with disabilities. She considers women with impaired communication or developmental disabilities to be especially vulnerable to abuse. Doucette believes isolation and institutionalization to be major factors in the abuse experienced by women with disabilities.

342. Doucette, J. (1988). *Sexual assault & the disabled woman: Disabled? Sexually assaulted? Need help?* **Toronto: DAWN (DisAbled Women's Network) Canada.**

The author provides straightforward information to women with disabilities who have been sexually assaulted about what to do and how to report a sexual assault. The author includes telephone numbers and hours of police, medical, and counseling services along with information on accessibility relevant to individuals with various disabilities.

343. Dowd, A. (1993, November 5). Allow ailing child to die in peace, Maine school teachers told. *The Edmonton Journal,* **p. A5.**

This newspaper article reports the case of a 12-year-old Maine child who has cerebral palsy and progressive scoliosis. It states that teachers at the school where Corey Brown attends special education classes have been instructed to comply with a limited "do not resuscitate" policy should Corey stop breathing. This policy is in place because it is believed that this would prevent further suffering since it is reported that the child's organs are slowly being crushed due to the nature of her disease. While CPR is prohibited from being used by the school nurse or teachers, they are allowed to administer oxygen and clear the child's windpipe. This article also includes a discussion of school board policy and "do not resuscitate" requests.

344. Downey, R. (1992). Open to abuse. *Social Work Today, 23*(38), **15.**

This article suggests that disbelieving courts and reluctant prosecutors protect abusers of children with mental retardation.

345. Downie, D., & Snart, F. (1983). Bioethical considerations for teachers of the severe and profoundly retarded: A position paper. *Special Education in Canada, 58*(1), **3–4.**

This position paper presents two arguments, deontological and utilitarian, that deal with the bioethical considerations concerning people with mental disabilities. The deontological perspective considers people with disabilities to be as valuable to society as people who are gifted. The utilitarian perspective considers people with disabilities to only be useful for medical experimentation. This paper suggests that teachers of students with disabilities should work against the utilitarian perspective by teaching their students that they are valued members of society.

346. Dreyer, L., & Haseltine, B. (1987). *The Woodrow Project: A sexual abuse prevention curriculum for the developmentally disabled.* **Fargo, ND: Red Flag Green Flag Resources, Rape and Abuse Crisis Center. (Exceptional Child Education Resources Clearinghouse Accession No. EC 20 2190)**

This facilitators' manual is used in conjunction with a videotape and presents a comprehensive guide to organizing and implementing a sexual abuse prevention curriculum for use with people with developmental disabilities. The target groups include young adults, ages 15 to 25 years old, with an IQ range of 40–70. The authors suggest that the curriculum might also be effectively used with people whose IQ falls in the 70–80 range and possibly with children as young as 10 years of age. The curriculum is divided into eight sections and emphasizes reinforcement, small group instruction, and role playing. Appendices include a sample letter to parents and outlines for meetings with teachers and parents. (Copies of this manual are available from Red Flag Green Flag Resources, P.O. Box 298, Fargo, ND, 58108.)

347. Drucker, F. (1989). A review of *Sexual homicide: Patterns and motives. Journal of Forensic Science, 34*(3), **794.**

This book review examines *Sexual homicide: Patterns and motives* (Ressler, R. K., Burgess, A. W., & Douglas, J. E. [1989]. *Sexual homicide: Patterns and motives.* Lexington, MA: Lexington Books). The book is written by two FBI agents and a Professor of Psychiatric Mental Health Nursing. It is primarily for law enforcement personnel and discusses criminal personality profiling, an FBI technique for apprehending, identifying, and convicting sex murderers. Also, it deals with the following areas: the social, environmental, and behavioral antecedents to sexual murders; the relationship between the crime and the environment; the motivation for the crime; and the factors involved in legal and psychiatric investigations. This book is not intended for behavioral scientists, but it is recommended for law enforcement personnel, jurists, attorneys, mental health professionals, and others interested in learning about the application of behavioral knowledge to law enforcement.

348. Drummond, C. R. (1994). Stopping the cycle of abuse: Managing the service culture. In S. Hollins (Ed.), *Proceedings: It did happen here: Sexual abuse and learning disability: Recognition and action* **(pp. 49–51). London: St. George's Hospital Medical School, Division of the Psychiatry of Disability.**

This chapter discusses issues related to prevention of sexual abuse in service environments. It emphasizes the need for support for "whistle blowers," better monitoring, and additional research.

349. **Duce, R., & Jenkins, L. (1994, February 12). Families denounce Allitt case "whitewash." *The Times*, pp. 1, 2.**
This newspaper article reports that parents of children murdered or disabled by Nurse Beverly Allitt are demanding an inquiry into the hospital murders and maimings after denouncing Sir Cecil Clothier's findings of these events as superficial. These parents found that the Clothier report was not critical enough of hospital staff and procedures, in particular, the finding that Allitt could not have been detected earlier or stopped. Beverly Allitt was sentenced to 13 life sentences for the murder of 4 children and the attempted murder of 3 other children. Some of the 9 children who were attacked but not killed were left with permanent disabilities.

350. **Dugger, C. W. (1991, May 23). Sex-abuse case in Harlem leaves neighbors confused. *The New York Times*, pp. B1, B9.**
This newspaper article reports that 51-year-old Kodzo Dobosu of Harlem faces charges of sexually abusing his 14-year-old adopted daughter who suffers from mental retardation. Mr. Dobosu has been recognized for adopting 35 hard-to-place children over a period of 20 years. He currently lives with 18 children. Adoption was made possible by applying to various states for these children. This single man has been honored with the father of the year award by the National Father's Day Committee and has been featured on such programs as *West 57th* and *Frontline* for his commitment to adopting children with disabilities.

351. **Dugger, C. W. (1991, June 3). Puzzling turns in a life devoted to children. *The New York Times*, pp. B1, B2.**
This newspaper article describes the case of Kodzo Dobosu of Harlem, who is accused of sexually assaulting his adopted daughter with mental retardation, and it includes a detailed history of Mr. Dobosu's life. Mr. Dobosu has been recognized for adopting 35 hard-to-place children with disabilities over a period of 20 years.

352. **Dunn, M. (1991). *Testimony of the Division of Rehabilitation Psychology and the Committee on Disability Issues in Psychology of the American Psychological Association presented to the National Institute on Disability and Rehabilitation Research on the subject of research and dissemination needs & opportunities in the coming decade.* Washington, DC: American Psychological Association.**
As a representative for the Division of Rehabilitation Psychology and the Committee on Disability Issues in Psychology of the American Psychological Association, the author discusses promoting research, education, and training dealing with disability. The author discusses the following: community integration, physical and sexual abuse, the role of psychological services in rehabilitation, and dissemination of information to frontline staff.

353. **Dunne, T. P., & Power, A. (1990). Sexual abuse and mental handicap: Preliminary study of a community based study. *Mental Handicap Research*, 3(2), 111–115.**
This article describes a study of 13 victims of sexual abuse who had developmental disabilities. The authors found that behavior problems were often the most salient feature of responses to sexual abuse in this population, particularly in people with limited verbal abilities. The authors also point out that most features of sexual abuse are the same for people with and without disabilities.

354. **Dyer, K. (1993, January). Functional communication training: Review and future directions. *The Behavior Therapist*, pp. 18–21.**
This article discusses functional communication training for people who exhibit challenging behavior problems. Functional communication training teaches people with problem behavior to communicate in a more appropriate, more desirable way. This is accomplished by prompting appropriate responses and reinforcement. This article includes a detailed description of this training and suggests future directions for research.

355. **Dytrych, Z., Matejcek, Z., & Schuller, V. (1988). The Prague cohort: Adolescence and early adulthood. In H. P. David, Z. Dytrych, Z. Matejcek, & V. Schuller (Eds.), *Born unwanted: Developmental effects of denied abortion* (pp. 87–102). New York: Springer.**
This chapter deals with twice-denied abortion and discusses the long-term follow-up of children born from unwanted pregnancies (UP) and pair-matched children of accepted pregnancies (AP). This follow-up of 216 UP children and 215 AP children between the ages of 14 and 16 from the city of Prague shows significant differences between the two groups in the following areas: school achievement, personal qualities, and perceptions of parental attitude. An additional follow-up at ages 16 to 18 and 21 to 23 concludes that UP children are at increased risk for the following: social problems, personal mental health problems, aspiration-frustration in situations of stress, extroversion, and lack of satisfaction with life, work, and marriage.

356. **Dytrych, Z., Schuller, V., & Matejcek, Z. (1988). The wantedness-unwantedness continuum and responsible parenthood. In H. P. David, Z. Dytrych, Z. Matejcek, & V. Schuller (Eds.), *Born unwanted: Developmental effects of denied abortion* (pp. 31–36). New York: Springer.**
This chapter examines wanted and unwanted pregnancies. It uses information obtained from the Prague cohort of

women who were twice denied abortions and the subsequent development of the children born to these women. The continuum from extreme wantedness to extreme unwantedness is illustrated in 17 categories. This chapter discusses responsible parenthood and examines future considerations, with an emphasis on today's families.

•E•

357. Eckenrode, J., Munsch, J., Powers, J. L., & Doris, J. (1988). The nature and substantiation of official sexual abuse reports. *Child Abuse & Neglect, 12*(3), 311–319.

This article discusses a study that reviewed 796 sexual abuse reports from New York State in 1985 in order to determine the factors that influenced the decision to investigate these reports. It investigated the age, sex, and ethnicity of the child and the source of the report as predictors of the decision to investigate these cases. This review found that substantiation rates increased with the age of the child, although this was more valid as a characteristic of reports involving female rather than male victims. This study discovered the following: Reports involving female children were more likely to be substantiated than those involving male children, there was no significant relationship between the decision to investigate and the ethnicity of the child, the source of the report appeared to be a good indicator of case determination, and mandated reports were investigated more often than reports from nonmandated sources (13% higher rate).

358. Edwards, J. P., & Elkins, T. E. (1988). *Just between us.* Portland, OR: Ednick Communications.

This book is intended for parents and professionals and addresses issues of sexuality of children, adolescents, or young adults with developmental disabilities. It covers many topics in plain English and provides practical information in addition to discussing ethical principles, concerns, and issues. It includes a chapter on avoiding exploitation that emphasizes the following: teaching students to discriminate between public and private behavior, teaching students to recognize appropriate and inappropriate touching, teaching students to understand what types of touching are suitable for various levels of relationship, teaching students to say "no" to inappropriate interactions initiated by others, and teaching students to report attempts at exploitation.

359. Egeland, B. (1985). The consequences of physical and emotional neglect on the development of young children. In *Child Neglect Monograph: Proceedings*

from a Symposium, November 10, 1985 (pp. 7–19). Washington, DC: Clearinghouse on Child Abuse and Neglect Information.

This chapter discusses the impact of neglect on childhood development. Using data from the Minnesota Mother-Child Project, the author found the following: Of the 24 families identified as neglecting, all the neglected children suffered from severe developmental consequences. Assessments of these children conducted from infancy through kindergarten found that their development deteriorated.

360. Egeland, B. (1991). A longitudinal study of high-risk families: Issues and findings. In R. H. Starr, Jr. & D. A. Wolfe (Eds.), *The effects of child abuse and neglect* (pp. 33–56). London: Guilford Press.

This chapter discusses a longitudinal study that was conducted with families at risk for child abuse or neglect. Two hundred sixty-seven high-risk infants and their families were initially assessed while the women were in their third trimester. The mothers in this study had a mean age of 20.5 years and were predominantly single (62%). Pregnancies were unexpected in 86% of cases, with only 13% of the biological fathers still residing in the home 18 months after the birth of the child. Forty percent of mothers had not completed high school. The families were generally in the low socioeconomic range and had chaotic and disruptive living environments. The results of a 1-year follow-up indicate the following: 45% of infants were anxiously attached, more than 50% of the children in each grade were referred to special education, and 15% of children were either physically or sexually abused or physically or emotionally neglected. This chapter discusses the measurement selection, subject selection, and ethical issues of this study, and it examines the consequences of physical abuse, sexual abuse, and neglect.

361. Egeland, B., & Vaughn, B. (1982). Failure of "bond formation" as a cause of abuse, neglect, and maltreatment. *Annual Progress in Child Psychiatry and Child Development*, 188–196. (Reprinted from *American Journal of Orthopsychiatry*, 1981, *51*, 78–84)

This article reviews several studies that support the increased likelihood of abuse and neglect following initial separation of infant and mother during the immediate postpartum period. The authors critically review these studies and investigate certain conditions related to early separation. For example, from a study that used a sample of 267 women receiving prenatal care, 32 mothers who were reported to abuse, neglect, or mistreat their infants were compared to 33 mothers who offered high-quality care. The information obtained from detailed medical records provided no evidence to support the link between early separation due to premature birth, prenatal problems, or other indices of limited contact with abuse, neglect, or mistreatment by mothers. The authors found no evidence to support a critical bonding period between mother and child immediately following birth. However, they suggest that early and extended contact between the mother and her infant may enhance their relationship; and hospital procedures that aim to make the mother feel more comfortable and competent in caring for her infant will enhance the development of maternal bonding.

362. Egginton, J. (1989). *From cradle to grave: The short lives and strange deaths of Marybeth Tinning's nine children.* **New York: William Morrow.**
This factual account is about Marybeth Tinning and the mysterious deaths of her nine children, one of whom was adopted. The first child died of natural causes. All of the other children's deaths were attributed to causes such as SIDS or Reye's syndrome, but circumstantial evidence points to the mother intentionally smothering her children. These nine children died between January 3, 1972 and December 20, 1985. Marybeth was tried and convicted for the death of her last child. Circumstantial evidence also suggests that Marybeth Tinning committed several acts of arson and petty thefts and poisoned her husband, Joe Tinning.

363. Ehlers, W. H., Prothero, J. C., & Langone, J. (1982). *Mental retardation and other developmental disabilities: A programmed introduction* **(3rd ed.). Columbus, OH: Charles E. Merrill.**
This book presents 14 lessons that introduce mental retardation and developmental disabilities in a programmed learning format. Each unit includes an outline of objectives, a narrative text, a programmed section, and review questions. A list of relevant readings concludes each lesson. This book covers the following topics: an introduction to the concept of developmental disabilities (DD); the history of mental retardation (MR) and DD; intelligence measurement, adaptive behavior measurement, learning problems and DD; the affective characteristics of the DD; the role of heredity and environment in intellectual functioning; special education for people with MR and DD; counseling people with DD and their families; community resources; independent living skills; and vocational rehabilitation and employment. This book also includes a glossary of terms.

364. Einfeld, S. L. (1984). Clinical assessment of 4,500 developmentally delayed individuals. *Journal of Mental Deficit Research, 28,* **129–142.**
This article discusses a study that analyzed data from the clinical assessments of 4,500 children with developmental delays over a 12-year period at the Grosvenor Diagnostic and Assessment Clinic. The clinic is operated by the New South Wales Department of Health in Sydney, Australia. The patients (42.7% female) ranged in age from birth to 20, with an average age of 5 and an average IQ of 40. The results of this analysis indicate the following: 161 patients (3.6%) were not diagnosed with

mental retardation, patients with mild and borderline mental retardation and IQ scores between 52–85 (n=909) had a high incidence of mental retardation of unknown origin (48%), patients with moderate to severe retardation and IQ scores between 20–52 showed an increase in minor congenital abnormalities, and patients with profound retardation had a high incidence of mental retardation due to trauma and hypoxia and overt brain pathology. This article also discusses some additional findings.

365. Elkind, P. (1989). *The death shift: The true story of Genene Jones and the Texas baby murders.* **New York: Onyx.**
This book provides a comprehensive account of LVN Genene Jones and the deaths of children in her care. Genene was an adopted child with three adopted siblings. She appeared to be strongly attached to her adopted brother, who is described as having had a learning disability and who accidently killed himself with a homemade bomb at age 14. Genene, then 16, appeared to have difficulty resolving her feelings of grief. As a nurse in the pediatric intensive care unit of the University of Texas Hospital in San Antonio, she seemed to be attracted to emergencies. Many children in her care had cardiac arrests, respiratory arrests, seizure crises, and unexplained seizure emergencies. These appeared to be associated with very large overdoses of succinylcholone, Dilantin, or heparin. Suspected in the epidemic of bizarre deaths, she was forced to leave the hospital, but she was given good references for a new nursing job. She then went to work in a pediatrician's office where the epidemic of deaths and life-threatening crises continued. Fired by the pediatrician and under investigation by the police in regard to multiple child murders, Genene Jones was hired by a Texas State School to provide nursing care to adults with mental retardation. Although Jones was convicted of only one child murder and aggravated assault involving a second child, she is suspected to have been responsible for many more (perhaps as many as 60) deaths. Several but not all of the children involved had disabilities. The children without disabilities who were murdered and assaulted generally were under 2 years of age, but the children with disabilities were significantly older (up to 8 years old). Jones received a total sentence of 159 years. One hospital administrator was fined $100 for contempt of court for failing to cooperate with the investigation.

366. Elks, M. A. (1993). The "lethal chamber": Further evidence for the euthanasia option. *Mental Retardation, 31*(4), **201–207.**
This article provides some of the history of the debate about the euthanasia of people with mental retardation. This article is written primarily as a response to the position that euthanasia was never seriously discussed in the United States. It presents examples of three basic positions using historical documents. First, some sources dismissed or rejected euthanasia as an option. Second, some sources presented ambivalent views. Third, some sources clearly supported euthanasia. This article

presents 1940s and 1950s' texts on mental retardation as examples of strong pro-euthanasia statements. The author suggests that the large, disease-infested institutions of the first half of the 20th century represented a form of passive euthanasia. He suggests that these institutions represented a form of "lethal chamber" that was acceptable to the general population.

367. Elmer, E., & Gregg, G. S. (1967). Developmental characteristics of abused children. *Pediatrics, 40*(4, Pt. I), 596–602.

This article discusses an evaluation of 50 children admitted to hospitals for injuries due to physical abuse years after the abuse in order to determine their development. Of the original 50 children, five could not be studied because they had been admitted to institutions for people with mental retardation. It could not be determined whether their severe mental retardation preceded or followed their injuries as the developmental level of the children was not systematically evaluated at the time of admission to hospital. Overall, the reevaluation showed that 50% of the children were classified as having mental retardation; however, due to the absence of information gathering on admission to the hospital, it was not possible to state whether the intellectual impairment occurred due to the abuse or precipitated the abuse. In either case, the authors predicted that due to their impairments one quarter of these children will become wards of the state and several others may only be able to remain in the community if kept in a sheltered environment.

368. Elvik, S. L., Berkowitz, C. D., Nicholas, E., Lipman, J. L., & Inkelis, S. H. (1990). Sexual abuse in the developmentally disabled: Dilemmas of diagnosis. *Child Abuse & Neglect, 14,* 497–502.

The authors of this article feel that it is difficult to evaluate people with developmental disabilities for physical signs of sexual abuse because this group is at risk for all types of abuse. This article discusses a study in which 35 females with mental retardation were examined by the child abuse medical team at Harbor/ UCLA Medical Center after an inpatient was found to be pregnant. These patients ranged in age from 13 to 55 (average age was 26). This examination found that 13 patients had genital findings consistent with prior vaginal penetration. The authors claim that dilemmas arose concerning the significance of healed genital lesions and the implications of these findings for the residential facility where these women lived. The authors recommend a team approach because it decreases the work load and frustration of the practitioner and provides support for the findings.

369. Elwood, J. H., & Darragh, P. M. (1981). Severe mental handicap in Northern Ireland. *Journal of Mental Deficit Research, 25,* 147–155.

The authors of this article discuss a study that estimated the prevalence and examined the medical determinants of severe mental disability in Northern Ireland for a period ranging from 1950 to 1969. This study analyzed records of persons in special care services, and it identified 4,701 individual cases of severe mental disability, which suggested a rate of 3.67 cases per 1,000 live births for the general population. The authors examine the causes attributed to genetic, environmental, and unknown variables and note an increase in genetically determined causes and a decrease in unknown causes of severe mental disability, which they attribute, in part, to better medical treatment. The most frequently seen determinants include: Down syndrome, pregnancy and birth associated disorders, and family.

370. Emery, J. L. (1985). Infanticide, filicide, and cot death. *Archives of Disease in Childhood, 60,* 505–507.

This article examines the pathology of filicide and discusses the subject with regard to sudden infant death syndrome (SIDS) or cot (crib) deaths. The author suggests that anywhere from 1 in 10 to 1 in 50 SIDS deaths is the result of filicide.

371. Emery, J. L. (1986). Families in which two or more cot deaths have occurred. *Lancet, 1,* 313–315.

This article presents 12 case studies involving families with two or more children who died of cot (crib) deaths or sudden infant death syndrome (SIDS). The author states that filicide was the probable cause of death for five of these families; in two additional cases, the author suggests that neglect was a factor in the children's health and their care. In three families, the author feels that the SIDS deaths involved familial or hereditary determinants. The author could not explain the SIDS deaths in two cases.

372. Emslie, G. J., & Rosenfeld, A. (1983). Incest reported by children and adolescents hospitalized for severe psychiatric problems. *American Journal of Psychiatry, 140*(6), 708–711.

This article discusses a study that assessed 65 children and adolescents who were admitted over a 6-month period to the Child and Adolescent Psychiatric Inpatient Unit of San Jose Hospital in California for psychiatric problems in order to determine the frequency of molestation by family members. The results of this study reveal the following: 22 patients (10 female, 12 male) were found to have a psychosis; 40 patients (16 female, 24 male) were found to have no psychosis; 3 male patients had an unknown diagnosis; of the 26 females admitted, 7 had been sexually abused by family members; all but 1 of the female patients came from the nonpsychosis group; and of the 39 males, 3 had been victims of incest. A comparison of teenage girls with a history of incest as opposed to those without showed significant differences. The authors suggest that severe family disorganization and the following ego impairment are the precursors to a psychopathology that results in hospitalization, and although incest could be a part of the family dysfunction, it is not necessarily present in all cases.

373. Endicott, O. R. (1980). Can human rights legislation help people who are mentally handicapped? *Canadian Human Rights Reporter, 1,* C32–C34.

This article discusses human rights for people with mental disabilities. It examines those rights that have been denied to people with mental disabilities and proposed provincial legislation to rectify these human rights violations. Also, this article discusses the Canadian Charter of Rights and Freedoms and the protection of people with mental disabilities.

374. Endicott, O. R. (1981). Will Emerson Bonnar get his "day in court"? *Canadian Journal on Mental Retardation, 31(1),* 17–18.

This article relates the case of Emerson Bonnar, a man with mental retardation who spent 15 years in a psychiatric institution (the maximum security wing of the Restigouche Hospital Centre in Campbellton, New Brunswick) because he was found unfit to stand trial on a charge of purse snatching. His case came to the attention of the National Legal Resources Service of the National Institute on Mental Retardation after Bonnar's story appeared on *Ombudsman,* a CBC television program. After the discovery of his case, two independent psychiatric assessments found that Mr. Bonnar was fit to stand trial, was not a dangerous person, and that institutionalization, and not a previous disorder, is probably responsible for his current mental status. The National Legal Resources Service of the National Institute on Mental Retardation recommended that a program of treatment and rehabilitation be initiated for Mr. Bonnar to help him reintegrate back into society. Although the Board of Review for New Brunswick accepted the recommendations, it disagreed on Mr. Bonnar's fitness to stand trial and his lack of dangerousness. Mr. Bonnar is held under a Lieutenant Governor's Warrant that allows for temporary transfer of Mr. Bonnar to a different facility. The warrant stands until Mr. Bonnar is fit to stand trial, yet the Crown does not have enough evidence for a new case; consequently, a new trial could technically never occur. The National Legal Resources Service of the National Institute on Mental Retardation is continuing to advocate for Mr. Bonnar.

375. Endicott, O. R. (1988). Is it still a capital offense to have Down syndrome? *Entourage, 3(3),* 17–24.

This article discusses the practice of withholding medical treatment from people with mental disabilities, paying particular attention to infants with Down syndrome. The author uses Canadian and United States court rulings to illustrate this issue.

376. Endicott, O. R. (1989). The right to raise children. *Entourage, 4(4),* 10.

This article addresses the parental rights of parents with intellectual disabilities. It claims that the court removes children from parents with intellectual disabilities because it believes that it is in the children's best interests. This article examines the court's belief and the guaranteed rights of people with intellectual disabilities to raise their biological children, which is included in the Canadian Charter of Rights and Freedoms.

377. Endicott, O. R. (1991). The liberty which seeks to understand the minds of others. *Entourage, 6(4),* 10.

This article summarizes the case of Justin Clark, a man with cerebral palsy who wanted to leave an institution. According to this article, Justin's father wanted to be appointed legal guardian of his son and have the court declare Justin legally incompetent, which would prevent Justin from leaving the institution. This article summarizes Justin's address at the 1991 Canadian Association for Community Living conference, where he discussed the importance of independence and the right to make decisions.

378. Endicott, O. R. (1991). Not out of the woods yet. *Entourage, 6(1),* 9.

This article discusses the 1987 Parliamentary bill that amended the Canada Evidence Act. It examines some of the implications of this bill for people with disabilities: For example, this bill removes some of the restrictions concerning the testimony in court of a person with disabilities. According to this amendment, people with disabilities, especially mental disabilities, are required to demonstrate that they understand what it is to tell the truth before they are allowed to testify. Also, this article examines some additional implications of the bill for people with disabilities.

379. Endicott, O. R. (1992). People First scores landmark victory in Ontario Court of Appeal. *Entourage, 7(1),* 6.

This article summarizes the proceedings of an Ontario Court of Appeal ruling that gave People First full access to court papers concerning an inquest against the Christopher Robin Home and the Brandwood Development Centre. The court ruled in favor of People First because it felt this group could not properly prepare a submission without complete documentation.

380. Englade, K. (1988). *Cellar of horror: The true story.* New York: St. Martins Press.

This true crime book details the abductions, rapes, tortures, and murders committed by Gary Heidnik in Philadelphia in the 1980s. Heidnik had originally aspired to be a military police officer, but instead, he trained to become a nurse. Later he became a minister in a church that he founded specifically to serve the spiritual needs of people with mental and physical disabilities. Heidnik preyed on marginalized women. While most of his victims were mentally retarded, he also victimized prostitutes and other woman of low status. He kept a number of slaves chained in his basement whom he repeatedly tortured and raped. At least two of these women died. He also kept a van parked across from a large institution where he took women to assault them. Because of errors by law enforcement and generally low priority given to these cases, police failed to act even when neighbors complained about the smell of burning flesh from his house, even when the family of one of his missing victims had identified him as the likely abductor, and even though he had a previous conviction for the abduction and sexual assault of a woman with mental retardation. He finally was arrested after one of his prisoners escaped and went to the police. After conviction, Heidnik was sentenced to death and 320 years in prison.

381. Engman, K. (1989, May 26). Foster dad sexually abused paralysed, speechless boy. *The Edmonton Journal*, p. B1.
This newspaper article discusses a case of sexual abuse involving a speechless quadriplegic boy and his foster father. It notes that the charges of sexual abuse have been stayed. While the Edmonton boy has been removed from the residence, the child was found to be unable to act as a witness due to his emotional and psychological frailty. This article points out that there have been three other cases of abuse against people with disabilities involving this same foster parent.

382. Engman, K. (1992, June 17). Teens get probation for torture of handicapped man. *The Edmonton Journal*, p. A1.
This newspaper article describes the case of two teens involved in torturing a man with mental disabilities who later died as a result of his beatings. The teens were given probation and community work by an Edmonton court. The adult in this case received 6 years in prison.

383. Engman, K. (1992, June 26). Crown appeals probation for beating of disabled man. *The Edmonton Journal*, p. B1.
This newspaper article reports that an appeal has been made by the Attorney General's Department concerning the light sentences given to two teenagers (ages 15 and 16) who pleaded guilty to the beating of Paul Devereaux, a man with developmental disabilities. The two teenagers were each sentenced to probation and community work. The assault on Paul Devereaux resulted in his death several days later.

384. Engman, K. (1993, January 20). Mom admitted smothering baby, ex-boyfriend says. *The Edmonton Journal*, p. B1.
This newspaper article reports that Patricia Just, age 28, is on trial in Edmonton, Alberta, for aggravated assault stemming from a smothering incident involving her 6-month-old son. The infant suffered severe brain damage and visual impairment as a result of the assault. The infant was put on life support and died from meningitis 11 months later. Ms. Just smothered the boy with a pillow to stop his crying. Ms. Just's boyfriend testified that she revealed the true cause of her son's death in a phone conversation.

385. Engman, K. (1993, June 6). Jason left blind, disabled by abuse. *The Edmonton Journal*, p. A3.
This newspaper article reports that Theresa and Rod Lenny have been convicted of aggravated assault against a 21-month-old infant who was placed in their care by Social Services. Jason Carpenter and his older sister were taken from their natural mother who resided in a drug and prostitution house and were placed into foster care with the Lennys on July 25, 1990. Six weeks later, Jason was rushed to the hospital with bruises and severe brain damage. Currently, Jason lives on life support, is visually impaired, and is unable to communicate as a result of his abuse. Sentencing will be forthcoming. The Lennys were acquitted of aggravated assault stemming from abuse of Theresa Lenny's son 2 years prior to the Carpenter case.

386. Engman, K., & Crockatt, J. (1992, June 18). Anger rises over youths' probation in fatal beating of handicapped man. *The Edmonton Journal*, p. B1.
This newspaper article describes the public anger over the leniency in sentencing two youths charged in the torture and fatal beating of Paul Devereaux, a 24-year-old Edmonton man with developmental disabilities. The two youths were sentenced to probation and community work. Two others involved in the beating were convicted and sentenced at an earlier time.

387. Engman, K., & Tanner, A. (1993, June 11). Jason's own mother isn't a saint, but was never cruel—relative. *The Edmonton Journal*, pp. A1, A9.
This newspaper article provides some background information on Glenda Carpenter, Jason Carpenter's biological mother who lost custody of her children for raising them in a drug and prostitution house. Jason Carpenter ended up in foster care with Theresa and Rod Lenny, who severely abused him and caused permanent brain damage and visual impairment. Theresa Lenny's background is also discussed.

388. Enhances personal freedom: Trial run a success, disabled driving school officially open. (1992, June 26). *The Edmonton Sun*, p. 10.
This newspaper article reports that a driving school for people with disabilities has officially opened for business. The Nissan Performance Driving School at Shannonville Motorsport Park, near Belleville, Ontario, runs six 1-day courses at a subsidized cost of $138 Canadian. The course for people with physical dis-

abilities is run in conjunction with the Hugh MacMillan Rehabilitation Centre in Toronto. Students will learn such maneuvers as skid control, emergency reactions, and crash avoidance. The driving school's phone number is (613) 962-5588.

389. Epstein, M. A., Markowitz, R. L., Gallo, D. M., Walker Holmes, J., & Gryboski, J. D. (1987). Munchausen syndrome by proxy: Considerations in diagnosis and confirmation by video surveillance. *Pediatrics, 80*(2), 220–224.

This article discusses a case of Munchausen syndrome by proxy that involves a mother and her 18-month-old infant. This mother used laxatives to induce tractable diarrhea in her son. The discovery of the inducement was made using video surveillance. The mother's medical history included approximately 15 psychiatric hospitalizations.

390. Erickson, M. F., Egeland, B., & Pianta, R. (1989). The effects of maltreatment on the development of young children. In D. Cicchetti & V. Carlson (Eds.), *Child maltreatment: Theory and research on the causes and consequences of child abuse and neglect* (pp. 647–684). Cambridge: Cambridge University Press.

This chapter focuses on how different types of child maltreatment (such as physical abuse, hostile/verbal abuse, physical neglect, emotional neglect, and sexual abuse) affect a child's development. It discusses the findings of the longitudinal prospective study conducted by the Minnesota Mother-Child Interaction Project. This study follows up children at risk for maltreatment by their first-time mothers. Two hundred sixty-seven mothers constituted the original sample group. The maltreatment subject group, identified when the children were 2 years of age, consisted of children from 24 physically abusive, 19 hostile/verbally abusive, 24 neglectful, and 19 psychologically unavailable mothers. A nonmaltreated group of 85 high-risk children from mothers in the original sample constituted a control group. The study obtained outcome measures from infancy through preschool. This study found the following: 1) physically abused children were aggressive, noncompliant, and exhibited acting out behavior; 2) the high degree of overlap in the physically and hostile/verbally abused groups contributed to the similarity in responsive behaviors for these children; 3) these children showed negative affect, low self-esteem, and avoidance behaviors with regard to mother-child interaction; 4) the neglected children were characterized by their negative affect, noncompliance, anger, and avoidant, nonaffectionate mother-child interaction, although they relied on their mothers for assistance and support; and 5) the children in the psychologically unavailable group were most noted for their anxious avoidant behavior, negative affect, anger, and noncompliance. When the children were 6 years of age, the study evaluated the following groups: 16 physically abused children, 17 ne-

glected children, 16 psychologically neglected children, and 11 sexually abused children were compared with a control group (65) of nonmaltreated high-risk children with regard to school adjustment. This comparison revealed the following: 1) the physically abused children were characterized by highly aggressive, disruptive, noncompliant behavior, and they exhibited poor comprehension and social emotional health; 2) compared to the control group, the neglected group was found to be more anxious, withdrawn, showed diminished sensitivity, was inattentive, and was academically limited; 3) psychologically neglected children were less socially and academically competent and more aggressive and nervous than controls; and 4) the sexually abused children were more withdrawn, obsessive-compulsive, inattentive, and exhibited a strong desire for closeness.

391. Ernhart, C. B., Sokol, R. J., Ager, J. W., Morrow-Tlucak, M., & Martier, S. (1989). Alcohol-related birth defects: Assessing the risk. *Annals of the New York Academy of Sciences, 562,* 159–172.

The authors of this article describe a study that assessed the risk of birth defects after prenatal exposure to alcohol using a cohort group comprising 239 mother-infant pairs. This study found the following: Severe alcohol consumption during pregnancy (defined as three drinks per day or greater) increased the risk of anomalies in neonates, the craniofacial anomalies that were associated with heavy drinking are representative of fetal alcohol syndrome, and neonates of women who were occasional drinkers were not noticeably different from those whose mothers abstained from alcohol consumption during pregnancy.

392. Etmanski, A. (1983). Exploring the boundaries of social change: Reflections on the Stephen Dawson court proceedings. *Canadian Journal on Mental Retardation, 33*(3), 6–13.

This article discusses a March 1983 decision brought down by the British Columbia Supreme Court in favor of Stephen Dawson, a man with a mental disability who needed an operation that would release pressure on his brain. The role of advocacy for people with disabilities in bringing about social change is discussed in light of these proceedings.

393. Ewingman, B., Kivlahan, C., & Land, G. (1993). The Missouri child fatality study: Underreporting of maltreatment fatalities among children younger than five years of age, 1983 through 1986. *Pediatrics, 91*(2), 330–429.

This article describes a study that attempted to estimate the incidence of child abuse and neglect (CAN) fatalities in Missouri during a 3-year period. Three hundred eighty-four children under the age of 5 were grouped into one of the following five categories: definite maltreatment, probable maltreatment, possible maltreatment, nonmaltreatment, and inadequate information. The results of this study indicate a distribution of 121 positive, 25 probable, and 109 possible cases of maltreatment. Of the total number of positive maltreatment cases, only 47.9% were recorded as maltreatment. The Division of Family Services claimed that 79.3% of the positive cases were abuse or neglect fatalities, while the Federal Bureau of Investigation Uniform Crime Reports database listed 38.8% (n=47) of these cases as homicide. Forty-six criminal convictions were recorded, of which one case resulted in two convictions. The authors conclude that underreporting of child abuse fatalities in Missouri exists due to lack of information sharing among agencies, inaccurate reporting procedures, concealment of abuse, and nonregulated definition of what constitutes maltreatment.

394. Ex-nurse probed in two deaths. (1988, April 3). *The Washington Post*, p. A16.
This newspaper article describes the investigation of an ex-nurse who worked at the Medical University of South Carolina and at the Charleston Memorial Hospital in South Carolina who is implicated in the deaths of two patients. Each terminally ill patient under the nurse's care was administered a lethal dosage of potassium and Demerol. It is believed that these killings were deliberate acts of malice, not acts of mercy.

395. Ex-nursing home aide gets life term in 5 patient killings. (1989, November 3). *The New York Times*, p. A13.
A former nurse's aide charged with the murder of terminally ill patients at the Alpine Manor Nursing Home was sentenced to life in prison. Gwendolyn Graham and Catherine Wood were both implicated in the deaths of several patients, killed by means of suffocation. Ms. Graham received a life sentence, and Ms. Wood received 20 to 40 years in prison.

396. Execution in Texas blocked; Missouri commutes penalty. (1993, June 3). *The Washington Post*, p. A16.
This newspaper article reports that Lewis Shaw had his execution sentence commuted by the Governor of Missouri several days before he was to be executed. His sentence has been changed to life in prison for the stabbing death of a prison guard. Lewis Shaw has mental retardation and is found to be suffering from mental illness. Gary Graham, another death row inmate in Texas, has also had his sentence commuted because he was convicted under a law that did not take into consideration his age (17) at the time of the offense.

•F•

397. Fahs, J. J. (1992). *Habilitative psychopharmacology (1985–1991): A reference guide.* Kingston, NY: National Association on the Dually Diagnosed.
This annotated bibliography provides references and abstracts for hundreds of books, articles, and chapters on the use of psychoactive drugs with people with disabilities. It is a rich source of information on the use and misuse of these medications. For those concerned with abuse issues, there are citations on treatment acceptability, legal issues, scientific fraud, antilibidinal drugs, electroconvulsive shock treatment (ECT), and the harmful and therapeutic effects of drugs.

398. Faller, K. C. (1993). *Child sexual abuse: Intervention and treatment issues.* McLean, VA: National Center on Child Abuse and Neglect, U.S. Department of Health and Human Services.
This manual is written for professionals working in the area of child sexual abuse. It covers the personal impact this work may have on professionals and discusses coping strategies. It includes definitions and examines the scope, the effects, and the indicators of child sexual abuse. Two sections are dedicated to the investigation and interviewing process, and an additional section is dedicated to sexual abuse treatment and its associated issues.

399. Fallon, P., & Coffman, S. (1991). Cognitive behavioral treatment of survivors of victimization. *Psychotherapy in Private Practice, 9*(3), 53–65.
The consequences of physical and sexual abuse are discussed in this article. It defines and illustrates the following cognitive behavioral treatment approaches used to assist survivors of abuse: activity scheduling, automatic thoughts identification, and personal schema elucidation.

400. Famularo, R., Kinscherff, R., & Fenton, T. (1992). Parental substance abuse and the nature of child maltreatment. *Child Abuse & Neglect, 16,* 475–483.
This article examines parental substance abuse and the nature of child maltreatment. Of 190 randomly selected physical and sexual child maltreatment cases from a juvenile court, 127 (67%) cases involved parents who were substance abusers. Alcohol abuse was significantly related to physical maltreatment, while cocaine abuse was significantly related to sexual maltreatment. It notes that maltreatment of either type lends itself to the probability of the other form of maltreatment; consequently, legal custody of the children in the 190 cases was given to the state.

401. Famularo, R., Kinscherff, R., Fenton, T., & Bolduc, S. M. (1990). Child maltreatment histories among runaway and delinquent children. *Clinical Pediatrics, 29*(12), 713–718.
The authors of this article discuss a study that examined the history of child maltreatment and focused on the physical or sexual abuse of 378 children under the age of

18 seen in juvenile court. One hundred and eighty-nine of these children exhibited criminal behavior, and 189 of the children exhibited noncriminal behavior, such as running away from home, truancy, or disobedience. A comparison of child maltreatment history showed that 42% of these children exhibiting criminal behavior and 52% of these children exhibiting noncriminal behavior had a history of abuse. A greater percentage of physical abuse was noted for the children who exhibited violent behavior (27%) when compared to the nonviolent children (14%), and a greater percentage of sexual abuse was noted for runaways (35%) as opposed to status offenders (5%). The authors conclude that child maltreatment could be a significant variable in future juvenile behavioral disorder.

402. **Fantuzzo, J. W., Jurecic, L., Stovall, A., Hightower, A. D., Goins, C., & Schachtel, D. (1988). Effects of adult and peer social initiations on the social behavior of withdrawn, maltreated preschool children.** *Journal of Consulting and Clinical Psychology, 56*(1), 34–39.
This article discusses a social initiation treatment program that was conducted with 39 maltreated preschoolers in order to increase their positive social behavior. The children were separated into three treatment groups: peer social initiation, adult social initiation, and a control group. The treatment consisted of two consecutive 15-minute play sessions in which play organization and sharing were the chosen initiations encouraged by the confederates. Both pretesting and posttesting of positive social behavior was conducted using behavioral analysis of the observed interactions. The results of this treatment program indicate that the greatest pre-post difference was found with the peer social initiation treatment group. There was no significant difference found between the adult and the control treatment group.

403. Farmer cleared of mercy killing. (1991, April 6). *The New York Times*, p. A25.
This newspaper article reports that Mr. Adelbert Ward, a 60-year-old farmer from Stockbridge, southeast of Syracuse, was acquitted of killing his brother William. Adelbert was originally charged with second-degree murder in William's suffocation death, which the district attorney described as a mercy killing. William had suffered from a head injury and blood poisoning resulting from a chain-saw accident 2 years earlier.

404. Fatout, M. F. (1990). Aggression: A characteristic of physically abused latency-age children. *Child and Adolescent Social Work, 7*(5), 365–376.
This article focuses on aggression and aggressive behavior as an outcome of the physical abuse of children. It details the expression of aggression in a therapeutic group and suggests treatment approaches.

405. Fatout, M. F. (1990). Consequences of abuse on the relationships of children. *Families in Society: The Journal of Contemporary Human Services, 71*(2), 76–81.
This article examines the impact of child abuse on relationship development. It defines factors that inhibit bonding, and it discusses the effects of child abuse on children's interactions with adults and peers in terms of characteristic behavior.

406. Favell, J. E., Azrin, N. H., Baumeister, A. A., Carr, E. G., Dorsey, M. F., Forehand, R., Foxx, R. M., Lovass, O. I., Rincover, A., Risley, T. R., Romanczyk, R. G., Russo, D. C., Schroeder, S. R., & Solnick, J. V. (1982). The treatment of self-injurious behavior. *Behavior Therapy, 13*(4), 529–554.
This article presents a review of the medical, psychodynamic, and behavioral approaches that are applied to the treatment of self-injurious behavior of people with developmental disabilities, in particular those with severe disabilities. It reviews research that supports the efficacy of each of the approaches, and it identifies a variety of self-injurious behaviors: for example, head banging, biting, face slapping, eye poking, and eating nonedible substances. It notes that self-injurious behavior has been associated with some medical disorders (e.g., Lesch-Nyhan syndrome, mental retardation), but it points out that, at present, medical treatment has not been developed or is not sufficient or necessary. It claims that the psychodynamic approach has not resulted in successful treatment approaches, especially for people with mental retardation. It reviews behavioral approaches that tend to view self-injury as operant behavior: for example, treatment by differential reinforcement of alternative behavior, treatment by rearranging antecedents, treatment by removing or withholding reinforcement for self-injury, and treatment by punishing self-injurious behavior. This article concludes that current evidence supports the behavioral strategies as the treatments of choice. This article includes a list of approximately 170 references.

407. Feigelson Chase, N. (1976). Institutional abuse. In *A child is being beaten: Violence against children, an American tragedy* (pp. 150–164). Dusseldorf: McGraw-Hill.
This chapter examines child abuse and neglect in government-funded institutions during the 1970s. It describes the deplorable conditions and abusive treatment of children and notes that institutionalization is a means of harboring some children while they wait to go to court in cases of physical or sexual abuse perpetrated by their parents. This chapter questions the rationale of a system that proposes to safeguard a child's welfare by taking the child out of an abusive situation and placing the child in an equally abusive institution; and it asks whether the abuse and neglect of children by parents is any less aversive than abuse and neglect perpetrated by institutional caretakers, guards, and inmates.

408. Feinmann, J. (1988). Corridors of fear. *Nursing Times, 84*(39), 16–17.
This article discusses women's claims of sexual harassment, rape, and abduction in psychiatric institutions. This article focuses on patient-patient abuse and discusses possible solutions.

409. Feldman, K. W., & Brewer, D. K. (1984). Child abuse, cardiopulmonary resuscitation, and rib fractures. *Pediatrics, 73*(3), 339–342.
This article discusses childhood rib fractures resulting from cardiopulmonary resuscitation (CPR). The conclusions drawn from a study of 41 child abuse victims, 50 CPR cases, and 22 rib fracture cases reveal that no fractures resulted from the administration of CPR. Of the 29 children with fractures, the study found that 14 (48%) were child abuse victims.

410. Feldman, M. (1990). Balancing freedom from harm and right to treatment for persons with developmental disabilities. In A. C. Repp & N. N. Singh (Eds.), *Perspectives on the use of nonaversive and aversive interventions for persons with developmental disabilities* (pp. 261–271). Sycamore, IL: Sycamore Publishing.
This chapter discusses the pros and cons of aversive conditioning for people with developmental disabilities who exhibit severe behavioral disorders. In addition, it suggests a treatment model that attempts to balance the patient's right to effective treatment and the right not to be harmed.

411. Feldman, W., Feldman, E., Goodman, J. T., McGrath, P. J., Pless, R. P., Corsini, L., & Bennett, S. (1991). Is childhood sexual abuse really increasing in prevalence? An analysis of the evidence. *Pediatrics, 88*(1), 29–33.
This review of the literature systematically compares data contained in 1970s and 1980s published studies with data contained in 1940s published studies in order to see if there has been an increase in the prevalence of child sexual abuse. Twenty studies that were conducted on the general population and focused on childhood sexual abuse were used for this analysis. This review used the following criteria to choose studies: quality of definitions, populations studied, and research design. Although the rate of disclosure of childhood sexual abuse has increased, the results of this review indicate that the prevalence of childhood sexual abuse has remained relatively the same for the last 40 years.

412. Fenigsen, R. (1989). A case against Dutch euthanasia. *Hastings Center Report, 19*(1), 22–30.
This article presents a Dutch cardiologist's view of euthanasia and assisted suicide as practiced in Holland. He points out that 76% of Dutch citizens supported euthanasia, and 77% supported involuntary euthanasia. Ninety percent of Dutch students in an undergraduate economics program approved of the compulsory euthanasia of unspecified groups of people to improve the economy. The Dutch media interpreted that support as a vote for human freedom and self-determination, but Fenigsen suggests that a careful review of the data shows that it was actually a "public acceptance of the view that life-saving treatment should be denied to the severely handicapped, the elderly, and perhaps to persons without families" (p. 23). He points to the legitimization of involuntary euthanasia by the acceptance of voluntary euthanasia, citing the case of a physician who was convicted of involuntary euthanasia of patients in "De Terp" old-age home in the Hague where secret killings of patients were exposed in 1985. This physician was under suspicion for killing 20 people and accused of 4 killings. Witnesses testified that some of the individuals killed were not ill or debilitated, but were only senile or uncooperative with the staff. Many other patients were threatened with euthanasia whenever they showed any sign of being uncooperative. Patients were killed with difficult to trace insulin overdoses. This doctor pleaded guilt to killing five patients and was convicted of three killings. A citizens committee was formed to support the physician, and the Board of Physicians felt this conviction might inhibit physicians or make them feel insecure in carrying out other euthanasia actions. A higher court dismissed the guilty pleas and declared him innocent. The punishment was abolished, and a civil court awarded the physician 300,000 guilders (about 150,000 U.S. dollars). Fenigsen also cites the cases of four nurses at the Free University Hospital in Amsterdam who secretly killed comatose patients. The Employees' Council defended them saying that they had been forced to take these actions by physicians who were too slow to order euthanasia. The court dismissed the charges because it found that they acted out of humane considerations. The Dutch society for voluntary euthanasia has supported the actions of physicians carrying out involuntary euthanasia and advocated for the involuntary euthanasia of various classes of people, including Thalidomide victims, unconscious individuals, and senile people. Its quarterly publication carried without comment a plea for killing all newborns with disabilities in order to build a stronger race. Fenigsen suggests that even in "voluntary" cases consent is often counterfeit or questionable, and it is inevitably linked to involuntary killing. He cites evidence that at least 300 infants with severe disabilities are passively euthanized by withholding care each year, a number that would be equivalent to about 5,000 per year in a population the size of the United States.

413. Ferguson, P. (1990). The social construction of mental retardation. In M. Nagler (Ed.), *Perspectives on disability* (pp. 203–211). Palo Alto, CA: Health Markets Research.
This chapter presents a position that social policy on disability should practically and conceptually meet the

needs of people with mental retardation. It suggests that people with severe and profound mental retardation have been ignored by social reforms that have helped other people with disabilities. The author provides a brief but interesting history of mental retardation and service reform that suggests that reformers achieved progress for those with less severe disabilities by maintaining a contrast class of "failures" who had more severe disabilities.

414. Ferreyra, S., & Hughes, K. (1982). *Table manners: A guide to the pelvic examination for disabled women and health care providers.* **San Francisco: Sex Education for Disabled People.**

This book, written by two women with physical disabilities, was designed for women with disabilities and health care providers. The authors advocate a cooperative approach to pelvic examinations: that is, the client with a disability works with the clinician to meet the client's specific needs. They point out that decisions (such as whether a women needs a sign language interpreter in the exam room or help transferring from a wheelchair) should be made by both the clinician and client. The authors conclude that a clinician does not have to be an expert in disabilities and a woman does not have to be an expert in pelvic examinations for this approach to work.

415. Fichten, C. S., Compton, V., & Amsel, R. (1985). Imagined empathy and attributions concerning activity preferences of physically disabled college students. *Rehabilitation Psychology, 30*(4), 235–239.

This article discusses a study that questioned 89 college students without disabilities about the activity preferences of male and female students with disabilities (wheelchair users) and students without disabilities. It examined imagined empathy and how it affected attribution and attitudes toward students with disabilities. In this study, the students completed a 20-question forced-choice questionnaire and the Attitude Toward Disabled Persons Scale. The questionnaire consisted of equally pleasurable activities but differed on variables of sociability and activity level. The results of this study indicate a discrepancy between the perceptions of students without disabilities regarding the activity preferences of students with disabilities. This study found that imagined empathy and prior contact with students with disabilities did not affect attribution patterns.

416. Fichten, C. S., Robillard, K., Judd, D., & Amsel, R. (1989). College students with physical disabilities: Myths and realities. *Rehabilitation Psychology, 34*(4), 243–257.

This article describes a study that examined the attitudes and self-concepts of college students with and without disabilities regarding mutual interaction and stereotypes about disability. The participants included 17 students who use wheelchairs, 15 students who are visually im-

paired, and 221 students with no physical disabilities. All of the participants were administered the Social Activity Questionnaire, the Social Avoidance and Distress Scale, the College Student Trait Checklists, and the Coopersmith Self-Esteem Inventory-Adult Form. The results of this study indicate the following: Students with and without disabilities are uncomfortable with others who have a disability different from their own; both groups use negative stereotypes for others with disabilities; and all of these students had similar results concerning self-esteem, social anxiety, dating anxiety, and dating behavior.

417. Field, T. (1987). Interaction and attachment in normal and atypical infants. *Journal of Consulting and Clinical Psychology, 55*(6), 853–859.

This article summarizes and critically evaluates research on attachment behavior during infancy and its long-term implications for the child. The author reviews articles that examine the effects of maternal alcohol consumption, premature infants, and abusive, neglectful, or depressed mothers on mother-infant attachment as well as attachment to inanimate objects. These articles seem to suggest the following: 1) early mother-infant interactions do not definitively predict later attachment classifications; 2) data on the predictive value of attachment classifications are equivocal; 3) atypical infants and normal infants differ on their interaction behaviors but not on attachment classifications, suggesting that the strange-situation behavior of the infant is not affected by premature infants or atypical infants; and 4) early interventions may affect interaction behaviors, but they do not seem to affect classifications of attachment. Despite these criticisms, the author notes that attachment between infants and caregivers is a significant process. However, the author suggests that a more complex paradigm than the strange-situation that would tap behavior in more ecologically meaningful situations in both stressful and nonstressful situations may provide more insight into the functional significance of attachment.

418. Fifield, B. B. (1984–1986). Ethical issues related to sexual abuse of disabled persons. *Sexuality and Disability, 7*(3/4), 102–109.

The author of this article focuses on ethical issues for health professionals and, in particular, on how ethical standards may be applied when one is confronted with situations involving sexual abuse of persons with disabilities.

419. Fine, M., & Asch, A. (1988). Disability beyond stigma: Social interaction, discrimination, and activism. *Journal of Social Issues, 44*(1), 3–21.

This article reviews the social psychological perspective used to examine disability over the past decade and challenges the assumptions that have shaped research and theory. These assumptions include the following: disability is primarily biological rather than sociological, all problems experienced by individuals with disabilities stem from their disabilities, people with disabilities are inherently victims, disability is a focal point of the self-concept of all people with disabilities, and all people with disabilities need help from people without disabilities. These assumptions are viewed as instrumental in developing the traditional views of researchers and professionals as well as the public and contributing to social policies such as those that permit the starving of or denial of medical care for labeled infants. This article proposes a return to Lewinian/minority group analysis on disability, and it provides some questions for future consideration.

420. Fine, M., & Asch, A. (Eds.). (1988). *Women with disabilities: Essays in psychology, culture, and politics*. Philadelphia: Temple University Press.
This book contains 13 essays that present the perspectives of women with disabilities. In addition, the introduction and epilogue provide valuable information and help integrating the results of the 13 chapters. The book is divided into three major sections: bodies and images, women with disabilities in relationships, and policies and politics. Sexual abuse and sexual assault as well as other forms of violence experienced by women with disabilities are not addressed as a separate chapter, but these topics are discussed in the introduction and in a number of chapters. Other topics related to the issue of abuse (e.g., attachment) are also discussed in this book.

421. Fine, M. J. (1986). Intervening with abusing parents of handicapped children. *Techniques*, 2(4), 353–363.
This article discusses a systems-ecological orientation for understanding and intervening with abusive families. As abuse of a child with disabilities is viewed as a dysfunction within the family, it is suggested that intervention be focused on the family. The author uses an example of a child with mild disabilities and his family to illustrate the dynamics of abuse and proposes a multilevel intervention model that integrates intervention at the levels of information input, belief/attitude change, skill acquisition, and behavior change. The author also stresses the need for ongoing family support and a sympathetic view of the parents.

422. Fine, S. (1989, December 23). Canada's "vulnerable adults": Their cries are seldom heard. *The Globe and Mail*, pp. D1, D2.
This newspaper article defines vulnerable adults as those who are dependant on others for their protection, safety, and care. Vulnerable adults include such populations as the elderly, former psychiatric patients, and people with disabilities. This article calls for the proper protection of and advocacy for people who are dependent on others. It points out that the need is great and government resources are limited; consequently, there has been an increase in the number of volunteer groups who advocate

for those who cannot speak for themselves, which is based on a referral system. Unfortunately, those people living in institutions or residences who are cut off from their families are seldom referred.

423. Fine, S. (1990, November 30). Coroner announces Brantwood inquest: Institution deaths to be probed. *The Globe and Mail*, pp. A1, A2.
This newspaper article reports that an inquest has been ordered into the deaths of 15 adults at the government-financed Brantwood institution for people with disabilities. It states that the adults died as a result of inadequate medical care while residing at Brantwood.

424. Fine, S. (1990, December 1). Children's deaths to be reviewed: Chief coroner calls for scrutiny of 2nd Ontario home for retarded. *The Globe and Mail*, p. A6.
This newspaper article reports that a review of the Christopher Robin Home in Oshawa, Ontario, has been ordered by Ontario's chief coroner. Thirteen deaths of former residents at the Christopher Robin Home, which occurred in 1 fiscal year, will be medically reviewed at the request of Ontario's chief coroner since the home for children with mental disabilities had only seven deaths in previous years.

425. Fine, S. (1991, October 4). Disabled women seek protection from abuse: Majority in survey report sexual assault. *The Globe and Mail*, p. A4.
This newspaper article discusses a questionnaire survey of women with disabilities concerning sexual assault conducted by the DisAbled Women's Network (DAWN) in Toronto, Canada. Questionnaires were delivered to members and agencies working with people with disabilities. Approximately 60 women responded to the questionnaires. The results indicate the following: almost 50% of the respondents had a history of sexual assault, defined as unwanted sexual acts; for almost 42% of the respondents, sexual assault occurred on more than one occasion; and 14% of the perpetrators had been charged with assault, and 6% were found guilty. Requests for more accessible services were made by the respondents, including wheelchair accessibility, sex education, women's shelters, abuse protection training, awareness training of legal rights, and counseling services. The study also concluded that 44% of the respondents who were abused blamed themselves for the abuse.

426. Fine, S. (1992, April 27). Findings on child molesters a shock. *The Globe and Mail*, pp. A1, A2.
This newspaper article discusses a report from the British Columbia Health Ministry on multiple child abuse offenders. This report states that 2,009 children were abused by 30 offenders. The average length of time of abuse is 10 years, with one offender abusing children over a period of 35 years. In half of the cases, the offender abuses only boys; in nine cases, only girls were

targeted; and in six cases, both boys and girls were abused.

427. Fine, S. (1992, December 7). Advocates would speak for society's powerless. *The Globe and Mail*, pp. A1, A8.
This newspaper article discusses Ontario's proposed legislation to develop an independent advocacy system to protect vulnerable adults. The article describes the 1987 death of Joe Kendall, who died from a beating he received for soiling his sheets at Cedar Glen nursing home in Orilla, Ontario, and from injuries he received from another resident during similar beatings.

428. Fine, S., & Allen, G. (1990, November 29). Ontario told about Brantwood in 1986: Warning preceded deaths at institution. *The Globe and Mail*, pp. A1, A10.
This newspaper article reports that information concerning serious problems with the Brantwood Centre for people with severe disabilities was known to the Ontario government two years prior to 15 deaths at the center. The deaths of 15 residents were a result of severe malnutrition, dehydration, and staff negligence. The Ontario Association for Community Living, which investigated Brantwood in 1986, noted their concerns about the center in a report to the Community and Social Services Ministry. It recommended an independent review of the residents and their needs and called for the monitoring of food and liquids.

429. Finger, P. (1990). Die Sterilisation geistig Behinderter nach 1905 BGB in der Fassung eines Entwurfs des Betreuungsgesetzes (BtG) [The sterilization of the mentally handicapped according to Paragraph 1905 BGB (civil code) in a draft of the Betreuungsgesetz]. *Praxis der Kinderpsychologie und Kinderpsychiatrie, 39*(4), 132–138.
This article discusses efforts to enact a sterilization law in contemporary Germany. It raises issues about the potential abuse of the law and traces the origins of this law to the eugenics of the Nazi era.

430. Fink, A. H. (1988). Education's responsibility for abused or neglected youth. *Pointer, 32*(4), 32–35.
This position paper discusses the need for educators to take an active and functional role in the rehabilitation of the abused child. Specific types of abuse and their developmental consequences are presented as well as a rationale for further involvement by the school system. The basis for this rationale includes: a moral mandate, an acknowledgment of the devastating effects abuse can have on the learning process, and an understanding that a teacher provides a consistent and caring adult model for a child. The fact that children with disabilities are at greater risk for abuse is very briefly mentioned.

431. Finkelhor, D. (1984). *Child sexual abuse*. New York: Free Press.
The author of this book proposes the following Four Preconditions Model of Sexual Abuse: 1) a potential offender has to have some motivation to abuse a child sexually, 2) the potential offender has to overcome internal inhibitions against acting on the motivation, 3) the potential offender has to overcome external impediments to committing sexual abuse, and 4) the potential offender or some other factor has to undermine or overcome a child's possible resistance to the sexual abuse. With regard to Precondition 3, factors predisposing to overcoming external inhibitors include the following: a mother who is not close to the child, social isolation of family, or unusual opportunities to be alone with the child. Factors predisposing to overcoming a child's resistance (Precondition 4) include the following: a child who is emotionally deprived, a child who lacks knowledge about sexual abuse, a situation of unusual trust between child and offender, and coercion. All of the above predisposing factors are applicable to children with disabilities, although the author does not specifically make this connection. He does, however, point out in his suggestions for further research that physical or emotional disabilities may compromise the child's ability to avoid abuse.

432. Finkelhor, D., & Baron, L. (1986). High-risk children. In D. Finkelhor, S. Araji, L. Baron, A. Browne, S. Doyle Peters, & G. E. Wyatt (Eds.), *A sourcebook on child sexual abuse* (pp. 60–89). Beverly Hills: Sage Publications.
This chapter characterizes risk factors associated with sexual abuse. It states that most studies agree that females are at greater risk for abuse than males. The age period most often associated with sexual abuse is between 8 and 12 years of age. There seems to be a relationship between sexual abuse and parental absence or unavailability, poor relationship between the child and parents, conflict between parents, and the presence of a stepfather in the household; but the authors have drawn no clear distinction regarding social class, ethnicity, social isolation, and sexual abuse. The authors also offer suggestions for future research.

433. Finkelhor, D., & Lewis, I. A. (1988). An epidemiologic approach to the study of child molestation. In R. A. Prentky & V. L. Quinsey (Eds.), *Human sexual aggression: Current perspectives* (pp. 64–77). New York: New York Academy of Sciences.
The authors of this chapter state that research on sexual assault in the last decade has moved from a criminological and clinical orientation to an epidemiological orientation and that there has been a shift to social psychological concepts. This chapter delineates the elements of these two approaches as applied to child molestation. It provides the results of a survey of undetected child molesters using an epidemiological approach (Randomized Response Technique) and suggests

possible social psychological concepts, such as male socialization, which can be applied to the problem of child molestation.

434. Firsten, T. (1990). *An exploration of the role of physical and sexual abuse for psychiatrically institutionalized women.* **Toronto: Ontario Women's Directorate.**
This paper discusses a study that investigated the histories and outcomes of abuse of 83 female psychiatric patients. The women in this study were drawn from 50 provincial psychiatric facilities and 33 general hospitals in Ontario. The results of this study indicate the following: 83% of the women reported experiencing one or more severe incidents of physical or sexual abuse, 48% did not have a record of abuse in their hospital admission charts, and the investigation of the relation between abuse histories and negative mental health consequences shows abuse to be an important component of the symptomatology of psychiatric patients.

435. Fisher, G. L., Jenkins, S. J., & Bancroft, M. J. (1985). *Teaching the mentally handicapped to avoid sexual exploitation.* **Reno, NV: Authors.**
The authors of this book claim that existing curricula developed for the prevention of sexual exploitation of children without mental disabilities are not appropriate for children with mental retardation. They discuss curricula specifically designed for students with special needs: the "Special Education Curriculum on Sexual Exploitation" for students who are mildly disabled and "Self-Protection for the Handicapped" for students who are moderately/severely mentally disabled. They point out that implementing the curricula in a school district requires the following: the approval of the administrator, inservice training for teachers, and an opportunity for parents to preview the curriculum materials and to discuss their concerns. They recommend that instruction should use the following format: a group setting rather than an individualized format, 30–45-minute sessions each day for 24 weeks, and the use of materials that are adapted to meet the needs of the particular students. They note that it is important that concepts and skills be mastered before discussing exceptions. The authors discuss an evaluation of the curriculum's efficacy, which was evaluated by placing trained and untrained students in potentially exploitative simulations. The results of this evaluation show that trained students performed significantly better than untrained students. The authors conclude that classroom training could be generalized to realistic situations.

436. Fitz-Gerald, D., & Fitz-Gerald, M. (1986). *Information on sexuality for young people and their families.* **Washington, DC: Gallaudet College, Pre-College Programs. (ERIC Document Reproduction Service No. ED 294 407)**
This book is written for young people who are hearing impaired or have difficulty with reading and language skills. The language used is straightforward, illustrations are composed of line drawings, and numerous aspects of sexuality are addressed (sexually transmitted diseases, abortion, sexual abuse and assault, and building relationships with others). This book includes the following: a glossary of 175 terms and expressions; a list of books for parents, preteens, teens, and children 7 to 10 years old; and a list of 11 free or inexpensive materials.

437. 5 accused of sex attack on retarded girl. (1989, May 26). *The Edmonton Journal,* **p. A15.**
This newspaper article reports that five members of the Glen Ridge High School football team in Glen Ridge, New Jersey, have been arrested and charged with the sexual assault of a teenage girl with mental retardation. Several other boys are considered witnesses in the case.

438. 5 youths held in sex assault on mentally impaired girl, 17. (1989, May 25). *The New York Times,* **pp. A1, A17.**
This newspaper article reports that five teenagers from Glen Ridge High School in New Jersey have been charged with conspiracy to commit sexual assault and aggravated sexual assault against a 17-year-old girl with mental impairments. Eight others were involved in witnessing the assault but were not charged. The five charged and the victim are White, and all of them knew each other. The sexual assault took place in the basement of two of the accused, twin brothers and cocaptains of the football team. The victim is believed to have been forced to perform several sexual acts and was penetrated by a broomstick handle and miniature baseball bat. The victim was brought to police by school officials three weeks after the assault took place. Three of those charged will be tried as adults.

439. Flavelle, D. (1990, June 11). Fighting for their safety. *The Toronto Star,* **pp. C1, C3.**
This newspaper article examines the victimization of people with disabilities. It cites a University of Alberta study that found that people with disabilities were 150% more likely to be victimized than people without disabilities after controlling for age and gender. This study concludes that offenders can be categorized into three major groups: relatives (30%), friends or acquaintances (30%), and paid caregivers (27%). This article points out that the resources most requested by people with disabilities concerning their protection include the following: emergency shelters and rape crisis centers geared toward people with disabilities, independent mediators to advocate for the rights of people with disabilities victimized in institutional settings, and education programs for people with mental disabilities dealing with sex education and appropriate and inappropriate sexual advances. This article includes a personal account of one family's experience.

440. Flecher, J. R., Holmes, P. A., Keyes, C. B., & Schloss, P. J. (Eds.). (1989). *Linking research and practice: An integrated approach to the treatment of the dually diagnosed* (1st ed.). Lexington, MA: Lexington Books.

This book states that the field of dual diagnosis is in its infancy, and the services as well as the training programs are meager. It suggests that fostering strong, constructive links between applied research and practice is likely to strengthen the field. It examines the barriers to such an integration, which include the following: 1) mental health and mental retardation have a well-established dichotomy between their researchers and practitioners; 2) their funding sources are different; 3) practitioners consider the results of research to be of little practical value or irrelevant; 4) researchers consider the practitioners too immersed in short-term problem solving and that they do not examine their successful techniques critically; and 5) researchers find it difficult to conduct research in community settings because the mental health problems of people with mental retardation come to the fore only when they enter a community agency, which is usually too small and thinly staffed to support a research effort. This book claims that methods of proper record-keeping in observable behavioral terms, measurement of the effectiveness of affective practitioner techniques, and dissemination of the effective treatment practice are some of the benefits of research for the practitioners. It suggests that practitioners can further research by identifying cases, by developing theories about affective treatment programs, by having access to resources necessary for conducting applied research, and by participating in the research. This book discusses intervention targets and the generation of reliable data using proper replicable methods and proper research designs that produce believable results. It claims professional societies can help bring the researcher and practitioner together and emphasizes the integration of research and practice. It suggests that the development of practice settings in the research culture and conducting research in community settings can foster this integration and help answer questions about the prevalence of psychiatric disorders in people with mental retardation. It can also help determine affective and practical assessment instruments for this population and the application of specific psychopharmacology and use of specific drugs for specific symptoms.

441. Flynn, D. (1988). The assessment and psychotherapy of a physically abused girl during in-patient family treatment. *Journal of Child Psychotherapy, 14*(2), 61–78.

This article discusses the assessment and psychotherapeutic treatment of a 7-year-old girl with a history of severe neglect by her mother and physical abuse by her stepfather. Psychotherapy was conducted at the inpatient treatment facility at the Cassel Hospital Families Unit. Having separated from her husband, the child's mother and her daughter underwent individual psychotherapy as a means for the mother to obtain permanent custody of the child. The major goal in this therapy consisted of building a strong relationship between the mother and her daughter. The child's thoughts, dreams, and fantasies expressed verbally and through illustrations were examined in therapy. This article discusses the issues relating to her prior history of maltreatment and the result of therapy.

442. Foley, G. M. (1985). Emotional development of children with handicaps [Special issue: The feeling child: Affective development reconsidered]. *Journal of Children in Contemporary Society, 17*(4), 57–73.

This article describes the emotional development of children with disabilities using the attachment-separation-individuation (ASI) theory. It presents a modified overview of the normal progression of ASI in light of current research. Using descriptive data on 17 mother-infant dyads followed clinically for 24 months, it suggests that children with disabilities are at risk for disordered patterns of interaction, delayed progression through the stages of ASI, and incomplete internalization of self-constancy and object constancy. It identifies specific interactional risk factors and describes patterns of ASI. It reviews methods of assessment, and it presents an intervention model for facilitating the progression of ASI by normalizing parent-child interactions.

443. Forest, M. (1984). Communicating: The way to freedom. *Canadian Journal on Mental Retardation, 34*(4), 29–33.

This article discusses the importance of teaching communication skills to people with developmental disabilities in order to facilitate their social development. It emphasizes diversity when teaching these skills.

444. Former foster parents on ill-treatment charges. (1991, October 16). *Otago Daily Times*, p. 26.

This newspaper article reports that a Palmerston North, New Zealand, husband and wife are currently standing trial for 11 counts of willfull ill-treatment of six boys who were in their foster care from 1984 to 1987. Allegations against the former foster parents include beatings, severe punishment, and neglect. The boys ranged in age from 3 to 10 years while in foster care. The husband and wife were approached about their disciplinary techniques by a Department of Social Welfare senior social worker on several occasions while they were foster parents. In 1987, the couple resigned from fostering but reapplied 2 years later in Auckland. Lawyers for the couple argue that the boys are conspiring against the couple and deny all allegations.

445. Forssman, H., & Thuwe, I. (1988). The Goteborg cohort, 1939–77: A 35-year follow-up of 120 persons born in Sweden after refusal of application for therapeutic abortion. In H. P. David, Z.

Dytrych, Z. Matejcek, & V. Schuller (Eds.), *Born unwanted: Developmental effects of denied abortion* (pp. 37–45). New York: Springer.

This chapter describes a follow-up study that compared 120 children (66 boys, 54 girls) born to women who were denied abortions with a control group of 120 children whose mothers did not apply for abortions. The results of this follow-up indicate significant differences between the mothers of the two groups, with the indexed group being older on average than controls and having a lower socioeconomic status. The comparison of the children at age 21 noted that the indexed children came from unstable households, required more public assistance, and were less educated. A follow-up at age 35 showed a general minimization of differences between the two groups.

446. Franchi, L. M. (1991). *Final results of the needs assessment of deaf and hard of hearing children for a sexual abuse prevention program.* **Vancouver, BC: Greater Vancouver Association of the Deaf.**

This report summarizes the results of a needs assessment of children who are deaf and hard of hearing in terms of sexual abuse. The children in this study were between 8 and 15 years of age. This study used the presentation skits on "bad touches." The children in this study expressed a variety of negative feelings in response to the skits. Twenty-one adults who are deaf and hard of hearing (19 to 69 years of age) were also interviewed. Fifty-one percent of the adults reported being subjected to unwanted sexual touching during childhood. Sixty-eight resource people who work with children who are deaf and hard of hearing were also interviewed. Sixty-two percent of these resource people had experience dealing with child sexual abuse. Seventy-seven percent of these resource people felt that children who are deaf/hard of hearing are at higher risk of sexual abuse than children without disabilities.

447. Frank, Y., Zimmerman, R., & Leeds, N. M. D. (1985). *Neurological manifestations in abused children who have been shaken.* **Developmental Medicine and Child Neurology, 27, 312–316.**

This article discusses four case histories of infants who were severely shaken. Retinal hemorrhages were found in all four cases, but no other evidence of external battery was noted. Three infants were permanently impaired with severe brain damage, spasticity, and blindness. The authors discuss the infants' computerized tomographies and neurologic abnormalities.

448. Fraser, G. (1993). *Going to court.* **NAPSAC (National Association for Prevention of Sexual Abuse of Children and Adults with Learning Disabilities) Bulletin, 6, 7–10.**

This article provides a case study of a child who was originally referred to a counselor because of phobic responses to the doctor and dentist but later disclosed

sexual abuse by a male staff member in her group home. This young girl was able to give an explicit, convincing, and detailed account of the abuse. She also indicated feelings of betrayal toward other adults who failed to protect her from being abused. She was frightened of the offender who had threatened to kill her and her family if she told about the abuse. The counselor provided therapy aimed at reducing her anxiety, building her self-esteem, and encouraging expression of her feelings about being abused. Police pressed charges after DNA testing matched a semen sample found on the carpet with the alleged offender, but this evidence would only be useful to corroborate the child's allegation. The court made several accommodations for this child (e.g., members of the court wore normal clothes instead of robes, screening her from the offender), and although she was anxious, she testified successfully. The author stresses the importance of preparing witnesses with disabilities for the courtroom.

449. Freeman, J. M. (1987). *If euthanasia were licit, could lives be saved?* **In R. C. McMillan, H. T., Englehardt, Jr., & S. F. Spicker (Eds.),** *Euthanasia and the newborn: Conflicts regarding saving lives?* **(pp. 153–168). Boston: D. Reidel.**

This chapter presents a case for euthanasia, arguing that legalization of euthanasia would lead to control of what is now a covert activity. The author argues that legalizing euthanasia would have many advantages: More individuals would be afforded a "death with dignity, quick and without pain" (p. 165); initial treatment would often be more vigorous if physicians knew that the option of euthanasia would be available later if the results of treatment were less than satisfactory; the process would be open and rationale, while it is now covert and uncontrolled; and fewer abortions would be needed since it would be possible to wait until after the child is born to decide whether or not it should be allowed to live. He proposes that families and physicians should have the power to determine euthanasia provided the decision is reviewed by a hospital ethics review committee. (Editors' note: While the arguments presented here are contrary to the basic theme of preventing violence against people with disabilities, it is important to understand this point of view in order to discuss it rationally.)

450. Freeman, R. J., & Roesch, R. (1989). *Mental disorder and the criminal justice system: A review.* **International Journal of Law and Psychiatry, 12, 105–115.**

This article looks at offenders with developmental disabilities and their treatment in the criminal justice system. It examines people with developmental disabilities in the community, their processing in the judicial system (e.g., arrest and trial), and offenders in custody. Also, this article discusses the issue of returning the offender to the community.

451. French, L. (1987). *Victimization of the mentally ill: An unintended consequence* of **deinstitutionalization.** *Social Work,* *32*(6), 502–505.

This article describes the victimization of people who are mentally ill and living on the streets. It argues for greater recognition of the problem and a responsive clinical network and justice system to deal with this victimization.

452. Fresco, F., Philbin, L., & Peters, K. (1992). The design and evaluation of a sexual assault support group for women with mild developmental disabilities. *Canadian Journal of Human Sexuality,* *1*(Suppl. 4), 5–13.

This article describes a sexual assault support group for women with mild developmental disabilities. The group consists of seven clients, ranging in age from 21 to 31; most of these women have a childhood history of sexual abuse, and all of them have a history of multiple sexual assaults in adulthood. A psychometrist, a social worker, and a supervising psychologist work with the group. All of these women were pretested and posttested for personality functioning using the Prout-Strohmer Personality Inventory (PSPI) and the Strohmer-Prout Behaviour Rating Scale (SPBRS). A sexual assault interview was initiated with these women to assess their sexual assault experiences and to establish a supportive relationship. This program consists of eight weekly sessions lasting 1.5 hours. This article describes the session topics, purpose, and techniques used in this program. No significant differences were noted for these women on personality functioning as measured by the PSPI and SPBRS; however, staff members have noted improvement in clients' assertiveness, self-confidence, acceptance of one's sexuality, and assessment of personal safety.

453. Fresco, F., Philbin, L., & Peters, K. (1992). A sexual assault support group for women with developmental disabilities. In *Crossing new borders* **(pp. 179–182). Kingston, NY: National Association for the Dually Diagnosed.**

This chapter discusses the role of support groups for women with disabilities who have been sexually assaulted. It states that group advantages include: context for sharing experiences, opportunities for modeling adaptive behavior, peer confrontation regarding attitudes and behavior under controlled conditions, expression of emotions, experience of group acceptance, and maximization of human resources. The authors describe a program consisting of eight, topically sequenced, 90-minute sessions for seven women with mild developmental disabilities who had been sexually abused as children (5) or sexually assaulted as adults (2). Group members rated their experience as positive and helpful, and staff members reported improvements in the assertiveness, self-confidence, and personal safety skills of the women participating in the group. Pretesting and posttesting of personality functioning, however, showed no significant changes. The authors recommend more sessions for future groups.

454. Fried, E. R. (1986, May). *A multi-modal treatment of developmentally disabled sex offenders.* **Paper presented to the Fourth National Conference on the Sexual Victimization of Children, New Orleans.**

This paper describes treatment strategies used by the Moderate Security Counselling & Treatment Unit (MSU) for sex offenders with developmental disabilities. The MSU program provides an alternative to prison, and this program offers help to pedophiles, rapists, and people with developmental disabilities who have been victims of incest. This program emphasizes the following: the exploration and recapitulations of childhood, comprehensive behavior modification, understanding social mores, and the acquisition of positive leadership skills.

455. Friedberg, J. B., Mullins, J. B., & Sukiennik, A. W. (1992). *Portraying persons with disabilities: An annotated bibliography of nonfiction for children and teenagers.* **New Providence, NJ: R. R. Bowker.**

This book provides a wealth of information on how people with disabilities are portrayed in nonfiction for children and teenagers. Books have been selected for inclusion based on their perceived value in fostering acceptance and understanding, appropriateness of content, and accessibility of reading level for young readers. This bibliography would be useful for anyone wanting to identify readings about individuals with disabilities for children and young adults. It is indexed by subject, author, and title to make the selection process easy for the reader.

456. Friedrich, W. N., Einbender, A. J., & Luecke, W. J. (1983). Cognitive and behavioral characteristics of physically abused children. *Journal of Consulting and Clinical Psychology, 51*(2), 313–314.

The study discussed in this article compared 11 preschool children with a history of physical abuse to 10 nonabused preschoolers. All of the children were male and matched for age, family income, maternal age, and education. Both groups of children were administered the McCarthy Scales of Children's Abilities and the Wide Range Achievement Test. In addition, the children's behavior was noted while they were completing different tasks. The results of this study indicate the following: the abused children performed significantly poorer on the Verbal and Memory scales of the McCarthy Scales of Children's Abilities in comparison to nonabused children; and no significant differences were noted in behavioral observations concerning the children.

457. Frisch, L. E., & Rhoads, F. A. (1982). Child abuse and neglect in children referred for learning evaluation. *Journal of Learning Disability, 15*(10), 538–541.

This article discusses 430 children from Oahu, Hawaii, who were referred to a central school problem clinic for evaluation of learning problems during the 1977–1978 school year. The proportion of these children (6.7%) who had been independently reported to the state child abuse agency was compared, after age adjustment, to the rate of such reporting for all children on the island and was found to be 3.5 times higher. The types of abuse and/or neglect reported were similar for the children with learning problems and for other island children. The authors feel that these findings strengthen the argument for a link between child maltreatment and developmental disabilities.

458. Frost, B. (1994, February 11). Ex-nurse given nine life sentences for string of sex attacks. *The Times*, p. 3.
This newspaper article from Dorset, England, reports that a former psychiatric nurse was sentenced to nine concurrent life sentences for sexually assaulting women with mental retardation. Michael Fox, age 50, pleaded guilty to five counts of kidnapping, three counts of rape, and one count of attempted rape. He has also asked the court to consider three additional kidnappings, three attempted kidnaps, two indecent assaults, and one attempted rape. Between June 1988 and December 1991, Fox abducted and assaulted his victims before abandoning them. Fox is also currently being questioned in the death of Jo Ramsden, a 21-year-old girl with Down syndrome who was found buried in a shallow grave in Dorset.

459. Fryers, T. (1992). Epidemiological research related to mental retardation. *Current Opinion in Psychiatry*, 5, 650–655.
This article examines the underlying causes of mental retardation. It discusses adverse influences on measured intelligence and performance: for example, nutrition, breastfeeding, alcohol exposure in utero, lead exposure, and low birth weight. Also, this article examines specific etiological groups and their frequencies: for example, Down syndrome, X-linked syndromes, phenylketonuria (PKU), cytomegalovirus, and some rarer syndromes like Retts and Prader-Willi.

460. Fulcher, G. (1989). *Disabling policies: A comparative approach to education policy*. London: Falmer Press.
This book discusses educational policies and how these policies affect the integration of people with disabilities. It compares educational policies from Scandinavia, the United States, England, and Australia. This book concludes that the objectives of policy and legislation differ and often conflict within each jurisdiction and policy often acts to handicap individuals with disabilities in society.

461. Furey, E. M. (1989). Abuse of persons with mental retardation: A literature review. *Behavioral Residential Treatment*, 4(2), 143–454.

This literature review examines the abuse of people with mental retardation in residential settings. It examines the causes for abusive behavior in relation to the following: organizational variables, staff characteristics, and client characteristics. This article includes recommendations for reducing the incidence of residential abuse.

462. Furey, E. M. (1994). Sexual abuse of adults with mental retardation: Who and where. *Mental Retardation*, 32(3), 173–180.
This article discusses an analysis of 461 cases of sexual abuse of adults with mental retardation. This analysis found the following: 1) most of the victims (72%) were female; 2) males with mild mental retardation were underrepresented and males with severe mental retardation were overrepresented in the sample, which suggests that males with severe disabilities may experience greater risk; 3) females with mild mental retardation were more common in the abused sample; 4) facility neglect was a major factor in 24.6% of sexual abuse cases; 5) other individuals with mental retardation were responsible for 42% of the sexual abuse cases; 6) paid service providers were responsible for 19% of the sexual abuse cases; 7) family members were responsible for 12% of the sexual abuse cases; 8) other individuals known to the victims were responsible for 13% of the sexual abuse cases; and 9) the offender was unknown in only 8% of the cases.

463. Furey, E. M., &. Haber, M. (1989). Protecting adults with mental retardation. *Mental Retardation*, 27(3), 135–140.
This article describes a Connecticut statute designed to protect adults with mental disabilities from abuse and neglect. The statute requires the following: those involved in the care of individuals with mental disabilities must report abuse and neglect without fear of reprisal; full access to client records must be given to investigative authorities; and should abuse or neglect be found, the victim must be provided immediate protective services. This article presents a breakdown of abuse cases reported within a 3-year period following enactment of the statute. It suggests that there was a highly significant increase in the reporting of such incidents within a 1-year period, that the majority of abuse occurred within the victims' living arrangements, and that paid staff were by far the main perpetrators of the abuse or neglect. This article provides recommendations for further research in this area.

464. Fyffe, C., & Thompson, D. (1991). The impact of misleading post-event information on the memory for events of people with intellectual disabilities. *National Coalition on Intellectual Disability: Interaction*, 5(4), 42–46.
This article discusses a study that tested the effect of misleading post-event information on the recall of subjects with and without mental retardation. The results of this study reveal the following: Both people with and

without mental retardation demonstrated some misinformation effect, people with mental retardation recalled less information than people without mental retardation under all test conditions, and people with mental retardation were no more likely to be misled by misinformation than people without mental retardation.

•G•

465. Gadeken, G. (1989, Spring). The Ray Charles syndrome: Distorted images of disabled people in the mass media. *Dialogue, 28,* 55–60.
This article claims that the mass media image of Ray Charles as a successful person with a visual impairment is a distorted view of most ordinary people with a visual impairment. It states that the public's perception becomes distorted by unrealistic representations of ability that people with disabilities find difficult to match. This article suggests that the expectations and perceptions of disability held by people without disabilities are influenced by this mass media image.

466. Gagne, R. J. (1994). A self-made man. In V. J. Bradley, J. W. Ashbaugh, & B. C. Blaney (Eds.), *Creating individual supports for people with developmental disabilities: A mandate for change at many levels* (pp. 327–334). Baltimore: Paul H. Brookes Publishing Co.
This chapter is a firsthand account of the life experiences of a man with cerebral palsy who spent much of his childhood in a state institution. He describes the general deficiencies of institutional life, including the physical abuse, but he seems more concerned about the universal insensitivity of staff than the occasional beatings.

467. Gair, D. S., Hersch, C. & Weisenfeld, S. (1980). Successful psychotherapy of severe emotional disturbance in a young retarded boy. *Journal of the American Academy of Child Psychiatry, 19*(2), 257–269.
This article presents a case study of a boy who, at the age of 6, was diagnosed with "an emotional form of retardation" and "psychosis," and it discusses an adult follow-up of this boy in order to demonstrate the importance of psychotherapy in the treatment of children with mental retardation. Initially, the boy was untestable for IQ, but ultimately, he tested low in the mildly retarded range. At the time of referral, he showed severe deficiencies in ego development. The boy improved following several years of psychotherapy and concurrent casework with the parents. At the age of 27, he is still mildly retarded, but he is able to support himself and is free of significant personality disabilities.

468. Gallagher, H. G. (1990). *By trust betrayed: Patients, physicians, and the license to kill in the Third Reich.* New York: Henry Holt.
This book examines the treatment of people with disabilities in Nazi Germany and in various cultures and times. The chapter entitled "Aktion T-4 at Hadamar" (pp. 9–23) deals with the extermination of adults and children with developmental disabilities at the Hadamar Psychiatric Institute in Germany during World War II. As part of the Third Reich's Aktion T-4 program, people with developmental disabilities were gassed or received lethal injections at the institute by hospital staff, and their bodies were cremated in the hospital's crematorium. The chapter entitled "The handicapped in other times and places" (pp. 24–44) examines the attitudes and treatment of people with disabilities in different cultures and societies. It discusses studies of disability and societal attitudes toward disability, and it compares these attitudes with the treatment of people with disabilities in Nazi Germany. The physician-patient relationship is addressed with regard to the medical profession's emphasis on the physical condition rather than the whole person. This chapter also examines the medical establishment's authoritarian stance toward patients and factors that relax this stance, for example, a patient's economic and social status. The chapter entitled "Aktion T-4 and the doctors" (pp. 178–204) examines Aktion T-4, the German euthanasia policy of killing psychiatric patients and others with developmental disabilities during the Nazi regime. This chapter emphasizes the resistance of some medical professionals during this time. It features individual case stories of doctors and nurses who resisted the government-sanctioned policy of killing patients with disabilities, and it examines the climate for physicians and health care during the Third Reich. Also, this chapter discusses the motivational factors that resulted in physicians cooperating with the Nazi movement.

469. Galleno, H., & Oppenheim, W. L. (1982, January/February). The battered child syndrome revisited. *Clinical Orthopaedics and Related Research, 162,* 11–19.
This article discusses a study that examined the early diagnosis and prevention of child abuse by orthopedic surgeons. In this study, a cohort of 66 physically abused children (50% were below the age of 3) were examined, and it found that 82% of these children had soft tissue injuries, while 21% had fractures. The results of this study show that the fractures that indicated abuse had common features: for example, metaphyseal corner fractures, lower extremity fractures in nonweight-bearing children, and bilateral acute fractures. The authors suggest that in order to detect the physical abuse of children more attention should be paid to the specific nature of the fractures rather than the different healing stages.

470. Garbarino, J. (1987). The abuse and neglect of special children: An introduction to the issues. In J. Garbarino, P. E. Brookhauser, & K. J. Authier (Eds.),

Special children-special risks: The maltreatment of children with disabilities (pp. 3–14). New York: Aldine de Gruyter.

This book examines the social context of abuse in order to determine ways in which the factors that produce or prevent abuse in the lives of children without disabilities children operate for children with disabilities. If being disabled elicits greater nurturance, surveillance, and resources being brought to bear upon a child's family, then the child in such a situation might be at less risk than a child without disabilities in the same family. Nevertheless, comprehension and communication difficulties and greater dependence on caregivers might make a child with disabilities less able to seek protection from maltreatment when it does occur. Therefore, in looking at the problem, the author is interested in knowing what differences the differences make, not just "what are the differences?" It must be recognized that disabling conditions may be linked to other factors that are the real cause of maltreatment. Research has identified five broad categories of risk: 1) characteristics of parents, 2) characteristics of the child, 3) aspects of the relationship between a particular adult and child that produces a deteriorating pattern of interaction, 4) elements of the immediate situation that stimulate abuse, and 5) any feature of the culture or society that encourages maltreatment or permits it to occur. The author feels that children with disabilities may be at risk for abuse because of any or all of these factors. The goal of this book is to protect children with disabilities by preventing conditions under which they are at special risk and by correcting problems when they do occur.

471. Garbarino, J. (1989). The incidence and prevalence of child maltreatment. In L. Ohlin & M. Tonrey (Eds.), *Family violence. Crime and justice: A review of research* (Vol. II, pp. 219–261). Chicago: University of Chicago Press.

This chapter examines the incidence and prevalence of child maltreatment. Governmental action regarding child maltreatment is discussed as well as research and policy issues. This chapter pays special attention to juvenile delinquency, previous history of maltreatment, and the lack of abuse reports from practitioners.

472. Garbarino, J., Brookhouser, P. E., & Authier, K. J. (Eds.). (1987). *Special children-special risks: The maltreatment of children with disabilities*. New York: Aldine de Gruyter.

This comprehensive book contains chapters relating to the following topics: 1) factors that contribute to maltreatment of children with disabilities; 2) the way in which supporting and strengthening families contributes to preventing maltreatment; 3) the relationship of the child with disabilities with siblings and peers without disabilities and their potential effects on the child's well-being and development; 4) the role of educators in prevention and identification of maltreatment; 5) the in-

cidence of abuse in residential settings and implications for its prevention; 6) the role of the federal government in regard to legislation affecting children with disabilities who are abused; 7) therapeutic issues, including a discussion of the long-term effects of abuse, intervention, the client, the therapist, and therapeutic methods; 8) medical issues, including indicators of physical and sexual abuse; 9) special legal problems in protecting children with disabilities; 10) children within the criminal justice system; and 11) a discussion of model community approaches for bringing together the concerns, knowledge, resources, and efforts of the systems that may separately address the problems of child abuse and disabling conditions. This book briefly discusses the detection, effects, reporting, and prevention of sexual abuse.

473. Garbarino, J., Guttman, E., & Wilson Seeley, J. (1986). Assessing the causes and effects of maltreatment. In J. Garbarino, E. Guttman, & J. Wilson Seeley (Eds.), *The psychologically battered child: Strategies for identification, assessment, and intervention* (pp. 71–104). San Francisco: Jossey-Bass.

This chapter deals with the assessment of children who have been psychologically maltreated. It uses psychometric instruments consisting of different evaluation scales in order to assess the child's psychological maltreatment, the family's social environment, and the family context or climate. This article points out that it is necessary to identify the areas of concern before beginning intervention. The authors describe different assessment instruments and suggest various interventions.

474. Garfield, E., & Welljams-Dorof, A. (1990). The impact of fraudulent research on the scientific literature—The Stephen E. Breuning case. *Journal of American Medical Association, 263* (10), 1424–1426.

This article focuses on the potential value of citation indexes for limiting the spread of falsified research. The citation indexes can make readers aware of explicit retraction notices, provided these are published in a suitable indexing format. The research impact of scientific fraud was studied by the citation analysis of 20 publications for Stephen E. Breuning, who published a number of studies through "misleading, deceptive practices" between 1980 and 1984 on the use of drugs to control hyperactive children with mental retardation. These publications received 200 citations of Breuning, and 40% were self-citations. Self-citations peaked during the first 2 years and declined later, while nonself-citations peaked after 1985, which coincided with the criticisms of Breuning's study. An examination of citation contexts in 101 instances showed that 33 were negative (disagreed with findings or methods), 10 were positive (agreed), and 58 were neutral (no evaluation).

475. Gartner, A., & Joe, T. (Eds.). (1987). *Images of the disabled, disabling images.* **Westport, CT: Praeger.**

Mass media's portrayal of people with disabilities is discussed in this book. It examines the means by which this characterization influences public decisions about education, employment, and everyday life for people with disabilities.

476. Garwick, G. B., & Jurkowski, E. (1992). Evaluation of HIV prevention and self-protection training programs. In A. C. Crocker, H. J. Cohen, & T. A. Kastner (Eds.), *HIV infection and developmental disabilities: A resource for service providers* **(pp. 171–179). Baltimore: Paul H. Brookes Publishing Co.**

This chapter examines ways of assessing programs that teach HIV prevention and self-protection training to people with mental disabilities. It addresses ways in which these programs can be improved and offers future considerations for program assessment.

477. Gast, D. L., Collins, B. C., Wolery, M., & Jones, R. (1993). Teaching preschool children with disabilities to respond to the lures of strangers. *Exceptional Children, 59*(4), 301–311.

The study discussed in this article examined the effectiveness of a personal safety training program for preschoolers with disabilities that focused on the lures of strangers. This study employed a constant time delay procedure to allow for generalization of response. The children ranged in age from 3 years, 5 months, to 5 years of age. All the children were developmentally delayed and were receiving speech therapy. Both probe and training sessions were used with the children and involved 26 graduate students acting as "strangers" unknown to the children. Probe sessions were conducted in different settings such as parks, on the street, parking lots, alleyways, and the local YMCA and involved the use of a stranger approaching a child while the child's trainer was within a minimum of 5 feet. The stranger would attempt to lure the child away during this time. Lures consisted of general requests, authoritarian statements, and incentives. Training sessions were conducted in various areas in the preschool and in vivo training sessions followed daily probe sessions using the same site. Training sessions consisted of three massed trials, where all three lures were presented randomly. Children were informed about the importance of saying "no" to strangers, demonstrated the correct response, and role played correct responses. The results of this study indicate that in vivo training generalized the correct responses to the lures of strangers across different settings, strangers, and lures.

478. Gaylin, W. (1993, May). The "she asked for it" defense. *Mirabella,* **pp. 112–114.**

This article examines the "she asked for it" defense used in the trial of four Glen Ridge High School football players accused of sexually assaulting a 17-year-old girl with mental retardation. The assault took place in the basement of a house where one of the players lived. The assault involved foreign objects being inserted into the girl's vagina.

479. Geelhoed, G. C., & Pemberton, P. J. (1985, October 14). SIDS, seizures or esophageal reflux? Another manifestation of Munchausen syndrome by proxy. *Medical Journal of Australia, 143,* 357–358.

The case history of a 14-week-old boy with episodes of cyanosis is presented in this article. After extensive investigation, it was deduced that the boy's 17-year-old mother induced symptoms in the infant by asphyxiation. The mother's desire to attract attention using her son's seizures suggests Munchausen syndrome by proxy. The falsification of the mother's personal history and the child's medical history highlights the importance of obtaining accurate background information in order to prevent unnecessary and sometimes invasive medical intervention, which unduly abuses the patient.

480. Gelles, R. J. (1975, January). Violence and pregnancy: A note on the extent of the problem and needed services. *The Family Coordinator,* **pp. 81–86.**

The topic of violence toward pregnant women by their mates is discussed in this article. It describes factors associated with this violence and examines the services needed to curb it. The author suggests four strategies to combat this type of family violence: planned parenthood, preparation for parenthood, establishment of family crisis centers as an avenue of reprieve, and fulfillment of a family's basic needs to survive.

481. George, J. D. (1988). Therapeutic intervention for grandparents and extended family of children with developmental delays. *Mental Retardation, 26*(6), 369–375.

This article describes a family support group for grandparents and extended family members of children with developmental delays. The program provides unique opportunities for the group members to discuss adjustment reactions, develop supportive roles with one another, and strengthen the entire family constellation.

482. Georgia nurse, a focus in 16 deaths, is charged with one killing. (1991, August 22). *The New York Times,* **p. B12.**

This newspaper article reports that Joseph Dewey Akin, a former nurse, has been charged in the death of a patient at the Cooper Green Hospital in Alabama. Akin is also implicated in 15 deaths at the North Fulton Regional hospital in Atlanta.

483. Gerard, W. (1992, July 11). Molesters prey on "passive" disabled women. *The Toronto Star,* **pp. A1–A2.**

This newspaper article reports that a woman with cerebral palsy was victimized and sexually assaulted by Jacques Perron, a transit service operator for people with disabilities. The Freedom Machine operator was found guilty of three counts of sexual assault and one count of unlawful confinement. His background includes 25 prior convictions involving break-and-enters, fraud, and armed robbery. As a transit operator, he had a position of authority and trust, while the victim was socialized to passivity and compliance. Perron received 9 years in prison.

484. Gers, D. (1984). "Lernbehinderte" früher und heute—Eine Unterrichtseinheit [Learning handicapped past and present: A historical description]. *Behindertenpädagogik, 23*(2), 98–125.

This article examines the treatment of children with developmental and physical disabilities in Germany during the early 20th century. It pays particular attention to treatment during the Nazi era and focuses on the sterilization and extermination of these children. It includes a case history of one family's ordeal during World War II, during which they saw their son with an emotional disorder being denied food and eventually institutionalized until his death. It presents comparative data involving families with and without children with disabilities. This comparison found the following: Families with a child with a disability usually had fewer rooms in the house, had fewer children with their own rooms, and had more single-parent households. Also, this article examines current assessment measures used in Germany to assess children with learning disabilities. (This article is written in German.)

485. Gething, L. (1991). Generality vs. specificity of attitudes towards people with disabilities. *British Journal of Medical Psychology, 64*, 55–64.

This article describes a study that assessed general versus specific attitudes toward people with disabilities using the Interaction with Disabled Persons Scale (IDP Scale). The IDP Scale assesses discomfort in social interaction. This study assessed 482 subjects (49.3% men, 50.7% women) with a mean age of 40–49. The participants in this study were asked to rate their agreement with a given statement on a 5-point scale: For example, "I try to act normally and ignore the disability." This study also administered 12 parallel forms of the scale; 11 of these scales dealt with different disabilities: AIDS, alcohol dependence, Alzheimer's disease, visual impairment, cerebral palsy, diabetes, Down syndrome, drug dependency, epilepsy, paraplegia, and schizophrenia. The 12th scale was a generalized version addressing the concept of disability. The participants in this study completed only one questionnaire and were not informed about the parallel forms. The results of this study indicate that type of disability did not affect response; however, prior contact did significantly influence response. This article concludes that these findings support the generality of attitudes toward disability.

486. Gil, E. (1979). *Handbook for understanding and preventing abuse & neglect of children in out of home care.* San Francisco: San Francisco Child Abuse Council, San Francisco County Department of Social Services, Office of Child Abuse Prevention.

This handbook provides information on child abuse and neglect in institutional and residential care. The first chapter examines the incidence of child abuse and neglect, with descriptions of different types of abuses. Chapter 2 addresses institutional child abuse, and Chapter 3 examines the causes of child abuse and neglect in out-of-home care. Chapter 4 discusses the response to the maltreatment of children in out-of-home care and examines the evaluation and assessment of the situation and the interview process. The last chapter features issues concerned with reporting abuse and neglect in out-of-home care. The appendix includes suggested questions for screening potentially abusive clients.

487. Ginath, Y. (1993). Report of the committee assigned to investigate the protection of hospitalized mental patients against sexual assault and abuse—A critical review. *Medicine and Law, 12*, 375–379.

This article provides a critical review of a report investigating the protection of Israeli hospitalized psychiatric patients from sexual assault and abuse perpetrated by other patients. The special committee assigned to this investigation was nominated by the Israeli Deputy Minister of Health. The committee concluded that abuses were taking place, but the frequency of those abuses was not examined. Following Israeli criminal law, no psychiatric patient is able to give consent; therefore, all instances of sexual assault or abuse must be considered rape. Responsibility lies with the hospital and staff for the protection of patients. The committee recommended that all psychiatric wards be converted to unisex wards. In response, the author notes that currently most wards are integrated, resulting in reduced sexual and aggressive behavior. Most patients are admitted voluntarily and would be considered competent regarding consent if brought before a court of law. Given that individuals adjust their behavior to society's expectations, viewing patients as irresponsible might result in irresponsible behavior. Staff should be able to provide protection to patients from sexual assault or abuse without resorting to unisex wards. The author does support the use of some unisex wards in every region of the country to provide services to patients who request them.

488. Glaser, D., & Bentovim, A. (1979). Abuse and risk to handicapped and chronically ill children. *Child Abuse & Neglect, 3*, 565–575.

This article claims that there is an overrepresentation of neglect and abuse of children who are disabled and physically ill. It examines the abuse factors of these children within their own families since there is an ongoing concern about parental attitudes and reactions toward children who are chronically ill and disabled and the potential for abuse in this context. This article compares patterns of abuse in children who are chronically ill or disabled and children who are not chronically ill or disabled. It suggests that there are clear differences between these groups: Children without disabilities are more likely to suffer abuse by commission rather than by omission of care and are more likely to suffer from neglect and failure to thrive; and the abused group with disabilities is more likely to suffer omission of care and overt signs of rejection. This article explores the degree and severity of abuse in the two groups, and it examines the potential ages for abuse and the social/emotional disturbance in the family.

489. Glasgow, D. V. (1993, June). Factors associated with learning disabilities demanding special care during sexual abuse investigations and interviews. *NAPSAC (National Association for Prevention of Sexual Abuse of Children and Adults with Learning Disabilities) Bulletin, 4,* 3–7.

This article discusses interviewing and investigation techniques that can be used with people with disabilities who have been sexually abused. It stresses that proper techniques need to be used in order to facilitate communication and to minimize distress to the interviewee. The author suggests three factors that influence communication between people with learning disabilities and others: 1) idiosyncratic nonverbal mannerisms, for example, lack of eye contact or apparent lack of concern on the part of the victim, which may be interpreted by the interviewer as signs of an illegitimate claim of abuse; 2) idiosyncratic or limited receptive communication, that is, the limited response or lack of response of the interviewee to questions that are complex; and 3) limitations or idiosyncrasies of expressive communication, that is, the limited ability of the interviewee to respond verbally to a question due to a limited vocabulary. The author suggests that questions should reflect the cognitive abilities of the interviewee not the interviewer. The author also addresses interviewer effect on the interviewee and the inclusion of a possible third party to help facilitate the interview process.

490. Godschalx, S. M. (1983). Mark: Psychotherapy with a developmentally disabled adult. *Image: The Journal of Nursing Scholarship, 15*(1), 12–16.

This article illustrates the use of psychotherapy with an adult with developmental disabilities. It states that the treatment goals are to increase frustration tolerance, self-esteem, and responsibility for self-care. It describes how to achieve these goals: by facilitating trust, balancing flexibility and directiveness, and communicating empathy. This article discusses countertransference and includes recommendations for future research.

491. Goetting, A. (1988). When parents kill their young children: Detroit 1982–1986. *Journal of Family Violence, 3*(4), 339–346.

This article examines parents or guardians who kill the children in their care. It supplies demographic information for 36 parents or guardians who were arrested for killing their children. Thirty-four children under the age of 6 were the victims in these crimes. Twenty-one primary caregivers were convicted of murder or manslaughter, and 1 was convicted of cruelty. Of the convicted felons, 18 were sentenced to prison terms. The author provides a character profile for perpetrator and victim and notes that homicide by beating was the most prevalent form of abuse.

492. Goffman, E. (1961). *Asylums: Essays on the social situations of mental patients and other inmates.* Garden City, NY: Anchor Books.

This book, a collection of four interrelated essays, presents Goffman's classic treatment of total institutions. This book states that total institutions are isolated from the mainstream of society, and as such, they develop social structures and values that often are distinct from the surrounding culture. It suggests that inmates are dehumanized and devalued, and individuals are subordinated to the needs of the institution. Also, this book explores the medical model and the occupational relationship (along with its assumptions and ideals) between staff and patients.

493. Goffman, E. (1963). *Stigma: Notes on the management of spoiled identity.* Englewood Cliffs, NJ: Prentice-Hall.

This book presents Goffman's classic treatment of stigma and its role in influencing social relationships. It includes examples and discussions of stigma associated with physical and mental disability as well as race, religion, conviction for a crime, and other devaluing labels. This book concludes that stigmatized people are viewed as less than human and that they might be taught to devalue themselves and subsequently expect and allow their own victimization.

494. Goldberg, B. (1986). Broken noses, sex abuse and devils on shoulders: A twenty-five year experience with mentally disabled adolescents. *International Journal of Adolescent Medicine and Health, 2*(3), 179–191.

This article describes an interdisciplinary model used to diagnose, evaluate, and treat children with mental retardation at a regional center in London, Ontario. It presents three cases in order to illustrate this model and considers community-oriented treatment and some current ethical issues affecting treatment.

495. Goldberg, R. T. (1987). The "right" to die: The case for and against voluntary passive euthanasia. *Disability, Handicap and Society, 2*(1), 21–39.

This article explores arguments for and against voluntary passive euthanasia. The author concludes that real voluntary choice is the fundamental principle that must be present; therefore, passive euthanasia is not appropriate for individuals who are not competent to make the choice.

496. Golding, J., Limerick, S., & MacFarlane, A. (1985). *Sudden infant death: Patterns, puzzles and problems.* **Somerset, England: Open Books.**

This book examines some of the patterns, puzzles, and problems associated with sudden infant death syndrome (SIDS). It compares the medical histories of 164 siblings of infants who suffered SIDS with the siblings of 308 control infants. After controlling for similar social and maternal background, the results of this study indicate the following: the risk of SIDS for siblings of infants who suffered SIDS was three times greater when compared to controls; there were three siblings with mental retardation and one sibling with epilepsy, although the exact origin of these disorders, whether prenatal or postnatal, is unknown; and mothers of SIDS infants had a greater rate of postmortality mental disorders than mothers of controls.

497. Golding, J. M. (in press). Sexual assault history and physical health in randomly-selected Los Angeles women. *Health Psychology.*

This article discusses a study of 1,610 women in Los Angeles that was conducted to examine sex abuse histories and physical disabilities. The results of this study reveal the following: Women with physical disabilities and some other chronic health conditions were significantly more likely to be victims of sexual assault; and women with "neurological disease" were more than twice as likely to report having been sexually assaulted. The increase of "medically explained" symptoms suggests that many symptoms are not psychogenic. The nature of the study did not allow determination of which health conditions existed prior to the sexual assaults and which emerged after the abuse.

498. Golding, J., & Peters, T. J. (1985). What else do SIDS risk prediction scores predict? *Early Human Development, 12,* **247–260.**

This article describes a study that attempted to discover what SIDS prediction scores predict. Using data from the British Births 1970 Survey, which included the medical and social history of 12,743 children born during a 6-day period in the United Kingdom, this study reassessed this data 5 years post in order to obtain a Carpenter score and a New score. These scores were used to determine their diagnostic value in predicting the degree of risk for SIDS. The reassessment found that children at risk for SIDS also had an increased risk for pneumonia, nonaccidental injury, and repeated or prolonged hospitalization. It also found that substandard living conditions and social dis-

ruption were significantly related to an increased risk for SIDS.

499. Goldstein, D. P. (1987). Annotated bibliography of sexuality and communication disorders. *ASHA (American Speech-Language-Hearing Association), 29*(12), **33–34.**

This bibliography provides 28 annotated references on the subject of sexuality and communication disorders. It includes references about people with developmental disabilities and sexuality, sex education, and psychosexual disturbance.

500. Gomez, C. F. (1991). *Regulating death: Euthanasia and the case of the Netherlands.* **New York: Free Press.**

This book describes euthanasia as it is practiced in Holland and discusses implications of the system for potential implementation in other places. The author finds that no clear definitional or operational differences exist between euthanasia, mercy killing, medical killing, and assisted suicide. Although some forms of euthanasia may remain illegal, this remains completely unenforceable under current euthanasia law. Under current laws, which make euthanasia a private event, even the number of cases each year is unknown. Estimates range from a low of less than 200 to a high of 20,000 euthanasia deaths per year. Most estimates are between 3,000 and 10,000 in a country of about 16 million people. The author discusses the involuntary euthanasia of a 2-day-old baby with Down syndrome.

501. Goodill, S. W. (1987). Dance/movement therapy with abused children. *The Arts in Psychotherapy, 14,* **59–68.**

This article describes dance and movement therapy, which is used as a multidisciplinary treatment approach for helping abused and neglected children to communicate and express their experiences. It states that the symbolic, nonverbal expression of dance and movement therapy is used to develop a positive body image, personal strength, trust, and a new awareness of appropriate adult behavior. A case illustration of a 11-year-old girl with a history of sexual abuse demonstrates some of these techniques.

502. Goodwin, J. M., & Fine, C. (1993). Mary Reynolds and Estelle: Somatic symptoms and unacknowledged trauma. In J. M. Goodwin (Ed.), *Rediscovering childhood trauma: Historical casebook and clinical applications* **(pp. 119–131). Washington, DC: American Psychiatric Press.**

This chapter gives an account of two historical cases involving girls who exhibited somatic symptoms in response to severe childhood trauma. Mary Reynolds was 8 years old when she fled with her family to the American frontier. The family left England because of religious persecution and discrimination and the religious riots of 1791 and 1793 in Birmingham. In 1810, Mary was found unconscious in a field. It was discovered that both her visual and auditory senses were inhibited and would remain so for the next 6 weeks. After another unconscious episode, Mary regressed back to infancy. A shifting between these states persisted for the next 13 years. A third state developed that reflected a more adult version of the second state. Here, Mary had no recollection of Birmingham. Mary's more serious somatic symptoms included: pseudoseizures, hysterical blindness and deafness, inability to read or write, and catatonia. The second case involves Estelle, an 11-year-old Swiss girl with numerous physical ailments. She could tolerate only the touch of her mother and aunt, was bedridden, and was very selective about food. Her history consisted of a personal brush with death from measles, the death of her father from cholera, and the near death of her mother and sister from cholera. Daydreaming, hallucinations, amnesia, and preoccupation with thoughts of death were some of Estelle's presenting symptoms. Estelle's somatic symptoms included: hysterical paralysis; chronic pain; head, abdominal, and chest aches; and a nervous cough. Her treatment consisted of hydro therapy, electrical treatment, and hypnosis, which put her in a trance-like state. During this state, several personalities were predominant, including one of four angels that, when dominant, was physically active and emotional. In both cases, reconstruction of the trauma did not occur during psychotherapy, but it was reenacted through transference, which resulted in the alleviation of her somatic symptoms.

503. **Goodwin, O., Zouhar, M. S., & Bergman, R. (1982). Hysterical seizures in adolescent incest victims. In J. Goodwin (Ed.), *Sexual abuse: Incest victims and their families* (pp. 101–108). Littleton, MA: John Wright-PSG.**
This chapter discusses six cases of hysterical or conversion seizures occurring in female adolescents who had been victims of incest. All of these adolescents experienced sexual problems, had histories of running away from home, and had attempted suicide. All of them experienced relief from the hysterical seizures as a result of psychodynamic intervention. The hysterical movements repeated actions related to sexual stimulation and actions related to resisting sexual assault. This chapter discusses the defensive functions of hysterical seizures, and it recommends that physicians take a complete sexual history when pseudoseizures are in the differential diagnosis. In addition, the authors recommend a complete neurologic examination, including electroencephalography.

504. **Gorman-Smith, D., & Matson, J. L. (1992). Sexual abuse and persons with mental retardation. In W. O'Donohue & J. H. Geer (Eds.), *The sexual abuse of children: Theory and research* (Vol. 1, pp. 285–306). Hillsdale, NJ: Lawrence Erlbaum Associates.**
This chapter focuses on sexuality and the sexual abuse of people with mental retardation. It provides definitions for sexual abuse, physical abuse, and mental retardation, and it examines the prevalence of abuse and the vulnerability of people with disabilities to abuse. In addition, the authors look at the effects of sexual abuse on victims and address assessment and treatment issues. This chapter includes suggestions for developing a prevention program for people with developmental disabilities.

505. **Gostin, L. (1987). Ammonia up the nose, compressed air in the face: Abuse or therapy? *Social Work Today, 19*(12), 16–17.**
This article describes aversive treatments used at the Behavior Research Institute. Miraculous claims have been made for the effectiveness of these treatments, but these claims have been poorly substantiated. In fact, the treatments appear to violate basic principles of human rights.

506. **Gostin, L. (1987). Human rights in mental health: A proposal for five international standards based upon the Japanese experience. *International Journal of Law and Psychiatry, 10*, 353–368.**
This article addresses human rights as they apply to people with mental illness. It proposes an international standardization of human rights concerning people with mental illness, adopting five principles from the International Forum on Mental Health Law Reform, which was jointly organized by the Japanese Society for Psychiatry and Neurology and the International Academy of Psychiatry and Law in Kyoto, Japan: 1) the right to humane, dignified, and professional treatment; 2) voluntary admission being encouraged whenever treatment is necessary; 3) the right to a full and impartial judicial hearing before involuntary loss of liberty; 4) the right to a free and open environment and free communication; and 5) the right not to be discriminated against on grounds of mental illness. This article provides a detailed examination of each principle.

507. **Gould, A. M. (1985, August/September). Physician heal thyself: How a Kingston court upheld the rights of the patients. *The Canadian Forum, 12*, 14–18.**
This article deals with a 1984 court case that involved patients' rights. The case was brought against a doctor at the Ongwanada Hospital in Kingston, Ontario, who felt it unnecessary to obtain consent for medical treatment from patients with mental and physical disabilities. The issue of consent was raised by the doctor's medical students who were at the institution for clinical work with the residents.

508. **Gowdey, C. W., Coleman, L. M., & Crawford, E. M. (1985). Ocular changes and phenothiazine derivatives in long term residents of a mental retardation center. *Psychiatric Journal of the University of Ottawa, 10*(4), 248–253.**

This article examines the corneal and lens opacities associated with the long-term use of chlorpromazine. In a study of 55 long-term residents of an institution who were on long-term phenothiazine derivative medication, 14 of them were found to have lesions of cornea and lens. The lens changes included the following: pigment dust, stippling, hazy or starshaped opacities, and scattered anterior brownish granular opacities. The total intake of phenothiazine derivatives by the residents varied from 104 gm to 2,180 gm. The mean intake of chlorpromazine by 12 of 14 residents in the lesion group was significantly higher than those without lesions. The residents in the group without lesions were predominantly treated with methotrimeprazine, with amounts ranging from 59 gm to 1,836 gm. Piperidinyl phenothiazines were taken by a majority of residents in both groups, and the mean intake by the lesion group was significantly greater. A significantly greater proportion of residents in the lesion group had taken more chlorpromazine than those without the lesions, and the mean intake per month was significantly higher in the lesion group. The results suggest that apart from chlorpromazine other phenothiazines may also be associated with lens changes. This article points out that a concomitant use of hepatic enzyme-inducing drugs may afford some protection.

509. Graber, B., Hartmann, K., Coffman, J. A., Huey, C. J., & Golden, C. J. (1982). **Brain damage among mentally disordered sex offenders.** *Journal of Forensic Sciences, 27*(1), 125–134.

This article describes a pilot study on structural brain dysfunction that was conducted with a group of sex offenders with mental disorders. This study used computerized tomography (CT scans), regional cerebral blood flow (rCBF), and neuropsychological tests to determine whether there was a significantly higher incidence of dysfunction. The results of this study indicate that 50% of the sexual offenders tested in the project showed brain dysfunction.

510. Grant, L. J. (1983). **Assessment of child sexual abuse: Eighteen months' experience at the child protection center.** *American Journal of Obstetrics and Gynecology, 148*(2), 617–620.

In this article, the author assesses 150 cases of sexual abuse allegations in the province of Manitoba. The results are analyzed in terms of age, sex, type of assault, relationship to assailant, and incidence of gonorrhea and pregnancy. The statistical findings in this report corroborate those of other investigators in terms of age, sex distribution of the victims, and relationship to offender. Also, this article discusses assessment problems in cases with sexually abused children and the complexity of the investigative process.

511. Gray, J. A. (1987). **The neuropsychology of emotion and personality.** In S.

M. Stahl, S. D. Iversen, & E. C. Goodman (Eds.), *Cognitive neurochemistry* (pp. 171–190). Oxford, England: Oxford University Press.

This chapter suggests that there are three important and separate neuropsychological systems that control emotional behavior: the approach system, the fight/flight system, and the behavioral inhibition system. Mainly, this chapter uses data from animal experiments to support this theory. It provides an explanation of these three systems and the interactions between them, and it provides a model illustrating these interactions. This chapter concludes that personality dimensions that focus on behavior reflect the interactions of the three neurologic systems, and it provides a model illustrating this idea.

512. Grayson, J. (1992, Fall). **Child abuse and developmental disabilities.** *VCPN, Virginia Child Protection Newsletter, 37,* 1, 3–7, 10, 12–13, 16.

This article discusses several topics dealing with the abuse of children with disabilities. It provides statistics that show the prevalence of abuse of children with disabilities and the incidence of developmental disabilities in abused children. Using the results of various studies, it discusses five broad categories of factors that relate to the increased risk for abuse or neglect of children with disabilities. It suggests a victim profile based on data collected from a sample of 500 children who have moderate to profound mental retardation. It discusses the problem of whether abuse preceded or succeeded the disability, detection and reporting of abuse, and assessment and investigation of abuse. This article also discusses treatment considerations, prevention ideas, and problems that might arise when identifying and investigating abuse.

513. Graziano, A. M., & Mills, J. R. (1992). **Treatment for abused children: When is a partial solution acceptable?** *Child Abuse & Neglect, 16,* 217–228.

This article stresses the need to focus more attention on the direct psychological treatment needs of physically abused children. A review of the literature notes that success has been achieved with treating similar psychological problems of nonabused children. This article examines the psychological characteristics of abused children, and it defines treatment goals, such as anger management, social skills training, and increased self-esteem. While the direct psychological treatment of abused children is only a partial solution to the problem of child abuse, which encompasses a multitude of contributing variables, the authors note that the significance of this treatment is measured in its contribution to overall personal functioning of the abused child.

514. Green, A. H., Voeller, K., Gaines, R., & Kubie, J. (1981). **Neurological impairment in maltreated children.** *Child Abuse & Neglect, 5,* 129–134.

This article examines neurologic impairment in maltreated children. It compares 60 physically abused children without head injuries, 30 neglected children, and 30 nonmaltreated children in order to study the effects of abuse on neurologic impairment. The results of the physical and neurologic examinations show that 115 children in the abused and neglected group had significantly more impairment than the nonmaltreated group. In fact, over half of the abused children were moderately or severely impaired.

515. Green, F. C. (1977). What will it cost the child if I don't report? In M. A. Thomas (Ed.), *Children alone: What can be done about abuse and neglect* (pp. 61–67). Reston, VA: Council for Exceptional Children.

This chapter discusses the physical, developmental, and socioemotional consequences of failing to report child abuse. Physical injuries that are not treated may result in scarring due to burns, misshapen or shortened limbs from unattended fractures, or neurologic deficits that accrue from repeated head injuries. Children who remain in maltreatment situations may suffer from developmental delays or damage (e.g., failures in social, language, and motor development), which in turn may require long-term intervention and, at worst, long-term institutionalization. This chapter views child abuse and neglect as a cyclical syndrome, which means that children who are abused will grow to become abusing parents. In the interim, such children may be hostile, isolated, and have difficulty establishing relationships with others. As they act out and their behavior becomes socially unacceptable, society may label them as delinquent and criminal. This leads to segregating them in institutions with other sociopaths, which reinforces antisocial behavior. The author concludes that the costs of failing to report child abuse are so great that failure to report is intolerable.

516. Green, L. (1989, May 19). Grand jury rejects murder count: Teary father not charged in death of comatose boy. *Los Angeles Times*, Part I, pp. 1, 21.

This newspaper article describes the case of Rudolfo Linares, a man who took his infant son off life support while keeping hospital staff at bay with a gun. Linares was not charged in his son's death. This ruling was brought down by a Cook County grand jury in Chicago. Their decision was largely shaped by the medical examiner's decision to classify the infant's death as undetermined. The infant suffered brain damage after a balloon became lodged in his throat.

517. Greenland, C. (1980). Mentally retarded sex offenders. In D. E. Zarfas & B. Goldberg (Eds.), *Aggression, mental illness, mental retardation: Psychobiological approaches* (pp. 206–213). London, ON: University of Western Ontario.

This chapter, presented at the Clarence M. Hinks Memorial Lectures at the University of Western Ontario in 1978, examines the relationship between mental disability and sexual aggression. It presents unpublished findings from a 1973 study that examined data collected from 28 dangerous sex offenders, 9 of whom were mentally disabled. Of these sex offenders with mental disabilities, three of them were within the mild range of intellectual disabilities, and six of them were classified as having borderline intellectual disabilities.

518. Greenland, C. (1987). CAN deaths in Ontario—A cohort study. In C. Greenland (Ed.), *Preventing CAN deaths: An international study of deaths due to child abuse and neglect* (pp. 38–72). London: Tavistock Publications.

This chapter discusses the analysis of child abuse and neglect deaths during a 10-year period in Ontario. The epidemiological study uses the records of 100 children, 95 of whom were under the age of 6. This study found the following: head and brain injuries were the causes of death in 57 cases, previous injuries were found in 63 of the children, the natural parents murdered their children in 63% of the cases, battered child syndrome was determined for 60 children, neglect was found in 20 cases, and homicide was the cause of death for 12 children.

519. Greenland, C. (1987). CAN deaths in the USA—Epidemiological studies. In C. Greenland (Ed.), *Preventing CAN deaths: An international study of deaths due to child abuse and neglect* (pp. 38–72). London: Tavistock Publications.

This chapter reviews the literature dealing with child abuse and neglect deaths in the United States. It cites hospital, community, and national studies from such locations as Texas, New York, and Los Angeles. This chapter examines such variables as socioeconomic status, family stress, and ethnicity. The author suggests that the incidence of child abuse and neglect deaths in the United States depends on the population sampled.

520. Greenley, D., & Zander, T. K. (1986). New legal protection for persons with mental handicaps. *Wisconsin Bar Bulletin, 59*(4), 9–11, 60.

This article examines the specifics of the Watt case, a precedent-setting case in the Wisconsin Supreme Court that greatly increased the rights of people who are disabled and elderly and who are protected under Chapter 55 of the Wisconsin Statutes. It discusses the Protective Services Law, which attempts to protect people with mental disabilities from abuse, neglect, and exploitation and to ensure their constitutional rights.

521. Griffith, J. L. (1988, December). The family systems of Munchausen syndrome by proxy. *Family Process, 27*, 423–437.

This article discusses two case studies of Munchausen syndrome by proxy (MSBP) in terms of family systems. The perpetrators in both cases were women in their mid-20s, and the victims were a 2-week-old girl and a 3-year-old boy. The family history, psychiatric evaluation of the parents, and the systemic evaluation of the family are discussed for both cases. This article examines the perpetrators, their family background, and possible treatment strategies. Somatoform disorder was noted in both mothers since childhood. The author discusses some of the shortcomings of the data-gathering process and suggests some management guidelines for MSBP.

522. Griffiths, D. (1992). Vulnerability: What makes people with developmental disabilities more vulnerable to abuse. In *Crossing new borders* (pp. 1–2). Kingston, NY: National Association for the Dually Diagnosed.

This chapter discusses some major factors in the vulnerability of people with developmental disabilities. It examines the following: the role of offenders' perceptions of people with disabilities, depersonalization, clustering of potential offenders with vulnerable individuals, and failure to screen or otherwise control potentially abusive caregivers.

523. Griffiths, D., & Hingsburger, D. (1985). Appropriately inappropriate. *Journal of Practical Approaches to Developmental Handicap, 9*(2), 5–7.

This article examines the rights of people with disabilities after the enactment of the 1985 Canadian Charter of Rights. In particular, the article focuses on the concept of normalization with regard to age appropriateness and people with disabilities. The concept of age appropriateness has changed our perspective of people with developmental disabilities. It has provided services to people with disabilities that are adult appropriate in terms of goals and programs; but outside the context of normalization, the concept has been used to deny people with disabilities the right to choose to act age inappropriately. This article examines the implications of the concept of age appropriateness for service providers working with people with developmental disabilities regarding intervention with age-inappropriate activity.

524. Groothuis, J. R., Altemeier, W. A., Robarge, J. P., O'Connor, S., Sandler, H., Vietze, P., & Lustig, J. V. (1982). Increased child abuse in families with twins. *Pediatrics, 70*(5), 769–773.

This article discusses a retrospective study that compared the prevalence of child abuse in 48 families of twins with the prevalence of child abuse in 124 single-birth families. All of the subjects in this study were matched on such variables as hospital of delivery, birth date, maternal age, race, and socioeconomic status. The two hospitals involved in the study were the St. Vincent Hospital and Medical Center in Toledo, Ohio, and the Nashville General Hospital in Nashville, Tennessee. The results of

this study indicate that twin status is more predictive of abuse than any other variable: For example, there were reports of abuse and severe neglect for three singleton families (2.4%) and nine twin families (18.7%). This study also found that twins had significantly longer nursery stays, lower birth weight, and lower Apgar scores and that greater feelings of parity among mothers of twins were significant when compared with singleton mothers.

525. Grossman, L. S., & Cavanaugh, J. L. (1989). Do sex offenders minimize psychiatric symptoms? *Journal of Forensic Science, 34*(4), 881–886.

This article states that denial of paraphilia is common among sex offenders. This article examines whether sex offenders have severe psychopathology as well as paraphilia and if they minimize these symptoms when undergoing forensic examination. After administering the MMPI to 36 sex offenders, the authors note that subjects who denied paraphilia were more likely to minimize psychopathology than those who admitted paraphilia, and subjects who faced no legal charges showed more psychopathology than those who faced charges. The most frequent forms of psychopathology found outside of paraphilia include the following: antisocial attitudes, somatization, thought disorder, and depressive features.

526. Grothaus, R. S. (1985). Abuse of women with disabilities. In S. Browne, D. Connors, & N. Stern (Eds.), *With the power of each breath* (pp. 124–128). Pittsburgh, PA: Cleis Press.

This chapter discusses the problem of abuse of women with disabilities. It points out that abuse is a personal problem as well as a political problem because women with disabilities are discriminated against not only based on their disability but also on their gender. This chapter makes 10 recommendations as a starting point for discussion and potential corrective action: 1) increased attention by policy makers, 2) increased enforcement of disability nondiscrimination laws, 3) increased funding for programs, 4) education by people with disabilities of workers in all violence-oriented programs, 5) development of resource lists in programs that provide specialized assistance, 6) better education of staff in medical facilities, 7) provision of adequate equipment in medical facilities, 8) recognition by the disability civil rights movement that women with disabilities face double discrimination, 9) recognition by the feminist movement that women with disabilities are being excluded by inaccessible meeting places and by ignorance, and 10) agitation by women with disabilities to demand that their concerns be considered and that their needs be met.

527. Guberman, C. (1989). *Sexual abuse prevention programs and mental handicap.* Toronto: The G. Allan Roeher Institute.

This report discusses an evaluation by an Advisory Committee coordinated by The G. Allan Roeher Institute, Toronto, of nine North American sexual abuse prevention programs to determine their usefulness with people with developmental disabilities. This evaluation was intended to be an initial step toward the development of criteria for a comprehensive and appropriate prevention program suitable for use by a range of individuals, families, and professionals throughout Canada. The report outlines the six criteria believed by the evaluation team to reflect the critical elements of any effective sexual abuse prevention program for people with disabilities: values, accuracy in representing the reality of sexual abuse, appropriate language and concepts for a range of individual abilities, a balance of positive and negative messages, empowerment, and reduction of individual isolation and corresponding increase in community awareness and participation. It provides the profiles of the nine programs and includes individual program descriptions and composite evaluations derived from the evaluation team's review. The findings are summarized in terms of general trends noted across the program evaluations, and these are discussed in relation to the criteria considered necessary for an effective sexual abuse prevention program. Comprehensive and thoughtful recommendations regarding the development of future sexual abuse prevention programs are provided in light of the evaluation team's conclusion that none of the nine programs adequately met all the stated criteria. A copy of the evaluation form used to complete this study is included in an appendix to this report.

528. Guess, D., Helmstetter, E., & Turnbull, H. R., III (1987). *Use of aversive procedures with persons who are disabled: An historical review and critical analysis.* **Seattle, WA: The Association for Persons with Severe Handicaps.**

This monograph provides a discussion of the use of punishment and negative reinforcement procedures, particularly as applied to people with severe intellectual impairment. It suggests that these procedures have been frequently used to increase compliance and that the procedures have been used more frequently with individuals with mental disabilities than with prisoners or individuals with psychiatric impairments because people with severe intellectual disabilities have been less able or less effective in protesting against their use. It reports a number of studies in which electric shock, slaps, or other aversive stimuli are used as "treatment" to gain more compliant behavior.

529. Guntheroth, W. G., Lohmann, R., & Spiers, P. S. (1990). **Risk of sudden infant death syndrome in subsequent siblings.** *Journal of Pediatrics, 116,* 520–524.

This article describes a study that attempted to determine the recurrence rate of sudden infant death syndrome (SIDS) by examining the siblings of SIDS infants. This study linked birth and death certificates for 251,124 live births from 1975 to 1984 in the state of Oregon. It found a recurrence rate of 11.9 per 1,000 live births in the next subsequent siblings ($n=3/253$) and a rate of 13 per 1,000

in all subsequent siblings ($n=5/385$) born following a SIDS infant. The study also found that the risk of death by causes other than SIDS for siblings of SIDS infants was calculated to be 20.8 per 1,000.

530. Gutis, P. S. (1988, January 5). Traces of muscle drug are found in body in nurse inquiry on L. I. *The New York Times,* **p. B4.**

This newspaper article describes the case of Richard J. Angelo, a former nurse at the Good Samaritan Hospital in West Islip who was held on charges of assault following the suspicious deaths of approximately 10 patients at the hospital. Angelo's unauthorized injections of drugs that bring about muscle paralysis were found in some of the exhumed bodies.

531. Gutis, P. S. (1989, October 20). Former patient points to nurse in murder trial: Man accused of killing 4 by fatal injections. *The New York Times,* **p. B3.**

This newspaper article is a follow-up of the case of nurse Richard Angelo of the Good Samaritan Hospital in West Islip, Long Island. Richard Angelo has been identified by an eyewitness, former patient Gerolam Kucich, 77, of Yugoslavia. Mr. Kucich identified Mr. Angelo as being responsible for injecting something into his intravenous tubing that causes paralysis. Before paralysis set in, Mr. Kucich was able to summon another nurse for help. Nurse Lauren Ball is still waiting to testify. The muscle relaxant drug Pavulon was later identified as having caused the paralysis. Richard Angelo is indicted on four counts of murder and three counts of assault. One count of assault involves Mr. Kucich, and the others involve former patients whose deaths could not be directly attributed to the the drug Pavulon. In total, 33 bodies of former patients have been exhumed.

•H•

532. Haaven, J., Little, R., & Petre Miller, D. (1990). *Treating intellectually disabled sex offenders: A model program.* **Orwell, VT: Safer Society Press.**

This book attempts to identify the most effective treatment components and teaching modalities for sex offenders with intellectual disabilities, and it describes the Social Skills Program at the Oregon State Hospital. Part I provides the framework for an indepth understanding of the various treatment components in the program. This section provides a history of the program, and it discusses the treatment milieu and the differences between treating sex offenders with and without disabilities. Part II presents the details of the program components and a case study of one subject's background and orientation. It discusses orientation techniques and a review of this subject's inhouse treatment and transition treatment and general transition practices. Also, it provides a chapter on general inhouse practices. A second case study is used to discuss treatment outcomes. Worksheets, schedules, activities, and other sample materials from the project are provided in the appendices.

533. Haddock, M. D., & McQueen, W. M. (1983). Assessing employee potentials for abuse. *Journal of Clinical Psychology*, *39*(6), 1021–1029.

This article discusses a study that assessed an employee's potential for abuse using the Child Abuse Potential Inventory (CAP-I), Minnesota Satisfaction Questionnaire (MSQ), and a general information form: The CAP-I assesses adults for their potential for child abuse, and the MSQ screens employees for job satisfaction. This study assessed 21 abusive and 21 nonabusive employees (controls) who had experience working in out-of-home care institutions. This assessment correctly identified 86% of the abusers and 100% of the nonabusers; in total, 93% of the abuser and nonabuser employees were correctly identified.

534. Hagberg, B., Hagberg, G., Lewerth, A., & Lindberg, U. (1981). Mild mental retardation in Swedish school children. II. Etiologic and pathogenetic aspects. *Acta Paediatrica Scandinavica*, *70*, 445–452.

This article describes a Swedish study (Gothenburg, Sweden) that examined 91 school-age children with mild mental retardation (MMR) in order to determine the etiology and pathogenetic aspects of MMR. In this study, 9% of the children had cerebral palsy, 12% had epilepsy, and 31% had psychiatric disorders. The results of this study suggest the following causes of MMR: 23% prenatal, 18% perinatal, 2% postnatal, and 55% unknown. This study found that 8% of the prenatal cases were the result of alcohol fetopathy.

535. Hagberg, B., & Kyllerman, M. (1983). Epidemiology of mental retardation: A Swedish survey. *Brain Development*, *5*, 441–449.

This article discusses an examination of the epidemiology of mental retardation in Swedish school-age children using data obtained from five epidemiological studies on populations from five Swedish counties. This examination found the following: the incidence of severe (SMR) and mild (MMR) mental retardation was 0.3% and 0.4%, respectively; the causes of MMR were determined to be 55% prenatal, 15%–20% perinatal, and 18% untraceable brain pathology; the causes of SMR were found to be 23% prenatal, 18% perinatal, and 55% untraceable determinants; Down syndrome was the most common factor in SMR; and fetal alcohol syndrome was detected in 8% of urban MMR cases. This article also includes information on chromosomal errors and fragile X.

536. Hahn, H. (1981). The social component of sexuality and disability: Some problems and proposals. *Sexuality and Disability*, *4*(4), 220–233.

This article discusses social problems experienced by people with disabilities in their sexual relationships. These problems include the following: a pervasive social taboo against sexual contact with people with disabilities, vulnerability, and depersonalization. The author suggests that little systematic research has been done to explore these problems, and more research is needed in this area.

537. Hahn, H. (1993). Can disability be beautiful? In M. Nagler (Ed.), *Perspectives on disability* (pp. 217–226). Palo Alto, CA: Health Markets Research.

This chapter describes the social history of disability and compares it with the social history of other minorities. The author suggests that stigma and rejection associated with disability will be improved only when positive attributes of disability are recognized and emphasized, "equivalent to the 'Black is beautiful' phenomenon" (p. 311). The chapter includes an interesting section on "the history of subversive sensualism" (p. 312) that discusses how disability has been valued or eroticized by various cultures. The author challenges us to question whether the contemporary sexual objectification described in feminist literature may be better than the asexual objectification experienced by people with disabilities, suggesting that erotic objects are valued even if they are depersonalized (Editors' note: Eroticized images of disability remain as a common undercurrent in contemporary society: For example, many men are sexually interested in women with amputated limbs. Erotic or pornographic materials featuring amputees are regularly published. Such interests are generally disparaged as deviant fetishes, but some women with disabilities have spoken out against such disparagement. They argue that their physical differences are apparent and pretending they do not exist is dishonest. They argue that it is better to be valued than devalued for their differences.)

538. Haldopoulos, M. A., & Copeland, M. L. (1991). Case studies of child care training volunteers found to be at risk for abuse. *Early Child Development and Care*, *68*, 149–158.

This article describes a 100-hour screening and training program that was offered to women in a small post-industrial city who were interested in child care. The program includes an interview by a clinical psychologist working in the area of child abuse and early childhood who uses open-ended questions to examine prior experience with physical or sexual abuse and/or mental illness. This program screens trainees for their potential to commit emotional abuse and neglect and examines them about their expectations of children. Also, the program asks trainees about anger, employment failures, and reasons for choosing child care and compares this information with training observations. The screening found that 10% of applicants (over 100 African-American, Latino, and White women in 3 years) were considered inappropriate for the training program. This article includes six case examples to illustrate some of the characteristics of those women who did not gain entry into the program.

539. Hall, J., Payne, T., & Simpson, J. (1986). *Legal rights & intellectual disability: A short guide.* **Redfern, Australia: Redfern Legal Centre.**
This book discusses protecting the civil rights of people with disabilities and taking action against any wrongs perpetrated against people with developmental disabilities in New South Wales, Australia. This book examines the following: protecting rights, discrimination, personal relationships, sheltered workshops, housing, guardianship and money management, crime and people with intellectual disabilities, consumer protection, and caregivers.

540. Haller, J. S. J. (1989, March). The role of physicians in America's sterilization movement, 1894–1925. *New York State Journal of Medicine, 89,* **169–179.**
This article presents a historical account of the American sterilization movement from 1894 to 1925. It examines the sterilization of people with developmental disabilities and criminals. The author states that this movement was initiated by the concern that "defective classes" were multiplying at a greater rate than the rest of the population. The author points out that it was believed that heredity instead of environment was the primary cause of disabilities and criminal behavior; consequently, preventing those classified as defective from reproducing was thought integral to the preservation of the society as a whole.

541. Hampson, R. B. (1988). Special foster care for exceptional children: A review of programs and policies. *Children and Youth Services Review, 10,* **19–41.**
This article reviews programs and policies concerning foster care of children with special needs. It examines program components: for example, screening and selection of special foster parents, training for foster parents, matching foster child to foster home, continuing education and professional follow-up, and professional status for foster parents. This article includes an evaluation of special foster care programs, and the results of this evaluation reveal the following: lower treatment costs for parent-therapist homes versus institutions, greater developmental improvements for the children, and greater frequency of long-term placement.

542. Hanley, R. (1989, August 19). 2 more charged in Glen Ridge attack. *The New York Times,* **p. A26.**
This newspaper article reports that two additional students from Glen Ridge High School have been charged in connection with the sexual assault of a 17-year-old girl with a mental disability. One of the teenagers is the son of the the town's police detective. In total, seven teenagers have been charged with conspiracy to commit sexual assault, aggravated sexual assault, and aggravated criminal sexual contact. The charges stem from an incident involving the accused, five other teenagers, and the victim. The victim was reportedly forced to perform several sexual acts and was penetrated by a broomhandle and a miniature baseball bat. All of those involved were acquainted with each other since elementary school. The author notes that the victim lacked the mental capacity to consent.

543. Hannaford, S. (1985). *Living outside inside: A disabled woman's experience: Towards a social and political perspective.* **Berkeley, CA: Canterbury Press.**
This collection of articles, essays, letters, and notes focuses on disability and the adversity faced by people with disabilities as a result of "societal reaction and nonaction." Susan Hannaford, who contracted multiple sclerosis in 1976, presents a series of personal accounts and theoretical/academic perspectives, written over a 2-year period. She insightfully portrays life experienced by those on the "abnormal divide of society" and challenges blatant inequities. She notes parallels in the treatment of women and people with disabilities and addresses specific issues faced by women with disabilities. Hannaford challenges entrenched attitudes regarding the value and humanity of all people (or the perceived lack of humanity). Hannaford's belief in the importance of self-advocacy is demonstrated by her political activism and role as a founder of Sisters Against Disablement (S.A.D.). Hannaford concludes that all people have the fundamental right to belong to their society.

544. Hannah, J. (1993, June 29). String of childrens' deaths sparks questions about adoptive couple. *The Edmonton Journal,* **p. A4.**
This newspaper article reports a story out of Cedarville, Ohio, that describes the deaths of five adopted children with disabilities at one home. Although 5 of the 10 children in care died within 9 months, it was acknowledged that most of the children were at risk for a short life span due to the severity of their disabilities. In one of the deaths, the adoptive parents pleaded guilty to the charge of neglect of a minor. The child had gotten into some household bleach and burned her lungs as a result of inhaling the fumes. An inquest is being conducted for three of the five deaths.

545. Hannah, M. E., & Midlarsky, E. (1987). Differential impact of labels and behavioral descriptions on attitudes toward people with disabilities. *Rehabilitation Psychology, 32*(4), **227–238.**
This article discusses two studies that were conducted to determine if preferred social distance was affected by the characterization of different disabilities such as visual impairment, severe mental retardation, and psychosis.

Both of these studies referred to the social, mental, or physical disabilities using labels (e.g., alcoholic, amputee, blind person, deaf person, diabetic, epileptic, ex-convict, mildly mentally retarded person, neurotic, psychotic, severely mentally retarded person, and person with an ulcer), descriptions, or labeled descriptions. The first study examined attitudes toward people with disabilities using preferred social distance and administered a questionnaire to 140 undergraduate university students. These students were given nine choice responses of social distance to a variety of people with social, mental, and physical disabilities: for example, marriage partner, close kin by marriage, neighbor, casual friend, fellow employee, would keep away from, would keep institutionalized, would send out of the country, and would sentence the person to death. This study also used the Attitudes Toward Disabled Persons Scale (ATPD) to assess the students' predisposition to people with disabilities. The second study administered a labeled description questionnaire to 209 undergraduate students. All other aspects of this study were similar to the first study. The results from both studies indicate that individuals respond differently to labels versus descriptors versus labeled descriptors of people with disabilities. These studies provide powerful evidence of how disability labels can increase social distance, but they also cast doubt on the idea that replacing labels with more descriptive information substantially improves attitudes.

546. Hansen, C. (1980). Child abuse: A cause and effect of mental retardation. In M.K. McCormack (Ed.), *Prevention of mental retardation and other developmental disabilities* (pp. 549–568). New York: Dekker.
This article reviews the literature linking cerebral palsy to abuse. It also discusses the long-term effects of abuse and neglect on children.

547. Hansen, D. J., & Warner, J. E. (1992). Child physical abuse and neglect. In R. T. Ammerman & M. Hersen (Eds.), *Assessment of family violence: A clinical and legal sourcebook* (pp. 123–147). New York: John Wiley & Sons.
This chapter discusses assessment procedures using a multimodal approach to assess a variety of dysfunctions in physical child abuse and neglect cases. It describes the use of psychometric tests and provides a case example.

548. Hanson, R. (Ed.). (1982). *Institutional abuse of children and youth.* New York: Haworth Press.
This book contains 14 articles written by various authors on topics related to the abuse and neglect of children in out-of-home care situations. The first section deals with defining institutional abuse and includes articles that address out-of-home care using a family systems perspective and the role of defining children's rights in the prevention of abuse. The second section discusses the relationship between religious values and child abuse. It also addresses the newspaper coverage of corporal punishment in schools. The third section deals with in-patient treatment and includes articles addressing the neglect of the health needs of juveniles, children's rights when entering therapeutic institutions, and abuse resulting from attempting to treat the untreatable. The fourth section discusses responses to the problem of abuse in institutional settings. The topics discussed in these articles include the following: advice to would-be reporters of institutional abuse, the attitudes of direct-care workers toward the use of physical force on children, and the use of standards in prevention. The last section of this book deals with meta-abuse, that is, the inadvertent reabuse of children by professional helping agencies.

549. Hard, S. (1986, October 22). *Sexual abuse of the developmentally disabled: A case study.* Paper presented at National Conference of Executives of Associations for Retarded Citizens, Omaha, NE.
This case study discusses a study that was conducted with 65 adults with developmental disabilities who were registered with the Indian Wells Valley Association for Retarded Citizens (ARC) work activity center. This study used an assessment questionnaire, and case records were also used in the analysis of data. Thirty-four female and 31 male subjects between the ages of 17 and 48 years participated in the study. Of the total number of women who participated in the study, 18 functioned at a mild level, 12 had moderate impairments, and 4 had severe impairments. For men, 24 had mild impairments, 5 had moderate impairments, and 2 had severe impairments. The results of this study reveal the following: sexual abuse was reported by 83% of women and 32% of men; the perpetrator was most often male (97%), and the abuse was most often perpetrated by an individual known to the victim; 55% of the sexual abuse involved incest; 50% of victims were abused on more than one occasion; women disclosed their abuse to others more often than men, but they were believed less than half the time; and the male victims were all believed upon disclosure. This case study discusses additional findings, sex education, and recommendation concerning the findings of this study.

550. Hargrave, M. C. (1991). Sexual incidents in residential treatment. *Child and Youth Care Forum, 20*(6), 413–419.
This article describes the nature and frequency of sexual incidents as reported by staff in three residential treatment centers for children and youths. It categorizes incidents as heterosexual, homosexual, child-to-staff initiated, singular, deviant, and miscellaneous. The results of this investigation indicate a developmental pattern of sexual activity, with homosexual experiences predominating among younger children and heterosexual experiences predominating in youth activity. The author provides a foundation for analysis of sexual activity among children and youths that includes: characteristics of children (cognitive, social, developmental), history of past abuse, staff behavior, and agency policy.

551. Harris Cohn, A., & Daro, D. (1987). Is treatment too late: What ten years of evaluative research tell us. *Child Abuse & Neglect, 11,* 433–442.

This article examines research on child abuse and neglect treatment programs. It reviews four government-funded multiyear studies that evaluated 89 different treatment programs and collected data on 3,253 families served by these programs. The first study was initiated in 1974, with consecutive studies running until 1982. The treatment programs incorporated the following: counseling, family therapy, self-help groups, educational and developmental courses, and other supportive services. The review concludes that treatment programs were generally unsuccessful, with at least one third of parents maltreating their charges while receiving treatment and more than 50% of families deemed to be at high risk for continuous abuse following treatment. Greater success was noted in cases of sexual abuse and the treatment programs dealing with sexual abuse.

552. Harrison, E., & Shryer, T. (1989, April 27). Weeping father pulls gun, stops infant's life support. *The Los Angeles Times,* Part I, pp. 1, 44.

This newspaper article describes the case of Rudolfo Linares, a man who, on Wednesday, April 27, 1989, walked into the Rush Presbyterian-St. Luke's Medical Center in Chicago and unplugged his infant son's life support, keeping nursing staff at bay with a gun. The father surrendered after his son died. The infant was on life support after having suffered irreversible brain damage as a result of having a balloon lodged in his trachea blocking oxygen to his brain. The father had attempted to disconnect his son's life support on one other occasion but was subdued by hospital staff. Linares was charged with murder.

553. Harvey, D. C., & Trivelli, L. U. (1990). *HIV education for persons with mental disabilities: AIDS Technical Report, No. 1.* **Washington, DC: National Association of Protection and Advocacy Systems.**

This technical report is part of a series on AIDS/HIV. This report is intended to help link together various legal advocacy organizations that provide services to people with mental illness or developmental disabilities. It claims that adolescents are at risk for exposure to HIV as they may unknowingly engage in high-risk sexual behavior. In addition, adolescents suffer high rates of sexual abuse and may self-medicate. This report encourages advocates to: consult with AIDS service organizations in order to develop HIV education programs; conduct a needs assessment for these services in the disability community; design the program by considering staff and agency needs; and use creative strategies that employ service providers, the press, and politicians. This report describes the Michigan Protection Advocacy Service program and discusses goals, objectives, issues surrounding AIDS/HIV presentations, training programs, the budget, recruitment of trainers and staff, scheduling, evaluation, and education of primary consumers. This report includes the following: a list of 27 references; 22 additional resources; and 12 associations, videos, and manuals.

554. Haseltine, B., & Miltenberger, R. G. (1990). Teaching self-protection skills to persons with mental retardation. *American Journal on Mental Retardation, 95*(2), 188–197.

This article describes a study that examined the effectiveness of a curriculum (presented in nine half-hour sessions) for teaching self-protection skills to eight adults with mild mental retardation in a small group format. In situ assessments were conducted to determine successful acquisition of appropriate skills, which were demonstrated by seven of the eight participants. A discussion of the findings highlights the importance of actual skill acquisition in simulated real-life situations as distinct from knowledge acquisition only. This article acknowledges the difficulties in generalizing these findings to situations of sexual abuse involving perpetrators known to the individual, and it emphasizes the need for further research in this particular area.

555. Haslam, R. H. A. (1980). Should the handicapped child be allowed to survive? *Mental Retardation, 30*(3), 38–41.

This article presents excerpts from the Child and Society Conference held in 1979 concerning issues of restricted medical treatment and children with disabilities. It focuses on arguments against restrictive or passive medical treatment and offers suggestions to parents that might help them cope with a child with disabilities.

556. Hass, C. A., & Brown, L. (1989). *Silent victims: Canada's criminal justice system and sexual abuse of persons with a mental handicap.* **Calgary, AB: Sexual Assault Committee.**

This report examines the Canadian criminal justice system and its handling of sexual assault cases involving victims with developmental disabilities. This report provides a literature review and statistical data concerning the prevalence and incidence rates of sexual assault and how it applies to people with disabilities. It addresses society's attitudes toward people with disabilities and the reflection of these attitudes in laws concerning sexual abuse. It discusses the following areas: caregivers and potential abuse by caregivers, alternative means of communication, legal status involving issues of consent, and criminal case examples involving the victimization of people with developmental disabilities. This report also examines the roles of police and prosecutors during an investigation of abuse, and it provides recommendations for future research.

557. Hatch, F. W., & Maietta, L. (1991). The role of kinesthesia in pre- and perinatal

bonding. *Pre and Peri Natal Psychology Journal, 5*(3), 253–270.

The authors of this article claim that movement made and felt throughout pregnancy by mother and infant is a fundamental component of parent-infant bonding. If this touch-guided motion is disrupted after birth by separation for a prolonged period of time, the authors feel that parent-infant bonding may be affected, but they also believe that parent-infant bonding may be enhanced by teaching parents and infants once again how to respond to each other's movement. They state that kinesthetic bonding is enhanced when parents become skilled at adjusting the time, space, or effort element of motion to match the movements of the infant. The authors suggest several ways of enhancing parent-infant relationships: knowledge of the relationship between human function and motion, the use of handling and positioning to optimize the infant's functional development, and organizing the physical environment to compensate for body size differences.

558. Haugaard, J. J. (1992). Epidemiology and family violence involving children. In R. T. Ammerman & M. Hersen (Eds.), *Assessment of family violence: A clinical and legal sourcebook* (pp. 89–107). New York: John Wiley & Sons.

The epidemiology of family violence involving children is discussed in this chapter. It examines methodological issues and study findings from community- and national-based studies, case studies from social agencies, and studies involving college students. It also includes studies that profile children as aggressors, and it concludes that there is a high incidence of family violence in society.

559. Havranek, J. E. (1991). The social and individual costs of negative attitudes toward persons with physical disabilities. *Journal of Applied Rehabilitation Counseling, 22*(1), 15–21.

This article discusses the social and individual cost of negative attitudes toward people with physical disabilities. It contains a literature review that examines cultural differences associated with accepting people with disabilities: for example, the role of stigma and other variables associated with attitudes toward people with physical disabilities; demographic data, obtained from general governmental statistics, government-funded rehabilitation agencies, and worker injury statistics concerning people with physical disabilities; coping responses to disability; and the economical aspects of physical disability and its impact on both the labor market and the individual. The author suggests that people with physical disabilities are just as able to adapt to their environment and overcome obstacles as people without disabilities, and that negative attitudes affect not only people with disabilities, but all of society.

560. Hayes, S. (1993). *People with an intellectual disability and the criminal jus-*

tice system: *Appearances before local courts* (Report No. ISSN 0817-7570). Sydney, Australia: New South Wales Law Reform Commission.

This report discusses a study that was conducted in New South Wales, Australia, to determine if people with intellectual disabilities were overrepresented in the criminal justice system. This study focused on four Local Courts in New South Wales that served a diverse socioeconomic and ethnic population. Individuals over the age of 18 who were asked to appear before the Local Court were asked to participate in this study. One hundred twenty people volunteered for the study and completed the Matrices section of the Kaufman Brief Intelligence Test (K-BIT), an abbreviated version of the Mini-Mental State Examination (MSE), and supplied personal demographic information. The results of this study indicate the following: 14.2% of the participants were in the mildly intellectually disabled range in cognitive ability; 8.8% of the participants were borderline as measured by the K-BIT; and for 31% of the participants, further assessment of mental state was indicated as measured by the MSE. Given the performance on one or both assessment measures, this study concludes that 30% of the participants would encounter difficulty in understanding or dealing with court proceedings.

561. Healy, K., Kennedy, R., & Sinclair, J. (1991). Child physical abuse observed: Comparison of families with and without history of child abuse treated in an in-patient family unit. *British Journal of Psychiatry, 158*, 234–237.

This article discusses the assessment, between May 1986 and October 1987, of 14 families with a history of physical child abuse and 13 families without a history of physical child abuse during their participation in a inpatient psychotherapy program at the Cassel Hospital Families Unit. The two groups were compared on the following variables: parental history, quality of the parental relationship, and changes made during the treatment program. This comparison found that those families with a history of abuse were more often headed by single mothers who were younger in age, were in contact with more professional agencies, and had personal histories of child abuse and disturbed adolescence than mothers from nonabusive families. Successful treatment was characterized by the mothers' positive relationships during treatment and in their personal histories. More benefit was also gained by those families who admitted to abuse than in those families where abuse was not admitted but was suspected.

562. Heckler, S. (1994). Facilitated communication: A response by child protection. *Child Abuse & Neglect, 18*(6), 495–503.

This article provides a case study of allegations of sexual abuse of a 7-year-old girl that arose through facilitated communication (FC). The child protection team attempted to test the validity of FC. Two controlled tests yielded no correct responses. A third test asked for answers to questions that the facilitator was not supposed to know. Although most of these questions were answered incorrectly or ambiguously, 3 of 14 questions were answered specifically and correctly, lending some support to validity. The author concludes that facilitation was working at least some of the time. He argues that FC evidence should not be ignored, but it should not be considered conclusive in itself. Heckler feels this evidence should be considered as part of a larger investigatory process. (Editors' note: Heckler's [1994] letter to the editor included in this same issue provides an updated and more negative perspective based on further case experience.)

563. Heckler, S. (1994). Letter to the editor. *Child Abuse & Neglect, 18*(6), 539–540.

This letter appears as an epilogue to the *Child Abuse & Neglect* special issue on facilitated communication (FC). A lead article by the same author in this issue provides some degree of support for FC. After writing the first article, Heckler was part of a child protection team that investigated several other reports of abuse resulting from FC disclosures. This team developed a protocol for evaluating the communication. None of the cases revealed any evidence to support FC. Many cases demonstrated responses that showed that the FC communications originated with the facilitator and not the presumed communicator. While Heckler is careful not to conclude that FC can never work for any child, he warns strongly about the potential harm of assuming that it is real until it is validated in each individual case.

564. Heifetz, L. J. (1989). From Munchausen to Cassandra: A critique of Hollander's "Euthanasia and mental retardation." *Mental Retardation, 27*(2), 67–69.

This article presents a critical analysis of Russell Hollander's paper, "Euthanasia and mental retardation: Suggesting the unthinkable" (*Mental Retardation, 27*, 53–61). Heifetz objects to several aspects of this article: the terminology, the content, and the conclusion.

565. Heinrichs, P. (1992, February 16). State "tortured" family. *The Sunday Age*, pp. 8–9.

This article details the case of a family who had their daughter taken away by Social Services on the basis of charges of sexual abuse made via facilitated communication. Only after the parents went to court to regain custody of their daughter did the court require objective validation of the facilitation. Tests showed that communication was originating with the facilitator and not their daughter. The daughter was then returned to her parents. Ironically, after the allegations were shown to be false, the facilitators indicated that through facilitation the young woman admitted that she had lied.

566. Heise, L. (1989). International dimensions of violence against women. *Response to the Victimization of Women and Children, 12*(1), 3–11.

This article claims that rape and other forms of violence violate a woman's basic human rights. It discusses the following areas: domestic violence, dowry deaths, the patriarchal family, preference for male children, and female genital mutilation. This article suggests that the elimination of female-targeted violence involves several components, including: exposing the violence, challenging the legal framework that supports male violence, and challenging the social inequities and cultural values that reinforce the economic dependence of women.

567. Helm, R. (1990, October 27). Study finds abusers of disabled often their helpers. *The Edmonton Journal*, p. C3.

This newspaper article reports that the findings of a University of Alberta study on abuse and disability notes that abusers of people with disabilities are commonly caregivers who are funded by the government. In addition, approximately 40% of those abused and 40% of nonabusing staff are reluctant to come forward with abuse issues for fear of reprisal or retribution from administrators in the from of reduced support. Amendments have been proposed to the Ombudsman Act, which will offer protection from retribution for anyone who comes forward with complaints of abuse.

568. Helm, R. (1994, May 12). Doctor reprimanded for judgement during delivery. *The Edmonton Journal*, p. A1.

This article describes the disciplining of a physician by the College of Physicians and Surgeons of Alberta who was found guilty of "unbecoming conduct" for telling the mother of an infant that the child was dead when delivered. In reality, the infant, born at 22 weeks gestation, had a heartbeat but was simply allowed to die with no effort to start breathing. He was reprimanded and assessed $2,831 in costs for the hearing. The doctor indicated that his reason for lying to the parents while letting their baby die was his belief that the baby could not be saved and his desire to spare the parents grief. The identity of the surgeon was protected by the disciplinary hearing. The reprimand credited the doctor with his genuine concern for the feelings of the parents, but parents reacted with outrage when they subsequently learned the true fate of their baby.

569. Helpern, M. (1976, March). Fatalities from child abuse and neglect: Responsibility of the medical examiner and coroner. *Pediatric Annals, 5*, 42–57.

The responsibilities of the medical examiner or coroner in investigations and postmortem examination of fatal child abuse or neglect cases are examined in this article. It states that erroneous reporting, mislabeling, or unlabeling is evident in cases of child abuse fatalities. This article discusses case examples, highlighting various obstacles encountered when dealing with suspected cases of child abuse fatalities.

570. Hendin, H., & Klerman, G. (1993). Physician-assisted suicide: The dangers of legalization. *American Journal of Psychiatry, 150*(1), 143–145.
This article discusses the issue of physician-assisted suicide and emphasizes the probability of abuses that will occur under legalization. The authors present several cases as examples of such abuses.

571. Hendricks, S. E., Fitzpatrick, D. F., Hartmann, K., Quaife, M. A., Stratbucker, R. A., & Graber, B. (1988). Brain structure and function in sexual molesters of children and adolescents. *Journal of Clinical Psychiatry, 49*(3), 108–112.
This article describes a study that examined the computerized tomography (CT scans) and regional cerebral blood flow (rCBF) of 16 male sex offenders in a state psychiatric facility. The study found that subjects have thinner and less dense skulls and lower rCBF values compared to controls. This article concludes that cerebral dysfunction may play an etiological role in deviant sexual behavior.

572. Hentoff, N. (1993, March 2). Dangerous misrepresentations in *The New York Times*. *Village Voice*, pp. 22–23.
This article criticizes *The New York Times* coverage of the Dutch euthanasia law in addition to the law itself and its application. Hentoff suggests that the new law makes it easier for physicians to kill people with disabilities with or without their consent and that consent guidelines are frequently ignored. He cites the Dutch government's 1991 Remmelink Report, which disclosed that at least 1,040 people die each year in the Netherlands as a result of involuntary euthanasia.

573. Herbert, M., Sluckin, W., & Sluckin, A. (1983). Mother-to-infant "bonding." *Annual Progress in Child Psychiatry and Child Development*, 63–84. (Reprinted from *Journal of Child Psychology and Psychiatry*, 1982, *23*(3), 205–221)
This article examines the concept of maternal "bonding" (i.e., rapid mother-to-neonate attachment), which appears frequently in psychiatric, pediatric, and social work discussions of childhood psychopathology and child abuse. Bonding is used as a diagnostic concept related etiologically to postpartum contact and separations of mother and infant. This article explores bonding's empirical basis and the implications for application in practice. It suggests that the term *bonding* is often misleading because of a tendency to simplify attachment phenomena. Also, it claims that there are no indications from animal or human studies that directly support the notion of a "sensitive period" in the formation of mother-infant attachments. This article discusses the negative implications of using this concept in social work and clinical practice, and it suggests alternative ways of conceptualizing these early parent-child events.

574. Herbst, D. S., & Baird, P. A. (1983). Nonspecific mental retardation in British Columbia as ascertained through a registry. *American Journal of Mental Deficiency, 87*(5), 506–513.
This article describes a study that examined the British Columbia Health Surveillance Registry in order to determine the prevalence of nonspecific mental retardation in British Columbia. Nonspecific mental retardation refers to mental retardation with no known etiology. A rate of 4.4 per 1,000 people was estimated for those age 15 to 29. From a 1952 to 1965 birth cohort, this study found an incidence rate of 5.2 per 1,000 live births for males and 4.0 per 1,000 live births for females. In 73% of people with mild mental retardation and 26.9% of people with profound mental retardation, this study found no other associated disability.

575. Herrenkohl, R. C., Herrenkohl, E. C., Egolf, B. P., & Wu, P. (1991). The developmental consequences of child abuse: The Lehigh longitudinal study. In R. J. J. Starr & D. A. Wolfe (Eds.), *The effects of child abuse and neglect: Issues and research* (pp. 57–81). London: Guilford Press.
This chapter concentrates on the developmental effects of child abuse as measured by the Lehigh Longitudinal Study. This study included the following components: the preschool-age study, school-age study, structural equation modeling study, and study of resilient children. This chapter examines methodology and findings and discusses future prospective activities for the Lehigh Longitudinal Study.

576. Hess, P. M. (1987). Parental visiting of children in foster care: Current knowledge and research agenda. *Children and Youth Services Review, 9*(1), 29–50.
This article reviews research on the relationship between parents and their children in a group of parents who visited their children while their children were in foster care. The results of this review indicate that parental contact is necessary but not sufficient for identification with the natural parent, and the frequency of parental visiting was not a significant predictor of change in the parent's perceived attachment to the child. Several studies also examined the relationship between the number of visits and child-parent well-being. In general, the well-being of children is enhanced by frequent visiting; however, in these studies, well-being is not defined consistently, and samples studied are small and fairly homogeneous. The author suggests caution in generalizing these findings. Relationships between parental well-being and frequency of parent-child contact during placement showed a positive correlation between the number of visits and parent well-being. Also, the author examines the following: the effects of varied access arrangements on children's and parents' well-being in divorcing families; the relationship between frequency of parental

visiting and discharge of children from foster care; and data relevant to caseworker contact, case investment, and its relationship to frequent visiting. This article identifies gaps in present knowledge and provides suggestions for future research.

577. Hevesi, D. (1988, July 3). Hospital deaths: Waiting for trial. *The New York Times*, p. I25.

This newspaper article describes the continuing case of nurse Richard Angelo and the hospital murders at the Good Samaritan Hospital in West Islip, Long Island, which is currently at an impasse. While Mr. Angelo has confessed in writing and on videotape to the lethal injections of former patients under his care, those confessions were obtained while he was experiencing 24 hours of constant interrogation. The accused is currently indicted with three counts of murder and one count of assault involving a patient who survived the ordeal. More charges are pending as more bodies are exhumed. In total, Richard Angelo is suspected in the murder of more than 10 patients. This article suggests that the motive for the crimes was the status derived from assisting these patients while they were experiencing an emergency, which was the direct result of the lethal injections.

578. Hewitt, S. E. (1987). The abuse of deinstitutionalized persons with mental handicaps. *Disability, Handicap and Society, 2*(2), 127–135.

This article advocates for the humane treatment of people with mental disabilities who are deinstitutionalized. It examines the strong likelihood of the abuse of these individuals, especially sexual abuse, and it reviews legislative efforts to protect people with mental disabilities, paying special attention to a 1986 Massachusetts law that established a Disabled Persons Protection Commission.

579. Hewitt, S. E. K. (1989). The sexual abuse of young persons with a mental handicap. *Medicine and Law, 8*, 403–414.

In this article, the author addresses the problem of legislative neglect and maltreatment of people with developmental disabilities who have been sexually abused. This article pays particular attention to case examples from the United Kingdom. The author provides recommendations for legal reform and social service improvements to better assist people with developmental disabilities.

580. Hill, G. (1987). Sexual abuse and the mentally handicapped. *Child Sexual Abuse Newsletter, 6*, 4–5.

This article discusses the importance of self-protection education for people with mental disabilities because such education greatly reduces the chances of being exploited. It points out that materials have been developed specifically for teaching sexuality concepts and self-protection to people with mental disabilities. The Seattle Rape Relief Developmental Disabilities Project is one

such program: Level 1 of this program is designed for children ages 6–11 and addresses incest and molestation; Level 2 is designed for ages 12 and up, and it focuses on self-protection in social and home situations and assertiveness training. This article states that 88% of people with mental disabilities are exploited and that only 12% are exploited if they have received self-protection education. Using these figures, the author suggests that education is the key helping people with mental disabilities avoid exploitation.

581. Hindle, R. (1994). Therapeutic work with children with learning disabilities who have been sexually abused. *NAPSAC (National Association for Prevention of Sexual Abuse of Children and Adults with Learning Disabilities) Bulletin, 7*, 7–10.

This article describes the author's counseling work with children with developmental disabilities who have behavior problems and often have been sexually abused. She suggests attempting to separate behavior problems into those associated with normal development, learning problems, and separation and loss issues (often associated with being separated from their natural families and being placed in alternative care). The author uses flow charts to develop schematic images of the child's life as an aid in understanding how events may have led to behavior problems. She also includes other practical suggestions.

582. Hingsburger, D. (1985). From culture to culture: Issues in deinstitutionalization. *Journal of Practical Approaches to Developmental Handicap, 9*(1), 8–11.

This article uses a comparative perspective to examine community living and institutionalization for people with developmental disabilities. It focuses on the following areas: space, social skills, responsibility, acceptance, activity level, number of people, environmental cues, sexual freedom, and the burden of gratitude.

583. Hingsburger, D. (1989). Logotherapy in behavioral sex counseling with the developmentally handicapped. *The International Forum for Logotherapy Journal of Search for Meaning, 12*(1), 46–56.

This article examines the use of logotherapy in behavioral sex counseling for people with developmental disabilities. Logotherapy's philosophy stems from the belief that humankind's primary motivational force is the search for meaning and that an individual's basic needs are secondary to this motivational force. In therapy, this philosophy is realized in the following ways: respect for the patient, a nondirective treatment approach, compatibility with behavior therapy, and compatibility with the philosophy of normalization. This article examines some of the goals of sex counseling: recognition of personal responsibility, participation in goal planning, training in decision making, and delineation of personal values.

584. Hingsburger, D. (1989). Motives for coprophilia: Working with individuals who had been institutionalized with developmental handicaps. *Journal of Sex Research, 26*(1), 139–140.

The author of this article presents the case of an institutionalized adult male with developmental disabilities who engaged in coprophilia combined with coprophagia. This behavior was deemed deviant until it was viewed within an environmental context. With privacy at a minimum and staff reprisals or reprimands feared, masturbation for this man was quick and vigorous. This resulted in bleeding due to the force, after which masturbation ceased until healing took place. This man was afraid of blood and reprimands from the doctor for masturbating; consequently, he used his feces as a lubricant to eliminate bleeding and cleaned his fingers with his mouth, again afraid of being reprimanded for masturbating. This patient's coprophilia disappeared after it was suggested he use a store-bought lubricant.

585. Hingsburger, D. (1989). Relationship training, sexual behavior, and persons with developmental handicaps. *Psychiatric Aspects of Mental Retardation Reviews, 8*(5), 33–37.

This article discusses relationship training for people with developmental disabilities. It addresses the differences between friendships, love relationships, sexual-love relationships, and staff/professional relationships and examines such issues as rights and responsibilities that are fostered by relationships. This article includes counseling and education techniques for relationship training.

586. Hingsburger, D. (1990). *I contact: Sexuality and people with developmental disabilities.* **Mountville, PA: VIDA.**

This book provides the personal perspective of a sexuality counselor and educator working with people with disabilities. Hingsburger uses anecdotal accounts and humor to make powerful points about how we must reconceptualize our interactions with and expectations of people with disabilities.

587. Hingsburger, D. (1992). Cautions and considerations for providing sex education for people with developmental disabilities who live within group homes. *Journal on Developmental Disabilities, 1*(1), 42–47.

This article outlines cautions that should be considered when implementing sex education in group homes for people with developmental disabilities. It discusses the following issues: possible conflict between agency policies regarding sexual expression and the implementation of appropriate education for those served by the agency; adequate preparation and informed, voluntary consent of students; and the ongoing nature of education regarding sexuality. This article recognizes the vulnerability of those in residential care to sexual victimization by supposed caregivers, and the author feels this must be dealt with in a sensitive manner when providing relevant and effective education.

588. Hingsburger, D. (1992). Erotophobic behavior in people with developmental disabilities. *The Habilitative Mental Healthcare Newsletter, 11*(5), 31–35.

In this article, erotophobic behavior is defined as the persistent and general negative emotional response to sexual cues: for example, nudity, one's own genitalia, or sexual behavior. This article presents 10 manifestations of erotophobia, and it provides a summary of a treatment strategy that includes the following: changing the person's attitude, delving into the person's past to assess how he or she developed this fear, and systematic desensitization.

589. Hingsburger, D. (1992). Human rights and HIV/AIDS: Recommendations concerning the rights of people with developmental disabilities. *SIECCAN (Sex Information & Education Council of Canada) Newsletter, 47* (4), 18–23.

This article examines the possible violation of rights of people who are or may be HIV-positive in agencies or facilities providing services to people with developmental disabilities. It discusses the following issues: freedom from punishment, the right to sex education, the right to privacy, and the right to generic services. This article includes recommendations for change and policy development.

590. Hingsburger, D. (1993). *I openers: Parents ask questions about sexuality and children with developmental disabilities.* **Vancouver, BC: Family Support Institute.**

This book uses parents' questions about sexuality and their children with disabilities to explore a number of sexual health issues. Some issues about abuse and exploitation are directly addressed, but the main value of the book is in encouraging healthy attitudes about sexuality that tend to discourage abuse.

591. Hingsburger, D. (in press). Working with hustlers/prostitutes with a developmental disability. *The Habilitative Mental Healthcare Newsletter.*

This article addresses the issue of hustlers and prostitutes with developmental disabilities and the challenges they pose to agencies that support them. Five individuals (three male, two female) with developmental disabilities were contacted by means of agencies and were questioned concerning their decision to work in the sex trade. For the males, money, social network, autonomy, and atmosphere were the main attractions for them to continue hustling. To a lesser degree, the same reasons were true for the women, although they had the additional consideration of a pimp. The need for affection and self-esteem were also noted to be positive influences for the women who viewed their pimps as boyfriends. For most of the individuals, hustling/prostitution was introduced to them by others in the trade. Most of the individuals had run away from group homes. Some of the hazards of hustling/prostitution are the uncertainty of work, fear of arrest, being ripped off, being forced to participate in something undesired, and disease. Therapeutic goals that would meet the clients' needs consisted of reducing their dependence on the sex trade for meeting their daily needs and finding alternative ways of expressing sexuality while pursuing different goals. These people were taught safer sex techniques, including condom training and teaching how to differentiate between low-risk and high-risk sexual behavior. This article notes that there will be follow-up papers on the approaches for meeting goals.

592. Hingsburger, D., Griffiths, D., & Quinsey, V. (1991). Detecting counterfeit deviance: Differentiating sexual deviance from sexual inappropriateness. *The Habilitative Mental Healthcare Newsletter, 10*(9), 51–54.

This newsletter is written for health care providers, and it examines sexual deviance and sexual inappropriateness. This article presents 11 hypotheses to explain the etiology of sexually inappropriate behaviors: structural, modeling, behavior, partner selection, inappropriate courtship, sexual knowledge, perpetual arousal, learning history, moral vacuum, medical, and medication side effect. It uses examples to illustrate each hypothesis. This article includes treatment objectives and depicts real sexual deviance.

593. Hingsburger, D., & Ludwig, S. (1993). *Homosexuality.* **East York, ON: SIECCAN (Sex Information & Education Council of Canada).**

This is the 10th book in a 17-part series on sexuality education for young adults and adults with developmental disabilities. This book discusses homosexuality using illustrations, Blissymbols, and script. It makes a distinction between gays, lesbians, and homosexual behavior; this book also discusses safe sex, AIDS, gay pride, and community services. A glossary of key words and Blissymbols is included in this book.

594. Hingsburger, D., & Ludwig, S. (1993). *Male masturbation.* **East York, ON: SIECCAN (Sex Information & Education Council of Canada).**

This is the 5th book in a 17-part series on sexuality education for young adults and adults with developmental disabilities. This book discusses male masturbation, ejaculation, semen, lubrication, and sexually explicit material using illustrations, Blissymbols, and script. It considers masturbation a personal sexual choice for everyone. It makes distinctions between appropriate public and private behavior and sexual expression. A glossary of key words and Blissymbols is included in this book.

595. Hingsburger, D., & Ludwig, S. (1993). *A man's body.* **East York, ON: SIECCAN (Sex Information & Education Council of Canada).**

This is the 3rd book in a 17-part series on sexuality education for young adults and adults with developmental disabilities. This book discusses male anatomy using illustrations, Blissymbols, and script. The developmental stages of puberty are discussed with relation to body growth; this book also covers the male reproductive system, masturbation, ejaculation, and intercourse. It makes distinctions between appropriate public and private behavior and sexual expression. A glossary of key words and Blissymbols is included in this book.

596. Hingsburger, D., & Ludwig, S. (1993). *Sexual self-advocacy.* **East York, ON: SIECCAN (Sex Information & Education Council of Canada).**

This is the 14th book in a 17-part series on sexuality education for young adults and adults with developmental disabilities. This book discusses sexual self-advocacy using illustrations, Blissymbols, and script. It focuses on people in residential care settings and how they can become involved in advocating their right to sexual expression. It also emphasizes the right that everyone has to equality and freedom of choice and that courage is needed to bring about change in policy. A glossary of key words and Blissymbols is included in this book.

597. Hingsburger, D., & Moore, L. (1991). Client-initiated sexual contact with caregivers. *The Habilitative Mental Healthcare Newsletter, 10*(1), 1–4.

The authors of this article suggest a protocol for helping staff and agencies working with people with developmental disabilities deal with incidents involving client-initiated sexual contact with caregivers. This protocol encourages staff to report all incidents and assess the client's behavior. During assessment, it is necessary to address four questions that deal with the client's behavior and the meaning it holds for him or her: Has the client participated in sex education? Were there any predisposing conditions before the incident? Have there been additional incidents experienced by other staff? and Have other clients been molested? The authors provide nine suggestions for the prevention of future reoccurrences.

598. Hite, M. C., Kleber, D. J., & Simpkins, K. E. (1985, April 15–19). *Family constellations of mentally retarded individuals: The changing role of the school psychologist.* **Paper presented at the 63rd Annual Convention of the Council for Exceptional Children, Anaheim, CA.**

In this paper, the needs of parents of children with mental retardation are discussed, and the authors propose that school psychologists can promote more effective parent-school relationships. Two case studies are provided to illustrate the concerns of families with adolescents who are moderately mentally retarded. The authors present interventions to provide immediate, short-term solutions for these families, and they describe the primary function of the special education school psychologist. The authors describe and discuss major role changes: for example, consultation for both home and school behavior, providing teachers with inservice training on family dynamics, group counseling and education that focuses on stress management, counseling individual families as a means of crisis intervention, and referral to other mental health professionals.

599. Ho, H. K. (1988). A survey on sex education problems of mentally retarded children. In F. C. Chen, A. S. Fraser, K. R. Lyen, D. Oon, D. Tan, & M. K. Wong (Eds.), *Proceedings from the 8th Asian Conference on Mental Retardation* (pp. 241–246). Singapore: AFMR (Asian Federation for Mental Retardation).
This article discusses a study that administered the Sex Education Questionnaire to 149 elementary (53 male, 96 female) and 30 junior high school teachers (6 male, 24 female) who taught children with mental retardation in the Republic of China. The study examined sex education problems of children with mental retardation. The results of this questionnaire show the following: teachers are most concerned with the easy exploitation of children with mental retardation for sex crimes, sex education should emphasize self-defense knowledge for females and sex hygiene knowledge, and most of these teachers believe that sex education should be taught starting in the fifth grade.

600. Ho, T. P., & Kwok, W. M. (1991). Child sexual abuse in Hong Kong. *Child Abuse & Neglect, 15*(4), 597–600.
Although this article claims that child sexual abuse is a rare problem in Chinese or Asian societies, it points out that there is little research and/or professional concern in this area. This article investigates the sociocultural factors related to the infrequency of child sexual abuse. This article presents three case studies of sexually abused Chinese children (in Hong Kong). This article notes that the three reported cases of intrafamilial child sexual abuse are not much different from those reported in the West; however, child sexual abuse remains a taboo, and even in identified cases, secrecy is a common factor. This article states that traditional Chinese tend to keep shameful secrets within the family circle more than Western families. It suggests that the absolute authority of the parents over children and a demand for unquestioned obedience may be factors that allow adults to use children for sexual gratification. This article also suggests that

low professional awareness of the sexual abuse of Chinese children might account for the low report rates.

601. Hobbs, C. J. (1984). Skull fracture and the diagnosis of abuse. *Archives of Disease in Childhood, 59*, 246–252.
This article describes a study that examined skull fractures in 89 children 2 years of age or younger. For 29 children, nonaccidental injury stemming from abuse was determined at onset of the study for comparison with the group consisting of accidental injury. Twenty fatalities were recorded, 19 of which were abused children. The skull fractures in the abused group were most often characterized by multiple or complex fractures and associated intracranial injury. Accidental skull fractures were narrow and linear, affecting the parietal bones.

602. Hobbs, C. J. (1989). Burns and scalds. *British Medical Journal, 298*, 1302–1305.
In this article, the author talks about the association between burns and scalds and child abuse. The author claims that 1% to 16% of children presented with burns or scalds at hospitals are victims of child abuse. The article discusses the different kinds of thermal injuries and the depths of injuries and makes a distinction between accidental and intentional burns. As well, it notes parental and child characteristics. This article describes differential diagnosis in cases of burns or scalds.

603. Hobbs, C. J. (1989). Fractures. *British Medical Journal, 298*, 1015–1018.
This article examines fractures resulting from child physical abuse. It discusses the detection of nonaccidental injury in terms of six particular patterns of fractures seen in cases of physical abuse: a single fracture with multiple bruises; multiple fractures in different stages of healing, sometimes with no bruises or soft tissue injuries; metaphysial-epiphysial injuries; rib fractures; new periosteal bone; and a skull fracture with intracranial injury. Also, it includes medical illustrations. The author states that the prevalence of fractures from physical abuse is most common in children under the age of 3, and accidental fractures are most often seen in school-age children.

604. Hobbs, C. J. (1989). Head injury. *British Medical Journal, 298*, 1169–1170.
This article discusses physical child abuse resulting in head injury with or without fractures. It describes the detection of head injury resulting from abuse, including: fractures, intracranial injuries, and retinal hemorrhages. Different manifestations of fractures resulting from accidents are compared to fractures from nonaccidental head injury. Medical illustrations and photographs are included, along with descriptions of various types of head injuries.

605. Hochstadt, N. J., Jaudes, P. K., Zimo, D. A., & Schachter, J. (1987). The medical and psychosocial needs of children

entering foster care. *Child Abuse & Neglect, 11,* 53–62.
This article describes a study that was conducted to determine the medical and psychosocial needs of children entering foster care so that provisions could be made to provide better health care service for this population. One hundred forty-nine children (49% male, 51% female) with histories of abuse and neglect entering the Cook County foster care system in Illinois were assessed at the La Rabida Children's Hospital and Research Centre. This study obtained information from the following: personal histories, physical examinations, the Denver Developmental Screening Text, the Vineland Adaptive Behavior Scale, and the Louisville Behavior Checklist. Parental (biological or foster) information was also obtained. The most prevalent reasons for removal of the children from their biological home was neglect (49.7%), physical abuse (28.9%), and abandonment (22.1%), with some children belonging to more than one category. It was noted that the foster children had an increased prevalence of chronic medical problems, were developmentally delayed, weighed less than the general population, were significantly shorter than the general population, and exhibited behavior problems.

606. Hodgins, S. (1992, June). Mental disorder, intellectual deficiency, and crime: Evidence from a birth cohort. *Archives of General Psychiatry, 49,* 476–483.
This article discusses a Swedish study that examined the relationship between mental disorders and crime and intellectual deficiency and crime. The subject cohort consisted of 7,362 men and 7,039 women born in 1953 and still living in Stockholm in 1983. Those admitted to a psychiatric ward were placed into three categories: major mental disorder (82 men, 79 women), alcohol/drug abusers (156 men, 98 women), and other mental disorders (64 men, 124 women). Subjects with developmental disabilities were considered people never admitted to a psychiatric ward, but who did receive special education in high school (113 men, 79 women). In 1983, criminal records from the Swedish National Police Register were collected for the subjects involved in the study. Controls consisted of those people who were not former psychiatric patients and had no developmental disabilities. The results of this study indicate the following: 1) men with major mental disorders were 2.5 times more likely to be criminally convicted and 4 times more likely to be convicted of a violent offense than men in the control group, 2) women with major mental disorders were 5 times more likely to be criminally convicted and 27 times more likely to be convicted of a violent offense compared to women in the control group, 3) men with developmental disabilities were 3 times more likely to be criminally convicted and 5 times more likely to be convicted of a violent offense compared to men in the control group, and 4) women with developmental disabilities were 4 times more likely to be criminally convicted and 25 times more likely to be convicted of a violent offense compared to women in the control group.

607. Hoeksma, J. B., Koomen, H. M., & Koops, W. (1987). Responsiviteit en hechting: Een enquete bij ouders van kinderen met en kinderen zonder een schisis [Responsiveness and attachment: A study with parents of children with and without cleft lip and/or palate]. *Nederlands Tijdschrift voor de Psychologie en haar Grensgebieden, 42(6),* 282–290.
This article examines the attachment development of infants with disabilities. Fifty-four normal male and female Dutch parents of "normal" children and 53 normal male and female Dutch parents of children with cleft lip and/or palate were questioned by letter about five topics dealing with the attachment development of their 4- to 22-month-old children: 1) recognizing and responding to signals, 2) perceived insecurity, 3) hospitalization, 4) feeding, and 5) play. Also, the authors discuss the psychometric analyses of the questionnaire.

608. Hofer, M. A. (1987). Early social relationships: A psychobiologist's view. *Child Development, 58(3),* 633–647.
This article outlines a strategy for studying early social relationships in relatively simple animal model systems. Using studies on early social attachment in 2-week-old rats and their acute and long-term responses to separation from their mothers, this article illustrates some of the differences in approach between neuroscientists and human developmentalists in dealing with the same research problems. It describes a mechanism that mothers use to regulate the physiological and behavioral systems of the infant and suggests that infant hyperactivity in response to separation can be moderated using artificial thermal, olfactory, and tactile maternal cues. It claims that long-term and acute effects of separation are two distinct processes. Also, this article discusses studies on the organization of nursing that reveal an unexpected degree of synchrony and reciprocity.

609. Holburn, C. S. (1990). Rules: The new institutions. *Mental Retardation, 28(2),* 89–94.
This article provides a critique of the bureaucracy in residential environments for individuals with developmental disabilities. It examines the harmful effects of a heavily regulated residential environment and suggests that excess rule following may produce staff indifference, inefficiency, and lack of caring.

610. Holburn, C. S. (1990). Symposium: Rules in today's residential environments. *Mental Retardation, 28(2),* 65–66.
This article examines the ICF-MR Guidelines that specify quality assurance rules for residential care facilities and concludes that these guidelines are an example of bureaucratic interventions that emphasize regulation compliance over enhanced quality of life for residents.

611. Holden, R. H. (1972). Prediction of mental retardation in infancy. *Mental Retardation, 10*(1), 28–30.
This article discusses a study that examined the mental ability of infants in order to help predict their mental development at a later age. This study examined children (*n*=117/2,875) participating in the Child Development Study at Brown University (which is part of the National Collaborative Study of Cerebral Palsy and other Neurological Diseases, National Institute of Neurological Diseases, and Stroke) who were 1 month below average on the Bayley Mental Scale, the Bayley Motor Scale, or both of these scales: These children made up Experimental Group I. A follow-up was conducted with these children at ages 8 months and 4 years. Experimental Group II consisted of 115 additional children with the same delays. A follow-up was conducted with the participants of Experimental Group II and 115 controls at ages 8 months, 4 years, and 7 years: Follow-up at age 4 was done using the Stanford-Binet Form L-M, and the follow-up at age 7 was done using the Wechsler Intelligence Scale for Children. The results of this study indicate the following: At ages 8 months and 4 years, Experimental Groups I and II did not differ significantly from each other, but both did significantly differ from controls; variability in IQ scores for all three groups was noted; at age 4, three times as many children in the experimental groups were developmentally delayed when compared to controls; and at the follow-up at age 7, the developmental delays noted at age 4 were still present.

612. Hollander, R. (1986). Mental retardation and American society: The era of hope. *Social Service Review, 60*(3), 395–420.
This article examines the origins of public policy concerning people with mental retardation in mid–19th-century America. It places the initial efforts to help this population within the social/historical context of a larger mission that existed among philanthropists to encourage a moral transformation within society. It identifies major forces that influenced the development of social policy: the fear of people with mental retardation, a religious duty to help them, an aesthetically based dislike of them, and public apathy. This article discusses the ongoing debate between advocates of short-term schooling and long-term incarceration; in addition, it describes how the question of providing for an adult with mental retardation became a focal point for resolving the debate.

613. Hollander, R. (1989). Euthanasia and mental retardation: Suggesting the unthinkable. *Mental Retardation, 27*(2), 53–61.
This article examines the United States's eugenics movement in the late 19th and early 20th century and its effect on people with developmental disabilities. This article focuses on the policy of euthanasia, which was proposed along with incarceration and sterilization as a means of controlling mental retardation. Also, this article examines the support for this policy that existed among members of the medical establishment and other service providers and the move toward incarceration of people with developmental disabilities.

614. Hollander, R. (1989). Response to Wolfensberger and Heifetz. *Mental Retardation, 27*(2), 71–74.
This article is a response to Wolfensberger and Heifetz's critique of Hollander's "Euthanasia and mental retardation: Suggesting the unthinkable" (*Mental Retardation, 27*[2], 53–61). Hollander defends his article by examining and discrediting the criticisms against it.

615. Hollins, S., & Roth, T. (1994). *Hug me: Touch me.* **London: St. George's Mental Health Library.**
This book is designed primarily for nonreaders and contains 33 pictures that tell a story without text. It is the story of a young woman who wants to be touched but does not understand whom it is okay to touch or what kinds of touch are appropriate for various relationships. She experiences rejection and frustration as a result of her inappropriate attempts to touch and hold others, but with guidance from a friend, she begins to learn appropriate ways to meet her needs. Separate picture captions at the end of the book tell the story of the pictures for people who can read.

616. Hollins, S., & Sinason, V. (1992). *Jenny speaks out.* **London: St. George's Mental Health Library.**
This is one of two companion books (the other book is entitled *Bob tells all*) by Hollins and Sinason written for people with learning disabilities. It is designed to help facilitate disclosure of sexual abuse, and it uses text and illustrations to tell a story of disclosure of sexual abuse by a young women when she moved to a group home. This book illustrates Jenny's initial unhappiness, her reaction to memories of the abuse, disclosure to friends, and her healing.

617. Hollins, S., & Sinason, V. (1993). *Bob tells all.* **London: St. George's Mental Health Library.**
This is one of two companion books (the other book is entitled *Jenny speaks out*) by Hollins and Sinason written for people with learning disabilities. This book is designed to help facilitate disclosure of sexual abuse, and it uses text and illustrations to tell a story of disclosure of sexual abuse by a young man when he moved into a group home. This book illustrates Bob's initial unhappiness, his reaction to memories of the abuse, disclosure to friends, and his healing.

618. Hopkins, J. (1990). The observed infant of attachment theory. *British Journal of Psychotherapy, 6*(4), 460–470.
This article reviews empirical findings in infant and child developmental research using Bowlby's (1980) attachment theory. It describes attachment behavior (AB) as an example of instinctive behavior that decreases the risk of

danger and increases safety. It suggests that the role of fathers and mothers in shaping AB are different and that attachment patterns are dependent on the nature of mothering received in the first year. It claims data support the intergenerational transmission of AB and that from these early attachment patterns internalized working models of the self, the other, and interpersonal relationships are constructed that guide later behavior. This article concludes that early intervention with parent-infant psychotherapy can help resolve dysfunctional AB patterns before they are internalized.

619. Hopper, D. (1989). Intellectually handicapped victims of abuse: Doubly victimized? *Autism Society Canada, 7*(4), 1, 3.

This article discusses a case in Canada in which a sexually assaulted woman with mental disabilities was not allowed to testify in court on her own behalf. Although the offender confessed, the case will not go to court.

620. Horne, M. D. (1988). Modifying peer attitudes toward the handicapped: Procedures and research issues. In H. E. Yuker (Ed.), *Attitudes toward persons with disabilities* **(pp. 203–222). New York: Springer.**

This chapter discusses programs designed to modify peer attitudes toward school-age children with disabilities. The author examines contact with and information about people with disabilities and how this contact and information affects attitudes. This chapter describes the combination of both contact and information in different structured settings and examines cooperative and competitive instruction and the teaching of social skills to children with disabilities. In addition, it discusses the following techniques: role playing; peer tutoring; bibliotherapy, which incorporates identification with a character, catharsis, and finally insight; game playing; media presentation; and educational material. This chapter also examines classroom organization and environment.

621. Horner, R. (1992, June 9). Vandalism at handicap school. *Cardston Chronicle,* **p. 3.**

This newspaper article reports that several 4- to 6-year-old children were apprehended at the Cardston and District Association for the Handicapped School building by a member of the community. It appears that the children instigated an act of vandalism at the school, causing damage to the building and a recycling vehicle. The cost of the broken windows in the school and those on the truck amount to approximately $700 Canadian. The children were turned over to their parents and the Royal Canadian Mounted Police.

622. Howard, A. C. (1986). Developmental play ages of physically abused and nonabused children. *American Journal of Occupational Therapy, 40*(10), 691–695.

This article discusses a study that examined the developmental play level of 12 physically abused and 12 nonabused children. Both groups had similar economic backgrounds, and in 42% of the cases, children of the same gender were paired together. All of these children came from either a women's support shelter or from a child-care center. The average ages for the abused and nonabused group were 3.6 years and 3.5 years, respectively. Race was not examined. The Preschool Play Scale was used to determine the developmental play level for each child. The four subsections of the scale consisted of the following: space management, material management, imitation, and participation. The results of this study show that a significant number, 11 in the abused group compared to 6 in the nonabused group, had developmentally lower play ages when compared to their chronological ages. The major difference in scores was found on the imitation subsection, which also incorporates imagination: The abused group obtained lower scores in this section. This article discusses certain limitations concerning the interpretation of the results.

623. Howell, D. (1991, April 19). Legal protection urged for disabled people who report abuse. *The Edmonton Journal,* **p. B3.**

This newspaper article reports the call for provincial legislation to protect victims of abuse, in particular, people with disabilities who have been abused. This protection would include independent advocacy for people with disabilities who have been abused in institutions and the report of these abuses to police. These recommendations were made by Dr. Dick Sobsey from the University of Alberta to the Premier's Council on the Status of Persons with Disabilities. As it stands, any abuses that occur in institutions do not need to be reported to police.

624. Howells, G. (1986). Are the medical needs of mentally handicapped adults being met? *Journal of the Royal College of General Practitioners, 36,* 449–453.

This article describes a survey of people with developmental disabilities who attended adult training centers in England and Wales that was conducted to determine if their medical needs were being met. The results of this survey indicate that common ailments in this population were not identified or treated, including: vision problems, auditory problems, and Down syndrome. This study found that consultation rates for people with developmental disabilities were lower than those for the general population. This article concludes that communication between patient and practitioners is a major component in improving medical services for people with developmental disabilities, and it suggests ways to improve services.

625. Howing, P. T., Wodarski, J. S., Gaudin, J. M. J., & Kurtz, D. (1989). Clinical

assessment instruments in the treatment of child abuse and neglect. In J. T. Pardeck (Ed.), *Child abuse and neglect: Theory, research and practice* **(pp. 69–82). New York: Gordon and Breach Science Publishers.**

This chapter discusses screening for potential child abuse and neglect in child welfare situations. It examines and describes numerous assessment tools: for example, parent assessment measures, child assessment measures, family assessment measures, marital assessment measures, stress assessment measures, social support assessment measures, and ecological assessment measures. These different measures incorporate the following techniques: self-report inventories, behavior rating scales, structured interviews, and observational coding schemes. This chapter includes references for all of the assessment measures.

626. Howze, D. C., & Kotch, J. B. (1984). Disentangling life events, stress and social support: Implications for the primary prevention of child abuse and neglect. *Child Abuse & Neglect, 8,* **401–409.**

Although it has been suggested that there is a link between child abuse, neglect, and stress, this article claims that empirical data do not support the body of literature that links child abuse, neglect, and stress. It suggests that this research is problematic for several reasons. It discusses Garbarino's ecological model, which examines interactions between parent and child characteristics and intrafamilial and extrafamilial stressors and social-cultural context. It suggests that this model is used infrequently in empirical research because of its methodological weaknesses and the absence of a systematic theoretical framework for the role of stress. This article concludes that the perception of stresses, social support, interpersonal resources, and the necessity of prevention are important at all levels in this ecological model.

627. Hubbard, R. (1985). Prenatal diagnosis and eugenic ideology. *Women's Studies International Forum, 8*(6), **567–576.**

This article discusses the links between new reproductive technologies and eugenics. While new reproductive technologies have been promoted as empowering women and giving them choices, some women are now having misgivings and feel that their choices have been taken away. German feminists have begun to take a strong stand against prenatal diagnosis because it is inevitably associated with intrusion on their choices about whether to complete their pregnancies.

628. Hughes, H. M., & DiBrezzo, R. D. (1987). Physical and emotional abuse and motor development: A preliminary investigation. *Perceptual and Motor Skills, 64,* **469–470.**

This article discusses a study that compared women from a battered women's shelter with women from the community on results from a self-report problem checklist regarding their children. The study group consisted of 65 families from the shelter, involving 52 boys and 65 girls, and 50 families from the community, involving 49 boys and 45 girls. All of the children were between the ages of 2 and 12. The problem checklist pertained to areas of cognitive, motor, and language development. It was hypothesized that the mothers from the shelter would select more items denoting learning disabilities in their children than the mothers from the community. The results indicate the following: the shelter children (18%) had significantly more learning difficulties than the comparison group (7%); and when the physically abused shelter children were compared with the nonphysically abused shelter children, 23% of the abused children had learning difficulties compared to 11% of the nonabused group.

629. Huitt, K., & Elston, R. R. (1991). Attitudes toward persons with disabilities expressed by professional counselors. *Journal of Applied Rehabilitation Counseling, 22*(2), **42–43.**

This article discusses a study that examined whether rehabilitation counselors, school counselors, and mental health counselors in the Commonwealth of Kentucky had different attitudes toward people with disabilities. This study mailed a questionnaire package that included the Attitudes Toward Disabled Persons Scale, Form A to 200 rehabilitation counselors, school counselors, and mental health counselors. It analyzed 86 packages. This study found no significant differences among the three counselor groups concerning their attitudes toward people with disabilities; instead, it found that all of the participants had positive attitudes.

630. Hume, J. (1991). The unremembered holocaust: How doctors ran a programme to kill people with disabilities (Part I). *New Zealand Disabled, 11*(5), **61–63.**

In Part I of this two-part article, Hume briefly examines the sanctioned euthanasia of people with disabilities in Nazi Germany. She describes the development of policies and laws that resulted in the government-sanctioned killing of people with disabilities. She shows how, with the blessing of Germany's most influential and respected academics, intellectuals, psychiatrists, physicians, teachers, public servants, philosophers, and researchers, the Nazi regime moved from sterilization programs of people with disabilities to a secret euthanasia program.

631. Hume, J. (1991). The unremembered holocaust: German doctors' "mercy" killings of people with disabilities (Part II). *New Zealand Disabled, 11*(6), **64–65.**

In Part II of this two-part article, Hume describes the particular case of the extermination center called Hartheim. She describes the deception used in the extermination of 14,000 people with disabilities at this hospital. She concludes that by protecting the rights of people with disabilities society is protecting the rights of all its citizens.

632. Hume, S. C., & Hiti, J. A. (1988). A rationale and model for group art therapy with mentally retarded adolescents. *American Journal of Art Therapy, 27(1), 2–12.*
This article presents a group treatment model that was developed for 13 adolescents with mental retardation and emotional impairments. Art therapy and group discussion that encouraged self-exploration and interpersonal learning formed the core of this group treatment model. The students involved in the treatment were divided into two groups according to their levels of functioning. This article describes the group structure and issues discussed by the group members in detail.

633. Hunfeld, J. A. M., Wladimiroff, J. W., Passchier, J., Uniken Venema-Van Uden, M., Frets, P. G., & Verhage, F. (1993). Emotional reactions of women late in pregnancy (24 weeks or longer) following the ultrasound diagnosis of severe or lethal fetal malformation. *Prenatal Diagnosis, 13,* 603–612.
This article reports on the emotional responses of 41 women at the time of being given a diagnosis of a birth defect and again 3 months after the birth of their babies. The results of this study indicate the following: the time of being given diagnosis was often associated with powerful psychological and psychosomatic symptoms; mothers improved significantly after their babies were born; and the results suggest strong differences between the responses of mothers whose babies had died and mothers whose babies had survived (including those who would probably die soon), suggesting limits to applying a grief paradigm to disability.

634. Hunter, E. (1993). The snake on the caduceus: Dimensions of medical and psychiatric responsibility in the Third Reich. *Australian and New Zealand Journal of Psychiatry, 27(1),* 149–156.
This article explores the role of psychiatrists in the Nazi sterilization and extermination programs. It points out that psychiatrists were most often the physicians with primary responsibility for deciding who should be killed and that psychiatrists were involved with every aspect of the ideology and practice of medical killing.

635. Hunter, R. S., Kilstrom, N., & Loda, F. (1985). Sexually abused children: Identifying masked presentations in a medical setting. *Child Abuse & Neglect, 9,* 17–25.
This article discusses a study that compared sexually abused children with overt presentations of abuse ($n=31$) with sexually abused children with covert presentations of abuse ($n=50$). The 79 females and 9 males in this study had an average age of 9.2 years and were assessed by the North Carolina Memorial Hospital maltreatment team. The presenting complaints of the overt group of children consisted of alleged sexual abuse. The covert group of children presented with physical or behavioral symptoms without disclosure of sexual abuse. The main complaints consisted of genital symptoms ($n=18$), psychosomatic and behavioral problems ($n=12$), pregnancy-related conditions ($n=7$), sexually transmitted diseases ($n=5$), asymptomatic sibling of victim ($n=5$), and miscellaneous ($n=3$). Eight of the nine males belonged to the covert group. Children in the covert group were more likely to have a history of sexual abuse, school problems, and psychosomatic complaints. In addition, these children's abusers were most often immediate family members. This article provides four case examples.

636. Hurley, A. D. (1989). *Behaviour therapy for psychiatric disorders in mentally retarded individuals.* **Lexington, MA: Lexington Books.**
This book examines the use of behavior therapy for psychiatric disorders in people with mental retardation. It claims that behavior therapeutic procedures are successfully used for phobic states, depression, and anorexia nervosa, not only for individuals with normal intelligence, but also for those with mental retardation. This book claims that the scope of behavior therapy has extended into the intrapsychic states to include thoughts and feelings apart from the modification of observable behavior and that systematic desensitization in phobias and cognitive behavior therapy in depression and anorexia nervosa have been well documented. The book reviews the application of behavior therapy techniques for individuals with mental retardation who experience phobias, depression, and anorexia nervosa. The patients reviewed in this book had mild mental retardation. This book states that persons with mental retardation have the same range of fears as those with normal intelligence but differ in the sense that they tend to follow the pattern of children's phobias. It states that counterconditioning and desensitization have been successful for alleviating these phobias. The book examines depression and notes that it is one of the most common psychiatric disorders noticed in persons with mental retardation. In addition to drug therapy and psychotherapy, it suggests that cognitive behavior therapy is highly successful for treating person who are mentally impaired and who experience depression. This book includes cases resistant to drug therapy. For example, anorexia nervosa, which has been lately recognized in persons with mental retardation. In the case of anorexia nervosa discussed in this book, the person was moved from the dormitory to the school infirmary. Privilege to attend classes depended on the patient showing a weight gain. The therapists ignored inappropriate eating behaviors and recognized normal eating behaviors. This patient underwent weekly cognitive behavior therapy sessions and began to gain weight. The author concludes that the treatment time was no longer for people with mental retardation than for persons with normal intelligence and the persons treated showed improvement.

637. Hvizdala, E. V., & Gellady, A. M. (1978). Intentional poisoning of two siblings by

prescription drugs. *Clinical Pediatrics, 17*(6), 480–482.

This article describes the intentional poisoning of a 4-year-old boy and his 7-year-old sister by their mother. The mother's intentional poisoning of her children with prescription drugs is discussed, and while Munchausen syndrome by proxy is not mentioned, it is described.

638. Hyson, G. (1988). Police involvement: What are the problems? *Interaction, 2*(4), 13–14.

This article discusses a New South Wales, Australia, study that asked people with intellectual disabilities to participate in a questionnaire survey to determine what attitudes they held toward the police, to uncover their knowledge of legal rights, and to identify any issues deemed helpful to people with intellectual disabilities concerning their arrest or questioning. The survey consisted of two questionnaires: one was designed for people with intellectual disabilities who had no prior experience with the police (*n*=76); and the second questionnaire was designed for people with intellectual disabilities with prior experience with the police, for example, arrests or questioning for a criminal offense (*n*=14). The participants in this study were diagnosed with mild (53%), moderate (41%), and severe (6%) intellectual disability. The results from the first questionnaire indicate the following: the majority would seek help from the police if they needed assistance (66%), the majority of respondents were not aware of their legal rights, and 93% of those surveyed stated that they would prefer to be accompanied by someone known to them should they be required to appear at a police station. The results from the second questionnaire indicated the following: 57% of respondents found communication with the police difficult when interrogated/arrested, and 78% of those taken to the police station signed documents without understanding their content. The author concludes that when people with intellectual disabilities become involved with the police they need the following: a better understanding of their legal rights, and support from someone known to them during police procedures.

•I•

639. Ibrahim, F. A., &. Herr, E. L. (1982). Modification of attitudes toward disability: Differential effect of two educational modes. *Rehabilitation Counseling Bulletin, 26*(1), 29–36.

This article describes a study that examined how two different educational approaches affected the attitudes of potential helping professionals toward persons with disabilities. This study used a sample of 50 undergraduate students from an introductory clinical speech course, and they were assigned to the following groups: 20 participants were in an experiential group, 20 participants

were in an informational group, and 10 participants were controls. The experiential group used role play to act out a specific speech or hearing disability. The informational group was shown films, slides, and given written personal accounts of people with communication disabilities. The results of this study indicate the following: The two educational strategies had a positive effect on attitudes toward people with communication disabilities, and these positive attitudes were present at posttest. The authors include recommendations for future research.

640. Igric, L., Sikic, N., & Burusic, D. (1990). Effects of Gestalt therapy and drug therapy in hyperactive severely mentally retarded children. In A. Dosen, A. Van Gennep, & G. J. Zwanikken (Eds.), *Treatment of mental illness and behavioral disorder in the mentally retarded: Proceedings of the International Congress, May 3rd & 4th, 1990* **(pp. 339–350). Leiden, the Netherlands: Logon Publications.**

This paper discusses a study that attempted to determine the effects of Gestalt therapy when used with hyperactive children with severe mental retardation. Children undergoing Gestalt therapy were compared to similar children receiving drug therapy. There were three children in each group, ranging in age from 6.5 to 14.10 years. All of the children were diagnosed with prenatal brain injury, except for one child who suffered postnatal injury due to infection. The five male children and one female child were all residents at the Centre for Rehabilitation, Stancic, near Zagreb, and they received regular rehabilitation treatment. Children in the Gestalt therapy group received therapy once a day for 20–30 minutes and their regular antiepileptic therapy. Therapy consisted of establishing trust through physical contact and the development of physical activities that would enhance self-perception, self-respect, and self-responsibility. Children in the drug therapy group received neuroleptics regularly; in addition, two children also received their regular antiepileptics. All of the children were observed during a 3-month period for 18 time slots. Hyperactive behavior was observed and estimated using six hyperactivity variables. This paper features case studies for each of the six children. The results of this study indicate the following: both groups displayed some improvement in certain aspects of hyperactivity; the Gestalt therapy did not transfer to other situations; and while the drug therapy group was not expected to display any changes, it did due to unknown reasons.

641. Invalid allowed to remove device: Georgia court says breathing machine may be taken off. (1989, November 22). *The New York Times*, **p. A18.**

This newspaper article reports that the Georgia Supreme Court ruled that Larry McAfee, a quadriplegic, has the constitutional right to have his respirator terminated. Mr. McAfee was involved in a motorcycle accident 4 years earlier that left him paralyzed and requiring the assistance of a respirator. Mr. McAfee also obtained the right to sedatives for relieving pain during the shutting-down procedure.

•J•

642. Jacobs, R., Samowitz, P., Levy, J. M., & Levy, P. H. (1989). Developing an AIDS prevention education program for persons with developmental disabilities. *Mental Retardation, 27*(4), 233–237.

The importance of developing and implementing appropriate AIDS prevention education programs for people with developmental disabilities and their caregivers is discussed in this article. While acknowledging the lack of specific data regarding the prevalence of HIV infection among this particular population, the authors emphasize the need to take immediate preventative action to minimize the threat to individuals at risk. This article outlines five specific obstacles that make it difficult to deliver AIDS education programs to all populations: It is necessary to discuss death, a subject that makes most people uncomfortable; it is difficult to discuss sexual behavior, a topic that often creates anxiety; it is difficult to discuss intravenous drug use, a topic that is not often taught to personnel working with people with developmental disabilities; information about AIDS is often confusing or misleading; and AIDS is associated with stigmatized groups, which overshadows the fact that AIDS is associated with "risk behaviors" and not "risk groups." The authors discuss principles for developing and adapting prevention programs so that these programs will be effective for individuals with developmental disabilities. In particular, this article examines the Health Belief Model because it has been successfully adapted for use in AIDS prevention education. It also describes the New York Young Adult Institute Model for AIDS education and presents practical strategies for effective education.

643. Jacobson, A. (1989). Physical and sexual assault histories among psychiatric outpatients. *American Journal of Psychiatry, 146*(6), 755–758.

This article describes a study that used a semistructured interview to gather complete histories of the physical and sexual assaults of 31 psychiatric outpatients. The results of this study reveal the following: 68% of these outpatients report having experienced major physical and/or sexual assaults, and most of the assaults had not been disclosed to past therapists. This article compares the assault histories of outpatients and inpatients and relates the findings of this study to clinical practice.

644. Jacobson, A., Koehler, J. E., & Jones-Brown, C. (1987). The failure of routine

assessment to detect histories of assault experienced by psychiatric patients. *Hospital and Community Psychiatry, 38*(4), 386–389.

This article describes a study that used structured interviews to uncover incidences of sexual or physical abuse among psychiatric patients. The results of this study reveal the following: Of 151 assaults reported, only 9 were recorded in patients' charts; and the information given in the chart often did not provide information about the assault beyond the fact that it occurred. The authors suggest that underreporting is due to not actively questioning patients about assault.

645. Jacobson, A., & Richardson, B. (1987). Assault experiences of 100 psychiatric inpatients: Evidence for the need for routine inquiry. *American Journal of Psychiatry, 144*(7), 908–913.

This article describes a study that interviewed 100 psychiatric inpatients about their history of physical and/or sexual assault. This study used assault scales and gathered detailed histories. This study found that 81% of these patients had experienced major physical and/or sexual assaults. The authors suggest that routine inquiries should be made into patients' assault history.

646. Jacobson, J. W. (1990). Regulations: Can they control staff compliance in human services systems? *Mental Retardation, 28*(2), 77–82.

This article suggests that current regulatory practices need to be complemented by management practices and policies that promote staff performance and compliance. It focuses on some management techniques, for example, promoting generalization and stimulus control.

647. Jacobson, J. W., & Ackerman, L. J. (1989). Psychological services for persons with mental retardation and psychiatric impairments. *Mental Retardation, 27*(1), 33–36.

This article presents the results of a study that examined the patterns in services provided to people with mental retardation and psychiatric impairments. The results of this study suggest that these services focus on clinical history, observation, and behavior checklists for diagnosis, and therapeutic efforts that address diverse aspects of interpersonal and social adjustment. The authors conclude that the benefits derived from these services were greater for people with mild or moderate retardation.

648. Jacobson, J. W., & Janicki, M. P. (1983). Observed prevalence of multiple developmental disabilities. *Mental Retardation, 21*(3), 87–94.

This article discusses the prevalence of autism, cerebral palsy, epilepsy, and mental retardation in a population of 43,692 people with developmental disabilities. Twenty-seven percent of these cases had two or more reported conditions. The authors estimate the prevalence of these conditions in the general population and describe the procedure for making this estimation.

649. Jacobson, J. W., & Otis, J. P. (1992). Limitations of regulations as a means of social reform in developmental disabilities. *Mental Retardation, 30*(3), 163–171.
This article discusses the power and limits of regulations and regulatory agencies to improve living conditions for people with mental retardation. The authors provide a brief history of the growth of regulation in New York State. They point out that regulations can create greater order in a system, but they often fail to improve human interactions or ensure justice. They suggest that regulations often provide short-term solutions to specific problems, but they can also cause long-term problems by inhibiting positive and spontaneous human behavior.

650. Jaffe, P. G., Sudermann, M., & Reitzel, D. (1992). Child witnesses of marital violence. In R. T. Ammerman & M. Hersen (Eds.), *Assessment of family violence: A clinical and legal sourcebook* (pp. 313–331). New York: John Wiley & Sons.
This chapter discusses child witnesses of family violence and presents background information regarding this area of research. Assessment approaches are examined as they relate to behavioral adjustment, subtle effects of witnessing spousal violence, and post-traumatic stress disorder. The authors also illustrate legal issues using a case history.

651. James, D. H. (1986). Neuroleptics and epilepsy in mentally handicapped patients. *Journal of Mental Deficiency Research, 30*, 185–189.
This article discusses a retrospective study that examined the hospital records of a group of 217 people with moderate and severe mental retardation, who had been in the hospital for more than 20 years, in order to determine if the prescription of neuroleptics had any effects on the occurrence of seizures. Of the 217 people reviewed in this study, 126 had received neuroleptic medication, and 39 out of this 126 had a history of epileptic seizures. Twenty-seven of these people had epilepsy prior to admission, 5 had epilepsy before receiving neuroleptics, and 4 had history of epilepsy in infancy and childhood. One person had seizures from a cerebrovascular accident. The results of this study indicate the following: neuroleptic treatment did not precipitate seizures in patients without a past history of convulsions, and neuroleptic treatment increased the number of seizures in certain patients with a history of epilepsy who were receiving inadequate anticonvulsant medication or whose seizures were poorly controlled despite adequate anticonvulsant levels. This article suggests certain guidelines for clinical practice based on the findings of this study.

652. Janicki, M. P., & Jacobson, J. W. (1982). The character of developmental disabilities in New York State: Preliminary observations. *International Journal of Rehabilitation Research, 5*(2), 191–202.
This article examines the population characteristics of people with developmental disabilities living in New York. The Developmental Disabilities Information Survey (DDIS) was used to survey 36,334 people with developmental disabilities (34% children, 66% adults) or who received developmental services. The findings of this survey indicate the following: people with developmental disabilities more often lived in community settings rather than institutions, most of these people had mental retardation, more children than adults had secondary conditions such as cerebral palsy or epilepsy, and approximately 50% of these people had physical disabilities.

653. Janofsky, J. S. (1986). Munchausen syndrome in a mother and daughter: An unusual presentation of folie a deux. *Journal of Nervous and Mental Disease, 174*(6), 368–370.
The author of this article describes the presentation of Munchausen syndrome by proxy in a mother and daughter. Both the mother and the daughter reported similar complaints when admitted to the same hospital. The physician who referred them both for neurologic services was the mother's son.

654. Jarde, O., Marc, B., Dwyer, J., Fournier, P., Carlier-Pasquier, H., & Lenoir, L. (1992). Maltreatment of the aged in the home environment in northern France: A year survey (1990). *Medicine and Law, 11*, 641–648.
This article reports the result of a survey of 25 home care nursing units and two hospitals in the northern region of France. Fifty-five cases of abuse were recorded: 12 women, and 43 men. Alcohol use was a precipitating factor in 19 cases. The physical consequences of the abuse include the following: bruises, blisters, superficial burns, and fractures of the ribs and skull. None of the offenses resulted in penal consequences for the offenders.

655. Jason, J., & Andereck, N. D. (1983). Fatal child abuse in Georgia: The epidemiology of severe physical child abuse. *Child Abuse & Neglect, 7*, 1–9.
In this article, 51 child abuse deaths that occurred over a 4-year period were compared to abuse cases and the general population in Georgia. This comparison shows the following: Children of families in receipt of Aid to Families with Dependent Children were 3.7 times at greater risk of abuse-related fatality than the comparison cases, and families of the fatality cases were characterized by the young age of the child and parents and the family's socioeconomic status. This article states that these varia-

bles were comparable to those found in the literature on severe child abuse cases.

656. Jaudes, P. K., & Diamond, L. J. (1985). The handicapped child and child abuse. *Child Abuse and Neglect, 9*(3), 341–347.

This article claims that the growth and development of children with disabilities can be affected by abuse (including sexual abuse) and neglect. By examining the experience of 37 children with cerebral palsy who have been maltreated and reviewing the literature in related areas, the authors identified the following four problems as crucial to the study of abuse and neglect of the child with disabilities: 1) abuse that causes disabilities, 2) abuse that occurs to the child with disabilities, 3) compromises in care that can occur when the child with disabilities becomes involved with the medical and legal systems, and 4) arrangements for foster care or other out-of-home placement for the child with disabilities. The authors conclude that the very systems designed to protect and care for the child often fail, leaving the child with disabilities without the opportunity to reach developmental potential. In light of these observations, they recommend that the pediatrician not only be aware of the existence of abuse and neglect of children with disabilities, but they should also serve in the dual role of coordinator of services and advocate for these children.

657. Jaudes, P. K., & Diamond, L. J. (1986). Neglect of chronically ill children. *American Journal of Diseases of Children, 140,* 655–658.

This article describes the results of a retrospective chart review (1977–1984) of a Chicago hospital. This review found that 61 children with chronic illnesses had been reported to the State Protection Agency as neglected. Forms of neglect included the following: medical care neglect (65%), educational neglect (8%), abandonment (14%), emotional neglect (4%), and physical neglect (9%). Although the nature of the data does not allow estimates of incidence, the authors conclude that neglect is a serious concern for many children with chronic illnesses.

658. Jeffs, A. (1993, February 12). Mother's rare disorder puts child in jeopardy, Alberta gov't alleges. *The Edmonton Journal,* p. A8.

This newspaper article reports that Alberta Family and Social Services is trying to gain custody of a 21-month-old girl with cerebral palsy whose mother is believed to have Munchausen syndrome by proxy. This syndrome is characterized by frequent medical visits and treatment concerning the child that are unnecessary and sometimes lead to induced illness in the child, constituting child abuse.

659. Jehu, D. (1992). Adult survivors of sexual abuse. In R. T. Ammerman & M. Hersen (Eds.), *Assessment of family*

violence: A clinical and legal sourcebook (pp. 348–370). **New York: John Wiley & Sons.**

This chapter examines the case history and assessment of an adult survivor of sexual abuse who has psychological problems. The author discusses post-traumatic stress reaction, mood disturbances, interpersonal problems, and sexual dysfunction and examines the legal issues surrounding this case.

660. Jellinek, M. S., Murphy, M. J., Poitrast, F., Quinn, D., Bishop, S. J., & Goshko, M. (1992). Serious child mistreatment in Massachusetts: The course of 206 children through the courts. *Child Abuse & Neglect, 16,* 179–185.

The authors of this article describe a study that followed 206 children through the Boston Juvenile Court system. During 1985 and 1986, 206 seriously neglected or physically abused children under the age of 13 were followed prospectively over a 4-year period. These children had all been brought before the Boston Juvenile Court on care and protection petitions. The average age of the children was 4.2 years, with an almost equal distribution of boys and girls, and 67% of the the children were minorities. The average length of stay in temporary foster care for these children was 2.3 years. The results of this study include the following: Substance abuse for at least one parent was evident in 43% of cases, 84% of the parents had psychiatric disorders, and 81% of the parents had been reported to the Department of Social Services because of the abuse and neglect of their children. The court's decision to return the child to his or her parents depended on the parents' compliance with court-ordered services.

661. Jenkins, E. J., Bell, C. C., Taylor, J., & Walker, L. (1989). Circumstances of sexual and physical victimization of Black psychiatric outpatients. 93rd Annual Convention & Scientific Assembly of the National Medical Association (1988, Los Angeles, California). *Journal of the National Medical Association, 81*(3), 246–252.

This article discusses a study that examined African-American psychiatric outpatients who had been victims of sexual assault or physical assault. The results of this study indicate the following: Women were more likely to report that they were victimized as adults than men, men were more likely to report that they were victimized as children, childhood assault typically occurred before the onset of psychiatric symptoms, and adult assault typically took place after psychiatric difficulties had been identified. The authors conclude that mental illness increases vulnerability to victimization and that childhood victimization may contribute to later psychiatric difficulties.

662. Jennings, S. (Ed.). (1987). *Drama-therapy: Theory and practice for teach-*

ers and clinicians. **London: Brookline Books.**

This book is intended for clinical practitioners or teachers who want to use role playing in their therapeutic work. It contains 12 chapters on dramatherapy: "Dramatherapy and groups" (Jennings), "Playing on many stages: Dramatherapy and the individual" (Gordon), "Dramatherapy and play" (Gersie), "Dramatherapy and drama" (Powley), "Dramatherapy and psychodrama" (Davies), "A systems approach to dramatherapy" (Shuttleworth), "Dramatherapy and the teacher" (Courtney), "Dramatherapy with disturbed adolescents" (Jennings & Gerse), "Dramatherapy with people with a mental handicap" (Brudenell), "Dramatherapy in a psychiatric day centre" (Whitelock), "Dramatherapy with elderly people" (Langley), and "Dramatherapy in in-patient psychiatric settings" (Mitchell). This book includes a list of training courses, associations, and journals associated with dramatherapy, and it contains a few chapters dealing with the use of dramatherapy with people who are mentally retarded and have behavioral disturbances and psychiatric impairments.

663. Jernberg, A. M. (1979). *Theraplay: A new treatment using structured play for problem children and their families.* **San Francisco: Jossey-Bass.**

This book presents theraplay, a new form of psychotherapy to treat emotional disturbances experienced by children and adults. Theraplay has its roots in psychoanalysis, developmental psychology, and nursery school practice. It is presented as a practical approach because it demonstrates quick visible results. This book contains 13 chapters: "Theraplay—History and method," "Theraplay sessions and instructions for the therapist," "Individual theraplay for children," "Group theraplay for children," "Family theraplay," "Special settings for treatment", "Underactive and overactive children," "Handicapped children," "Autistic children," "Adolescents," "Adults," "Selecting and training therapists," and "Future directions."

664. Johnson, P. J., & Rubin, A. (1983). Case management in mental health: A social work domain? *Social Work,* **28(1), 49–55.**

The authors of this article recommend the use of case management as an approach to caring for the multiple needs of people with disabilities. This approach is considered particularly important as a strategy in the context of deinstitutionalization. In the case management approach, one worker, specifically the case manager, links the client to the complex service delivery system. It is the case manager's responsibility to ensure that the client receives appropriate services. The authors discuss the difficulty in simultaneously integrating psychotherapeutic and sociotherapeutic orientations to social work practice that also fit case management and the specific needs of the client with chronic mental disability. They also discuss the problematic nature of concluding that social work can claim case management

as part of its domain. The authors conclude that case management and its impact need to be more clearly understood and it will be necessary to determine which practitioners want to or may be best suited to implement the requisite assortment of tasks.

665. Johnson, P. R., Grant, D., & Wilson, J. S. T. (1983). Group sexuality counselling: Further research findings. *Journal of Practical Approaches to Developmental Handicap,* **7(2), 14–18.**

This article discusses the effectiveness of a 10-week group sexuality counseling program for people with mental disabilities. It describes the preassessments and postassessments conducted with the 15 participants, who were between 22 and 45 years of age, using the Sexuality Development Index. It includes procedural aspects of the program and the results of the assessments.

666. Johnson, T. F., O'Brien, J. G., & Hudson, M. F. (1985). *Elder neglect and abuse: An annotated bibliography.* **Westport, CT: Greenwood Press.**

This bibliography features 144 annotations of articles and books dealing with the subject of elder abuse and neglect. For most annotations, topic, objective, methods, and conclusions are clearly denoted. It also includes an additional unannotated bibliography and a directory of organizations that provide services to the elderly living in the United States. The Model Adult Protective Services Act prepared by the Senate Select Committee on Aging is included in the Appendix.

667. Jones, E. E. (1984). *Social stigma: The psychology of marked relationships.* **New York: W. H. Freeman.**

This book uses a social/psychological analytic approach to examine the relationship between "marked" and normal people and the stigmatizing conditions concerning that relationship. The term *marked* refers to people with disabilities or people who are disfigured.

668. Jones, J. W., Joy, D. S., & Martin, S. L. (1990). A multidimensional approach for selecting child care workers. *Psychological Reports,* **67, 543–553.**

This article consists of a series of validation studies that examine the use of the Personnel Selection Inventory as a screening and selection tool for child-care workers. The inventory consists of five psychological scales assessing honesty, drug avoidance, nonviolence, emotional stability, and safety, and an additional distortion scale assesses respondent candidness. The participants consisted of the following: child-care workers who worked with children with disabilities in a nursing home setting, adult child-care volunteer workers, and adults convicted of sexual abuse and rape of children. Cross-validation was conducted using the following measurement tools: the EMO Questionnaire, which assesses for emotional maladjustment; the Minnesota Multiphasic Personality Inventory; the Maudsley Personality Inventory; and the

Child Abuse Potential Inventory. The results indicate that the Personnel Selection Inventory correlated with child-care workers' job performance and identified sex offenders.

669. Judge acquits nurse charged in deaths of three patients. (1988, June 23). *The New York Times*, **p. A20.**
This newspaper article reports that Jane Bolding, a nurse charged in the deaths of three patients by means of lethal injection, was acquitted by Judge Joseph S. Casula on the grounds of insufficient evidence. It states that no witnesses were found to support the case against Bolding. An investigation was initiated when records showed that Ms. Bolding was the primary care nurse on duty when 57 patients experienced cardiac arrest.

670. Jullian-Reynier, C., MacQuart-Moulin, G., Moatti, J. P., Loundou, A., Aurran, Y., Chabal, F., & Ayme, S. (1993). Attitudes of women of childbearing age towards prenatal diagnosis in southeastern France. *Prenatal Diagnosis, 13,* **613–627.**
This article reports the results of a survey of 514 French women in 1990 concerning their attitudes toward prenatal diagnosis. Most (78%) of these women indicated that they would want an amniocentesis and consider abortion if they had a 1% chance of having a baby with trisomy 21. Women who already knew and had established relationships with children with Down syndrome were less likely to want an amniocentesis or to consider abortion. Women who had more positive estimations regarding the capabilities of children with Down syndrome were also less likely to want amniocentesis or to consider abortion.

671. Jurkowski, E., & Amado, A. N. (1993). Affection, love, intimacy, and sexual relationships. In A. N. Amado (Ed.), *Friendships and community connections between people with and without developmental disabilities* **(pp. 129–151). Baltimore: Paul H. Brookes Publishing Co.**
This chapter describes the sexuality and the sexual needs of people with developmental disabilities. It is primarily concerned with showing that the sexuality of people with developmental disabilities is normal and acceptable. It stresses that many of society's difficulties with the sexuality of people with developmental disabilities is the result of a history of labeling, segregation, and differential treatment of people with developmental disabilities. Even though the authors address the risks of exploitation, abuse, and violence associated with community integration and normalization, they provide a balanced context, suggesting that these risks are better controlled by preparing people to make reasonable choices and exercise reasonable caution rather than by restricting personal rights in the hope of reducing risks.

(Editors' note: Several studies support the contention that community integration decreases risk of abuse and that isolation associated with segregation and institutionalization increases risk.)

672. Justice, B., & Justice, R. (1990). *The abusing family* **(rev. ed.). New York: Plenum.**
The authors of this book present a social environmental model of abusive families. While there is little specific discussion about children with disabilities, the authors state that differences exist across societies regarding how children with disabilities are treated and that treatment of children with disabilities depends partially on the social valuation of such children.

•K•

673. Kaeser, F. (1992). Can people with severe mental retardation consent to mutual sex? *Sexuality and Disability, 10*(1), **33–42.**
This article addresses the issue of consent to mutual sex and people with severe mental retardation in an institutionalized setting. It examines the need to protect the individual from harm versus the right of the individual to express himself or herself. This article discusses the redefinition of consent and illustrates aspects of a management plan.

674. Kahn, G., & Goldman, E. (1991). Munchausen syndrome by proxy: Mother fabricates infant's hearing impairment. *Journal of Speech and Hearing Research, 34,* **957–959.**
This article features the case of a mother's fabrication of her 11-month-old daughter's sensorineural hearing loss. It presents a summary of the child's medical records as well as a review of the mother's actions during the ordeal. The authors stress the need to combat this type of abuse by obtaining documented medical reports for the confirmation of case histories.

675. Kalichman, S. C., Craig, M. E., & Follingstad, D. R. (1990). Professionals' adherence to mandatory child abuse reporting laws: Effects of responsibility attribution, confidence ratings, and situational factors. *Child Abuse & Neglect, 14,* **69–77.**
This article discusses a study that examined the association between attribution of responsibility and reporting of child abuse among licensed psychologists. Two hundred ninety-five psychologists from South Carolina (147) and Georgia (148) completed a questionnaire containing vignettes dealing with child sexual abuse. The vignettes differed with regard to the gender of the child

and with the admittance of guilt by the father. After reading the vignettes, the psychologists were asked to rate the degree of relative responsibility pertaining to the father, mother, child, and society for the child abuse situation. The psychologists were also asked to rate both their likelihood to report the child abuse and their confidence in knowing that abuse had taken place on a 6-point Likert scale. The results of this study indicate the following: mothers were more often attributed greater blame if the father denied any allegations of abuse; reporting child abuse was not predicted by the attribution of responsibility; confidence in knowing that abuse had taken place was related to greater likelihood of reporting child abuse; and male psychologists attributed more responsibility for the abuse to the father than female psychologists, who blamed the mothers more frequently than the fathers.

676. Kallen, E. (1989). *Label me human: Minority rights of stigmatized Canadians.* **Toronto: University of Toronto Press.**
This book discusses human rights for alcoholics, people with disabilities, and gays and lesbians. It examines the formation of stigma and the attachment and removal of stigmas. The author offers some strategies in order to ensure greater recognition and protection for minority groups who are stigmatized.

677. Kaminer, Y., Feinstein, C., & Barrett, R. P. (1987). Suicidal behavior in mentally retarded adolescents: An overlooked problem. *Child Psychiatry and Human Development, 18*(2), 90–94.
The authors of this article suggest that suicide and suicidal behavior are overlooked in people with mental retardation. They discuss three cases of suicidal behavior in inpatient adolescents with mental retardation, and they note that cognitive deficits do not imply a decreased risk for suicide.

678. Kantrowitz, B. (1993, August 2). Wild in the streets. *Newsweek,* **pp. 40–49.**
This article discusses the growing violence of teenage gangs, especially assaults and murder. One particular story in this article involves a 55-year-old man, Charles Conrad from Atlanta, who suffered from multiple sclerosis. Mr. Conrad's mobility was limited to the use of a walker or wheelchair. Coming home one early evening, he confronted or was confronted by three teenagers ages 14, 15, and 17, who were in the process of burglarizing his home. The three teenagers tortured Mr. Conrad over the next few hours. Mr. Conrad's injuries consisted of stab wounds made by a knife and barbecue fork, beatings with a hammer and a shotgun barrel, and strangulation by rope. At one point, believing the victim to be dead, one of the youths poured salt into the wounds. Mr. Conrad finally died after being hit over the head by a brass eagle. The boys drove off in his van and were arrested the next day by police.

679. Kastner, T., DeLotto, P., Scagnelli, B., & Testa, W. R. (1990). Proposed guidelines for agencies serving persons with developmental disabilities and HIV infection. *Mental Retardation, 28*(3), 139–145.
This article proposes procedural guidelines to reduce the risk for HIV infection for agencies caring for individuals with developmental disabilities. These guidelines attempt to ensure that individuals with developmental disabilities who are infected with the HIV virus have access to appropriate services. They describe the HIV procedures used by the Association for Retarded Citizens (Arc): A multidisciplinary committee was developed and recommended policy and guidelines related to HIV issues; procedures had to be applicable in every possible services setting, interpretable to several staff members, and flexible in order to accommodate the various disabilities of the clients; and procedures were meant to minimize the risk of transmission of the HIV virus.

680. Katz, H. (1994, Spring). Abuse & women's mental health: Recognizing long-term effects. *Abilities, 18,* 41–42.
This article discusses the relationship between violence against women and the mental health status of women who experience violence. It reviews a number of studies that link mental health difficulties in women with experiences of child abuse, sexual assault, or other forms of violence.

681. Katz, I., Glass, D. C., Lucido, D., & Farber, J. (1979). Harm-doing and victim's racial or orthopedic stigma as determinants of helping behavior. *Journal of Personality, 47*(2), 340–364.
This article describes three experiments that were carried out to determine whether unintentional harm doers would be more inclined to make restitutions to victims stigmatized by race, physical disability, or neither. The first experiment examined African-American versus White victims. In the second experiment, the victims either did or did not use a wheelchair. The last experiment involved a person with a disability and a person without disabilities. This article describes the method used for all three experiments. The results of these experiments indicate that nonintentional harm doers were more inclined to make restitutions to stigmatized victims than nonstigmatized victims.

682. Katz, I., Hass, R. G., & Bailey, J. (1988). Attitudinal ambivalence and behavior toward people. In H. E. Yuker (Ed.), *Attitudes toward persons with disabilities* (pp. 47–57). **New York: Springer.**
This chapter reviews ambivalence theory research, particularly the work of Katz and his colleagues. Ambivalence theory suggests that social attitudes toward marginalized people (e.g., people with disabilities, racial and ethnic minorities, and senior citizens) tend to be characterized by dual perceptions (i.e., deviant and dis-

advantaged). Positive responses to their disadvantaged status are common under many conditions, but other conditions, such as stress, result in predominantly negative responses. As a result, response amplification takes place. In response amplification, attitudes are extremely empathetic and behavior is extremely accommodating until conditions shift, and then attitudes and behavior rapidly become very negative.

683. Katz, J. (1992). Abuse of human beings for the sake of science. In A. L. Kaplan (Ed.), *When medicine went mad: Bioethics and the holocaust* (pp. 233–270). Totawa, NJ: Humana Press.

This chapter provides a concise history of some of the worst abuses in medical experimentation before, during, and after the notorious Nazi human experiments. People who were economically disadvantaged or disabled were often the subjects in such experiments: For example, in 1963, two physicians at a Brooklyn Hospital injected active cancer cells into 22 chronically ill and debilitated patients without their consent or knowledge. Although the two physicians were disciplined for failure to obtain informed consent, their peers elected one of the two vice presidents of the American Association for Cancer Research the following year and elected him president the year after his tenure as vice president.

684. Katz, M. B. (1986). Child-saving. *History of Education Quarterly, 26*(3), 413–424.

This article reviews recent literature that discusses the historical movement of child welfare reform in turn-of-the-century America and England. It presents several interpretations of differing social service, institutional, and family preservation movements. The author points out that a paradigm shift occurred in conjunction with a qualitative shift in the perception of children. Where formerly children were considered simply miniadults, the influence of Darwin led the way for children to be considered intrinsically unique and worthy in themselves.

685. Kaufman, B., & Wohl, A. (1992). *Casualties of childhood: A developmental perspective on sexual abuse using projective drawings.* New York: Brunner/Mazel.

This book uses a developmental perspective to explore childhood sexual abuse as it is reflected in the drawings of both abused children and adult survivors. Using the developmental perspective, the authors use normative latency goals, expectations, and tasks to probe the long-term sequelae of childhood sexual trauma.

686. Kaye, K., Elkind, L., Goldberg, D., & Tytun, A. (1989). Birth outcomes for infants of drug abusing mothers. *New York State Journal of Medicine, 89*(5), 256–261.

This article discusses a study that examined the birth outcomes for infants of drug-abusing mothers. In this study, 585 mother-infant cohorts who were recognized for maternal drug use were compared to a like number of controls. It divided the drug users into five categories representing the type of drug abuse: opiates without cocaine ($n=79$), cocaine without opiates ($n=382$), cocaine plus opiates ($n=96$), crack cocaine without opiates ($n=106$), other cocaine without opiates ($n=276$), and unspecified drug abuse ($n=28$). The results of this study indicate the following: Drug-exposed infants were significantly lower in birth weight and mean gestational age than controls; polydrug abuse during pregnancy was more detrimental to the infant's birth weight, gestational age, and hospital stay than single drug use during pregnancy; and crack-cocaine-exposed infants had lower birth weights and more adverse neurologic signs than infants exposed to other types of drugs.

687. Kaye, N. S., Borenstein, N. M., & Donnelly, S. M. (1990). Families, murder, and insanity: A psychiatric review of paternal neonaticide. *Journal of Forensic Sciences, 345*(1), 133–139.

This article examines paternal neonaticide, that is, the killing of a newborn less than 24 hours old by his or her father. It presents two historical case studies and two new case studies. A psychodynamic explanation is used to explain this type of behavior, and the authors suggest a new categorical subdivision of infanticide that would incorporate three subtypes characterized by the age of the newborn.

688. Kazak, A. E. (1986). Families with physically handicapped children: Social ecology and family systems. *Family Process, 25,* 265–281.

This article uses a social ecological perspective (which looks at the relationship between people and their environment) to examine research on families with children with physical and developmental disabilities. The first part of the article includes a review of the literature that identifies methodological difficulties in past studies. The second part of the article examines stress on the family, the child, parental roles, the marital relationship, and siblings (microsystem) and offers suggestions for future research. The third part of this article discusses the social support networks of families with children with physical and developmental disabilities (exosystem). This article also addresses the implications of a social ecological perspective on family assessment and intervention.

689. Kazmin, A. L. (1989, November 16). Judge negates $7.5 million for victim of rape. *Los Angeles Times,* pp. B1, B8.

This newspaper article reports on a rape case where Judge David M. Schacter of the San Fernando Superior Court ruled that there was insufficient evidence to prove that Andrea Nerpel suffered any damages or that the Laurelwood Convalescent Hospital, a North Hollywood nursing home, was negligent in her care. Ms. Nerpel, age 38, has been paralyzed and unable to communicate since a car accident at age 19. While a resident at the nursing home, she was raped and impregnated. This led to a subsequent abortion and her sterilization. The perpetrator was never identified. The $7.5 million in damages awarded by the jury to the plaintiff was negated by Judge Schacter.

690. Keilitz, I., & Van Duizend, R. (1986). Current trends in the involuntary civil commitment of mentally disabled persons. *Rehabilitation Psychology, 31*(1), 27–35.
This article examines current trends in involuntary civil commitment of people with developmental disabilities. In particular, it discusses two current trends: cooperation among legal and psychosocial professionals, and the use of informal proceedings imposed by the courts concerning involuntary civil commitment. This article concludes with a call on psychologists to play a greater role in this process.

691. Kelleher, M. E. (1987). Investigating institutional abuse: A post-substantiation model. *Child Welfare, 66*(4), 343–351.
This article describes a state's reaction to reported incidents of abuse at a child residential care facility. Using a postsubstantiation model geared toward institutional abuse, a team of investigators endeavored to address program problem areas and strengths instead of using a traditional investigation of isolated abuse and abuser. This article describes the reaction of the institutional staff to this method of investigation as cooperative but critical. Also, this article discusses implications for future policy development.

692. Kelley, S. J. (1994). Abuse of children in day care centres: Characteristics and consequences. *Child Abuse Review, 3*(1), 15–25.
This article reviews information on abuse of children in child-care centers. The author summarizes data from four studies of abuse in child-care settings. This article provides information about abuse in organized caregiving settings that has potential relevance for children with disabilities who are abused in service settings. Abuse in child-care settings is commonly accompanied by threats to preserve silence for participation in sexual relations between children and ritual abuse (in about one third of cases). Perpetrators include staff (45%), relatives of staff (25%), directors or owners (16%), nonchild-care staff (8%), and occasionally others (5%).

693. Kelly, L. (1992). The connections between disability and child abuse: A review of the research evidence. *Child Abuse Review, 1*, 157–167.
This article discusses the two major connections between child abuse and disability. It states that disability can be an outcome of abuse, and it also points out ways that disability may be linked to increased vulnerability. The author asserts that the exact nature of the connection

remains unclear from currently available evidence and discusses many problems with existing research. More and better research is recommended as a means of clarifying the relationship between abuse and disability and guiding future efforts to protect children.

694. Kelly, L. (1992). The evidential experience of children with disabilities. *Child Abuse Review, 1*, 188–190.
This article discusses the failure of the justice system to accommodate the needs of children with disabilities as crime victims and witnesses. It describes the process of criminal prosecution and how a child abuse victim is treated in this system. The author also discusses how families are treated by the system and argues for greater accommodation of the needs of children with disabilities and their families.

695. Kempe, C. H., Silverman, F. N., Steele, B. F., Droegemueller, W., & Silver, H. K. (1980). The battered-child syndrome. In G. J. Williams & J. Money (Eds.), *Traumatic abuse and neglect of children at home* (pp. 89–101). Baltimore: The John Hopkins University Press.
This chapter examines the battered child syndrome. It discusses neglect, bone fractures, subdural hematoma, failure to thrive, soft tissue injury, sudden death, and discrepancy between the medical diagnosis and the child's history provided by the parents. The authors stress that the physician's responsibility is to the child when there is a suspicion of child abuse.

696. Kempton, W. (1983). Teaching retarded children about sex. *PTA Today, 8*(6), 28–30.
This article discusses how parents can prepare children with mental retardation to cope with their emerging sexuality, not only in terms of biology, but in terms of emotional and social development.

697. Kempton, W., Gordon, S., & Bass, M. (1986). *Love, sex and birth control for mentally handicapped people: A guide for parents* (rev. ed.). Philadelphia: Planned Parenthood Association of Southeastern Pennsylvania.
The booklet offers parents of children with mental retardation suggestions for comfortably discussing sexuality with their children. In addition to discussing specific facts about reproduction, sexual intercourse, and the differences between male and female, this booklet addresses human sexuality, including the following: feelings, attitudes, behavior, and the manner in which people relate to both themselves and others. This booklet is divided into sections that address the following: sex education, what children should be told and how, preparation for puberty, homosexuality, dating, masturbation, intercourse, contraceptive methods, sexually transmitted diseases, birth control, abortion, vasectomy or tubal ligation, marriage and parenthood, and women with disabilities as mothers.

This booklet also includes a section on how to protect children with mental retardation from being sexually abused or exploited and includes detailed anatomical illustrations of a sexually developed young man and woman, fetuses at various stages of development, the birth of a baby, and birth control items.

698. Kendall Tackett, K. A., Meyer Williams, L., & Finkelhor, D. (1993). Impact of sexual abuse on children: A review and synthesis of recent empirical studies. *Psychological Bulletin*, *113*(1), 164–180.

This review of the literature examines 45 studies dealing with sexually abused children and the consequences of that abuse. These children generally display a variety of symptoms: post-traumatic stress disorder, anxiety, behavioral dysfunction, and self-esteem problems. This review notes age-specific symptoms and points out that 30% of this population does not display any symptoms, and it concludes that symptoms decrease over an extended period of time for more than half the victims.

699. Kennedy, M. (1989). The abuse of deaf children. *Child Abuse Review*, *3* (1), 3–6.

This article summarizes a survey that was conducted to examine how social workers and teachers of children who are deaf cope with the sexual abuse of these children. This survey highlighted the needs of these professionals, examined the difficulties of implementing prevention programs for children who are deaf, and drew attention to the need for awareness of the child abuse of children who are deaf. The most common response from these professionals was their lack of confidence while dealing with the sexual abuse of children who are deaf.

700. Kennedy, M. (1989). Child abuse—Disabled children suffer too. *Childright*, *60*, 18–20.

This article discusses the specific needs of children with disabilities that should be incorporated into services designed for treating abused children. It points out the difficulties children with disabilities face in reporting abuse, and it focuses on the similarities of treatment models for children with and without disabilities and the differences in implementing these programs. The author suggests that training should include the nature and implications of disabilities and communication difficulties.

701. Kennedy, M. (1989). The deaf child as a double victim. *Social Work Today*, *21*(4), 18–20.

This article reports the results of a 1988 study that surveyed social workers and teachers of children who are deaf. This survey indicates the following: Children who are deaf and sexually abused have low self-esteem, and they feel isolated and confused not only as a result of the abuse, but because of the disability as well. This article points out that children who are deaf feel that they have

been abused because of their disability. The author suggests that these children need to be taught that deafness and abuse are two different issues.

702. Kennedy, M. (1989, March). Sexual abuse: A survivor's story. *Soundbarrier*, pp. 10–11.

This article summarizes the childhood sexual abuse experience of a woman who is deaf. In this article, she explains how her disability and abuse resulted in low self-esteem and a suicide attempt. She describes her suffering and feelings of betrayal and her stages of recovery. This article also includes guidelines for detecting different types of abuse.

703. Kennedy, M. (1989). The silent nightmare. *Soundbarrier*, 22, 9.

This article discusses the need to pay closer attention to the abuse of children who are deaf. It claims that most services (e.g., sexual abuse prevention programs, phone help-lines, and diagnostic treatment techniques) are not appropriate for children who are deaf. This article concludes that it is necessary to prioritize the services for children who are deaf.

704. Kennedy, M. (1990). The deaf child who is sexually abused—Is there a need for a dual specialist? *Child Abuse Review*, 4(2), 3–6.

This article emphasizes the importance of communication between the counselor and children who are deaf. It suggests that counseling should be done in the child's mode of communication, and a child who is deaf receives better help from a professional who is trained both in sexual abuse and deaf issues, in other words, a dual specialist. This article applies Finkelhor's model to children who are deaf in order to describe and explain negative outcomes of abuse.

705. Kennedy, M. (1990). No more secrets— Please. *Deafness*, 6(1), 10–12.

This article presents the goals of Keep Deaf Children Safe (KDCS) and highlights the reasons for the vulnerability of children who are deaf. It emphasizes the urgent need to address the lack of services for children who are deaf and their families, and it points out that this lack of services may lead to increased stress levels for these families, which might also increase the probability of child abuse.

706. Kennedy, M. (1992). Children with severe disabilities: Too many assumptions. *Child Abuse Review*, 1, 185–187.

This article describes how two children with severe disabilities were affected by sexual abuse and how their behavior and adaptive functioning improved after they were taken into care. It also discusses the general issues of how children with severely impaired communication may not be considered competent witnesses and how they may be excluded from access to appropriate treatment services.

707. Kennedy, M. (1992). Not the only way to communicate: A challenge to voice in child protection work. *Child Abuse Review, 1,* 169–177.

This article is written for child protection workers and features different communication techniques and tools available for use with abused children with disabilities. The augmentative communication techniques examined in this article include the following: sign language for use with children who are hearing impaired or hearing impaired/visually impaired, Makaton symbols over text for use with children with language disorders, and communication boards and computers for use with children with cerebral palsy or multiple disabilities.

708. Kennedy, M., & Kelly, L. (1992). Inclusion not exclusion. *Child Abuse Review, 1*(3), 147–149.

This guest editorial provides an introduction to the articles in the issue that focus on abuse and disability. It also discusses the exclusion of children with disabilities from child abuse prevention and intervention services. The authors acknowledge that some progress has been made toward inclusion, but they suggest that much more is still needed and urge all involved to create service parity for children with disabilities.

709. Kent, J., Cartwright, D., & Ossorio, P. (1990). Attitudes of peer groups toward paraplegic individuals. In M. Nagler (Ed.), *Perspectives on disability* (pp. 601–607). Palo Alto, CA: Health Markets Research.

This chapter describes a study that used two experiments to assess the attitudes of peer groups toward paraplegic individuals. The first experiment employed an unstructured interview where 10 university students without disabilities were questioned about their beliefs, feelings, and concerns regarding paraplegics. The results from the interviews were represented by two factor groups: those issues discouraging friendship and those issues encouraging friendships. In the second experiment, 30 students were asked to complete Form A of the Attitudes Toward Disabled Persons Scale (ATDP Scale). After completing Form A, the students viewed a 28-minute film portraying the life of a person with disabilities. This was followed by Form B of the ATDP Scale. The results from the second experiment indicate an increase in positive attitudes toward people with disabilities following the film. The authors suggest that there is a degree of role uncertainty for individuals without disabilities when interacting with individuals who have disabilities, and they feel that experience with and education about people with disabilities is one means by which this relationship can be strengthened.

710. Kent, J. T. (1980). A follow-up study of abused children. In G. J. Williams & J. Money (Eds.), *Traumatic abuse and neglect of children at home* (pp. 291–303). Baltimore: The Johns Hopkins University Press.

This chapter discusses a study on child abuse that examined intervention and the effects of child abuse independent of socioeconomic status (SES). This study included 219 nonaccidental trauma (NAT) and 159 gross neglect (NEG) children under court protection in Los Angeles County. As well, 185 families who requested protective services (PS) from the County Department of Public Social Service (DPSS) made up a nonabused group with evidence of family dysfunction and low SES. The data for this study were collected with a survey questionnaire filled out by a case worker using information gained from DPSS records, hospital records, police investigation reports, foster home reports, and school reports. The results of this study indicate the following: The children in the two abused groups gained weight and height while in foster care; both abused groups improved on most problem behavior variables and academic and peer relation variables in school after intervention; when compared to the PS group, the two abused groups displayed greater behavior problems when entering foster care; and when compared to the abused groups, the PS group functioned better academically when entering foster care. This chapter concludes that the effects of an abusive environment on children is independent of SES and family dysfunction and that intervention alleviates some of the effects of abuse.

711. Kent Public Schools. (1985). *Self-protection for the handicapped: A curriculum designed to teach handicapped persons to avoid exploitation.* Seattle, WA: Author. (ERIC Document Reproduction Service No. ED 263 705)

This curriculum is a modification of the Curriculum for Developing an Awareness of Sexual Exploitation and Teaching Self-Protection Techniques developed by the Developmental Disabilities Project of Seattle Rape Relief Center. The self-protection curriculum contains one level instead of the two contained in the original curriculum: This design change was instituted so that younger children (ages 8 to 13) or students with more disabilities could be taught the first five units during the first few presentations of the curriculum; the vocabulary has been simplified and some lessons omitted, while others have been added; where possible, third-person characteristics have been changed to first person in the narrative stories, making them easier to identify with; references to rape and sexual exploitation have largely been omitted because the self-protection curriculum deals with exploitation in general rather than specifically with sexual exploitation, and since many students have little knowledge of sexual intercourse, the concept of rape would have no meaning for them; where the original curriculum refers to a victim as being raped, the self-protection curriculum refers to the victim as being "hurt"; and this curriculum discusses appropriate and inappropriate touching. This curriculum has been evaluated and selected as a model program for use in the state of Washington.

712. Kiernan, C. (1988). **Child abuse: A case for change.** *British Journal of Special Education,* *15*(4), 140–142.
This article discusses procedures for handling allegations of physical or emotional abuse of residential school children enrolled in special education programs. This article examines the placement system used to decide where these children will live, focusing on placement in private and voluntary centers and the regulation of the centers. The author offers suggestions for ensuring the rights of these children.

713. The killing of Kevin Thorpe. (1989, August 8). *The New York Times,* p. A18.
This editorial concerns Keven Thorpe, a 31-year-old Brooklyn man with mental retardation who suffocated while being restrained by 10 police officers. It questions the policemen's handling of Mr. Thorpe and the department's handling of the case. In particular, it asks why department guidelines for the handling of emotionally disturbed individuals were not followed.

714. Kinzl, J., & Biebl, W. (1991). **Sexual abuse of girls: Aspects of the genesis of mental disorders and therapeutic implications.** *Acta Psychiatrica Scandinavica,* *83,* 427–431.
This article discusses a study that assessed 33 women with a history of sexual child abuse for mental disorders. This study performed psychiatric assessments, gathered biographic information, and conducted a structured interview with each of the women treated at the Psychosomatic Division of the Department of Psychiatry at the University Clinics of Innsbruck in 1989. The women ranged in age from 17 to 44, with an average age of 27. Mental and psychosomatic disorders were categorized according to the *Diagnostic and Statistical Manual of Mental Disorders (DSM-III-R).* The results of this study indicate the following: 1) anxiety disorders were the most frequent presentations among these women; 2) 87% of these women experienced very severe sexual abuse in childhood; 3) fathers (48%) and stepfathers/male companions (24%) perpetrated most of the abuse; 4) these women came from families with a large number of children in the household, with 54% of families having more than four children; and 5) these women came from families where the mother experienced chronic depression and tranquillizer abuse and the fathers abused alcohol. The authors conclude that the high frequency of anxiety disorders in these women who had experienced childhood sexual abuse is caused by ego weakness resulting from helplessness and betrayal in situations of separation.

715. Kisabith, K. L., & Richardson, D. B. (1985). **Changing attitudes toward disabled individuals: The effect of one disabled person.** *Therapeutic Recreation Journal,* *19*(2nd quarter), 24–33.
The integration of a person with a spinal cord injury into an instructional sports class with 41 university students is examined in this article. It claims that a positive change in attitudes resulted from this integration. This article concludes that people with disabilities must take an active role in helping to change attitudes toward people with disabilities.

716. Kleinman, P. K. (1987). *Diagnostic imaging of child abuse.* Baltimore: Williams & Wilkins.
This book provides a wealth of information for physicians on the use of imaging techniques to identify child abuse. Chapter 8, "Head trauma," is of particular interest and provides a review of studies that suggest that mental retardation and other developmental disabilities often result from child abuse: For example, one of the cited studies found that 64% of all head injurics of 84 infants between 3 weeks and 11 months of age admitted to the hospital with a diagnosis of head injury or abnormal CAT scan (computerized tomography) and 95% of the most serious injuries were secondary to child abuse.

717. Kline, D. F. (1982). *The disabled child and child abuse.* Chicago: National Committee for Prevention of Child Abuse.
This document discusses the relationship between child abuse and disability, and it addresses the problems of multiple placements. It points out that there are an estimated 8 million children with disabilities in the United States, 7% of whom acquired the disability after birth. This document discusses the following topics: educational neglect, the relationship between abuse and the presence of a child with a disability in the family, prevention, and help for parents.

718. Kline, D. F., & Kline, A. C. (1987). *The disabled child and child abuse.* Chicago: National Committee for Prevention of Child Abuse.
This booklet on children with disabilities and child abuse addresses some of the issues concerned with abuse resulting in disability and abuse of children with disabilities. The authors touch on the incidence of disability in infants and examine some factors that could lead to an increase in child abuse of children with disabilities. Also, the authors suggest some prevention measures.

719. Kloeppel, D. A., & Hollins, S. (1989). **Double handicap: Mental retardation and death in the family.** *Death Studies,* *13,* 31–38.
Using four case studies, the authors examine the expression of grief or bereavement in people with mental retardation in response to the loss of a family member. The case studies feature the reactions of people with developmental disabilities who are in a residence, in an institution, and live at home. The case studies feature the loss of a parent, a sibling, and a relative. The authors

offer suggestions for bereavement intervention techniques that might be used with people with mental retardation.

720. Knutson, J. F., & Sullivan, P. M. (1993). Communicative disorders as a risk factor in abuse. *Topics in Language Disorders, 13*(4), 1–14.

This article reviews the literature on the relationship between communicative disorders and child abuse and provides additional data on this relationship collected at the Boys Town National Research Hospital in Omaha, Nebraska. While the authors warn that their data are not a representative sample of children and, therefore, the application of findings based on these data may be limited, they present a number of tentative findings. First, the abuse of children with impaired communication appears to be more severe than the abuse of other children. Second, impaired communication interferes with the interview process required for investigation of abuse. Third, the risk for sexual abuse appears to be elevated even more than the risk for other forms of abuse for children with impaired communication. Fourth, the risk of extrafamilial abuse appears to increase more than the risk for intrafamilial abuse for this group. The authors make a number of recommendations for professionals working with children with impaired communication based on these findings.

721. Kocur, M. (1993). Amanda was not believed. *ARCH•Type, 10*(6), 14–15.

This article describes the abuse of a blind woman by adolescents in her neighborhood. Although she reported the abuse to police, they told her that there was little that they could do unless she could visually identify the offenders.

722. Koegel, P. (1986). You are what you drink: Evidence of socialized incompetence in the life of a mildly retarded adult. In L. L. Langness & H. G. Levine (Eds.), *Culture and retardation: Life histories of mildly mentally retarded persons in American society* **(pp. 47–63). Dordrecht, the Netherlands: D. Reidel.**

This chapter examines nonnormative behavior displayed by people with developmental disabilities that is not a physiologically exclusive product, but is a process of socialization. The author addresses deviance theory and then focuses on a case example of an adult male with developmental disabilities to help illustrate how family attitudes, expectations, and exposure to new experiences help shape behavior.

723. Kord, D. (1982, March 29–April 2). *A family-oriented approach to the treatment of developmentally-delayed preschoolers.* **Paper presented at the 59th Annual Meeting of the American Orthopsychiatric Association, San Francisco.**

This paper presents the role of family therapy in a clinic for preschoolers with developmental delays. Two types of families are believed to benefit from the use of a family therapy approach: families in which the needs of the child are misunderstood or misread, and families with dysfunctional transactional patterns that antedated the child's difficulties. It describes the process of the initial screening and assessment sessions and presents the approaches used by the family therapist to "seduce" the family into therapy. The author concludes that the family therapist needs to collaborate with other therapists and requires considerable sophistication concerning child development.

724. Kottke, J. L., Mellor, S., & Schmidt, A. C. (1987). Effects of information on attitudes toward and interpersonal acceptance of persons who are deaf. *Rehabilitation Psychology, 32*(4), 239–244.

This article discusses a study that examined 225 university students concerning how information affects attitudes toward and interpersonal acceptance of people who are deaf. In this study, students were first asked to complete the Attitudes Toward Disabled Persons Scale (Form O) and the California F-scale, and then, they were presented with two gender-neutral cover stories concerning a student's application for university: one story involved one of two deaf conditions and the other story involved a nondeaf condition. After reading the cover story, the Interpersonal Judgement Scale and Attitudes Toward Deafness Scale were completed by the students. Those students who read a cover story involving a deaf-label condition were more positive in their attitudes than those students who read a cover story involving the deaf-description condition and the nondeaf condition. The study found that more information led to a less positive attitude toward people who are deaf, although this finding was not significant. Also, this study found no support for the idea that information affected interpersonal acceptance.

725. Krantz, J., & Frank, C. (1990). Institutional approaches to child abuse. *Journal of Child and Youth Care, 4*(6), 35–43.

The authors of this article approach the problem of institutional child abuse from a systematic perspective. They believe that looking at specific individual cases of abuse masks the contribution of the organization as a whole to the incidence and maintenance of child abuse. They discuss how hierarchical staffing, environmental neglect, and lack of leadership in integrating the facility may initiate and exacerbate the problem. The authors briefly outline two case studies of residential care facilities that approached and reduced the problem of child abuse in divergent but equally effective ways.

726. Kravitz, R. M., & Wilmott, R. W. (1990). Munchausen syndrome by proxy presenting as factitious apnea. *Clinical Pediatrics, 29*(10), 587–592.

This article presents a case study of Munchausen syndrome by proxy (MSBP) with recurrent apnea. In this case, a 26-year-old woman sought medical help for her 14-day-old son because of recurrent apnea. The study follows the infant's development up to the age of 6 months. It notes that both parents graduated from a special education high school and includes a more defined personal history of the infant's mother. After a complete psychiatric evaluation, the mother was diagnosed with schizoid affective disorder with major depression and acute anxiety. This article includes a literature review that discusses the characteristics of MCBP in terms of the presentation of symptoms, the mother's behavior, and parental dynamics. The authors also address possible treatment for this form of child abuse.

727. Krenk, C. J. (1984). Training residence staff for child abuse treatment. *Child Welfare, 63*(2), 167–173.
This article describes a curriculum for the identification and counseling of children who are victims of sexual abuse and who are living in a residential treatment center. It describes the training of child-care counselors, teachers, psychologists, and social workers in a number of areas, including: group therapy, interviewing techniques, and the development of treatment plans. After this training, the staff reported several positive effects of the training, including: appropriate emotional reactions to child disclosure and improved identification of victim symptomatology.

728. Krents, E., Schulman, V., & Brenner, S. (1987). Child abuse and the disabled child: Perspectives for parents. *Volta Review, 89*(5), 78–95.
This article describes several important aspects of familial child neglect and abuse, including sexual abuse. The authors note the overwhelming prevalence of the problem and suggest characteristics that may be typical of an abuser. They state that there is growing research to suggest that children with disabilities are increasingly at risk for abuse due to a number of factors: for example, frustrated parental expectations and added pressure on the family unit. They suggest a list of signs for identifying a child victim as well as guidelines for schools and parents to use in preventing child abuse. The authors include a parents' and children's bibliography.

729. Krieg, K. C., & Goodwin, J. M. (1993). The Dora syndrome: Attempts to restructure childhood in adult victims of child abuse. In J. M. Goodwin (Ed.), *Rediscovering childhood trauma: Historical casebook and clinical applications* (pp. 169–183). Washington, DC: American Psychiatric Press.
This chapter examines the Dora syndrome. The name Dora syndrome is derived from Freud's Dora case, which involved a young woman with numerous psychosomatic symptoms resulting from her abusive childhood. Dora's

earnest request for treatment was confounded by her resistance to the therapeutic process. The authors use case examples to focus on child abuse in order to illustrate four themes of the Dora syndrome: the client's noncompliance with treatment, reconstruction of the parents, reconstruction and completion of childhood, and chronic rage.

730. Krueger-Pelka, F. (1988, March). Abuse: A hidden epidemic. *Mainstream*, pp. 9–13.
This article examines sexual and physical abuse of people with disabilities. The author presents some case examples of maltreatment and looks at some of the obstacles encountered when people with disabilities try to obtain help. These obstacles usually involve inadequate resources at women's shelters and social service agencies for people with disabilities.

731. Krugman, R. D. (1985). Fatal child abuse: Analysis of 24 cases. *Pediatrician, 12*, 68–72.
This article describes a study that analyzed 24 cases of fatal child abuse from the Kempe Nation Center. In this study, 11 children were under 1 year of age, 10 were between 1 and 3, and 3 were between 3 and 6. The results of this analysis indicate that the majority of deaths were due to head trauma ($n=17$), with the perpetrators usually being the biological parent ($n=9$) or live-in boyfriend ($n=8$). It notes that false case histories and a delay in seeking medical attention were present in all of these cases. This article points out that civil prosecution was taken for 17 cases and criminal prosecution for 20 cases.

732. Kuhse, H., & Singer, P. (1985). *Should the baby live? The problem of handicapped infants*. Oxford: Oxford University Press.
This book presents arguments for killing babies with birth defects such as Down syndrome or other conditions associated with mental retardation. This book is based on Singer's "utilitarianism" and suggests that such killings are morally acceptable. Utilitarian arguments suggest that it is inconsistent for society to accept the aborting of babies with disabilities shortly before birth, but not accept the killing of the same babies shortly after birth even though in the case of premature babies they may be less developed. It also suggests that it is cruel to passively let these babies die while denying them the mercy of a quick and relatively painless death. Kuhse and Singer also argue that killing babies when they are very young is morally superior to allowing them to live to develop greater self-awareness when death would be a more severe loss because of their further development. The authors present arguments for euthanasia, suggesting that the infants' interests are served as well as those of families and society as a whole. This book provides an excellent example of the philosophy and rationale that drive the current movement for euthanasia of people with disabilities.

•L•

733. Labaton, S. (1993, December 29). Battle over discrimination against disabled is opened. *The New York Times*, p. A7.
This newspaper article reports that legal action has been initiated by the Justice Department against the state of Illinois and the city of Aurora concerning employment discrimination against police officers and firefighters with disabilities. At issue are pension benefits that are being denied to former city employees due to such conditions as diabetes and chronic back problems.

734. Ladimer, I. (1982). The role of the arbitration process in changing mental illness and mental retardation systems. *Psychiatric Quarterly, 54*(2), 123–137.
This article examines arbitration awards given in cases of alleged institutional abuses against patients by staff in psychiatric hospitals. The case examples detail the alleged abuses and the resulting arbitration verdicts. This article discusses the types of arbitration awards, and it examines the legal review systems for patient abuse and the influence of arbitration on the improvement of patient care. This article describes a proposed project that would gather information from employment records and related data in order to design an assessment tool for risk management and quality assurance.

735. Lamb, M. E., Gaensbauer, T. J., Malkin, C. M., & Schultz, L. A. (1985). The effects of child maltreatment on the security of infant-adult attachment. *Infant Behavior and Development, 8*(1), 35–45.
This article discusses a study that assessed how maltreatment affects the security of infant-parent attachment. In this study, 32 maltreated children ages 8.7 to 31.8 months (average age was 18.4 months) were compared with nonmaltreated children matched on sex, age, ethnic background, and parent occupation and education. The study divided the maltreated children into four groups: children maltreated by mothers and living with their mothers, children maltreated by mothers living in foster care and observed with foster mother, children maltreated by mothers living in foster care and observed with biological mother, and children maltreated by a person other than biological mother. The children were videotaped during separation and reunion events and were rated for the following: proximity and contact seeking, contact maintaining, and resistance avoidance, search, and distance during interaction. This study classified the infants as either securely (B), avoidantly (A), or resistantly (C) attached. The results of this study indicate the following: A significantly higher number of infants behaved insecurely in groups where they were maltreated by and seen with mothers and in groups where they were maltreated by mothers and seen with foster mothers; and there was no increase in the number of children behaving insecurely when the source of maltreatment was un-

known or by someone other than the mother. The authors conclude that similar findings are required in independent samples before results of this study can be considered reliable.

736. Lamond, D. A. P. (1989). The impact of mandatory reporting legislation on reporting behavior. *Child Abuse and Neglect, 13*(4), 471–480.
This article states that in 1987, in New South Wales, Australia, teachers and other school professionals were added to the list of professionals required by law to report suspected cases of child sexual abuse to the Department of Family and Community Services. This article points out that this mandatory-reporting legislation resulted in a significant increase in the number of reports made by teachers, but the overall quality of reports by teachers remained the same. This increase in reports provides further evidence that laws requiring the reporting of abuse improve reporting practices.

737. Lang, R. E., & Kahn, J. V. (1986). Teacher estimates of handicapped student crime victimization and delinquency. *Journal of Special Education, 20*(3), 359–365.
This article discusses an American study in which 75 special education teachers identified the most common violent and property crimes among their special education students. These teachers also provided estimates of crime victimization and delinquency among these students. The findings of this study indicate the following: a need for more federal and state crime reporting methods and a need for education aimed at reducing the vulnerability of students with disabilities, both as victims and perpetrators.

738. Lang, R. E., & Kahn, J. V. (1989). Effects of an experimental special-education crime-prevention intervention: A time-series study. *Journal of Clinical Child Psychology, 18*(3), 263–270.
This article discusses a study that examined the effects of an experimental special education crime prevention program using 42 students in special education enrolled in four elementary schools. These students had the following disabilities: learning disabilities, mental retardation, or behavior disorders. The results of this crime prevention intervention show that the students' violent and property crime victimization and criminal exploitation rate dropped significantly over time. The authors emphasize the need for this type of education for this group of children.

739. Large, T. (1990). The effects of attitudes upon the blind: A reexamination. In M. Nagler (Ed.), *Perspectives on disability* (pp. 165–168). Palo Alto, CA: Health Markets Research.
The effects of positive and negative attitudes on people who are blind are examined in this chapter. It describes a

study that was conducted using people (eight men, eight women) who were blinded after age 6 and had successfully accepted their visual impairment. These people were questioned about how other people's attitudes affected their adjustment. The results of this study indicate that family attitudes and relationships seemed to exert the most influence on these people's adjustments to blindness.

740. Larsson, G., Bohlin, A. B., & Sten-backa, M. (1986). Prognosis of children admitted to institutional care during infancy. *Child Abuse & Neglect, 10*(3), 361–368.

This article presents a Swedish follow-up study of infants in institutional care. This study analyzed three groups of infants following institutionalization: infants who remained with their biological mother, infants who were raised in foster care, and infants who were adopted. The authors found that children raised by their biological mother had significantly more psychological disturbances than children raised in adoptive homes. They conclude that the experience of institutional care alone did not appear to put the child at risk for developmental problems; however, permanency and quality of care seemed to be factors that affected later development.

741. Laterza, P. (1979). An eclectic approach to group work with the mentally retarded. *Social Work with Groups, 2*(3), 235–245.

This article examines the use of group therapy for people with developmental disabilities. In therapy, the emphasis is placed an group interaction, modeling, and action-oriented practice to encourage role learning. Behavior contracts and the use of transactional analysis are incorporated into therapy, as is structure, to provide a learning environment for problem solving and adult role behavior. The author recommends a flexible, eclectic approach for working with people with developmental disabilities.

742. Laufer, P. (1994). *A question of consent: Innocence and complicity in the Glen Ridge rape case.* **San Francisco: Mercury House.**

This book provides a history and analysis of the Glen Ridge, New Jersey, sexual assault case. The author suggests that the underlying issues of consent and social position are reflected in the social responses of the community and explores the rationalizations for this sex crime. Attitudes about mental retardation, disability, and marginalized people are viewed as key factors in legitimizing sexual assault.

743. Laurance, J. (1994, February 12). Allitt's victims could have lived. *The Times*, p. 2.

This newspaper article suggests that the deaths of four children and the injury to nine others by Nurse Beverly Allitt could have been prevented if doctors, nurses, and managers had not overlooked medical evidence at the Grantham and Kesteven general hospitals in England. An inquiry into the deaths on Ward Four by Sir Cecil Clothier (Clothier Report) identifies senior management and ward managers as indecisive and sloppy and staffing levels as inadequate. In addition, abnormalities in chest X-rays showing rib fractures resulting from violence were missed by doctors. Twelve recommendations are suggested, including: reference checks on employees, identification of applicants with personality or behavioral disorders, postmortem examination of any child death that occurs unexpectedly, and servicing equipment that monitors the breathing of patients and sounds an alarm if the patient stops breathing.

744. Lauter, H., & Meyer, J. E. (1982). Mercy killing without consent: Historical comments on a controversial issue. *Acta Psychiatrica Scandinavica, 65*, 134–141.

This article discusses mercy killing or euthanasia without the consent of the patient, involving people with developmental disabilities. It includes a historical review that examines Social Darwinism (a social theory that uses the concepts of evolution and natural selection) and the eugenics movement in Europe during the late 19th and early 20th centuries. It discusses the application of Social Darwinism by the Nazi regime and the sterilization and extermination of children and adults with developmental disabilities in Germany. It addresses nonconsenting euthanasia for people with developmental disabilities and its relationship to psychiatry and the family's responsibility in the decision-making process. The authors point out that this decision-making process might also be carried out by a commissioned board of representatives. The authors also discuss the absence of free will on the patient's part in nonconsenting euthanasia and examine the meaning of "meaningful life," a concept that is used to make these decisions.

745. Lauter, H., & Meyer, J. E. (1984). Active euthanasia without consent: Historical comments on a current debate. *Death Education, 8*(2/3), 89–98.

This article outlines the historical background and context of active euthanasia, concentrating on the senile or the chronically insane, and reviews the concept of Social Darwinism and the actions of Nazi Germany. It describes the steps that led to the "mercy killing" of the incurably ill or insane by the Nazis. The authors point out that contemporary advocates of euthanasia believe that the "extermination of valueless life" under Hitler's government was an extension of the myth about the purity of the "volk" and that it should be seen as related to the "final solution" of the "Jewish problem" and to the measures taken against gypsies. The authors conclude that the belief that the question of benevolent euthanasia must be decided without personal consent transforms euthanasia into extermination.

746. The Law Commission. (1993). *Mentally incapacitated adults and decision-making: A new jurisdiction* (Consultation Paper No. 128). **London: HMSO Books.**

This is the first consultation paper from the Law Commission that addresses the need for law reforms concerning people with developmental disabilities. This consultation paper deals with reforms that will establish private law jurisdiction concerning issues related to personal care and welfare of people with developmental disabilities: for example, family and caregivers' limited authority in decision making for people with disabilities in their care, defining the client group, administrative and judicial decision making, financial decision making, personal care and welfare decision making, enduring powers of attorney, and procedures to appoint a power of attorney before becoming incapacitated.

747. The Law Commission. (1993). *Mentally incapacitated adults and decision-making: Medical treatment and research* (Consultation Paper No. 129). **London: HMSO Books.**

This is the second consultation paper from the Law Commission that addresses the need for law reforms concerning people with developmental disabilities. This paper discusses the issue of consent for medical treatment of people with developmental disabilities. This paper provides a description of the incapacitated patient and current treatment of the patient with respect to medical treatment decisions. It makes suggestions for a judicial forum that would deal with questions from persons in the position to give consent for others concerning medical treatment. It examines procedures for appointing a medical treatment attorney before an individual becomes incapacitated and situations that might warrant a second opinion for medical treatment decisions. This paper also examines the present Mental Health Act and reform proposals to the act concerning the treatment of people with mental disorders.

748. The Law Commission. (1993). *Mentally incapacitated and other vulnerable adults: Public law protection* (Consultation Paper No. 130). **London: HMSO Books.**

This is the third consultation paper from the Law Commission that addresses the need for law reforms concerning people with developmental disabilities. This paper deals with public law reforms concerning local public authorities and social services. The client group who might be affected by these reforms to public authorities include incapacitated people and vulnerable people. It addresses the powers that public authorities might require: for example, the investigation of abuse, assessment of services, and short-term intervention for vulnerable or incapacitated persons. This paper also discusses guardianship and the proposed new jurisdiction and its use by local authorities.

749. Leaning, J. (1993, February 6). German doctors and their secrets. *The New York Times*, p. I21.

This newspaper article reports that the World Medical Association's newly elected president, Dr. Hans Joachim Sewering, has resigned his position due to the exposure of his Nazi past. It notes that Dr. Sewering was a member of the SS and the attending physician at Eglfing-Haar Hospital, where 203 patients with disabilities were sent to their deaths. While some German doctors closed ranks after the disclosure of this evidence, others protested Sewering's election and petitioned for his removal.

750. Lebovici, S. (1989). John Bowlby [Special issue: The men who marked psychiatry in the 20th century]. *Psychiatrie Francaise, 20*(2), 29–35.

This article examines the psychoanalytic thought of British psychoanalyst John Bowlby, including his role at the Tavistock Clinic and his attachment theory. It describes Bowlby's studies concerning the psycho-pathogenic effects of the lack of maternal care on children from many different countries, and it discusses his appeal to Darwinism to justify his theories. Although Bowlby defines himself as a psychoanalyst and agrees with Freud that an early childhood trauma constitutes the prototype for and ultimate cause of adult psychopathology, this article concludes he challenged psychoanalytic drive theory and favored empathy, rather than detachment, as the appropriate psychoanalytic stance.

751. Lederer, S. E. (1992). Orphans as guinea pigs: American children and medical experimenters, 1890–1930. In R. Cooter (Ed.), *In the name of the child: Health and welfare 1880–1940* (pp. 96–123). **London: Routledge.**

This chapter examines the practice of medical experimentation on orphan children between 1890 and 1930 in the United States. It claims that these healthy children were used as guinea pigs for unproven vaccines and diagnostic tests and were exposed to such viruses as small pox, measles, and tuberculosis and such procedures as lumbar punctures, all in the name of medical advancement. This chapter includes historical accounts of these practices and examines the opposition to using orphans for experimentation.

752. Lee, D. A. (1979). Munchausen syndrome by proxy in twins. *Archives of Disease in Childhood, 54*, 646–647.

A case report of twins who were physically abuse by their mother is described in this article. It states that Munchausen syndrome by proxy was determined to be the cause of the abuse following the discovery that the mother had induced the symptoms in her children. This article notes that both parents were known to the Social Service Department because of nonaccidental injuries to their children from previous marriages.

753. Lee, H. C. B., & Cheung, F. M. (1991). The attitudes toward rape victims scale:

Reliability and validity in a Chinese context. *Sex Roles, 24(9/10),* **599–603.**
This article discusses two studies that were conducted to determine the cross-cultural applicability of the Attitudes toward Rape Victims Scale (ARVS). The first study administered the ARVS, the Attitudes Toward Women Scale, and the Traditionality-Modernity Factor Scale to 202 Chinese university students and found that the ARVS was reliable and valid. In the second study, reliability and validity of the ARVS was examined using the known-group method: That is, this study compared the scores of 299 adults from four different professional groups. The results of this second study indicate that women held more favorable attitudes toward rape victims than the men in this study. The authors conclude that the ARVS shows promise as a cross-cultural research tool.

754. LeGrand, A. L. (1990). Training of social skills with mildly mentally retarded persons with severe behavioral disorders. In A. Dosen, A. Van Gennep, & G. J. Zwanikken (Eds.), *Treatment of mental illness and behavioral disorder in the mentally retarded: Proceedings of the International Congress, May 3rd & 4th, 1990* **(pp. 315–323). Leiden, the Netherlands: Logon Publications.**
This article describes a social skills training program for people with mild developmental disability who have severe behavioral disorders. This program involves a group of five clients and two trainers, and it runs from 30 to 35 sessions once a week for 2 hours. Nine specific skills are taught during the program: self-introduction, requesting something, refusing a request, discussion of something, criticizing something, being criticized, coping with disappointment, coping with anger, and giving compliments. In order for clients to be admitted into the program, they must meet the following criteria: IQ must be equal or greater than 70, scores on the Screeninglist Social Skills and Behaviour Assessment Instrument must be acceptable, they should have some reading and writing skills, they should have some self-awareness of one's own restricted social skills, they should have good motivation, they should demonstrate they can participate, they should have been institutionalized at least 6 months, and they must have an interview with a trainer. This article discusses the training procedure and the influence of psychopathology and/or psychiatric disturbances on participation, and it concludes that clients (ages 21 to 35) who participated in the program showed improvement in the development of specific social skills and assertive behavior.

755. LeGrand, C. (1984). Mental hospital regulation and the safe environment. *Law, Medicine & Health Care, 12(6),* **236–242.**
This article addresses the emerging legal issue of institutions that fail to protect staff and clients from sexual assault. It suggests that institutions are liable for sexual assaults only if they contribute to the assault through negligence, and it points out that courts focus on whether the institution had any specific information about the assailant or victim that made the attack foreseeable and preventable. At least seven such lawsuits by clients raped in mental institutions have been heard in court. In three successful lawsuits, regulatory infractions were cited as contributing factors.

756. Leitschuh, C., & Brotons, M. (1991, April). Recreation and music therapy for adolescent victims of sexual abuse. *JOPERD (Journal of Physical Education, Recreation & Dance),* **pp. 52–55.**
This article summarizes an 11-week recreation and music therapy program. This program is designed for sexually abused adolescents with severe emotional problems, and it uses music and a safe environment to help adolescents who are verbally inexpressive creatively express their feelings.

757. Levett, A., & Kuhn, L. (1991). Attitudes towards rape and rapists: A White, English-speaking South African student sample. *South African Journal of Psychology, 21(1),* **32–37.**
This article discusses a study that investigated the effects of a sexual assault offender's race and class on the offender's responsibility to the victim, sentencing of the offender, and perceptions of the victim. This study used a vignette method to assess these variables. The participants of the study were White South African students enrolled in an English-speaking university. This study found the following: White students suggested harsher punishment for a Black offender and a working class offender than for a White offender, attitudes toward the victim remained the same regardless of the offender, and White female students were more influenced by the offender's race and class than the male students across all offender conditions. This article includes a literature review that examines attitudes toward rape and class and race prejudices in an apartheid society. (This article is written in Afrikaans.)

758. Levine, E. M. (1986). Sociocultural causes of family violence: A theoretical comment. *Journal of Family Violence, 1(1),* **3–12.**
The author of this article notes that during the last decade family violence has become a favorite topic for research and academic investigation. This article presents a theoretical analysis of the major sociocultural changes that might lead to an increase in violence and a weakening of moral standards. This article discusses the following areas: development of industrialization, residential mobility, the growth of individualistic values, decline of school and parental authority, and the impact of the media and popular culture.

759. Levine Powers, J., Mooney, A., & Nunno, M. (1990). Institutional abuse: A review

of the literature. *Journal of Child and Youth Care, 4*(6), 81–95.
This literature review examines the abuse of children in institutions. It describes institutional maltreatment and discusses the incidence of abuse in residential facilities. According to the authors, abuse stems, in part, from inadequate resources and insufficient training of staff members for handling stressful situations and the difficulty of managing and caring for these institutionalized children.

760. Levitas, A., & Gilson, S. F. (1989). *Psychodynamic psychotherapy with mildly and moderately retarded patients*. Lexington, MA: Lexington Books.
This book claims that the cognitive deficits of people with mental retardation overshadow their emotional and personality traits. It states that the standard techniques used in adult psychotherapy may not be applicable for persons with mental retardation and as models for child psychotherapy because of the concreteness of this therapy; it also suggests that appropriate psychotherapeutic techniques are not used for persons with mental retardation because there is a lack of knowledge about their personality development and social adaptive lives. Although there are reports in the literature since the 1950s about the use of psychotherapeutic techniques with people who have mental retardation, this book claims that the absence of self-reliance in people with mental retardation makes them unsuitable for psychotherapy. In this book, the clinical challenges are illustrated with case reports involving the following: poor diagnosis, how mental illness can also affect people with mental retardation, how they can recover given the right type of environment, different types of symptoms of mental illness in people with mental retardation, the role of anxiety in totally disorganizing a person with mental retardation, and the diagnostic overshadowing. According to the authors, the first major step is to establish communication with a person in whom the capacity for abstract and formal thought is limited. The traits common to individuals with mental retardation include: passivity, self-absorption, repetitiveness, lack of interests or pursuit of novelty, inflexibility, and simple emotions. Consequently, these traits call for the therapist to play a more active part in the therapy. The predictable crisis points in the lives of people with mental retardation (for parents and/or the individuals with mental retardation) include the following events: when mental retardation becomes a reality; birth of siblings; starting school; puberty and adolescence; sex and dating; being surpassed by younger siblings; emancipation of siblings; end of education; out-of-home placement and residential moves; changing staff-client relationships; inappropriate expectations from parents and supervisors; aging, illness, and death of parents; death of peers; loss of friends; medical illness; and psychiatric illness. The authors suggest that the next step in the process of psychotherapy is to determine whether the patient has a problem or if the systems in which the patient is involved are creating a problem. While a person with mental retardation may not cope with the subtleties of in-depth psychotherapy, the authors claim that explanations, reassurance, and environmental manipulation can bring about a change. The authors discuss in detail the issues of transference, deepening therapeutic alliance, the resistance to psychotherapy, and countertransference issues, including resolution of dependency and the termination process in psychotherapy. According to the authors, it is the therapist's and the patient's shared task to uncover the truth of the patient's situation, to allow and empower the patient to take responsibility for what is within his or her power, and to come to terms with the shortcomings of the various agencies that deal with him or her.

761. Li, A. K. F. (1981). Play and the mentally retarded child. *Mental Retardation, 19*(3), 121–126.
This article describes the play characteristics of children with mental retardation and presents arguments supporting the importance of play for these children. It uses a brief, critical review of the scarce literature concerning play and children with mental retardation to suggest the need for more research on the use of play for these children. Also, the author outlines the procedures to be used in the therapeutic use of play with children with mental retardation who also have emotional or behavior problems.

762. Libow, J. A., & Schreier, H. A. (1986). Three forms of factitious illness in children: When is it Munchausen syndrome by proxy? *American Journal of Orthopsychiatry, 56*(4), 602–611.
This article describes five manifestations of Munchausen syndrome by proxy. It discusses these five manifestations and how they are expressed by the three subtypes of primary caregivers who manipulate their children for their own gains. The authors state that the help seekers, active inducer, and the doctor addict all have unique styles and are characterized by the age of the child and maternal affect of the mother.

763. Lieberman, A. F. (1985). Infant mental health: A model for service delivery [Special issue: Mental health services to children]. *Journal of Clinical Child Psychology, 14*(3), 196–201.
This article describes the Infant-Parent Program, an infant mental health service that provides assessment and treatment for infants and families with potential or actual child abuse, neglect, and disorders of attachment or socioemotional functioning. This program has established a collaborative network with pediatric care, Child Protective Services, and community agencies serving infants and families at risk. This article describes the methods of assessment and treatment and how this program interacts with other child services.

764. Lifton, R. J., & Hackett, A. (1990). Physicians, Nazi. In I. Gutman (Ed.),

Encyclopedia of the holocaust (Vol. 3, L–R, pp. 1127–1132). New York: Macmillan.

This chapter provides a chilling account of the corruption of physicians under the Third Reich. Rationalization of extermination programs required the medicalization of death making and elaborate propaganda efforts. Physicians played a vital role in all such activities, helping to portray national socialism as applied social and genetic biology. Physicians were the creators of much of the Nazi medical mythology, and they were also among those who became the most ardent believers and among those who benefitted most by it. Prior to the rise of the national socialist party to power, a large percentage of German physicians and medical school professors were Jews. As Jewish physicians were boycotted, terrorized, and eventually barred from medical practice, a great deal of upward mobility was created for other physicians. The increased need for physicians created by the war effort and the dependence on the medical profession to legitimize the mass extermination programs further contributed to their rising status under Hitler. The proportion of physicians (45%) with memberships in the Nazi party was higher than the proportion for almost any other profession. Their participation in the sterilization and euthanasia programs was not only horrific in itself, but critical to the development and justification of the subsequent mass murder of Jews and other ethnic and religious groups. The euthanasia program fathered the mass extermination program through four direct links: 1) it shared the same philosophy and "biomedical vision" (p. 1127) of racial healing; 2) it corrupted both direct participants and, to a lesser extent, the general population to a tolerance for killing; 3) it developed the prototype technology of gas chambers, controlled starvation, lethal injection, and a variety of other mass killing methods; and 4) it provided trained personnel. The initial rationale for the euthanasia program came from Karl Binding, a lawyer, and Alfred Hoche, a psychiatrist, in their 1920 book, *The Permission to Destroy Life Unworthy of Life.* Hospitals and institutions held lectures and demonstrations for government officials, professionals, the press, and the general public to convince them that the euthanasia program was justified. Dramatic and documentary films were produced by Nazi propagandists to convince Germans that the killing of people with disabilities was justified, humane, and even valorous. These propaganda activities were so effective that families sometimes began requesting the euthanasia of their children. Initially, institutions and hospitals were encouraged simply to neglect their patients. Inadequate medical care, food, and supervision resulted in many deaths, but this was too slow and undependable. Dr. Hermann Pfannmüller, at Eglfing-Haar, 1 of 30 centers set up primarily to kill children with disabilities, perfected systematic starvation methods. The program for exterminating children with disabilities started before the adult program and continued after the adult program was partially dismantled in 1941.

765. Light, M. J., & Sheridan, M. S. (1990). Munchausen syndrome by proxy and apnea (MBPA). *Clinical Pediatrics, 29*(3), 162–168.

This article discusses a questionnaire survey of 127 apnea programs conducted to determine how many patients in the program were victims of Munchausen syndrome by proxy. The results of this questionnaire found 54 cases of Munchausen syndrome by proxy reported from 51 apnea programs. The study obtained additional information on 32 of the reported cases and discovered that 83% of these cases involved apnea. Of these, three cases involved fatalities, one case developed severe brain damage, and five siblings of these index cases were also sudden infant death syndrome (SIDS) cases.

766. Lindner-Middendorp, C. J. M. (1990). Psychotherapy of multiply handicapped persons. In A. Dosen, A. Van Gennep, & G. J. Zwanikken (Eds.), *Treatment of mental illness and behavioral disorder in the mentally retarded: Proceedings of the International Congress, May 3rd & 4th, 1990, Amsterdam, the Netherlands* **(pp. 355–360). Leiden, the Netherlands: Logon Publications.**

This article examines the possibility of treating the emotional or behavioral disorders of people with multiple disabilities. Instead of claiming that psychotherapy for people with multiple disabilities is possible, this article states that psychotherapy for people with multiple disabilities is not impossible. It supports this statement by: examining multiple disabilities, supplying examples of emotional or behavioral problems in which multiple disabilities are important factors, and discussing ways to make various psychotherapeutic methods available for people with multiple disabilities. The article concludes that psychotherapy for people with multiple disabilities is not impossible if the following conditions are met: knowledge about how multiple disabilities affect an individual, experience with people with multiple disabilities, use of communication and/or language styles understood by the client, and use of aids that are adapted for the client.

767. Livesay, S., Erhlich, S., Ryan, L., & Finnegan, L. P. (1989). Cocaine and pregnancy: Maternal and infant outcome. *Annals of the New York Academy of Sciences, 562,* **358–359.**

This article describes a study that compared three groups of women matched for age, socioeconomic status, cocaine use, and parity in order to determine maternal and infant outcome. The results of this comparison of cocaine users ($n=93$), noncocaine drug users ($n=83$), and nondrug users ($n=63$) indicates that the infants of cocaine users and other drug users had poor outcomes in growth, gestational age, and Apgar scores. Also, this study found that infants who were exposed to cocaine in utero had the poorest outcomes for growth, gestational age, and Apgar scores.

768. Loewenstein, R. J. (1993). Anna O: Reformulation as a case of multiple personality disorder. In J. M. Goodwin (Ed.), *Rediscovering childhood trauma: Historical casebook and clinical applications* (pp. 139–167). Washington, DC: American Psychiatric Press.
This chapter describes the case of Anna O., also known as Bertha Pappenheim. She is famous in the history of psychiatry and psychoanalysis because she was a patient of both Breuer and Freud. This chapter examines her history from early childhood to adulthood and the theories that suggested childhood abuses contributed to the development of her multiple personalities.

769. Lombardo, P. A. (1985). Three generations, no imbeciles: New light on *Buck v. Bell. New York University Law Review, 60*(1), 30–62.
This article discusses the contributions of three men to the famous *Buck v. Bell* eugenic sterilization case. This article alleges and provides some evidence that Irving Whitehead, who acted as Carrie Buck's lawyer, was in collusion with Aubrey Strode, the lawyer for the other side, and acted to ensure that his client would lose and the sterilization law would be upheld. The account of the history of Carrie Buck (the focus of the famous sterilization trial) is very enlightening. She was a normal child who did well in school and showed no indication of developmental disability. Her foster parents wanted her institutionalized because she was unwed and pregnant, which was embarrassing for them. The pregnancy was a result of a rape by their nephew.

770. Longmore, P. K. (1985, Summer). Screening stereotypes: Images of disabled people. *Social Policy*, pp. 31–37.
This article examines the portrayal of people with disabilities in television and film. It discusses a variety of disabilities, the frequency of characterization of people with disabilities, stereotypes, and the social and cultural functions of disability images using examples from 1970s and 1980s popular television programs and films. The author concludes that the positive portrayal of people with disabilities in commercials and other programs highlights a changing social climate and shows that the creators of television programs and films are more conscious of the new emerging sociopolitical clout of the disability civil rights movement.

771. Longo, R. E., & Gochenour, C. (1981). Sexual assault of handicapped individuals. *Journal of Rehabilitation, 47*, 24–27.
In this article, 11 case studies are described that examine the sexual assault of people with disabilities. The case studies cover a range of topics: insensitivity of the case worker in handling the reported incident, the victim as an object of aggression, the child victim, and abuse by the residential caregiver. The authors discuss six intervention techniques that may assist those working with people with disabilities.

772. Lonsdale, S. (1990). *Women and disability: The experience of physical disability among women.* London: Macmillan Education.
Although this book notes that the experiences discussed in it may have a broader application, its major focus is women with physical and sensory disabilities. It discusses the effects of disability in the following areas: historical and social contexts, invisibility, dependency/independence, employment, financial consequences, discrimination, and self-image. It examines self-image in relation to issues of sexuality. It discusses the vulnerability of women with disabilities to sexual abuse in terms of a double vulnerability, that is, reporting abuse by a caregiver threatens the person's independence and the possibility of institutionalization raises the potential risk of further abuse. Also, it discusses issues such as the "regulation of fertility" and points out the irony of simultaneously experiencing social isolation and invasion of privacy, which leads to the denial of humanity and sexuality. This book also includes a bibliography.

773. Lovett, H. (1987). People to people. *Entourage, 2*(2), 36–42.
This article addresses the inappropriateness of aversive conditioning for controlling behavior. Using case studies, this article illustrates how this form of conditioning results in pain and suffering for the patient. The author suggests that support and understanding are more viable means for controlling behavior.

774. Loyie, F., & Staples, D. (1994, April 2). The brutal death of a gentle spirit. *The Edmonton Journal*, pp. G1–G2.
This article describes the life and death of Joyce Cardinal, a 34-year-old Native American woman with severely impaired speech who was burned to death by an unknown assailant. She lived for 22 days after being knocked unconscious, drenched with gasoline, and set ablaze in Edmonton, Alberta, in November of 1993.

775. Loyie, F., & Staples, D. (1994, April 2). A cruel killer—The perfect victim. *The Edmonton Journal*, p. A1.
This article describes the continuing investigation of the murder of Joyce Cardinal, a 34-year-old woman who was covered with gasoline and set on fire on November 28, 1993. Ms. Cardinal was a Native American woman with severely impaired speech and was sometimes believed to be mentally disabled, although those closest to her report that she was not mentally disabled. The lack of public interest in the case is contrasted with the overwhelming public interest in another murder in the same area, and this article raises questions about whether the lack of interest in Joyce Cardinal's murder may be related to her disability or Native American status.

776. Luckasson, R. (1992). People with mental retardation as victims of crime. In R. W. Conley, R. Luckasson, & G. N. Bouthilet (Eds.), *The criminal justice system and mental retardation: Defendants and victims* (pp. 209–220). Baltimore: Paul H. Brookes Publishing Co.

This chapter discusses crime victimization of people with disabilities, particularly people with mental retardation. Luckasson points out that the U.S. National Crime Survey does not provide information on disability but that other smaller studies suggest that the prevalence of crime is high among people with disabilities. Crimes committed in institutional settings are not included in the National Crime Survey. She suggests that the use of terms such as *abuse* to describe crimes committed against people with disabilities that would be recorded as assault if committed against people without disabilities also conceals and trivializes the extent of the problem. Luckasson suggests seven factors that increase vulnerability for people with mental retardation, including exposure to high-risk environments and differential treatment by law enforcement and the courts. She suggests strategies for improving legal responses to victimization of people with disabilities and for enhancing victim assistance to this group.

777. Ludwig, S., & Barrett, M. (1993). *Sexuality and physical disability*. East York, ON: SIECCAN (Sex Information & Education Council of Canada).

This is the 11th book in a 17-part series on sexuality education for young adults and adults with developmental disabilities. This book discusses sexuality and physical disability and the means by which a person with disabilities can attain a sexually gratifying life. It discusses intimacy, masturbation, safe sex, birth control, and intercourse using illustrations, Blissymbols, and script. It makes distinctions between appropriate public and private behavior and sexual expression. A glossary of key words and Blissymbols is included in this book.

778. Ludwig, S., & Hingsburger, D. (1989). Preparation for counselling and psychotherapy: Teaching about feelings. *Psychiatric Aspects of Mental Retardation Reviews, 8*(1), 1–7.

This article examines the Feelings Curriculum, a teaching tool used in group counseling to assist people with developmental disabilities to recognize and identify feelings and emotions. The Feelings Curriculum is appropriate for people with mild to moderate developmental disabilities. This tool identifies four states of emotion: glad, sad, mad, and scared. This tool uses drawings of faces expressing these emotions and teaches some facts associated with feelings. Analysis of emotional responses in varying situations are used to discuss group differences and similarities. The authors conclude that the group format allows for the sharing of responses,

teaches listening skills and respect, and fosters a sense of identity with group members.

779. Ludwig, S., & Hingsburger, D. (1993). *Adolescence*. East York, ON: SIECCAN (Sex Information & Education Council of Canada).

This is the 4th book in a 17-part series on sexuality education for young adults and adults with developmental disabilities. In this book, adolescence and the developmental changes that occur during this period are discussed using illustrations, Blissymbols, and script. It makes distinctions between appropriate public and private behavior and sexual expression. A glossary of key words and Blissymbols is included in this book.

780. Ludwig, S., & Hingsburger, D. (1993). *AIDS*. East York, ON: SIECCAN (Sex Information & Education Council of Canada).

This is the 13th book in a 17-part series on sexuality education for young adults and adults with developmental disabilities. This book discusses acquired immuno deficiency syndrome (AIDS). It defines AIDS and its development and describes its prevention. It examines safe activities that do not promote the spread of the disease using illustrations, Blissymbols, and script. It makes distinctions between appropriate public and private behavior and sexual expression. A glossary of key words and Blissymbols is included in this book.

781. Ludwig, S., & Hingsburger, D. (1993). *Being sexual teaching manual*. East York, ON: SIECCAN (Sex Information & Education Council of Canada).

This is the last book in a 17-part series on sexuality education for young adults and adults with developmental disabilities. It is the teaching manual for the *Being Sexual* series. It supplies background information on the series, examines its potential use as an educational tool, and defines its use of Blissymbols. Also, it discusses the key symbols used in the series in the Appendix.

782. Ludwig, S., & Hingsburger, D. (1993). *Birth control*. East York, ON: SIECCAN (Sex Information & Education Council of Canada).

This is the 9th book in a 17-part series on sexuality education for young adults and adults with developmental disabilities. It discusses family planning and birth control options for both men and women using illustrations, Blissymbols, and script. A glossary of key words and Blissymbols is included in this book.

783. Ludwig, S., & Hingsburger, D. (1993). *Female masturbation*. East York, ON: SIECCAN (Sex Information & Education Council of Canada).

This is the 6th book in a 17-part series on sexuality education for young adults and adults with developmental disabilities. This book discusses female masturbation, sexual arousal and pleasure, and orgasm using illustrations, Blissymbols, and script. It considers masturbation a personal sexual option for everyone. It makes distinctions between appropriate public and private behavior and sexual expression. A glossary of key words and Blissymbols is included in this book.

784. Ludwig, S., & Hingsburger, D. (1993). *Heterosexual intercourse*. East York, ON: SIECCAN (Sex Information & Education Council of Canada).
This is the 7th book in a 17-part series on sexuality education for young adults and adults with developmental disabilities. This book discusses intimacy, heterosexual intercourse, different sexual positions, orgasm, and shared feelings and communication using illustrations, Blissymbols, and script. It makes distinctions between appropriate public and private behavior and sexual expression. A glossary of key words and Blissymbols is included in this book.

785. Ludwig, S., & Hingsburger, D. (1993). *Human reproduction*. East York, ON: SIECCAN (Sex Information & Education Council of Canada).
This is the 8th book in a 17-part series on sexuality education for young adults and adults with developmental disabilities. This book discusses human reproduction and examines intercourse, fertilization, gestation, birth, and nursing using illustrations, Blissymbols, and script. Also, it discusses miscarriage, pregnancy counseling, abortion, premature births, and birth by Caesarean section. A glossary of key words and Blissymbols is included in this book.

786. Ludwig, S., & Hingsburger, D. (1993). *Sexual abuse*. East York, ON: SIECCAN (Sex Information & Education Council of Canada).
This is the 15th book in a 17-part series on sexuality education for young adults and adults with developmental disabilities. This book discusses sexual abuse using illustrations, Blissymbols, and script. It defines what constitutes sexual abuse, and it examines a person's emotional response to sexual abuse. Also, it discusses the procedure to follow when one has been sexually abused: the need to tell a trusted individual about the abuse, the medical examination, and the legal process. A glossary of key words and Blissymbols is included in this book.

787. Ludwig, S., & Hingsburger, D. (1993). *Sexuality and aging*. East York, ON: SIECCAN (Sex Information & Education Council of Canada).
This is the 16th book in a 17-part series on sexuality education for young adults and adults with developmental disabilities. This book discusses sexuality and aging using illustrations, Blissymbols, and script. It examines the physiological changes the body undergoes and issues of intimacy, sexual expression, and relationships when

one ages. It makes distinctions between appropriate private and public sexual behavior and includes a glossary of key words and Blissymbols.

788. Ludwig, S., & Hingsburger, D. (1993). *Sexually transmitted diseases*. East York, ON: SIECCAN (Sex Information & Education Council of Canada).
This is the 12th book in a 17-part series on sexuality education for young adults and adults with developmental disabilities. This book discusses the detection, prevention, and treatment of sexually transmitted diseases using illustrations, Blissymbols, and script. It makes distinctions between appropriate public and private behavior and sexual expression. A glossary of key words and Blissymbols is included in this book.

789. Ludwig, S., & Hingsburger, D. (1993). *A woman's body*. East York, ON: SIECCAN (Sex Information & Education Council of Canada).
This is the 2nd book in a 17-part series on sexuality education for young adults and adults with developmental disabilities. This book discusses a woman's body using illustrations, Blissymbols, and script. The stages of puberty are discussed, and it focuses on menstruation, female reproductive organs, masturbation, reproduction, and childbirth. It makes distinctions between appropriate public and private behavior and sexual expression. A glossary of key words and Blissymbols is included in this book.

790. Lujan, C., DeBruyn, L. M., May, P. A., & Bird, M. E. (1989). Profile of abused and neglected American Indian children in the Southwest. *Child Abuse & Neglect, 13*, 449–461.
This article describes a study that assessed children from 53 families who were identified by the Child Protection Team of the Southwest Indian Health Service Hospital for abuse and/or neglect between December 1982 and March 1985. This study obtained data on general demographics, history of abuse, neglect, alcohol and/or substance abuse, and medical and disabling conditions in children using intake forms: one form for the children ($n=117$) and the other form for the parents ($n=88$) and the grandparents ($n=78$). The children (59% boys, 41% girls) in this study ranged in age from several months to 21 years, with an average age of 8 years. The results of this study indicate that alcohol abuse by the parents/grandparents was a prevalent factor in the neglect of 88% of the children who were neglected and in the abuse of 68% of the children who were abused, with 65% of the cases reporting both abuse and neglect. The authors note that the abuse and neglect of these children occurred within the context of multidysfunctional families.

791. Lukawiecki, T. (1991). *Elder abuse bibliography*. Ottawa, ON: Health and Welfare Canada.

This bibliography from the National Clearinghouse on Family Violence brings together books, government documents, reports, articles, and films from the 1980s on the topic of elder abuse. The references include Departmental Library call numbers, number of pages, keywords, and notes, and the information is provided in both French and English.

792. Lusthaus, E. W. (1981). Prevention perverted. *Canadian Journal on Mental Retardation, 31*(3), 30–32.

In this article, the prevention of intellectual disability by means of amniocentesis and abortion is questioned by the author, a mother of a child with Down syndrome. Instead, she suggests focusing on nutrition, environmental and social awareness, and education as ways in which to prevent intellectual disability.

793. Lusthaus, E. W. (1985). "Euthanasia" of persons with severe handicaps: Refuting the rationalizations. *Journal of the Association for Persons with Severe Handicaps, 10*(2), 87–94.

This article presents arguments against euthanasia of people with severe disabilities. The author argues that the underlying rationale for euthanasia is based on the belief that these individuals are less than human. She refutes this contention along with the secondary rationale that people with severe disabilities have no potential for quality of life, and therefore, killing them is in their best interest.

794. Lusthaus, E. W. (1991). Drastic actions: The results of viewing people as less than human. *Developmental Disabilities, 19*(1), 28–48.

This article discusses society's negative attitudes toward people with developmental disabilities and the discrimination and abuse that results from these negative attitudes. It reviews the literature in order to illustrate some of the unjustified actions against people with disabilities that result from the perception that they are less than human: for example, sterilization, segregation, institutionalization, abuse, and neglect. The author describes how the move away from institutional settings in the early 1960s brought about problems, which were also encountered by institutions, that were usually the result of a lack of support services. The author concludes that the poor treatment of people with disabilities will persist if society continues to view people with developmental disabilities as less than human.

795. Lutzker, J. R. (1990). Behavioral treatment of child neglect. *Behavior Modification, 14*(3), 301–315.

Child neglect and the behavioral treatment of neglected children is discussed in this article. It examines several different areas of dysfunction caused by this neglect: personal cleanliness, nutrition, and home safety and cleanliness. This article uses case examples drawn from referrals to the Illinois Department of Children and

Family Services Project 12 Ways, and it examines primary prevention issues related to health, stimulation, and affect.

796. Lynch, B., Molloy, D., Sullivan, M., Turner, T., & Representatives of the Mount Cashel Residents. (1991). Unfinished business: The Mount Cashel experience. *Journal of Child and Youth Care, 6*(1), 55–66.

This article provides a chronological account of the events immediately prior to, during, and following the closure of Mount Cashel. It was written by former staff and residents of the institution and outlines the feelings and concerns of those affected by the disclosures of 1989. This article expresses confusion and a sense of injustice, due in part to the negative attitude of the media and community toward the affair. Also, it describes an alternative program set up for boys forced to leave Mount Cashel at the time of closure.

797. Lyons, M. (1990). Enabling or disabling? Students' attitudes toward persons with disabilities. *American Journal of Occupational Therapy, 45*(4), 311–316.

This article discusses a study that assessed the attitudes of 223 undergraduate occupational therapy and 326 undergraduate business students at an Australian university in order to determine how they perceived people with disabilities. The participants of this study were asked to complete the Attitudes Toward Disabled Persons Scale, Form A and were questioned about any prior contact with people with disabilities (prior contact was categorized into valued social contact ($n=275$) and other contact ($n=274$). Those students who experienced valued social contact were significantly more positive in their attitudes concerning people with disabilities than students without such contact. However, this study found that, overall, there was no significant difference in the attitudes of both groups.

•M•

798. MacDonald, J. (1990, September 27). Camp will check beefs over medical, personal care. *The Edmonton Journal,* p. B3.

This newspaper article reports that officials at Camp Health, Hope, and Happiness, which is run by the Northern Alberta Crippled Children's Fund, are currently investigating complaints concerning inadequate medical and personal care for adults and children with disabilities residing in the camp. The complaints came from three institutions who send their residents to camp each summer. The investigation is in response to five senior citizens, one who fell out of bed due to the absence of side rails and was found to have a plugged catheter tube, and four who were not receiving their full medication. The camp serves more than 700 campers.

799. Mackenzie, T. B., Collins, N. M., & Popkin, M. E. (1982). A case of fetal abuse? *American Journal of Orthopsychiatry, 52*(4) 699–703.
This article examines a case of fetal abuse involving a 34-year-old woman with a history of alcohol and phenobarbital abuse. This woman also reported experiencing abuse from her husband. The woman exhibited no suicidal tendencies, and she was not psychotic. No fetal damage was noted, and a healthy infant was delivered at term. The authors include a discussion of the medical and legal rights of the fetus and of the patient.

800. Macklin, R. (1992). Which way down the slippery slope? Nazi medical killing and euthanasia today. In A. L. Kaplan (Ed.), *When medicine went mad: Bioethics and the holocaust* **(pp. 173–199). Totawa, NJ: Humana Press.**
This chapter discusses the common aspects of the Nazi euthanasia program and current proposals for assisted suicide and euthanasia. Macklin provides a restrained argument that shows concern for the current proposals for assisted suicide and euthanasia. She points out that many different definitions of assisted suicide and euthanasia are currently in use, creating a blurred concept of what is being proposed. She quotes Leo Alexander, U.S. Counsel for War Crimes at the Nuremberg trials, as saying that the horrific Nazi T4 atrocity started with a subtle change in the attitudes of physicians. She also cites parallels with the current concept promoted by some advocates of euthanasia, which states that withholding nutrition or medicine is morally superior to actively killing another human being. She quotes Hermann Pfannmüller, the Nazi physician credited with the perfecting techniques for starving children with disabilities, as saying, "We do not kill...with poison, injections, etc....No, our method is much simpler and more natural" (p. 191).

801. MacLean, N. M. (1992, February/March). Abuse issues for people with mental handicaps. *Transition,* **pp. 7–8.**
This article contains an interview with Kim Lyster, Community Relations Director of the British Columbia Association for Community Living (BCACL), on the issue of abuse and people with developmental disabilities. The BCACL is the provincial advocacy group for people with disabilities and their families. The interview addresses such issues as types of abuses, the increased prevalence of abuse perpetrated against people with developmental disabilities, legal concerns involving prosecution and lawyers, and resource and educational material for advocates.

802. MacLeod, R. (1992, February 15). Former operators charged after probe of
"rest home." *The Globe and Mail,* p. A10.
This newspaper article reports that 23 criminal charges have been laid against four former employees of the Gromley Rest Home in Richmond Hill, Toronto. The home is a privately run residence for former psychiatric patients. Charges include neglect, assault, and forcible confinement, and they cover a 6-year period.

803. MacNamara, R. D. (1988). *Freedom from abuse in organized care settings for the elderly and handicapped: Lessons from human service administration.* **Springfield, IL: Charles C Thomas.**
This book provides a good summary of Roger MacNamara's personal perspective on institutional abuse and also draws on some formal research. While MacNamara's perspective is largely based on his own experience, 25 years as a superintendent of various residential institutions have led to many apparent insights. He suggests that stress, isolation, depersonalizing environments, lack of care in selecting paid caregivers, habituation of violence, leadership failures, and a number of other factors contribute to chronic residential abuse. This book includes an interesting list of attributes MacNamara associates with caregivers likely to commit abuse. This list represents one of the first attempts at profiling abusive caregivers.

804. Madhavan, T., & Narayan, J. (1991). Consanguinity and mental retardation. *Journal of Mental Deficiency Research, 35,* **133–139.**
This article discusses a study conducted in India that examined the role of consanguinity in mental retardation. This study examined 517 people with mental retardation and their families. One hundred sixty children were born of consanguineous marriages, and 357 were born to nonconsanguineous marriages. The findings of this study indicate the following: the risk of mental retardation is very significant in children of parents in a consanguineous marriage who have a family history of mental retardation, and those most at risk for mental retardation in offspring are uncle-niece consanguineous marriages.

805. Maher, T. F. (1989). The psychological development of prelinguistic deaf infants. *Clinical Social Work Journal, 17*(3), 209–222.
This article discusses the psychological development of an infant with hearing impairments and focuses on the infant's interaction with the environment. It examines attachment and object relations and their part in the psychological development of the infant. It reviews the research in these areas and concludes that the emotional availability of the caregiver in infancy seems to be the most important growth-promoting feature of the early rearing experiences. It states that the studies of deaf infants indicate that hearing impairments in infants as well as the caregiver's reaction to the impairment influences "infant-parent" relationships. It claims that the limited

communication skills of the child with hearing impairments restricts expressions of affection that may affect mother-child bonding. It suggests that, eventually, mothers may withdraw from children with hearing impairments who seem less active in the absence of maternal stimulation and, as a result, lack initiation. Also, it proposes that the stressful caregiver-infant relationship interferes with preverbal communication skills, and as a result, children with hearing impairments lag behind their peers in emotional and cognitive development. In addition, children with hearing impairments have a higher risk of developing psychological disorders. This article provides a case history of a 16-year-old boy with hearing impairments who has a psychiatric disorder. It describes the treatment of this disorder using the Fraiberg intervention model, which consists of intensive psychotherapy, developmental guidance, and supportive treatment. The author concludes that therapeutic interventions need to be more widely available and offered at an earlier stage in the development of a child with hearing impairments.

806. Makas, E. (1988). Positive attitudes toward disabled people: Disabled and nondisabled persons' perspectives. *Journal of Social Issues,* **44**(1), 49–61.

This article discusses a study conducted to assess what constitutes positive attitudes toward people with disabilities. This study questioned people with and without disabilities about their views on people with disabilities. This study used the Issues in Disability Scale to assess these perspectives. The participants in this study included people with disabilities (n=92), "good attitude" individuals without disabilities chosen by the participants with disabilities for their positive attitudes toward people with disabilities (n=96), and students without disabilities (n=83). The students without disabilities filled out the questionnaire twice: The first time they completed it honestly, and the second time they tried to fake a good attitude. The results of this study indicate that the participants with disabilities and the participants without disabilities differed on what constitutes positive attitudes toward people with disabilities. The participants with disabilities felt that a positive attitude was evident when they were treated as an individual, with no specialized treatment offered due to their disability. For the participants without disabilities, a positive attitude was characterized by a desire to be helpful and nice, which, according to the author, tends to reduce the person with disabilities to a helpless or needy role.

807. Man guilty of assaulting mentally disabled adults. (1989, September 22). *The Globe and Mail,* **p. D13.**

This newspaper article reports on the outcome of the trial of Jean Thibault, former owner of the Cedar Glen Home for adults with mental disabilities. Mr. Thibault was convicted of 11 counts of assault and acquitted on 14 other charges. Nineteen witnesses told how the owner abused residents in the home by means of assault, criminal negligence causing bodily harm, assault with a weapon, uttering death threats, and unlawful confinement.

808. Mansell, S., & Sobsey, D. (1993). Therapeutic issues regarding the sexual abuse of people with developmental disabilities. *Revue Sexologique,* **1**(2), 139–159.

This article examines sexual abuse issues involving people with developmental disabilities. Selected findings from a University of Alberta survey study on sexually abused people with developmental disabilities are presented and addressed with regard to the following: accessibility, availability, and appropriateness of sexual abuse treatment for people with developmental disabilities. This study found that people with developmental disabilities who have been sexually abused have trouble gaining access to resource centers and resources. According to the authors, inadequate training and experience among professionals in treating sexually abused people with developmental disabilities and professional pessimism toward adapted therapy for people with developmental disabilities has limited the development of suitable treatment approaches. Examples of appropriate sexual abuse treatment strategies for use with people who have disabilities are provided for practitioners.

809. Mansell, S., Sobsey, D., & Calder, P. (1992). Sexual abuse treatment for persons with developmental disabilities. *Professional Psychology: Research and Practice,* **23**(5), 404–409.

Using data collected by the Sexual Abuse and Disability Project at the University of Alberta with a survey of 119 sexual abuse victims with developmental disabilities, the authors discuss sexual abuse treatment for people with developmental disabilities. The authors found that treatment services for people with developmental disabilities are usually inaccessible, unavailable, and inappropriate. They feel that inadequate treatment services are the result of a lack of qualified professionals in the area of sexual abuse treatment and the slow development of appropriate treatment programs. They examine therapy approaches for use with people with developmental disabilities and provide examples of sexual abuse treatment programs used with children and women who were abused as children. In addition, the authors discuss sexual abuse treatment issues for people with developmental disabilities.

810. Mansour, G., Zernitsky-Shurka, E., & Florian, V. (1987). Self-reported assertion of males with and without a physical disability: A cross-cultural study. *International Journal of Rehabilitation Research,* **10**(2), 167–174.

The cross-cultural study discussed in this article was conducted with males with and without disabilities in order to assess levels of assertion. This study obtained self-reports from Israeli Arabs (n=42) and Israeli Jews (n=40) with physical disabilities and Israeli Arabs (n=58) and Israeli Jews (n=49) without disabilities (controls) using the Assertion Inventory. The results of this study indicate that Arabs without disabilities had the least amount of assertion when compared to the other three groups. This article included further discussion of different cultural demands and social behavior.

811. Marais, E., & Marais, M. (1976). *Lives worth living: The right of all the handicapped.* **London: Souvenir Press.**

The book uses a historical perspective to examine the lives of people with mental disabilities in England. It examines the services available to this population and discusses future trends in care. The first section presents a definition of mental disability, reviews various types of disabilities, and explores the emotional aspects of the lives of people with mental disabilities. The second section presents a historical overview of changing attitudes and practices. The third section describes the education of people with mental disabilities and emphasizes the following: language and communication, music, social training, play therapy, and preparation for employment. The fourth section discusses people with mental disabilities in the community and the use of leisure time and the role of the social worker. The fifth and final section presents the trends in services and discusses areas in which interested lay and professional persons can provide help. This book includes a bibliography and various addresses of societies and organizations in England as well as suppliers of goods.

812. Marchant, C. (1993). A need-to-know issue. *Community Care,* **990, 11.**

This article discusses sex education for young adults with mental retardation. The author argues that these individuals need to know about sexuality in order to help protect them from abuse.

813. Marchant, R. (1991). Myths and facts about sexual abuse and children with disabilities. *Child Abuse Review,* **5(2), 22–24.**

This article provides basic information about sexual abuse of children with disabilities by presenting widely held mythical beliefs (e.g., children with disabilities are asexual beings, and no one would abuse such vulnerable children) and contrasting them with the grim realities of abuse.

814. Marchant, R., & Page, M. (1992). Bridging the gap: Investigating the abuse of children with multiple disabilities. *Child Abuse Review,* **1(3), 179–183.**

This article addresses the child abuse of children with multiple or severe disabilities. It pays particular attention to the investigation process used by child protection workers when they investigate allegations of abuse. The authors suggest techniques that stem from their investigative work with 15 children with disabilities, ages 7 to 17, who were suspected of having been abused. They emphasize meeting the needs of the child, in part, by

using alternative communication systems. The authors discuss assessing suspected abuse and preparing for the investigative interview, and they describe general factors found useful during the interview process.

815. Marchant, R., & Page, M. (1993). *Bridging the gap: Child protection work with children with multiple disabilities.* **London: National Society for the Prevention of Cruelty to Children.**

This monograph discusses the challenges of including children with severe and multiple disabilities in the full range of child abuse prevention and intervention services, and it identifies priorities for improving service for these children. In addition to introduction and conclusion sections, there are chapters on the following areas: "When to investigate," "How to investigate," "Interviewing: Preparation and practical issues," "Conducting the interview," "Therapeutic work," and "Preventive work." The authors identify communication impairment as the greatest obstacle to prevention, law enforcement, and treatment services, and they suggest some strategies for improving communication. The authors conclude that there is a need for cooperative efforts among professionals, particularly those with skills related to the needs of people with disabilities and those with skills related to child protection.

816. Marchetti, A. (1987, May). *Abuse of mentally retarded persons: Characteristics of the abused, the abuser, and the informer.* **Paper presented at the 111th Annual Meeting of the American Association on Mental Deficiency, Los Angeles. (ERIC Document Reproduction Service No. ED 286 313)**

This paper discusses possible causes of abuse of people with mental retardation living in institutions by residence staff. The database comprised all abuse cases reported between January 1984 and September 1986 in residential facilities in the state of Alabama, and a review of these data reveal the following: The abused group is identified as having higher IQs and demonstrating more adaptive behavior compared to nonabused residents; age, sex, and racial factors yielded no significant differences; staff profiles suggest that the abuse was committed primarily by direct care personnel who are less educated and less well paid than other staff members; and abuse tended to be reported by professionals and administrative staff. The author suggests that direct care staff should receive more instruction regarding behavior management and aggression control techniques and that staff should be rotated on a regular basis to less stressful areas of the residence. Also, the author feels that more professional and administrative staff should be assigned to residential areas, and abuse should be reported and tracked.

817. Marchetti, A. G., & McCartney, J. R. (1990). Abuse of persons with mental

retardation: Characteristics of the a-bused, the abusers, and the informers. *Mental Retardation, 28*(6), 367–371.

This article analyzes the reports of abuse or neglect from four residential facilities for persons with mental disabilities. The authors found that the vast majority of abuse was perpetrated by nonprofessional direct care staff on the second shift and was directed toward individuals with mild, moderate, and severe disabilities. Nonprofessional direct care staff also reported most of the incidents, although there were reports from indirect and professional staff as well. The analysis reveals that male staff were more likely to abuse, but equally likely to report as compared to female staff. It also suggests that the resident's age, gender, and race are not significant factors in risk for abuse.

818. Margolin, L. (1991). Child sexual abuse by non-related caregivers. *Child Abuse & Neglect, 15,* 213–221.

This article describes the nature of contacts between child abuse victims and their nonrelated perpetrators. Although abuse was identified in a variety of settings under a number of caregiving arrangements, the author found that most of the abuse was perpetrated by a regular caregiver in the child's own home. Perpetrators were generally male, with a mean age of about 18. A key finding was that parents' lack of action in response to allegations of abuse by their children contributed to the continuation of the abuse.

819. Margolin, L. (1992). Child abuse by mothers' boyfriends: Why the overrepresentation? *Child Abuse & Neglect, 16,* 541–551.

This article examines the overrepresentation of mothers' boyfriends in child abuse cases when compared to other nonparental caregivers. The data for this study were obtained from single mothers and cases of child physical abuse from the Iowa Department of Human Services. The results of this examination indicate that mothers' boyfriends who perform minimal child-care services are responsible for more child abuse than other nonparental caregivers. It discusses the conditions that result in this overrepresentation: the location of child care in single-parent families; gender of the perpetrator, with more abuse being perpetrated by males; nongenetic relationship between the abused child and the perpetrator; the perpetrator being viewed as an illegitimate caregiver by family members, themselves, their partners, and society; and rivalry between the child and the mother's boyfriend.

820. Marinelli, R. P., & Dell Orto, A. E. (Eds.). (1984). *The psychological and social impact of physical disability* (2nd ed.). New York: Springer.

This book addresses the psychological and social impact of physical disability on the individual with physical disabilities and his or her associates. It examines the personal meaning and interpersonal significance of a dis-

ability and discusses attitudes, attitude change, and social acceptance of people with disabilities.

821. Marino, R. V., Scholl, T. O., Karp, R. J., Yanoff, J. M., & Hetherington, J. (1987). Minor physical anomalies and learning disability: What is the prenatal component? *Journal of the National Medical Association, 79*(1), 37–39.

This article describes a study that compared 30 children with learning disabilities who did not have mental retardation, ranging in age from 7 to 11, who attended special education classes with 30 controls matched for age and gender. Each child was examined for physical or neurologic characteristics of fetal alcohol exposure. The authors found that the group with learning disabilities was 7.25 times more likely to exhibit characteristics of fetal alcohol exposure than controls.

822. Marks, P. (1993, April 22). Man is held in abandoning of his handicapped son, 9. *The New York Times,* p. B6.

This newspaper article reports the case of a 9-year-old Long Island boy with cerebral palsy who was abandoned in a bowling alley by his father because the father was unable to obtain care for his son. The unemployed father, Warclaw Dobkowski, dropped his son off at a bowling alley, telling one of the employees that he was too much trouble. The employees chased after the father, but they were unable to convince him to take back his son. The father was charged with abandonment of a child, with bail set at $5,000. Mr. Dobkowski has also been ordered not to have any contact with his son after he threatened to leave his son in the middle of traffic if he was forced to take care of him. Custody of the boy was given to his mother.

823. Martin, E. D., Jr., & Gandy, G. L. (1990). *Rehabilitation and disability: Psychosocial case studies.* **Springfield, IL: Charles C Thomas.**

This book provides disability-oriented case studies for use in a variety of disciplines involved with therapeutic counseling, both rehabilitation and psychological counseling. The case studies were designed to permit the development of multiple perspectives, depending on the discipline or theoretical orientation. Part 1 contains three chapters that discuss the following: the philosophical foundations and aspects of the rehabilitative process, the social and psychological aspects of disability as it relates to rehabilitation, and a guide to help the practitioner evaluate disability. Part 2 presents psychosocial case studies of people who have disabilities such as rheumatoid arthritis, blindness and visual disability, cardiovascular disease, back injury, chronic obstructive pulmonary disease, deafness and hearing impairment, learning disability, mental retardation, personality disorder, seizure disorder, mood disorder, spinal cord injury, and substance abuse disorder. In each case, the social evaluation provides an overview and context for the medical, psychological, educational, vocational, and economic assessments. This book includes discussion questions after each case.

824. Martin, H. P. (1976). Neurologic status of abused children. In H. P. Martin (Ed.), *The abused child: A multidisciplinary approach to developmental issues and treatment* **(pp. 67–82). Cambridge, MA: Ballinger.**
This article describes a 5-year follow-up study of 58 abused children. This sample of children represented less severely injured children than many other studies done around this time. Of the children with no previous history of head injury, 43% manifested some neurologic trauma. The author emphasizes the importance of using a multidisciplinary approach when treating the victims of child abuse.

825. Martin, J. A., & Elmer, E. (1992). Battered children grown up: A follow-up study of individuals severely maltreated as children. *Child Abuse & Neglect,* *16*, **75–87.**
The long-term follow-up study of 19 battered children is described in this article. The results of this follow-up indicate a complex relationship between childhood maltreatment and adult functioning. According to the authors, the varied outcomes for these adults make it impossible to generalize.

826. Martin, K. (1992, April 23). Judge decries attack on disabled woman. *The Calgary Sun,* **p. 12.**
This newspaper article reports that Bertram Floyd Johnson, a 54-year-old resident-manager for the Calgary Association for the Mentally Handicapped nursing home, was given a 3-year jail term for sexually assaulting a resident. A 39-year-old female with Down syndrome used anatomically correct dolls and limited gestures and verbal communication to describe her ordeal.

827. Martin, N., & Martin, B. (1992). Sexual abuse: Special consideration for teaching children who have severe learning difficulties. *Mental Handicap Bulletin,* *86*(4), **13–17.**
This article discusses factors that make children with mental retardation more vulnerable to sexual abuse, and it includes recommendations for personal safety and sex education: for example, teaching children that some parts of the body are private, teaching children that they have the right to say "no," and teaching children to tell a trusted person what has happened. The authors also stress the responsibility of teachers to recognize and report signs of abuse, and they present some strategies for teachers to use in teaching children with severe disabilities about abuse prevention.

828. Martorana, G. R. (1985). Schizophreniform disorder in a mentally retarded adolescent boy following sexual victimization [Letter to the editor]. *American Journal of Psychiatry, 142*(6), 784.
This letter to the editor is a comment on an earlier article in the journal about three female adolescents who developed psychoses after sexual assault and their subsequent treatment. This letter tells of a case involving a 14-year-old male with mental retardation who was sexually assaulted and developed a psychosis after the attack. This letter describes the child's subsequent treatment and recovery.

829. Mash, E. J., & Terdal, L. G. (Eds.). (1988). *Behavioral assessment of childhood disorders* **(2nd ed.). New York: Guilford Press.**
This book uses a behavioral perspective for the assessment of specific disorders in children and families. It contains 18 chapters that provide a detailed analysis of the disorder, and it examines specific methods used for assessment: "Behavioral assessment of child and family disturbance" (Mash & Terdal), "Attention deficit disorder with hyperactivity" (Barkley), "Conduct disorders" (McMahon & Forehand), "Childhood depression" (Kazdin), "Fears and anxieties" (Barrios & Hartmann), "Social skill deficits" (Hops & Greenwood), "Mental retardation" (Crnic), "Autism" (Newsom, Hovanitz, & Rincover), "Learning disabilities" (Taylor), "Brain-injured children" (Fletcher), "Chronic illness and pain" (Johnson), "Childhood obesity" (Foreyt & Goodrick), "Tic disorders and Gilles de la Tourette syndrome" (Barkley), "Elimination problems: Enuresis and encopresis" (Fielding & Doleys), "Child abuse and neglect" (Wolfe), "The sexually abused child" (Wolfe & Wolfe), "Family conflict and communication in adolescence" (Foster & Robin), and "Anorexia nervosa and bulimia" (Foreyt & McGavin).

830. Masuda, S. (1988). 22 million for transition houses—But can we use them. *Thriving,* *1*(1), 1. (*Thriving* is a publication of DAWN Canada.)
This article points out that although the Canadian government is undertaking an initiative to create more shelters for battered women there is no requirement that these shelters be accessible to women with disabilities.

831. Masuda, S., & Riddington, J. (1990). *Meeting our needs.* **Vancouver, BC: DAWN (DisAbled Women's Network) Canada.**
This document includes the following: 1) background information about sexual, physical, and emotional abuse of women with disabilities; 2) a survey of accessibility of Canadian transition houses for battered women; and 3) guidelines for improving the accessibility of transition houses. An introduction, written by Jillian Ridington, includes information on the nature and prevalence of offenses committed against women with disabilities. The accessibility survey includes useful ratings of shelters in each province and territory. The guidelines for improving

accessibility include much useful information to assist service providers.

832. Matas, R. (1992, February 21). Child abuse kills 5,000 each year, MD says. *The Globe and Mail*, **p. A4.**
Dr. Richard Krugman, who spoke at the World Congress on Child Health, reports that approximately 1 to 2.5 million children are abused in the United States each year, 5,000 of whom die as a result of the abuse. Dr. Krugman elaborates on his personal research involving a study of 70 fatal abuse cases carried out by the Kempe National Centre for the Prevention of Child Abuse and Neglect in Denver, Colorado. In addition, Dr. Gallo spoke to Congress about the magnitude of HIV-infected infants and predicted that in Africa alone a quarter of a million infants will be born with the HIV virus in 1992.

833. Matson, J. L. (1984). Psychotherapy with persons who are mentally retarded. *Mental Retardation, 22*(4), 170–175.
The author asserts the importance of professionals paying greater attention to the emotional problems of people who have mental retardation. According to the author, although over the years a wide variety of therapies have been used with people with mental retardation, these therapies have had differing degrees of success and empirical rigor. These therapies include: dynamic therapy, group therapy, behavioral therapy, and play therapy. This article examines crucial questions in psychotherapy research, for example, the generalizability of treatment effects and the criteria used to assess successes that are both clinically and statistically significant. It asserts that it is important for mental health professionals to use psychotherapeutic approaches with clients with mental retardation who have emotional problems. The author concludes that the increasing knowledge of psychotherapy and the development of new approaches and technological advances in more established therapy methods may make therapy more viable for people who have mental retardation.

834. Matson, J. L. (1989). *Social learning approaches to the treatment of emotional problems.* **Lexington, MA: Lexington Books.**
This book describes how social learning procedures (such as modeling, role playing, social reinforcement paired with tokens, and feedback on performance of desired behaviors) and instructions for effectively performing particular skills can be used to correct a wide range of emotional problems in persons with mental retardation. It illustrates the successful management of depression, phobias, obsessive compulsive behaviors, psychosomatic complaints, and decreasing inappropriate verbal behavior in persons with chronic schizophrenia using assessment and empirically validated treatment approaches. The data suggest that these methods have potential for ameliorating the problems of persons with mental retardation and mental illness. The author feels that the nature, degree, and type of emotional problems in persons with

mental retardation may vary as a function of intellectual level and concludes that the presence of additional physical disabilities may further complicate these emotional problems.

835. Matson, J. L. (1989). Social learning approaches to the treatment of emotional problems. In R. Fletcher & F. J. Menolascino (Eds.), *Mental retardation and mental illness* **(pp. 141–155). Lexington, MA: Lexington Books.**
This chapter discusses social learning approaches to the treatment of emotional problems in adults with mild developmental disabilities. It features case examples for the following emotional problems: depression, psychosomatic complaints, obsessive compulsive behavior, phobias, and the verbal behaviors of schizophrenia. This chapter also includes a discussion of the following assessment and treatment techniques: modeling, role playing, social reinforcement, token economies and other forms of feedback, and instructions.

836. Matson, J. L., & Senatore, V. (1981). A comparison of traditional psychotherapy and social skills training for improving interpersonal functioning of mentally retarded adults. *Behavior Therapy, 12,* **369–382.**
This article discusses a comparison study conducted with 32 outpatients with mild to moderate mental retardation in order to examine interpersonal functioning. The 11 females and 21 males ranged in age from 28 to 49. Each participant was randomly assigned to one of three conditions: psychotherapy ($n=11$), social skills training ($n=11$), and a no treatment condition ($n=10$). Treatment involved a 1-hour session twice a week for 5 weeks and involved three to five people per group. In psychotherapy, group cohesion and self-expression of feelings were emphasized. The social skills training focused on such target behaviors as reducing complaint statements and increasing positive statements. Both treatments used events and the workshop as reference. Preassessments and postassessments were conducted using the following: role play scenes rated after listening to an audiotape of the participants' responses, group meetings, the Nurses' Observation Scale for Inpatient Evaluation, and the Social Performance Survey Schedule. Target behaviors consisted of the following: appropriate statements of one word, appropriate statements of more than one word, inappropriate statements, and general social skills. The results of this study indicate that the participants in the social skills treatment program showed significantly more improvement in their interpersonal function than participants in the other two treatment programs.

837. Matsushima, J. (1990). Interviewing for alleged abuse in the residential treatment center. *Child Welfare, 69*(4), 321–331.
The author of this article makes a series of recommendations for people conducting interviews in order to determine abuse in residential facilities. The author sug-

gests that the interviewer should support both the child accuser and staff and should incorporate the use of open-ended questions in order to uncover the circumstances and context of the alleged abuse. Also, the author stresses the need for collaboration and specifics in child testimony as there is a likelihood of unsubstantiated claims.

838. Matthews, G. F. (1983). *Voices from the shadows: Women with disabilities speak out.* **Toronto: Women's Educational Press.**

The author, Gwyneth Ferguson Matthews, describes this book as "a somewhat informal mixture of interview and autobiography." In response to a request by the Government of Nova Scotia in 1981, the International Year of Disabled Persons, Matthews interviewed 45 Canadian women with a range of social, economic, and educational backgrounds and needs. The purpose of the research was to identify and address the issues and difficulties faced by women with disabilities. Ironically, the government was unwilling to publish the findings on the grounds that it was "too depressing." Dissatisfied with the government's reaction to the reality lived by women with disabilities, Matthews arranged for publication of her findings in this volume. She provides a personal perspective on areas such as education, sexuality, motherhood, home, accessibility (both physical and social), employment, finance, and friendship. She discusses and challenges traditional myths and discrimination in all aspects of life, and she emphasizes the need to advocate for changes that would enable all women to lead decent lives. This book includes a resource guide that contains a bibliography and a list of Canadian self-help and advocacy groups.

839. Mayer, M. A. (1992). Rights & responsibilities—Choices & consequences: The new skill domains. In *Crossing new borders* **(pp. 64–67). Kingston, NY: National Association for the Dually Diagnosed.**

This chapter describes the shift from teaching people with disabilities to be compliant to teaching them about their rights and how to make their own choices. The author discusses some issues for professionals and provides practical suggestions for implementing training on rights, responsibilities, choices, and consequences. A personal "Bill of Rights and Responsibilities" is described to clarify each individual's rights, choices, and responsibilities.

840. Mayer, P., & Brenner, S. (1989). Abuse of children with disabilities. *Children's Legal Rights Journal, 10*(4), 16–20.

This article provides a brief overview of research that examines the prevalence of child abuse involving children with disabilities. It offers suggestions that attempt to explain why these children are more likely to be abused than children without disabilities. This article discusses the challenges for the legal profession when working with people with disabilities who have been abused, and

it provides information about services for children and adults with disabilities.

841. McAfee, J. K., & Gural, M. (1988). Individuals with mental retardation and the criminal justice system: The view from states' attorneys general. *Mental Retardation, 26,* 5–12.

This article deals primarily with people with mental retardation who are accused of criminal offenses; however, some of the problems cited with defendants also are of concern to victims. The authors conclude that police, prosecutors, and judges typically lack information about people with disabilities.

842. McArther, S. (1989). Crime risk education is essential for the disabled. *Rehabilitation Digest, 19*(4), 20–21.

This article discusses crime prevention material designed for use by people with disabilities. This material addresses the following areas: accessibility to 911 emergency services; Ontario laws regarding physical, verbal, and sexual abuse; how to get help; residential security; and safety in the streets. These materials were developed by Crime Risk Education is Essential for the Disabled (CREED). CREED was developed by the Ontario Federation for the Cerebral Palsied (OFCP). This article also makes reference to a crime survey conducted by CREED in the Toronto area, a crime survey that indicates that people with disabilities are more often victimized than people without disabilities. This article mentions the workshops held by CREED throughout Ontario and CREED's coordination for the Ontario Women's Directorate of an education program entitled "Local Sexual Assault Education Initiatives."

843. McCabe, M. P., & Cummins, R. A. (no date). *Sexual abuse among people with intellectual disabilities: Fact or fiction.* **Unpublished manuscript. Melbourne, Australia: Deakin University.**

This article discusses a study conducted to uncover sexual abuse among 30 people with mild mental retardation and 50 people without disabilities. The results of this study indicate the following: 1) people with mild mental retardation were more likely to be victims of sexual assault, 2) people with mild mental retardation were more likely to commit sexual assault, 3) people with mild mental retardation were 3.6 times as likely to have been raped, 4) people with mild mental retardation were 2.4 times as likely to have had unwanted sexual contact on more than one occasion, 5) people with mild mental retardation were 1.8 times as likely to have had sexual contact with a relative, and 6) people with mild mental retardation were also much more likely to lack sex education and other critical personal safety information.

844. McCaffrey, M. (1979). Abused and neglected children are exceptional children. *Teaching Exceptional Children, 11*(2), 47–50.

This article discusses the role of a teacher when child abuse or neglect is suspected. According to the author, the teacher has the responsibility to report suspected cases of child abuse (including sexual abuse) and neglect. The teacher also has a professional responsibility: A teacher should find out what resources are available to him or her both in and out of school; school staff should be given inservice training on the problem of child abuse and neglect; teachers can organize policy development or program development even without inservice training; staff should provide follow-up assessment and evaluation and support services once a case has been reported; and teacher should recognize children in potential high-risk situations, for example, children who are premature, disruptive, or have disabilities.

845. McCann, I. L., Sakheim, D. K., & Abrahamson, D. J. (1988). Trauma and victimization: A model of psychological adaptation. *The Counseling Psychologist,* *16*(4), 531–594.

This article presents an extensive review of the different variables involved in the course and aftermath of victimization. A review of the literature focuses on the prevalence of victimization and the different response patterns among victims. Of these response patterns, this article closely examines the emotional, cognitive, biological, behavioral, and interpersonal responses. It suggests some theories to explain the reactionary response of the victim and discusses cognitive schemas using case examples to demonstrate the victim's psychological adaptation to his or her experience. This article also discusses some of the therapeutic implications.

846. McCartney, J. R. (1992). *Abuse in public residential facilities for persons with mental retardation.* **Tuscaloosa, AL: The Association for Retarded Citizens of the United States and the Alabama Department of Mental Health and Mental Retardation.**

This report discusses a survey that was conducted in 23 state institutions serving people with developmental disabilities in order to collect information on abuse. This study used a control group of randomly selected clients and staff for comparison purposes, and it compared the data from 401 abused participants and 409 controls. The average age for the abused group was 34.94 years, and it was 36.88 years for controls. The study group was 60% male and 40% female, and the participants were predominantly White. The findings of this study indicate the following: physical abuse occurred most frequently between 3 P.M. and 6 P.M.; abusive incidents increased in May to June and decreased in November to December; incidents of abuse occurred more frequently in residential versus nonresidential areas; victims had most likely been victimized previously and exhibited maladaptive behavior; and perpetrators were most commonly male, new to the job, had a history of abusing, and worked the second shift. This report suggests abuse prevention and reduction strategies.

847. McCelland, C. O., Rekate, H., Kaufman, B., & Persse, L. (1980). Cerebral injury in child abuse: A changing profile. *Child's Brain,* *7*(5), 225–235.

This article presents case review data on 21 children admitted to the hospital over a 1-year period with skull or cerebral injuries as the result of child abuse. It describes a broad profile of resulting central nervous system sequelae and examines several injuries: whiplash shaken infant syndrome, cerebral contusions, severe spinal cord injuries resulting in paresis, skull fractures, and miscellaneous injuries. It points out that computer tomography (CAT scan) has proved to be valuable in the location of subdural-intracerebral hematomas and posterior fossa lesions as well as in providing longitudinal assessment of sequelae related to head trauma. This article also discusses the role of the child protection team.

848. McClain, P. W., Sacks, J. J., Froehlke, R. G., & Ewigman, B. G. (1993). Estimates of fatal child abuse and neglect, United States, 1979 through 1988. *Pediatrics,* *91*(2), 338–343.

The authors of this article estimate the number of child abuse and neglect (CAN) fatalities using death certificates of children ages birth to 17 from 1979 through 1988. They classified the deaths using the *International Classification of Diseases* (9th rev.). Three models, consisting of six coding categories, were used, ranging from being very conservative to being more inclusive. The coding categories explaining the cause of death were: 1) overt (CAN deaths), 2) homicide, 3) undetermined, 4) accident, 5) sudden infant death syndrome (SIDS), and 6) natural. For categories 2 to 6, research studies and crime data were used to help determine the estimated number of CAN deaths. The results of this evaluation indicate that the mean annual number of CAN deaths ranged from 861 to 1,814 for those children 4 years of age or younger and 949 to 2,022 for those children ages 17 years or younger, depending on the model. It found that children ages 5 years or younger constituted 90% of CAN deaths, and infants constituted 41% of CAN deaths. The authors note that approximately 85% of CAN deaths were misrecorded as being the result of other causes.

849. McCord, J. (1983). A forty year perspective on effects of child abuse and neglect. *Child Abuse & Neglect,* *7,* 265–270.

The author of this article conducted a 40-year perspective study of 232 males whose case records date back to the early 1940s. Four categories, "Neglected," "Abused," "Rejected," and "Loved," were used to distinguish how these men were raised by their parents. The subjects in the four categories were similar in socioeconomic status. During the late 1970s, a follow-up was conducted with 98% of these cases in order to assess the long-term effects of child abuse and neglect on developmental outcome. State records were accessed and interviews were conducted. The results of this analysis indicate that 45% of the males who had a prior history of abuse or neglect had criminal convictions, abused alcohol, were mentally ill, or had died at an early age. It found that males in the "Loved" category had the lowest rate of juvenile delinquency when compared to the other three categories. The author found that these four groups had similar problems with alcoholism, divorce, and occupational success.

850. McCrone, D. E. (1981). Preventing child abuse: A bibliography of information professionals should know to protect deaf children. *Perspectives for Teachers of the Hearing Impaired, 3*(5), 11–13.
This article includes sections on sexual abuse, institutional abuse, legal responsibilities, characteristics of offenders and potential offenders, hiring and training personnel, prevention programs, and treatment programs. It includes a bibliography of resources related to the abuse and neglect of children who are deaf.

851. McFarlane, A. C. (1988). Posttraumatic stress disorder and blindness. *Comprehensive Psychiatry, 29*(6), 558–560.
This article discusses four cases of post-traumatic stress disorder in people who are blind. It examines the following topics: the importance of visual imagery in the processing of traumatic events and the disruption of selective attention in post-traumatic stress disorder.

852. McFarlane, A. H. (1986). "The place of attachment in the life events model of stress and illness": Comment. *Canadian Journal of Psychiatry, 31*(8), 792–793.
This article comments on the article by West et al. (West, M., Livesley, W. U., Reiffer, L., & Sheldon, A. [1986]. *Canadian Journal of Psychiatry, 31*[3], 202–207) that examines the role social ties play in protecting against the development of depression and neurosis. It argues that West's model neglects the fact that life events precipitate a specific social need that leads to anxiety and then sets in motion predetermined attachment behaviors.

853. McFarlane, J. (1989). Battering during pregnancy: Tip of an iceberg revealed. *Women and Health, 15*(3), 69–84.
Battery during pregnancy and the adverse effects it has on the fetus are discussed in this article. It cites studies on etiology and incidence and describes a community-based educational prevention program promoting health and safety during pregnancy.

854. McGee, J. J. (1990). Toward a psychology of interdependence: A preliminary study of the effect of Gentle Teaching in 15 persons with severe behavioral disorders and their caregivers. In A. Dosen, A. Van Gennep, & G. J. Zwanikken (Eds.), *Treatment of mental illness and behavioral disorder in the mentally retarded: Proceedings of the International Congress, May 3rd & 4th, 1990, Amsterdam, the Netherlands* (pp.

45–70). Leiden, the Netherlands: Logon Publications.
This article describes the use and effect of Gentle Teaching with 15 people with severe behavioral disorders and their caregivers. It describes the five assumptions that govern Gentle Teaching: the meaning and power of value-centered interactions can be taught to people who do not respond to positive reinforcement; continuous delivery of noncontingent value-centered interactions is necessary for reducing severe behavioral patterns; reducing the use of punishment, restraint, and so forth helps break down the barriers that restrict social interactions such as bonding, friendship, and so forth; the caregiver's value giving and assistance leads to the person's ability to accept, seek out, and initiate human valuing; and although the use of punishment, restraint, and so forth might reduce severe maladaptive behavior, these treatments do not foster feelings of union and interdependence. This article investigates Gentle Teaching in four areas: 1) the reduction of severe and life-threatening behaviors; 2) the acceleration of positive client/caregiver interactions; 3) the reduction of punishment, restraints, and so forth; and 4) the acceleration of value giving. The author concludes that Gentle Teaching results in substantial changes in the client and the caregiver.

855. McGrath, T. (1991). Overcoming institutionalized child abuse: Creating a positive therapeutic climate. *Journal of Child and Youth Care, 6*(4), 61–68.
The purpose of this article is to characterize the child-care worker who may be at risk for perpetrating acts of abuse. It describes this care worker as a senior member of the staff who feels alienated or "burned out" and is able to negatively influence more inexperienced members of the team. The author offers recommendations about how staff members can create and maintain a positive, healthy working environment.

856. McGraw, S., & Sturmey, P. (1994). Assessing parents with learning disabilities: The parental skills model. *Child Abuse Review, 3*(1), 36–51.
This article reviews issues related to the parenting skills of people with mental retardation. The authors present a parental skills model that considers the parents' skills and abilities, personal and family history, and support and resources in determining potential for child care and support. They recognize that institutionalization and other atypical childhood experiences may threaten parenting skills more than any inherent limitations imposed by disability.

857. McGuire, T. L., & Feldman, K. W. (1989). Psychologic morbidity of children subjected to Munchausen syndrome by proxy. *Pediatrics, 83*(2), 289–292.
This article describes six case reports that address the psychological morbidity of Munchausen syndrome by proxy victims. Cases two and three and cases five and six involve siblings. Case one was the fourth child in a

family in which three older siblings were previously abused. All of the children in these cases had developmental behavior problems.

858. McKague, C. (1985). The competency of a mentally handicapped person to testify. *Just Cause, 3*(2), 19–22.

This article examines the five criteria that need to be met by persons with developmental disabilities in order to be considered competent to testify: displaying sufficient intelligence, a capacity to observe the event in question, a capacity to recall events, a capacity to narrate, and feeling a duty to tell the truth. This article includes four case examples that illustrate how to determine competence.

859. Mckenzie, L. (1983). *Reasons for judgement in the matter of Steven Dawson.* Toronto: National Institute on Mental Retardation.

This paper examines the reasons for a decision made by British Columbia Supreme Court Judge Lloyd G. McKenzie in the case involving Stephen Dawson, a 6-year-old child with a severe mental disability. This child required corrective surgery to repair a blocked shunt. Stephen's parents objected to the surgical intervention and went to court to prevent it.

860. McKinley, J. C., Jr. (1989, August 5). Officers implicated in report on death of a retarded man. *The New York Times*, pp. A1, A29.

This newspaper article reports the suffocation death of Kevin Thorpe, a 31-year-old Brooklyn man with mental retardation who suffocated while being restrained by police officers. The police were called to the home of Esther Thorpe, Kevin's mother, who required assistance because her son was hitting her. The two police officers who arrived were unable to restrain Mr. Thorpe and called for assistance. In total, 10 officers are implicated in the death of Kevin Thorpe, who suffocated due to the weight of the officers on his back.

861. McKinley, J. C., Jr. (1989, August 6). Family says retarded victim couldn't heed officers. *The New York Times*, p. A28.

This newspaper article follows the continuing story of Kevin Thorpe, a 31-year-old Brooklyn man with mental retardation who suffocated while being restrained by police officers. Mr. Thorpe is described by family members as a man with a small vocabulary and hyperactivity. His lack of understanding concerning commands made by police led to Mr. Thorpe's ultimate restraint by up to 10 police officers. Restraint consisted of having officers sitting or lying on Mr. Thorpe. This article asks whether or not police followed departmental guidelines concerning the handling of emotionally disturbed people. One of the guidelines calls for the use of an emergency services officer, who was not called in this particular case. Another guideline states that arrest of the subject should not be

attempted unless the subject poses a danger or threat to himself/herself or to others.

862. McLaren, J., & Brown, R. E. (1989). Childhood problems associated with abuse and neglect. *Canada's Mental Health, 37*(3), 1–6.

This article reviews the literature dealing with physically abused, sexually abused, and neglected children in order to determine the indicators of child abuse. This article concludes that there are a variety of childhood disorders associated with abuse and neglect and that different forms of maltreatment lead to similar problems.

863. McMullen, R. J. (1986). Youth prostitution: A balance of power? *International Journal of Offender Therapy and Comparative Criminology, 30*(3), 237–244.

The article describes a study conducted in central London, England, that examined the experiences of young people who become prostitutes. This study found the following factors believed to lead to a life of prostitution: feelings of powerlessness, histories of childhood sexual abuse, running away from home, feelings of worthlessness, and social attitudes. This article includes a discussion of STREETWISE, a therapeutic intervention program.

864. McPherson, C. (1984, February 6). Vulnerable victims of assault. *The Toronto Star*, pp. B1, B2.

This newspaper article gives an overview of the problem of sexual assault of persons with disabilities. While there are virtually no statistics on the rate of assault and crime against people with disabilities, most experts say that crime against this population is no more frequent than crime against people without disabilities. According to this article, people with disabilities are clearly more vulnerable: For example, attacks on people with disabilities can have more severe consequences than attacks on people without disabilities; people with disabilities cannot communicate to authorities as readily as people without disabilities, especially if the victim is deaf or blind; the victim with disabilities feels that if the crime is reported there may be repercussions, such as, losing a job or some other benefit; people with disabilities have a poor self-image; and if a person with disabilities is sexually assaulted, the chance for a conviction is low because, in court, a victim with mental retardation has his or her credibility attacked as do other victims. This article points out that there is a review of the court process and its availability to people with disabilities being done by a member of the Ontario judiciary.

865. McPherson, C. (1990). Concerns around the gaps in legislation re: The assault and sexual assault of people with disabilities. *Victims of Violence Report, 1*(2), 40–42.

This article offers several recommendations for filling the gaps in the legislation regarding the assault and sexual assault of people with disabilities: 1) extend provisions of C-15 to all vulnerable victims, not just children; 2) remove the requirement for understanding an oath; 3) provide interpreters for all victims who require them; 4) establish clearer guidelines for the misuse of authority under § 265 (3) (d) of the criminal code, which establishes that teachers, health service providers, or other caregivers of people with disabilities are misusing authority when they have sex with a service consumer unless the care provider can clearly demonstrate unprejudiced, informed consent on the part of the service consumer; 5) mandate reporting of abuse of people with disabilities; 6) provide whistle-blower protection measures; 7) allow hearsay when it is the best available source; 8) require complete abuse protocols for all agencies serving vulnerable populations; 9) screen all employees before hiring to agencies serving vulnerable populations; 10) provide an emergency substitute guardian who can consent to examination when the current guardian is suspected of abuse; 11) provide independent advocates for all people living in institutions; 12) provide emergency placement for vulnerable adults in danger of abuse; 13) provide money through criminal injuries compensation boards to fund victim treatment services or special accommodations required to make these services accessible and appropriate; 14) use civil proceedings to direct compensation to victims in order to fund treatment; 15) lengthen the time for suing for damages related to incest, sexual abuse, and sexual assault; 16) strengthen professional standards and regulations exercised by professional associations; 17) provide a Medicare diagnostic classification of child abuse and wife assault in order to assist in gathering more data; 18) provide mandatory testing for sexually transmitted diseases in alleged abusers; 19) reduce the length of time before cases are heard since delay may reduce the chances of the victim with a disability remembering or testifying; 20) ensure that the best forensic evidence possible is available in cases with victims who have disabilities since challenges to their testimony may make this evidence more vital to successful prosecution; 21) and enact mandatory arrest laws that require the police to charge suspected abusers.

866. McPherson, C. (1990). *Responding to the abuse of people with disabilities.* **Toronto: ARCH (Advocacy Resource Centre for the Handicapped).**
This booklet is intended to assist people with disabilities and others who advocate for them to recognize and respond to abuse. It provides a clear explanation of Canada's criminal justice system and its implications for crime victims. Although many of the details of this booklet are specific to Canada, its organization and clarity make it potentially useful for those preparing a similar guide for other jurisdictions.

867. McQueen, P. C., Spence, M. W., Garner, J. B., Pereira, L. H., & Winsor, E. J. T. (1987). Prevalence of major mental retardation and associated disabilities in the Canadian Maritime provinces. *American Journal of Mental Deficiency, 91*(5), 460–466.
This article discusses a study that examined the prevalence of major mental retardation in children 7 to 10 years of age living in the Canadian Maritime provinces. The study group consisted of 167 children from New Brunswick, 118 children from Nova Scotia, and 22 children from Prince Edward Island. The results of this study indicate the following: prevalence of major mental retardation was 3.65 per 1,000 children; variation in prevalence appeared to be associated with the age of the mother, greater population density, and the number of physicians per capita; and the major associated disabilities were speech and behavior disorders and epilepsy.

868. Mead, J. J., & Westgate, D. L. (1992). *Investigating sex crimes against children.* **Chino, CA: For Kids Sake.**
This book is an informative guide to investigating sex crimes against children. It supplies descriptive characteristics of both victim and perpetrator. It provides a sexual assault medical evaluation outline and suggests interviewing techniques for use with victims of sexual abuse.

869. Meadow, K. P., Greenberg, M. T., & Erting, C. (1984). Attachment behavior of deaf children with deaf parents. *Annual Progress in Child Psychiatry and Child Development,* 176–187.
This article discusses a study where 17 children who are deaf, all of whom had parents who were both either deaf or hard of hearing, were videotaped to assess development of secure attachment with and independence from their parents. Videotapes consisted of 30-minute sequences comprising three segments. The findings of this study were similar to previous studies of children with normal hearing. These children with hearing impairments did not show significant signs of delays in the development of attachment with their parents. The authors suggest that discrepancies between this study and previous studies may be the result of parental characteristics, history, and environment rather than the development of the child with a hearing impairment.

870. Meadow, R. (1977). Munchausen syndrome by proxy: The hinterland of child abuse. *The Lancet, 2,* 343–345.
In this article, two case histories of mothers who induced recurrent illnesses in their children in order to obtain unwarranted medical services are discussed in terms of Munchausen syndrome by proxy (MSBP). The first case history involves a 6-year-old girl and her mother. The child's induced symptoms began at 8 months of age. The second case involves a boy who received medical treatment for recurrent illnesses from the age of 6 weeks. At age 14 months, this child died as a result of his mother's symptom induction, which involved the ingestion of large dosages of sodium. This article describes similari-

ties in both cases: falsification of the children's case histories, the tampering of specimens by the mothers, and the pleasant and cooperative nature of the two women. Both women had been labeled hysterical personalities and had a tendency toward depression.

871. Meadow, R. (1982). Munchausen syndrome by proxy. *Archives of Disease in Childhood,* **57, 92–98.**
This article describes the presence of Munchausen syndrome by proxy (MSBP) in 17 families that included 19 children under the age of 7. Two of the children died, eight were taken from the home, and nine were left in the custody of the parents. The abuse was perpetrated by the mother in all cases. This author discusses the warning signs of MSBP and explains the rationale behind this behavior and its association with nonaccidental injury, iatrogenic injury, and parent-induced injury.

872. Meadow, R. (1989). Epidemiology. *British Medical Journal,* **298, 727–730.**
Types of child abuse, the prevalence of abuse, and its etiology are discussed in this article. It includes pictorial examples of the different kinds of abuse, from punching and lashing to severe neglect and sexual abuse.

873. Meadow, R. (1989). Munchausen syndrome by proxy. *British Medical Journal,* **299, 248–250.**
This article discusses Munchausen syndrome by proxy, a form of child abuse characterized by a fictitious disorder in a child fabricated by a primary caregiver, usually the mother. The abuse stems from the direct actions of the mother and the prescribed treatment of the doctors. Telltale signs include: perceived illness in the child, doctor shopping, induced disability in the child, and fabrication of symptoms. This article describes types of fabricated illnesses and factual causality, warning signs for these cases, and action to be taken by medical personnel who suspect abuse.

874. Meadow, R. (1989). Poisoning. *British Medical Journal,* **298, 1445–1446.**
This article examines the intentional poisoning of children. It discusses the detection of intentional poisoning of children and the analysis of the type of poison used in this type of child abuse. The author notes that the victims in these cases are usually less than 2.5 years old and that accidental poisoning usually occurs in toddlers between the ages of 2 and 4.

875. Meadow, R. (1989). Suffocation. *British Medical Journal,* **298, 1572–1573.**
This article examines the association between asphyxia by means of smothering and child abuse. It describes clinical features and indications of smothering and differential diagnosis like apnea and sudden infant death syndrome (SIDS). The author believes that 2% to 10% of infants who died of SIDS are actually victims of child abuse.

876. Meadow, R. (1990). Suffocation, recurrent apnea, and sudden infant death. *Journal of Pediatrics,* **117(3), 351–357.**
This article reviews the cases of 27 children who had been suffocated by their mothers. Of this study group, nine children died from their abuse, and one child developed severe brain damage as a result of the abuse. Twenty-four children experienced recurrent episodes of apnea, cyanosis, or seizures. Eleven children were victims of Munchausen syndrome by proxy. Thirty-three siblings were associated with the study group, of which 18 had died at an early age. Similar medical presentations were given for 13 of the siblings who had died, although most were diagnosed with SIDS.

877. Measures, P. (1992, January 30). Abuse: The disability dimension. *Social Work Today,* **pp. 16–17.**
This article alerts social workers to the problem of violence against people with disabilities. It is intended as an introduction to the topic, and it raises questions about how violence is linked to disability and what social workers need to do in order to address the needs of clients with disabilities who experience abuse.

878. Mehta, M. N., Lokeshwar, M. R., Bhatt, S. S., Athavale, V. B., & Kulkarni, B. S. (1979). "Rape" in children. *Child Abuse & Neglect,* **3, 671–677.**
This article describes a study that examined 130 individual child rape cases in India in order to determine the relevant factors associated with child rape in India. The Indian cultural context provides a perspective on the treatment of rape and provides a comparison with Western culture. The study examines the incidence of rape and the socioeconomic and familial backgrounds of victims. This article also discusses the results of this study.

879. Meier, J. H., & Sloan, M. P. (1982). *Acts of God or rites of families: Accidental versus inflicted child disabilities.* **Beaumont, CA: Children's Village, USA. (ERIC Document Reproduction Service No. ED 234 891)**
In this document, child abuse is studied in terms of a multifactorial model in which neglect dynamics play a central role. It pays particular attention to the operation of these dynamics between parents and a child with disabilities. It discusses the role of reproductive pay-off in the neglect of a weaker or less fit child, and it considers the effects of removing a child as a factor in the dissolution of the family or the begetting of a new infant. The authors suggest interdisciplinary family-oriented intervention to help parents resolve the conflicts surrounding the damaged parent-child relationship.

880. Meier, J. H., & Sloan, M. P. (1984). The severely handicapped and child abuse. In J. Blacher (Ed.), *Severely handicapped young children and their families* **(pp. 247–274). Orlando, FL: Academic Press.**

The authors of this chapter point out the uncertainty of the relationship between the contribution of abuse to developmental delays and the contribution of developmental delays to abuse. This chapter's primary focus is on physical abuse, not sexual abuse, but many of the issues raised appear to generalize across these two forms of abuse. The authors point out that the majority of children who are victims of physical abuse have developmental disabilities.

881. Meinhold, P. M., & Mulick, J. A. (1990). Counter-habilitative contingencies in institutions for people with mental retardation: Ecological and regulatory influences. *Mental Retardation, 28*(2), 67–75.

According to this article, reinforcement practices that do not result in adaptive behavior or habilitation are called counter-habilitative. This article examines some counter-habilitative contingencies in institutions for people with mental retardation. It uses study data from a residential facility to demonstrate the influence of various counter-habilitative regulatory contingencies affecting residents. This article concludes that the interaction between agency regulations, social ecology of the institution, and residents' individual needs may produce contingencies that might be counter-habilitative for staff members and residents.

882. Meinhold, P. M., & Mulick, J. A. (1991). Counter-habilitative contingencies in residential institutions. In S. R. Schroeder (Ed.), *Ecobehavioral analysis and developmental disabilities: The twenty-first century* (pp. 105–121). New York: Springer-Verlag.

This chapter examines the counter-habilitative contingencies that affect staff and resident behavior in residential institutions for people with mental retardation. The effects of the physical and social environment of the institution on the conduct of staff and residents is both direct and indirect. The analysis of the institutional ecology on resident behavior suggests that the systems that are in place to foster habilitation and independence could be counter-habilitative. Recommendations are made for further analysis of institutional policies and regulations concerning their affect on residents.

883. Meins, W. (1990). Psychotropic drug use in mentally retarded adults—Prevalence and risk factors. In A. Dosen, A. Van Gennep, & G. J. Zwanikken (Eds.), *Treatment of mental illness and behavioral disorder in the mentally retarded: Proceedings of the International Congress, May 3rd & 4th, 1990, Amsterdam, the Netherlands* (pp. 299–305). Leiden, the Netherlands: Logon Publications.

The study discussed in this chapter examined the prevalence and risk factors of psychotropic drug use in adults with mental retardation. Eleven hundred fifty-four (1,154) people from Hamburg, Germany, were categorized into three age groups: 19–40 years of age (*n*=422), 41–59 years of age (*n*=503), and 60 years or older (*n*=229). There were 664 males and 490 females, with 765 institutionalized and 389 noninstitutionalized participants in this study. The results of this study indicate the following: 1) 22% of the participants were prescribed psychotropic drugs, two thirds of which were neuroleptics; 2) the prescription of psychotropic drugs was correlated with age, gender, and setting, with younger subjects, male subjects, and institutionalized subjects receiving more psychotropic drugs in general and more neuroleptics specifically; 3) 43% of the participants received several psychotropic drugs simultaneously; and 4) anticonvulsants were also correlated with age and setting, with greater prescribed use for young participants and institutionalized participants. In addition, 692 participants of this study were assessed for aggressive behavior as defined by aggressive behavior directed toward a person or object within the last 4 weeks. Of this sample, 109 participants met this criterion and were further examined. The results of this examination reveal the following: psychotropic drug treatment was more often prescribed if the participants were younger, displayed greater motor skills, displayed fewer self-help skills, and if staff had difficulty discerning the onset of aggressive behavior; and neither frequency nor severity of aggressive behavior was correlated with drug treatment.

884. Melberg, K. (1984). Mentally retarded easy prey. *Spokesman, 17*(19), 5–6, 14.

This article discusses how myths commonly held about women are applied to people with mental retardation (e.g., people with mental retardation are devalued in the same way that women are devalued).

885. Melling, L. (1984). Wife abuse in the deaf community. *Response to Violence in the Family and Sexual Assault, 7*(1), 1–2, 12.

This article focuses on wife abuse in the deaf community. It points out the following: 1) violence against women who are deaf is inflicted by men who are deaf as well as by men who are not deaf; 2) for the woman who is hearing impaired, all the problems facing battered women are exacerbated by communicating with those who do not speak her language and the critical lack of information and services available to her; 3) the woman who is deaf has special problems in that there is an information gap between herself and others; and 4) there is the community factor, that is, the deaf community is extremely close, strong, and insular, and the wife has a greater dependence on this community and is afraid of threatening this support system. This article discusses the responses of professionals, whose approach operates on three levels: to educate those working with domestic abuse victims about the special needs of women who are deaf, to educate people with hearing impairments about the problem of domestic violence, and to train those working with people who are deaf to identify and assist battered women.

886. Mellon, C. A. (1989, Winter). Evaluating the portrayal of disabled characters in juvenile fiction. *Journal of Youth Services in Libraries, 2,* 143–150.

This article examines the characterization and stereotyping of people with disabilities in juvenile literature. It presents a more realistic portrayal of people with disabilities using examples from fiction and nonfiction.

887. Melton, G. B. (1987). Special legal problems in protection of handicapped children from parental maltreatment. In J. Garbarino, P. E. Brookhauser, & K. J. Authier (Eds.), *Special children-special risks: The maltreatment of children with disabilities* **(pp. 179–193). New York: Aldine de Gruyter.**

This chapter points out that parents have a legal duty to care for their children, and when the child is disabled, the state requires that the child receives a free, appropriate education, including appropriate related services. Currently in the United States, the legislative trend is toward expanding jurisdiction for state intervention to protect children from maltreatment. The primary purpose of state intervention is prevention. The question then arises of whether Child Protective Services can be used to prevent disabling conditions. This chapter suggests that primary and secondary prevention of disabilities are prone to substantial practical, ethical, and legal problems: for example, competency to testify, proof of harm, dispositional planning, and termination of parental rights.

888. Melton, G. B., & Greenberg Garrison, E. (1987). Fear, prejudice, and neglect: Discrimination against mentally disabled persons. *American Psychologist, 42* **(11), 1007–1026.**

This article examines federal legislation that pertains to the advocacy of people with mental disabilities. The authors use legal cases to illustrate both historical and present federal antidiscrimination statutes.

889. Menolascino, F. J. (1989). Overview: Promising practices in caring for the mentally retarded-mentally ill. In R. Fletcher & F. J. Menolascino (Eds.), *Mental retardation and mental illness* **(pp. 3–13). Lexington, MA: Lexington Books.**

This chapter presents an overview of the practices of caring for people with mental retardation who are mentally ill. This overview reveals that people with mental retardation suffer from the same range of mental illnesses as the general population. The reasons for the high incidence of mental illness in people with mental retardation include: reduced capacity to withstand stress, poor ability to resolve mental and emotional conflicts, lack of competence, and emotional instability. This chapter notes that the diagnosis of psychiatric problems in people with mental retardation may not be possible with the traditional diagnostic methods; consequently, it suggests that it is necessary to consider the atypical features that are unique and individualized. This chapter states that reliance on the signs rather than the symptoms will help in the diagnosis. According to this chapter, one of the major steps in the management of mental illness in people with mental retardation is the establishment of bond between the caregiver and the individual requiring care. This chapter recommends the following introduction to Gentle Teaching: ensuring and teaching the value of human presence by preventing the occurrence of the maladaptive behavior, use of adaptive tasks to focus the client's attention, and teaching the meaning of reward. It suggests that psychoactive medication should be used as an adjunct to the whole treatment process and should be phased out based on how much the client is stabilized. Community care with placement of the person in specialized group homes forms the final part of the total rehabilitation. The author suggests links with community mental health programs and feels that professionals working for the welfare of people with mental retardation who are mentally ill should act as agents for social change by bringing these people back into the family and community.

890. Mercer, J., Andrews, H., & Mercer, A. (1983). The effects of physical attractiveness and disability on client ratings by helping professionals. *Journal of Applied Rehabilitation Counseling, 14*(4), 41–45.

This article discusses a study in which graduate and undergraduate students in personal and guidance counseling, rehabilitation counseling, or social work rated a client on 22 bipolar adjectives, which were later factored into six orthogonal factors: social attractiveness, prognosis, physical attractiveness, personal evaluation, severity of presenting problem, and adjustment. Also, these students rated a female confederate in one of four conditions: attractive with physical disability, attractive without physical disability, unattractive with physical disability, and unattractive without physical disability. A multiple analysis of variance procedure indicates the following: the attractive confederate was rated more favorably; and the client with a disability received higher ratings on all six factors, with the exception of the severity of the presenting problem. According to the authors, these findings indicate that a positive stereotype for a female with a disability exists.

891. Mercer, M. (1982). Closing the barn door: The prevention of institutional abuse through standards. In R. Hanson (Ed.), *Institutional abuse of children and youth* **(pp. 127–132). New York: Haworth Press.**

This chapter recommends the implementation of standards, instead of case by case investigation, for helping prevent institutional abuse. It examines the following issues: prevention theory, staffing and supervision, programming, community support, and disciplinary action.

892. Meyer, J. E. (1988). "Die Freigabe der Vernichtung lebensunwerten Lebens" von Binding und Hoche im Spiegel der deutschen Psychiatrie vor 1933 ["Release for elimination of those unworthy of living" by Binding and Hoche: The response of German psychiatry prior to 1933]. *Nervenarzt, 59*(2), 85–91.

The author of this article addresses German psychiatry prior to 1933 by examining the book "Die Freigabe der Vernichtung lebensunwerten Lebens" (Release for elimination of those unworthy of living), written in 1920 by German psychiatrists K. Binding and A. Hoche. Binding and Hoche advocated the elimination of people with developmental disabilities. The author examines reactions to this book by reviewing the psychiatric literature of that time and notes that there was little reaction from the psychiatric profession in response to the publication of this book; in fact, this topic was rarely discussed. The author questions why German psychiatrists did not see the danger of this attitude toward people with disabilities. Also, the author discusses the role of Social Darwinism and the Weimer Republic.

893. Meyer, J. E. (1988). The fate of the mentally ill in Germany during the Third Reich. *Psychological Medicine, 18*(3), 575–581.

This article examines measures used against adults and children with disabilities by the Nazi regime under Hitler during World War II. It discusses these measures, which included the sterilization and extermination of psychiatric patients to ensure that those who were considered incurable did not reproduce. Approximately 350,000 people, mostly with psychiatric disorders, were sterilized between 1934 and 1939. It discusses the "Aktion" program, a German term much like the English word "operation" when used in the military sense, which was responsible for the extermination of children with disabilities. The "Aktion" program was initiated as part of the extermination plan against people with disabilities in 1939 and resulted in the death of approximately 5,000 children under the age of 17. It describes the "Aktion T4" program, which ran from 1939 to 1941 and was responsible for the death of approximately 70,000 adult psychiatric patients. This program was stopped because of public uneasiness about this program. This article discusses the Second Phase of Nazi euthanasia, or Wild Euthanasia, that killed approximately 70,000 patients up to 1945. This Second Phase involved the "Aktion 14 f 13" program, in which doctors who had worked on "Aktion T4" were moved to concentration camps in order to identify prisoners who were deemed unworthy of life. It discusses Operation Brant, named for Hitler's personal physician, in which the Nazis removed and exterminated

patients from mental hospitals in order to make room for war casualties. The author addresses some of the possible social and political determinants for the movement against people with disabilities and the response of German psychiatrists to these programs.

894. Meyer-Lindenberg, J. (1991). The Holocaust and German psychiatry. 143rd Annual Meeting of the American Psychiatric Association: International Scholars Lecture Series (1990, New York, New York). *British Journal of Psychiatry, 159*, 7–12.

This article examines the role of German psychiatry and psychiatrists during the Holocaust and the effect that the Holocaust had on German psychiatry. It pays particular attention to the role of psychiatry in the extermination, sterilization, and institutionalization of people with developmental disabilities. During the first few years of the Nazi regime, 1,200 university professors, one third of them from the field of medicine, were removed from their positions, and anyone who opposed the Nazi ideology was placed in indoctrination camps. Jewish doctors were initially denied the right to practice in 1933, and in 1938, they were stripped of their licenses and expelled from the country. This article states that one third of those medical professionals left in Germany were believed to be sympathetic to the Nazi ideology. It also describes the heroic efforts of some German psychiatrists in opposing the Nazi regime and assisting those in need. This article examines the impact of compliance to the state on medical ethics.

895. Michaud, S. G., & Aunesworthy, H. (1989). *Ted Bundy: Conversation with a killer.* **New York: Signet.**

This book provides extensive interviews with serial killer and rapist Ted Bundy conducted shortly before his execution. Although readers should use caution regarding Bundy's credibility since he remains manipulative and evasive throughout the interviews, his own statements provide testimony to the power of alcohol, depersonalization, and pornography in disinhibiting horrendous urges of fused sexuality, violence, and control. Bundy also discusses the need to raise his self-esteem by beating the system. His episodes of shoplifting, car theft, and savage murders all served to temporarily boost his self-image, which was severely threatened by pervasive feelings of inadequacy and failure.

896. Michelin, L. (1993, May 3). Vulnerable need firmer protection, says group. *The Red Deer Advocate*, **p. B1.**

This newspaper article reports that critics of the Vulnerable Persons Protection Act, a private-member's bill proposed to the Alberta legislation, would like additional changes to the bill in order to offer greater protection from abuse for people with disabilities. The bill currently does not address issues concerning behavior therapies that utilize electric shocks, cold showers, or time outs. The bill does give institutions and group homes the responsibility for the protection of its residents and protects employees from recrimination resulting from the disclosure of patient abuse. In addition, the bill makes it mandatory to inform outside sources of institutional abuses.

897. Miles Patterson, P. (1991). *Doubly silenced: Sexuality, sexual abuse and people with developmental disabilities.* **Madison: Wisconsin Council on Developmental Disabilities.**

This book provides a helpful guide for frontline workers, case managers, family members, advocates, and guardians associated with people with developmental disabilities. It outlines a variety of ways in which concerned individuals can help support people with developmental disabilities in making responsible decisions regarding their sexuality, help provide support to those who have been sexually abused, and provide intervention with individuals with developmental disabilities who are sexual abuse offenders. It discusses the development and expression of sexuality of people with developmental disabilities and the environmental barriers to this development and expression of sexuality. Also, this book includes chapters that examine sexuality, policies about sexuality and education, sexual assault, survivors, and offenders.

898. Millard, L. (1994). Between ourselves: Experiences of a women's group on sexuality and sexual abuse. In A. Craft (Ed.), *Practice issues in sexuality and learning disabilities* **(pp. 135–155). London: Routledge.**

This chapter describes the author's work in counseling a group of women with learning difficulties. Although the group was not set up as an abuse survivors' group, many group members had been sexually abused, and one was raped during the time that the group meetings were taking place. As a result, dealing with sexual violence became a central focus for the group. The author stresses the need for wholistic counseling that deals with the individual's whole life and does not focus merely on abuse issues.

899. Miller, C., & Boe, J. (1990). Tears into Diamonds: Transformation of child psychic trauma through sandplay and storytelling. *The Arts in Psychotherapy, 17,* **247–257.**

The Tears into Diamonds treatment program for child psychic trauma is discussed in this article. Two modalities, fairy tale storytelling and sandplay, are used in this treatment program in order to give the abused child the means to communicate his or her trauma and fears. In sandplay, projective play is initiated by the child who metaphorically communicates to the staff member a personalized experience using miniature figures in sand. In the second modality, story and fantasy tales are chosen by the staff that metaphorically represent themes that simulate the trauma experienced by the child, for example, aggression, abuse, fear, abandonment, and so forth. The child can communicate his or her experience with reference to the story. The staff responds to the storytelling within the same context. The sharing of experience is conducted within a nurturing environment, which includes a personal nursing staff member.

900. Miller, T. (1988, June 15). *Helping the survivors of sexual assault.* **Paper presented at the Sexual Assault and the Mentally Handicapped 2nd Annual Conference, The Blackfoot Inn, Calgary, AB.**

The author of this paper provides recommendations for assisting people with developmental disabilities who have been sexually assaulted. This paper includes a list of counseling goals, and it discusses procedural guidelines for caregivers, parents, counselors, and therapists to follow when helping the individual deal with the assault. The author examines prevention issues, including self-protection against sexual assault for young people.

901. Millington, R. (1992, September). Waiting for the trial. *National Association for the Protection from Sexual Abuse of Adults and Children with Learning Disabilities, 1,* **9–10.**

This article describes the sexual abuse of a young woman with a learning disability, examines the legal investigation of this abuse, and discusses the ensuing court proceedings. The article is written from the perspective of the young woman and discusses her unsupportive family and her court anxiety.

902. Miner, M. H., Marques, J. K., Day, D. M., & Nelson, C. (1990). Impact of relapse in prevention in treating sex offenders: Preliminary findings. *Annals of Sex Research, 3,* **165–185.**

This article describes a study conducted by the Sex Offender Treatment and Evaluation Project (SOTEP) in California to determine the effectiveness of their Relapse Prevention intervention program for sex offenders. This study examined 50 treated cases (volunteers), 48 controls (volunteers), and a group of involuntary offenders who did not enter the program. Their offenses included the following: child molestation (boys only, girls only, both genders) and rape of adult women. The intervention consisted of a cognitive behavioral approach that addressed the following: cognition, decision making, and development of coping skills. Using the Multiphasic Sex Inventory, this study found that those offenders who had completed the program were significantly more inclined to accept responsibility for their actions than controls. Using the Minnesota Multiphasic Personality Inventory, the Carlson Psychological Survey, and two Locus of Control assessment tools, this study found that those offenders who had completed the program accepted responsibility for their life circumstances. It found that cognitive distortions, justification for criminal behavior, and deviant sexual arousal were also reduced among treated offenders. Using the Sex Offender Situational

Competency Test, this study found that treated offenders appeared better able to cope in high-risk situations. In addition, this study found that post-release criminal activity was less frequent in treated offenders than in controls and nonvolunteers.

903. Minford, A. M. B. (1981). Child abuse presenting as apparent "near-miss" sudden infant death syndrome. *British Medical Journal, 282,* **521.**
This article presents the case history of a 4-month-old boy with an apneic episode and his 27-year-old mother. The mother had induced the apneic episode by smothering the child. During pregnancy, the mother had suffered depression and had suicidal thoughts while being hospitalized for bronchiectasis.

904. Minnesota Program for Victims of Sexual Assault. (1983). *Are children with disabilities vulnerable to sexual abuse?* **St. Paul: Author.**
This pamphlet is designed to acquaint parents of children with disabilities about the problem of sexual abuse. This pamphlet focuses on prevention.

905. Mitchell, E. A., Taylor, B. J., Ford, R. P. K., Stewart, A. W., Becroft, D. M. O., Thompson, J. M. D., Scragg, R., Hassall, I. B., Barry, D. M. J., Allen, E. M., & Roberts, A. P. (1992). Four modifiable and other major risk factors for cot death: The New Zealand study. *Journal of Paediatrics and Child Health, 28*(Suppl. 1), S3–S8.
This article describes a New Zealand study on major risk factors for sudden infant death syndrome (SIDS) that compared 485 SIDS infants to 1,800 controls using obstetric records and parent interviews. Four factors were found to be significant in accounting for 82% of infant deaths associated with SIDS: having the infants sleep in the prone position, bed sharing with the infant, maternal cigarette smoking, and not breastfeeding. This study also confirmed risk factors cited by other studies.

906. Mitchell, E. A., Thompson, J. M. D., Stewart, A. W., Webster, M. L., Taylor, B. J., Hassal, I. B., Ford, R. P. K., Allan, E. M., Scragg, R., & Becroft, D. M. O. (1992). Postnatal depression and SIDS: A prospective study. *Journal of Paediatric Child Health, 28*(Suppl. 1), S13–S16.
This article describes a prospective study from New Zealand that was conducted to examine risk factors involved in postneonatal mortality. Thirty-three mothers of sudden infant death syndrome (SIDS) children and 174 mothers of control infants were compared on measures of postpartum depression measured at 4 weeks. Forty-six percent of the mothers of SIDS children were found to be depressed, compared with 16% of the mothers of con-

trols. Postnatal depression and SIDS were found to be highly correlated even after controlling for confounding variables.

907. Mitscherlich, A., & Mielke, F. (1962). *The death doctors.* **London: Elek Books.**
This book is an English translation of a book first published in 1949 in German. It describes some of the most frightening medical experiments conducted by physicians in the Third Reich in Germany, which were conducted along with the mass sterilization and euthanasia programs. This book is primarily a compilation of exerpts and quotes from 260 documents and testimony given at the Nuremberg trials. Testimony at Nuremberg by Karl Brandt, a defendant and physician who was put in charge of developing the euthanasia program, detailed how, in 1939, the father of a child with physical, mental, and sensory disabilities requested permission for "mercy killing " (p. 234), and this request was used to provide a rationale for a major program that ended the lives of many thousands. The legal basis for these actions had already been enacted in the 1933 "Law for the Prevention of Hereditarily Diseased Posterity" (p. 233) which permitted the elimination of both "undesirable national elements and undesirable invalids" (p. 233). While the decree was explicit, many of the organizations and activities set up to carry it out remained camouflaged. For example, three major groups set up to carry out the elimination program were "The National group for Study of Sanitoria and Nursing Homes, The Foundation for the Care of Institutions in the Public Interest, and the Limited Company for the Transport of Invalids in the Public Interest" (p. 236). Each of these units had a children's section that specifically concentrated on the euthanasia of children. The rationale given for secrecy was that if patients knew in advance "they would become excited" (p. 238). Terms such as "final medical assistance in the case of incurable invalids" (p. 239) were commonly used to legitimize mass murder as euthanasia, palliative care, or assisted suicide. Participants in the program were sworn to secrecy under penalty of death. Large-scale killing began at Grafneck Castle in March 1940, "though the male staff started somewhat earlier" (p. 240). About 75 people were killed each day there by gassing and lethal injection. These murder victims included adults diagnosed with mental illness and children with mental disabilities. Relatives were informed of the deaths with a form letter stating that the cause of the sudden and unexpected deaths was brain tumors or appendicitis and stated that life had been a torment due to their relative's mental disability and that the family should be happy that death had brought a relief to the suffering. The letters went on to explain that since the institution was threatened by an epidemic, it was necessary to cremate the body immediately for public health reasons. In spite of secrecy, however, Brandt described how blunders that resulted from the speed and scale of the murders led to suspicions among the general public. Some families received two different death notices for their relatives listing different causes and times of death; others actually received two urns with the ashes of their loved ones or were notified of the death of their loved one

occurring at a time when that individual was still alive and seen by relatives. Brandt estimated the total number of mentally ill killed as 60,000, but admittedly, he based this on a proportion of the total population (elsewhere this number is estimated at well over 100,000) and offers no estimates of the numbers of people with other disabilities who were eliminated. Brandt defended his work against charges that it might have been cruel, unethical, or immoral, indicating that the "underlying motive was the desire to help individuals who could not help themselves and were thus prolonging their lives in torment" (p. 266). Brandt was convicted at Nuremberg and sentenced to death. Hitler ordered an end to the mercy killing of adults in 1941 because of public criticism of the program, but the euthanasia of children with disabilities continued to the end of the war.

908. Moglia, R. (1986, March). Sexual abuse and disability. *SIECUS (Sex Information & Education Council of the United States) Report*, **pp. 9–10.**
This article tells the true story of a girl with disabilities who was sexually assaulted by her stepfather. This story is only one of numerous cases. It provides a review of the statistics available on sexual assault of people with disabilities and briefly discusses a general overview of the problem.

909. Monat-Haller, R. K. (1992). *Understanding & expressing sexuality: Responsible choices for individuals with developmental disabilities.* **Baltimore: Paul H. Brookes Publishing Co.**
This book was designed to help both parents and practitioners accept the sexual needs and feelings of people with developmental disabilities and mental retardation. In addition, the book is intended to provide people with developmental disabilities and mental retardation with information and counseling so that they might understand and express their own developing sexuality. This book presents a pragmatic perspective that outlines both successful and unsuccessful techniques. The author views people with mental retardation or developmental disabilities as sexual human beings with various levels of development, adaptive behavior, and coping skills. The first part of the book addresses the development of an individualized education/counseling program and the fundamental aspects of sexuality education and counseling. It discusses the principles underlying education and counseling as they relate to the following activities: self-stimulation, same-sex and opposite-sex activity, and marriage and parenthood. The final part of the book examines the following community issues: sexual abuse and exploitation, sex offenders, and undesirable sexual behavior. The appendices include organizational resources, a curriculum for inservice training, instructional aids and suggestions, and assessment tools. In addition, this book provides a glossary of terms, a list of approximately 175 written materials, a list of films, and a list of anatomical doll manufacturers.

910. Money, J. (1980). The syndrome of abuse dwarfism (psychosocial dwarfism or reversible hyposomatotropinism): Behavioral data and case report. In G. J. Williams & J. Money (Eds.), *Traumatic abuse and neglect of children at home* **(pp. 365–374). Baltimore: The Johns Hopkins University Press.**
This chapter examines the behavioral characteristics of psychosocial dwarfism and the case report of a 21-year-old male. Maltreatment was first recognized when the subject was 2.5 months old, with preventive action initiated at age 16. Severe intellectual and motor impairment was diagnosed as well as physical growth retardation. It includes a biography of the abuse and eventual reeducation of this man. As a result of treatment, this man's intelligent quotient increased from 51 to 79, and his height and weight also increased.

911. Monfils, M. J. (1984). New challenges in social work practice with the mentally retarded. In F. J. Menolascino & J. A. Stark (Eds.), *Handbook of mental illness in the mentally retarded* **(pp. 385–397). New York: Plenum.**
This chapter focuses on social workers and their role as service providers for people with developmental disabilities. The author states that because of the confirmation of human rights for people with developmental disabilities it is necessary to examine their access to appropriate resources concerning mental health. The author believes that the social worker who addresses the needs of people with developmental disabilities in both institutional and community settings should become involved in the following activities: social group work, boundary work such as coordinating discharge-planning efforts, family support services, consultation, and community development.

912. Monfils, M. J. (1985, March). Theme-centered group work with the mentally retarded. *Social Casework: The Journal of Contemporary Social Work*, **pp. 177–184.**
The author of this article reviews the theme-centered interactional model and provides suggestions for its application in work with people who have developmental disabilities. The theme-centered interaction model consists of group counseling that is centered around a central theme. Its versatility is in its variability of theme, which depends on the subject group. This article examines the following areas: common themes that can be used with clients with disabilities, group composition, group purpose, therapeutic techniques, and leadership style.

913. Monfils, M. J. (1989). Group psychotherapy. In R. Fletcher & F. J. Menolascino (Eds.), *Mental retardation and mental illness: Assessment, treatment and service for the dually diagnosed* (pp. 111–125). Lexington, MA: Lexington Books.

This chapter addresses group psychotherapy for people with developmental disabilities. It contains a literature review and discusses the advantages of group therapy. It examines the following areas: important variables that need to be considered for group therapy for people with developmental disabilities (group composition, goals, group structure, rules, procedures), techniques of therapy (types of interventions, awareness of reality, stress), and leadership style. This chapter also discusses some common themes that occur in therapy with people who have developmental disabilities.

914. Monfils, M. J. (1989). *Group psychotherapy*. Lexington, MA: Lexington Books.

This book describes group treatment approaches that form an important part of the comprehensive treatment-management approach for people with mental retardation who have psychiatric disorders. It states that group treatment approaches have been practiced since the late 1940s in the management of adolescents with mental retardation, and these include: role play, films, parties, psychodrama, and pantomimes. This book traces the history of the use of group therapeutic techniques in the management of the psychiatric disorders of persons with mental retardation. The mastering of assertion skills in persons with mental retardation is emphasized since they are frequently victimized because they cannot speak for themselves. The advantages of group therapy include: sharing of information and experiences, peer and therapist modeling, confrontation, group support and encouragement, problem solving, cohesion, and efficient use of resources. According to the author, therapists who work with persons with mental retardation need to carefully consider the composition of the group and each individual's strengths and difficulties. Optimally, a group functions with about six to eight members. Group members need to possess some motivation for change, have some verbal expression abilities, and have some degree of insight. Those in acute psychotic excitement may be excluded, but people with severe and profound mental retardation should not be excluded. A clear understanding with group members about the group's purposes and goals is necessary; this understanding could be in the form of a contract. The group structure and the therapeutic techniques should be tailored to the intellectual and verbal comprehension levels of the clients, and the rules and procedures should be specified. In the techniques involved, establishing a relationship with the group and self-disclosure are important. Denial should be adequately handled. Directive approach may be used for people with severe and profound mental retardation. The techniques for the relationship group and social skills group are described. Reality awareness is emphasized in psychotic, primitive, and minimally verbal persons. Many of the techniques used in group therapy are aimed toward stress management. An active and directive style of leadership is indicated. The common themes that recur in the group therapy sessions include: inadequate self-image, sexual problems, handling emotions, feelings about being retarded, and adjustment problems when separating from the family and moving into community residences and vocational placement. The author suggests mental health professionals should be excited about using group therapeutic procedures for persons with mental retardation.

915. Monfils, M. J., & Menolascino, F. J. (1983). Mental illness in the mentally retarded: Challenges for social work. *Social Work in Health Care, 9*(1), 71–85.

The study discussed in this article was conducted to determine the prevalence and nature of mental disorders in people with mental retardation who lived in the community. The authors feel information obtained might help determine which social work treatment strategies would be most effective for meeting the needs of these people. Of 168 people referred for psychiatric evaluation, 114 of them were assessed with both mental illness and mental retardation and were included in the study. Participants ranged in age from 6 to 76 (66% male), with 6% under the age of 10, 43% teenagers, and 51% adults, and they were all assessed between January 1976 and June 1979 by the Eastern Nebraska Community Office of Retardation. The participants' psychiatric disorders consisted of the following: schizophrenia, personality disorders, psychoneurotic anxiety reaction, adjustment reactions, and organic brain syndrome. This article discusses psychiatric disorders, accompanying clinical descriptors, and treatment techniques.

916. Monfils, M. J., & Menolascino, F. J. (1984). Modified individual and group treatment approaches for the mentally retarded-mentally ill. In F. J. Menolascino & J. A. Stark (Eds.), *Handbook of mental illness in the mentally retarded* (pp. 155–169). New York: Plenum.

This chapter discusses individual counseling and group counseling for people with developmental disabilities. It examines both therapist and client characteristics that might predict successful outcomes and discusses treatment goals, intervention techniques, and common themes in therapy.

917. Moore, T., Pepler, D., Weinberg, B., Hammond, L., Waddell, J., & Weiser, L. (1990). *Research on children from violent families*. Toronto: York University Family Problem-Solving Project.

This book discusses research on children and family violence and the psychological impact of being a victim of or witness to this type of family interaction. It discusses the strengths and weaknesses that the child possesses to cope with such situations, the mother-child relationship, the sibling relationship, and peer relations and adjustment problems experienced by children from abusive homes. Recognizing that situations of family dysfunction are different, the authors point out that affective responses in children are also different.

918. Morey, M. A., Begleiter, M. L., & Harris, D. J. (1981). Profile of a battered fetus. *The Lancet, 2,* 1295–1296.
This article presents a case report of prenatal battery. This case involves a woman who had three pregnancies, with one successful delivery. Physical abuse during pregnancy was present for all pregnancies. The infant who was delivered by means of caesarean section died within a few hours. An autopsy revealed intraventricular hemorrhaging. According to the authors, fetal battery resulting in stillbirths or dying neonates is not a rare occurrence.

919. Morgan, S. R. (1987). *Abuse and neglect of handicapped children.* San Diego: College-Hill Press.
This books states the following: Children with disabilities are victims of abuse at least as often as other children, some children acquire disabling conditions as a result of abuse, premature infants are abused and neglected significantly more than others, infants with birth defects are more likely to be victims of gross life-threatening neglect, and alcohol is noted as a factor in child sexual abuse and other forms of abuse. This book examines the following areas: societal attitudes toward people with disabilities, the definition of child abuse and neglect, the question of cause and effect between disabilities and abuse, the characteristics of parents who abuse, and abuse by professionals.

920. Morris, A. (1982). *A curriculum guide: Social and self-protection skills for the severely handicapped.* Washington, DC: Molly Roeseler Anderson.
This is an appropriate guide for teaching nonverbal students about self-protection skills in order to prevent abuse. This guide can be used independently of other written material or audiovisuals.

921. Morris, S. (1993, June). Healing for men. *NAPSAC (National Association for Prevention of Sexual Abuse of Children and Adults with Learning Disabilities) Bulletin, 4,* 11–13.
This article describes the author's experience working with a group of sexually abused young men with mental retardation. He describes his initial feelings of uncertainty and uneasiness working with these clients and suggests that discussing the work with others was helpful in overcoming these feelings. Sexual abuse is often a manifestation and symptom of the greater powerlessness experienced by people with disabilities. Healing requires addressing the broader life issue of disempowerment. The therapist must help clients gain power over all aspects of their lives, but he or she must be careful not to encourage a false sense of power that will likely result in failure. The therapist should choose an environment that is private and encourages a sense of confidence and con-

trol, a place that will be relatively free from intrusion from others. Clients' living environments also require consideration to help develop a sense of safety; any unsafe conditions that led to the abuse (e.g., access of perpetrator) must be controlled before treatment can be expected to be successful. The group of abused men needed to express their anger about the way they had been treated before their anger could be resolved. In the early stages, expression of anger was frequently expressed as violent fantasy. The therapist permitted and encouraged these expressions in early stages, then began to selectively encourage more appropriate expressions of anger. The therapist also used natural objects (e.g., wood, stones) to practice nonthreatening positive experiences with touch. Many other ideas are presented based on the author's personal experiences as a therapist.

922. Morris, S. (1994). How to best support the disclosure-survivor: "The most horrible present in the world." In S. Hollins (Ed.), *Proceedings: It did happen here: Sexual abuse and learning disability: Recognition and action* (pp. 37–42). London: St. George's Hospital Medical School, Division of the Psychiatry of Disability.
This chapter provides a description of Respond, a counseling and support service for people with mental retardation who have been sexually abused. It also provides guidelines and rationale for these types of services.

923. Morrison, E. F. (1991). Victimization in prison: Implications for the mentally ill inmate and for health professionals. *Archives of Psychiatric Nursing, 5(1),* 17–24.
This article reports the results of a qualitative study of mentally ill inmates in prison. The author concludes that mentally ill inmates are often victimized because of their isolation from social support, failure to comply with prison norms, and need for attention.

924. Morrison, J. M., & Ursprung, A. W. (1990). Children's attitudes toward people with disabilities: A review of the literature. In M. Nagler (Ed.), *Perspectives on disability* (pp. 158–164). Palo Alto, CA: Health Markets Research.
This literature review examines the attitudes of children toward people with disabilities. The studies reviewed used children of various ages in attitude-testing situations where self-evaluation and evaluation of others were conducted. Evaluation procedures involved displaying slides and tapes of children with disabilities versus children without disabilities to the subject groups. The subjects' reactions were rated using an adjective checklist denoting stereotypic attitudes. The results of these studies indicate the flexibility and impressionability of children's attitudes toward people with disabilities. This article pre-

sents suggestions for changing children's attitudes, and this review discusses methodological problems in the studies and future research implications.

925. Morton, M. (1992). Not being able to speak doesn't mean I can't tell: Facilitated communication and disclosures of abuse. *NRCCSA (National Resource Center on Child Sexual Abuse) News, 1*(4), 7, 12.

This article examines facilitated communication for individuals with apraxia and disclosure of abuse. The challenges presented to the different support systems and the legal system when faced with disclosure are discussed in terms of the reliability of the statements and the ownership of those statements.

926. Move for abandoned boy. (1993, April 23). *The New York Times*, p. B6.

This newspaper article reports that a 9-year-old Long Island boy who was abandoned by his father in a bowling alley because he required too much care has been placed in residency at the school he regularly attends.

927. Moysa, M. (1991, May 11). Disabled women, kids targets of more assaults, expert says: Self-defence courses needed, Banff conference told. *The Edmonton Journal*, p. A7.

This newspaper article discusses a conference on Women and Mental Health-Women in a Violent Society in Banff, Alberta, that examined the physical and sexual abuse of women and children with disabilities. This article notes the following: 1) women and children with disabilities were 1.5 times more likely to become victims of abuse than the rest of society; 2) females are more often victimized, while the majority of perpetrators are male; 3) the greater the degree of disability, the greater likelihood of being victimized more than once; 4) the greater number of disabilities, the greater likelihood of suffering violence; 5) victim competence to testify was found to be the greatest obstacle to overcome with regard to laying charges against the perpetrator and having the case go to trial; 6) offenders were commonly found to be family, strangers, or caregivers; and 7) self-defense training, sex education training, and a revision of the judicial system were areas that needed improvement to help better protect women and children with disabilities.

928. Mrazek, D. A., Casey, B., & Anderson, I. (1987). Insecure attachment in severely asthmatic preschool children: Is it a risk factor? *Journal of the American Academy of Child and Adolescent Psychiatry, 26*(4), 516–520.

This article compares the attachment ratings of 26 children with severe asthma (ages 37–69 months) and 17 healthy children (ages 38–70 months). It states that 42% of the children with asthma were rated as insecurely attached compared with 14% of the comparison children. It examines the differences in the behavioral scores among the securely attached children with asthma, the insecurely attached children with asthma, and the healthy children. This article demonstrates the significant differences between all three groups, and it suggests that the quality of the child's attachment to the mother may serve as a potential risk or protective factor for the subsequent development of psychopathology.

929. Muccigrosso, L. (1991). Sexual abuse prevention strategies and programs for persons with developmental disabilities. *Sexuality and Disability, 9*(3), 261–271.

This article addresses the need for effective education in the prevention of sexual abuse of individuals with developmental disabilities. The vulnerability of people with developmental disabilities is attributed to an overprotected life environment, which may increase the risk of sexual abuse. The author recognizes the importance of community education as well as education directed toward individuals at risk and notes various inadequacies in existing community sexual abuse prevention and treatment services in meeting the needs of people with disabilities: for example, inadequate funding, lack of appropriate services, and limiting attitudes. Several recommendations are made regarding prevention strategies and education programs. This article provides seven examples of long-term programs suitable for implementation by teachers and staff members working closely in an ongoing capacity with students. It includes three examples of short-term, intensive programs provided by visiting professionals on a periodic basis. In addition, six resources useful for both long-term and short-term programs are described, as are specific teaching strategies for their successful implementation. A consistent, ongoing effort by all concerned is recommended to ensure the success of prevention programs for individuals with developmental disabilities.

930. Mulick, J. A., & Meinhold, P. M. (1992). Analyzing the impact of regulations on residential ecology. *Mental Retardation, 30*(3), 151–161.

This article examines the rules and regulations for residential programs and how they affect the behavior of service providers. The authors suggest that the generalized nature of these regulations minimizes their application to individual needs and specific environmental conditions. They believe an ecobehavioral analysis of regulatory rules would uncover the disparity between the intended effect versus actual effect of regulations, and once known, this disparity could be addressed by revising the rules and regulations.

931. Mullan, P. B., & Cole, S. S. (1991). Health care providers' perceptions of the vulnerability of persons with disabilities: Sociological frameworks and empirical analyses. *Sexuality and Disability 9*(3), 221–241.

Mullan and Cole examine the perceptions of health care providers about professional responsibility for persons with disabilities, their perceptions of the risk of sexual exploitation for people with disabilities, and the consequences of sexual exploitation for people with disabilities and their care providers. The authors found that health care professionals felt that different categories of disability pose different risks for sexual exploitation: For example, people with cognitive impairments were considered to be most at risk for sexual exploitation. This study also shows that professionals had the least confidence in their ability to detect sexual exploitation and the most confidence in their ability to report and conduct follow-up of incidents of sexual exploitation. The authors also discuss the implications for training and policy formulation.

932. Mullins, J. B. (1986). The relationship between child abuse and handicapping conditions. *Journal of School Health,* *56*(4), 134–136.

This article explores the relationship between child abuse and disability. It discusses the factors contributing to the likelihood of abuse, including: intragenerational abuse, characteristics of the child, and expectations of parents. According to this article, the evidence suggests that many disabling conditions, such as cerebral palsy or developmental disability, may have their origin in childhood trauma. This trauma may include forms of abuse such as severe head shaking or burn injury. It notes that children who are disabled appear to be at greater risk for subsequent abuse than do their peers without disabilities. This article recommends that school personnel and community members should be included in the identification and remediation of this problem.

933. Munro, J. D. (1985). Counseling severely dysfunctional families of mentally and physically disabled persons. *Clinical Social Work Journal,* *13*(1), 18–31.

This article claims that some families who have a member with a mental or physical disability behave in self-destructive or resistant ways, and "severely dysfunctional families" may present a considerable obstacle to the habilitation of a person with a disability. It points out that such families may be extremely frustrating to work with and, as a result, receive very little professional assistance. It discusses the probable causes of severely dysfunctional family behavior and presents examples of several maladaptive family patterns. Also, this article presents practical treatment strategies for helping these dysfunctional families.

934. Murder charges dismissed in death of deformed baby. (1988, January 10). *The New York Times,* p. A20.

This newspaper article reports that the murder charges against a father who killed his newborn son due to the infant's deformities have been dropped. Dr. Daniel McKay of Harvey, Illinois, pleaded temporary insanity to explain why he flung his son to the delivery room floor.

935. Murder outstrips traffic as killer of U.S. babies. (1989, March 1). *The Calgary Herald,* p. A18.

This newspaper article reports that researchers at the John Hopkins University claim that more American infants under the age of 1 are killed as a result of infanticide than from traffic accidents. From 1980 to 1985, there were 1,250 infant deaths resulting from infanticide in the United States. This converts to a rate of 5.7 infanticides per 100,000 infants per year: One third of these infants died of injuries resulting from child abuse such as battery, 11% were victims of strangulation or suffocation, 6.5% were victims of willful neglect or abandonment, 5% were victims of firearm injuries, 3% were victims of drowning, and another 3% were victims of stabbings. The remaining deaths were unspecified.

936. Murphy, J. M., Jellinek, M., Quinn, D., Smith, G., Poitrast, F. G., & Goshko, M. (1991). Substance abuse and serious child mistreatment: Prevalence, risk, and outcome in a court sample. *Child Abuse & Neglect,* *15,* 197–211.

This article examines parental substance abuse and its relationship with child abuse and neglect cases brought before the Boston Juvenile Court in order to determine the related judicial outcome factors involved in child maltreatment cases. In 43% of the 206 child abuse or neglect cases brought before the court, substance abuse was documented for at least one of the parents. Alcohol, cocaine, and heroin were rated as being the most abused substances. Those parents with histories of substance abuse were significantly more likely to have been referred to the child protective agencies than nonsubstance-abusing parents. They were also more likely to lose custody of their children, to be rated by the court as being at higher risk for subsequent child abuse or neglect, and to reject court-ordered services when compared to nonsubstance-abusing parents. The authors note that alcohol abusers were more often repeat offenders.

937. Murphy, L., & Della, S. (1987). Abuse and the special child. *Special Parent/Special Child,* *3*(1). (ERIC Document Reproduction Service No. ED 288 323)

The major focus of this article is on education and increasing adult awareness of the problem of abuse of children with disabilities. It emphasizes the vulnerability of these children to abuse. It provides guidelines about how to collect information when a child discloses and how to evaluate changes in the child that suggest abuse. It outlines report procedures as well as signs of physical and sexual abuse. Also, it includes a list of things for parents to do and not to do.

938. Murphy, M. (1989, October 31). Home operator gets 5 1/2 years for assaults. *The Toronto Star,* p. A10.

This newspaper article reports that Jean Thibault, former owner of the Cedar Glen Home for adults with mental disabilities, was sentenced to 5.5 years in jail for assault against residents at the home. The former construction worker was accused by former employees and residents of beating and kicking residents and found guilty of assault.

939. Murry, M. (1990, May 2). Disabled abused "almost daily" group charges. *The Toronto Star*, p. A9.
This newspaper article reports on findings from a study on people with disabilities who were abused. The study was prepared by Dr. Dick Sobsey from the University of Alberta and includes 150 cases of abuse perpetrated against people with disabilities. This study found that people with disabilities have a 2 to 10 times greater risk of abuse than the general population, with abuse often occurring in institutional settings.

940. Murti Rao, J., Cowie, V. A., & Mathew, B. (1989). Neuroleptic-induced Parkinsonian side effects in the mentally handicapped. *Journal of Mental Deficiency Research, 33*, 81–86.
This article discusses the Parkinsonian side effects of chlorpromazine in a group of 67 people with mental disabilities. A 19-item scale to rate Parkinsonism was devised to measure the severity of the side effects. The results of this study indicate the following: 1) 85% of the participants had a mild disturbance of movement; 2) 15% had a moderate disturbance of movements; 3) there were more people with involuntary face, hand, and feet movements; 4) 59% had disorders relating to face and tongue; 5) 40% had disorders relating to wrist and fingers; 6) 36% had disorders relating to toe and ankle; 7) rigidity and tremors characterized these disorders; 8) significant correlations were seen between the Parkinsonism scale score and age; 9) none of the demographic and pharmacologic variables (such as cumulative chlorpromazine and anticholinergic doses, current chlorpromazine and anticholinergic doses, and sex and age) predicted the scores on the Parkinsonism scale; and 10) those with overt brain damage did not seem to be at greater risk for developing Parkinsonian side effects.

941. Musick, J. L. (1984). Patterns of institutional sexual assault. *Response to Violence in the Family and Sexual Assault, 7*(3), 1–2, 10–1.
This article describes an analysis of sexual assaults in psychiatric settings. The assault accounts were provided by 26 former patients with mental illness and 39 facility staff members. From these accounts, several common institutional practices emerged: allowing male staff to care for and escort female patients; inadequate supervision and control of male patients in coed spaces; inadequate supervision of heavily medicated, restrained, or isolated female patients; and inadequate supervision and absence of security in isolated spaces. This article describes factors that increase patient vulnerability: incapacitation by chemical or physical restraints, social powerlessness, social isolation, and objectification by staff. It points out that when abuse is detected the supervisory staff often allow the "staff-assailants" to resign with no notation on

their records; therefore, the employee can seek work at another institution. It suggests that this method of dealing with the problem fails to provide a strong deterrent to others. The results from the analysis of the accounts indicate the following: a number of patient-perpetrator assaults were committed by men known to be violent but who had nevertheless been admitted to general and coed psychiatric units; reports of assault/abuse are often not taken seriously by staff, who believe most complaints are false; and when police are called in, they often take the attitude that the problem is an internal one that the institution should deal with itself. The author concludes that unless patient reports are treated as criminal complaints the acts cannot be treated as crimes, and assailants cannot be deterred or punished.

942. Myers, B. A. (1991). Treatment of sexual offenses by persons with developmental disabilities. *American Journal on Mental Retardation, 95*(5), 563–569.
The author of this article describes a case study of a young man with a mild mental disability who was diagnosed as a paraphiliac, specifically, a pedophile. This young man was given variable doses of medroxyhprogesterone acetate (MDA), a medication used in the treatment of sexual offenders, in order to determine the drug's effect on subsequent sexual behavior. The results of this study indicate that the treatment was effective in distinguishing sexual interest and had the potential to prevent further pedophiliac behavior. There is a brief discussion about the ethics of such a treatment program as it pertains to persons with developmental disabilities. This is an important but somewhat limited section of the article since the drug appears to ameliorate all sexual interest, which can reinforce the myths concerning the asexuality of individuals with mental disabilities.

943. Myers, J. E. B. (1994). The tendency of the legal system to distort scientific and clinical innovations: Facilitated communication as a case study. *Child Abuse & Neglect, 18*(6), 505–513.
This article provides a legal analysis of the use of facilitated communication (FC) in the courts. The author suggests that the adversarial system is ill suited to determining the actual value of FC. Myers concludes that there are too many unanswered questions about the legitimacy, reliability, and validity of FC, and it should not be allowed in the courtroom until these issues are resolved.

944. Myhrman, A. (1988). The northern Finland cohort, 1966–82: A follow-up study of children unwanted at birth. In H. P. David, Z. Dytrych, Z. Matejcek, & V. Schuller (Eds.), *Born unwanted: Developmental effects of denied abortion* (pp. 103–110). New York: Springer.
This chapter describes a follow-up study conducted on a cohort of children from unwanted pregnancies (UP), accepted pregnancies (AP), and later pregnancies (LP).

The study initially assessed 11,737 pregnant women regarding their feelings about being pregnant. Depending on their response, the women were categorized as 63% AP, 25% LP, and 12% UP. The children were assessed at age 28 days, 8 years, 14 years, and 16 years. The findings of this study indicate that children in the UP cohort obtained a significantly higher infant mortality rate (24 deaths per 1,000 live births) and significantly higher rate of cerebral palsy and mental retardation when compared to children in the AP category. The author notes that the socioeconomic status was lowest for the UP group.

•N•

945. Nagler, M. (Ed.). (1990). *Perspectives on disability: Text and readings on disability.* Palo Alto, CA: Health Markets Research.

This book is a collection of articles that examines the concerns of people with disabilities in North America. It concentrates on 10 areas, which include: social attitudes, sexuality, employment, and the meaning of being different.

946. Nagler, M. (Ed.). (1993). *Perspectives on disability* (2nd ed.). Palo Alto, CA: Health Markets Research.

This book is a collection of readings on the sociology of disability. Most of the articles have been previously published in a variety of journals. The compilation of these articles into a single volume provides an intensive reader for anyone interested in advocacy for people with disabilities, deviance, social labeling theory, human rights, and a number of related issues. The articles have been carefully selected and grouped into major categorical areas. Nagler, a leading authority on social aspects of disability, has included his own brief commentaries to introduce major sections of the book. Some of the articles directly address violence, abuse, "involuntary euthanasia," or other closely related topics, and almost all of them address the underlying issue of the cultural attitudes toward disability that disinhibit maltreatment.

947. Narayan, J., Madhavan, T., & Surya Prakasam, B. (1993). Factors influencing the expectations of parents for their mentally retarded children. *Journal of Intellectual Disability Research, 37,* 161–168.

This article describes a study that examined the influence of age, gender, literacy, locality of living, level of retardation, and duration of follow-up on parental expectations for children with developmental disabilities. This study examined the following issues: treatment for cure, education, training, and general information. The parents

of 100 children (mean age between 11 and 13) attending home-based training at the National Institute for the Mentally Handicapped in Secunderabad, India, participated in the study. All of the parents were interviewed using open-ended questions concerning their expectations for their children. The findings of this study indicate that parental expectations are influenced by the child's age and the duration of follow-up.

948. National Center on Child Abuse and Neglect (DHEW). (1980). *Child abuse and developmental disabilities: Essays.* Washington, DC: Author.

This document presents expert opinion and research on the relationship between developmental disabilities and child abuse. It discusses the following topics: cooperation between professionals working in these two areas, parent reactions to developmental disabilities in their children, advocacy, the identification of high-risk infants, the use of community resources, efforts by Parents Anonymous, and the development of counseling and referral skills.

949. National Deaf Children's Society and Keep Deaf Children Safe Project. (no date). *You choose.* London: Author.

This book is designed to help children who are deaf to learn about safety and how to ask for help in dangerous situations. This book contains sentences or questions illustrated by sign language, and it reinforces the concepts with color illustrations in which the answer is covered by a paper flap. This book provides working notes at the beginning of each section for adults to use when they to go through the book with children.

950. National Institutes of Health. (1989). *Treatment of destructive behaviors in persons with developmental disabilities. Consensus Development, 7(9),* 15.

This article is a consensus statement from the National Institutes of Health that focuses on the treatment of destructive behaviors in people with developmental disabilities. It defines destructive behavior as behavior that is a danger to self, others, or property. It describes the following treatment approaches: behavioral reduction and enhancement, educational/skills acquisition, ecological and stimulus-based treatments, and pharmacologic treatments. It examines the efficacy of treatment approaches and assesses the risks and benefits. This article includes recommendations for each treatment approach and discusses future research in this area.

951. National Society for the Protection from Sexual Abuse of Adults and Children with Learning Disabilities. (1994). *Annotated bibliography.* Nottingham, England: University of Nottingham Medical School.

This annotated bibliography includes annotations from 257 sources related to sexual abuse of people with learning disabilities (Editors' note: *Learning disabilities* as used here and generally in the United Kingdom refers to intellectual or cognitive disabilities that result in impairment of adaptive behavior.) This book is well indexed by subject and author name. It also includes a list of sources for policy and guidelines on abuse in the United Kingdom. This annotated bibliography is international in scope, but it is more comprehensive in cataloguing sources from the United Kingdom.

952. Neal, S., & Michalakes, S. (1992). Developing self-esteem and assertiveness skills in special needs populations. In *Crossing new borders* (pp. 96–99). Kingston, NY: National Association for the Dually Diagnosed.

This chapter describes the need to teach self-esteem and assertiveness skills to people with disabilities and provides some examples of practical activities to use in teaching. The authors suggest training groups employing two facilitators and 10 to 16 students, and they provide a number of physical activities, games, and role-playing simulations to help develop self-esteem and assertiveness.

953. Neistadt, M. E., & Freda, M. (1987). *Choices: A guide to sex counseling with physically disabled adults*. Malabar, FL: Robert E. Krieger.

This book provides useful basic information for occupational therapists and other health care professionals who may provide occasional counseling on sexuality to adults with physical disabilities. It stresses positive attitudes toward sexuality and flexibility in finding appropriate expressions of sexuality and intimacy for people with disabilities.

954. Nesbit, W. C. (1991). Emotional abuse: Vulnerability and developmental delay. *Developmental Disabilities Bulletin, 19*(2), 66–80.

This article discusses the emotional abuse of children with special needs at home and at school and the different symptoms of emotional abuse. Also, it examines the Psychological Abuse Scale for Teachers, which is designed to assist teachers in recognizing emotional abuse.

955. Nesbit, W. C., & Karagianis, L. D. (1982). Child abuse: Exceptionality as a risk factor. *Alberta Journal of Educational Research, 28*(1), 69–76.

This article defines child abuse and neglect as physical or mental injury, sexual abuse, and negligent treatment or maltreatment. It states that it is clear that abuse can cause a disabling condition, but it is not clear whether disability antedates abuse or results from it. It claims that it is extremely difficult to unravel the matrix and assign a weighting to a specific disability as a causal factor for abuse. This article reviews the literature on a disabling condition as a causal factor for abuse and how the community, school, and teacher can help prevent child abuse associated with exceptionality.

956. New South Wales Law Reform Commission. (1992). *People with an intellectual disability and the criminal justice system* (Report No. ISSN 1031-0002). Sydney, Australia: Author.

This issue paper was initiated by the Law Reform Commission of New South Wales, Australia, in order to identify relevant issues concerning people with intellectual disabilities. It examines the following issues: definitions of intellectual disability; crime and people with intellectual disabilities; the police and police procedures; the courts and court proceedings; sentencing, custody, and release; establishing specialist units in the courts or police for dealing with people with developmental disabilities; and mental illness. This paper includes suggestions for further discussion at the end of each chapter.

957. New South Wales Law Reform Commission. (1993). *People with an intellectual disability and the criminal justice system: Consultations* (Report No. ISSN 0817-7570). Sydney, Australia: Author.

This review of the criminal justice system as it pertains to people with intellectual disabilities was conducted by the Law Reform Commission of New South Wales, Australia. This review included consultations with 45 people (30 men, 15 women) with mild to borderline mental retardation, ranging in age from late teens to retirement. The participants' experience with the criminal justice system ranged from being suspects, offenders, victims, or witnesses to having no experience. The participants were asked to suggest reforms for the criminal justice system with regard to people with intellectual disabilities. This review describes the consultation process, and it includes case illustrations. This review includes the following suggestions: better training for police, lawyers, court personnel, and judges about people with intellectual disabilities; and more information for people with developmental disabilities about the criminal justice system and how to report crimes.

958. New York State Commission on the Quality of Care for the Mentally Disabled. (1987). *Abusing the unprotected: A study of the misuse of aversive behavior modification techniques and weaknesses in the regulatory structure*. Albany, NY: Author. (ERIC Document Reproduction Service No. 301 989)

This report describes events at Opengate, an intermediate care facility for people with mental retardation. At the time of investigation, the facility served 30 residents, many of whom also had psychiatric diagnoses or significant behavior problems. The facility used straightjackets, handcuffs, a "time-out chair," and seclusion along with a variety of aversive techniques to control behavior that it indicated was severe, unmanageable, and dangerous. Residents were also denied visits from family because the Opengate administration viewed these visits as disruptive. Investigation showed that many illegal practices were being employed, and aversive procedures were used for minor infractions of rules that posed no danger. The requirement to attempt to control behavior with non-aversive methods before using aversive methods was routinely ignored: For example, one client's management plan calling for the use of a straightjacket, hand restraints, being hit on the palms of the hands, a time-out helmet, ammonia fumes, and water spray contained no indication that any less aversive strategies were attempted. Since this aversive program was written and implemented on the resident's first day of admission, it was apparent that no other interventions had been attempted. These procedures were used without the consent of residents or their families. When the facility was cited for violating state regulations, the executive director of Opengate insisted that such procedures were absolutely necessary. When the board of directors failed to back his position and ordered him to comply with state regulations, the executive director resigned and was replaced with management that implemented nonaversive procedures. When nonaversive procedures replaced the previous aversive procedures, behavior of the 30 Opengate residents improved rather than deteriorated, indicating that, at least in this case, nonaversive methods were more effective than aversive methods.

959. New York State Commission on the Quality of Care for the Mentally Disabled. (1987). *Child abuse and neglect in New York mental hygiene facilities.* **Albany: Author. (ERIC Document Reproduction Service No. ED 301 990)**

This document describes a study by the New York State Commission on Quality of Care for the Mentally Disabled that examined child abuse and neglect reports taken from mental health and mental retardation residential facilities. This examination found that the annual report rate of abuse and neglect in the New York City facilities was found to be more than twice the annual rate for the state of New York. The commission identified trends in the characteristics of children most at risk and defined terms of highest risk in an effort to better offer specific recommendations for improved reporting, investigation, and prevention of abuse and neglect in these facilities. This document includes tabular statistics of abuse as well as the response of state offices to the reports of abuse in the appendices.

960. Newbern, V. B. (1989). Sexual victimization of child and adolescent patients. *Image: The Journal of Nursing Scholarship, 21*(1), 10–13.

This article describes a study that administered the Patient Abuse Questionnaire, developed by the author, to 272 respondents working in acute care institutions, nursing homes, state institutions for people with mental illness or mental retardation, public health or home health agencies, and military hospitals or mental health centers. Respondents included registered nurses, licensed practical nurses, nursing aides, psychologists, social workers, physiotherapists, and occupational therapists. This study

examined three categories of abuse: physical, psychological, and socially acceptable. The results of this study reveal the following: All three forms were reported as occurring as often as three times a week or more; 8% of the sample reported sexual abuse where sexual abuse was narrowly defined as "forcible rape, whether completed or attempted"; and the sexual abuse of children and adolescents occurred in many health care settings, including emergency rooms, drug rehabilitation programs, pediatric hospitals, physicians' offices, mental health centers, and state institutions for people with mental illness or mental retardation. This article includes case reports to supplement the study, and it discusses the methodological limitations of the study. The author recommends that research should be conducted in the area of sexual abuse of children and adolescents in health care settings.

961. Newlands, M., & Emery, J. S. (1991). Child abuse and cot deaths. *Child Abuse & Neglect, 15*(3), 275–278.

This article describes a study that attempted to identify links between families with children who had died with the diagnosis of sudden infant death syndrome (SIDS) and those registered with the Child Protection Registry in Southern Derbyshire. This study reviewed 288 registered children born between January 1, 1984 and June 30, 1988 in order to determine whether they had any siblings who had died due to SIDS. The children who were registered were either at risk for abuse or had been abused. The results of this review indicate that during this period 9 registered SIDS cases were siblings of the 288 registered children. With 95 registered SIDS cases reported during this time period, this represents a 9.5% association of SIDS deaths with abusing families for the Southern Derbyshire region.

962. Nibert, D., Cooper, S., & Crossmaker, M. (1989). Assaults against residents of a psychiatric institution: Residents' history of abuse. *Journal of Interpersonal Violence, 4*(3), 342–349.

This article describes a study that examined abuse and assault histories of institutionalized psychiatric patients. Fifty-eight chronic psychiatric patients (30 women, 28 men) from a Midwestern state run psychiatric institution volunteered for this study, which also included an assault prevention training program. All of the participants were interviewed about their personal experience with physical and sexual assault. The results of this study indicate the following: 60% of the women and 36% of the men reported at least one incidence of rape during their lifetime, 71% of the participants received threats of violence while institutionalized, 53% of the participants experienced physical assault while institutionalized, 38% of the participants experienced sexual assault while institutionalized, other residents were the perpetrators of both physical and sexual assaults more than 50% of the time, and staff members were the offenders in 39% of the physical and 27% of the sexual assaults against those participants who reported a history of assault. The authors recommend further research on the relationship between sexual assault and mental health problems as well as education and training for institutional staff.

963. Nicholls, R. (1988). Who are we to change the attitudes of others. *Interaction: The Australian Magazine on Intellectual Disability, 2*(1), 24–28.
The author of this article claims that the negative attitudes of professionals concerning people with disabilities influences society. This article uses a historical perspective to examine negative attitudes and some of the common stereotypes of people with disabilities: for example, the view that people who have disabilities are diseased or are less than human. The author notes the influence of Wolf Wolfensberger's work on this article. In particular, this article emphasizes Wolfensberger's concept of normalization, also known as social role valorization, a concept that looks at human services practices and the effects they have on social devaluation.

964. Nicholson, E. B., Horowitz, R. M., & Parry, J. (1986). Model procedures for child protective service agencies responding to reports of withholding medically indicated treatment from disabled infants with life threatening conditions. *Mental and Physical Disability Law Reporter, 10*(3), 221–249.
This article discusses model procedures designed to assist American states in the development of written policies to respond to reports of the withholding of medically needed treatment from infants with a disability who have a life-threatening condition. These procedures were developed by the American Bar Association's National Resource Center of Child Advocacy and Protection and Commission on the Mentally Disabled in response to the American Child Abuse Amendments of 1984. This model addresses the following: definition of terms, planning by child protection agencies, intake procedure, preliminary investigation, on-site investigation, the decision-making process, and follow-up.

965. Nova Scotia, Department of the Attorney General and Department of Solicitor General. (1991). *Protocol for investigation and prosecution of cases involving persons with special communication needs.* Halifax, Nova Scotia: Author.
This protocol for police and prosecutors is designed to help ensure that witnesses and crime victims with disabilities receive equitable treatment. It is based on the principles of equal access to justice and accommodation of individual needs. It provides guidelines for investigative interviews, including the audio- and video-taping of interviews whenever possible. It discusses the inclusion of a support person in the interview and provides guidelines for prosecutors on ensuring that people with impaired communication can participate in court.

966. Nuernberg Military Tribunals. (1946). *Trials of war criminals before the Nuernberg Military Tribunals under Control Council Law No. 10: Vols. I and II. The medical case.* Washington, DC: U.S. Government Printing Office.
These two volumes contain about 1,400 pages of information about the Nazi euthanasia program and medical experiments prosecuted as crimes against humanity. They indicate how the murders of 200,000 to 300,000 people with disabilities could take place as an open secret under the legitimization of assisted suicide and mercy killing. The case against physician Karl Brandt is particularly well documented. Brandt, who took orders directly from Hitler, had authority over much of Germany's medical system during World War II. While he admitted a role in the euthanasia program, he insisted that his goals were humanitarian and that much of the killing extended far beyond the limits that he had established for the program. The testimony and documents included indicated the close relationship between the ethnic genocide and euthanasia programs. Many of the Jews killed in concentration camps were killed under genocide orders after being declared unfit for work. Brandt was found guilty of crimes against humanity for his role in the euthanasia program. From the inception of the program, the questionnaires used to determine if people were suited for euthanasia included information on ethnic status, particularly if they were Jewish, Black, or mixed race. In many cases, the so-called medical examinations of ethnic groups was speeded up, although even for "Arayan" Germans the examination seemed a mere formality. For example, one physician is reported to have taken the whole morning to find almost 105 Germans unfit to live, while he was able to make the same decision for 1,200 Jews in the afternoon. Most of the medical experts never actually saw the people that they condemned to death, merely rubber-stamped piles of questionnaires. The only real factor in these life-or-death decisions was the capacity for doing work that could be exploited by the government.

967. Nunno, M. A., & Motz, J. K. (1988). The development of an effective response to the abuse of children in out-of-home care. *Child Abuse & Neglect, 12*(4), 521–528.
This article discusses differences in the investigation of maltreatment in the family situation and in the out-of-home care situation. It discusses the following aspects of investigation: the essential components of an investigation, identification, reporting, assessing risk factors in the initial report, the gathering of evidence, levels of culpability, and approaches to corrective actions. The authors point out that the protection of children in out-of-home care falls almost exclusively in the hands of child protective agencies. They suggest that specialized investigation units may better suit these cases.

968. Nunno, M., & Rindfleisch, N. (1991). The abuse of children in out-of-home

care. *Children & Society,* 5(4), 295–305.

This article addresses child abuse in out-of-home care. It provides an overview of maltreatment and examines administration, environment, personnel, and child residents. It examines American legislation, policy, and programs, including the work of the National Center on Child Abuse and Neglect (NCCAN), and focuses on the Child Abuse Prevention and Treatment Act. It discusses the findings of a survey of state representatives to the NCCAN that indicate the need for changes to the statutory definitions of maltreatment, specifically concerning children in out-of-home care. Other findings of this survey indicate the following: an estimated rate of 42 children per 100 in out-of-home care are maltreated annually in the United States; investigation into child out-of-home maltreatment is usually conducted by state child protection agencies, which could result in conflict of interest; and current prevention efforts involve training and screening of personnel, although no comprehensive prevention effort for out-of-home child maltreatment has been adopted by any state.

969. Nurse convicted in four killings at L. I. hospital: Guilt in fatal injections could draw 50 years. (1989, December 15). *The New York Times,* p. B2.

This newspaper article reports that former nurse Richard Angelo of the Good Samaritan Hospital in West Islip, Long Island, has been convicted of two counts of murder, one count of manslaughter, and one count of criminally negligent homicide in the lethal injection of former patients. A maximum sentence of 50 years in jail is possible.

970. Nursey, A. D., Rohde, J. R., & Farmer, R. D. T. (1991). Ways of telling new parents about their child and his or her mental handicap: A comparison of doctors' and parents' views. *Journal of Mental Deficiency Research,* 35, 48–57.

This article describes a study that was conducted to assess differences between parents' and doctors' views concerning the disclosure to parents that their child has a developmental disability. One of two versions of a questionnaire was hand delivered to 132 families who had a child with developmental disabilities. Another version of the questionnaire was mailed to 197 doctors who worked with people who have developmental disabilities and their families. The questionnaire consisted of a series of statements concerning views about the depth of information provided, timing of disclosure, frankness, and roles in the decision-making process. The participants rated their views on a 4-point Likert-type scale. The results of this study indicate the following: 61% of the parents (*n*=79) and 37% of doctors (*n*=73) returned their questionnaires; of those parents who responded, 30% had children with developmental disabilities under the age of 10; the majority of parents had children between the ages of 11 and 21; parents preferred to be told about their child's condition at an early stage; doctors felt parents should be

told at a later stage; parents considered themselves the primary decision makers with regard to their children; and neither parents nor doctors differed in their views about the depth or frankness of the information provided about the child's disability.

•O•

971. Oates, R. K. (1991). Child physical abuse. In R. T. Ammerman & M. Hersen (Eds.), *Case studies in family violence* **(pp. 113–134). New York: Plenum.**

In this chapter, a case study of shaking infant syndrome is described that involves a young female infant who was healthy at birth but developed severe cerebral palsy, blindness, intellectual impairment, and spastic quadriplegia as a result of abuse. This chapter discusses medical, legal, social, and family issues concerning the case and presents some treatment options. It also includes a general description of physical abuse, historical background, incidence, and types of injuries.

972. Oates, R. K., & Peacock, A. (1984). Intellectual development of battered children. *Australia and New Zealand Journal of Developmental Disabilities,* 10(1), 27–29.

This article discusses a study that compared 38 children who had been admitted to the hospital due to battering on an average of 5.5 years earlier with a matched control group on current test scores achieved on the Wechsler Intelligence Scale for Children-Revised (WISC-R) and the Wechsler Preschool and Primary Scales of Intelligence (WPPSI). Although the severity of the injuries initially leading to hospitalization could not account for the lower scores, the battered group had significantly lower scores. The authors conclude that long-term treatment is necessary in view of the long-term effects of child battering.

973. Oates, R. K., Peacock, A., & Forrest, D. (1984). The development of abused children. *Developmental Medicine & Child Neurology,* 26, 649–656.

This article describes a follow-up study that reviewed and compared 39 abused children (24 boys, 15 girls) who were admitted to the Royal Alexandra Hospital for Children approximately 5.5 years earlier with a comparison group. The mean age of the abused group and comparison group was 8.9 and 9.0 years of age, respectively. The children in the study were matched according to gender, age, social class, and ethnicity. The most common diagnosis for the abused group was bruising, followed by bone fractures, skull fractures, and severe neglect. Cognitive and verbal abilities were measured by the Wechsler Intelligence Scale for Children-Revised (WISC-R), a verbal language development scale, a reading ability test, and the Children's Personality Questionnaire. The results of this study indicate that the intelligence and verbal language development of the abused group was significantly poorer than the comparison group.

974. Oates, R. K., Peacock, A., & Forrest, D. (1984). Development in children following abuse and nonorganic failure to thrive. *Archives of Disease in Childhood, 138,* **764–767.**
This article discusses a follow-up study that reviewed and compared 39 abused children (24 boys, 15 girls) who were admitted to hospital approximately 5.5 years earlier and 14 children (8 boys, 6 girls) who were admitted to hospital approximately 13 years earlier with nonorganic failure to thrive (NOFTT) with comparison groups. The children in the study were matched according to gender, age, social class, and ethnicity. The study indicates that the abused and the NOFTT children were significantly delayed in language development, reading age, and verbal intelligence in relation to the comparison groups. Also, the abused group was significantly delayed in general intelligence, interpersonal relations, and self-concept.

975. O'Brien, J. (1991, November). Against pain as a tool in professional work on people with severe disabilities. *TASH Newsletter,* **pp. 16–17.**
This is the first part of a two-part article on the use of pain as a tool in the professional work with people who have severe disabilities, and the author examines how pain is used as a treatment tool in behavior management. The author questions the use of electric shock, aversive odors or noises, neglect, or impoverishment as means of eliciting appropriate behavior in clients. The author also questions the choice of using pain as a treatment option by professionals and the justification for this choice.

976. O'Brien, J. (1991, December). Against pain as a tool in professional work on people with severe disabilities. *TASH Newsletter,* **pp. 10–11.**
This is the second part of a two-part article that examines the use of pain as a tool in professional work with people who have severe disabilities. The author suggests ways to decrease the use of pain as a treatment option: recognizing the danger of depersonalization and over-dependence on others, setting guidelines for professional practices, allowing for reconciliation between offenders and victims, and building enduring relationships.

977. O'Brien, J., O'Brien, C., & Schwartz, D. (Eds.). (1990). *What can we count on to make and keep people safe? Perspectives on creating effective safeguards for people with developmental disabilities.* **Syracuse, NY: Human Policy Press.**
Selections from background papers and excerpts from discussions with participants in the Pennsylvania De-velopmental Disabilities Planning Council Annual Retreat are presented in this document. It discusses the creation of effective safeguards for people with developmental disabilities in light of their vulnerability and the inadequacies of present service-oriented methods for keeping people safe. It states that such formal, professional efforts may actually weaken the spirit of community commitment necessary for the development of caring relationships among people. Two alternative approaches to personal safety are compared in terms of their respective contributions, limitations, costs, and effectiveness: namely, the predominant administrative regulation and related legal advocacy approach and a life-sharing/personal commitments alternative. It outlines strategies to increase people's safety: work for social change; work to change the service system; and support families and friends so that individuals with disabilities have the opportunity to establish meaningful relationships with others, have opportunities for community participation and association, and gain power over their daily lives. It presents and discusses options for action. This document provides historical and current perspectives concerning an individual's safety, and it emphasizes the need to strengthen community commitment and make necessary assistance more relevant and effective.

978. O'Day, B. (1983). *Preventing sexual abuse of persons with disabilities.* **St. Paul: Minnesota Department of Corrections, Program for Victims of Sexual Assault.**
This manual presents sexual abuse prevention curricula for students with hearing impairments, physical disabilities, blindness, or mental retardation. Each curriculum contains lessons that basically cover the following: vocabulary, types of touching, myths and facts about sexual abuse, acquaintance rape, what to do if you are victimized, reactions and feelings of victims, personal safety, and assertiveness. There are some variations in the curricula, depending on the group being addressed. Accompanying each lesson, information is provided in terms of objectives, materials to be used, and presentation instructions. This 181-page manual also contains a parent's guide, a teacher's guide, exercises, and 20 posters illustrating aspects of the lessons.

979. O'Day, B. (1983). *A resource guide for signs of sexual assault: A supplement to: Preventing sexual abuse of persons with disabilities: A curriculum for hearing impaired, physically disabled, blind and mentally retarded students.* **St. Paul: Minnesota State Department of Corrections. (ERIC Document Reproduction Service No. ED 277 213)**
This manual is part of a curriculum on preventing sexual abuse of people with disabilities and is intended to assist instructors presenting material to people with hearing impairments. It presents illustrations of signs in sign

language for legal terms and terms for sexual victimization.

980. O'Hagan, K. (1983). The story of Kerry. *Social Work Today, 14*(31), 10–14.
This article presents a case history of the abuse of one child with a disability. The child sustained an injury believed to be nonaccidental. The author discusses the implications of this case study for child protection services.

981. Okla. retarded man is killed. (1994, June 12). [*Associated Press* wire story].
This article describes the Salina, Oklahoma, murder of Robert Ballard, a 33-year-old man with mental retardation who was beaten to death by two assailants who broke into his home in the middle of the night. Although he tried to flee, the assailants ran after him and beat him with a board, a toilet seat, and his "talk-back" electronic device. The 14-year-old and 17-year-old who confessed to the beating have not presented a plausible motive; robbery has been ruled out, and although one claimed they were angry because of a lewd remark that Ballard had made to a young woman who lived in the area, she claims the incident never occurred. The other assailant would only say that they did it because they were drunk.

982. Oliver, J. E. (1975). Microcephaly following baby battering and shaking. *British Medical Journal, 2,* 262–264.
This article discusses three cases of microcephaly that resulted in mental retardation in previously normal children. Because detailed social and psychiatric information was taken, the diagnosis of child abuse could be made; otherwise, the three children would have become part of the large group of institutionalized individuals whose deficits are of unknown origin.

983. Oliver, J. E. (1983). Dead children from problem families in NE Wiltshire. *British Medical Journal, 286,* 115–117.
This article examines 147 families with known neglect or maltreatment histories over two generations for the incidence of childhood fatalities. Both the parents and the children in these families were exposed to abuse or neglect. In 21 years, 560 children were born to these families, with 531 children suffering maltreatment. Forty-one children within this time period died before the age of 8, of whom 32 died before the age of 1. The rate of fatality for this group of children was 47.1 per 1,000 live births. This article describes the causes of death for 41 cases of childhood fatalities.

984. Ombudsman of British Columbia. (1987). *The use of criminal record checks to screen individuals working with vulnerable people* **(Public Report No. 5). Victoria: Queen's Printer for British Columbia.**
The Ombudsman of British Columbia proposed several guidelines for screening individuals who work with

vulnerable people: 1) all employees whose work assignments bring them into contact with vulnerable people must authorize disclosure of police records; 2) positions of trust to be monitored must be clearly defined and monitored; 3) vulnerable people must be clearly defined; 4) criminal record screening must be performed on every employee meeting the definition; 5) criminal record screening must be performed on prospective employees prior to employment; 6) criminal record screening must be mandated for private as well as public employees; 7) there must be a mechanism for checking agency and individual compliance; 8) information must be released to both employee and employer; 9) past conduct confirmed by conviction or admission of guilt in diversions or discharges must be included, and offenses for which pardons have been granted shall not be released; 10) rules must be established for the party who bears the cost of criminal record screening; 11) information received must be assessed on the basis of relevancy; 12) the agency must consider that if the behavior is repeated whether it will pose a threat to client safety or welfare, interfere with duties, or pose other specific threats; 13) the agency must consider the circumstances of the charge (e.g., offender's age); 14) the agency must consider the recency of the charge; 15) they must allow the employee to provide supplemental information related to the area of concern; 16) decisions must be made consistently; 17) the privacy of the individual who is being checked must be maintained; 18) information obtained should not be available for other purposes; 19) permanent records of information disclosed must not be maintained except in exceptional cases and by mutual agreement; 20) appeal procedures must be developed, available, and explained to employees asked to make disclosures; and 21) data should be maintained to monitor complaints of abuses of criminal record checks as well as the benefits of policy. As criminal records may be incomplete because of errors, exclusion of juvenile offenders (58% of all pedophiles commit their first offense as adolescents), and so forth, the Ombudsman made several recommendations: 1) caution must be exercised so that checks do not perpetuate racial or class bias; 2) because Canadian provinces have varying policies, training and certification agencies should incorporate these procedures or inform individuals seeking training that they will be required to undergo checks later on; 3) those administering the process must be trained; 4) consent forms should specify the information sought, how it will be used, how the information will be available to the prospective employee, and assure confidentiality; 5) adverse decisions based on these records should be communicated in writing to the individual affected, explaining the reasons and outlining the appeal process; 6) these procedures must be recognized as limited and not be expected to replace other safeguards, including other screening procedures; and 7) no information should be released that cannot be verified.

985. Ombudsman of British Columbia. (1992). *Complaints regarding allegations of abuse of students at Jericho Hill*

Provincial School for the Deaf: Interim public report. Victoria: Author.

This report reviews the results of the investigation that took place after allegations of abuse at the Jericho Hill Provincial School for the Deaf. The government of British Columbia was accused of not responding properly to these allegations. The investigation team examined the transcripts of children's statements and interviewed the children's therapists and advocates and the alleged victims. This report focuses on the response of the government to the allegations.

986. Orelove, F. P. (1990). Courage and dignity: What people with severe handicaps have taught me. *Entourage, 5*(2/3), 21–24.

This article relates the author's experience with three people with mental disabilities. It describes observations about this experience and knowledge gained from this personal interaction.

987. Oren, J., Kelly, D. H., & Shannon, D. C. (1987). Familial occurrence of sudden infant death syndrome and apnea of infancy. *Pediatrics, 80*(3), 355–358.

In this article, the authors examine the infants of families with two or more infants who have died of sudden infant death syndrome (SIDS) or had apnea of infancy or unusual polygraph or pneumogram recordings. Twenty-eight infants had two or more siblings who had previously died of SIDS. The authors point out that the results of evaluations and clinical data did not predict whether an infant would die from SIDS.

988. O'Shaughnessy, H. (1994, April 2). Murder and mutilation supply the human organ trade. *The Edmonton Journal*, p. G2.

This newspaper article raises more questions about the sacrifice of people with disabilities to supply the lucrative human organ transplant trade. This article discusses a series of abuses of the system. It suggests that some people are getting children with disabilities from orphanages in eastern Europe and killing them for their hearts or other body parts. This article suggests that these individuals adopt regardless of the nature of the disability provided that they make certain that the adopted child's heart or other vital organs are in good working order.

989. Osnes, P. G., & Stokes, T. F. (1988). Treatment of child abuse and neglect: The role of functional analyses of observed interactions. *Journal of Child and Adolescent Psychotherapy, 5*(1), 3–10.

The authors of this article state that a functional analysis of behavior and environment is an integral step in treating family members who abuse or neglect their children. The authors examine the assessment of target behaviors in children and their caregivers and the home

environment, and they discuss treatment options for families who abuse or neglect their children and illustrate these treatment approaches using case examples.

990. Oswin, M. (1979). The neglect of children in long-stay hospitals. *Child Abuse and Neglect, 3*(1), 89–92.

This article discusses the institutional abuse of children in terms of emotional deprivation, deprivation of normal childhood experiences, and physical neglect, including lack of therapy for their disabilities and lack of warm nurturing contact.

991. Oustend, C., Oppenheimer, R., & Lindsay, J. (1980). Aspects of bonding failure: The psychopathology and psychotherapeutic treatment of families of battered children. In G. J. Williams & J. Money (Eds.), *Traumatic abuse and neglect of children at home* (pp. 498–509). Baltimore: The Johns Hopkins University Press.

This chapter discusses a study that examined treatment and intervention techniques for families of battered children, bonding failure, and child abuse. This study examined two groups of subjects: The first group consisted of 86 referred families with a child who was treated at the Park Hospital for Children, and group two included 24 selected mothers who were outpatients being treated because they were afraid of injuring their babies. The treatment for group one consisted of a confirmed diagnosis of child battering, other diseases in the child, and an examination of family background and family relationships. Both mother and child were then admitted to a specialized unit that allowed for the organization of a safe therapeutic environment. The study noted an improvement in family relationships. The outpatient service for the second group included group therapy and play therapy for both mother and child. In addition, the mothers were asked to record their own behavior in a diary and were given the opportunity to contact the social worker during a crisis. This study noted that those who attended regularly showed improved relations between mother and child.

992. Overholser, J. C. (1990). Fetal alcohol syndrome: A review of the disorder. *Journal of Contemporary Psychotherapy, 20*(3), 163–176.

The adverse effects of alcohol consumption during pregnancy and fetal alcohol syndrome (FAS) are reviewed in this article. It presents the diagnostic criteria for FAS and discusses the effects of alcohol on the fetus at different gestational ages. It also discusses the direct and indirect biomechanics of cause and effect. This article suggests that the severity of fetal impairment is related to the severity of maternal alcohol consumption; consequently, it includes a brief discussion of preventive measures.

•P•

993. PACER Center. (1990). *Let's prevent abuse: A prevention handbook for early childhood professionals and families with young children with special emphasis on needs of children with disabilities.* **Minneapolis, MN: Author.**

This manual is written for parents and service providers, and the first section of it discusses the importance of the U.S. Education of the Handicapped Act of 1970, PL 91–230, which addresses the educational needs of children with disabilities up to the age of 5. This manual discusses the following areas: definition of child abuse, indicators of child abuse, risk factors of child abuse, and federal laws related to reporting abuse.

994. Pallone, N. J., & Chancles, S. (Eds.). (1990). The clinical treatment of the criminal offender in outpatient mental health settings: New and emerging perspectives. *Journal of Offender Counseling, Services & Rehabilitation, 15(1).*

This journal presents a wide-ranging effort to gain new, useful, and appropriate perspectives on the clinical treatment of the criminal offender in outpatient mental health and social service settings. These articles examine the interaction between the "traditional" interests of corrections professionals and the outpatient mental health care community, in particular, those involved in domestic violence, alcohol abuse, and substance abuse. The following articles are included in this journal: "'Privatizing' the treatment of criminal offenders" (Demone & Gibelman), "Men who abuse their spouses: Social and psychological supports" (Davidovich), "Men who abuse their spouses: An approach to assessing future risk" (Goldsmith), "Treating abusive parents in outpatient settings" (Otto), "Treatment needs and services for mothers with a dual diagnosis: Substance abuse and mental illness" (Morris & Schinke), "Drug use and felony crime: Biochemical credibility and unsettled questions" (Pallone), "Outpatient treatment for substance-abusing offenders" (Hirschel & Keny), "Alcohol abuse and the young offender: Alcohol education as an alternative to custodial sentencing" (Greer, Lawson, Baldwin, & Cochrane), "The convergence of the mentally disordered and the jail population" (Snow & Briar), and "Outpatient treatment of the sexually motivated murderer and potential murderer" (Schlesinger & Revitch).

995. Palmer, E. (1992, March). Withdrawing treatment raises dilemmas. *New Zealand Disabled,* **p. 64.**

This Australian article discusses the withholding of medical treatment from a man with cerebral palsy. This factual account was presented at the National Conference of the Australian Society for the Study of Intellectual Disability and the National Council on Intellectual Disability. According to this article, the man's fight to stay alive after the hospital removed a feeding tube resulted in the reinsertion of the tube. With the patient's health worsening after returning home, he eventually died. This article addresses questions about medical treatment and patient consent in those cases where the patient is unable to advocate for himself or herself.

996. Parish, R. A., Myers, P. A., Brandner, A., & Templin, K. H. (1985). Developmental milestones in abused children, and their improvement with a family-oriented approach to the treatment of child abuse. *Child Abuse & Neglect, 9(2), 245–250.*

This article examines the effect of the Family Development Center Program on preschool children who have been abused and their parents. While in the program, children attend a therapeutically oriented playschool on a daily basis, and their parents participate in group therapy and anger management technique training. Using the Learning Assessment Technique Profile, the authors found that 79% of the 53 children tested demonstrated improved developmental skills. The greatest improvement was seen in fine motor and language skills, areas that were initially significantly delayed for the group as a whole. The authors also plan to follow the children tested over a 5-year period.

997. Parker, H., & Parker, S. (1986). Father-daughter sexual abuse: An emerging perspective. *American Journal of Orthopsychiatry, 5(4), 531–549.*

This article reports on factors associated with incest behavior in fathers. The factors described in this article include the following: fathers who had greater involvement in activities of early care of their daughters were much less likely to commit incest, and fathers' perception of their own treatment by parents also differentiated incestuous and nonincestuous fathers. This article describes less powerful factors: fathers' education, biological fatherhood status, use of drugs and alcohol, time spent at home (abusive fathers spent less time at home), frequency of membership in secular organizations, and number of close friends. Together, these factors account for 43% of variance between abusive and nonabusive fathers.

998. Parker, T., & Cooper, R. M. (1984, May 27–31). *Family therapy as a treatment model for families with a mentally retarded child.* **Paper presented at the 108th Annual Meeting of the American Association of Mental Deficiency, Minneapolis, MN.**

This paper discusses the assessment and treatment implications of family therapy for people with mental retardation. It examines parental reactions to the initial diagnosis of mental retardation and special parental problems that require assessment and treatment, for example, parental inadequacies and emotional problems. It claims that the need for supportive family counseling at the point of diagnosis and interpretation is critical, and it presents three areas for treatment intervention: within the developmental life stages of families with a child with retardation, through the hierarchical familial structure, and inside the central triangle (mother, father, and child with a disability) of the child's family. It includes case studies that illustrate each intervention and presents diagrams of family dysfunction commonly found in families with children with mental retardation. Also, this paper discusses the role of the professional in attempting to promote functional intrafamilial relationships through the restructuring of the familial hierarchy and familial role assignments.

999. Parker, T., Hill, J. W., & Miller, G. (1987). Multiple family therapy: Evaluating a group experience for mentally retarded adolescents and their families. *Family Therapy*, 14(1), 43–51.

For the families of adolescents with mental retardation, the developmental period of increasing independence approaching adulthood can be marked by apprehension. This article describes a multiple family therapy group treatment model that was designed to evaluate the effectiveness of this model for families with an adolescent. The group provided an opportunity to share with other families facing similar emotional issues concerning the independence of their adolescent with mental retardation in a therapeutic environment. The study's findings using this model tend to support the premise that independence presents developmental issues for both the individual and the family system. Three families, each with an adolescent with mental retardation, participated in the multiple family therapy group experience.

1000. Parness, J. A. (1988). The abuse and neglect of the human unborn: Protecting potential life. In D. J. Besharov (Ed.), *Protecting children from abuse and neglect: Policy and practice* (pp. 141–158). Springfield, IL: Charles C Thomas.

This chapter discusses the shortcomings of present abuse and neglect laws concerning the unborn human and suggests possible changes to those laws. The most prevalent issue involves the implementation of criminal charges that can be laid against individuals who perpetrate an act of assault against the unborn. This chapter presents and discusses some court cases.

1001. Partington-Richer, M. (1993, December 8). Abuse takes many forms. *Slave Lake Lakeside Leader*, p. A2.

This newspaper article discusses a seminar that was sponsored by the town's Family and Community Support Services department concerning the abuse of people with disabilities. It examines several forms of abuse: for example, physical abuse, sexual abuse, neglect, emotional abuse, psychological abuse, and verbal abuse. This article notes that research indicates that most abusers are male, and abuse stems from the need to gain power and control.

1002. Patients left in lurch: Peacekeepers launch Bosnia mercy mission. (1993, November 15). *The Edmonton Sun*, p. 2.

This newspaper article reports that 570 patients at two psychiatric hospitals in Fojnica and Bakovici, in Bosnia-Herzegovina, have been left unattended by staff because of heavy fighting in the area between Croats and Muslims. United Nations peacekeepers from Canada and Denmark are currently safeguarding the two hospitals that house both children and adults with developmental disabilities. It states that the patients are in control of the wards although fighting has broken out among the patients.

1003. Patterson, P. M. (1991). *Doubly silenced: Sexuality, sexual abuse and people with developmental disabilities*. Madison: Wisconsin Council on Developmental Disabilities.

This book aims to encourage people with developmental disabilities to make responsible decisions regarding sexuality and survive the effects of sexual abuse and gives suggestions to service providers for effective intervention. The first half of the book covers topics such as sexuality, sex education, and policies about sexuality. This book also discusses sexual assault, the effects of sexual abuse on the victim, and treatment strategies for offenders.

1004. Paulson, J. A., & Rushforth, N. B. (1986). Violent death in children in a metropolitan county: Changing patterns of homicide, 1958 to 1982. *Pediatrics*, 78(6), 1013–1020.

This article examines trends in child homicide for children 15 years of age and younger from 1958 to 1982. The authors found the following: Children ages 4 or younger were more often victims of filicide when the means of the assault resulting in death was a blunt instrument, firearm injuries resulting in death were most prevalent for those between the ages of 10 and 14, higher rates of homicide occurred in the city than the county or suburbs, and homicide rates were higher for boys of color.

1005. Pava, W. S. (1994). Visually impaired persons' vulnerability to sexual and physical assault. *Journal of Visual Impairment & Blindness*, 88, 103–112.

This article reports on a national survey of 161 women and men with visual impairment regarding their perceptions of vulnerability to sexual and physical assault. Although women were much more likely to consider themselves as vulnerable, there were no significant differences in unsuccessful or successful assaults. Unsuccessful assaults had been attempted against 29.7% of the women and 29.4% of the men. Successful assaults had been perpetrated on 16.2% of the women and 11.8% of the men. Martial arts training was significantly associated with failure of attempted assaults for both women and men.

1006. Pava, W. S., Bateman, P., Appleton, M. K., & Glascock, J. (1991, December). Self-defense training for visually impaired women. *Journal of Visual Impairment & Blindness,* **85, pp. 397–401.**

This article is written for educators and adults with disabilities, and it discusses two self-defense and rape prevention courses for women with visual disabilities. It examines the following self-protection skills: physical resistance, safety precautions, and shaping emotional response to attempted rape. These courses provide several discussions and rehearsals of "rape scenarios" to increase problem-solving skills and physical resistance. This article states that self-defense courses for women with low vision and women who use guide dogs are also being developed.

1007. Pavulon discovered in six more bodies of nurse's patients. (1988, February 10). *The New York Times,* **p. B3.**

This newspaper article reports that the case of homicide involving former nurse Richard Angelo of the Good Samaritan Hospital in West Islip has been expanded after the discovery of drugs in six additional exhumed former patients. In total, eight former patients have now been identified as having died under the care of Mr. Angelo. All of these patients had traces of the muscle relaxant drug Pavulon in their bodies.

1008. Pawelski, C. E. (1992). The world of disabilities. *NRCCSA (National Resource Center on Child Sexual Abuse) News,* **1(4), 3, 10.**

The author of this article suggests some guidelines for appropriate interaction when one enters the world of disabilities, including: the importance of the individual as a person; not to be misled by acronyms or jargon when talking about the world of disabilities; be open to the whole spectrum of specializations within this world; and become more informed about it through literature, the media, and any other means.

1009. Pawelski, C. E., Wallis, P. J., Crocker, M., & McGaughey, J. (1990). *Summary of strategies and information presented at a workshop on child abuse and disabilities.* **Jackson Heights, NY: Child Abuse and Disabled Children Program, The Lexington Center.**

This paper summarizes a workshop on "Child Abuse and Disabilities" that was held by the Child Abuse and Disabled Children Program at the Lexington Center. In this workshop, interviewers are taught to use a number of charts that are designed to help children with disabilities talk about incidents of sexual abuse. In order to familiarize the interviewer with the person being

interviewed, this workshop provides a list of questions (presented in a chart) that attempt to determine the child's level of understanding. Also, this workshop provides a disability checklist used to assess the child's strengths and weaknesses. This paper also provides interviewing strategies.

1010. Payoffs demanded for participants. (1993, December 29). *The Edmonton Journal,* **p. B8.**

This newspaper article discusses the need for federal compensation to people who were fed radioactive food as part of an experiment during the 1940s and 1950s. This article reports that 19 teenage boys with mental retardation were involved in studies funded by the Atomic Energy Commission and the Quaker Oats Company. Energy Secretary Hazel O'Leary and her department are trying to establish whether or not the researchers violated the 1974 Nuremberg Code, which was established in response to Nazi human experimentation during the second World War. It pays particular attention to the following: whether the participants were completely informed about the project, whether they gave their consent voluntarily, and whether everything was done to protect them from harm.

1011. Pearson, P. (1994). Murder on her mind. *Saturday Night, 109*(5), 46–53, 64.

This article explores the ideas of leading criminologist Candice Skrapec. Skrapec suggests that sexual sadists, medical murderers, mercy killers, and other serial killers are only superficially different and are fundamentally similar: That is, they are driven by the same overwhelming need for control and violence.

1012. Pell, D. M. (1983). The Supreme Court limits the rights of the handicapped by narrowly construing federal statutes intended to assist them. *Whittier Law Review,* **5, 435, 455–456.**

This article examines 1970s' U.S. federal legislation that provided rights to people with disabilities. It concludes that the rights of people with disabilities have been restricted by the narrow interpretation of these rights by the Supreme Court. This article uses the evidence drawn from several cases to examine this restriction of rights.

1013. Pelton, L. H. (1978). Child abuse and neglect: The myth of classlessness. *American Journal of Orthopsychiatry,* **48(4), 608–617.**

Although it is an increasingly popular view that the problems of neglect and child abuse are not restricted to a particular class, this article suggests that there is little evidence to support the idea that child neglect and abuse is distributed evenly throughout all classes. This article claims that there is a strong relationship between child abuse and neglect and poverty and that the belief that child neglect and abuse is equally distributed among all classes is a myth. It suggests that the persistence of this myth allows the problems of abuse and neglect to be couched in terms of a psychodynamic or medical model rather than as a sociological and poverty-related problem. This article concludes that poverty-related stressors may be an important factor in the prevalence of child abuse and neglect among the poor.

1014. Pendler, B., & Hingsburger, D. (1990). Sexuality: Dealing with parents. *The Habilitative Mental Healthcare News-letter, 9*(4), 29–34.

The authors of this article suggest that the topics of sexuality and sex education are often sensitive issues for agencies serving people with developmental disabilities to discuss with parents. This article recommends some procedural guidelines for using a group approach with parents on these issues. The group approach consists of five 75-minute sessions, each designed to meet one goal. These goals include the following: the sharing and validation of concerns, fostering parental acceptance, learning that sex is part of being human, setting realistic goals, and offering support and information. Also, this article provides further detail about the sessions.

1015. Penfold, P. S. (1982). Children of battered women. *International Journal of Mental Health, 11*(1/2), 108–114.

This article examines 16 children with multiple dis-abilities (ages 2 – 11) of abused mothers who were referred to a child psychiatry center (1 child had an abused father). It identifies several problems: for example, be-havior and learning problems, hyperactivity, overde-pendence, anxiety, bizarre behavior, and asthma. The author concludes that the effects on children of mothers who are abused and the detection of woman battering when children are referred as patients are hampered by stereotypical attitudes that preserve male prerogatives and veil violence toward women and by pervasive beliefs that mothers are to blame for their children's problems.

1016. Peraino, J. M. (1990). Evaluation of a preschool antivictimization prevention program. *Journal of Interpersonal Vio-lence, 5*(4), 520–528.

This article describes a study that examined an anti-victimization program conducted for preschoolers. In this program, preschoolers were taught abuse concepts, for example, sexual, physical, and stranger abuse. This study used a 4-factor design to assess the preschoolers' anti-victimization knowledge. In this study, there were 46 preschoolers from different socioeconomic levels and races and the mean age was 59.5 months. This study administered a follow-up test 6.5 weeks after the end of the program to 19 of the preschoolers. It found that preschoolers who received the program scored significant-ly higher at posttest than preschoolers who were not involved in the program. Although race, sex, and/or socioeconomic status (SES) did not appear to affect the results, this study found that male and low SES pre-schoolers had less knowledge about abuse than other preschoolers prior to the program.

1017. Perlin, M. L. (1987). State constitu-tions and statutes as sources of rights for the mentally disabled: The last frontier? *Loyola of Los Angeles Law Review, 20*(4), xi–xiv, 1249, 1326–1327.

This article discusses the "golden age" in federal litiga-tion (1972–1978) concerning people with mental disabilities, a period in which there was considerable pro-gress in the advocacy for people with mental disabilities. It provides evidence of this "golden age" in terms of important federal institutional changes and litigation decisions, for example, the state patients' bill of rights and the advocacy of equal rights for people with disabilities.

1018. Perlman, N., & Ericson, K. (1992). Interviewing developmentally handicap-ped persons: The ability of develop-mentally handicapped individuals to ac-curately report on witnessed events. In J. Casselman (Ed.), *Law and mental health* (pp. 202–206). Belgium: Leuven.

According to the authors of this chapter, very little research has been conducted to examine the capacity of people with developmental disabilities to provide competent eye-witness testimony in a legal setting. The authors describe a study conducted to determine the competency of people with developmental disabilities in some specific areas of memory that deal with reporting events. The study involved 30 individuals with developmental disabilities and 30 individuals without disabilities between ages 17 and 26. The participants viewed a short film that depicted a failed murder attempt and were asked questions from a variety of formats. This chapter reports the results from three of these question formats: Question format 1 used contextualized questions requiring short answers, question format 2 used very specific questions requiring a yes or a no answer, and question format 3 used statements that included a yes/no question. The results suggest the following: people with mild developmental disabilities are as competent as people without disabilities to answer structured specific questions, structured questions about entities present during an entire sequence, and questions about events or circumstances central to the critical action or plot. The authors conclude that this research has practical implications for law, clinical psychology, and psychiatry.

1019. Perlman, N., & Ericson, K. (1992). Is-sues related to sexual abuse of persons with developmental disabilities: An overview. *Journal on Developmental Disabilities, 1*(1), 19–23.

This article reviews the literature and issues concerning the sexual abuse of people with intellectual disabilities. In particular, it examines the vulnerability of people with intellectual disabilities.

1020. Perlman, N., Millar, C., & Ericson, K. (1993). Therapy for sexually abused young children. *Infants and Young Children,* **5(3), 43–48.**
This article discusses issues related to the diagnosis and treatment of young children, preschool to latency age, who have been sexually abused. It uses a developmental perspective in order to highlight the problems associated with decisions about intervention. It includes case histories, and although the accounts of adult survivors of childhood sexual abuse are considered a major source of information, the authors point out that the anecdotal nature of this information suggests caution when making decisions about intervention. The authors call for more research in the area of the sexual abuse of young children.

1021. Perlman, N., & Sinclair, L. (1992). Play and psychological assessment of a sexually abused child with developmental disabilities. In *Crossing new borders* **(pp. 176–178). Kingston, NY: National Association for the Dually Diagnosed.**
This chapter presents a case study of a 7.5-year-old girl with a mild developmental disability referred because medical findings suggested sexual abuse. Through play, she revealed extreme anxiety, age-inappropriate sexualized behavior, disassociative reactions, fear of men, and association of victimization with female figures.

1022. Perske, R. (1972). The dignity of risk and the mentally retarded. *Mental Retardation,* **10(1), 24–27.**
The author of this article examines the ways in which Denmark and Sweden have empowered people with developmental disabilities to take risks in their daily lives. These risk-taking experiences fostered by the Danes and Swedes encompass community, industry, heterosexual relationships, and building design. Community risk-taking experiences involve social training exercises such as asking for directions, making one's own way around town, and excursions out of town. In industry, people with developmental disabilities perform tasks at a work station using similar equipment as other workers. The emphasis is on proper safety and equipment instructions, not on the modification of equipment for use by people with developmental disabilities. Relationships are accommodated by less segregation of genders in dormitories and supportive assistance from professionals. Changes in building and house designs are now more stylized with regard to comfortable living, rather than "super safe" structures. This entails more windows, glass, and brightly colored fixtures. These changes highlight a change in attitude toward people with developmental disabilities.

1023. Perske, R. (1980). Some haunting questions surrounding the refusal to repair Phillip Becker's heart. *Mental Retardation,* **30(4), 35–37.**
This article discusses the U.S. Supreme Court case of Phillip Becker, a 13-year-old boy with Down syndrome.

In 1980, the issue of Phillip's need for corrective surgery and his parents' refusal to allow medical treatment to help repair Phillip's heart was brought before the United States Supreme Court, which decided in favor of the parents. This article discusses this decision.

1024. Perske, R. (1991). *Unequal justice? What can happen when persons with retardation or other developmental disabilities encounter the criminal justice system.* **Nashville, TN: Abingdon Press.**
This book provides biographical accounts of people with developmental disabilities who are facing possible execution for crimes. These accounts make a powerful case that many of these people are innocent, and others, although guilty of the offenses, have been treated unfairly by the criminal justice system. This book is written in a journalistic style, but it includes a good bibliography for those who want to research this topic more deeply.

1025. Peters, Y. (1992, February/March). The silent epidemic. *Transition,* **pp. 11, 14.**
This article is an excerpt from a speech given at "The proceedings of the Coalition of Provincial Organizations of the Handicapped's (COPOH) workshop on disabled women's issues," and it deals with the abuse of women with disabilities. This article addresses such factors as dependency and passivity, which are seen to contribute to women's vulnerability. According to this article, because law enforcement officials do not trust the credibility of women with developmental disabilities, these women have been reluctant to report abuse; consequently, there is a lack of information and services for abused women with disabilities. This article examines the theory of domination as an explanation for violence, and it discusses the law and equality. This article suggests that gender neutrality in law could restrict women by not recognizing that certain experiences are unique to certain groups of individuals.

1026. Peterson, C. L. (1986). Changing community attitudes toward the chronic mentally ill through a psychosocial program. *Hospital and Community Psychiatry,* **37(2), 180–182.**
This article describes a training program that assists formerly institutionalized chronically mentally ill patients in learning basic trades and social skills. Through the use of a psychosocial rehabilitative program entitled the Highlands Clubhouse, former patients are taught interpersonal communication skills, grooming, manners, and budgeting in order to make it easier for these patients to rejoin and be accepted by the community. The program emphasizes nonpatient roles and is run out of the Highlands Community Counseling Center in Abingdon, Virginia.

1027. Peterson, D. R., Chinn, N. M., & Fisher, L. D. (1980). The sudden infant

death syndrome: Repetitions in families. *The Journal of Pediatrics, 97*(2), 265–267.

This article examines the incidence rate of sudden infant death syndrome (SIDS) among subsequent siblings of infants who have died of SIDS. A questionnaire was filled out by 1,263 SIDS families, of which 1,194 were families with singleton births. These 1,194 families had 839 children born subsequent to the SIDS infant. Of these 839 children, 582 were the next subsequent child. With 11 SIDS deaths occurring in this group, an incidence rate of 19 per 1,000 live births for the next subsequent sibling of a SIDS infant was calculated. In total, there were 18 subsequent SIDS deaths in the 839 children, which converts into a incidence rate of 21 per 1,000 live births for any subsequent sibling of a SIDS infant.

1028. Peterson, D. R., Sabotta, E. E., & Daling, J. R. (1986). Infant mortality among subsequent siblings of infants who died of sudden infant death syndrome. *Journal of Pediatrics, 108,* 911–914.

This article describes a study conducted to assess the infant mortality rate among subsequent siblings of infants with sudden infant death syndrome (SIDS) in the state of Washington between 1969 and 1984. The incidence rate of SIDS for next subsequent siblings of SIDS infants was calculated to be 7.1 per 1,000 live births and 7.4 per 1,000 for all subsequent siblings of SIDS infants. A computerized database, which linked birth and death files on infants, was used for this study. A control cohort of 2,774 subjects and 1,256 subsequent siblings was used for comparison. The incidence rates for next subsequent siblings and all subsequent siblings was calculated to be 4.3 and 4.0 per 1,000 live births, respectively.

1029. Pfadt, A. (1990). Diagnosing and treating psychopathology in clients with a dual diagnoses: An integrative model. In A. Dosen, A. Van Gennep, & G. J. Zwanikken (Eds.), *Treatment of mental illness and behavioral disorder in the mentally retarded: Proceedings of the International Congress, May 3rd & 4th, 1990* (pp. 217–224). **Leiden, the Netherlands: Logon Publications.**

This paper describes a formal analytic model of psychopathology. This model consists of a three-dimensional gird design made up of 168 cells incorporating a temporal dimension, social systems levels, and behavioral and experimental domains: temporal dimensions consist of past, present, and future; social systems levels consist of biological, psychological, interpersonal, small group, social ecological, organizational, and cultural; and the behavioral and experimental domains consist of outsider and insider points of view. The author suggests that the utility of this model stems from its integrative perspective, which will assist in the

conceptualization of the whole individual regardless of one's theoretical point of view.

1030. The Phillip Becker case. (1981). *The Canadian Journal on Mental Retardation, 31*(1), 20–22.

This article discusses the Phillip Becker case, which involved a United States Supreme Court ruling concerning medical treatment for Phillip, who has a mental disability and requires heart surgery. The court ruled in favor of the parents, who requested that no medical intervention should be initiated by the doctors. This article also features three case studies of parents who have children with mental disabilities.

1031. Pillemer, K. (1985). The dangers of dependency: New findings on the domestic violence against the elderly. *Social Problems, 33,* 146–158.

This article reviews research related to dependency as a factor in elder abuse. It suggests that dependency of the elder victim on the abuser is not adequate to explain the abuse; instead, mutual dependency, typically physical dependency of the victim on the abuser and financial dependency of the abuser on the victim, appears to be a critical factor in elder abuse. The author feels that this finding might be applied to caregiver abuse since paid caregivers depend on their victims for their income.

1032. Pillemer, K., & Finkelhor, D. (1989). Causes of elder abuse: Caregiver stress versus problem relatives. *American Journal of Orthopsychiatry, 59,* 179–187.

This article reports research results from a study designed to determine the relative importance of caregiver stress and caregiver personality problems for predicting elder abuse. This study found that problem caregivers accounted for abuse to a much larger extent than dependency of the victim or family stress.

1033. Pinderhughes, E. E., & Rosenberg, K. F. (1990). Family-bonding with high risk placements: A therapy model that promotes the process of becoming a family. *Journal of Children in Contemporary Society, 21*(3/4), 209–230.

This article suggests that families that adopt children who are high risk, emotionally disturbed, and developmentally disabled require adoption services that help the process of becoming a family. In response to the number of referrals of adoptive families in crisis requiring adoptive services, this article presents a preventive psycho-educational model created by family therapists at a mental health facility. This family-bonding model is based on a conceptualization of the phases of adjustment and attachment that adoptive families are thought to experience. The authors provide examples of some of the interventions and techniques used by the therapist to help families in the following areas: making attachments, acknowledging separate histories, and enhancing communication. They present the results of a study conducted to understand what factors influenced families' participation in the family-bonding sessions. This model is viewed as one preventive service, and the authors conclude that other diverse services are needed throughout the life cycle of the adoptive families and should be developed to assist these families.

1034. Pivato, E. (1986). Community living and the denormalization of the family. *The Mental Retardation and Learning Disability Bulletin, 14*(2), 62–66.

This article looks at government-supported services that allow children with severe disabilities to reside at home. It offers suggestions for the improvement of these services.

1035. Police prejudice and negligence helped Beck escape detection. (1993, February 9). *The Times,* p. 5.

This newspaper article reports that a government inquiry into the Leicestershire child abuse case involving Frank Beck concluded that the Leicestershire County Council and police neglected to act on serious allegations of abuse that occurred at the residential homes for disturbed children. The report by Andrew Kirkwood criticizes social service managers and police officers for not acting on allegations of child sexual abuse and ignoring warning signs. In addition, child-care strategies and monitoring of residential homes for children were not in place during the time when Beck was employed by the homes.

1036. Pontius, A. A. (1988). Introduction to biological issues, with neuropathological case illustrations. In R. A. Prenky & V. L. Quinsey (Eds.), *Human sexual aggression: Current perspectives* (pp. 148–153). New York: New York Academy of Sciences.

In this chapter, the author presents a summary of two clinical case studies of two sex offenders that seem to indicate that they suffer from two types of limbic system dysfunction in the frontal and temporal lobes. EEGs, neuropsychological examinations, and brain electric activity mapping (BEAM) were conducted on these offenders. One offender had temporal lobe epilepsy, and the other offender had psychotic trigger reaction. Both dysfunctions share the similar symptom of episodic dyscontrol.

1037. Pontius, A. A. (1988). Limbic system-frontal lobes' role in subtypes of "atypical rape." *Psychological Reports, 63,* 879–888.

This article suggests that two subtypes of fronto-limbic dysfunctioning (temporal lobe epilepsy and limbic psychotic trigger reaction) are implicated in certain cases of "atypical rape," that is, rapes that are committed without intent or control and involve extreme changes in the

perpetrator's sexual preference in areas such as the victim's gender, age, or sexual act. This article provides two case studies to illustrate the role of limbic system-frontal lobes in "atypical rape."

1038. Pope, K. S. (1987). Preventing therapist-patient sexual intimacy: Therapy for a therapist at risk. *Professional Psychology Research and Practice, 18*(6), 624–628.

This article summarizes research findings in the area of therapist-patient intimacy. It points out that this phenomenon appears to be a major problem for the profession. Research findings suggest that many therapists feel sexual attraction for their clients and are uncomfortable with it. The author emphasizes the need for the development of various intervention models enabling therapists to accept and understand this attraction and, as a result of this intervention, avoid acting it out. Using a fictional case study, the author suggests a preliminary approach to developing an intervention model. This model addresses such issues as confidentiality, the use of contracts, education, covert modeling, and cognitive-behavioral techniques.

1039. Pope, K. S. (1988). How clients are harmed by sexual contact with mental health professionals: The syndrome and its prevalence. *Journal of Counseling and Development, 67*(4), 222–226.

This article discusses therapist-patient sexual intimacy in terms of its prevalence, types, consequences, and contributing factors. It discusses the potential for this phenomenon to form into a distinct syndrome, and it describes some of the symptoms in the therapist: guilt; feelings of emptiness and isolation; sexual confusion; impaired ability to trust; identity, boundary, and role confusion; emotional lability; suppressed rage; increased risk for suicide; and difficulties in concentration and attention.

1040. Pope, K. S., Keith-Spiegel, P., & Tabachnick, B. G. (1986). Sexual attraction to clients: The human therapist and the (sometimes) inhuman training system. *American Psychologist, 41*(2), 147–158.

This article discusses therapist attraction to clients and how therapists react to and handle these feelings. It suggests that 95% of male therapists and 76% of female therapists had experienced some sexual attraction to a client on at least one occasion, and about 5% to 10% of male therapists and 1% to 2% of female therapists admitted to actually having a sexual relationship with one or more clients. It discusses the traumatic effects of these sexual contacts on the clients: anger, distrust, and fear. It suggests that therapist training regarding attraction to clients is generally inadequate and underresearched. This article recommends that this issue be dealt with by training therapists in order to cope with this situation more effectively.

1041. Powers, J. L., Mooney, A., & Nunno, M. (1990). Institutional abuse: A review of the literature. *Journal of Child and Youth Care, 4*(6), 81–95.
This article reviews the literature pertaining to institutional child abuse. It suggests that the maintenance of abuse may be related to lack of an operational definition of abuse, which leads to severe underreporting. The authors state that abuse may operate on three levels: overt direct care abuse, program abuse, and system abuse. They claim that staff morale, working conditions, and proximity of children to society should be considered contributing factors to institutional abuse. The authors include recommendations for investigating institutional maltreatment.

1042. Presscott, J. W. (1990). Affectional bonding for the prevention of violent behaviors: Neurobiological, psychological and religious/spiritual determinants. In L. J. Hertzberg, G. F. Ostrum, & J. R. Field (Eds.), *Violent behavior: Vol. I. Assessment & intervention* (pp. 95–124). Greatneck, NY: PMA.
This chapter outlines Prescott's SAD (somatosensory affectional deprivation) theory. This theory states that the primary cause of human violence is failure to develop normal primary affectional bonds between parents and children in early childhood. The failure of this bonding is believed to interfere with the development of secondary affectional bonding when these children reach adulthood. The author cites a number of human and animal studies. The primary emphasis of this chapter is an extensive analysis of various cultures that correlates the levels of violence with practices inconsistent with bonding.

1043. Price Byrne, J., & Valdiserri, E. V. (1982). Victims of childhood sexual abuse: A follow-up study of a noncompliant population. *Hospital & Community Psychiatry, 33*(11), 938–940.
This article discusses the investigation of a noncompliant population of families who did not return for follow-up appointments concerning the sexual abuse of their child. Of 79 children under the age of 14 seen at the Thomas Jefferson University Hospital's pediatric sexual assault clinic, 34 (6 male, 22 female) failed to return for follow-up. The mean age of the noncompliance group was 7.7 years, with 47% of the cases involving incest. This is compared to a mean age of 8.3 years for the compliant group (13 male, 32 female), with 24% of these cases involving incest. Racial distribution was similar for both groups. Both telephone and written contact with noncompliant families was initiated and appointments were rescheduled. In 15 cases, follow-up of noncompliant

families was not possible, 11 families failed to keep their reappointments, and 2 families refused. Six families did not reschedule appointments.

1044. Proctor, R. (1988). *Racial hygiene: Medicine under the Nazis.* Cambridge, MA: Harvard University Press.
This book provides a detailed account of medicine in the Third Reich. While Proctor acknowledges the role of the Nazi ideology and leadership in bringing about the Aktion T-4 euthanasia program, he also provides clear evidence that the physicians and scientists were the real force behind eugenics and that the Nazi regime merely validated their beliefs and legitimated their actions.

1045. Proctor, R. N. (1992). Nazi biomedical policies. In A. L. Kaplan (Ed.), *When medicine went mad: Bioethics and the holocaust* (pp. 23–42). Totawa, NJ: Humana Press.
This chapter briefly describes Nazi biomedical policies, including sterilization, euthanasia, and medical experimentation on involuntary subjects. The author points out that the euthanasia program was never intended to be euthanasia, but rather, it was intended to be triage that would free medical resources for other purposes, particularly the war effort. This was further necessitated because 60% of Germany's physicians prior to the Third Reich had been Jewish. The euthanasia program was generally popular in the community, and deliberate efforts were made to ensure that parents of children with disabilities would feel embarrassment and shame: "Hospital archives are filled with letters from parents writing to health authorities requesting that their children be granted euthanasia" (p. 36). The Nazi architects of the sterilization program estimated that 10%–15% of the German population was defective and would require sterilization, and methods of sterilization were developed (e.g., injection of supercooled carbon dioxide to damage the fallopian tubes, X-rays) that would allow a staff of 10 to sterilize 1,000 women per day. The author points out that historians are only beginning to fully acknowledge the links between the euthanasia program and the racial and ethnic extermination programs: For example, in the fall of 1941, when most of the mass extermination of people with severe disabilities had been completed, the gas chambers at Germany's psychiatric hospitals were dismantled and shipped to Majdanek, Auschwitz, and Treblinka, where they were reassembled and put into service exterminating Jews and other ethnic minorities. Many doctors and nurses who ran the euthanasia program went along with the equipment and ran the new programs.

1046. Project IMPACT Special Strategy Session On Sexual Abuse of Children and Adolescents With Disabilities. (1988). *Proceedings from special strategy session for dealing with the sexual abuse of children and adolescents with disabilities.* St. Paul, MN: Author.

(Available from Project IMPACT: Government Training Service, 202 Minnesota Building, 46 East Fourth Street, St. Paul, MN 55101) This paper summarizes the 1-day strategy session on sexual abuse of children with disabilities that was presented by the Department of Human Services and Project IMPACT. It discusses the following issues: the way the sexual abuse of children with disabilities is handled by the criminal justice system, ways to improve reporting and investigation, testimony and protection of abused children, treatment of offenders with disabilities, and corroborating evidence. It also includes suggestions and strategies developed during the workshop.

1047. Pross, C. (1991). Breaking through the postwar coverup of Nazi doctors in Germany. *Journal of Medical Ethics, 17*(Suppl.), **13–16.** This article reviews the role of physicians in the Nazi Aktion T-4 euthanasia program as well as other war crimes. Only 1 of 14 doctors who directly staffed the killing hospitals was prosecuted. Most of these doctors continued to practice medicine under false names, protected by their colleagues. Others were protected by other physicians who declared them too sick to stand trial, using "false diagnoses" (p. 14).

1048. Protective services for disabled children. (1986). *Mental and Physical Disability Law Reporter, 10*(4), **303–304.** This document discusses two court case rulings regarding the abuse and neglect of children with mental and physical disabilities.

1049. Protzman, F. (1989, April 18). Killing of 49 patients by 4 nurse's aides stuns the Austrians. *The New York Times,* **pp. A1, A11.** This newspaper article reports the case of four nurse's aides from Pavillion V of Lainz Hospital in Vienna, Austria, who confessed to killing 49 elderly patients. It states that Maria Gruber, Irene Leidolf, Waltraud Wagner, and Stefanie Mayer were placed under arrest but had not been formally charged. It is suspected that the killings started in 1983 and could possible involve as many as 300 patients. This article suggests that Maria Gruber is the one responsible for most of the murders.

1050. Protzman, F. (1991, March 31). Hospital aides in Vienna convicted of killing 42. *The New York Times,* **p. A12.** This newspaper article reports that the four nurse's aides charged with the murder of at least 42 elderly patients from Lainz Hospital in Vienna, Austria, were convicted and sentenced. Waltraud Wagner and Irene Leidolf each received life sentences. Stefanie Mayer received 20 years, and Maria Gruber received 15 years in jail. The patients were murdered by lethal injection or by water being forced into their lungs.

1051. Pueschel, S. M. (1991). Ethical considerations relating to prenatal diagnosis of fetuses with Down syndrome. *Mental Retardation, 29*(4), **185–190.** Because of the legal and ethical considerations created by the technological advances in prenatal diagnosis of genetic and chromosomal abnormalities, the author presents the debate between proponents of prenatal diagnosis and selective abortion and those who feel that physical and intellectual disabilities do not constitute valid reasons for abortion. The author suggests that prospective parents of fetuses with chromosomal abnormalities need to receive appropriate counseling, information, and support in order to make independent decisions on this matter.

1052. Pugh, R. J. (1978). The battered fetus. *British Medical Journal, 2,* **858.** The author of this editorial questions the rationale behind the common practice of ignoring the battered fetus as a topic of concern as important as other areas of maltreatment and abuse. The writer relates personal experiences, including an insightful statement made by a mother who associated her child's deformities with the physical assault she suffered while she was pregnant.

1053. Putnam, M. (1981). *Mentally handicapped love.* **Madeira Park, BC: Harbour Publishing.** This mostly autobiographical account reveals the events in the life of a young woman with an intellectual disability who desires to be a published author. Her views are supported with some fictional accounts.

1054. Pynoos, R. S., & Eth, S. (1986). Witness to violence: The child interview. *Journal of the American Academy of Child Psychiatry, 25*(3), **306–319.** This article discusses a technique appropriate for interviewing a traumatized child who has been a witness to an act of extreme violence. It discusses the three stages of the interview: drawing and storytelling, discussion of the experience and any associated feeling perceived by the child, and discussion of the aftermath of the experience and any consequential effects it might have for the child. This interviewing method has been used with children who have been witnesses to many forms of assault and victimization as well as suicide and accidental death.

1055. Quadriplegic wins right to end his own life. (1989, September 7). *The Toronto Star,* **p. A16.**

This newspaper article reports that Larry James McAfee has won the right to refuse medical treatment. Mr. McAfee is a quadriplegic who is dependent on the use of a ventilator to assist his breathing. His battle with the courts to obtain the right to have his ventilator disconnected has lasted 4 years. Mr. McAfee became paralyzed as a result of a motorcycle accident. The former civil engineer, hunter, and athlete felt his life to be hopeless and wanted to remove the responsibility for switching off the ventilator from his family and friends. In response to this, he devised his own device which he could personally trigger to shut the ventilator off. Currently, Mr. McAfee is unsure of his decision to follow through with the disconnection.

1056. Quast-Wheatley, L. (1988). Sexual victimization: A trauma needing the attention of educators. *The Pointer, 32*(4), 11–14.

Due to an overrepresentation of sexually abused children in special education classes, the author of this article feels that it has become necessary for educators to amend their traditional role. This article discusses the means by which educators may identify a victim of sexual abuse in their classrooms. Steps and guidelines for reporting are presented as well as information for the prevention of future abuse and school-based intervention. Finally, it supplies suggestions for an appropriate curriculum and a list of relevant materials that can be used in the classroom.

1057. Quill, T., Cassell, C., & Meier, I. E. (1992). Care of the hopelessly ill: Proposed clinical criteria for physician-assisted suicide. *New England Journal of Medicine, 327*(19), 1380–1384.

This article suggests criteria for permitting physician-assisted suicide. The authors urge a public policy permitting physicians to assist people to die when they have an incurable (but not necessarily terminal) condition associated with unrelenting suffering. The authors stress that the patient must understand his or her condition and choose death.

1058. Quinlan, B. (1992). Ethical dilemmas for institutional service providers. *Journal on Developmental Disabilities, 1*(1), 24–28.

This article describes a review of patient files at the coed Adult Occupational Centre for people with developmental disabilities in Edgar, Ontario, conducted to determine what treatment programs needed to be established to meet their needs. In particular, it examines the needs of those patients who were admitted due to deviant sexual behavior. This article also discusses issues concerning the development of a treatment program, for example, ethical issues.

•R•

1059. Rabb, J., & Rindfleisch, N. A. (1985). Study to define and assess severity of institutional abuse/neglect. *Child Abuse and Neglect, 9*(2), 285–294.

This article discusses an empirical study that addressed the need for the development of operational definitions of institutional abuse and neglect. Six hundred thirty respondents rated 24 instances of child maltreatment in institutions in terms of their degree of harmfulness. The respondents included direct caregivers, managers in institutions, public child welfare workers, foster parents, board members of caregiving facilities, and children in care. The results of this study indicate the following: Situations were judged to be harmful more often than they were judged to be instances of abuse or neglect; generally, judgments about out-of-home care were not different from judgments about in-home care; and different negative sequelae for the child resulted in different harm ratings and judgments of abuse or neglect.

1060. Rabinovitch, D. (1992, June 10). The innocent who finally won justice. *The Guardian*, p. 23.

This newspaper article reports that Craig Williamson, an employee for Mencap, a mental health charity organization, was sentenced to 3.5 years for sexually assaulting a client in his care. Nicole Boniface, a 23-year-old woman with a learning disability, testified in court against her attacker. This case is unique since it came to trial and resulted in a conviction. Two barriers that confront cases involving victims with developmental disabilities are the victim's understanding of having to tell the truth in court and the ability of the victim to withstand cross-examination. Nicole's mother has organized a charity group, VOICE, that will lobby the government to change legislation concerning the law as it applies to people with developmental disabilities testifying in court. Currently, only juveniles are allowed to testify using video link in cases involving sex or violence.

1061. Radford, J. P. (1991). Sterilization versus segregation: Control of the "feeble-minded," 1900–1938. Fourth International Symposium in Medical Geography: Medical geography: A broadening of horizons (1990, Norwich, England). *Social Science and Medicine, 33*(4), 449–458.

This article provides a case study of Langdon colony, developed in the 1930s as an extension of England's Starcross institution for people with mental retardation. According to the author, the development of this colony is associated with the eugenic philosophy and the debate over sterilization or institutionalization as the preferred method of controlling the reproduction of the "unfit."

1062. Rafter, N. H. (1992). Claims-making and socio-cultural context in the first

U.S. eugenics campaign. *Social Problems, 39*(1), 17–34.

This article provides a constructionist analysis of the development of American institutions for the "feeble-minded." It raises many questions about the eugenic campaign and why it focused primarily on women. It uses historical analysis to identify the roles of social construction of gender, deviance, and institutionalization.

1063. Ragg, M., & Lesperance, M. (1990, October). *Group treatment for intellectually limited adolescent sex offenders in community residential care: A parallel group model for the offenders and their caregivers.* **Paper presented at the Twelfth Annual Symposium for the Advancement of Social Work with Groups, Miami, FL.**

This paper discusses the techniques that can be used in group treatment for adolescent sex offenders with intellectual disabilities. These techniques attempt to enhance the offenders' self-understanding, increase their social and sexual skills, and instill victim empathy in them. This paper encourages the participation of caregivers in the treatment process, and it lists the possible reasons for caregiver resistance to the treatment program.

1064. Ralph, S. (1989). Using videotape in the modification of attitudes toward people with physical disabilities. *Journal of the Multihandicapped Person, 2*(4), 327–336.

The author of this article suggests that it is evident that portraying people with disabilities positively (e.g., being capable and competent) positively influences the way people think about disability. This article discusses information gathered from adult educators who viewed a videotape of a woman with neurofibromatosis. The women in the story does her own narrating and relates her daily activities in a realistic, positive manner, including any obstacles encountered by her. The author reports that the response to the videotape was generally very positive; in particular, the respondents found the presenter a very effective advocate for her own story.

1065. Rantakallio, P., & Went, L. V. (1986). Mental retardation and subnormality in a birth cohort of 12,000 children in northern Finland. *American Journal of Mental Deficiency, 90*(4), 380–387.

This article discusses a study that examined the incidence of mental retardation and subnormality in a 1-year birth cohort of 12,058 children born in Oulu or Lapland, Finland, in 1966. The children were followed up to the age of 14, with 14 children unaccounted for from the original cohort. The children's health, development, and school performance were assessed using questionnaires filled out by public health nurses and family members. The findings of this study indicate that the cumulative incidence rate of severe mental retardation, mild mental retardation, and mental subnormality was 7.4, 5.5, and 13.4 per 1,000 children, respectively, with corresponding prevalence rates of 6.3, 5.6, and 13.7 per 1,000 children.

1066. Reece, R. M. (1990). Unusual manifestations of child abuse. *Pediatric Clinics of North America, 37*(4), 905–921.

This article presents case reports of unusual manifestations of child abuse and discusses the indicators of this abuse. It examines the following manifestations: aspiration of poisons and so forth, burns, dehydration, ingestion of poisons and so forth, lacerations, tin ear, and Munchausen syndrome by proxy.

1067. Reece, R. M. (1993). Fatal child abuse and sudden infant death syndrome: A critical diagnostic decision. *Pediatrics, 91*(2), 423–429.

This article focuses on the issues of fatal child abuse and sudden infant death syndrome (SIDS). It defines SIDS and examines the incidence and epidemiology of SIDS. The difference between SIDS and fatal child abuse is supported by literature reviews. The author states that cases of abuse in SIDS deaths are primarily determined using autopsies, radiographic studies, death scene investigation, and prior medical history investigation. The author discusses child death review teams and suggests 13 recommendations for investigating and determining the cause of death.

1068. Reece, R. M. (Ed.). (1994). *Child abuse: Medical diagnosis and management.* **Philadelphia: Lea & Febiger.**

This book contains a wealth of valuable information about child abuse from a medical perspective. Chapters on head trauma, sudden infant death syndrome, photo-documentation, Munchausen syndrome by proxy, conditions mistaken for child abuse, and genetic disorders that mimic child abuse are of particular interest.

1069. Reid, J. G. S. (1992). Abuse: An international practice. *ILSMH (International League of Societies for Persons with Mental Handicap) News, 13,* 1, 3.

This article reviewed the discussion of abuse that took place at the 1990 World Congress of the International League of Societies for Persons with Mental Handicap in 1990 in Paris. Much of the discussion focussed on reported abuse in an institution in Leros, Greece. Problems in developing countries and eastern Europe were also discussed. A copy of the ILSMH official policy statement, "The right of persons with mental handicap to be protected against abuse and mistreatment" is also included.

1070. Reid, J. G. S. (1992). Abuse: A sad world tour. *ILSMH (International League of Societies for Persons with Mental Handicap) News, 13,* 5–6.

This article presents examples of the abuse of people with mental disabilities around the world. While there is some mention of sexual abuse, this article focuses primarily on physical abuse.

1071. Residents abused at home, former employee tells trial. (1989, September 20). *The Globe and Mail*, p. A16.
This newspaper article reports on abuse at the Cedar Glen Home for adults with emotional disabilities. Jean Thilbault, owner of the Cedar Glen Home at Jackson's Point in Ontario, faces 25 counts of violence against residents at the home. In addition, Mary Jane Thilbault, wife of the accused, pleaded guilty to four counts of assault against residents at the home. The assaults took the form of beatings. A former employee and residents at the home testified against Mr. Thilbault.

1072. Retarded man slain in home. (1994, May 3). [*Associated Press* wire story].
This wire story describes the murder of Robert Ballard, a 33-year-old man who was beaten to death with his electronic communication device by two teenage boys who kicked down his door and entered his home in Salina, Oklahoma. According to a police investigator who ruled out robbery as a motive, the 17-year-old and 14-year-old "just picked on him because he was an easy target." Ballard was living alone but ate and washed at the nearby home of his aunt, who said that he had been harassed on previous occasions and that "drunks" had tried to break into his house at night on previous occasions. Ballard had tried to flee from his attackers but was chased down and beaten to death. His body was found the following afternoon in a ravine 50 yards from his home.

1073. Retarded teens used in testing. (1993, December 27). *The Edmonton Sun*, p. 33.
This newspaper article reports that during the 1940s and 1950s researchers at Harvard University and the Massachusetts Institute of Technology were involved in radiation testing using teenagers with mental retardation. Thirty-six boys between the ages of 15 and 17 were fed low levels of radioactive calcium so that researchers could determine how it was being digested. The research was funded by the Quaker Oats Company and the United States Atomic Energy Commission. No follow-up studies were reported to determine the welfare of these boys.

1074. Reyome, N. D. (1990). Executive directors' perceptions of the prevention of child abuse and maltreatment in residential facilities. *Journal of Child and Youth Care*, 4(6), 45–60.
This article describes a study that examined executive directors' perceptions of factors that are most important in the prevention of institutional child abuse and maltreatment. Using information from recent literature, the author developed a survey that targeted 107 agencies in the New York State area. The findings of this survey indicate the following: Staff supervision was deemed most important in the prevention of child abuse, follow-

ed by professionalism in child care, organizational issues, staff recruitment, treatment services, staff retention, and environmental issues. Executive directors also indicated that the use of a team approach and the inclusion of families were effective protectors against abuse. The author notes that low salaries were consistently cited as an obstacle for adequate staffing and subsequent quality of care.

1075. Richards, J., & Goodwin, J. M. (1993). Electra: Revenge fantasies and homicide in child abuse victims. In J. M. Goodwin (Ed.), *Rediscovering childhood trauma: Historical casebook and clinical applications* (pp. 27–38). Washington, DC: American Psychiatric Press.
This chapter discusses the Electra complex (which is a daughter's desire to kill her mother and marry her father) in terms of Electra's childhood abuses rather than the Oedipal urges that are thought to characterize sexual development. This mythical story is examined in relation to a case involving a 15-year-old girl who was sexually, emotionally, and physically abused by her father. Also, this chapter defines the symptoms of the Electra complex: the Cinderella syndrome, a history of abuse, unresolved grief regarding the loss of a parental figure, feelings of helplessness and hopelessness, and a mother figure who herself was abused.

1076. Richardson, M., & Keeran, C. V. (1990). The responsibility of scientists in shaping public policy. *Mental Retardation*, 28(2), 63–64.
This guest editorial suggests that science has an important responsibility and role in the political process and in shaping public policy for people with mental retardation and their families. The authors claim that scientists have not yet learned the important lessons about political activism from people with mental retardation and their advocacy movement, and they believe that it is critical for advocates, scientists, and policy makers to work together in order to shape future policy for people with mental retardation.

1077. Richwald, G. A., & McCluskey, T. C. (1985). Family violence during pregnancy. In D. B. Jelliffe & E. F. P. Jelliffe (Eds.), *Advances in international maternal and child health* (Vol. 5, pp. 87–96). Oxford: Clarendon Press.
This chapter discusses physical violence against a woman during pregnancy. Although some studies are presented to establish incidence rates, the authors point out that the prevalence of this type of abuse is not exactly known at this time. The authors examine possible adverse prenatal outcomes of wife battering during pregnancy and suggest possible theories that try to explain this form of abuse.

1078. Riddington, J. (1989, March). *Beating the "odds": Violence and women with*

disabilities (Position paper 2). Vancouver, BC: DAWN (DisAbled Women's Network) Canada.

This 45-page position paper reports results from a survey of 245 women with disabilities. It reports that 40% had experienced some form of abuse, about 12% had been raped, and 15% had been assaulted. For 56%, sexual or physical abuse began after the onset of their disability, and for another 26%, abuse occurred both before and after the onset of disability. For 19%, abuse had occurred before but not after the onset of disability. Some form of violence or sexual assault was experienced by women in all disability categories, and there was some evidence that multiple disabilities increased risk. Perpetrators of abuse, rape, or assault included spouses and ex-spouses (37%), parents (15%), strangers (28%), service providers (10%), boyfriends or dates (7%), and the remainder by other relatives, neighbors, or their own children. Reports were made to police, social service agencies, parents, teachers, or spouses in 43% of the cases, and the author points out that this rate may be high because more than half of the respondents in this sample were members of consumer groups with disabilities, and more than 40% were members of women's advocacy groups. The most common reasons cited for not reporting were fear and dependency. Only about 10% of the sample had used shelters or other services, about 15% reported that no services were available or that they tried unsuccessfully to obtain services, and 55% did not attempt to obtain services at all. This report also includes much more information on the DAWN Canada study and several others.

1079. Riddington, J. (1989). *Who do we think we are? Self-image and women with disabilities.* **Vancouver, BC: DAWN (DisAbled Women's Network) Canada.**

This report discusses the results of a survey that examined the positive self-image of women with disabilities. Two hundred forty-five women participated in this 1988 study. In particular, this survey examined those issues that inhibit the formation of positive images of self for women with disabilities.

1080. Ridgeway, S. M. (1993). Abuse and deaf children: Some factors to consider. *Child Abuse Review, 2*(3), 166–173.

This article describes three cases of abuse of deaf children. It provides an analysis of these cases and discusses risk factors, communication issues, and implications for training.

1081. Riffenburgh, R. S., & Lakshmanan, S. (1991). The eyes of child abuse victims: Autopsy findings. *Journal of Forensic Sciences, 36*(3), 741–747.

In this article, autopsies on 77 pairs of eyes from suspected cases of child abuse were examined for retinal hemorrhages. Forty-seven cases of retinal hemorrhages were determined, of which 23 cases were accompanied by additional physical findings of abuse. The results of these examinations indicate that hemorrhages are more characteristic of younger cases and occurred more often in cases with intracranial injury, which suggests shaking infant syndrome. For three cases of retinal hemorrhages, the author rules out abuse.

1082. Rindfleisch, N., & Baros-Van Hull, J. (1982). Direct care worker's attitudes toward use of physical force with children. In R. Hanson (Ed.), *Institutional abuse of children and youth* **(pp. 115–125). New York: Haworth Press.**

This chapter describes a survey conducted to investigate the attitudes of direct care workers about the use of physical force with children in institutions. One hundred direct care workers were selected from 42 living units representing small public, small private, large public, and large private institutions. There were 25 care workers surveyed in each of the four categories. A five-part self-administered questionnaire, which featured role-playing techniques, was completed by each participant. The results of the survey indicate that willingness to use force was associated with several factors: the degree of resentment toward children, management of routines within the organization, degree of participation in decision making, size of the community in which the caregiver was raised, and the age of the caregiver.

1083. Rindfleisch, N., & Bean, G. J. J. (1988). Willingness to report abuse and neglect in residential facilities. *Child Abuse & Neglect, 12,* 509–520.

This article discusses a study conducted to identify factors that characterize residential care workers who would willingly report cases of abuse or maltreatment and those workers who would not report these types of cases. This study gathered information from 598 individuals working in 24-hour residential care facilities. Sixty-two facilities in 33 counties in five states were involved in the study. It used a factorial survey approach, incorporating two vignettes illustrating hypothetical situations, and it analyzed seven variables using a hierarchical regression model. The results of this study indicate that staff were more willing to report cases of sexual and physical abuse and more reluctant to report cases involving restraint or control, moral behavior of the staff, and cases of neglect. The authors note that the position of the staff perpetrator, support for reporting incidences of abuse, and assessment of the severity of the incident were less important factors influencing a staff member's willingness to report.

1084. Rindfleisch, N., & Hicho, D. (1987). Institutional child protection: Issues in program development and implementation. *Child Welfare, 66*(4), 329–342.

This article discusses a survey of 48 states and the District of Columbia conducted to determine the procedures for handling complaints of abuse and neglect of children in institutions. It summarizes findings on statutes and policies, prevention programs, reporting, investigation, and efforts to reduce conflicts of interest. Site visits to four states were conducted to verify survey information. The authors suggest that a checklist could serve as a tentative framework for viewing child protection services in the different states.

1085. Rindfleisch, N., & Rabb, J. (1984). How much of a problem is resident mistreatment in child welfare institutions? *Child Abuse and Neglect, 8*, 33–40.

This article provides information collected since 1980 by the Institutional Children Protection Project about mistreatment in child welfare residential institutions. In the 1,700 facilities surveyed, there are about 69,000 children and youths. Maltreatment in the survey meant abuse and neglect. The definition of abuse and neglect used in the survey was the respondent's own subjective view. As a result, the authors believe the data represent incidents of a generally more serious nature, but the survey does not give a breakdown of the specific type of abuse. Rates of utilization vary from 8 reports per 10,000 to 19 per 10,000 children and youths in the population among Health and Human Services regions. The average rate is 12 per 10,000. The survey also included visits to sites to confirm the results. Observations of site visitors suggest that only one out of five complainable situations may be reported to child protection agencies. A list of complainable occurrences that come to the attention of site visitors is included to document the problem. This list includes incidents of sexual abuse. The authors believe residential complaint rates may be twice as large as intrafamilial complaint rates.

1086. Rinear, E. E. (1985). Sexual assault and the handicapped victim. In A. W. Burgess (Ed.), *Rape and sexual assault* (pp. 139–145). New York: Garland Publishing.

This chapter discusses the problem of sexual assault of people with disabilities. It claims that people with disabilities are more vulnerable to sexual assault and may also face a number of additional problems: For example, individuals with emotional disabilities may find that others fail to believe that they were actually assaulted or victimized, individuals with physical and perceptual disabilities may be targeted as victims of sexual offenders because of their restricted abilities, people with disabilities are limited in the type and amount of resistance that they are able to mount against their assailants, and individuals with disabilities who are dependent on others may be exploited by offenders who manipulate the victim's dependence. This article discusses the coping behaviors used by rape victims, and they can be viewed as comprising three distinct phases: the threat of attack, the attack itself, and the period immediately after the attack. This article also discusses possible methods of prevention of the victimization of people with disabilities: for example, self-defense classes for people with disabilities, crisis centers and support group

availability, education of the public and prosecutors, and educational programs implemented in institutions.

1087. Rioux, M. H. (1990). Sterilization and mental handicap: A rights issue. *Journal of Leisurability, 17*(3), 3–11.

This article discusses the issue of sterilization of people with mental disabilities. It examines the different stances on sterilization held by the Supreme Court of Canada and the British House of Lords and their influence on the rights of people with mental disabilities.

1088. Rioux, M. H. (1991). Exchanging charity for rights: A challenge for the 1990s. *Entourage, 6*(2), 3–5.

This article questions the use of the charitable model in the allocation of goods and services to people with disabilities. Instead, it suggests that the allocation of goods and services should be based on the human rights model. This article points out that the following aspects of the present allocation of goods and services will need to be changed: for example, the social conformity and paternalism that informs income, employment, and services will have to be replaced; the role of professionals as experts and their role in the decision-making process will need to be reexamined; and disability and poverty must be viewed as the results of politics and economics, not as an outcome of individual behavior.

1089. Ritchie, S. (1992, March 15). Doctor describes practices in deaths of disabled kids. *The Toronto Star*, p. B4.

This newspaper article describes the testimony of Dr. David Sliwowicz, medical director of the Christopher Robin Home in Ajax, Ontario, who testified in court regarding the deaths of 15 children with disabilities who were treated at the residence. The doctor stated that it was an unwritten practice to provide palliative care to those children with disabilities. Large dosages of morphine were administered to relieve pain, regardless of any respiratory problems suffered by the children. (Morphine represses respiratory activity.) Lack of parental consultation and the home's "Do Not Resuscitate" policy have been questioned.

1090. Rivera, B., & Widom, C. S. (1990). Childhood victimization and violent offending. Annual Meeting of the American Society of Criminology (1988, Chicago, Illinois). *Violence and Victims, 5*(1), 19–35.

This article describes a study that investigated the relationship between childhood victimization and aggressive offenses. This study compared official criminal records for 908 substantiated cases of physical and sexual abuse and neglect between the years 1967 and 1971 with a matched control group of 667 subjects that did not have any official record of abuse or neglect. The subjects in this study were between 16 and 33 years of age. This study examined the following: sex-specific and race-specific effects of childhood victimization, chronicity, age of onset, temporal patterns, and continuity. This study found the following: victimization during childhood appeared related to violent offending, especially for males and African Americans; abused and neglected subjects appeared to begin delinquent careers earlier than the controls; and childhood victims were about the same age at their first arrest for violence, and they were no more likely to continue committing aggressive offenses when compared to the controls.

1091. Robb, J. C. (1990). The dilemma of the mentally disabled sexual abuse victim. *Developmental Disabilities Bulletin, 18*(2), 1–12.
This article addresses some of the issues faced by people with mental disabilities who have been sexually abused and wish to prosecute the offender. It pays particular attention to the restrictions in the Criminal Code concerning people with mental disabilities and the problem of providing admissible evidence proving the reality of sexual abuse.

1092. Roberts, J., Golding, J., Keeling, J., Sutton, B., & Lynch, M. A. (1984). Is there a link between cot death and child abuse? *British Medical Journal, 289,* 789–791.
This article describes a study from an obstetrics unit in Oxford that attempted to determine whether certain factors obtained through obstetric notes, which are indicative of child abuse, could predict the likelihood of sudden infant death syndrome (SIDS). This study matched and compared 55 abused infants and 146 controls who died between the ages of 8 days and 2 years. The results of this study indicate that four of the five factors (i.e., whether the mother was ages 20 or younger, emotional disturbance of the mother, referral to social worker, or admittance of the infant to a special care unit) did not help predict SIDS. The authors note that concern over parental ability did distinguish between the two groups.

1093. Robertson, D. E. J. (1992). *Portraying persons with disabilities: An annotated bibliography of fiction for children and teenagers.* **New Providence, NJ: R. R. Bowker.**
This book provides a wealth of information on how people with disabilities are portrayed in literature for children and teenagers. The author points out that many lifelong attitudes are developed in the formative years and that old stereotypes about disability are often replaced by new ones. She suggests that many but not all of the earlier negative stereotypes in the literature have been eliminated in the literature of the last decade and that equally unrealistic stereotypes of people with disabilities as beyond human frailties are replacing them. Many of the cited stories deal with violence, child abuse, or sexual abuse in conjunction with disability. Generally, people with disabilities are portrayed as victims, and abuse is most frequently associated with emotional disabilities.

1094. Rode, S. S., Chang, P. N., Fisch, R. O., & Sroufe, L. A. (1982). Attachment patterns of infants separated at birth. *Annual Progress in Child Psychiatry and Child Development,* 182–187 (Reprinted from *Developmental Psychology,* 1981, *17*[2], 188–191)
The authors of this article evaluate 24 cases of an infant's attachment to the caregiver when separation occurred immediately following birth because of prematurity or extreme health problems. This evaluation assessed infants at 12 to 19 months of age using the Ainsworth Strange Situation assessment and the Bayley Scales of Infant Development. The results of this evaluation indicate that the attachments of the infants in this study were comparable to the attachments of infants in previous studies who had not been separated for an extended period of time. It found no significant differences between this group and previous groups on Bayley scores, height, weight, gestational age, birth weights, days of hospitalization, or parental visiting patterns. The authors conclude that early days are important, but attachment is a process that evolves during the first year of life.

1095. Rodning, C., Beckwith, L., & Howard, J. (1989). Prenatal exposure to drugs and its influence on attachment. Conference of the Behavioral Teratology Society, the National Institute on Drug Abuse, and the New York Academy of Sciences: Prenatal Abuse of Licit and Illicit Drugs (1988, Bethesda, Maryland). *Annals of the New York Academy of Sciences, 562,* 352–354.
This article discusses a study that compared the attachment behavior of 18 toddlers who had been prenatally exposed to drugs with 57 high-risk preterm and 20 full-term toddlers. It assessed influence on attachment in a laboratory using the Ainsworth Strange Situation. The results of this study indicate the following: Drug-exposed toddlers displayed less interactive behaviors; exhibited less strong feelings of pleasure, anger, and distress; showed higher proportions of insecure attachments; and had significantly lower developmental quotients. Also, the study found that the postnatal rearing environment was a significant factor in mitigating, to some degree, the effects of prenatal drug exposure. The authors suggest that further investigations are required into the relationship between the physiological and behavioral effects of prenatal drug exposure.

1096. Rodriguez: Autonomy & vulnerability must both be protected. (1993, Fall). *Abilities, 16,* 77–78.
This article describes a court battle involving Ms. Rodriguez, who has progressive amyotrophic lateral sclerosis (ALS), also known as Lou Gehrig's disease, and the Attorneys General of British Columbia and Canada. It concerns the issue of assisted suicide for people with disabilities. Ms. Rodriguez argues that the current pro-

hibition against assisted suicides is discriminatory against persons with disabilities and wants the law to be struck down. This article discusses the implications of this case.

1097. The Roeher Institute. (1988). *The language of pain: Perspectives on behaviour management.* **Toronto: Author.**
This book examines the use of aversive techniques as a means of behavior management for people with mental disabilities. It includes accounts of and expresses concerns with aversive techniques used by professionals.

1098. The Roeher Institute. (1988). *Vulnerable: Sexual abuse and people with an intellectual handicap.* **Toronto: Author.**
This book examines the prevalence of sexual abuse of people with mental disabilities in institutions and the community. It uses a literature review and a survey of community services in order to examine some of the important issues concerning the sexual abuse of people with mental disabilities. It also discusses the following: the treatment of victims of abuse, the effects of abuse, and people with mental disabilities who are sex offenders.

1099. The Roeher Institute. (1989). *Sexual abuse prevention programs and mental handicap: A report prepared by the Roeher Institute.* **North York, ON: Author.**
This booklet evaluates nine sexual abuse prevention programs and assesses their suitability or adaptability for use with people who have developmental disabilities. Three of these programs are generic programs, and the rest of them target children with developmental disabilities. This booklet includes standards for an effective prevention program: In short, an effective prevention program needs to include people with developmental disabilities, their families, teachers, legal and medical professionals, and counselors all across the country.

1100. The Roeher Institute. (1991). *Research by/for/with women with disabilities.* **Toronto: Author.**
This book discusses prospective Canadian research that focuses on women with disabilities. It is written for those doing research in the fields of women's studies and disability. It provides a general outline concerning research methods dealing with women with disabilities.

1101. The Roeher Institute. (1991). *The right to control what happens to your body: A straightforward guide to issues of sexuality and sexual abuse. Know your rights, seek true justice, gain real power.* **North York, ON: Author.**
This book addresses the sexuality and sexual abuse of people with mental disabilities and is written for the self-advocate. It discusses a person's rights over his or her body and supplies information concerning procedural guidelines for dealing with sexual abuse.

1102. The Roeher Institute. (1992). *No more victims: A manual to guide counsellors and social workers in addressing the sexual abuse of people with a mental handicap.* **North York, ON: Author.**
This manual is written for counselors and social workers in order to inform them about sexual abuse and people with mental disabilities. It examines the following topics: recognition of abuse, legal aspects, appropriate response to abuse, counseling people with mental disabilities who have been abused, and prevention of sexual abuse in the community and institutions.

1103. The Roeher Institute. (1992). *No more victims: A manual to guide families and friends in addressing the sexual abuse of people with a mental handicap.* **North York, ON: Author.**
This manual is part of the *No More Victims* series from the Roeher Institute, and it is designed to inform families and friends about sexual abuse and people with mental disabilities. It discusses the following topics: indications of abuse, legal concerns, responding to abuse issues, and prevention.

1104. The Roeher Institute. (1992). *No more victims: A manual to guide the legal community in addressing the sexual abuse of people with a mental handicap.* **North York, ON: Author.**
This manual is part of the Roeher Institute's *No More Victims* series, and it is written in order to inform the legal community about the sexual abuse of people with mental disabilities. It discusses the Criminal Code and the Canada Evidence Act in relation to people with mental disabilities who have been abused. It also provides additional information about the following: prevalence, identification of sexual abuse, and prevention.

1105. The Roeher Institute. (1992). *No more victims: A manual to guide the police in addressing the sexual abuse of people with a mental handicap.* **North York, ON: Author.**
This manual focuses on the prevention and treatment of sexual abuse of people with disabilities. The first part of the manual contains information on people with intellectual disabilities. The second part of the manual discusses the sexual abuse of people with intellectual disabilities: for example, the indicators of abuse, reporting, legal procedures, prevention, and services. This manual illustrates the sexual abuse of people with intellectual disabilities using personal stories.

1106. Roessler, R. T., & Lewis, F. D. (1984). Conversation skill training with mentally retarded and learning disabled sheltered workshop clients. *Rehabil-*

itation Counseling Bulletin, 27(3), 161–171.

This article discusses the results of a social skills training program. Three employees of a sheltered workshop participated in a social skills training program that was designed to improve their conversational skills. The program comprised 10 lessons, and the training package focused on cognitive inoculation (how to handle rejection in social conversations), discrimination (when to start a conversation), and target skills (greeting and opening question). The last two components of the program were taught by using modeling, role playing, and feedback. An overall skill review was included in the training package. The results of the small-group multiple-baseline study indicate the following: The participants improved their use of targeted conversational skills over the course of training; and they maintained their skills in role-playing situations, but they experienced difficulty generalizing some of the target behaviors to other individuals. The authors note the need for additional in vivo practice and training on aspects of nonverbal communication.

1107. Rogeness, G. A., Amrung, S. A., Macedo, C. A., Harris, W. R., & Fisher, C. (1986). Psychopathology in abused or neglected children. *Journal of the American Academy of Child Psychiatry, 25*(5), 659–665.

This article describes a study that compared 377 boys and 162 girls with emotional problems under the age of 16 who had either a history of abuse, a history of neglect, or no history of abuse or neglect in order to determine if there were any differences in psychopathology or cognitive ability. All of the children in this study were admitted to a children's psychiatric hospital and were diagnosed using the *Diagnostic and Statistical Manual of Mental Disorders (DSM-III)*. This study used the Wechler Intelligence Scale for Children (WISC) to assess the children's cognitive ability. This study examined 60 boys and 39 girls in the abuse group, 100 boys and 27 girls in the neglect group, and 217 boys and 96 girls in the group that had not been abused or neglected. The findings of this study indicate the following: neglected boys have lower verbal IQs than boys in the other two groups, abused boys and neglected boys were more frequently diagnosed with conduct disorder than boys with no history of abuse or neglect, abused girls were more often diagnosed with conduct disorder than girls in the other two groups, and abused girls and neglected girls both obtained lower verbal and performance IQ scores than girls who had not been abused or neglected.

1108. Rogers, R. G. (1990). *Reaching for solutions: The report of the Special Advisor to the Minister of National Health and Welfare on Child Sexual Abuse in Canada*. Ottawa, ON: Health and Welfare Canada, National Clearinghouse on Family Violence. (Department of Supply and Services Catalogue No. H.74-28/1990E)

This report provides recommendations for dealing with the problem of child sexual abuse in Canada: 1) a Children's Bureau should be established within Health and Welfare Canada with a mandate for a broad range of children's interests, including combating child abuse, child-care concerns, and many other functions; 2) a National Resource Centre on Child Abuse should be established within the Children's Bureau; 3) five to seven Regional Resource Centers for the Prevention of Child Abuse should be established across Canada; 4) each province should develop an interministerial mechanism to coordinate efforts of various provincial departments relevant to child abuse; 5) the Canadian Medical Association should assume an increased role in prevention, detection, and treatment of child abuse; 6) each local community should develop interdisciplinary and inter-jurisdictional protocols for prevention and treatment; 7) each province should develop and/or maintain a mechanism for monitoring child protection and other relevant services (an ombudsman model is suggested); 8) appropriate audiovisual materials should be developed or obtained and distributed to increase public awareness; 9) federal and provincial governments should continue to support public education as community-based primary prevention; 10) the Minister of Justice should review legislation that will address the protection of children from the harmful effects of pornography; 11) the Canadian Radio and Television Commission (CRTC) should assume a more active role in regulating the amount of violence and sexually exploitive material broadcast; 12) all relevant professional associations should develop policies that describe the role of their members in prevention, detection, and treatment; 13) all organizations (including churches) and agencies within Canada should further develop their efforts to prevent child abuse within their agencies; 14) policies should set out guidelines on selection, screening, and training of leaders and staff as well as investigation and reporting of any reports of abuse; 15) each law enforcement jurisdiction should develop a clear policy for charging and prosecuting offenders; 16) local protocols should not delay treatment of the offender pending resolution of criminal proceedings; 17) all police officers should receive multidisciplinary training; 18) the federal government should fund and assess model programs and collect and disseminate information; 19) the federal Department of Justice should monitor and defend Bill C-15; 20) further reforms should be made to the legislation governing child sexual abuse prosecutions in order to permit qualified experts to testify on the reliability of testimony, to permit witnesses to testify about out of court statements made by a child, to permit judges to require accused individuals to vacate the premises as a condition of bail, to permit an adult to accompany a child in the witness stand, and to permit the use of videotaped statements by any child witness in a child abuse prosecution; 21) the appointment of counsel to protect the needs of child victim witnesses should be considered; 22) provincial governments should take steps to effectively implement the provisions of Bill C-15; 23) those responsible should ensure that policies on expert witnesses show sensitivity to the needs of those professionals; 24) scheduling priority should be given to child sexual abuse cases; 25) a commission should be developed to study the development of architectural designs for courthouses sensitive to the needs of children and other sensitive witnesses; 26) the national Judicial Education Centre and provincial organizations should ensure that education programs include child sexual abuse and capabilities of child witnesses; 27) a model ethics code should be developed for dealing with children and other vulnerable witnesses; 28) victim impact statements and information about the long-term effects of child sexual abuse should be imparted to sentencing judges and included as part of judicial education programs; 29) departments of corrections should make treatment available to convicted child abusers; 30) federal legislation should be amended to allow judges to order treatment services to be made available; 31) postcharge programs for offenders should be established on an experimental basis and carefully evaluated; 32) the criminal code should be revised to allow extended probation (up to life terms) for those convicted of child sexual offenses; 33) parole legislation should be amended to allow longer periods of supervision; 34) provincial and territorial governments should amend legislation to facilitate evidence given by children in civil cases at least to the extent currently provided under Bill C-15; 35) police and child protection investigators should have special training in the dynamics of abuse allegations in the context of parental custody disputes; 36) provincial and territorial legislation should be amended to permit civil damages to adult survivors of child sexual abuse; 37) Criminal Injury Compensation Boards should develop legislation and policy that support compensation of victims of sexual abuse; 38) compensation as restitution should be considered as part of the offender's sentence; 39) Health and Welfare Canada should support programs that assist voluntary organizations in reducing the risk for abuse, including guidelines for supervision and screening of volunteers, and that all such agencies should have clear policies and procedures regarding the prevention, detection, and reporting of abuse; 40) federal and provincial government agencies should ensure that policy and procedure make possible the release of the criminal records of individuals applying for and working in paid or voluntary positions with children; 41) government and private agencies should develop and implement appropriate staff screening procedures; 42) provincial and territorial governments should establish mechanisms for identifying and registering abusers; 43) addressing the needs of adult survivors of sexual abuse should be an important priority for provinces and territories; 44) provincial and territorial governments should address the current gaps in services; 45) federal, provincial, and territorial governments should study the special needs of rural and isolated communities and develop initiatives for meeting those needs; 46) nonoffending members of families should be considered and included in treating victims; 47) the federal government should fund research and evaluation of treatment for victims, families, and offenders; 48) the Expert Advisory Committee on Healing and Treatment should develop a long-range plan for effective offender treatment in order to ensure that frontline specialists are available; 49) the Canadian Association of Chiefs of Police and the Royal Canadian Mounted Police should review policy and practice related to investigation and the expertise and resources needed to support policies; 50) the Canadian Police College should require senior police officials to take an orientation program on child abuse; 51) Canadian law schools should ensure that all students acquire a basic understanding of family violence and child sexual abuse and that interested students should have the opportunity to take more advanced classes; 52) provincial Attorneys General should offer a week-long training program for Crown Attorneys on child victim witness preparation and related matters; 53) probation and parole officers should receive specialized training in child sexual abuse; 54) Health and Welfare Canada should ensure that appropriate training regarding identification and treatment of victims is available and encouraged; 55) professional schools and colleges should ensure that those who work with children can recognize child sexual abuse and respond appropriately; 56) federally funded projects in child abuse should include research and evaluation components; 57) Health and Welfare Canada should maintain an ongoing dialogue with scholars, researchers, clinicians, and other stakeholders; 58) the proposed Children's Bureau of Health and Welfare Canada should develop common definitions so that a national statistical database can be established; 59) the federal government should establish an Aboriginal Expert Advisory Committee; 60) the proposed Children's Bureau of Health and Welfare Canada should establish a special task force to examine the issues of child abuse for very young children, children in institutional settings, children with disabilities and disturbances, and new Canadians; 61) the proposed Children's Bureau of Health and Welfare Canada should establish a special task force to examine the issues of child abuse in rural and remote settings; and 62) the federal government should publish an annual report that describes progress in combating child abuse. (Editors' note: During the fall of 1990, Canada's Prime Minister, Brian Mulroney, announced the establishment of a Children's Bureau during United Nations meetings on the rights of children.)

1109. Root, I. (1992). Head injuries from short distance falls. *American Journal of Forensic Medicine and Pathology,* *13*(1), 85–87.

This article reviews the literature on head injuries to children in short distance falls, with special attention to resolving apparent discrepancies. While some studies suggest that skull fractures can occur in falls from heights as low as 33 inches, such skull fractures are not typically associated with significant brain injury.

1110. Rose, E., & Hardman, M. L. (1981). The abused mentally retarded child. *Education and Training of the Mentally Retarded Child, 16*(2), 114–118.

The authors of this article review research in the area of child abuse and mental disabilities. This review reveals a higher incidence of mental disabilities in children as a result of abuse or neglect. The authors point out that it is difficult to interpret the research because definitions of mental retardation and child abuse are not standardized across studies. The authors also discuss ways of breaking the abused child/abusing parent cycle and methods of treatment.

1111. Rosen, C. L., Frost, J. D., Bricker, T., Tarnow, J. D., Gillette, P. C., & Dunlavy, S. (1983). Two siblings with recurrent cardiorespiratory arrest: Munchausen syndrome by proxy or child abuse? *Pediatrics, 71*(5), 715–720.

This article examines the case histories of two siblings, a 7-month-old girl and 4-year-old boy, both with histories of recurrent episodes of cardiorespiratory arrest, who were the victims of child abuse perpetrated by their mother. Polygraphic monitoring and a hidden camera were used to discover the cause of these recurring episodes. A psychological evaluation of the mother revealed that she had a narcissistic personality disorder.

1112. Rosen, D. A., Rosen, K. R., Elkins, T. E., Andersen, H. F., McNeeley, S. G., & Sorg, C. (1991). Outpatient sedation: An essential addition to gynecologic care of persons with mental retardation. *American Journal of Obstetrics and Gynecology, 164*(3), 825–828.

This article points out that it is difficult to provide outpatient gynecologic examinations to people with mental retardation because of a lack of cooperation. This article discusses a study that evaluated the safety and efficacy of oral ketamine and/or midazolam for sedating difficult-to-manage patients with mental retardation in an outpatient gynecologic setting. The participants in this study were people who needed general anesthesia to have a pelvic examination. In this study, ketamine alone (4-10mg/kg), midazolam alone (0.1 to 0.4 mg/kg), or both ketamine and midazolam were administered either orally or intranasally by an anesthesiologist, and vital parameters along with sedation level were measured every 15 minutes. This study was conducted over a period of 18 months. Out of 275 patients referred to the clinic, 61 (22%) were scheduled for examination with sedation protocol, and 81% of these women were successfully examined. No adverse effects caused by the medications were noted. The authors conclude that sedating difficult-to-examine women with mental disability can be safely performed in the outpatient setting, thus avoiding the need for general anesthesia and its inherent risks.

1113. Rosen, T. S., & Johnson, H. L. (1988). Drug-addicted mothers, their infants, and SIDS. *Annals of the New York Academy of Sciences, 533,* 89–95.

This article discusses a study that examined drug-addicted mothers, their infants, and sudden infant death syndrome (SIDS). This study screened 111 pregnant women for drug use during their pregnancy and categorized into them three groups: methadone (*n*=25), multidrug (*n*=42), and controls (*n*=44). After delivery, the researchers conducted physical and neurological examinations of the neonates. Also, it conducted follow-up assessments of the infants at age 2 months, 4 months, 6 months, and 12 months. The results of this study indicate the following: There was a greater frequency of premature labor and fetal heart rate abnormalities for the methadone and multidrug users; these two groups also contained more women smokers; and infants in the methadone group had lower birth weight, smaller head circumference, and more neurologic abnormalities than the other two groups. In total, four infants died of SIDS in this study: one from the methadone group and three from the multidrug group.

1114. Rosenbaum, J. D., Rosenberg, K. F., & McDonnell, C. (1990). Treatment staff as perpetrator: Sexual abuse within an agency. *Residential Treatment for Children & Youth, 7*(3), 87–94.

This article examines the clinical, systemic, and social issues concerning the sexual abuse of children by staff or caregivers working in residential treatment centers. It pays particular attention to clinical work, staff anxiety, litigation, community, and perpetrators. It also discusses the healing process for both agency and staff after an abuse incidence.

1115. Rosenberg, D. A. (1987). Web of deceit: A literature review of Munchausen syndrome by proxy. *Child Abuse & Neglect, 11,* 547–563.

This review of the literature features the compilation of 117 Munchausen syndrome by proxy (MSBP) cases. The analysis of these cases indicates the following: mothers were the only perpetrators in this form of child abuse; bleeding (44%) and seizures (41%) were found to be the most common symptoms and signs of this type of abuse; short-term morbidity, acute pain, and/or illness were present in 100% of the cases; approximately 70% of the symptoms in the children were produced in the hospital setting by the mothers; and loneliness and isolation were common problems for these mothers. This article offers medical and procedural recommendations to social services and the courts when dealing with suspected MSBP cases.

1116. Rosenberg, D. A. (1988). Recent issues in child maltreatment. In D. C. Bross, R. D. Krugman, M. R. Lenherr, D. A. Rosenberg, & B. D. Schmitt (Eds.), *The new child protection team handbook* **(pp. 113–125). New York: Garland.**

Munchausen syndrome by proxy (MSBP) and fetal abuse are discussed in this chapter. It features the distinguishing characteristics of each type of abuse and presents a case example of MSBP. This chapter includes some recommendations for medical professionals.

1117. Rosenberg, D. A. (1994). Munchausen syndrome by proxy. In R. M. Reece (Ed.), *Child abuse: Medical diagnosis and management* (pp. 266–278). Philadelphia: Lea & Febiger.

This chapter provides an extensive description of Munchausen syndrome by proxy based on research and clinical accounts. In Munchausen syndrome by proxy, a parent or other caregiver fakes, simulates, or causes an illness or injury to a child in order to meet the caregiver's social or psychological needs. While the condition is apparently rare and only about 250 cases have been well documented, it seems likely that the condition has been underdiagnosed, and many more cases go undetected. Mothers have most frequently been identified as offenders, but fathers, other relatives, babysitters, and nurses have also been identified. Victims are most frequently infants or toddlers because they have limited communication abilities (the condition is likely to exist at later ages in children and even adults who have impaired communication). Although data are too limited to generalize, one series of cases suggests that 75% of cases involve at least some production of real illness or injury, while the other 25% involve only falsified information. This chapter also includes 14 detailed suggestions for medical investigation and intervention.

1118. Rosenberg, M. S., & Giberson, R. S. (1991). The child witness of family violence. In R. T. Ammerman & M. Hersen (Eds.), *Case studies in family violence* (pp. 231–253). New York: Plenum.

This chapter discusses the psychological issues surrounding a case of a child witness to marital violence. A case report is presented describing the situation and resulting problems. It discusses issues relating to medical, legal, social, and family parameters; as well, it discusses an assessment of psychopathology and its findings. This article suggests treatment options.

1119. Rosenberg, S. A., & McTate, G. A. (1982). Intellectually handicapped mothers: Problems and prospects. *Children Today, 11*(1), 24–26.

The authors of this article feel that parents who have mental retardation and provide inadequate care for their children can become more effective caregivers. They suggest that improvements in parenting may depend, to a great extent, on the availability of services that are adapted to the needs of adults who learn slowly and on the desire of the parents to improve their caregiving skills. For parents in the borderline and mildly retarded range of intelligence, they stress that IQ scores are not particularly good predictors of ability to parent. The authors discuss several intervention strategies: home visits, group sessions, and individual counseling.

1120. Rosenhan, D. L. (1973, January). On being sane in insane places. *Science, 179*, 250–257.

This article discusses a study in which eight pseudopatients (a psychology graduate student, three psychologists, a psychiatrist, a pediatrician, a painter, and a housewife) were admitted to a psychiatric ward after complaining of hearing voices. On the ward, these pseudopatients displayed normal behavior. The results of this study indicate that the behavior of psychiatric patients is rarely viewed within the context of the environment; instead, the behavior of psychiatric patients is attributed to personal characteristics, a practice that results in the labeling and depersonalization of patients.

1121. Rosenthal, G., & Bar, O. D. (1992). A biographical case study of a victimizer's daughter's strategy: Pseudoidentification with the victims of the Holocaust. *Journal of Narrative and Life History, 2*(2), 105–127.

This article provides a case study of a 59-year-old woman who was the daughter of a Nazi euthanasia physician. She suffered from intense fears of extermination, which were interpreted as a pseudo-identification with the victims of her father. This pseudo-identification was seen as a defense that she used to avoid feelings of identification with her father and the euthanasia program.

1122. Rosenthal, J. A., Motz, J. K., Edmonson, D. A., & Groze, V. (1991). A descriptive study of abuse and neglect in out-of-home placement. *Child Abuse & Neglect, 15*, 249–260.

This article describes a study that gathered information on 290 incidents of maltreatment from foster homes, group homes, residential treatment centers, and institutions and categorized them as physical abuse, sexual abuse, and neglect. The results of this study indicate that the most prevalent form of maltreatment is physical abuse (55%), followed by sexual abuse (24%) and neglect (21%). It discovered that foster homes and residential treatment centers report the most number of abuse cases (38% each), and 92% of the incidents occurred on the property. In two thirds of reported incidents, perpetrators denied responsibility for the charges. Both perpetrators and victims were predominantly male. Twenty-seven percent of the perpetrators had been involved in prior incidences of abuse.

1123. Ross, A. L., & Grenier, G. L. (1990). Moving beyond the evil empire of institutional abuse—May the organizational force be with you. *Journal of Child and Youth Care, 4*(6), 23–33.

This article focuses on the theory of acculturation and the need for institutions to move from child protection and control toward the facilitation of child growth and development. The philosophical basis for this shift in focus is outlined, with an emphasis on growth and wisdom principles and a conception of the organization as a cultural unit. The authors note that the chief executive officer's role in the new organization is one of servant leader, visionary, and integrator.

1124. Ross, A. L., & Hoeltke, G. (1987). An interviewing tool for selection of residential child care workers: A follow-up report. *Child Welfare, 66*(2), 175–183.
This article discusses the statistical validation of the Child Care Perceiver Interview (CCPI), a screening device for residential child-care workers. This article claims that the CCPI can be used to predict a worker's performance using open-ended questions. In order to back up this claim, several validation studies were conducted to examine the following areas: content, construct, and predictive and concurrent validity. These studies found that the CCPI is a predictively valid assessment tool and performs independently with regard to race, age, or gender. (Editors' note: See the following reference for a more detailed description of the Child Care Perceiver Interview: Ross, A. L., & Hoeltke, G. [1985]. A tool for selecting residential child-care workers: An initial report. *Child Welfare, 64*[1], 46–54.)

1125. Rosser, K. (1990). A particular vulnerability. *Legal Service Bulletin, 15*(1), 32–34.
This Australian article examines the sexual assault of women with developmental disabilities and the problems associated with these victims giving evidence in court. It addresses some of the reasons why this crime goes unreported and explores other disability-related sexual offences found in the Crimes Act of New South Wales, Australia. The author describes the pros and cons of special legislation versus prosecuting these offences under general sexual assault statutes and concludes that there is a need for more study.

1126. Roth, S. (1991). Silent pain. *Nursing Times, 87*(6), 62–65.
This article discusses the story of a young woman with Down syndrome and a mild developmental disability who was sexually assaulted. It examines the effects of this assault on the woman's behavior and on her family and explores how nurses might assist a victim of sexual assault and his or her family through this type of experience. Also, this article discusses proactive sex education and the victim's and family's possible emotional reactions to sexual assault.

1127. Roumasset, E. G. (1991). Early experiences, affect organization, and separation anxiety in adolescent females with the self-mutilation syndrome. *Dissertation Abstracts International, 51*(10), 5039B–5040B.
This abstract describes a study that attempted to define the self-mutilation syndrome and distinguish it from suicidal behavior. This study compared 15 female self-mutilators with 15 female suicide attempters. All of these subjects were psychiatric inpatients between the ages of 12 and 25. This study excluded those individuals who were psychotic or had mental retardation. For the purposes of this study, self-mutilation was defined as any self-destructive act that was performed without expressing the intention to commit suicide and was limited to breaking or bruising the skin, and a suicide attempt was defined as any self-destructive act performed after expressing the intention to commit suicide. The girls and women in this study were assessed using three sets of variables: histories of sexual and physical abuse, early childhood medical trauma, sado-masochistic thoughts, and current violence; control of depression, hostility, and anxiety; and patterns of attachment and separation anxiety. The results of this study indicate the following: 1) self-mutilators had more negative life experiences and more severe pathological symptoms than those who attempt suicide; 2) on a self-report questionnaire, self-mutilators had more incidents of physical abuse, incest, sexual assault, and sado-masochistic thoughts than those who attempt suicide; 3) on the Beck Depression Inventory (BDI), self-mutilators were more depressed than those who attempt suicide; 4) on the Depressive Experiences Questionnaire (DEQ), self-mutilators had more periods of depression than those who attempt suicide; 5) on the Beck Anxiety Inventory (BAI), self-mutilators were more anxious than those who attempt suicide; 6) on the Hostility and Direction of Hostility Questionnaire, self-mutilators were more hostile than those who attempt suicide; and 7) on the Adolescent Separation Anxiety Test, self-mutilators showed significantly more evidence of anxious attachment than those who attempt suicide. The author suggests that self-mutilating behavior has its roots in pathological interactions between the child and primary caregivers during the pre-verbal and early childhood periods of development, which results in the inadequate development of integrated, internalized, object relations. The author contends that self-mutilation is best viewed as a symptom of attachment disorder and as an attempt to gain control over past abuse. The author suggests that future research should investigate the link between self-mutilation and incest as well as other forms of physical and sexual abuse, borderline personality disorder, and unconscious mental functioning and that epidemiological factors related to self-mutilation could be studied using a large, multisite, collaborative study.

1128. Rowe, W. S., Savage, S., Ragg, M., & Wigle, K. (1987). *Sexuality and the developmentally handicapped: A guidebook for health care professionals.* Queenston, ON: Edwin Mellen Press.
This book, written in two parts, is designed for health care professionals and deals with sexuality and people with intellectual disabilities. The first part of the book addresses issues of knowledge, attitudes, and skills regarding human sexuality. The second part of the book applies this information to the four main concerns of sexuality and people with intellectual disabilities: masturbation, homosexuality, aversive sexual behavior, and sexual variations. Also, this book provides case examples and suggestions for counseling.

1129. Rozovsky, L. E., & Rozovsky, F. A. (1990). Mental health: Rights of property and person. In CCH Canadian Limited (Ed.), *Canadian health facilities law guide* (pp. 6071–6074). Don Mills, ON: CCH Canadian Limited.

This chapter discusses codified rights of patients in mental health facilities: for example, the right not to be detained without consent or cause, the right to be informed of one's rights, and the right to communicate with others.

1130. Rue, V. M. (1985). Death by design of handicapped newborns: The family's role & response. *Issues in Law & Medicine, 1*(3), 201–225.

The psychological and emotional variables involved in refusing treatment for newborns with disabilities or the abortion of fetuses with disabilities are discussed in this article. The author concludes that infanticide, whether it takes the form of refusing treatment or abortion, reveals the following: national antichild prejudice; hatred of suffering, dependency, ugliness, and imperfection; and attitudes of prejudice toward and discrimination of those who are different or have disabilities.

1131. Ruff, K. (1986). Hospital Riviere-des-Prairies—Not a place to call home. *Entourage, 1*(1), 6–13.

This article discusses the efforts of the parents of children with disabilities living in Hospital Riviere-des-Prairies, in Montreal, Quebec, to stop the maltreatment and abuse occurring at the hospital. It describes their fight to acquire community services that would allow their children to live in the community. This article examines these parents' fight for the rights of their children and the responses to this fight for rights.

1132. Ruff, K. (1986). Sterilization without consent. *Just Cause, 3*(4), 22–25.

This article uses case examples to examine the sterilization without consent of three females with developmental disabilities who were 10, 12, and 24 years of age. In all three cases, the court authorized non-therapeutic hysterectomies. This article discusses the legal rights of these females.

1133. Ruffner, R. H. (1990). The invisible issue: Disability in the media. In M. Nagler (Ed.), *Perspectives on disability* (pp. 143–146). Palo Alto, CA: Health Markets Research.

This chapter discusses the portrayal of people with disabilities in the media. It examines the lack of recognition people with disabilities receive from the media, apart from medical issues and human interest stories. It states that people with disabilities want to be recognized by the media and the public as an issue, and they not want to be ignored or shielded from mainstream society. The author suggests that using the power of the media to change public opinion about people with disabilities will foster greater acceptance.

1134. Rusch, R. G., Hall, J. C., & Griffin, H. C. (1986). Abuse-provoking characteristics of institutionalized mentally retarded individuals. *American Journal of Mental Deficiency, 90*(6), 618–624.

This article examines the abuse-provoking characteristics of institutionalized individuals with mental retardation. It discusses possible explanations for higher rates of abuse directed against certain types of patients and suggests recommendations for reducing abuse of patients with mental retardation through improved staff training, reconsideration of the practice of grouping aggressive residents together, and the provision of incentives to staff members working with aggressive clients.

1135. Russell, D. E. H. (1984). The prevalence and seriousness of incestuous abuse: Stepfathers vs. biological fathers. *Child Abuse & Neglect, 8*, 15–22.

This article describes a study that attempted to determine the incidence and seriousness of sexual abuse perpetrated by biological fathers as opposed to stepfathers. The study conducted interviews with 930 adult women in order to determine whether or not they had been sexually abused. Although the combined noncompliance and non-respondent rate totalled 50%, 42 women reported a history of sexual abuse. The results of this study indicate that biological fathers were the abusers in 60% of cases, while stepfathers were the abusers in 33% of cases. When the study examined the total number of respondents who lived with their stepfathers, 17% of these women had been abused as opposed to 2.3% of women who lived with their biological fathers. The author points out that stepfathers were most often implicated in the most severe forms of abuse when compared to biological fathers.

1136. Russell, M., Czarnecki, D. M., Cowan, R., McPherson, E., & Mudar, P. J. (1991). Measures of maternal alcohol use as predictors of development in early childhood. *Alcoholism: Clinical and Experimental Research, 15*(6), 991–1000.

This article discusses a study that assessed alcohol intake prior to pregnancy and indications of problem drinking in 547 women during prenatal visits. A 6-year follow-up of 152 children of those women who were initially assessed was conducted to measure the children's development, in particular growth and cognition. The alcohol intake group was categorized by abstainers ($n=39$), light/moderate drinkers ($n=97$), heavy drinkers ($n=11$), and very heavy drinkers ($n=5$). The results of this follow-up found that greater consumption of alcohol was related to shorter height, smaller head circumference, and increased dysmorphology. It also noted that problem drinking was related to increased fetal alcohol syndrome facial features and decreased verbal IQ and Token Test scores.

1137. Russell, T., & Boswell, C. F. (1986). A comparison of selected demographic, educational, and behavioral factors among adolescent mentally retarded offenders and adolescent mentally retarded nonoffenders. *Journal of Offender Counseling, Services & Rehabilitation, 10*(3), 5–24.

This article discusses a study that examined the predictive significance of selected demographic, educational, and behavioral variables in identifying potential offenders among juveniles with mental retardation. The authors suggest that identifying juveniles with mental retardation who are likely to become offenders before they get into trouble and come into contact with the criminal justice system would simplify delinquency prevention programs. This study included 40 identified offenders with mental retardation and 40 identified nonoffenders with mental retardation from the Tuscaloosa, Alabama, school system. This study used multiple regression analysis to analyze the relationship between the dependent variable (offender/nonoffender) and 21 independent variables. The results of this study indicate the following: only 3 of the 21 independent variables assessed (number of siblings with court referral, number of days in school, and standard score spelling) could significantly discriminate between offenders and nonoffenders: That is, offenders tended to have at least one sibling with court referral, to have a fewer number of days in school, and to have poorer spelling skills than nonoffenders.

1138. Russo, H. (1988). Daughters with disabilities: Defective women or minority women. In M. Fine & A. Asch (Eds.), *Women with disabilities: Essays in psychology, culture, and politics* (pp. 139–171). **Philadelphia: Temple University Press.**

This chapter addresses the relationship between women with disabilities and their parents. It focuses particularly on the role of parents' attitudes and expectations and their daughters' sexual behavior and adjustment. The author suggests that the family may try to keep the daughter with a disability in the role of a child and therefore view her as asexual. Families may also fear that fostering sexuality in their daughter with a disability will lead to rejection, exploitation, or abuse. They may also believe the stereotypes that suggest women with disabilities will bear children with disabilities or be unable to rear them. The author points out that parents also have difficulties when they try to determine prospective spouses for their daughters: They seemed unable to imagine anyone desirable (as a spouse or son-in-law) being attracted to their child.

1139. Rutter, M. (1989). Intergenerational continuities and discontinuities in serious parenting difficulties. In D. Cicchetti & V. Carlson (Eds.), *Child maltreatment: Theory and research on the causes and consequences of child abuse and neglect* (pp. 317–348). **Cambridge: Cambridge University Press.**

In this chapter, parenting is viewed multidimensionally, incorporating a variety of variables that interact in the dyadic relationship between parent and child. This chapter examines the effects of institutionalization on parental bonding. The results of this examination indicate that women who were reared in institutions had difficulty dealing with severe social stresses due to their limited repertoire; consequently, they exhibited greater parental breakdowns during times of severe stress. It found that these women's attempts to parent well met with limited success due to their limited ability to see their child's wants and needs. This chapter also discusses marriage, and it suggests that successful marriages occur after careful planning. This planning is defined as positive reasons for living together and familiarity with each other for at least 6 months prior to cohabitation. It claims that dysfunctional relationships result when the cohabitation of the institutionalized woman and her mate occurs because of pregnancy or the female's desire to leave an unhappy home (institution). It also found the following: Planners were more likely to choose functional spouses than nonplanners, and marital support was a key variable in successful parenting, with those women who were planners receiving more support. This chapter concludes that planning is the result, in part, of positive school experiences.

1140. Ryan, J., & Thomas, F. (1987). *The politics of mental handicap.* **London: Free Association Books.**

This book provides an ethnographic, social, political, and historical perspective on the treatment of people with intellectual disabilities. It analyzes institutional care as a method of social control that is rationalized as care and protection but in reality leads to depersonalization and inevitable abuse. In this chapter, the historical background provides an excellent discussion about some of the stigmatizing myths about disability, tracing their origins back through the centuries to their likely sources in the distant past.

1141. Ryerson, E. (1984). Sexual abuse and self-protection education for developmentally disabled youth: A priority need. *SIECUS (Sex Information & Education Council of the United States) Report, 13*(1), 1–3.

The author of this article states that the reporting rate of sexual abuse among people with developmental disabilities is lower than that of the general population. The explanation given is that 99% of the abusers are relatives or care providers, and therefore, the victim is either unaware that he or she is being exploited or is very confused about the sexual activity and the intent of the offender. The offender often leads the victim to believe that theirs is a "special" relationship or convinces the victim to keep the activity a secret. The Developmental Disabilities Project's curriculum for preventing sexual exploitation is available to schools, but due to economic issues and the sensitivity of the subject matter, it is not being used by many schools. The author stresses that self-protection education is of critical importance and should be a priority, overriding economic concerns and embarrassment.

•S•

1142. Sabotta, E. E., & Davis, R. L. (1992). Fatality after report to a child abuse registry in Washington State, 1973–1986. *Child Abuse & Neglect, 16,* 627–635.

This article assesses the incidence of fatality for 11,085 children registered over a 13-year period with the Washington State child abuse registry. When compared to the general population, this assessment found that registered children were almost 3 times as likely to die and 20 times as likely to die from homicide. When compared to the general population, this assessment found that infants 12 months old or younger had the highest fatality rate, while adolescents were most at risk for fatality resulting from abuse.

1143. Salyer, K. M., Holmstrom, R. W., & Noshpitz, J. D. (1991). Learning disabilities as a childhood manifestation of severe psychopathology. *American Journal of Orthopsychiatry, 61*(2), 230–240.

This article discusses a study that examined the severity and nature of psychopathology in children with learning disabilities. Twenty-four boys with learning disabilities, ranging in age from 7 to 10.11 years, were compared to a control group of children matched for age, gender, race, and IQ. All of these children were assessed using the Child Behavior Checklist, the Rorschach, the Roberts Apperception Test for Children, and the Wide Range Achievement Test-Revised. In addition, controls received the Slosson Intelligence Test, while the indexed group received the Wechsler Intelligence Scale for Children-Revised (WISC-R) verbal scale and the Stanford Binet. The indexed children were all receiving special education in school, and nine children were diagnosed with attention-deficit/hyperactivity disorder. The results of this study indicate the following: children with learning disabilities exhibit a greater degree of psychopathology than controls, emotional and ego functioning were specifically identified, and the degree of psychopathology was not related to the degree of underachievement.

1144. Salzinger, S., Feldman, R. S., Hammer, M., & Rosario, M. (1991). Risk for physical child abuse and the personal

consequences for its victims. *Criminal Justice and Behavior, 18*(1), 64–81.

This review of the literature focuses on the risk and resulting developmental effects of physical child abuse. A path analysis model is used to describe the association between family violence and physical child abuse. This article examines behavioral dysfunction resulting from the abuse in the following domains: neurologic functioning, intellectual impairment, affective and social behavior, and social cognition.

1145. Salzinger, S., Feldman, R. S., Hammer, M., & Rosario, M. (1993). The effects of physical abuse on children's social relationships. *Child Development, 64,* 169–187.

This article describes a study that compared 87 physically abused children with a matched control group of 87 non-abused children on variables of social behavior and peer status. All of the children in this study were between the ages of 8 and 12. This study gathered information in classrooms, through interviews with the children and their mothers, and by ratings from parents and teachers. It assessed peer ratings, social networks, family variables, and behavior problems, and the results of this study indicate that the abused children had lower peer status and had more socially inappropriate behavior than controls.

1146. Samuels, M. P., McClaughlin, W., Jacobson, R. R., Poets, C. F., & Southall, D. P. (1992). Fourteen cases of imposed upper airway obstruction. *Archives of Disease in Childhood, 67,* 162–170.

This article discusses the covert video surveillance used to determine the cause of recurrent cyanotic episodes in 14 infants. This surveillance found that intentional smothering was responsible for the upper airway obstructions in these infants. Twelve mothers, one father, and one grandmother were implicated in the abuse.

1147. Sandgrund, A., Gaines, R. W., & Green, A. H. (1974). Child abuse and mental retardation: A problem of cause and effect. *American Journal of Mental Deficiency, 79*(3), 327–330.

This article discusses a study that compared the cognitive development of 60 physically abused, 30 neglected, and 30 nonabused children in order to determine the effects of child abuse. All of the children were matched according to gender, age, and socioeconomic status and were between 5 and 12.9 years of age. The children were assessed and interviewed by a psychiatrist and psychologist. The assessment employed the Wechsler Preschool and Primary Scale of Intelligence (for ages 5 to 6.6 years), the Wechsler Intelligence Scale for Children, the Rorschach, the Bender Gestalt, the Human Figure Drawings, the Children's Apperception Test (Card #1, 4, 7, 10, 5-s), and the Rosenzweig Picture Frustration Test. Although the authors point out that it is difficult to determine an exact cause-effect relationship between retardation and abuse and neglect using the results of this study, the results indicate that both the abused and the neglected children had significantly lower IQ scores than nonabused children and that both the abuse and neglect of children seems to be related to cognitive impairment.

1148. Sapon-Shevin, M. (1983, January). Teaching children about differences: Resources for teaching. *Young Children, 38,* **24–32.**
Educating children about the differences between people, especially with regard to disabilities, is examined in this article. It addresses the different media of communication available, such as curriculum materials, books, and television.

1149. Sardella, S. (1994, April). Disabled children vulnerable to abuse. *A P A (American Psychological Association) Monitor,* **p. 37.**
This article reviews a number of issues related to the abuse of children with disabilities. The author cites studies that indicate children with disabilities are at increased risk but suggests that the reasons for increased risk remain unknown. She also quotes several psychologists who work with children with disabilities, including Judith Levey and Vasilios Legos, whose chapter on "Vulnerable populations: Children with disabilities" is included in Volume II of the American Psychological Association's Violence and Youth report (to be published in the last half of 1994). This article also lists potential prevention and treatment strategies.

1150. Satcher, J., & Dooley Dickey, K. (1992). Attitudes of human-resource management students toward persons with disabilities. *Rehabilitation Counseling Bulletin, 35*(4), **248–252.**
This article discusses a study that was conducted with 143 human resource management students (53% women) from three Mississippi universities to determine their attitudes toward people with disabilities. The premise of this study states that human resource management professionals would be less inclined to support people with disabilities in employment positions or to help them maintain employment if they held negative attitudes about people with disabilities. This study assessed variables regarding gender, race, prior contact, anticipated type of business occupation, and anticipated size of occupational setting and administered the Attitudes Toward Disabled Persons Scale, Form O, to 75 White, 62 African-American, and 6 Latino, Native American, and international students. The results of this study indicate that gender and race were significant variables in determining attitudes toward people with disabilities. It found the following: White women had the most positive attitude, Whites were more positive than African Americans, White men were more accepting than African-American men or African-American women, and African-American women were the least accepting of people with disabilities. Also, this study found that prior contact did

not significantly influence attitudes toward people with disabilities.

1151. Saunders, E. J. (1988). A comparative study of attitudes toward child sexual abuse among social work and judicial system professionals. *Child Abuse & Neglect, 12,* **83–90.**
This article examines the attitudes of five groups of social workers and judicial professionals toward child sexual abuse. The attitudes examined include the following: victim culpability, victim credibility, offender culpability, and the crime and punishment of child sexual abuse. While there were statistically significant differences between the survey results of these groups, this examination found no statistically significant differences among the five groups on the issues of victim culpability, offender culpability, and crime seriousness. This article concludes that the attitudes of professionals in this study were consistent with their perceived roles: for example, police and social workers were strong advocates for victims, public defenders were strong advocates for alleged offenders, and judges held more neutral attitudes toward victims and offenders.

1152. Savage, D. G. (1989, June 27). Executing young killers is upheld: High court OK's death penalty for 16-year-olds, the mildly retarded. *The Los Angeles Times,* **p. 1.**
This newspaper article reports a United States Supreme Court ruling that decided being 16 years old or having mild mental retardation does not protect you from the death penalty under the Eighth Amendment, which disallows "cruel and unusual punishment." The Supreme Court voted 5–4 in favor of this ruling that will affect approximately 24 of the 2,200 inmates currently on death row. While the public generally supports capital punishment, they are opposed to the current ruling, as measured by public opinion polls. This newspaper article discusses case examples of young offenders and offenders with mental retardation given the death sentence.

1153. Savage, H. S. (1980). The relevance of the fitness to stand trial provisions to persons with mental handicap. *Autonomy, 1*(2), **3–9.**
This article discusses the relevance of the Fitness to Stand Trial provisions under Canada's Criminal Code for people with developmental disabilities. The process for determining Fitness to Stand Trial under the Criminal Code is examined, as are other issues: for example, options for the trial judge on remand and on unfitness to stand trial, the insanity clause, the role of the Board of Review and the Lieutenant Governor, the review process, the issue of due process and of treatment under the Lieutenant Governor's Warrant, the applicability of the Canadian Bill of Rights, due process of law, equality before the law, arbitrary detention, and cruel and unusual treatment or punishment.

1154. Savells, J. (1983). **Child abuse in residential institutions and community programs for intervention and prevention.** *Child Abuse and Neglect, 7*(4), 473–475.

This article examines specific problems areas in the approach taken by residential care facilities toward child care: for example, the alienation of community officials, staff shortages, overcrowding leading to abuse or objectionable means of control, the repression of spontaneity, and few alternatives to institutionalization. This article discusses possible solutions (e.g., change in priorities, community involvement).

1155. Saxton, M., & Howe, F. (Eds.). (1987). *With wings: An anthology of literature by and about women with disabilities.* **New York: Feminist Press.**

Thirty women writers contributed to this anthology of stories, poems, and essays in an attempt to overcome invisibility and to challenge traditional stereotypes and discrimination of women with disabilities. In recognizing that their lives are doubly constrained and subject to oppression because of their gender and disability, the writers address the "historical silencing" of their experience. The material is presented in three thematic parts: The physical and emotional experience of disability is addressed in Part 1; Part 2 discusses interpersonal relationships, especially the myths, stereotypes, and discrimination faced by women with disabilities with regard to sexuality and the right and ability to have and take care of children; and Part 3 focuses on overcoming internal barriers and reevaluating traditional attitudes regarding disability as experienced by women. The editors note their initial hope for the broadest representation of the many types of experiences faced by women with different disabilities and acknowledge the difficulty in achieving this representation; nevertheless, the material presented in the anthology has broad application for all readers.

1156. Schaeffer, R. (1989). **Grausamkeit in christlicher tradition [Cruelty in the Christian tradition].** *Analytische Psychologie, 20*(4), 257–281.

This article explores the psychological implications of the Christian images displayed at a monument at a mass grave in Irsee, Bavaria, of mental patients exterminated during the Third Reich. The author interprets the images to illustrate a subconscious cultural fascination with suffering and death. The murder of people with disabilities is seen as a consistent part of such a world view.

1157. Schaffer, J., & Sobsey, D. (1991). **A dialogue on medical responsibility.** In L. H. Meyer, C. A. Peck, & L. Brown (Eds.), *Critical issues in the lives of people with severe disabilities* (pp. 601–606). **Baltimore: Paul H. Brookes Publishing Co.**

This dialogue on medical responsibility between Dick Sobsey and Jim Schaffer focuses on the specific case of Indiana Baby Doe, an infant chosen for selective nontreatment because of the infant's surgically correctable defect and diagnosed Down syndrome. This dialogue examines the rights of parents regarding medical treatment for their children and the rights of children to medical treatment. As well, it describes a case history of Indiana Baby Doe and Dr. Schaffer's involvement in trying to obtain medical services for this infant.

1158. Schaffner, P. E. (1985). **Specious learning about reward and punishment.** *Journal of Personality and Social Psychology, 48*(6), 1377–1386.

This article presents the result of a study in which subjects were asked to rate the value of punishment and reinforcement strategies that they applied during a computer simulation. In fact, neither punishment nor reinforcement had any effect on the randomly distributed data that they received; however, subjects consistently considered punishment to be more effective. The reason for their unfounded confidence in using punishment appeared to be a regression phenomenon. Since punishment was applied after "bad" behavior, behavior was more likely to improve immediately after punishment was applied. Since reward was applied after "good" behavior, behavior was more likely to get worse, immediately after reward was applied. The author discusses how the same type of regression influences our perception of punishment and reward in actual clinical practice and empirical research.

1159. Scheer, J., & Groce, N. (1988). **Impairment as a human constant: Cross-cultural and historical perspectives on variation.** *Journal of Social Issues, 44*(1), 23–37.

This article examines the variation in the attention given to people with physical disabilities using cross-cultural and historical perspectives. The author concludes that the presence of people with disabilities has remained constant in society, yet the attention given to them has been variable and has depended on the times and social context.

1160. Schei, B., Sameuelsen, S. O., & Bakketeig, L. S. (1991). **Does spousal physical abuse affect the outcome of pregnancy?** *Scandinavian Journal of Social Medicine, 19*(1), 26–31.

This article examines spousal abuse during pregnancy and the adversive outcome for the neonate. It discusses a study that assessed 66 battered women and 114 controls. This study found that spousal violence occurred in 40 of the 306 pregnancies, and a significant number of spontaneous abortions occurred in the abused group. The mean birth weight of neonates born to the abused group was also found to be lower than that of the control group, although smoking during pregnancy was not used as a variable.

1161. Schild, S. (1982). Beyond diagnosis: Issues in recurrent counseling of parents of the mentally retarded. *Social Work in Health Care, 8*(1), 81–93.

This article points out that most of the social work literature that discusses counseling parents of children with mental retardation deals with the initial period around the time of diagnosis. This article suggests that parent counseling may be necessary following the period of initial diagnosis because parents may experience problems of a different nature: for example, parent expectations, value dilemmas, life transitions, and environmental transactions. This article defines practice issues and discusses these issues in relation to the dual-world realities faced by these parents: that is, their children's delayed learning and developmental progress, the inherent uncertainties in the situation, and the problems encountered when helping parents with the inevitable crises that occur during their lifetime.

1162. Schilling, R. F., Kirkham, M. A., & Schinke, S. P. (1985). *Coping, social support, and the prevention of maltreatment of handicapped children: Final report.* Seattle: Washington University, Child Development and Mental Retardation Center.

This report discusses a study that compared nonabusing families with low-income and single-parent families. All families in the study had a child with a disability. This study gathered data using questionnaires and interviews. The results of this study indicate the following: socioeconomic status differentiated families on measures of stress; the child's specific disability and level of functioning were not predictive of the parent's coping style or appraisal of stress; in general, no relationship existed between marital status, age of the parent or the child, and stress, coping, or social support; for both groups, economic worries were general in nature and did not revolve around the child with a disability (however, parents with more effective personal coping responses reported greater use of social supports); and compared to mothers, fathers showed less optimism about the future, used a narrower range of coping devices, and had fewer social supports.

1163. Schilling, R. F., Kirkham, M. A., & Schinke, S. P. (1986). Do child protection services neglect developmentally disabled children? *Education and Training of the Mentally Retarded, 21,* 21–26.

This article examines the relationship between child protection services and children with developmental disabilities. In spite of data suggesting that children with developmental disabilities are more likely to be abused, this article points out that they are underrepresented in the caseloads of child protection workers. The authors feel that child protection agencies may consider children with disabilities to be outside their mandate and assume they are served by other agencies. In their survey of child protection service workers, the authors found that 82% believed that developmental disability increased risk of abuse, but 84% had never served a client with a developmental disability (12% had only served one, and 4% had only served two).

1164. Schilling, R. F., & Schinke, S. P. (1984). Maltreatment and mental retardation. In J. M. Berg & J. M. de Jong (Eds.), *Perspectives and progress in mental retardation: Social, psychological, and educational aspects* (Vol. 1, pp. 11–22). Baltimore: University Park Press.

The authors of this chapter state that children with mental retardation are at greater risk for abuse and neglect since ordinary care standards are inadequate for this group. Children with mental retardation may have unique requirements for feeding, clothing, prosthetics, and attention to safety. There is also a higher risk of emotional neglect by parents who are unable to accept their child's limitations. Some children with mental retardation have behavioral characteristics, such as tantrums, aggressiveness, and noncompliance, that negatively affect the parents. In general, the physical, emotional, and financial burden of raising a child with a disability causes family stress and increases the risk of abuse. In regard to intervention, parents can be taught coping skills and how to enhance their social supports. The authors conducted pilot studies of group training for families. The results show more self-control, calmness, positive self-talk, and self-praise among the participants. In their discussion of people with mental retardation in the community, the authors state that as people with mental retardation gain greater freedom they will be at greater risk for exploitation since their relative dependency puts them in a vulnerable position. People with mental disabilities may have difficulty grasping community standards of sexuality (e.g., conversation, touching, and public masturbation) and therefore may find themselves in exploitive situations. The authors feel that prevention of sexual abuse includes training in appropriate sexual behavior, meaning both rights and responsibilities.

1165. Schilling, R. F., & Schinke, S. P. (1989). Mentally retarded sex offenders: Fact, fiction, and treatment. *Journal of Social Work and Human Sexuality, 7*(2), 33–49.

This article discusses the right of persons with intellectual disabilities to normal sexual functioning and the tendency to view the sexuality of people with intellectual disabilities as deviant. Also, this article examines the research that suggests people with intellectual disabilities are at higher risk for committing sexual offenses. This article includes treatment strategies for offenders with intellectual disabilities and provides recommendations for future research.

1166. Schilling, R. F., Schinke, S. P., & Kirkham, M. A. (1985). Coping with a

handicapped child: Differences between mothers and fathers. *Social Science and Medicine, 21*(8), 857–863.

In this article, research on the differences in coping styles between mothers and fathers of children with developmental disabilities is reviewed. This research review found the following: mothers turn to both internal and external coping sources, fathers rely primarily on internal means of coping, and gender-related coping differences may function in a complementary or a conflicting manner in the family where there is a child with a disability.

1167. Schinke, S. P., Blythe, B. B., Schilling, R. F., & Barth, R. (1981). Neglect of mentally retarded persons. *Education and Training of the Mentally Retarded, 16*(4), 299–303.

The authors of this article feel that it is necessary for professionals to be aware of and address the psychological needs of people with mental retardation. In an effort to facilitate data collection in treatment environments, the authors present a framework for defining the physical and emotional neglect of people with disabilities, and they discuss the following ideas: primary caregivers should have social, educational, and health services made available to them in order to remediate and prevent neglect; early assessment and intervention are critical in upgrading the skills of parents, siblings, group home staff, and institutional attendants; the natural environment is the preferred teaching environment for instructing caregivers; human services workers must redefine neglect as it relates to their target population; and in the case of mental retardation, workers must regularly reevaluate rehabilitation programs.

1168. Schirmer, B. R. (1986, April). *Child abuse and neglect: Prevalence, programs and prevention with the hearing impaired*. Paper presented at the 70th Annual Meeting of the American Educational Research Association, San Francisco. (ERIC Document Reproduction Service No. ED 270 954)

This paper reviews literature related to abuse and neglect of children who are hearing impaired and the services available to them. The findings of this literature review indicate that children with preexisting disabling conditions seem to be at higher risk for child abuse and neglect, but no particular groups of children with disabilities were found to be more at risk than others. The author suggests, however, that the communication deficits of children with hearing impairments may increase the child's vulnerability to be abused and neglected. Although a nationwide survey of the United States did not uncover any existing prevention programs for children with hearing impairments, this paper identifies the components of an effective prevention program: parent education, parent support groups, and periodic respite care.

1169. Schloesser, P., Pierpont, J., & Poertner, J. (1992). Active surveillance of child abuse fatalities. *Child Abuse & Neglect, 16*, 3–10.

This article discusses a review of 104 cases of infant or early childhood (ages birth to 4) deaths in order to determine the underlying causes of these deaths and to propose prevention strategies for reducing these types of deaths. This review correlated information on birth and death certificates with information received from the child abuse registry of the Kansas Department of Social and Rehabilitation Services by means of Limited or Partial Active Surveillance. This review found that: 85% of fatalities occurred with children who were less than 2 years of age, 65% of these children were age 12 months or less, and 60% of those who died were girls. It was noted that low birth weight was common among the victims. This review also suggests that: prenatal care for the mothers was inadequate; complications during pregnancy were more prevalent; and mothers were most often young at the onset of childbearing, were single, and had a limited amount of education. The authors propose active surveillance as an intervention strategy in preventing child abuse fatalities.

1170. Schmidt, G. (1985). *Vom Rassenmythos zu Rassenwahn und Selektion* [From racial myth to racial psychosis and persecution]. *Nervenarzt, 56*(7), 337–347.

This article is written by a physician who lived through the euthanasia and genocide of the Nazi era. The author finds troubling parallels with contemporary attempts to legitimatize assisted suicide. The author argues that making death easier for people with terminal illness does not require extraordinary death-making procedures, and such procedures are an essential step toward involuntary extermination of people with disabilities.

1171. Schneider, C. J. (1982). The Michigan Screening Profile of Parenting. In R. H. Starr (Ed.), *Child abuse prediction: Policy implications* (pp. 157–174). Cambridge, MA: Ballinger.

This chapter discusses the Michigan Screening Profile of Parenting (MSPP), a self-report inventory designed to identify attitudes about the following: childrearing, parental self-awareness, and parental self-control. The author suggests that this inventory can be used to screen new adoptive or foster parents for potential child abuse or child neglect.

1172. Schneider, J. W., & Chasnoff, I. J. (1992). Motor assessment of cocaine/ polydrug exposed infants at age 4 months. *Neurotoxicology and Teratology, 14*, 97–101.

This article discusses a study that compared 74 cocaine/ polydrug-exposed infants with 50 nondrug-exposed infants on their performance on the Movement Assessment of Infants test at age 4 months. The test assessed the infant's risk for motor dysfunction. The results of this study found that drug-exposed infants were at greater risk for motor dysfunction than nondrug-exposed infants. It also found that exposed infants were more developmentally impaired in areas of muscle tone, primitive reflexes, and volitional movement.

1173. Scholz, J. P., & Meier, J. H. (1983). Competency of abused children in a residential treatment program. In J. E. Leavitt (Ed.), *Child abuse and neglect: Research and innovation* (NATO Advanced Sciences Series, pp. 211–234). The Hague, the Netherlands: Nijhoff.
This chapter discusses the results of a study that found that more than half of the child abuse victims tested suffered significant developmental delays.

1174. Schopler, E. (1986). Treatment abuse and its reduction. *Journal of Autism and Developmental Disorders, 16(2)*, 99–104.
This article discusses ways in which oversimplification leads to confusion between the merit of a therapeutic technique for the treatment of children with disabilities and factors affecting the vulnerability of parents to unsubstantiated claims for cure or relief. It notes the following: For cases of crisis with incompletely understood illness or behavior, certain experimental therapy techniques that are easily abused may offer the best intervention; and the risks of abuse can be significantly reduced by early intervention and family support, examining other treatment options, and improving legislative protection against abuse and malpractice.

1175. Schor, D. P. (1987). Sex and sexual abuse of developmentally disabled adolescents. *Seminars in Adolescent Medicine, 3(1)*, 1–7.
This article discusses aspects of sexuality and sexual abuse of adolescents who are developmentally disabled. These adolescents have difficulty achieving maturation and independence, partly due to being dependent on others for physical care. As well, caregivers and school personnel may be overprotective and inhibit these children's acquisition of self-care and social skills. This article uses Finkelhor's ([1984]. *Child sexual abuse.* New York: Free Press) Four Preconditions of Sexual Abuse model to explain the victimization of adolescents with disabilities. This model suggests the presence within the potential offender of a motivation to sexually abuse a child that acts to overcome internal and external inhibitions against acting on this motivation as well as helping to overcome the child's resistance. In applying the model, the author points to motivational factors of the perpetrator, such as attraction to the child-like behavior of certain adolescents with mental retardation and satisfaction in engaging in an adult relationship without an adult emotional interaction. It may be easier for the perpetrator to overcome internal (societal) inhibitions to abuse in a society that devalues people with mental disabilities. Since people with mental disabilities are often stereotyped as having abnormal sex drives, prohibitions may be further weakened. Overcoming external (situational) inhibitions may be easier because adolescents with mental disabilities have fewer situational safeguards to protect them from sexual exploitation. These adolescents lead more isolated lives and are often cared for by surrogates who can restrict access to outsiders. Typically, the child is unaware of how to obtain help if a problem arises. Characteristics of people with mental disabilities can contribute to the perpetrator overcoming the child's resistance. They are often more easily led and have a greater need to please others. Often, they are lacking attention and affection. They may have had no sex education. In addition, they may face being disbelieved or may lack communication skills to report abuse. The author discusses prevention, noting that programs to prevent sexual abuse of adolescents with developmental disabilities are rare; however, information on this group is readily available for caregivers. There has also been an increased awareness of stresses placed on families with children with disabilities, and many physicians recognize that some children are at greater risk for abuse due to their individual behavior. Activities or programs to assist in attaining independence and social competency can reduce vulnerability. The author concludes that sex education, including abuse prevention, can serve to protect many adolescents with developmental disabilities.

1176. Schreiber, M. (Ed.). (1983). *Siblings of mentally retarded and developmentally disabled persons: Proceedings of the Annual National Seminar (1st, New York, N.Y., May 19–20, 1983).* New York: Association for the Help of Retarded Children.
These proceedings present papers from a May 1983 seminar on siblings of people with mental retardation and developmental disabilities. The contributors to these proceedings include parents, siblings, and professionals from social work, nursing, and psychology. The following papers are included in these proceedings: "Life with an older sister" (Miller & Kalish), "Raising a family and dealing with differences in children: A parent's view" (Moore), "Normal siblings of retarded persons" (Schreiber), "Siblings' feelings: A need for expression" (Neel), "Groups for normal siblings of developmentally handicapped children" (Mates), "Modification of sibling interaction in families with a mentally retarded child" (Vespo), "Explaining differences to children" (Giglio), "A developmental perspective of the siblings of handicapped children" (Feigon), "A family systems look at the developmentally disabled" (Jaffe-Ruiz), and "The parent perspective" (Moore).

1177. Schuler, C. (1990, September 28). Camp manager plans action on his dismissal: Feels betrayed by administration. *The Edmonton Journal*, p. B3.

This newspaper article reports that a camp manager who brought forward allegations of abuse involving another counselor and adults with developmental disabilities at Camp Health Hope and Happiness is currently fighting his own dismissal by camp administrators. Emile van der Poorten approached camp administrators in 1989 with allegations that a counselor encouraged a resident to masturbate in front of others and kicked another resident in the posterior. After administrators' inaction, van der Poorten went to the Royal Canadian Mounted Police with his information. A few days later, van der Poorten was fired. The administrators' reason for the dismissal was because of van der Poorten's poor business management skills. The counselor accused of abuse denied all allegations and returned this year as a volunteer at the camp. The accused was released from duties last week because there was no more need for his services. A committee is investigating the allegations and camp policy and procedures regarding complaints.

1178. Schultz, G. L. (1981). Sexual contact between staff and residents. In D. A. Shore & H. L. Gochros (Eds.), *Sexual problems of adolescents in institutions* (pp. 90–103). Springfield, IL: Charles C Thomas.
This chapter discusses sexual contact that occurs between staff and adolescent residents of institutions. The questions of abuse and exploitation in these contacts are not fully addressed, and the focus is on the development of appropriate sexual and social relationships. (Editors' note: While the failure to address exploitative relationships is a serious omission, this chapter is worth reading. The described desexualization and enforced celibacy of adolescents in institutions may be important factors in increasing their vulnerability to sexual exploitation.)

1179. Schuman, D. C. (1986). False accusations of physical and sexual abuse. *Bulletin of the American Academy of Psychiatry and the Law, 14*(1), 5–21.
This article discusses seven cases of false accusations of child abuse in domestic litigation cases. It suggests that these accusations are most often found in cases that involve child custody and visitation rights. This article discusses aspects of parent and child regression and offers some recommendations for evaluators when dealing with these cases.

1180. Schutter, L. S., & Brinker, R. P. (1992). Conjuring a new category of disability from prenatal cocaine exposure: Are the infants unique biological or caretaking casualties? *Topics in Early Childhood Special Education, 11*(4), 84–111.
This article examines in utero exposure to cocaine and how it affects the mother, fetus, neonate, and infant. It includes a literature review that suggests there is little variability in behavior between those infants exposed to cocaine in utero and infants with neurologic impairments. The authors propose a new category for infants

exposed prenatally to cocaine, and they suggest intervention strategies to use with families with an infant exposed in utero to cocaine.

1181. Schwartz, D. B. (1992). *Crossing the river: Creating a conceptual revolution in community and disability.* Brookline, MA: Brookline Books.
This book covers many different areas related to improving the lives of people with disabilities based on the central thesis that natural human networks, such as families and communities, are inherently better than institutional approaches to care. Chapter 10, "What really keeps people with disabilities safe in society?" deals most directly with issues of abuse and regulatory safeguards. It suggests that regulatory control may have deleterious effects on safety because it directs efforts away from the real issues and may conflict with the natural safeguards by presenting barriers to healthy and safe processes as well as institutional ones.

1182. Schwier-Melberg, K. (1989, October). Parents must take first step to recognize sexual abuse as reality. *Dialect: Newsmagazine of the Saskatchewan Association for Community Living,* p. 11.
This article discusses Charlene Senn's book, *Vulnerable,* but it goes beyond a review to discuss underlying issues related to sexual abuse of people with intellectual impairments. This article urges parents to recognize the risks and work toward controlling these risks by ensuring that their children receive appropriate social, sexual, and assertiveness skills training.

1183. Schwier-Melberg, K. (1990). *Speakeasy: People with mental handicaps talk about their lives in institutions and in the community.* Austin, TX: PRO-ED.
This book is a series of interviews with people with mental disabilities concerning their personal experiences in institutions and in the community. It concludes that overcoming social barriers is still a very valid concern for people with mental disabilities.

1184. Scott, C. S., Lefley, H. P., & Hicks, D. (1993). Potential risk factors for rape in three ethnic groups. *Community Mental Health Journal, 29*(2), 133–141.
This article reports on risk factors for rape among nonLatino White, Latino, and African-American women. Of the 881 rape victims surveyed, 51% had no identified risk factors. The remaining 49% had one or more of the following risk factors: mental disability, prior history of sexual assault or incest, tourist or visitor status, and homelessness. The presence of various risk factors appeared to interact strongly with ethnic status, suggesting a strong cultural component in these risk factors.

1185. Scott, K. D. (1992). Childhood sexual abuse: Impact on a community's mental health status. *Child Abuse & Neglect,* *16,* 285–295.

This article discusses an epidemiological study that was conducted to determine the effect of child sexual abuse on community mental health through the use of impact or attributable fractions. A total sample of 3,131 individuals from the Los Angeles Epidemiologic Catchment Area were divided into sampling units for testing. All individuals were over the age of 17. Psychiatric disorders were assessed using the National Institute of Mental Health Diagnostic Interview Schedule. The results of this study indicate the following: a history of child sexual abuse increases one's probability of developing a psychiatric disorder, an affective disorder, substance abuse and dependency, drug abuse or dependence, alcohol abuse or dependence, obsessive-compulsive disorder, phobia, and major depression; and child sexual abuse is estimated to contribute to 74% of psychiatric cases with a history of child sexual abuse and 3.9% of all psychiatric cases.

1186. Scott, W. J. (1980). Attachment and child abuse: A study of social history indicators among mothers of abused children. In G. J. Williams & J. Money (Eds.), *Traumatic abuse and neglect of children at home* **(pp. 130–142). Baltimore: The Johns Hopkins University Press.**

This chapter discusses a study that was conducted to determine if mothers of abused children were different from mothers of nonabused children with regard to attachment. It obtained the social history for 30 mothers of abused children and 29 mothers of nonabused children. Three areas of attachment were examined: childhood experiences related to attachment, affiliative behavior carried into adolescents and adulthood, and subsequent parental behavior. The results of this study indicate the following: Mothers of abused children differed on 14 of 20 social indicators when compared to mothers of nonabused children; and the mothers of abused children had a history of separation from their parents as children, institutionalization as an adolescent, use of alcohol or drugs, assault by a significant male as an adult, problems with the police, illegitimate children, and psychiatric problems.

1187. Seagull, E. A., &. Scheurer, S. L. (1986). Neglected and abused children of mentally retarded parents. *Child Abuse & Neglect, 10,* 493–500.

The authors of this article followed 64 parents with mental disabilities who had been identified by a social service agency as abusive or neglectful toward their children. This article notes that most of the parents had come from an abusive or chaotic background. The authors found that the majority of children had been removed from the parents' home because the family did not respond to intense parenting intervention by community agencies. They conclude that parents with mental

disabilities are at risk for abusing or neglecting their children and may not profit from the traditional intervention assistance given to normally functioning parents. They recommended a foster care type of arrangement for the entire family in order to avoid dysfunction and break-up.

1188. Sears, J., Bishop, A., & Stevens, E. (1989). Teaching *Miranda* **rights to students who have mental retardation.** *Teaching Exceptional Children, 21*(3), 38–42.

This article addresses the need to teach students with developmental disabilities about their constitutional rights concerning self-incrimination and the *Miranda* warnings in case they are ever suspected of criminal activity. It provides teaching suggestions and an instructional scenario incorporating cued responses.

1189. Seattle Rape Relief Developmental Disabilities Project. (1982). *Special education curriculum on sexual exploitation: Level I Kit (Ages 6–11).* **Seattle, WA: Comprehensive Health Education Foundation.**

This special education curriculum on sexual exploitation consists of four filmstrips, a teacher's guide with written narrative, six pamphlets, and a body map. It is designed for students 6 to 11 years of age who have physical disabilities or learning disabilities or whose learning difficulties place them in the slow learner to educably retarded range. The focus of the curriculum is on awareness of the problem, how to avoid or prevent different kinds of sexual exploitation, and on where and how to report incidents. The teacher's guide includes specific lesson plans, pretests and posttests, and resource lists. The written narrative is made up of stories, role-play situations, and scripts for the filmstrips. A body map includes overlays. Three pamphlets provide information on sexual exploitation to parents and others involved with students who are disabled. The other three pamphlets describe the elementary-level curriculum to parents.

1190. Seattle Rape Relief Developmental Disabilities Project. (1982). *Special education curriculum on sexual exploitation: Level II Kit (Ages 12–19).* **Seattle, WA: Comprehensive Health Education Foundation.**

This special education curriculum on sexual exploitation consists of 20 filmstrips, a teacher's guide with written narrative, six pamphlets, and a body map. It is designed for students 12 to 19 years of age who have physical disabilities or learning disabilities or whose learning difficulties place them in the slow learner to educably retarded range. The focus of the curriculum is on awareness of the problem, how to avoid or prevent different kinds of sexual exploitation, and on where and how to report incidents. The teacher's guide includes specific lesson plans, pretests and posttests, and resource lists.

The written narrative is made up of stories, role-play situations, and scripts for the filmstrips. A body map includes overlays. Three pamphlets provide information on sexual exploitation to parents and others involved with students who are disabled. The other three pamphlets describe the secondary-level curriculum to parents.

1191. Seattle Rape Relief Developmental Disabilities Project. (1991). *Sexual assault awareness: The truth can help: For parents of youth with disabilities.* **Seattle, WA: Author.**
This booklet provides information about sexual assault legal issues and indicators of abuse, and it offers suggestions for caregivers and parents of people with disabilities who have been abused. Also, this booklet introduces "Project Action," a service that helps people with disabilities who have been sexually assaulted.

1192. Segal, U. A. (1992). Child abuse in India: An empirical report on perceptions. *Child Abuse and Neglect, 16*(6), **887–908.**
The author of this article points out that little attention has been paid to the nature and extent of child abuse in India; consequently, this article discusses the theoretical background of child abuse and examines the Western and Indian definitions of child abuse. This article describes a study that used Giovannoni and Becarra's ([1979]. *Defining child abuse.* New York: Free Press.) vignette pairs describing different categories of child maltreatment to measure the perceptions of child abuse held by 45 social workers, 46 professionals in other human services, and 42 people not involved in human services, all of whom were Indian nationals living in India. The results of this study reveal that these three groups of Indian nationals had similar perceptions of the severity of different forms of abuse. The author describes the differences in perceptions between Giovannoni and Becarra's U.S. study and this Indian study and discusses the implications of these differences.

1193. Seidelman, W. E. (1989). In memoriam: Confrontation with evil. *Hastings Center Report, 19*(6), **5–6.**
This article discusses the controversy about the continued use of skeletons and other specimens that were by-products of the the Nazi holocaust. The author indicates that cadavers used at the University of Heidelberg came from euthanasia victims at Hadamar Hospital and that skulls and other specimens used at the Max Planck Institute of Brain Research also came from the euthanasia program. This article also discusses the key role of medical professionals in the evolution of Nazi genocide.

1194. Seidelman, W. E. (1992). "Medspeak" for murder. In A. L. Kaplan (Ed.), *When medicine went mad: Bioethics and the holocaust* **(pp. 271–279). To-tawa, NJ: Humana Press.**

This chapter discusses how medical terminology has been developed and used to help depersonalize certain patients and make killing them acceptable. Nazi expressions such as "the great hospital" used to describe the gas chamber and crematorium and the "great therapy of Auschwitz" used to describe death in the gas chamber are chilling examples. The author points out that "murder was rationalized on the basis of clinical dehumanization" (p. 272). The author also explores current examples of medical expression such as "Gomer" and "vegetative" state as subtle forms of the same process.

1195. *Selected readings: Sexual offenders identified as intellectually disabled.* **(1989). Orwell, VT: Safer Society Press.**
These selected readings include seven articles on sex offenders with intellectual disabilities: "A comprehensive evaluation of an intellectually disabled sex offender" (Caparulo), "A multimodal treatment of developmentally disabled sex offenders" (Fried), "A summary of selected notes from the working sessions of the First National Training Conference on the Assessment and Treatment of Intellectually Disabled Juvenile and Adult Sexual Offenders, Columbus, OH, March 25–27, 1988" (Lackey & Knopp), "Sexual assault of handicapped children" (Longo & Gochenour), "Treatment and evaluation issues with the mentally retarded sex offender" (Murphy, Coleman, & Haynes), "The intellectually handicapped sexual offender" (Parsons), and "Selected bibliography: Sexual offenders identified as intellectually disabled" (Safer Society Program).

1196. Seligman, M., & Darling, R. B. (1989). Effects on the family as a system. In M. Seligman & R. B. Darling (Eds.), *Ordinary families, special children: A systems approach to childhood disability* **(pp. 83–110). New York: Guilford Press.**
This chapter examines how a child with disabilities affects the family as a system. It pays particular attention to the amount of stress placed on a family with a child with disabilities. Subtopics for this chapter include the following: stages of mourning; chronic burden of care; stigma; marital adjustment, divorce, and single parenthood; families with children with different disabilities; the severity of the disability; and other factors that affect the family. The authors note that research on the effects of disability on the family as a system has contained methodological shortcomings.

1197. Selim, M. (1993, June). Sexual abuse of children and young adults with learning disabilities among Pakistanis living in Pakistan and in the United Kingdom. *NAPSAC (National Association for Prevention of Sexual Abuse of Children and Adults with Learning Disabilities) Bulletin, 4,* **7–10.**

This article provides anecdotal accounts of sexual abuse of Pakistanis with developmental disabilities in Pakistan and in England. The author also provides some analysis of how cultural differences may influence the nature of the abuse and the response to abuse. In the mid-1980s in Pakistan, a young servant who was partially blind and had a mental disability was found to be pregnant by her master. As a result, she was convicted of having had illegal sexual intercourse and imprisoned, while no action was taken against her master. Media accounts of the case, however, brought strong protests from the public, and a higher court reversed her conviction on the "grounds of manifest injustice" (p. 7). The author provides other accounts of abuse in both family and institutional settings and suggests that the abuse problem is aggravated by the unwillingness to discuss sexuality in contemporary Pakistan. In Britain, abuse also occurs in Pakistani families, and there is no evidence to suggest that it is more or less frequent than in other English families. Nevertheless, the author points to a number of features of Pakistani culture that may result in particular patterns of abuse in Pakistani families. According to Selim, poor education, social isolation, and female disempowerment may make Pakistani mothers less likely to report suspected abuse. A strong cultural ethic of male dominance may add to this problem. Extended family structures may expose Pakistani children to more distantly related males, which could influence risk. The tradition of bed sharing with older children may also be a source of risk. Pakistani families are more likely to be isolated from the community and service providers, and the ethnic community may create more pressure to cover-up sexual misconduct than to confront it. Strong religious prohibitions against sexual expression may reduce the risk of abuse, but they might also encourage some kinds of abuse since there are few opportunities for "acceptable" expression of sexuality. The discrepancy between Pakistani and British mores may be another source of risk since Pakistanis in Britain have difficulty identifying with either culture. Selim emphasizes that these are merely hypotheses based on observations and have not been verified by systematic research.

1198. Sengstock, W. L., Magerhans Hurley, H., & Sprotte, A. (1990, September). The role of special education in the Third Reich. *Education and Training in Mental Retardation,* pp. 225–236.

This article examines the role of German special education for people with developmental and physical disabilities in Hitler's Third Reich. The Nazi government instituted cost-cutting measures that affected those considered inferior and too expensive to maintain for three reasons: the popularity of Social Darwinism, which emphasized the survival of the fittest in society; the poor state of the German economy; and high unemployment. To reduce the financial drain on the economy, the Nazi government reduced or eliminated schools and services for people with disabilities. It sterilized so-called "inferiors" because they thought they could ensure the survival of society by reducing the risk of inferiors bearing inferior

offspring. The authors note that special education under National Socialism (Nazi Party) had to conform to Nazi ideology: That is, people with disabilities who were considered trainable were sterilized and trained to perform unskilled labor, and those considered untrainable were institutionalized. Approximately 300,000 to 350,000 people with disabilities were sterilized during the Third Reich.

1199. Sengstock, W. L., & Ruttgardt, S. E. (1994). Rebuilding special education in Germany after World War II. *Education and Training in Mental Retardation and Developmental Disabilities,* 29(1), 69–81.

This article describes the redevelopment of special education in post-World War II Germany. The pre-war special education system in Germany had been quite advanced, but it remained segregated from mainstream schools and communities. This isolation contributed to the vulnerability of children with special needs under the Nazi regime. After World War II, the initial focus was to restore the system that had predominated in the 1920s and early 1930s. Services remained segregated until the late 1950s, when parents began to demand integrated services

1200. Senn, C. Y. (1988). *Vulnerable: Sexual abuse and people with an intellectual handicap*[Monograph]. Downsview, ON: G. Allan Roeher Institute. (ERIC Document Reproduction Service No. ED 302 975)

This monograph, prepared for the Family Violence Prevention Division of Health and Welfare Canada, provides a thorough treatment of sexual abuse and people with intellectual disabilities. The author summarizes a number of studies that appear to show increased risk of sexual abuse for people with intellectual impairments, though indicating caution in interpretation because of the estimates used by researchers. The author points out difficulties in obtaining data from institutional settings, but she presents indirect evidence of sexual abuse problems in institutions and explores developmental disabilities as a risk factor. She concludes that people with intellectual impairment experience at least equal risk for sexual abuse. Finkelhor's model of risk factors is used as a conceptual basis for explaining increased risk among children with intellectual impairments. Symptoms of child sexual abuse are discussed in relation to children with intellectual impairment. The author summarizes information on sexual offenders with disabilities, pointing out that many of these offenders had been sexually abused as children. She discusses legal issues related to consent, ability to testify in court, and Charter implications, and she includes detailed recommendations for prevention and treatment. This report includes a long list of references, including many unpublished and hard-to-find documents.

1201. Service, C. N. (1992, August 8). Dutch pediatricians back mercy killing of

handicapped newborns. *The Halifax Chronicle Herald*, **p. D20.**
This newspaper article reports that a panel of Dutch pediatricians requested clear guidelines governing mercy killings of infants with disabilities. Similar to the guidelines established with regard to euthanasia, they suggest that these guidelines should govern procedures involved in ending the lives of newborns while avoiding possible prosecution of doctors. It is estimated that approximately 10 infants per year could be termed mercy killings. Holland has an annual live birth rate of 200,000.

1202. Seton, C. (1991, November 30). Five life terms for head who abused children. *The Times*, **pp. 1, 18.**
This newspaper article reports that Frank Beck, former head of Leicestershire residential homes for children, was sentenced to five life terms for child abuse. Over a 13-year period, Frank Beck had assaulted approximately 200 children in his care. The life sentences stem from four guilty charges of buggering (anal intercourse) and one count of rape. In addition, Beck was given a total of 24 years for other counts of sexual and physical abuse involving minors.

1203. Seton, C. (1991, November 30). Therapy method made children ripe for abuse. *The Times*, **p. 3.**
This newspaper article focuses on the child abuse trial of Frank Beck, former head of three Leicestershire residential homes for emotionally disturbed children, and his use of regression therapy with children. With regression therapy, the children were encouraged to return to earlier stages of development by being treated as infants. This involved bottle feedings, cuddling, and being carried by staff members. Children were also verbally and physically abused in order to break them into submission, after which they would be nurtured. The prosecution argues that this form of therapy isolated the children and made them vulnerable to abuse.

1204. Seton, C. (1991, November 30). Why no action was taken against Beck. *The Times*, **p. 3.**
This newspaper article examines the overwhelming evidence that was available to social services 4 years prior to the resignation of Frank Beck, former head of three Leicestershire residential homes for emotionally disturbed children. Frank Beck was charged with numerous physical and sexual abuse charges against children in his care and against former care staff. Twelve incidents investigated by council resulted in no decisive action against Beck, and Leicestershire authorities did not mention allegations against Beck for child abuse in their reference of Beck to new employers.

1205. Sexual abuse prevention project for deaf/hard of hearing children. (1990). *Acehi Journal*, *16*(2), **146.**
This article discusses a sexual abuse prevention project for children who are deaf or hard of hearing. It describes an assessment of the information needed by 8-year-old to 15-year-old children to prevent sexual abuse conducted by the Greater Vancouver Association of the Deaf in British Columbia. It examines the association's plans to develop resources geared toward the learning needs of children who are deaf or hard of hearing and to create a distribution plan that will target members of the deaf community in need of further information on prevention strategies and safety issues.

1206. Sexual exploitation and abuse of people with disabilities. (1984). *Response to Violence in the Family*, *7*(2), **7–8.**
This article addresses the prevalence of sexual abuse among people with disabilities or special vulnerability. Also, it addresses the need for services for people with disabilities who are victims of rape and other forms of sexual abuse.

1207. Sgroi, S. M. (1989). Evaluation and treatment of sexual offense behavior in persons with mental retardation. In S. M. Sgroi (Ed.), *Vulnerable populations: Sexual abuse treatment for children, adult survivors, offenders, and persons with mental retardation* **(Vol. 2, pp. 245–283). Lexington, MA: Lexington Books.**
This chapter discusses assessing people with developmental disabilities for sexually abusive behavior. It suggests areas where it might be possible to identify sexually abusive behavior: mutual consent between those parties involved, a resident's sexual knowledge of interactive sexual behavior, the concept of privacy, and the identification of a power imbalance between those parties involved which precludes consent. It examines reporting sexually abusive behavior and the investigation of complaints using interviews. This chapter uses case examples to illustrate interviewing techniques and patterns of sexually abusive behavior in adults with mental retardation, and it suggests some treatment options.

1208. Sgroi, S. M., & Carey, J. A. (1989). A curriculum for adults with mental retardation. In S. M. Sgroi (Ed.), *Vulnerable populations: Sexual abuse treatment for children, adult survivors, offenders, and persons with mental retardation* **(Vol. 2, pp. 217–244). Lexington, MA: Lexington Books.**
This chapter examines a sex education training curriculum for adults with severe, moderate, and mild mental retardation. It describes three training sessions and the accompanying exercises. These sessions demonstrate appropriate social interaction and how to avoid sexual victimization.

1209. Sgroi, S. M., Carey, J. A., & Wheaton, A. B. (1989). Sexual abuse avoidance training for adults with mental retardation. In S. M. Sgroi (Ed.),

Vulnerable populations: Sexual abuse treatment for children, adult survivors, offenders, and persons with mental retardation (Vol. 2, pp. 203–216). Lexington, MA: Lexington Books.

This chapter addresses sexual abuse avoidance training for adults with mental retardation. The goal of this program is to teach adults with mental retardation to avoid sexual victimization. This chapter discusses the following procedural guidelines: participant selection, training site, staff participation, incentives for resident participation, rules for participation, contracts, observation of participant reactions, follow-up, evaluation, and frequency of training sessions. This chapter describes participant functioning levels for those clients with mild, moderate, or severe mental retardation, and it suggests different approaches to teaching and trainer preparation.

1210. Shah, A. K. (1992). Violence, death and associated factors on a mental handicap ward. *Journal of Intellectual Disability Research,* 36(3), 229–239.

This article presents the results of a 21-month study of violence by residents on a locked ward of a residential institution housing 20 "high-dependency adult males with mental retardation." Of the 26 residents of the ward, 18 were involved with at least some violence, and 8 were not involved with violence. Violent behavior was not associated with degree of mental retardation, psychiatric diagnosis, race, length of stay, diagnosis of epilepsy, physical illness, or sensory impairment. Residents were younger and were more likely to have abnormal electroencephalograph readings. Since the numbers in the violent and nonviolent groups were small, very large differences were required to demonstrate significant differences. The author recorded 620 violent incidents during the 21-month period: 284 involved violence against other residents, 126 involved self-directed violence, 69 involved violence against staff, and 141 involved destruction of property. Four patients were involved in 74% of the violent episodes. Two of these four patients died suddenly of unusual causes during the study. One patient died of a ruptured aorta, and the other patient died of a ruptured small intestine. As the author suggests, both are injuries that could have been caused by blows to the chest or abdomen. A third patient died of pneumonia shortly after the study. The author points out the need for more research on such deaths.

1211. Shah, S. A. (1989). Mental disorder and the criminal justice system: Some overarching issues. *International Journal of Law and Psychiatry,* 12, 231–244.

This article examines the criminal justice system and how it deals with offenders with developmental disabilities. It focuses on three issues: the medical and legal use of the terms *mental illness* and *mental disorder,* the rationale for the legal concern with mental disorders, and the confounding function of police power and therapeutic objectives.

1212. Shaman, E. J. (1986). Prevention programs for children with disabilities. In M. Nelson & K. Clark (Eds.), *The educator's guide to preventing child sexual abuse* (pp. 122–125). Santa Cruz, CA: Network Publications.

This chapter describes the resources, services, and staff training activities that were provided by the Disabilities Project of the Seattle Rape Relief Crisis Center. It also makes recommendations relevant to prevention programs and includes some data (e.g., compared to the 65% to 85% of victims without disabilities, people with disabilities that experience sexual assault know the offender in 99% of cases). It discusses problems with overemphasis on teaching children to obey authority, isolation, and the myth of the asexuality of people with disabilities, and there is a brief description of training programs. The author stresses the importance of clarifying the values and perceptions of those who will provide sex education, the necessity of a team approach, the recognition and accommodation of differences across individuals and cultures, and the cooperation and coordination of parents. A 4-paragraph description of the Disabilities Project is also included on pages 160–161 of this book.

1213. Shane, J. F. (1988). *Abuse against children with developmental handicaps: An annotated bibliography.* **Toronto: Ontario Association for Community Living.**

This annotated bibliography lists 32 items and is organized into five sections: causal factors, parents with developmental disabilities, legal issues, general information, and educational material. The focus of this bibliography is on the causal relationship between child abuse and developmental disabilities, and it includes research articles.

1214. Shapiro, J. P. (1993). *No pity: People with disabilities forging a new civil rights movement.* **New York: Times Books.**

This book describes the development of the modern disabilities rights movement. This book is written from a journalistic perspective and explores unresolved issues. Chapter 9, "No less worthy life," gives a good account of the Larry McAfee case. McAfee, who had been paralyzed in a motorcycle accident, asked to be assisted with suicide and the court approved. Disability rights activists protested, suggesting the courts willingness to assist him to die was based on his disability status and therefore people with disabilities did not have equal protection. They also pointed out that McAfee wanted to die because of the poor quality of care he received while being shuttled from one nursing home to another, and the activists felt the solution should be better care, not helping him die. The courts, however, supported McAfee, but by the time the case was settled, McAfee was receiving better care, was happier with his circumstances, and no longer wanted to die. This book also includes information about inhuman institutional conditions and misuse of aversive treatment. The author describes his visit to the Behavior Research Institute in 1989. He reports seeing "Janine" who had been featured on the television show *20/20* four years earlier as remarkably recovered as a result of aversive treatment. Now, after 4 more years of aversive treatment, she had regressed to her former state of uncontrollable self-injury.

1215. Sharpe, S. (1992, June 21). Victims don't fall through cracks in Alberta— They're pushed. *The Calgary Herald*, p. B4.

This newspaper article compares the lenient sentences for offenders who perpetrate crimes against women or people with disabilities with the severe sentence for a teenager who was sentenced to 6 weeks in jail for being in contempt of court for skipping school. The author questions the moral judgment in these sentences.

1216. Shaughnessy, M. F. (1984). Institutional child abuse. *Children and Youth Services Review*, *6*, 311–318.

The abuse of children residing in institutions and residential care centers and its causes are discussed in this article. It examines various types of abuses and their affects on treatment: for example, misdiagnosis, lack of treatment, medication, and frequent transferrals. This article also discusses personnel, clients, institutions, and financial support. This article claims that abuse stems from human, bureaucratic, and fiscal problems. It discusses the following problems: 1) organizational roadblocks to proper treatment (e.g., poor staff-administration relations, little accountability in large institutions, lack of cooperation between departments, policies that require specialized staff, heavy paperwork duties for therapists), 2) incompetent staff, 3) staff turnover, 4) a remote location that isolates children from parents, 5) inappropriate placement of children as a stopgap measure, 6) the use of medication as a form of social control, 7) premature discharge, and 8) inadequate follow-up. The author considers inadequate follow-up a form of abuse.

1217. Shereshewsky, B. (1993). Protection of hospitalized mental patients against sexual assault and abuse. *Medicine and Law*, *12*, 325–327.

The author of this article, a retired Justice of the Supreme Court of Israel, discusses the need to protect hospitalized psychiatric patients from sexual assault and abuse perpetrated by other patients. The author advocates the use of separate gender wards to minimize the possibility of abuse.

1218. Sheridan, M. S. (1989, February). Munchausen syndrome by proxy. *Health and Social Work*, pp. 53–58.

The role of social workers and their management of Munchausen syndrome by proxy (MSBP) cases is discussed in this article. It discusses the identification of MSBP, the psychodynamics of the family, and the management of these cases.

1219. Sherlock, R. (1987). *Preserving life: Public policy and the life not worthy of living*. Chicago: Loyola University Press.

This book provides an intense discussion of issues regarding the right to refuse treatment, suicide, assisted suicide, and involuntary euthanasia. This book provides a history of growing support for euthanasia in the United States and Great Britain prior to its repudiation that resulted as a reaction to Nazi policies. This book also explores practical policy-making and enforcement issues.

1220. Sherwood, S. N. (1980). *Play psychotherapy with socially maladaptive mentally retarded children using same-age and younger-age peers as therapists*. Athens, OH: Ohio University.

This book describes the results of a study that examined play therapy for 24 children with mental retardation and 24 adaptive peer therapists. The results of this study suggest that an optimal degree of therapeutic atmosphere and structure occurred in the younger age groups when the adult therapist and the younger peer therapist presented appropriate coping strategies and prosocial behaviors. The results of this study also indicate that same-age sessions had a competitive atmosphere.

1221. Shore, D. A. (1982). Sexual abuse and sexual education in child caring institutions. In J. R. Conte & D. A. Shore (Eds.), *Social work and child sexual abuse* (pp. 171–184). New York: Haworth Press.

The author of this chapter suggests that although sexual neglect and sexual abuse are problems in institutional care of children and youth, this topic has not been the subject of any research. Sexual neglect is discussed as the failure to provide appropriate role models, adequate sex education, or opportunities for appropriate sexual expression. Sexual neglect, in addition to being directly harmful, is viewed as contributing to the risk for sexual abuse.

1222. Showers, J. (1992). "Don't shake the baby": The effectiveness of a prevention program. *Child Abuse & Neglect*, *16*, 11–18.

This article examines the "Don't shake the baby" project. Because severe shaking of babies can result in permanent disability and death, the "Don't shake the baby" project was initiated to educate parents about the danger of shaking their infants. Six hospitals participated in the project, handing out a "Crying: What should I do" card to new parents. In total, 3,293 (21%) out of 15,708 parents of newborns returned the response card that accompanied the Crying Card. The results of this study indicate the following: 77% of those parents who returned the response card found the information package helpful,

49% of those parents who responded were less likely to shake their babies, and 91% of those parents who responded recommended that other parents should read the Crying Card. The article also includes demographic information.

1223. Shryer, T. (1989, December 27). Ex-officer gets bail in mercy killing. *The Los Angeles Times*, p. A4.
This newspaper article reports the case of a retired police officer who faces first-degree murder charges for killing his wife who had suffered from multiple sclerosis for 20 years. Alice Williams's health had deteriorated over the 6 months before the Christmas Eve shooting. Gerald Williams claimed that his wife had requested that he end her life, thereby ending her suffering. Williams was facing additional heart surgery and did not believe he could continue taking care of his wife. Williams was released on a $250,000 personal bond.

1224. Sigal, M. D., Altmark, D., & Carmel, I. (1986). Munchausen syndrome by adult proxy: A perpetrator abusing two adults. *The Journal of Nervous and Mental Disease, 174*(11), 696–698.
This article presents a single case study of Munchausen syndrome by proxy involving a 34-year-old man and his two female partners. Of the two women, a wife and girlfriend, the wife died due to the severity of the abuse, while the man's girlfriend was paralyzed. This article includes a short personal history of this man and the two women. It also discusses a psychiatric evaluation of this man that found he had a narcissistic personality disorder, which was characterized by loneliness, depression, and a constant search for unrequited maternal love.

1225. Sigelman, C. K. (1981). Asking questions of retarded persons: A comparison of yes-no and either-or formats. *Applied Research in Mental Retardation, 2*(4), 347–357.
This article discusses a study that examined the frequent tendency of people with mental retardation to respond in the positive to yes-no questions. This article also compares the use of the yes-no format with the either-or format.

1226. Sigelman, C. K. (1981). When in doubt, say yes: Acquiescence in interview with mentally retarded persons. *Mental Retardation, 19*(2), 53–58.
This article discusses a study that investigated the rates of acquiescence by people with mental retardation living in institutions or in the community to questions, regardless of their content. The results of this study indicate that participants with lower IQ scores tended to acquiesce more than participants with higher IQ scores. The author discusses the danger of relying on yes-no questions when working with this population.

1227. Sigelman, C. K. (1982). Evaluating alternative techniques of questioning mentally retarded persons. *American Journal of Mental Deficiency, 86*(5), 511–518.
This article examines the use of questions in interviewing people with mental retardation and discusses implications for question design. Question types were tested with preteens, teens, and adults with mental retardation. Open-ended questions were found to be unanswerable by many of the participants. Furthermore, the interviewers found that trying to clarify or enlarge upon such a question only resulted in increased response bias. Questions with a yes-no format yielded higher response rates, but they also introduced a serious acquiescence bias. However, multiple choice questions, particularly if used in conjunction with pictures, yielded valid answers from many of the participants.

1228. Sigelman, C. K. (1982). The responsiveness of mentally retarded persons to questions. *Education and Training of the Mentally Retarded, 17*(2), 120–124.
This article discusses a study that measured responsiveness to questions using an interview format with two groups of children and one group of adults with mental retardation. Questions with a yes-no format and questions requiring participants to choose among pictures consistently resulted in increased responsiveness as compared to questions with an either-or format. Verbal, multiple choice questions and open-ended questions resulted in the lowest levels of responsiveness.

1229. Sigelman, C. K., & Singleton, L. C. (1986). Stigmatization in childhood: A survey of developmental trends and issues. In S. C. Ainlay, G. Becker, & L. M. Coleman (Eds.), *The dilemma of differences: A multidisciplinary view of stigma* (pp. 185–208). New York: Plenum.
This chapter examines and follows the development of stigmatization in children from infancy. It discusses children's reactions to ethnic and developmental disability differences among peers.

1230. Silverman, D. (1987). *Communication and medical practice: Social relations in the clinic*. London: Sage Publications.
This book on medical communication includes a chapter called "Coercive interpretation in the clinic: The social constitution of the Down's syndrome child" that presents a qualitative study that compared how physicians communicate with parents of children with and without Down syndrome regarding heart surgery. Differences in content (e.g., presence versus absence of reassurance) and style of communication influence parents of children with Down syndrome to refuse surgery while influencing

the parents of children without Down syndrome to consent to surgery.

1231. Simpson, J. (1987). A six month sentence for stealing five dollars, and the nsw "missing services" report. *Interaction,* 1(1), 19–20.

This article presents the case of an Australian man with a developmental disability who was sentenced to 6 months in jail for stealing $5. The man had committed minor offenses before, including thefts and assaults against figures of authority, and he had spent time in jail. The author argues that the Australian criminal justice system is ill-equipped to deal with offenders with developmental disabilities and that the lack of services available for these offenders may result in the following: infringement of their personal rights, victimization in prison, and poorer adjustment once their prison term has been served. The author offers suggestions to better equip the justice system: training programs for police, lawyers, magistrates, judges, and Corrective Service Personnel; identification of offenders with developmental disabilities; appropriate counseling services and training programs for these offenders; and segregation from other prisoners of those offenders deemed especially vulnerable.

1232. Sinason, V. (1986). Secondary mental handicap and its relationship to trauma. *Psychoanalytic Psychotherapy,* 2(2), 131–154.

This article presents a position that some apparent mental disabilities are actually a defense against trauma. In such cases, the symptoms of disability are associated with a secondary gain for the patient, although the nature of the secondary gain may be well hidden. In other cases, opportunistic disabilities occur when primary disabilities are exacerbated by the effects of trauma. Sinason illustrates these ideas with clinical material from two cases.

1233. Sinason, V. (1988). Smiling, swallowing, sickening and stupefying: The effect of sexual abuse on the child. *Psychoanalytic Psychotherapy,* 3(2), 97–111.

By examining the process of small everyday abuse in a loving home, this article discusses the meaning of child sexual abuse and its effect on the child. This is done by means of extracts from a baby observation and by tracing in the twice weekly psychoanalytical psychotherapy of two children, a preadolescent boy and a 5-year-old girl, the infantile processes of smiling, swallowing, being sick, and becoming stupid. The study found that the trauma of sexual abuse played a part in the mental disability of the boy, who is seen moving from being a tragic victim of abuse to being an adolescent struggling against abusing, and that sexual abuse produced emotional and learning difficulties for the girl.

1234. Sinason, V. (1989). Uncovering and responding to sexual abuse in psychotherapeutic settings. In H. Brown & A. Craft (Eds.), *Thinking the unthinkable: Papers on sexual abuse and people with learning difficulties* (pp. 39–50). London: FPA Education Unit.

This chapter discusses the interpretation of indirect disclosures made by people with intellectual impairments who have been sexually abused. The author uses two case studies to illustrate the complexity of interpretation and other relevant points. The author concludes that although disability was already present, the extent of impairment was greatly increased as a result of abuse.

1235. Sinason, V. (1990). Individual psychoanalytical psychotherapy with severely and profoundly handicapped patients. In A. Sossen, A. Van Gennep, & G. J. Zwanikken (Eds.), *Treatment of mental illness and behavioral disorder in the mentally retarded: Proceedings of the International Congress, May 3rd & 4th, 1990* (pp. 71–80). Leiden, the Netherlands: Logon Publications.

This paper illustrates the use of psychoanalytical psychotherapy with two clients with severe mental retardation. The first case example features a 25-year-old woman who was referred due to her violent behavior to herself and others. Her father had passed away 1 year earlier, 6 months prior to the onset of the violent behavior. It was established that this woman started hearing a voice in her head with the death of her father. While the voice was friendly at first, it eventually told her to hurt others because she would not be returning home to live with her mother now that the father had died. The second case example concerns a 24-year-old male who was referred for self-injurious behavior, public anal masturbation, and depression. He was raised by his father who had died 2 years previously. It was determined that this man had been abused sexually by his father and by a staff member in a short-stay hospital unit. This paper includes several psychoanalytic psychotherapy findings from work with people with severe developmental disabilities.

1236. Sinason, V. (1993). The special vulnerability of the handicapped child and adult: With special reference to mental handicap. *Bailliere's Clinical Paediatrics,* 1(1), 69–86.

This article provides an overview of issues related to the increased vulnerability to abuse of people with disabilities. The author discusses estimates of increased risk and provides a description of the kinds of abuse often experienced by people with disabilities. She emphasizes the need for treatment and the typical lack of access to appropriate treatment for people with disabilities.

1237. Sinason, V. (1994). Working with sexually abused individuals who have a learning disability. In A. Craft (Ed.), *Practice issues in sexuality and learning disabilities* (pp. 156–175). London: Routledge.

This chapter provides clinical case study excerpts to illustrate how a psychoanalytic approach to counseling can be applied to people with learning disabilities who have been sexually abused. This chapter is based on the author's work at the Tavistock clinic and St. George's Hospital in London.

1238. Sinason, V., & Davies, R. (1994). What do staff do when a colleague is an alleged abuser. In S. Hollins (Ed.), *Proceedings: It did happen here: Sexual abuse and learning disability: Recognition and action* (pp. 47–48). London: St. George's Hospital Medical School, Division of the Psychiatry of Disability.

This chapter describes how staff react to allegations of sexual abuse that have been made against a colleague. It also provides advice on what staff should do when someone makes such allegations.

1239. Singer, L., Farkas, K., & Kliegman, R. (1992). Childhood medical and behavioral consequences of maternal cocaine use. *Journal of Pediatric Psychology, 17*(4), 389–406.

This review of the literature highlights the adverse effects of maternal cocaine use on the fetus. It describes the pharmacologic and medical effects of cocaine exposure in utero, and it discusses neurologic impairment (in terms of behavior and cognition) during childhood that can result from in utero exposure to cocaine. The article examines mother-child interaction and includes suggestions for improved future research and intervention.

1240. Single, T., & Henry, R. L. (1991). An unusual case of Munchausen syndrome by proxy. *Australian and New Zealand Journal of Psychiatry, 25*, 422–425.

This article discusses an unusual case of Munchausen syndrome by proxy involving a 11-year-old boy who was given a false history of cystic fibrosis. This article states that the fabricated medical history and symptoms were directly caused by the boy's father. It suggests that the father used the child to meet his financial and litigational needs. The father had on numerous occasions registered complaints to the child protection agency against his second and third wives for the abuse of his son from his first marriage.

1241. Siskind, A. B. (1986). Issues in institutional child sexual abuse: The abused, the abuser, and the system. *Residential Treatment for Children and Youth, 4*(2), 9–30.

This article reviews sexual abuse in residential institutions for children. It describes profiles of the abuser and the victim, and it suggests that the abuser and the victim must be understood outside of the residential institute before they can be understood within it. This article also discusses recommendations for treatment and prevention.

1242. Skuse, D. H. (1989). Emotional abuse and neglect. *British Medical Journal, 298*, 1692–1694.

This article defines the characteristics of emotional abuse and neglect. Consequential developmental and social and emotional delays are discussed in relation to the stages of development, from infancy through to school-age children. Key physical, developmental, and behavioral features are presented for each developmental stage.

1243. Sluyter, G. V., & Cleland, C. C. (1979). Resident abuse: A continuing dilemma. *American Corrective Therapy Journal, 33*(4), 99–102.

The authors of this article propose a system for dealing with physical abuse in residential settings. They feel that a standardized process for investigating reports of abuse must be developed, and they present a decision paradigm for administrators to use in determining what action should be taken: The decision paradigm takes into account whether there are demonstrable injuries or not, whether the client can or cannot testify on his or her own behalf, whether witnesses (if any) are reliable, and whether the suspect admits or denies guilt. The recommended action for the given circumstances is included in this article. The authors discuss some prevention measures: clients could be physically examined on admission so that any scars or lesions could be evaluated, new employees should be informed of the unacceptability of abuse and the consequences to be expected if it occurs, and keeping routine records of accidental injuries before an abuse situation arises may provide clues as to the perpetrator by checking frequency of injuries across dormitories and shifts when a complaint is registered.

1244. Smith, C., Algozzine, B., Schmid, R., & Hennly, T. (1990). Prison adjustment of youthful inmates with mental retardation. *Mental Retardation, 28*(3), 177–181.

This article examines the prison adjustment of young inmates with mental retardation and young inmates without mental retardation. It compares various infractions committed across the two groups as a measure of their adjustment. It indicates that the two groups of inmates do not adjust to prison life in the same way: For example, inmates with mental retardation generally had greater difficulty adapting to prison. This article also points out that behavioral measures were significantly different across the two groups.

1245. Smith, J. A. S., & Adler, R. G. (1991). Children hospitalized with child abuse and neglect: A case-control study. *Child Abuse & Neglect, 15*, 437–445.

This article discusses a study that reassessed risk factors involved in child abuse after minimizing the effect of social class. In this study, 45 hospitalized abused children were matched with controls. The results reveal that abused children were more likely to have younger parent households, fewer siblings, and a prior history of separation from their mothers within the first year of infancy. Parental history of abuse, dysfunctional relationship between the parents, and more stressful life events 1 year prior to assessment were also more common among abused children.

1246. Smith, J. D., & Polloway, E. A. (1993). Institutionalization, involuntary sterilization, and mental retardation: Profiles from the history of the practice. *Mental Retardation, 31*(4), 208–214.
For much of the 20th century, the practice of sterilization was a common accompaniment to institutionalization for individuals with mental retardation. Following the Supreme Court's decision in *Buck v. Bell* (1927) supporting the practice, numerous states passed legislation legalizing sterilization for institutionalized individuals, and consequently, over 60,000 individuals with mental retardation were sterilized in the United States. This article discusses a study that analyzed the data on 212 individuals in Virginia discharged between 1969 and 1989 who were sterilized. The focus of this study included gender, age at the date of sterilization, level of mental retardation, and the location of the individual's discharge. This article discusses the nature of these findings within the general context of the practice of sterilization.

1247. Smith, J. T., & Bisbing, S. B. (1988). *Sexual exploitation by health care and other professionals* **(2nd ed.). Potomac, MD: Legal Medicine Press.**
This monograph provides considerable information regarding the legal aspects of sexual exploitation by physicians, psychiatrists, psychologists, and a number of other professionals. It explores the issues of abuse of power and violation of trust, and it provides abstracts of many civil and criminal cases. Many of the cases involve patients with minor or major psychiatric diagnoses, and some had other types of disabilities. Most cases cited involve victims who were women, but some victims were male, and some were children. An interesting issue running through many of the court cases is the responsibility of hospitals and other institutions. The argument has frequently been made and sometimes been accepted that institutions do not carry responsibility for their employees since sexual misconduct is outside the scope of their practice.

1248. Smith, S. M. (1983). 134 battered children: A medical and psychological study. In R. J. Gelles & C. P. Cornell (Eds.), *International perspectives on family violence* **(pp. 83–96). Lexington, MA: D. C. Heath.**
This chapter discusses a study that examine the battering of 134 Canadian children. Fifty-three children admitted to emergency care with injuries not due to accident or trauma served as a control group. The results of this

study indicate the following: Battered children were younger than children in the control group and tended to have multiple injuries in various stages of healing; over one third of the battered children had intracranial hemorrhage due to violent whiplash shaking; and in general, battering was often found to result in permanent neurologic damage.

1249. Snart, F., & Maguire, T. (1986). Using puppets to increase children's knowledge and acceptance of handicapped peers. *Canadian Journal for Exceptional Children, 3*(2), 57–59.
This article examines the effectiveness of a puppet theater performance in educating children in grades 2 to 4 about children with disabilities. Skits (designed to help children without disabilities develop positive attitudes toward children with disabilities) were performed by the Kids on the Block puppet theater. Preassessment and postassessment questionnaires concerning heightened awareness and attitudinal change were handed out to 136 third graders who had watched the performance. This article discusses the methods used to assess these children's attitudes and examines the results of these assessments.

1250. Snipers gun down patients at Bosnian mental hospital: Canadians hear reports of chlorine gas being used in fighting. (1993, November 13). *The Edmonton Journal,* **p. A5.**
This newspaper article describes how patients from a mental hospital were gunned down by snipers in Bosnia-Herzegovina. Canadian peacekeepers are guarding two hospitals in the towns of Fojnica and Bakovici, which house several hundred patients with developmental disabilities. The hospital employees are escorted home at night, leaving the patients unattended. As a result of no supervision, several patients have been killed by snipers because they wandered outside at night.

1251. Sobsey, D. (1988). Research on sexual abuse: Are we asking the right questions? *Newsletter of the American Association on Mental Retardation, 1*(4), 2–3.
This article discusses some of the problems facing researchers of sexual abuse of victims with disabilities and attempts to establish a research agenda. It suggests that research should move away from questions of incidence and prevalence of abuse in special populations since adequate, although not very precise answers are currently available. It suggests that researchers move to more applied problems of prevention of sexual abuse and treatment of survivors.

1252. Sobsey, D. (1988). Sexual offenses and disabled victims: Research and implications. *Vis-a-Vis: A national newsletter on family violence, 6*(4), 2–3.
This article reports the results of a study that indicates that people with a wide range of disabilities are more

likely to experience sexual abuse or assault, are less likely to find appropriate treatment, and are less likely to see the offender convicted. The perceived vulnerability of people with disabilities is viewed as an important factor in increasing the risk for sexual abuse. Exposure to a large number of caregivers and isolated programs are also viewed as contributing factors. (This article is also available in French.)

1253. Sobsey, D. (1988). Sexual victimization of people with disabilities: Professional & social responsibilities. *Alberta Psychology, 17*(6), 8–9.
This article discusses the psychologist's role in preventing, identifying, and treating sexual abuse and sexual assault of victims with disabilities. It emphasizes current service inadequacies and makes suggestions for improving future services.

1254. Sobsey, D. (1990). Modifying the behaviour of behaviour modifiers: Arguments for counter-control against aversive procedures. In A. C. Repp & N. N. Singh (Eds.), *Perspectives on the use of nonaversive and aversive interventions for persons with developmental disabilities* (pp. 421–433). Sycamore, IL: Sycamore Publications.
This chapter examines B. F. Skinner's six criteria for the acceptable use of aversive techniques in behavior modification and argues against the use of aversive techniques with people who have developmental disabilities.

1255. Sobsey, D. (1990). Too much stress on stress? Abuse & the family stress factor. *Quarterly Newsletter of the American Association on Mental Retardation, 3*(1), 2, 8.
This article reviews research on the three-stage model of disability that claims disability creates family stress and family stress leads to abuse of the family member with disabilities. Several studies are cited that suggest that this model is incorrect or at least overemphasized in explaining abuse of people with disabilities.

1256. Sobsey, D. (1992). The research that shattered the myths: Understanding the incidence and nature of abuse and abusers. In *Crossing new borders* (pp. 3–7). Kingston, NY: National Association for the Dually Diagnosed.
This article presents 14 myths related to abuse of people with disabilities and provides evidence to contradict them: for example, people with disabilities provoke their own abuse, people with disabilities are eternal children, inappropriate behavior and psychological disturbances are direct outcomes of developmental disabilities, families of children with disabilities must assume the roles of paraprofessionals, and people with disabilities must be protected from society.

1257. Sobsey, D. (1992). What we know about abuse and disabilities. *NRCCSA (National Resource Center on Child Sexual Abuse) News, 1*(4), 4, 10.
This article discusses contemporary research in the area of abuse and disabilities. While some questions have been answered, more answers still need to be sought in such areas as risk for abuse for people with disabilities, reasons why children with disabilities are abused, the role of stress in abuse, and what types of prevention and treatment services are required to help individuals and families at risk.

1258. Sobsey, D. (1993). Disability, discrimination and the law. *Health Law Review, 2*(1), 6–10.
This article presents some general definitions of impairment, disability, and handicap, and it examines some of the legal issues faced by people with disabilities: reasonable accommodation, medical discrimination, access to education, right to refuse treatment, offenders with disabilities, agency responsibility, and equal protection of the law. The article also discusses Bill 218—the Vulnerable Persons Protection Act that was introduced in the Alberta Legislature in 1992. Bill 218 recommends the following: Individuals employed in the service system should be required to report abuses of people with disabilities, agencies serving this population should have policies in place for handling cases of abuse, those individuals who come forward with allegations of abuse should be protected from punishment, and new employees must be screened before working with people with disabilities.

1259. Sobsey, D. (1994). An integrated ecological model of violence against people with disabilities. In S. Hollins (Ed.), *Proceedings: It did happen here: Sexual abuse and learning disability: Recognition and action* (pp. 3–24). London: St. George's Hospital Medical School, Division of the Psychiatry of Disability.
This chapter describes the integrated ecological model of violence against people with disabilities. The author describes a number of factors that are affected by disability: counter-control, learned helplessness, attachment disruptions, appraisal of circumstances, social isolation, environmental differences, social learning, stress, depersonalization, and cultural attitudes. The author suggests that these factors associated with disability make people vulnerable to violence.

1260. Sobsey, D. (1994). Sexual abuse of individuals with intellectual disability. In A. Craft (Ed.), *Practice issues in sexuality and learning disabilities* (pp. 93–115). London: Routledge.
This chapter presents data on patterns of sexual abuse of 107 people with mental retardation. These data suggest that abuse tended to be chronic and severe, that signs of

emotional trauma were apparent in virtually all the victims, that convictions of perpetrators were infrequent, and that treatment services were often inaccessible or inappropriate.

1261. Sobsey, D. (1994). *Violence and abuse in the lives of people with disabilities: The end of silent acceptance?* **Baltimore: Paul H. Brookes Publishing Co.**
This book provides an extensive overview of the research and issues related to violence and disability. The first half of the book presents an overview of research to date and a review of historical examples of violence and abuse. The second half of the book presents prevention and intervention strategies based on an integrated ecological model of abuse. This model emphasizes environmental factors that connect disability with violence. There are 13 chapters in this book: 1) "Perspectives on the issue of abuse," 2) "Abuse, violence, and disability," 3) "Sexual abuse and sexual assault," 4) "Institutional abuse," 5) "For their own good...Caregiving or abuse?," 6) "An integrated ecological model of abuse," 7) "Empowering individuals to resist abuse," 8) "Families and other caregivers: Support and selection," 9) "Building safer environments," 10) "Law and law enforcement," 11) "Changing attitudes that disinhibit violence," 12) "Healing the consequences of abuse," and 13) "Prevention and intervention teams." This book is fully indexed and includes over 670 references.

1262. Sobsey, D., & Doe, T. (1991). Patterns of sexual abuse and assault. *Sexuality and Disability,* **9**(3), 243–259.
This article describes the patterns in the sexual abuse or assault of people with disabilities. The data for these trends were collected from 162 reports of victimization involving people with disabilities. It discusses frequent trends in the sexual abuse or assault of people with disabilities: repeated chronic victimization, significant injury suffered by the victim, and infrequent reporting of the crime to authorities. This article states the following: Perpetrators are most frequently paid service providers, with abuses occurring most often in service settings; perpetrators are most frequently male, with victims being predominantly female; charges against offenders are as rare as convictions; and it is difficult to obtain treatment services for victims with disabilities. The authors discuss an ecological model of abuse and suggest prevention strategies.

1263. Sobsey, D., Gray, S., Wells, D., Pyper, D., & Reimer-Heck, B. (1991). *Disability, sexuality, and abuse: An annotated bibliography.* **Baltimore: Paul H. Brookes Publishing Co.**
This annotated bibliography is a collection of books, articles, reports, and other forms of written text that address the issues of sexual abuse and the exploitation of people with disabilities. The annotated bibliography contains 1,123 annotations. Various disciplines are represented, including: psychology, medicine, special education, rehabilitation medicine, and law. It includes an introduction by Dick Sobsey that discusses research and clinical issues and a foreword by Sandra Cole that describes the development of research on sexual abuse and disability. One hundred ninety-eight of the entries are included in this current bibliography.

1264. Sobsey, D., & Mansell, S. (1990). The prevention of sexual abuse of people with developmental disabilities. *Developmental Disabilities Bulletin,* **18**(2), 51–66.
Existing and alternative sexual abuse prevention strategies for people with developmental disabilities are examined in this article. While acknowledging the importance of training programs for reducing risks of abuse, the authors recognize the potentially adverse effects of such programs; ironically, in placing the responsibility for prevention on potential victims rather than offenders, there may be a tendency to blame the victim and, thus, perpetuate the failure to address the underlying causes of abuse. The need for effective education of individuals with disabilities and their caregivers is discussed in terms of appropriate and comprehensive sexuality education as well as individual rights and assertiveness training, choice making, and communication skills training. Given the incidence of abuse within the human services delivery system, this article emphasizes the importance of administrative reform in facilitating prevention of systemic abuse. It discusses several key areas, including staff screening and agency responsibility for those they purport to serve. The reduction of isolation of individuals through integration into community settings and the responsible and thoughtful use of drug therapy and behavior management programs are also examined in terms of preventing abuse. The detection, reporting, prosecution, and treatment of sexual abuse are regarded as critical components of prevention programs for reducing the future incidence of abuse and for developing greater public and professional awareness of the issues. The power of attitudes and the changing of attitudes are discussed in relation to cultural myths regarding people with disabilities and their sexual abuse. Changing dehumanizing attitudes is advocated as an essential step toward the empowerment of people with disabilities, which in turn reduces the risk of individual abuse.

1265. Sobsey, D., & Mansell, S. (1992). Teaching people with disabilities to be abused and exploited. Part I. Blaming the victims for their abuse. *Active Treatment Solutions,* **3**(4), 1, 7–11.
This article examines abuse and people with disabilities. It states that a variety of explanations have been put forth to explain why people with disabilities have been found to be at heightened risk for abuse: For example, the dependency-stress hypothesis suggests that children with disabilities are more dependent on their caregivers, causing increased stress for parents who are unable to cope, which may result in abusive behavior. The authors

point to the inadequacies of this hypothesis and how it contributes to victim blaming. They claim that the relationship between parental stress and the abuse of children with disabilities has not been supported by research, and they believe that the view that children with disabilities are the cause of stress and abuse is discriminatory. An alternative ecological model is presented to explain abuse and disability. This model is adapted from previous models on child abuse and focuses on specific factors that directly influence abuse at the level of the relationship between abuser and victim, the level of social unit, and/or the level of culture. The key aspect of this model concerns the power inequity between abuser and victim.

1266. Sobsey, D., & Mansell, S. (1994). Sexual abuse patterns of children with disabilities. *International Journal of Children's Rights,* **2, 96–100.**
This article reports on the results of an analysis of 130 cases of sexual abuse of children with disabilities. Most of the victims (71%) were female, and most of them (55.8%) experienced chronic abuse. Only 18.3% of these children experienced abuse on only one occasion. Younger children (birth to 12) were more likely to be abused by family members, and older children were more likely to be abused by peers with disabilities. Abuse by paid service providers was frequent in all age categories.

1267. Sobsey, D., Mansell, S., & Wells, D. (1991). *Sexual abuse of children with disabilities and sexual assault of adults with disabilities: Prevention strategies.* **Edmonton: University of Alberta, Sexual Abuse and Disability Project.**
This report documents the work of the University of Alberta Sexual Abuse and Disability Project during 1990 and 1991 and its emphasis on the prevention and treatment of sexual offenses against children and adults with disabilities. Building on the findings of a previous project, in which the nature and extent of sexual offenses against people with disabilities were examined, this project provides guidelines for the prevention of such acts and the subsequent treatment of victims. A validation study was conducted in which 112 experts in the fields of sexual abuse and/or disability responded to a survey detailing prevention and treatment strategies considered useful in working with victims of sexual abuse who have developmental disabilities. The respondents were asked to rank items within 47 cluster categories in terms of their perceived importance within each cluster. The results of the statistical significance of rankings of specific clusters are provided; in general, most rankings indicate consistent priorities among the respondents and, as a result, provide formal validation for the prevention and treatment components specified in the study. These findings are discussed in terms of their application in the development of appropriate and effective prevention and treatment services at individual, agency, and community levels. The authors emphasize the need for significant reform and

change in a number of areas (e.g., legal processes and social/cultural attitudes) for empowering and valuing people with disabilities. The limitations of the study are noted (e.g., the strategies discussed have yet to be implemented and evaluated); however, the social validation represents a significant step in determining directions for future research in this area. Samples of the victims' survey and validation survey forms are included in the appendices, as is a list of the consultants who responded to the survey. Also, this report includes a French language annotated bibliography of literature related to disability, sexuality, and abuse.

1268. Sobsey, D., & Varnhagen, C. (1988). *Sexual abuse, assault, and exploitation of people with disabilities.* **Ottawa, ON: Health and Welfare Canada.**
This document contains a 13-page report and an annotated bibliography. This report of a study, commissioned by National Health Research and Development Program, includes a literature review, a survey of agencies serving Canadian survivors of sexual abuse and assault, and a survey of Canadian victims of sexual assault or abuse who are disabled. The authors conclude that people with a wide range of disabilities are at increased risk for sexual assault and sexual abuse and that current prevention and treatment programs do not respond adequately to the needs of people with disabilities.

1269. Sobsey, D., & Varnhagen, C. (1989). Sexual abuse of people with disabilities. In M. Csapo & L. Gougen (Eds.), *Special education across Canada: Challenges for the 90's* **(pp. 199–218). Vancouver, BC: Centre for Human Development & Research.**
This chapter reports and analyzes some data from a Canadian study on the sexual abuse and assault of people with disabilities. It goes beyond the data to discuss possible factors that result in the high rate of assault and abuse in special populations and suggests steps to reduce risks and provide more appropriate services for victims.

1270. Sobsey, D., & Varnhagen, C. (1991). Sexual abuse, assault, and exploitation of Canadians with disabilities. In C. Bagley (Ed.), *Preventing child sexual abuse* **(pp. 203–216). Toronto: Wall and Emerson.**
This chapter presents the results of an analysis of Canadian cases of sexual abuse of people with disabilities and makes recommendations for prevention, detection, and treatment.

1271. Sobsey, D., Wells, D., & Gray, S. (1989). *Sexual assault and abuse of people with disabilities: Networking directory.* **Edmonton: University of Alberta, Department of Educational Psychology, Severe Disabilities Program.**

This directory includes information about more than 100 people and organizations concerned about prevention and treatment of sexual abuse of people with disabilities. In addition to names, addresses, and phone numbers, the directory includes information on services provided and specific interest areas. Entries are listed alphabetically by name, with an interest area index and a professional discipline index to help readers locate information. Many of the entries are from Alberta, but some entries are included from across Canada and the United States.

1272. Socall, D. W., & Holtgraves, T. (1992). Attitudes toward the mentally ill: The effects of label and beliefs. *The Sociological Quarterly, 33*(3), 435–445.

This article describes a study that was conducted to determine if subjects would respond in the same manner to people labeled mentally ill as they would to people who were labeled physically ill and exhibited the same physical behaviors. The data for this study were obtained from 206 mailed questionnaires, which consisted of case vignettes describing a person with either a mental or physical disorder and with disorders ranging from low to moderate to high in severity. The participants were asked to respond to six social distance questions by rating them on a scale from 1 (extremely unwilling) to 7 (extremely willing). In addition, participants were questioned regarding their beliefs about the target's perceived dangerousness, violent tendencies, criminal tendencies, and emotional stability. As well, illness prognosis was examined in relation to the target's probability of becoming a welfare recipient, being a failure, not recovering, or being unemployed. The results of this study indicate that people who are mentally ill were rejected more often than people who were physically ill and displayed identical behavior to those people with mental illness and that people who are mentally ill were thought to be less predictable and thought to have poorer positive outcomes.

1273. Söder, M. (1990). Prejudice or ambivalence? Attitudes toward people with disabilities. *Disability, Handicap & Society, 5*, 227–241.

This article describes ambivalence rather than prejudice as the predominant social response to disability. Ambivalence theory suggests that society has both positive and negative attitudes toward disability and that social context determines whether positive or negative attitudes predominate. Söder suggests that positive attitudes are a result of the individual's identification with people with disabilities through the understanding that he or she could acquire a disability at any time. He suggests that negative attitudes are a result of the individual's fear of disability and rejection of the notion of personal vulnerability. These conflicting attitudes about disability are believed to result in positive attitudes toward individuals with disabilities under most circumstances but sudden shifts to negative attitudes when stress or threat becomes part of the context for interaction.

1274. Soeffing, M. (1975). Abused children are exceptional children. *Exceptional Children, 42*, 126–133.

Research in the area of abused children and disabilities is reviewed in this article. Several studies found that many abused children do have intellectual or physical disabilities. Research on disabilities as a result of abuse has reported a high incidence of mental, emotional, and physical disabilities. Implications for educators are discussed in terms of signs of abuse and school policy on reporting. Also, this article provides a summary of federal programs in the United States.

1275. Sohn, H. A. (1983, October). *Child abuse prevention and the mentally handicapped.* **Paper presented at a conference on "The Mentally Handicapped Parent," Chatham, ON.**

This paper addresses the question of whether children of parents with mental retardation are at greater risk for abuse. It cites literature reviews by other authors. The overall conclusion is that people with mental disabilities make unacceptable parents; however, the research reviewed is considered to be methodologically weak. The author concludes that more research is necessary since there is sufficient reason to be concerned about the relationship between child abuse and mental disabilities.

1276. Solnit, A. J. (1984). Theoretical and practical aspects of risks and vulnerabilities in infancy. *Child Abuse & Neglect, 8*, 133–144.

This article focuses on the parent-child relationship, especially the vulnerabilities and at-risk conditions that might influence the healthy development of a child. Vulnerabilities in the child are defined as weaknesses of the child, while at-risk conditions refer to environmental factors that interact with the child. The author recommends professional intervention, which would strengthen the parent-child bond and minimize the development of a high-risk environment and promote healthy development in the child. Some hypothetical and clinical cases are included to help illustrate some of the theoretical and practical aspects of the topics discussed in this article.

1277. Solomons, G. (1978). Developmental disabilities and child abuse. *Medical Newsletter, 30*(3), 12–17.

This article uses incidence studies to alert physicians to issues concerning abuse of children with developmental disabilities. It claims that low birth weight infants and children with disabilities are particularly vulnerable to abuse. It signals the high vulnerability of the infantile head, brain, and eyes and cites the following finding by Nelson and Ellenberg (1976) (Predictors of epilepsy in children who have experienced febrile seizures. *New England Journal of Medicine, 295*[19], 1029–1033): In a sample of 38,533 children with cerebral palsy, intracranial infection and head injury were the most common causes of acquired motor disability. This article also discusses the following: heavy parenting duties; parental guilt, anger, and denial; and parents' negative self-image. It includes recommendations to assist the physician in the detection of the potential for abuse in caregivers, including parents and professionals.

1278. Solomons, G. (1979). Child abuse and developmental disabilities. *Developmental Medicine and Child Neurology, 21*(1), 101–108.
This article reviews literature in the area of child abuse and developmental disabilities. This review reveals that disabilities both contribute to and result from abuse. As a member of the medical profession, the author stresses the importance of recognizing abuse in patients and offering assistance to families when abuse is discovered.

1279. Solomons, G., Abel, C. M., & Epley, S. A. (1981). Community development approach to the prevention of institutional and societal child maltreatment. *Child Abuse and Neglect, 5*(2), 135–140.
This article describes a community-institutional development (CID) system aimed at primary prevention of child maltreatment in institutions. The system emphasizes collaboration between the institution and the community. The CID team includes 20 to 30 people, half of whom are lay volunteers, and half of whom represent various disciplines related to the rights and care of residents in institutions. The team works with the institution to improve child treatment and performs periodic reviews assessing conditions contributing to institutional and societal maltreatment.

1280. Somander, L. K. H., & Rammer, L. M. (1991). Intra- and extrafamilial child homicide in Sweden 1971–1980. *Child Abuse & Neglect, 15*, 45–55.
This article discusses a study that examined the extent of intrafamilial and extrafamilial child homicide in Sweden over a 10-year period. In total, 79 cases involving 96 children under the age of 15 were recorded for this time period. This study found that intrafamilial homicide was characterized by homicide-suicide cases (*n*=58) and nonsuicide cases (*n*=26). It found that extrafamilial homicide (*n*=12) was characterized by its sexual abuse motive, male perpetrators, and school-age victims. This study also found that strangulation, shooting, and stabbing were the most common forms of violence. This article notes that 37 of the 47 perpetrators psychologically examined after the fact were found to be mentally ill.

1281. Sorenson, S. B., & Siegel, J. M. (1992). Gender, ethnicity, and sexual assault: Findings from a Los Angeles study. *Journal of Social Issues, 48*(1), 93–104.
This article describes a study that investigated the influence of gender and ethnicity (the participants in this study were Latinos and nonLatino Whites) on the chances of being sexually assaulted, the circumstances involved in a sexual assault, and its consequences. This study used a sample of 3,000 adults living in the community. This study found that Latinos and men had significantly lower rates of sexual assault than nonLatino Whites and women, but once assaulted, this study found that neither ethnicity nor gender was related to the chance of another assault. This study also found that people who were sexually assaulted were more likely than people who were not assaulted to have a mental disorder; however, it appears that this association is not affected by gender or ethnicity. Also, this study found that women were more likely than men to have specific emotional and behavioral problems associated with sexual assault and that, regardless of gender or ethnicity, sexual assault appears to be associated with an increased use of mental health and general health services.

1282. Southall, D. P., Stebbens, V. A., Rees, S. V., Lang, M. H., Warner, J. O., & Shinebourne, E. A. (1987). Apnoeic episodes induced by smothering: Two cases identified by covert video surveillance. *British Medical Journal, 294*, 1637–1641.
This article describes two case histories where covert video surveillance was used to reveal the asphyxiation of two infants by their mothers in a hospital setting. The first case involves a 22-month-old boy and his 22-year-old mother. The boy's recurrent cyanotic episodes began at 4 months of age. The boy's two older siblings had also been abused. The second case involves a 6-month-old girl with recurrent cyanotic episodes that began at age 3 weeks. Her mother was 22 years old and had another child who, at age 2, suffered burns to her body and upper extremity due to hot coffee. In both cases, the act of smothering was captured by hidden video surveillance. This article notes that both mothers were abused by their fathers during their teenage years and were very cooperative and unusually calm in the hospital setting.

1283. Souther, M. D. (1984). Developmentally disabled, abused and neglected children. In Department of Health and Human Services (Ed.), *Perspectives on child maltreatment in the mid 80's* (pp. 33–35). Washington, DC: Human Development Services.
This chapter points out that abused and neglected children are frequently at risk for developmental disabilities. It states that studies show that children who have been abused and neglected can become disabled because of their maltreatment.

1284. Spackman, R., Grigel, M., & MacFarlane, C. (1990). Individual counselling and therapy for the mentally handicapped. *Alberta Psychology, 19*(5), 14–18.
This review of the literature dispels the myth that counseling and psychotherapy are not appropriate ap-

proaches for clients with developmental disabilities. The authors point out that communication difficulties between client and therapist are often the greatest stumbling blocks to overcome in therapy, but they suggest that a variety of approaches can be used in therapy to assist people with developmental disabilities once the client and therapist have established communication. The authors provide examples of therapeutic approaches found in the literature, and they discuss some areas to consider when counseling clients with developmental disabilities: the need for trained counselors/therapists, ethical considerations, and the use of community-based services.

1285. Sparr, M. P., & Smith, W. (1990). Regulating professional services in ICFs/MR: Remembering the past and looking to the future. *Mental Retardation, 28*(2), 95–99.
The authors of this article review the history of regulations for intermediate care facilities for people with mental retardation. They suggest that the self-monitored quality assurance system was the product of both a resistance to change and a failure of the professional community to achieve excellence in its own area. This article concludes that this system set the stage for litigation and legislation and, ultimately, government intervention.

1286. Spector, S. (1990). Gas chambers. In I. Gutman (Ed.), *Encyclopedia of the Holocaust* **(Vol. 2, E–K, pp. 539–544). New York: Macmillan.**
This article traces the development and use of the gas chamber by the Nazis. The gas chamber was first used in December 1939 to kill Polish mental patients. In January 1941, Victor Brack, the head of the euthanasia program, adopted it for use at several "T4" institutions. These institutions also developed the practice of disguising the gas chambers as shower rooms.

1287. Speight, N. (1989). Non-accidental injury. *British Medical Journal, 298,* **879–881.**
Nonaccidental injury is discussed in this article. Characteristic features of physical abuse are detailed with the use of case studies and photographs. The article includes a profile of the roles of medical professionals involved when child abuse is suspected.

1288. Spragg, P. A. (1983, October 5–8). *Counseling approaches with retarded persons: Current status and an attempt at integration.* **Paper presented at the Region IV Conference of the American Association on Mental Deficiency, Snowmass, CO.**
This literature review examines counseling people with mental retardation. It identifies promising trends, proposes a counseling model, and discusses three areas that

appear necessary for counseling this population: counseling must meet measurable objectives, it must be cost effective, and it is important to have an integrated model. The author offers a definition of counseling that focuses on behavior change and reviews the literature dealing with the following approaches to counseling people with mental retardation: psychodynamic, behavior therapy, and nondirective and directive group counseling. According to the author, the conclusions of the research in this area are suspect because most of this research suffers from poor designs and/or methods. The author discusses current treatment trends for people with mental retardation: social skills training, social skills counseling models, self-management training, and emotional training. The author concludes that a useful counseling model includes the following: internal validity; consideration of the specific learning characteristics of the client with mental retardation; the use of techniques that have been validated in both the experimental and applied literature; the use of techniques that address cognitive, behavioral, and affective areas; and cost effectiveness.

1289. Spragg, P. A. (1984, May 27–31). *Counseling the mentally retarded: A psychoeducational perspective.* **Paper presented at the 108th Annual Meeting of the American Association on Mental Deficiency, Minneapolis, MN.**
This paper suggests that a psychoeducational or cognitive perspective can be valuable in counseling people who have mental retardation: for example, pretreatment assessments that emphasize process rather than product. It discusses the cognitive foundations of therapeutic communication and examines attention, memory and recall, and input organization. It describes aspects of the learning perspective: the influence of client expectations and motivation, the factors that influence the acquisition of behavior, and meta-cognitive treatment strategies. This paper also discusses the problems associated with measuring counseling outcomes with people who have mental retardation, and it examines the value of objectively rated criterion-referenced tests based on behaviorally anchored constructs most applicable to people who have mental retardation.

1290. Staff report on the institutionalized mentally disabled and a response from the Justice Department. (1985). *Mental and Physical Disability Law Reporter, 9*(2), 154–157.
This article describes selected parts of a report covering conditions in mental institutions, a review of the Justice Department's enforcement of the Civil Rights of Institutionalized Persons Act, and a response from former Assistant Attorney General W. B. Reynolds. The staff contends that abuse and neglect exist and that care and treatment must be provided in an atmosphere of dignity and respect and that the Justice Department activities suggest that the department is engaged in a concerted attempt to narrow the rights of the institutionalized people with mental disabilities. In spite of these conten-

tions, Reynolds states that the department is proud of its record of enforcement.

1291. Stahlecker, J. E., & Cohen, M. C. (1985). Application of the strange situation attachment paradigm to a neurologically impaired population [Special issue: Family development]. *Child Development, 56*(2), 502–507.

In this article, the authors examine attachment between 24 mothers and their infants between the ages of 12 and 26 months using the Ainsworth et al. (Ainsworth, M., Blehar, M., Waters, E., & Wall, S. [1978]. *Patterns of attachment: A psychological study of the strange situation*. Hillsdale, NJ: Lawrence Erlbaum Associates) Strange Situation procedure. The infants in this study were neurologically impaired or exhibited motor impairment or delay. The Bayley Scales of Infant Development was administered to assess the child's degree of impairment relative to children without disabilities. The Carolina Record of Individual Behavior (CRIB), the Rhythmic Habit Pattern, and the Social Responsiveness sections were used to assess atypical behavior patterns often associated with infants with disabilities. Five of the 24 infants could not be classified (e.g., exhibited uninterpretable differentiation of mother from stranger and little or no movement toward mother or stranger); seven infants were classifiable but lacked gross locomotion; and 12 infants were fully classifiable. When comparing general development, nonclassified infants were characterized as being the most impaired, and locomotive classifiable infants were the least impaired; however, this study found that the degree of motor or mental impairment was not significantly related to the quality of attachment between mother and child and that infants who rated higher on the social responsiveness measure were more likely to possess secure attachments than those receiving lower ratings. The authors suggest that the strange situation paradigm, with minor adaptions, may be useful in assessing attachment behaviors in children with physical disabilities and their parents, and they offer several avenues for further investigations.

1292. Stark, E., Flitcraft, A., & Frazier, W. (1979). Medicine and patriarchal violence: The social construction of a "private" event. *International Journal of Health Services, 9*(3), 461–493.

The contribution of medicine and social constructs to the incidence of wife battery is discussed in this article. It suggests, after the analysis of 481 women who were seen in emergency rooms, that there is an established pattern of events prior to the battery. It claims that medicine and its mechanized pattern of responses maintains the silence of battery and implies self-victimization on the woman's part, which can result in continued abuse. Patriarchal authority and the role it plays in medicine are also examined in this article.

1293. Starr, E. (1994). Facilitated communication: A response by child protection. *Child Abuse & Neglect, 18*(6), 515–527.

This article reviews the literature on facilitated communication (FC) and people with autism and provides a commentary on Heckler's (1994) case study. While the author points to some anecdotal and phenomenological support for the value of FC, she also stresses the dismal results of more objective, empirical studies. She analyzes the case study provided by Heckler (1994) in the same issue and concludes that this provides little evidence to support FC. Starr stresses the importance of objective validation of FC in any case where FC disclosures are critical to confirming allegations of abuse.

1294. Starr, R. H., Jr. (1982). A research-based approach to the prediction of child abuse. In R. H. Starr, Jr. (Ed.), *Child abuse prediction: Policy implications* (pp. 105–134). Cambridge, MA: Ballinger.

This chapter describes a study that attempted to identify variables that distinguish child-abusing families (*n*=87) from nonabusing families (*n*=87). This study recruited abusive families from those families who had a child admitted to the emergency room at the Children's Hospital of Michigan in Detroit and had been reported for suspected or actual child abuse to the Michigan Department of Social Services. The children in this study were all 5 years of age or younger. This study assessed the children and their families using the following methods: observations, interviews, and psychometric evaluation. This study used the following instruments: the Lanyon's Psychological Screening Inventory, the Wechsler Adult Intelligence Scale, the Cohler's Maternal Attitude Scale, Caldwell's Home Observation for the Measurement of the Environment Scale, the Bayley Scales, the McCarthy Scales, and the Bayley Behavior Profile. In addition, this study obtained additional information using medical records and 5-point Likert-type scales. A factor analysis did not uncover any statistically significant interrelationships between the majority of variables that might distinguish abusing families from nonabusing families. The results of this study indicate that family isolation and neglect were two characteristics that distinguished abusing families from nonabusing families.

1295. Starr, R. H., Jr., Dietrich, K. N., Fischhoff, J., Ceresnie, S., & Zweier, D. (1984). The contribution of handicapping conditions to child abuse. *Topics in Early Childhood Special Education, 4*(1), 55–69.

This article reviews the literature dealing with the contribution of low birth weight, prenatal problems, congenital disorders, and mental retardation to child abuse. While existing transactional and ecological theories suggest such child factors should contribute to abuse, this review found that a careful analysis of studies indicates disabling conditions are not major causal factors. It points out that results of prospective, longitudinal research suggest that minor deviations in child behavior rather than major disabilities are related to the occurrence of abuse. This article concludes that efforts to help families adjust to having a child with disabilities, while helpful in alleviating the stresses in such families, will not have a major impact on the incidence of abuse.

1296. Starr, R. H., Jr., MacLean, D. J., & Keating, D. P. (1991). Life-span developmental outcomes of child maltreatment. In R. H. Starr, Jr. & D. A. Wolfe (Eds.), *The effects of child abuse and neglect* **(pp. 1–32). London: Guilford Press.**

This chapter examines the long-term chronic effects of child maltreatment and abuse, and it focuses on intergenerational continuation of maltreatment, delinquency resulting from a history of abuse, and exhibition of distinctive psychological abnormalities resulting from an abusive childhood. This chapter reviews the literature and suggests that the probability of intergenerational continuation of abuse is less than 30%. It points out that a history of physical abuse and future risk of delinquency are highly correlated, although the risk of future delinquency and other forms of maltreatment such as sexual abuse or neglect is less clear. It claims that psychological dysfunction resulting from abuse is particularly difficult to assess due to such confounding variables as family dysfunction, parenting problems, inadequate social support, substance abuse, and psychopathology. This chapter includes suggestions for future research.

1297. Stavis, P. F. (1991). Harmonizing the right to sexual expression and the right to protection from harm for persons with mental disability. *Sexuality and Disability,* **9(2), 131–141.**

This article discusses the sexual rights of people with mental disabilities and suggests that treatment professionals and caregivers should acknowledge the legal rights of such persons. It discusses the following topics: consent, criminal law, civil law, and constitutional law. This article integrates seemingly disparate legal principles by suggesting a method to apply them consistently to persons with mental disabilities.

1298. Steinbach, A. (1991). The closing of an institution: Life in the William F. Roberts. *Entourage,* **6(3), 10–11.**

This article describes the experiences of a self-advocate while residing in the William F. Roberts Hospital School in New Brunswick. It explores the institutional abuse suffered by this advocate and the accompanying feelings of despair and frustration.

1299. Steiner, J. (1984). Group counseling with retarded offenders. *Social Work,* **29(2), 181–85.**

This article discusses group therapy for offenders with mental retardation. The author states that offenders who have mental retardation have special problems and needs that are magnified when they first enter jail and are

awaiting trial. This article examines a program that identified offenders with mental retardation and assigned them to a special holding area. This program supplies supportive services to help these inmates understand the legal process. Also, this program uses a local mental health center in order to provide specialized therapeutic services. This mental health center conducts group counseling sessions at the jail and attempts to help these offenders cope with their new environment by teaching them to develop problem-solving skills and to constructively use their resources. Of the 175 inmates who participated in the program, 53% were sentenced to prison, 39% were either released on probation or acquitted, and 8% were sent to a mental health institution. Also, 14% of the inmates who received both group and individual services continued to use supportive services compared to the inmates (32%) who only received individual services. The author recommends further research on the use of group therapy programs for offenders with mental retardation.

1300. Stevenson, R. D., & Alexander, R. (1990). Munchausen syndrome by proxy presenting as a developmental disability. *Developmental and Behavioral Pediatrics,* **11(5), 262–264.**

In this article, a case history of Munchausen syndrome by proxy is presented involving an 11-month-old girl and her mother. Multiple developmental disabilities in the infant, involving cerebral palsy, gastrotomy dependence, and feeding problems, were claimed by the mother. The true diagnoses was made by a interdisciplinary team after evaluation. This case is noteworthy for its complex presentation of multiple disabilities. Two siblings of this infant were also victims of abuse.

1301. Stewart Helton, A., McFarlane, J., & Anderson, E. T. (1987). Battered and pregnant: A prevalence study. *American Journal of Public Health,* **77(10), 1337–1339.**

The authors of this article interviewed 290 pregnant women from prenatal clinics in a large metropolitan area and found that 24 (8%) reported being physically battered during their current pregnancy. Forty-four women (15%) reported being battered before their pregnancy. The subject group ranged in age from 18 to 43, and 43.1% of the women were Latino, 32.1% White, 22.4% African American, and 2.4% American Indian or Asian. This article notes that the most frequent sites of abuse were the face and head.

1302. Stimpson, L., & Best, M. C. (1991). *Courage above all: Sexual assault against women with disabilities.* **Toronto: DAWN (DisAbled Women's Network) Canada.**

This book details the results of a 1990 Ontario study that examined the sexual abuse of women with disabilities. Three hundred women with disabilities were mailed questionnaires in this study, and taped interviews were also conducted with those women who had experienced a sexual assault. This book offers recommendations for dealing with the sexual abuse of women with disabilities.

1303. Straus, M. A., & Gelles, R. J. (1986). Societal change and change in family violence from 1975 to 1985 as revealed by two national surveys. *Journal of Marriage and the Family, 48, 465–479.*
The authors of this article describe a study that compared the physical child abuse and spousal abuse rates from 1975 and 1985 using data from 2,143 families in 1975 and 3,520 families in 1985. The results from this study show that the rates of abuse were lower in 1985 than 1975, although the incidence of abuse was still extremely high. The authors discuss several possible explanations for this reduction, including: different procedural methods for obtaining data, reluctance to report incidents of abuse, reduction in family violence as a result of preventive educational efforts, and reduction as a result of changing family patterns regardless of educational efforts.

1304. Streissguth, A. P., Randels, S. P., & Smith, D. F. (1991). A test-retest study of intelligence in patients with fetal alcohol syndrome: Implications for care. *Journal of the American Academy of Child and Adolescent Psychiatry, 30(4), 584–587.*
This article describes a study that compared the childhood and adolescent IQ scores of 27 subjects diagnosed with fetal alcohol syndrome and 13 subjects with fetal alcohol effect. The average test-retest interval for these subjects was 8 years. The results of this study indicate that these children and adolescents had neurologic impairments.

1305. Streissguth, A. P., Sampson, P. D., & Barr, H. M. (1989). Neurobehavioral dose-response effects of prenatal alcohol exposure in humans from infancy to adulthood. *Annals of the New York Academy of Sciences, 562, 145–158.*
This article discusses the adverse chronic effects of prenatal alcohol exposure using two studies. The first clinical study involved 58 patients with fetal alcohol syndrome and 34 patients with fetal alcohol effect. Patients ranged in age from 12 to 42 years and were assessed on measures of intelligence, achievement, and behavior. The second study incorporated a longitudinal prospective design involving a cohort of 250 children born to mothers who were heavy drinkers and smokers and 250 children born to mothers who either abstained from alcohol or were infrequent drinkers. These children were assessed on days 1 and 2, at 8 and 18 months, and at 4 and 7 years of age. The results from these two studies indicate that chronic cognitive and neurologic problems result from prenatal alcohol exposure.

1306. Stromland, K. (1990). Contribution of ocular examination to the diagnosis of fetal alcohol syndrome in mentally retarded children. *Journal of Mental Deficiency Research, 34, 429–435.*
The author of this article discusses a study that used ocular examinations on a cohort group of 28 children with mild mental retardation in order to discover if it was possible to determine the presence of fetal alcohol syndrome (FAS). In five of the six suspected cases of FAS, the author was able to make a positive diagnosis. In addition, it was possible to make two other FAS diagnoses. In total, 16 of the children were observed to have some form of ocular abnormalities, with the majority involving the face, outer eye region, and strabismus.

1307. Stromsness, M. M. (1991). Characteristics associated with the sexual abuse of adults with mild mental retardation. *Dissertation Abstracts International, 52(6), 3311–B*
This abstract describes a study conducted to estimate the prevalence of sexual abuse among adults with mental retardation and to examine the characteristics and experiences of sexual abuse among people with mental retardation. There were 27 primarily White community residents in this study (14 women and 13 men), and the mean age of the participants was 35.3 years. Eighty-two percent of the respondents were employed, 78% had received sex education, and 67% reported being sexually abused. This study used the Socio-Sexual Knowledge and Attitude Test to assess the participant' sexual knowledge and to elicit their words for sexual terms. This study also employed a 55-item structured interview. The results of this study indicate the following: Of the sexual abuse victims, 72% had told someone; nearly two thirds of the incidents of sexual abuse involved sexual contact (defined as anal, oral, or vaginal intercourse; fondling; or forced masturbation); the majority of offenders were known to their victims; incest (defined as sexual abuse by a biological, adopted, step, or foster family member) accounted for 33% of the sexual abuse; victims of sexual abuse were more likely than nonvictims to be in significant relationships; sex education did not appear to prevent sexual abuse, but it did appear to increase the likelihood of reporting sexual abuse; and the majority of victims received no medical, psychological, or legal help. The author points out that this study uncovered a higher rate of abuse than similar studies, and she suggests that this might be the result of different definitions of sexual abuse and the age, sex, and level of retardation of study subjects. Although the author offers several suggestions for further research, she suggests that future efforts to study people with mental retardation need the support of state and local agencies in order to be successful.

1308. Stuart, C. (1986). Helping physically disabled victims of sexual assault. *Medical Aspects of Human Sexuality, 20(11), 101–102.*
This article explains the approach a physician should take when dealing with a victim with physical disabilities of sexual assault. It suggests that the physician must be

aware of the two myths about sexual assault of victims with disabilities: people with disabilities are immune to sexual assault and only woman are raped. It discusses four stages of recovery: 1) shock, 2) anger, 3) understanding and acceptance, and 4) integration into life experience. This article states that victims with physical disabilities may have more difficulty negotiating these stages than victims without disabilities. It points out that the physician's role is to provide for the physical and emotional needs of the victim and to gather medical evidence for possible prosecution of the perpetrator. This article emphasizes that it is important to remember that people with disabilities have an additional need, which is to be allowed to make decisions for themselves. In this case, the decision involves the crime itself and how the victim will deal with it.

1309. Stuart, C. K., & Stuart, V. W. (1981). Sexual assault: Disabled perspective. *Sexuality and Disability, 4*(4), 246–253.

This article discusses sexual assault against people with disabilities with regard to common myths about sexual assault, defense against assault, rape, recovery from assault, and suggestions for assisting sexual assault victims with disabilities.

1310. Stuart, O. W. (1992). Race and disability: Just a double oppression? *Disability, Handicap & Society, 7*(2), 177–188.

The author of this article suggests that being both Black and disabled in Britain does not amount to double oppression; instead, it constitutes a single simultaneous experience of oppression. The author claims that Blacks with disabilities are oppressed in three distinct areas: They lack or have a limited sense of identity, they have unequal access to finite resources, and they are isolated from the ethnic minority community. The author claims that the medical model of disability and perceived cultural influences contribute to this oppression.

1311. Sturner, W. Q., Sweeney, K. G., Callery, R. T., & Haley, N. R. (1991). Cocaine babies: The scourge of the '90s. *Journal of Forensic Sciences, 36*(1), 34–39.

This article presents six case histories of infant deaths related to cocaine intoxication. It includes postmortem descriptions of the cases. This article notes that either the mother, the child, or both had a positive screening for cocaine.

1312. Sullivan, J. F. (1991, May 5). New Jersey high court sets rules on mental handicap in sex cases. *The New York Times,* p. A44.

This newspaper article reports that the New Jersey Supreme Court has established guidelines concerning persons with mental disabilities and sex cases. The guidelines define persons who are considered mentally defective as those who cannot differentiate sexual conduct

from other behaviors and those who cannot refuse to engage in sexual activity. Anyone who engages in sexual behavior with a person who is known to have a mental deficit or who should be aware of a mental deficit is liable to be charged with sexual assault. This ruling stems from the New Jersey High School case involving members of the football team and the sexual assault of a teenage girl with mental retardation. In addition, this article discusses a case involving the rape of a Passaic County girl with mental retardation.

1313. Sullivan, P. M., Brookhouser, P. E., Knutson, J. F., Scanlan, J. M., & Schulte, L. E. (1991). Patterns of physical and sexual abuse of communicatively handicapped children. *Annals of Otology, Rhinology, and Laryngology, 100*(3), 188–194.

This article examines the patterns of physical and sexual abuse of children with communication disabilities using data gathered from the Center for Abused Handicapped Children at Boys Town National Research Hospital in Nebraska. These data concern 482 children and adolescents (274 male, 208 female [84% of these children and adolescents were White]), ranging in age from infancy to 21, with a mean age of 7.5 years, who were referred to the center. These children and adolescents were subjected to the following forms of maltreatment: sexual abuse, physical abuse, emotional abuse, neglect, and a combination of one or more forms of maltreatment. These children and adolescents had the following disabilities: hearing impairments (n=212), speech and/or language impairments (n=87), mental retardation (n=74), behavioral disorders (n=43), and learning disorders (n=39). Ninety-seven percent of sexual abuse offenders were relatives or others entrusted with the child's care. The results of this examination indicate the following: males with disabilities were more likely to be sexually abused than males without disabilities in the general population, and children attending residential schools were at greater risk for sexual abuse than children who were mainstreamed.

1314. Sullivan, P. M., Mann, M., Scanlan, J. M., & Burley, S. K. (no date). Protocol for interviewing handicapped children and adults about abuse. Omaha, NE: Center for Abused Handicapped Children, Boys Town National Research Hospital.

This paper discusses interviewing children and adults with disabilities about abuse. It outlines issues related to interviewing in sexual abuse cases and establishing communication. This paper presents 22 general points about interviewing children and adults with disabilities about abuse.

1315. Sullivan, P. M., & Scanlan, J. M. (1987). Therapeutic issues. In J. Garbarino, P. E. Brookhauser, & K. J. Authier (Eds.), *Special children,*

special risks: The maltreatment of children with disabilities (pp. 127–159). **New York: Aldine de Gruyter.**
This chapter points out the lack of available treatment programs for children with disabilities and the staff to serve them. It suggests that research on the effects of abuse and outcome studies on efficacy of therapeutic methods are also lacking with regard to people with disabilities and that studies of the long-term effects of sexual abuse on children without disabilities have had conflicting results. The authors' own study of 67 victims of childhood sexual abuse show that all the children have more than one behavior problem as measured by the Child Behavior Checklist. This chapter addresses psychotherapeutic concerns regarding children with disabilities who have been abused. A review of the literature examines some of the long-term consequences of child maltreatment. This chapter discusses the following areas: involuntary patients, authoritative intervention, ancillary patients, location of the therapy, therapist's characteristics, therapeutic methods, treatment goals, and impediments to therapy.

1316. Sullivan, P. M., & Scanlan, J. M. (1990). Psychotherapy with handicapped sexually abused children. *Developmental Disabilities Bulletin, 8*(2), 21–34.
This article examines the psychotherapy treatment plans and counseling methods used with sexually abused children with disabilities at the Centre for Abused Handicapped Children. It discusses the manifestations of post-traumatic stress disorder, the long-term effects of sexual abuse, and the differences between individual and group therapy. This article presents 13 goals of the therapeutic program for people who have been sexually abused.

1317. Sullivan, P. M., Scanlan, J. M., Brookhouser, P. E., Schulte, L. E., & Knutson, J. F. (1992). The effects of psychotherapy on behavior problems of sexually abused deaf children. *Child Abuse & Neglect, 16,* 297–307.
This article describes a therapeutic psychotherapy intervention program conducted with sexually abused boys and girls who attended a residency school for the hearing impaired. Due to some parental noncompliance, only 21 boys and 14 girls participated in the program; the remainder made up the nontreatment comparison group. All the children were between the ages of 12 and 16, and the type of abuse consisted of the following: witnessing sexual abuse, fondling (forced), oral and digital penetration, and anal and vaginal intercourse. The perpetrators where dormitory staff members or older students. Both groups were randomly assigned to one of two assessment groups, which consisted of either pretreatment assessment (Child Behavior Checklist [CBC]) or no pretreatment assessment. The treatment involved 2 hours of individual therapy per week for 36 weeks and was conducted in sign language. Some of the treatment goals were related to the following issues: guilt, trust,

depression, expression of anger, interpersonal relationships, sexual preferences, maltreatment, emotional independence, and self-identity. All of the children were assessed using the Child Behavior Checklist 1 year after therapy. The results of the post-treatment assessment indicate that boys who underwent therapy obtained lower CBC scores in areas of Total, Internal, External, Somatic, Uncommunicative, Immature, Hostile, Delinquent, Aggressive, and Hyperactive variables than boys in the comparison group; and the girls who underwent therapy were lower in areas of Total, External, Depressed, Aggressive, and Cruel scores than nontherapy girls.

1318. Sullivan, P. M., Vernon, M., & Scanlan, J. M. (1987). Sexual abuse of deaf youth. *American Annals of the Deaf, 132*(4), 256–262.
The authors of this article cite four studies of sexual abuse of children who are deaf that indicate that 54% of boys who are deaf and 50% of girls who are deaf have been sexually abused, compared with 10% of hearing boys and 25% of hearing girls. Children who are deaf are especially unlikely to discuss sexual abuse unless asked. In addition to fear of rejection, loss of love, punishment, or blame, children who are deaf face another problem: The parent, teacher, or other caregiver may not know enough sexual signs to understand when the child reports sexual abuse. As with other children with disabilities, children who are deaf are taught to comply with authority and, therefore, are more susceptible to bribes and threats. They tend to be not only curious but also naive about sexual norms. In terms of reporting abuse, schools have historically handled the problem internally. The authors believe this is a serious error, leading to "ethical compromises of the worst sort." Often, the perpetrator is asked to resign and is promised a good recommendation if he or she does resign. Thus, the abuser finds another position in a school where he or she can abuse more children. Lecturing the abuser "not to do it again" is another unacceptable approach and is not a solution for such a serious problem as sexual abuse. The authors describe the legal, ethical, and professional statutes and standards to be followed when dealing with child abuse.

1319. Sullivan, R. (1993, October). The big picture. *Life,* pp. 10–11.
This magazine article features the story of Jenson, a 10-year-old boy who has no eyes. When he was 10 months old, Jenson was admitted to a hospital in Columbia for acute diarrhea. He came out of the hospital with bandaged eyes. The doctor told Jenson's mother that her son was dying. Another doctor in Bogota confirmed that his eyes had been removed, which allowed his corneas to be removed for transplant. This article states that the practice of trafficking in stolen body parts by doctors very seldom leads to criminal charges because the victims or witnesses are usually killed.

1320. Summit, R. C. (1983). The child sexual abuse accommodation syndrome. *Child Abuse & Neglect, 7,* 177–193.

This article describes the child sexual abuse accommodation syndrome. This syndrome involves the results of adult reactions to the child's disclosure of sexual abuse: disbelief, blame, and rejection from adults. The author states that the adult perception of appropriate behavior for children who have been sexually abused has been inappropriate and unrealistic and has resulted in further alienation of the child from protection and recovery. This article examines the five categories of the child sexual abuse accommodation syndrome: secrecy; helplessness; entrapment and accommodation; delayed, unconvincing disclosure; and retraction. The author proposes a model for this syndrome in order to assist clinicians working with sexually abused children.

1321. Sundram, C. J. (1984). Obstacles to reducing patient abuse in public institutions. *Hospital and Community Psychiatry, 35*(3), 238–243.

This article examines the problems that hinder the reporting, investigation, and prevention of patient abuse in public facilities. It claims that the reporting of minor abusive conduct is influenced by working conditions and that the reporting of major abusive conduct is influenced by powerful factors in the administrative and disciplinary structures of state institutions. The author suggests measures designed to decrease the incidence of abuse and to ensure the reporting of any such incidents.

1322. Sundram, C. J. (1986). Strategies to prevent patient abuse in public institutions. *New England Journal of Human Services, 6*(2), 20–25.

Although United States law requires an advocacy system and prosecutor in every state, this article suggests that advocacy systems must be independent of all service providers. It claims that institutions have chosen to neglect abuse problems, and abuse problems have not been high priorities for institutional administrations. Consequently, the author offers several recommendations: 1) eliminating abuse must be placed as the highest priority for institutional administrations, 2) staff screening and staff training are critical, 3) administrative and professional staff must be actively present in all institutional venues, 4) staff and residents must be impressed with the importance of reporting, 5) the code of silence must be broken, 6) reporting staff and employees must be protected from retribution, and 7) reporting and investigation procedures must differentiate between serious and less serious complaints.

1323. Svec, H. J. (1992). Multiple personality disorder or psychosis. In *Crossing new borders* **(pp. 28–29). Kingston, NY: National Association for the Dually Diagnosed.**

This article provides a review of the symptoms of and treatments for multiple personality disorder (MPD). The author describes his own clinical experience with MPD in dually diagnosed people with developmental disabilities and provides a case example.

1324. Swanson, C. K., & Garwick, G. B. (1990). Treatment for low-functioning sex offenders: Group therapy and interagency coordination. *Mental Retardation, 28*(3), 155–161.

This article examines the historical explanations for the lack of specialized therapy for sex offenders who are low functioning or have mental retardation, and it explores the abusive and inconsistent responses to such offenders. It claims that this group of offenders has historically been scapegoated for many crimes in society, and there have been many laws and policy restrictions regarding the social and sexual activities of this group. Increasingly, these policies have been loosened; however, this article notes that society's longstanding discomfort with this group hinders normalization and consistent treatment. Also, this article discusses the procedures of and results from an outpatient group treating sex offenders who are low functioning.

1325. Sweeney, J. (1993, Winter). Violence. *CTAT Field Report (University of Northern Colorado, Center for Technical Assistance & Training)*, **pp. 5–7.**

This article provides general information and discusses issues regarding violence against women with disabilities. It also provides a description of Denver's Domestic Violence Initiative for Women with Disabilities (DVI) that has operated since 1986. The DVI provides support, crisis intervention, advocacy, education, training, and technical assistance to community agencies.

1326. Swett, C., Surrey, J., & Cohen, C. (1990). Sexual and physical abuse histories and psychiatric symptoms among male psychiatric outpatients. *American Journal of Psychiatry, 147*(5), 632–636.

This article summarizes a study conducted in a psychiatric outpatient clinic for adults that examined the sexual and physical abuse histories and psychiatric symptoms of male psychiatric outpatients. This study involved 125 male patients, and the results of this study indicate the following: 48% of the men in this study had been sexually and/or physically abused, those men with histories of abuse scored higher on the global severity index of the SCL-90-R (a test that examines psychiatric symptoms) than those men without a history of abuse, and the psychiatric symptoms were more severe among male patients with histories of sexual abuse and/or physical abuse.

1327. Szivos, S. E., & Griffiths, E. (1990). Group processes involved in coming to terms with a mentally retarded identity. *Mental Retardation, 28*(6), 333–341.

This article presents an alternative approach to addressing the stigma of people with mental retardation. It suggests using group therapy based on the two paradigms of loss and consciousness raising, and it reports the experiences of seven adult group members as they passed through six overlapping phases: denial, statement, recognition, exploration, meaning, and acceptance.

1328. Szymanski, L. S., & Jansen, P. E. (1980). Assessment of sexuality and sexual vulnerability of retarded persons. In L. S. Szymanski & P. E. Tanguay (Eds.), *Emotional disorders of mentally retarded persons: Assessment, treatment and consultation* (pp. 111–127). Baltimore: University Park Press.
This chapter contains a variety of related topics dealing with the sexuality and sexual vulnerability of people with mental retardation: for example, natural sexual development; denial of sexual expression; the genetic threat of sexually active people with mental retardation; the sexuality of institutionalized people; the unconstitutionality of laws concerning people with mental retardation; and the management, assessment, treatment, and prevention of the sexual abuse of people with mental retardation.

1329. Szymanski, L. S., & Tanguay, P. E. (Eds.). (1980). *Emotional disorders of mentally retarded persons: Assessment, treatment, and consultation*. Baltimore: University Park Press.
This book is designed for mental health professionals who work with people with mental retardation. It includes 16 chapters that focus on the following areas: professional roles and training, assessment, treatment, and consultation. Chapter titles and authors are: "Professional roles and unmet manpower needs" (Cushna, Szymanski, & Tanguay), "Training of mental health professionals in mental retardation" (Tanguay & Szymanski), "The psychological definition of mental retardation: A historical review" (Cushna), "A field theory approach to understanding developmental disabilities" (Tanguay), "The biomedical components of mental retardation" (Crocker), "Psychiatric diagnosis of retarded persons" (Szymanski), "Cognitive development: Neuropsychological basis and clinical assessment" (Tanguay), "Early infantile autism and mental retardation: Differential diagnosis" (Tanguay), "Assessment of sexuality and sexual vulnerability of retarded persons" (Szymanski & Jansen), "Individual psychotherapy with retarded persons" (Szymanski), "Family adaptation to the diagnosis of mental retardation in a child and strategies of intervention" (Hagamen), "Group psychotherapy with retarded persons" (Szymanski & Rosefsky), "Psychopharmacology and the mentally retarded patient" (Rivinus), "Basic principles of behavior therapy with retarded persons" (Jansen), "Mental health consultations to educational programs for retarded persons" (Szymanski & Leaverton), and "Mental health consultations to residential facilities for retarded persons" (Szymanski, Eissner, & Rosefsky). This book provides a variety of perspectives concerning therapy and other assorted treatment approaches that can be used to address the emotional concerns faced by people with developmental disabilities and mental retardation.

•T•

1330. Talbot, Y., & Shaul, R. (1987). Medical students learn about attitudes and handicaps. *Entourage, 2*(3), 6–11.
This article describes the practice of having first-year medical students spend time with families of people with mental disabilities. This practice was initiated to help improve health care for people with disabilities by changing physicians' attitudes. This article discusses the students' experiences, attitude changes, and suggestions for implementing this type of course work in the regular curriculum.

1331. Tanner, A. (1993, June 6). Why did Social Services miss the early signs? *The Edmonton Journal*, pp. A1, A3.
This newspaper article reports that Rod and Theresa Lenny, the foster parents convicted of aggravated assault against 21-month-old Jason Carpenter, were investigated four times by Social Services for abuse against their own children prior to receiving Jason into their care. Jason Carpenter was assaulted by the Lennys while in their foster care and experienced severe and permanent brain injury. Two doctors and a neighbor voiced concern for children in the care of the Lennys. This tragedy has placed the Alberta welfare system under scrutiny for its handling of this case. Insufficient training for staff, large caseloads, and a short supply of foster care families are some of the issues noted in the breakdown of the child welfare system contributing to this case.

1332. Taylor, C. G., Norman, D. K., Murphy, J. M., Jellinek, M., Quinn, D., Poitrast, F. G., & Goshko, M. (1991). Diagnosed intellectual and emotional impairment among parents who seriously mistreat their children: Prevalence, type, and outcome in a court sample. *Child Abuse & Neglect, 15,* 389–401.
This article describes a Boston study that was conducted to determine the prevalence of intellectual and emotional impairment in parents of abused and neglected children. This study examined the court records of 206 child abuse and neglect cases. The mean age of the children in this study was 4.1 years, and there was an equal number of boys and girls. Information about the parents included the following: any court investigator or Department of Social Services reports, medical information, psychological testing, and psychiatric evaluation. Unfortunately, information was not available for all the parents, but the

information that was available indicates the following: more than 50% of the parents had either intellectual or emotional disorders; type of disorder did not predict type of abuse, greater risk of continued abuse, or court order removal of children from the home; those parents with significant psychopathology were more likely to lose custody of their children than parents who were less emotionally impaired; and parents with intellectual impairments were more inclined to accept court-ordered services.

1333. Taylor, E. M., & Emery, J. L. (1982). Two-year study of the causes of post-perinatal deaths classified in terms of preventability. *Archives of Disease in Childhood, 57,* **668–673.**
Infant deaths in Sheffield, England, during a 2-year period are addressed in this article. The authors classify the deaths using preventability as the basis for the classification. This study examined 65 infant deaths that occurred during the indexed period. Although 9 of these infants were without gross deformities or genetic abnormalities, this examination suggests that 35 of these deaths were unpreventable after the prenatal period. Of the remaining 30 infants, 20 died of diseases that are occasionally fatal, 2 infants died of nonaccidental injury, 3 infants were suspected of having died due to gentle battering, 4 infant deaths were true cot (crib) deaths, and 1 infant died due to an accident. This article includes a full discussion of these categories.

1334. Taylor, E. M., & Emery, J. L. (1990). Categories of preventable unexpected infant deaths. *Archives of Disease in Childhood, 65,* **535–539.**
This article reviews 115 registered unexpected infant deaths or sudden infant death syndrome cases that occurred in Sheffield, England. For 19 of the 115 infant deaths, this review found that true sudden infant death syndrome was the cause of death. For the other 83%, the categories of death include: poor prognosis ($n=7$), treatable disease ($n=45$), minor disease ($n=32$), probable accidental ($n=4$), and probable filicide ($n=8$). This article includes and discusses the demographics for families within each category.

1335. Taylor, R. B. (1981). Discarded children. In R. B. Taylor (Ed.), *The kid business: How it exploits the children it should help* **(pp. 38–66). Boston: Houghton Mifflin.**
This chapter examines institutional child abuse of children with and without disabilities in foster care. It presents case examples of abusive institutions or residential treatment facilities such as Willowbrook, the Kate School, the Green Valley School, Oak Creek Ranch, and Stockton State Hospital in order to help illustrate the many forms of abusive caregiving. Using these examples, this article examines the legal restrictions and regulations that hinder the expedient resolution of these cases and discusses future considerations for foster care.

1336. Taylor, R. B. (1981). The Kate School. In R. B. Taylor (Ed.), *The kid business: How it exploits the children it should help* **(pp. 220–259). Boston: Houghton Mifflin.**
In this chapter, the author describes a case of residential abuse of children with autism and children with developmental and emotional disabilities at the Kate School in California during the 1970s. It examines the case from the initial recognition of the punishment techniques and confrontational therapy practiced at the treatment facility to the final closure of the school.

1337. Taylor, S. J., & Bogdan, R. (1980). Defending illusions: The institution's struggle for survival. *Human Organization, 39*(3), **209–218.**
The authors of this article claim that organizational goals and structures act as legitimating myths that are used to gain support from external public groups on whom organizations depend for their survival. They describe a study conducted at four mental health institutions that examined how institutional professionals and administrative staff deal with the visible discrepancy between goals and practices. They discuss the following: 1) how institutional standard-bearers develop a worldview and deal with the discrepancy between goals and practices, 2) how administrators deal with the outside world, and 3) the defenses used to counteract outside criticism. The authors conclude that it is difficult to predict if mental health institutions can survive the outside criticisms being leveled at them and that it is difficult to predict what the crisis in mental health institutions (i.e., their inability to help their clients) will mean to the administrators and professionals who operate these institutions.

1338. "10 days of terror." (1994). *Dialog, 8*(1), **6–7.**
This article provides a brief case history recounting the experiences of a man with multiple sclerosis who encountered discrimination turning to violence. On three separate occasions in April 1992, this man was thrown out of an elevator in his wheelchair, threatened with a knife and punched, and beaten by people in his neighborhood who told him "you're a poor excuse for a human being." The man and his family were forced to move out of their apartment to a new residence in order to escape the violence.

1339. ten Have, H. A. M. J., & Welie, J. V. M. (1992). Euthanasia: Normal medical practice. *Hastings Centre Report, 22*(2), **34–38.**
This article discusses the practice of euthanasia in contemporary Holland. It reports Dutch statistics from the report of the Committee on the Study of Medical Practice Concerning Euthanasia (a committee chaired by a Dutch Attorney General of the Supreme Court, J. Remmelink). Each year in the Netherlands 130,000 people die. In 49,000 of these cases, decisions must be made regarding how long to continue care. Assisted sui-

cide occurs in just 400 cases, while some form of euthanasia takes place in about 2,300 cases. This number increases to about 8,100 if potentially lethal doses of pain medication are included. Approximately 1,000 cases of active euthanasia take place with no request at all. An additional 3,200 to 7,000 cases of passive involuntary euthanasia take place each year. About 9,000 people request euthanasia each year, but many of these requests are not honored.

1340. Terry, D. (1988, July 28). A retarded boy fatally beaten: Stepfather held. *The New York Times*, p. B3.
This newspaper article reports that an 8-year-old Brooklyn boy with mental retardation was fatally beaten by his stepfather, Alvin Marshburn, as a result of the father's frustration with the child's condition. An autopsy confirmed that Zarak Bendigo had endured previous beatings, which resulted in broken ribs, cord lacerations around the neck, genital lacerations, and peritonitis. The stepfather was charged with second-degree murder.

1341. Terry, D. (1994, February 3). 19 children found in squalid Chicago apartment. *The New York Times*, pp. A1, A12.
This newspaper article reports that on February 2, 1994, Chicago police investigating an inner-city apartment for drugs found 19 neglected children ranging in age from 1 to 14. Interestingly, only one child was found to have been abused in addition to being neglected. A 4-year-old boy with cerebral palsy had telltale abuse marks from a belt and cigarettes, in addition to other bruises and cuts. The boy currently remains in hospital. The other children have been taken into custody by the Department of Children and Family Services.

1342. Tharinger, D., Burrows Horton, C., & Millea, S. (1990). Sexual abuse and exploitation of children and adults with mental retardation and other handicaps. *Child Abuse & Neglect: The International Journal*, 14(3), 301–312.
This article examines the sexual abuse and exploitation of children, adolescents, and adults with developmental disabilities, and it addresses some of the legal aspects of this issue, including: class legislation that will protect the rights of people with disabilities, and legal consent. This article discusses the incidence of abuse and the increased vulnerability of people with disabilities, and it describes the acute and chronic effects of abuse, professional response to allegations of abuse, and therapeutic interventions.

1343. Thies, A. P. (1976). The facts of life: Child advocacy and children's rights in residential treatment. In G. P. Koocher (Ed.), *Children's rights and the mental health professions* (pp. 85–96). New York: John Wiley & Sons.

In this chapter, the author asserts that children's needs will become legal rights only when they are accepted as enforceable claims against other persons or institutions. Protection is not enough. Also, children rely on adult advocates no matter what the system, rules, or laws. The author concludes that anyone involved with the welfare of children must be aware of any conflict between their own interests and the child's interests.

1344. Thomas, B., & Mundy, P. (1991). Speaking out. *Nursing Times*, 87(6), 67–68.
This article describes the case of a young woman with developmental disabilities who had a history of sexual abuse. It examines the involvement of the police, social services, and the courts after this young woman's disclosure of incest.

1345. Thomas, D. (1993, July 4). Bodily harm. *The Edmonton Journal*, pp. C1–C2.
This special section examines both historical and current sterilization practices for people with disabilities in the province of Alberta, Canada. The author examines the Alberta Sexual Sterilization Act of 1928 and the impact it had on people with developmental disabilities. Until the repeal of the Sexual Sterilization Act in 1972, the provincial Eugenics Board ordered the sterilization of 2,844 individuals with developmental disabilities, Indians, and Metis, with or without consent. The board's pursuit of preventing defective children from being born seemed to have included not only people with disabilities, but also ethnic minorities. Operations were usually conducted at Alberta Hospital Ponoka and at a training school hospital now know as Michener Centre. The current climate concerning sterilization practices revolve around the "Eve" decision brought down by the Supreme Court of Canada in 1986. This decision states that sterilization without consent cannot be conducted except for "health" reasons. While tubal ligation is strictly for sterilization purposes, the more drastic hysterectomy could be argued to be for health reasons such as cancer control. This has resulted in a 15.5% increase in hysterectomies since the "Eve" decision. This article also discusses the impact of this decision on current sterilization practices involving people with disabilities.

1346. Thomas, G. (1988). *Journey into madness: Medical torture and the mind controllers*. London: Gorgi Books.
This book relates the true story of Dr. Ewan Cameron, a CIA-backed physician who was involved in medical projects that involved brainwashing and radical surgery. His patients were Canadian mental hospital referrals. The author delves deeper into the international trappings of medical torture by examining the techniques of behavioral control and concludes that both mind and body can be subject to state-sponsored terrorism and ideology.

1347. Thomas, G. (1990). Institutional child abuse: The making and prevention of an

un-problem. *Journal of Child and Youth Care, 4*(6), 1–22.
This article discusses the concept of institutional child abuse and claims that institutions should lay personal rather than systematic responsibility in cases of abuse or neglect. It suggests that facilities should be developmentally oriented rather than merely child protectionist. It outlines the current problems from an evolutionary perspective, which takes into account community apathy, older children in care, and legal and social service antagonism. It examines the traditional rationale for faulty care: *parens patriae*, lack of resources, and measures taken "in the child's best interest." These explanations are reconceptualized to reflect a child's developmental needs. The author suggests that an expected by-product of such a conceptual reform would be the extinction of institutional child abuse.

1348. Thombre, M. (1987). Attachment and infant feeding methods. *Journal of the American Academy of Child and Adolescent Psychiatry, 26*(4), 596.
In this comment on the work of G. A. Wasserman et al. ([1987]. Contributors to attachment in normal and physically handicapped infants. *Journal of the American Academy of Child and Adolescent Psychiatry, 26*[1], 9–15) on contributors to attachment in "normal infants" and infants with physical disabilities, the author of this article questions whether the difference found in maternal responsiveness in mothers of infants with disabilities was related to feeding methods. Although method of feeding was not reported in the study, the author feels that infants in the experimental group were probably less likely to have been started on the breast. The author suggests that there is reason to believe that there may be a biological difference in the motivation of mothers, triggered by oxytocin during breastfeeding, to respond to their infants.

1349. Thomson, M. (1992). Sterilization, segregation and community care: Ideology and solutions to the problem of mental deficiency in inter-war Britain. *History of Psychiatry, 3,* 473-498.
This article discusses the history of eugenics between World Wars I and II in Britain. This article points out that people with mental retardation only became defined as a separate category of "lunatics" in 1913 with the passage of the Mental Deficiency Act. This legislation was closely connected with a eugenic goal of sexual segregation and isolation to eliminate people with mental retardation from society.

1350. Thyer, B. A. (1987). Punishment-induced aggression: A possible mechanism of child abuse? *Psychological Reports, 60,* 129–130.
This article explores the possible application of a punishment-induced aggression paradigm to understanding child abuse. Punishment-induced aggression has been well documented in animal experiments and analysis of human behavior. Punishment-induced aggression occurs when an individual is exposed to aversive stimuli and responds with a generalized response of aggression in interactions with other individuals. The author argues that this provides a parsimonious explanation of child abuse that does not require mentalistic theories, such as attachment or caregiver personality. Even if punishment-induced aggression is not accepted as a sole explanation for child abuse, it may have value as a factor in understanding child abuse and a variety of other forms of violence.

1351. Ticoll, M. (1993). Responding to abuse—The need for protocols. *ARCH• Type, 10*(6), 18–19.
This article discusses the sexual assault of an adolescent with a developmental disability by a neighbor in Nova Scotia. Although this young woman was able to tell what had happened and the neighbor signed a confession, the case was never prosecuted because of a series of problems with the investigation. One positive outcome of this case, however, was the development of a protocol for police and prosecutors that should help in future cases.

1352. Tilley, S. (1994, May 12). Skull ID'd. *The Edmonton Sun,* p. 5.
This article recounts the events leading to the identification of a skull found in a remote area of Edmonton as Michelle Kshyk, a woman with a mental disability. She had been missing for 3 years after telling family and friends that she was going on a date with someone she met through a radio call-in dating service show. Police believe that foul play was involved. No other remains have been located.

1353. Titus, D. G. (1991). The effects of childhood sexual abuse on personality and ego development. *Dissertation Abstracts International, 52*(3), 1741B–1742B.
This abstract describes a study that examined the long-term effects of childhood sexual abuse on adult survivors. This study specifically investigated the long-term effects of sexual assault on ego and personality development and the presence of post-traumatic stress disorder (PTSD). After a review of the literature, this study hypothesized that there would be developmental lags and a high incidence of PTSD and borderline personality disorder (BPD) in adult survivors. The participants in this study included 30 adult survivors (20 female and 10 male) from three mental health centers. This study excluded people who had diagnoses of psychosis, bipolar disorder, organicity, mental retardation, active chemical dependence, multiple personality disorder, and those who committed sexual abuse. This study administered a structured interview to obtain information on sexual abuse and the presence of PTSD symptoms, and it used the Borderline Syndrome Index (BSI), the Millon Clinical Multiaxial Inventory-II (MCMI-II), and the Washington University Sentence Completion Test (SCT) to measure ego

development. The results from the structured interviews and the MCMI-II indicate the following: 1) all of the survivors had PTSD, 2) it was not possible to predict the level of ego development using any one sex abuse or family variable, 3) the presence of both sexual and physical abuse appears to predict lower ego development, and 4) adult survivors of sexual abuse have significantly higher levels of depression Also, this thesis discusses other findings and includes some treatment recommendations.

1354. Tobin, P. (1992). Addressing special vulnerabilities in prevention. *NRCCSA (National Resource Center on Child Sexual Abuse) News, 1*(4), 5, 14.

This article discusses the vulnerabilities that are a daily reality for people with disabilities, including: dependency on others, lack of personal boundaries and access to information, low self-esteem, lack of self-confidence, and compliance with anyone in authority. This article suggests that these vulnerabilities are fostered by the public's denial of a need for change and the belief that there is no abuse of people with disabilities. It stresses education as a means for reducing the vulnerability of people with disabilities.

1355. Tomlinson, D. (1993). Family violence & abuse: Independent living approach to prevention. *Abilities, 16,* 37.

This article examines the prevention of family abuse and abuse against people with disabilities. It discusses a prevention program sponsored by the Canadian Association of Independent Living Centers entitled "Creating Community Frameworks for Family Violence Prevention Among Citizens who have Disabilities." It describes three separate projects that have been initiated to meet the needs of different populations: a self-help program for youths with disabilities, a rural outreach program for elderly people with disabilities, and a national community education and information program. Also, this article includes information about Independent Living Trainers who will help implement these programs by developing training packages and guidelines for staff members.

1356. Too close for comfort: A self-advocate writes about her experiences with relationships. (1992). *Entourage, 7*(2), 10.

In this article, the author writes about her own experience with sexual abuse and how it has affected her relationships with men.

1357. Towfighy-Hooshyar, N. (1980). The characteristics of institutional settings which influence residents' development. *Mental Retardation Bulletin, 8*(3), 122–133.

This article examines the differences in institutional settings and characteristics that might be associated with the developmental differences of residents with intellectual disabilities. The author examines the literature in order to determine which institutional characteristics affect the development of residents.

1358. Travin, S., Cullen, K., & Protter, B. (1990). Female sex offenders: Severe victims and victimizers. *Journal of Forensic Sciences, 35*(1), 140–150.

This article notes the scarcity of research dealing with sexual offenses committed by females. It provides a review of the literature and describes nine case studies of female sex offenders and female sexual abusers. The case studies provide a psychological profile and examine the prevalence of personal victimization of these offenders. This review indicates that all of the female perpetrators had been subjected to some form of abuse, had low self-esteem, had few positive social relationships, and functioned at a marginal level. The authors suggest that more research should be conducted with this population and that clinicians should be more sensitive to the needs of female sex offenders.

1359. Trudell, B., & Whatley, M. H. (1988). School sexual abuse prevention: unintended consequences and dilemmas. *Child Abuse & Neglect, 12,* 103–113.

This article examines the role of elementary school personnel in sexual abuse prevention programs. It claims that the assumptions concerning elementary school sexual abuse programs have unintended consequences: They stress a simple solution to this complex social problem, and they contribute to victim blaming. This article contends that school prevention programs should not be overemphasized as they provide only a partial solution and cannot eliminate child sexual abuse because they do not focus on preventing offenders from offending. Instead, these programs may create the impression that children are responsible for preventing their own victimization and may feed into victim blaming. This article provides a critique of these programs and stresses the importance of getting educators to examine the assumptions and consequences of school prevention programs.

1360. Truesdell, D. L., McNeil, J. S., & Deschner, J. P. (1986). Incidence of wife abuse in incestuous families. *Social Work, 31*(2), 138–140.

This article discusses a study that questioned 30 women about the prevalence of wife abuse in incestuous families. The women in this study were between 24 and 52 years of age. All of these women had attended a mother's group that was part of an incest treatment program offered by the Texas Department of Human Resources. Illegibility for inclusion in the program was determined if a woman had a child who was considered a victim of incest. This study used a questionnaire, which included the Conflict Tactics Scale, to obtain data. The Conflict Tactics Scale was chosen for its ability to distinguish between milder forms of family violence and more serious forms of family violence. The results of this study indicate the following: 22 of the 30 women

(73%) reported at least one incidence of physical abuse; psychological abuse was also noted for the same number of women, but at a higher rate of incidence; 7 women (23%) reported life-threatening abuse; and the perpetrator of the abuse was the biological father or the stepfather of the child. The authors suggest that to continue to focus blame for the child's abuse on the mother is unjust, claiming that the mother herself is often abused. They discuss theories concerning incest and the roles attributed to individual parents, and they suggest changes for incest treatment programs.

1361. Truscott, D. (1990). Sexual exploitation in psychotherapy: II. Responding to disclosures of exploitation. *Alberta Psychology, 19*(5), 24.

This article examines the psychologist's legal, ethical, and therapeutic responsibilities when a client discloses sexual exploitation by a previous therapist. Unless the disclosure reveals violent behavior or child abuse, the author claims that the therapist's main legal and ethical responsibility in these cases is to avoid breaching the client's right to confidentiality. According to the author, the therapeutic responsibility of providing quality care is the therapist's main obligation when faced with disclosures of sexual exploitation by a previous therapist.

1362. Trute, B. (1990, July). Child and parent predictors of family adjustment in households containing young developmentally disabled children. *Family Relations, 39,* 292–297.

This article discusses a study that assessed 88 randomly chosen families with a young child with developmental disabilities in order to determine the adjustment of the child, the parent, and overall family functioning. This study administered (during an in-home interview that lasted approximately 2 hours) the Family Assessment Measure III, the Dyadic Adjustment Scale, the Colorado Childhood Temperament Inventory, and a specifically designed disability index. The average age of the children in the study was 5 (39% female, 61% male). Single-child families made up 32% of the sample, 27% of families had two children, and 41% of families had three or more children. The results of this assessment indicate that positive family adjustment was related to the degree of marital adjustment and the father's education level but not to such child attributes as gender, degree of disability, or temperament. The author concludes that existing social services and family practitioners should conduct assessments for marital stability, disability, and adequate family resources in order to discover how the family is adjusting to the presence of a child with disabilities.

1363. Trute, B., & Hauch, C. (1988). Building on family strength: A study of families with positive adjustment to the birth of a developmentally disabled child. *Journal of Marital and Family Therapy, 14*(2), 185–193.

This article describes a study that was conducted to examine the positive adjustment variables in families of infants born with developmental disabilities in Manitoba, Canada. The 36 families who participated in this study were screened using a file review system initiated by social workers and an independent screening by pediatricians; all of these professionals worked for a child development center. This study assessed three areas of adjustment: family adjustment, child emotional stability, and child development progress. The concordance rating between social workers and pediatricians was 91%. This study used the following assessment tools: the Family Assessment Measure III, the Dyadic Adjustment Scale, the Texas Social Behavior Inventory, the Beck Depression Inventory, and the Colorado Childhood Temperament Inventory. These scales were used to assess the mother's network density and support as well as the infant's degree of disability. The infants were mostly male (64%), with an average age of 3. Forty-four percent of infants had multiple disabilities, and 20% of them had severe disabilities. The results of this study indicate the following: Positive adjustment to the birth of a child with developmental disabilities was related to families with two parents and few other children in the household; parental subsystems and use of support networks were found to be associated with good adjustment; and the child's degree of disability, level of mobility, and family income were not related to adjustment.

1364. Trute, B., & Hauch, C. (1988). Social network attributes of families with positive adaptation to the birth of a developmentally disabled child. *Canadian Journal of Community Mental Health, 7*(1), 5–16.

This article discusses a study that examined the social network attributes of families who had positively adapted to the birth of a child with developmental disabilities. Positive adaptation was independently assessed in terms of family adjustment, child adjustment, and child developmental progress by social workers and staff pediatricians using case file reviews. Thirty-six successfully adapted families participated in personal interviews. Both parents were asked to generate a list of individuals who provided them with support. The mothers, who were the primary caregivers, were also asked to identify which individuals in their support network were acquainted with each other and associated independently with each other. Family member relationships and types of support were noted, and mothers were asked to complete the Family Coping Strategies Scale, the Perceived Social Support from Families and Friends, and the Marlowe Crowne Social Desirability Scale. The findings of this study indicate the following: successful families who adapted positively to the birth of a child with developmental disabilities had small social networks consisting of family and friends, mothers closely associated with other women, and the mothers had diverse support networks.

1365. Trute, B., Tefft, B., & Segall, A. (1989). Social rejection of the mentally ill: A

replication study of public attitude. *Social Psychiatry and Psychiatric Epidemiology,* 24, 69–76.

This article discusses a replication study from the University of Manitoba, in Winnipeg, Canada, that examined publicly held attitudes and beliefs about people with mental illness. This study conducted 548 interviews with randomly chosen households. It used a survey questionnaire that included the following: a social rejection scale, and a scale related to experience with and knowledge about mental illness. This replicated study was conducted a decade after an initial survey on public attitudes about mental illness. The initial study indicated that social attitude toward mental illness could be categorically divided into the following social relations: personal contact, and social responsibility that involves impersonal contact. The results from the replication study suggest the following: social relations rejection of people with mental illness is related to prior personal experience with and perceived dangerousness of mental illness and the respondent's age; and rejection of people with mental illness in situations of social responsibility was found to be related to the respondent's education. This study found that there were no significant differences in publicly held attitudes and beliefs about people with mental illness between the two survey studies.

1366. Turk, V., & Brown, H. (1992). Sexual abuse and adults with learning disabilities: Preliminary communication of survey results. *Mental Handicap,* 20(2), 56–58.

This article discusses a survey that was conducted in the South East Thames Regional Health Authority to determine the incidence and nature of sexual abuse of adults with disabilities during 1989 and 1990. The results of this study indicate the following: both genders were liable to be sexually victimized (73% women, 27% men); the average age of the victim was 31, but most of the victims were between the ages of 21 and 30; 60% of the victims were diagnosed with severe or profound learning disability, with almost 70% of victims having additional disabilities such as communication problems, behavioral problems, or multiple disabilities; most of the incidents of sexual abuse took place in staffed residences or family residences, with 95% of abuse involving physical contact; the perpetrators were predominantly men (97%), and cases of single perpetrators abusing more than one victim were noted; and in 95% of the cases, the perpetrator was known to the victim, with no legal action taken against the perpetrator in almost half the cases. Using the results of these data, the authors estimate that 950 new cases of sexual abuse would be reported per year.

1367. Turk, V., & Brown, H. (1993). The sexual abuse of adults with learning disabilities: Results of a two year incidence survey. *Mental Handicap Research,* 6(3), 193–216.

This article reports the results of a British survey of cases of sexual abuse of adults with mental disabilities. The authors review their findings along with the results of other research and make recommendations for prevention, intervention, and research.

1368. Turnbull, H. R. (1986). Incidence of infanticide in America: Public and professional attitudes. *Issues in Law & Medicine,* 1(5), 363–389.

This article discusses the selective nontreatment of infants with disabilities. It examines the attitudes of society and physicians regarding the care of these children, and it discusses the incidence of infanticide of newborns with disabilities.

1369. Turner, T. S. (1988, February). Human rights concerns in health care institutions. *The Spokesman,* pp. 17–18.

This article discusses the effect of institutionalization on the social, emotional, and legal status of those who enter them. The author points out that institutionalization is characterized by choicelessness, powerlessness, and vulnerability, and people typically adapt by becoming increasingly passive, dependent, and compliant. Although the author does not directly address abuse issues, such an individual as previously described is likely to be at risk for abuse and exploitation.

1370. Tuteur, M. (1993). Neo-Nazis & disability in Germany: Never again...once again! *Abilities,* 16, 64–65.

This article examines selected articles that appeared in German journals between 1992 and 1993 dealing with the victimization of people with disabilities. This examination found an increase in violence toward people with disabilities, especially in what was East Germany. This article concludes that the Neo-Nazi philosophy of intolerance toward people with disabilities appears to be more visible.

1371. 2 held in deaths at nursing home: Ex-nurse's aides are seized in Michigan and Texas—Bodies are exhumed. (1988, December 6). *The New York Times,* p. A26.

This newspaper article reports that two ex-nurse's aides are implicated in the deaths of former residents at the Alpine Manor Nursing Home in Walker, Michigan. Catherine May Woods is charged with two counts of murder involving terminally ill elderly patients. Gwendolyn Gail Graham is charged with the death of a former patient. Eight suspicious deaths appeared to be the result of suffocation. Ms. Graham is being held on $1 million bond.

1372. Tymchuk, A. J., & Andron, L. (1990). Mothers with mental retardation who do or do not abuse or neglect their children. *Child Abuse & Neglect,* 14, 313–323.

The authors of this article refute the notion that parents with mental disabilities are inherently at risk to neglect or abuse their children. They examined the histories of 33 mothers with mental disabilities to determine the variables that might predict abuse and/or neglect and removal of children from the home. The authors determined that some mothers with mental disabilities do provide adequate care for their children and that inadequate care generally takes the form of neglect rather than abuse. As well, they also suggest that IQ and other within-subject variables may not be as predictive of abusive situations as are family demographics and access to helping agencies.

1373. Tymchuk, A. J., Andron, L., & Barolek, S. J. (1990). *Nurturing program for parents with developmental disabilities and their children.* **Park City, CA: Family Development Resources.**
This activities manual for parents with special learning needs covers a variety of issues in childrearing: nurturing, giving praise, discipline, hygiene, recognizing needs, development, handling anger, punishment, communication, building children's self-esteem, and safety proofing the home. It also provides illustrations and a guide for facilitators.

•U•

1374. Ugent, W. D., Graf, M. H., & Ugent, A. S. (1986). Fetal alcohol syndrome: A problem that school psychologists can help recognize, treat and prevent. *School Psychology International, 7,* **55–60.**
This article discusses fetal alcohol syndrome (FAS) and fetal alcohol effect and focuses on the following: incidence of FAS; and the physical, neurologic, behavioral, and intellectual characteristics of FAS. This article highlights prevention and treatment issues.

1375. Ulicny, G. R., White, G. W., Brandford, B., & Mathews, R. M. (1990). Consumer exploitation by attendants: How often does it happen and can anything be done about it? *Rehabilitation Counseling Bulletin, 33(3),* **240–246.**
This article describes a survey that was conducted to determine the prevalence of consumer exploitation and abuse of people with physical disabilities who require the daily services of personal attendants in their homes. The questionnaire was administered over the phone by staff members from 15 randomly selected independent living centers. Ninety-one consumers responded to the questionnaire. The questionnaire consisted of open-ended questions and 12 forced-choice questions pertaining to be-

haviors that were hypothesized to be related to consumer exploitation. The results of this survey indicate that 40% of consumers (*n*=36) had been exploited by their personal attendants, and of these, 10% reported physical abuse at the hands of their attendants. The survey found that exploitation involved forged checks and the theft of jewelry, money, medication, clothes, and stereo/television equipment.

1376. United States Department of Health and Human Services, National Center on Child Abuse and Neglect. (1981). *Study findings: National study of the incidence and severity of child abuse and neglect* **(DHHS Publication No. [OHDS] 81-30325). Washington, DC: Author.**
This report summarizes and analyzes data obtained from a national study on the prevalence and severity of child abuse and neglect. It details and discusses estimates of abuse, demographics, and characteristics of cases brought to the attention of Child Protective Services agencies.

1377. U. S. experiments on people compared to Nazi atrocities. (1993, December 29). *The Edmonton Journal,* **p. B8.**
This newspaper article examines research ethics regarding the use of humans in scientific research. This article claims that experiments conducted in the United States from the 1940s to the 1970s were as unethical as the Nazi experimentation on humans during World War II. For example, some research involved the injection of plutonium into human subjects who had not given their consent. Children with mental retardation were deliberately injected with hepatitis, while African Americans with syphilis were led to believe that they were receiving treatment even though they were not receiving treatment. This article was written in response to the news about the use of children with mental retardation who were fed radioactive cereal, but who, like their parents, were unaware of this fact. The study was funded by the Atomic Energy Commission and Quaker Oats Company in the late 1940s and early 1950s.

•V•

1378. Vaillant, G. E. (1985). Loss as a metaphor for attachment. *American Journal of Psychoanalysis, 45(1),* **59–67.**
This article contends that psychopathology is not caused by separation and loss of those loved, but rather, it is caused by the failure to internalize those loved or those not loved at all. It suggests that taking the psychiatric view of separation and loss too literally and ignoring that grief can be a metaphor for attachment risks therapeutic rigidity. It claims that successful internalization allows people to be enriched by those they have loved and lost and that internalization is a shorthand way of discussing

the psychic metabolic process that assimilates split objects and leads to object constancy. It describes reanalyzed data from a study of adult development that followed 268 males from adolescence to middle age and found that the best and worst outcome groups in terms of chronic depression did not differ in relation to childhood parental loss. It suggests that traits of orality and dependence made it difficult for these people to grieve and that the etiology of these traits was having lived with inconsistent, immature, and incompatible parents rather than having lost good ones. It discusses the findings of Rutter ([1981]. *Maternal deprivation reassessed.* Harmondsworth, England: Penguin Books), whose study of the importance of separation and loss upon child development suggests that poor interpersonal relationships, conflicted parental relationships, exposure to conflict-ridden but enduring marriages, privation, and failure to form attachment bonds lead to emotional disabilities in children. This article illustrates these findings with case studies.

1379. Valenti-Hein, D. (1992). The development of sexual abuse policy statements. In *Crossing new borders* (pp. 169–172). Kingston, NY: National Association for the Dually Diagnosed.
This chapter discusses the development of policy statements that contain a concise but insightful analysis of why people with developmental disabilities experience increased risk for abuse. The author discusses a number of important factors to consider when developing policy and procedures: 1) national and regional laws, 2) ages of clients served by an agency, 3) legal status and competency of clients, 4) clients' rights to report and to privacy if they choose not to report, 5) to whom reports should be made, 6) time of disclosure (i.e., an immediate disclosure of sexual assault typically requires different responses than a long delayed disclosure), 7) provisions for maximizing client safety, and 8) considerations for addressing false or unsubstantiated disclosures.

1380. Valenti-Hein, D., & Schwartz, L. (1994). *The sexual abuse interview for the developmentally disabled.* Santa Barbara, CA: James Stanfield Company.
This interview protocol provides a standardized interview to use in the event of a disclosure or suspicion of sexual abuse. It includes developmental assessment items that help identify basic information and communication skills. It also provides basic tests of suggestibility and the ability to differentiate between fantasy and reality and between truth and lies. It includes scoring forms and a series of reproducible pictures to be used in the interview. This interview is designed for use as an aid to investigation and prosecution, but it could also be used to assess individuals for training.

1381. Valentine, D. P. (1990). Double jeopardy: Child maltreatment and mental

retardation. *Child and Adolescent Social Work, 7*(6), 487–499.
This article reviews three potential relationships between abuse and disability: 1) mental retardation is considered as a potential risk factor for abuse of children, 2) child abuse is considered as a potential cause of mental retardation, and 3) parent mental retardation is considered as a potential causal factor in child abuse.

1382. van Dalen, A. (1989). The emotional consequences of physical child abuse. *Clinical Social Work Journal, 17*(4), 383–394.
This article focuses on children's emotional responses to physical abuse. It proposes a model that suggests a relatively sequential series of emotional responses, consisting of nine incremental steps grouped into three levels of severity: conscious responses, unconscious responses, and denial and resignation. This article discusses and illustrates diagnostic and treatment implications.

1383. Van, I. M. H., & Kroonenberg, P. M. (1988). Cross-cultural patterns of attachment: A meta-analysis of the Strange Situation. *Child Development, 59*(1), 147–156.
This article examines almost 2,000 Ainsworth Strange Situation classifications obtained in eight different countries. Using correspondence analysis, it investigates the differences and similarities between distributions in classifications of samples. It claims that the aggregation of samples per country and continent allows for a firmer empirical basis for cross-cultural analysis and establishes substantial intracultural differences. In a number of instances, samples from different areas in one country resembled those in other countries more than they did each other. It states that the data suggest a pattern of cross-cultural differences, for example, avoidant classifications appear more prevalent in Western European countries and resistant classifications appear more frequent in Israel and Japan. This article notes that intracultural variation was nearly 1.5 times the cross-cultural variation.

1384. van Staden, J. T. (1979). The mental development of abused children in South Africa. *Child Abuse and Neglect, 3*(3/4), 997–1000.
This article describes a study that compared the scores of 30 abused White South African children, ranging in age from 6 months to 6 years, with a control group of 20 nonabused children using the Griffith's Mental Development Scale. Although the locomotor skills of abused children did not differ significantly from those of the control group, abused children were found to have severe interpersonal and practical deficits due to stunting of all other areas of mental development.

1385. Varley, C. K. (1984). Schizophreniform psychoses in mentally retarded adolescent girls following sexual as-

sault. *American Journal of Psychiatry, 141*(4), 593–595.

This article examines the cases of three females with mental retardation (ages 14 to 17) who developed schizophreniform psychoses following sexual assault. The author uses these cases to illustrate how female adolescents with mental retardation are particularly vulnerable to sexual exploitation and how their response to sexual assault may be qualitatively different from that of people without mental retardation. As the assault was not identified in any of the cases until the psychosis had been resolved through neuroleptic treatment and family therapy, the author states that psychiatrists should be aware that sexual assaults can contribute to a psychotic condition in adolescents with mental retardation and that there is a need for the development of prophylactic services through sex education for people with developmental disabilities.

1386. **Veelken, N., Ziegelitz, J., Knispel, J. D., & Bentele, K. H. P. (1991). Sudden infant death syndrome in Hamburg: An epidemiological analysis of 150 cases.** *Acta Paediatrica Scandinavica,. 80,* 86–92.

The authors of this article discuss an epidemiological study that retrospectively analyzed 150 cases of sudden infant death syndrome (SIDS) documented over a 5-year period in Hamburg, Germany. This study determined an incidence rate of 2.3 per 1,000 live births ($n = 150/65,876$) and noted regional differences with regard to incidence rates and seasonal differences. The results of this study indicate that the majority (82%) of infants died within the first 6 months of life. This study also isolated several risk factors: the age of the mother, birth weight of the infant, preterm infants, and the number of siblings.

1387. **Vesti, P., & Lavik, N. J. (1991). Torture and the medical profession: A review.** *Journal of Medical Ethics, 17*(Suppl.), 4–8.

This article reviews the role of physicians in torture. It concludes that evidence shows that physicians throughout history have taken part in both legitimized and illegal torture. The authors also identify links between physicians' roles in the annihilation of people with disabilities and torture. (Editors' note: This article is particularly relevant to the discussion of physicians' proposed roles in deciding when euthanasia is appropriate.)

1388. **Victims of Violence. (1986).** *Violent crime and the disabled: A Victims of Violence survey.* Ottawa, ON: Author.

This paper states that the research has not addressed the different aspects of mental health affected by the use of violence against people with disabilities. It suggests that future researchers and other professionals should recognize not only the effects of trauma on mental health, but the impact of dependency, fear, isolation, and credibility when people with disabilities have been abused.

1389. **Victims of Violence. (no date). Sexual assault and abuse of the disabled: The disabled sometimes victimized again by justice system. In** *Victims of Violence Report* **(pp. 31–33). Ottawa, ON: Author.**

This chapter focuses on the sexual abuse of people with disabilities. It claims that the majority of cases of sexual abuse of people with disabilities in Canada are never reported, and for this reason, people with disabilities are in the high-risk group. This chapter discusses the lack of research related to the mental health issues and legal aspects of violence against people with disabilities.

1390. **Vizard, E. (1989). Child sexual abuse and mental handicap: A child psychiatrist's perspective. In H. Brown & A. Craft (Eds.),** *Thinking the unthinkable: Papers on sexual abuse and people with learning difficulties* **(pp. 18–28). London: FPA Education Unit.**

This chapter includes general information on child sexual abuse as viewed by a child psychiatrist and a discussion of some of these issues as they specifically relate to children with intellectual disabilities. It examines some of the following issues: the increased vulnerability of children with disabilities, the sexualized behavior of child victims that may expose them to further sexual abuse and reinforce the false impression that they are to blame for their own abuse, the possibility that behavioral changes that result from sexual abuse may simulate or aggravate intellectual impairment, and the perception of children with disabilities as potential victims.

1391. **Vocational and Rehabilitation Research Institute. (1987).** *Sexual assault manual: Information and procedures following a sexual assault.* Calgary, AB: Author.

This manual provides procedural guidelines for handling sexual assault or sexual abuse situations involving people with mental disabilities. It discusses the following issues: emergency procedures, aspects of disclosure, legal information, and assessment of required services for victims.

1392. **Voeckler, C., Bilwes, M., Oswald, A., & Schneider, G. (1989). Schizophrenie et euthanasie [Schizophrenia and euthanasia. Symposium: The psychiatric evolution (1988, Saint-Maurice, France)].** *Evolution Psychiatrique, 54*(2), 387–395.

This article provides a case history of a family with six schizophrenic children who were killed under the Nazi euthanasia program. The authors suggest that schizophrenia in contemporary relatives of these children implies that a genetic factor is likely, but they point out that medicalized killing is unacceptable.

1393. von Dadelszen, J. (1987). *Sexual abuse study: An examination of the histories of sexual abuse among girls currently in the care of the Department of Social Welfare* **(Research series 7). Wellington, New Zealand: Department of Social Welfare.**

This report from the Department of Social Welfare in Wellington, New Zealand, examines the histories of sexual abuse among girls currently in the care of the department. One hundred thirty-six girls out of a total sample of 230 girls were interviewed for the study. The findings show that 71% of those interviewed and 33% of those not interviewed were known to have been abused. Forty-eight percent (*n*=46) of those who were interviewed and were abused reported more than one instance of sexual abuse unrelated to any previous experiences of abuse. A total of 169 experiences of sexual abuse were reported. Ninety-six percent of perpetrators were male, with a mean age of 28 years. The average age of the victim was 10. Fifty-one percent of sexual abuse experiences involved family members, and 37% involved people known to the victim or family. In 44% of the sexual abuse experiences, sexual intercourse was involved. Threats and/or force were used by the perpetrator 53% of the time, and alcohol was involved 33% of the time. Feelings of fear, shame, anger, and distrust of men and boys were shared by the majority of victims.

1394. von Ronn, P. (1991). Zum indirekten Nachweis von Totungsaktivitaten wahrend der zweiten Phase der NS-"Euthanasie" [Indirect proof of murderous activities during the second stage of the Nazi-"Euthanasia"]. *Recht and Psychiatrie, 9*(1), 8–13.

This article discusses the Nazi euthanasia program and how well it was hidden from the German public. The author points out that euthanasia was rarely detectable from other causes of death from medical records; however, a comparison of the records of patients labeled as troublesome or unproductive workers with patients without these labels reveals a disproportionate number of deaths in the low status group.

1395. Vondra, J. I., Kolar, A. B., & Radigan, B. L. (1992). Psychological maltreatment of children. In R. T. Ammerman & M. Hersen (Eds.), *Assessment of family violence: A clinical and legal sourcebook* **(pp. 253–290). New York: John Wiley & Sons.**

This chapter deals with the psychological or emotional maltreatment of children. It discusses the identification and assessment of mental injury in children in relation to the different developmental stages from infancy to adolescence. This chapter examines the legal issues surrounding the definition of psychological maltreatment and the resulting psychological dysfunction. Two case studies help illustrate the ambiguous nature of this form of maltreatment, the legal considerations involved, and ways to deal with the situation.

1396. Vriak, A., McMurchy, G., & Watson, R. (Eds.). (1992, February/March). Violence & women with disabilities [Special issue]. *Transition.*

This newsletter includes articles focusing on the different aspects of the problem of violence against women with disabilities: for example, rape trauma syndrome, abuse issues for women with intellectual disabilities, the reasons for vulnerability of women with disabilities, intervention and treatment, and ritual abuse.

•W•

1397. Wadsworth, J. S., & Harper, D. C. (1991). Grief and bereavement in mental retardation: A need for a new understanding. *Death Studies, 15,* 281–292.

This article examines the grief and bereavement of people with mental retardation. It claims that it is important to understand the comprehension or expression of grief and bereavement in people with mental retardation when assisting them to cope with the death of a family member or relative. Also, it suggests that positive coping strategies might prevent additional mental health problems that could result from this loss or other changes, for example, a change in residence. This article points out that there is little research concerning the variables associated with loss and grief among people with developmental disabilities, and as a result, it is difficult to tell which strategies are successful in helping people with developmental disabilities cope with the loss of a loved one.

1398. Wald, M. S., & Cohen, S. (1988). Preventing child abuse—What will it take? In D. J. Besharov (Ed.), *Protecting children from abuse and neglect: Policy and practice* **(pp. 295–319). Springfield, IL: Charles C Thomas.**

This chapter describes possible means for preventing child abuse. It discusses causality in child abuse and examines the application of these theories to treatment. Given that there are many variables involved in child abuse, this chapter points out that prevention programs may offer a variety of means for preventing child maltreatment. Consequently, this chapter evaluates several prevention programs: for example, early and extended contact programs, perinatal support programs, parent education classes, and counseling programs. The authors also discuss prevention strategies for the individual and the feasibility (i.e., the cost and critical value) of initiating a prevention program.

1399. Wales, J. K. H., Herber, S. M., & Taitz, L. S. (1992). Height and body

proportions in child abuse. *Archives of Disease in Childhood, 67,* 632–635. This article discusses a study that measured 91 children subjected to physical abuse and/or neglect for height and body proportion. The measurements were compared to 345 local children who were assessed on their height, sitting height, and leg length. This study found that a significant number of abused children were short in stature (*n*=31/91) when compared to the control group. Follow-up of 25 abused children who had undergone such social intervention as working with social workers, adoption, or foster care revealed a significant recovery in leg length.

1400. Walker, P. W. (1980). Recognizing the mental health needs of developmentally disabled people. *Social Work, 25*(4), 293–297. According to this article, many people with developmental disabilities and their families are denied adequate mental health services. It claims that this lack of services is the result of conflicts in bureaucratic priorities and mental health professionals' belief that many people with developmental disabilities do not respond directly to clinical services. It points out that the perspective of the mental health community might be the result of earlier ideas that suggested people with developmental disabilities did not have feelings and would not respond appropriately to traditional forms of therapy. This article provides two case studies to illustrate how the performance of developmental tasks of people with disabilities may be blocked or denied due to their families' habitual distortions or denial of this person's need for normalizing, growth-promoting activities. The author concludes that families with a child with developmental disabilities need counseling to help them address these habitual distortions and to help them overcome their tendency to excessively manipulate their relationships with their children.

1401. Walsh, A. (1990). Twice labeled: The effect of psychiatric labeling on the sentencing of sex offenders. *Social Problems, 37*(3), 375–389. This article describes a study that reviewed the files of 431 sex offenders in order to determine if psychiatric labels upon referral influenced their sentencing. This review found that 246 sex offenders were referred for psychiatric evaluation and were labeled: for example, pedophile, poor psychosexual development, polymorphous perverse, sexual psychopathy, inadequate personality, and so forth. It found that the prognosis for recovery was defined as poor, fair, or good. This study controlled for the seriousness of the crimes and prior record and found that sex offenders who were labeled were two times more likely to be incarcerated than sex offenders who were not labeled.

1402. Walsh, B. W., & Rosen, P. M. (1988). *Self-mutilation: Theory, research, and treatment.* **New York: Guilford Press.**

This book on self-mutilation is intended for a broad range of mental health professionals, and it is divided into three areas: theory, research, and treatment. Part I discusses the various forms of self-mutilative behavior reported in the literature, and it provides the incidence rates of self-mutilating behavior in several Western countries. Using theory and a review of the literature, it illustrates a critical distinction between suicide attempts and self-mutilative behavior. The authors assert that self-mutilation and suicide need to be understood and treated as separate clinical problems. In Part II, self-mutilation is described in relation to various clinical populations: adolescents and persons with borderline personality disorder, adolescents and persons with psychosis, adolescents and persons with retardation, and adolescents and persons with autism. In addition, the authors provide empirical evidence for the phenomenon of self-mutilative contagion. Part III provides specific guidelines for therapy for self-mutilators: cognitive-behavioral therapy, psychoanalytic therapy, family therapy, and group therapy. The authors also identify clinical strategies that are likely to be counterproductive to treatment, and they discuss the way in which various modalities may be integrated into a comprehensive, multimodal treatment program. Also, this book includes a bibliography with approximately 150 references.

1403. Walters, A. S., Barrett, R. P., & Feinstein, C. (1990). Social relatedness and autism: Current research, issues, directions. *Research in Developmental Disabilities, 11*(3), 303–326. This article reviews studies of social relatedness in autism. It examines studies that deal with attachment and social interest, recognition and communication of emotions, social cognition and communication, symbolic play, and the neuroanatomy and neurochemistry of social relatedness. This article concludes that progress has been made in behaviorally defining and measuring relevant subcomponents of social relatedness that are abnormal in autism, many previously held clinical generalizations about autism, particularly those concerning eye contact and attachment, have been called into question.

1404. Ward, A. (1992). Caring for other people's children. In W. Stainton Rogers, D. Hevey, J. Roche, & E. Ash (Eds.), *Child abuse and neglect: Facing the challenge* **(pp. 106–112). London: The Open University.** This chapter discusses children who are cared for by caregivers other than their biological parents. It examines factors that contribute to possible instances of neglect or abuse within the context of noted differences between caring for biological children and caring for nonbiological children. This chapter uses a case study to illustrate the issues. Also, the author discusses residential care issues.

1405. Ward, C. (1988). Stress, coping and adjustment in victims of sexual assault: The role of psychological defense mech-

anisms [Special issue: Stress counselling]. *Counselling Psychology Quarterly, 1*(2/3), 165–178.

This article discusses a study that was conducted to determine if psychological defense mechanisms were employed by 40 Indian, Malay, and Chinese victims of sexual assault (ages ranged from 12 to 19) to cope with sexual assault (primarily rape). This article notes that 15 of these children and adolescents were abused by close family members. This study used semistructured interviews, and the results of these interviews reveal that 90% of these children and adolescents used psychological defense mechanisms, for example, repression, emotional insulation, and rationalization. The author suggests that psychological defense mechanisms should be included in the interpretation of stress and coping processes in crisis theory, research, and counseling.

1406. Warren, A. C., Holroyd, S., & Folstein, M. F. (1989). Major depression in Down's Syndrome. *British Journal of Psychiatry, 155,* 202–205.

This article points out that there is a high rate of psychiatric disorders among people with mental retardation and that affective disorders have unusual presentations in people with severe and profound mental retardation. It claims that recognizing affective disorders in people with Down syndrome is complicated by their poor verbal skills. This article discusses a study that examined five people with Down syndrome who were referred for psychiatric evaluation of dementia. These people were found to have major depression. All of them had cognitive and behavioral deterioration. This article describes and contrasts the features of major depression and Alzheimer's disease. It concludes that affective disorders may present with severe cognitive disturbances and vegetative function, the course of behavioral deterioration may fluctuate, and delusions and hallucinations may be prominent. The authors recommend electroconvulsive shock therapy as an effective treatment of this disorder for people with Down syndrome.

1407. Washington State Department of Social and Health Services. (1983). *Sexual exploitation: What parents of handicapped persons should know.* **Olympia: Author. (ERIC Document Reproduction Service No. ED 258 408)**

This brochure defines the major areas of sexual exploitation under Washington State law. Changes in child behavior that may indicate victimization are discussed as well as immediate and long-term action that parents can take in the event of sexual exploitation. Also, this brochure describes the services offered by the Seattle Rape Relief Developmental Disabilities Project.

1408. Wasserman, G. A. (1986). Affective expression in normal and physically handicapped infants: Situational and developmental effects. *Journal of the American Academy of Child Psychiatry, 25*(3), 393–399.

The author of this article points out that studies of children with physical disabilities often report incidences of sadness, inhibition, passivity, social isolation, and withdrawal; consequently, this article examines 14 infants with a variety of orthopedic and facial malformations not usually associated with mental retardation and 14 healthy infants at 12, 18, and 24 months of age. The infants' interactions with their mothers, alone, and with strangers were videotaped and examined for open expression of positive and negative affect during 10-second coding intervals. Expressions of emotions depended on the situation for both groups of toddlers. During their second year, infants with physical disabilities were increasingly unwilling to engage a stranger in positive interactions, and they displayed delays in their ability to control their expressions of distress during maternal separation. The author concludes that diminished social skills of children with physical disabilities occurs earlier than has previously been reported and is not simply related to attachment but is one of several problems confronting these children.

1409. Wasserman, G. A., Green, A., & Allen, R. (1983). Going beyond abuse: Maladaptive patterns of interaction in abusing mother-infant pairs. *Journal of the American Academy of Child Psychiatry, 22*(3), 245–252.

This article discusses a study that assessed 12 abusing and 12 nonabusing mother-infant pairs in order to determine if there were any differences between the two groups on patterns of interaction between mother and child. The infants in this study were matched for age, gender, ethnicity, and socioeconomic status. The mother-infant pairs were assessed while at play for 10 minutes. The interaction was videotaped and scored using the Maternal Style Scale. For this scale, behavior is recorded every 10 seconds. The Bayley Mental Developmental Scale was also used to assess eight infants in each group. The presence or absence of behavior was coded according to items in one of four categories: control, stimulation, affective behavior, and proxemic behavior. The results of this assessment indicate the following: Abusing mothers tend to ignore their children more than nonabusing mothers, initiating less play activities and less verbal teaching; and nonabusing mothers exhibit more positive affect than abusing mothers. The authors note that abusing mothers display a lack of interaction with their infants, and this lack of interaction puts these infants' future cognitive and social development at risk.

1410. Wasserman, G. A., Lennon, M. C., Allen, R., & Shilansky, M. (1987). Contributors to attachment in normal and physically handicapped infants. *Journal of the American Academy of Child and Adolescent Psychiatry, 26*(1), 9–15.

This article investigates the elements that contribute to attachment in infants with physical disabilities and infants without physical disabilities. Thirty-six infants with congenital facial and orthopedic malformations and 46 infants without physical disabilities were videotaped in semistructured "strange situations" at 9 months and 12 months with their mothers. The results of this study indicate that control infants were significantly more responsive at 9 and 12 months; however, mothers of infants with disabilities were more available and positive at 12 months. This study found that mothers of both groups differ in behaviors used to encourage attachment, but the outcome was the same for both groups. Although early problems are apparent in the responsiveness of infants with disabilities, improvements in mother-infant relationships occurred after 9 months and by the end of the first year. The authors suggest that these improvements continue to have a positive influence on attachment, and high-risk interactions may be more adaptive than previously anticipated.

1411. Watson, G. (1992). The abuse of disabled children and young people. In W. Stainton Rogers, D. Hevey, J. Roche, & E. Ash (Eds.), *Child abuse and neglect: Facing the challenge* (pp. 113–118). London: The Open University.

This chapter discusses the abuse of children with disabilities. Children's disabilities are categorized under five different headings: physical disability; behavioral or emotional problems; learning difficulties; specific problems, including autism and epilepsy; and stigmatization. Factors that put these children at risk for abuse include: cultural factors, personal characteristics, stress, institutional abuse, lack of education, and the dilemmas of disability. The author suggests three ways to help children at risk for being abused: communication, openness, and education.

1412. Watson, M., Bain, A., & Houghton, S. (1992). A preliminary study in teaching self-protective skills to children with moderate and severe mental retardation. *Journal of Special Education, 26*(2), 181–194.

This article discusses a group-based self-protection skills training program for seven students with mental retardation. The five girls and two boys in this training program ranged in age from 6 to 8 and were instructed on how to respond to inappropriate advances from strangers. Three target behaviors were stressed during training: NO, refusal to comply with the stranger's request; GO, vacating the area of confrontation; and TELL, informing others who are trustworthy about the incident. The training consisted of 15 lessons involving different settings. The children were tested on five different occasions over a period of 9 weeks, and this testing involved hidden video- and audiotaping. The results of this testing indicate that self-protection skills improved for six of the seven children.

1413. Waxman, B. F. (1991). Hatred: The unacknowledged dimension in violence against disabled people [Special issue: Sexual exploitation of people with disabilities]. *Sexuality and Disability, 9*(3), 185–199.

This article suggests that crimes against people with disabilities are crimes of hate. It argues that such crimes should be acknowledged by the federal Hate Crimes Statistics Act, which at present does not recognize the disproportionately high rate of violence against this group as indicative of hate mongering. It claims that people with disabilities have been victimized by society because of the focus on the defective socialization of people without disabilities instead of on the characteristics of people with disabilities. This article presents historical and experimental research on attitudes toward people with disabilities.

1414. Waxman, B. F. (1994). Up against eugenics: Disabled women's challenge to receive reproductive health services. *Sexuality and Disability, 12*(2), 155–171.

This article discusses the lack of resources and services to support reproductive health and reproductive rights for women with disabilities. Waxman presents an argument that this lack results from society's devaluation of women with disabilities and an implicit philosophy of eugenics.

1415. Waxman, H. M., Astrom, S., Norberg, A., & Winblad, B. (1988). Conflicting attitudes toward euthanasia for severely demented patients of health care professionals in Sweden. *Journal of the American Geriatrics Society, 36*(5), 397–401.

This article reports the results of a survey of more than 1,000 workers in institutions concerning their attitudes toward euthanasia for patients with severe dementia. There was considerable disagreement about the appropriateness of euthanasia for people with severe dementia. Individuals who were less happy with their current job situations were more likely to endorse euthanasia.

1416. Webber, L. (1993, May 10). Convicted of raping a retarded adult: A video tape and hearsay evidence clinches the case. *Alberta Report*, p. 27.

This magazine article reports on the case of Daniel William Brennan, who was accused of the rape and assault of an adult with developmental disabilities he had hired to cut his lawn. Brennan was found guilty of two counts of sexual assault and sodomy, and he received 7 years in jail. The case against Brennan was made using a 30-second videotape obtained from Brennan's house showing the naked victim on Brennan's bed and hearsay evidence obtained from a crisis unit worker. This hearsay evidence pertained to semen stains found on the victim's clothes and welt marks found on the victim's back. No physical evidence of the assault was noted by police. The victim had a prior history of false sexual assault claims and public displays of sexual behavior.

1417. Weicker, L. J. (1987). Federal response to institutional abuse and neglect: The Protection and Advocacy for Mentally Ill Individuals Act. *American Psychologist, 42*(11), 1027–1028.
This article discusses the 1985 testimony before the Subcommittee on the Handicapped and the Appropriations Subcommittee on Labor, Health and Human Services, and Education by parents, advocates, journalists, employees, administrators, and residents of federal institutions for people with disabilities that revealed the abuse and neglect occurring in federal institutions. In response, a Senate investigation was initiated that assessed 31 facilities in 19 states over a 9-month period. This investigation involved the interview of 500 staff, residents, administrators, advocates, and officials. This investigation found that understaffing, inadequate training for staff, long work hours, low wages, overcrowding, and an ineffective certification system for institutions were some of the reasons for this abuse and neglect. Because of this investigation, a Protection and Advocacy for Mentally Ill Individuals Act was developed and became law in 1986. This law resulted in the expansion of existing protection and advocacy agencies, who were given the authority to investigate and take legal or administrative action against abusive or neglectful conditions involving people with disabilities.

1418. Weinbach, R. W., & Curtiss, C. R. (1986). Making child abuse victims aware of their victimization: A treatment issue. *Child Welfare, 65*(4), 337–346.
This article discusses theories dealing with increasing the awareness of the child who is an abuse victim. It discusses the different patterns of abuse of adolescents, and it examines the emotional after-effects of abuse. This article describes a descriptive study that assessed 195 men and 40 women at a South Carolina prison facility using a structured interview administered by graduate students. The people in this study were incarcerated for violent criminal offenses. Ninety of these people (38%) were abused in childhood. Abuse was defined as behavior that fell within the legal definition of child abuse. Out of this group of abused people, 75% did not feel abused as children. Theories as to the rationale behind this reaction are discussed in terms of the semantics of violence, socioeconomic status of the subjects, and denial. Treatment of the abused victim is discussed, with the emphasis on tailoring intervention to the needs of the client.

1419. Weinberg, J. K. (1988). Autonomy as a different voice: Women, disabilities, and decisions. In M. Fine & A. Asch
(Eds.), *Women with disabilities: Essays in psychology, culture, and politics* (pp. 269–296). Philadelphia: Temple University Press.
This chapter addresses the ways that legal and health care systems influence choices regarding sexuality and social behavior for women with mental disabilities. It specifically examines sexual and physical abuse in institutional settings. It points out that the role of communication problems in limiting the ability to report abuse is an important factor. The lack of standards for caregivers is also seen as a major contributor to the problem. The author suggests that existing statutes are inadequate and often limited to the protection of children or elderly people; therefore, these statutes exclude many people with disabilities.

1420. Weinberg, S., Jr. (1980). The transmission of psychopathology through four generations of a family. In G. J. Williams & J. Money (Eds.), *Traumatic abuse and neglect of children at home* (pp. 517–535). Baltimore: The Johns Hopkins University Press.
This chapter presents the history of four generations of a family known to the Jewish Board of Guardians, a social service agency. It examines the transmission of psychopathology in this family from one generation to the next, from 1928 to 1970, and it discusses some of the problems encountered by this family: severe neglect, abuse, psychopathology, and developmental disability.

1421. Weir, R. F. (1984). The law and handicapped infants. In *Selective nontreatment of handicapped newborns: Moral dilemmas in neonatal medicine* (pp. 116–142). New York: Oxford University Press.
This chapter discusses the law and selective nontreatment of infants with disabilities. It defines tort actions dealing with wrongful birth and wrongful life, and it illustrates these actions with case examples. Also, this chapter uses case studies to discuss federal law and the rights of people with disabilities.

1422. Weir, R. F. (1984). Options among ethicists. In *Selective nontreatment of handicapped newborns: Moral dilemmas in neonatal medicine* (pp. 143–187). New York: Oxford University Press.
In this chapter, several ethicists discuss five different views on the selective nontreatment of infants with disabilities: treat all nondying neonates, terminate the lives of selected nonpersons, withhold treatment according to parental discretion, withhold treatment according to quality of life projections, and withhold treatment judged not in the child's best interests. This chapter also discusses the general problems regarding ethical literature on selective nontreatment of infants with disabilities.

1423. Weir, R. F. (1984). **Pediatricians and selective nontreatment.** In *Selective nontreatment of handicapped newborns: Moral dilemmas in neonatal medicine* (pp. 59–90). New York: Oxford University Press.

In this chapter, seven pediatric specialists discuss the selective nontreatment of newborns with disabilities. This chapter includes case examples to highlight the position taken by each medical professional. These specialists reach an agreement on the consequences of selective nontreatment, but they concede that procedural contingencies are still open to debate.

1424. Weir, R. F. (1984). **Selective nontreatment and criminal liability.** In *Selective nontreatment of handicapped newborns: Moral dilemmas in neonatal medicine* (pp. 91–115). New York: Oxford University Press.

This chapter examines the legal liability of selective nontreatment of newborns with disabilities. This liability is of greatest concern to parents and physicians who have the right to select or withhold treatment. This chapter uses case examples to illustrate the issues, it discusses the legal status of selective nontreatment, it examines the present debate about the law, and it raises questions about changing the law.

1425. West, M. A., Richardson, M., Crimi, J. L., & Stuart, S. (1992). **Identification of developmental disabilities and health problems among individuals under protective services.** *Mental Retardation, 50*(4), 221–225.

This article describes a review of 150 case records referred to Child Protective Services and a protocol for screening case records for developmental disabilities and health problems. The results of this review indicate that 11% of the children in the sample had confirmed developmental disabilities and an additional 23% were suspected of having developmental disabilities. The authors found that information on health and developmental status of children was sparse and often lacking. They urge efforts to include this information in all child protective services case records.

1426. Westcott, H. L. (1991). **The abuse of disabled children: A review of the literature.** *Child: Care, Health and Development, 17,* 243–258.

This literature review addresses the abuse of children with disabilities. It points out that studies dealing with this topic have had their methodological shortcomings. In addition, society has failed to meet the needs of those children who are found to be at an increased risk for abuse. The author recommends new policies and additional research concerning the abuse of children with disabilities.

1427. Westcott, H. L. (1991). *Institutional abuse of children—From research to policy: A review* (Report No. ISBN 0 902498 30 4). London: National Society for the Prevention of Cruelty to Children.

This extensive report from the National Society for the Prevention of Cruelty to Children addresses the issues of institutional child abuse. It examines the following areas: the nature of institutional abuse; the protection of children in institutions; the role of society in institutional abuse; and policy and practice issues concerning staffing, investigation, and quality of care.

1428. Westcott, H. L. (1992). **Vulnerability and the need for protection.** In J. Gibbons (Ed.), *The Children's Act of 1989 and family support: Principles into practice* (pp. 89–100). London: Her Majesty's Stationery Office.

This chapter discusses the role of family support in the protection of children with disabilities from abuse. It describes a number of studies that indicate increased risk for children with disabilities and suggests a number of factors that increase vulnerability. Social factors are considered as the prime contributors to increased risk for children with disabilities being abused, and empowerment of people with disabilities and their families is discussed as a primary prevention strategy.

1429. Westcott, H. L. (1993). *Abuse of children and adults with disabilities.* London: National Society for the Prevention of Cruelty to Children.

This report discusses a study conducted by the London-based National Society for the Prevention of Cruelty to Children that examined the abuse of children and adults with disabilities. This study used interviews to collect data, and the results of these interviews indicate the following: Children with disabilities are at increased risk for abuse than children without disabilities; disclosure of abuse is difficult for all children, especially children with disabilities who might have additional communication difficulties; the effects of abuse are long-term, affecting relationships, development of trust, and self-esteem and instilling a sense of vulnerability; the participants in this study felt strongly about the stigma of having been abused as children and being viewed as the next generation of abusers; and counseling services were limited. This report includes samples of interviewee responses, and it provides recommendations concerning the findings of this study.

1430. Westcott, H. L. (1994). **The memorandum of good practice and children with disabilities.** *Journal of Law and Practice, 3*(2), 21–32.

This article reviews a British government protocol for investigative interviews involving children with disabilities as witnesses. It discusses issues of competency, credibility, compellability (i.e., the ability of the court to require a witness to testify), and availability for cross-examination related to various disabilities. The memorandum of good practice suggests a multistage interview. The first phase is designed to develop rapport and learn more about the child and the child's abilities and disabilities that may require accommodation. The second stage of the interview requests a free narrative account. The third stage consists of nonleading questions to get more details of the account. The fourth and final stage terminates the interview and reassures the child. The memorandum also suggests appropriate accommodations to the child's communication skills. The author suggests that the memorandum of good practice will have value in some cases but that it does not allow adequate accommodation for many other children, particularly those with severe disabilities.

1431. Westcott, H. L. (in press). Abuse of children and adults who are disabled. In S. French (Ed.), *On equal terms: Working with disabled people* **(pp. 190–205). London: Butterworth.**
This chapter provides a general discussion of abuse of children with disabilities from an ecological perspective. Westcott suggests that isolation, exclusion, discrimination, and increased dependency on caregivers for intimate care are factors that contribute to increased incidence of abuse of children and adults with disabilities. The author also provides information on the effects of abuse on children with disabilities and strategies to prevent abuse.

1432. Westen, D., Ludolph, P., Misle, B., Ruffins, S., & Block, J. (1990). Physical and sexual abuse in adolescent girls with borderline personality disorder. *American Journal of Orthopsychiatry, 60*(1), 55–66.
This article discusses a study that compared 27 female adolescents diagnosed with borderline personality disorder and a control group comprising 23 female adolescents for any history of sexual and/or physical abuse. All of the participants were inpatients at the adolescent unit of the University of Michigan Medical Center during 1983 and 1988. No significant differences were found between the two groups at the onset of the study, with the average age for both groups falling between 15 and 16, but the results of the study indicate the following: The borderline personality disorder group had a greater incidence of neglect and abuse than the control group; fathers were most often the perpetrators for both physical and sexual abuse in both groups, with most borderline personality disorder patients having more than one abuser; and a history of neglect was usually precipitated by a history of physical and sexual abuse. In terms of impulsiveness, a significant difference was noted between those individuals who were abused and those who were not abused, with the abused group being more impulsive.

1433. Westerlund, E. (1990). Thinking about incest, deafness, and counselling. *Journal of the American Deafness and Rehabilitation Association, 23*(3), 105–107.
This article is written for health care providers and women with disabilities. It discusses the longlasting, traumatizing effects of incest and the complexity of incest for women who are deaf. It examines the following psychological effects: stigma, self-blame, loss of self-esteem, confusion, powerlessness, inability to trust, and avoidance. This article concludes that the difficulties that already exist in the treatment of incest are greatly increased when the individual has a disability.

1434. Westra, B., & Martin, H. P. (1981). Children of battered women. *Maternal Child Nursing Journal, 10*(1), 41–54.
This article describes a study that assessed 20 children from 15 families who were residing with their mothers in shelters for battered women to determine if they exhibited any functional delays or dysfunctional behavior resulting from living in an abusive environment. The children ranged in age from 2.5 to 8 years. This study found the following: the developmental delays in verbal, cognitive, and motor abilities were significantly lower for children from the shelter when compared to a standardized population; and greater aggressive behavior was demonstrated by the children from the shelter. Demographics were obtained from all the families involved in this study.

1435. Wexler, D. B. (1982). Seclusion and restraint: Lessons from law, psychiatry, and psychology. *International Journal of Law and Psychiatry, 5,* 285–294.
This article provides a legal analysis of the right of people living in institutions to personal security and freedom from restraint and seclusion. Much of the analysis is based on a Supreme Court Decision, *Youngberg v. Romeo* (102 S. Ct. 2452 [1982]), a case in which Romeo, a man with mental retardation, sued administrators of Pennhurst State School and Hospital, a large institution where he lived. The U.S. Supreme Court ruled that he was entitled to personal security and freedom from bodily restraint, but it qualified those rights in several ways. For example, the court considered that it was sometimes necessary for institutions to use restraint to protect residents and ruled that institutions could not be expected to protect residents from all violence. It allowed significant latitude for clinical judgment of professionals in making judgments regarding when restraint or seclusion might be required. The court upheld the use of seclusion or restraint as acceptable in an emergency situation, but its use in nonemergency situations appears to be unacceptable unless the resident accepts it voluntarily. To be considered as an emergency, the behavior of the resident must pose a clear and substantial threat to someone's safety, and the seclusion or restraint must be used to terminate or control the threat, not as punishment when the threat is no longer present and apparent.

1436. Wexler, R. (1990). *Wounded inno-cents: The real victims of the war against child abuse.* **Buffalo, NY: Prometheus Books.**
This book presents a scathing indictment of "child-savers." Wexler suggests that children are often taken from their families because of unverified accusations of abuse and placed in foster care or institutional care that is truly abusive. This book includes many anecdotal accounts of abuse and neglect in care, including some involving children with disabilities, who often end up with the worst placements because they are excluded from many of the better possible placement alternatives. This book cites two studies from Kansas City. One study found that 57% of children placed in foster care were sent to settings that were high risk for abuse or neglect. The second study suggests that 25% of children placed in foster care were actually abused in the protective foster care settings. Two other studies found that 21% of abuse and neglect cases in Louisiana involved offenses committed in foster care and that 28% of children placed in foster care in Baltimore were abused while in care.

1437. White, J. W., & Sorenson, S. B. (1992). A sociocultural view of sexual assault: From discrepancy to diversity. *Journal of Social Issues, 48(1), 187–195.*
This article applies a sociocultural perspective to definitions of rape and to certain aspects of research: for example, methods used to assess sexual assault. The authors examine the relationship between certain sociocultural factors and reporting sexual assault: for example, the experience and reaction of victims to sexual assault, the motives of the perpetrator, and the response of society. The results of this examination support the idea that rape is a social act.

1438. White, R., Benedict, M. I., Wulff, L., & Kelley, M. (1987). Physical disabilities as risk factors for child maltreatment: A selected review. *American Journal of Orthopsychiatry, 57(1), 93–101.*
This article reviews the literature on child abuse and suggests that children with physical disabilities may be at increased risk for maltreatment or neglect. It evaluates theoretical, definitional, and methodological concerns and discusses research issues. The authors conclude that the reviewed literature supports, but does not confirm, linkages between children with disabilities and the risk of maltreatment.

1439. Whitehead, J., & Unger, L. (1991). Bringing the abusive employee back. *Journal of Mental Health Administration, 18(2), 143–147.*
This article describes the reintegration of abusive employees back into the work environment. It examines the circumstances of abuse accusations and the strained relations that are created between employee and employer. It discusses a survey of 10 employees accused of abuses

and their respective supervisors that was conducted to examine what system supports each required for continued relations at work. The authors informally interviewed the 10 pairs of employees and their supervisors in addition to administering the surveys. The authors point out that it is important to understand and manage this return process since most employees (75%) charged with abuse are found to be to some degree culpable, receive a penalty that does not terminate their employment, and return to work. Although their supervisors viewed these settlements as admissions of guilt, some of the employees viewed the negotiated settlement of charges against them as vindication. These employees felt that they had been treated unfairly and that their supervisors should now make it up to them with better treatment. Some other employees were ashamed or embarrassed by the charges against them, but even those who acknowledged their wrongdoing seemed uninterested in changing their behavior. This survey resulted in the creation of a reintegration process that focused on more structured reintegration, clearer communication between parties regarding expectations, and support for both employees and supervisors from upper management. A pilot project that incorporated this reintegration process was initiated with five employee/supervisor cases, and according to the authors, this project was successful.

1440. Whitney, C. R. (1993, January 16). Top German doctor admits SS past. *The New York Times,* **p. I3.**
This newspaper article reports that German doctor Hans Joachim Sewering, president-elect of the World Medical Association, is accused of sending a 14-year-old girl with tuberculosis to her death during the Nazi regime. Dr. Sewering has admitted that he was a member of the SS before World War II. An international campaign to remove Dr. Sewering from the post of president has been established by doctors.

1441. Whittaker, J. K. (1987). The role of residential institutions. In J. Garbarino, P. E. Brookhouser, & K. J. Authier (Eds.), *Special children-special risks: The maltreatment of children with disabilities* **(pp. 83–100). New York: Aldine de Gruyter.**
This chapter first examines what is known about the incidence of maltreatment in residential institutions. Next, internal and external factors relating to child maltreatment in institutional environments are discussed. In regard to internal factors influencing maltreatment, references are made to various sources that outline institutional policies that ensure residents' rights, appropriate treatment plans, and family involvement. The author points out the following: While good programs for institutions are available, they are useless without proper staff training; evaluation of programs and providing staff support are of great importance; and external factors that can help to prevent maltreatment in institutions are family involvement, strategies for community liaison, and citizen review.

1442. Widom, C. S. (1988). Sampling biases and implications for child abuse research. *American Journal of Orthopsychiatry, 58*(2), 260–270.

This article discusses a number of sampling biases that have influenced researchers' understanding of child abuse. At least four of these common sampling biases have probably contributed to the lack of recognition of abuse of children with disabilities. First, many studies have restricted their samples to children abused in their homes; consequently, institutional abuse is ignored. Since a much larger proportion of children with disabilities live in institutions than the proportion of children without disabilities living in institutions, much of the abuse affecting children with disabilities has been ignored. Second, some studies have limited their sample to children abused by biological parents. Since much of the abuse of children with disabilities is extrafamilial abuse, this has also led to underestimating the abuse of children with disabilities. Third, some studies have excluded children with cognitive or neurologic impairments, which obviously leads to underrepresentation of these children in the sample. Finally, many studies restrict their analysis to cases that have been officially substantiated. Substantiated cases, however, may not be representative of a larger number of unreported or unconfirmed cases. Children with disabilities that affect their ability to communicate or who are socially isolated as a result of their disabilities are probably less often among the substantiated cases than among the unreported or unconfirmed cases, and so, they are likely to be underestimated in research that focuses on substantiated cases. The author points out that no sampling method will be likely to overcome all of these problems, but she recommends that researchers clearly identify the potential limitations of their sampling methods. She suggests that a clearer understanding is most likely to result from the consideration of a variety of studies using varied sampling methods.

1443. Wiggin, C. (1994). Sexual abuse procedures. *NAPSAC (National Association for Prevention of Sexual Abuse of Children and Adults with Learning Disabilities) Bulletin, 7,* 11–14.

This article describes the development of a set of procedures for dealing with sexual abuse in a day-care setting for adults with developmental disabilities. This article is based on the experience of staff in one setting who developed procedures after a staff member in their agency was found to have sexually abused several service users and was convicted and sent to prison. The procedures developed are designed to guide staff who encounter allegations of abuse or suspect abuse. The author reports a summary of a review of the procedures 18 months after they were implemented. The review suggests that the procedures were beneficial but that unresolved issues required further attention.

1444. Wight-Felske, A. E., & Barnes, H. (1992). *The law and your rights: A plain language guide to your rights under the Individual's Rights Protection Act of Alberta.* **Edmonton: The Alberta Association for Community Living.**

This book examines Alberta's Individual's Protection Act as it relates to people with mental disabilities. It addresses individual rights as they appear in the act, and it discusses the Alberta People First advocacy group for people with disabilities.

1445. Wilgosh, L. (1990). Sexual assault and abuse of people with disabilities: Parents' concerns. *Developmental Disabilities Bulletin, 18*(2), 44–50.

This article presents a summary of parental concerns raised at the 1989 Sexual Assault and Abuse of People with Disabilities International Conference in Edmonton, Alberta. It recommends some procedural guidelines for dealing with sexual abuse, and it discusses prevention strategies.

1446. Wilgosh, L. (1994). Sexual abuse of children with disabilities: Intervention and treatment issues for parents. In S. Hollins (Ed.), *Proceedings: It did happen here: Sexual abuse and learning disability: Recognition and action* **(pp. 60–72). London: St. George's Hospital Medical School, Division of the Psychiatry of Disability.**

This chapter discusses sexual abuse concerns of parents of children with mental retardation. It provides considerable information about counseling and support for people with mental retardation who have been abused and makes specific recommendations to parents.

1447. Wilhelm, H. H. (1990). Euthanasia Program. In I. Gutman (Ed.), *Encyclopedia of the Holocaust* **(Vol. 2, E–K, pp. 451–454). New York: Macmillan.**

This article describes the euthanasia program under Hitler. The author points out that there was a tradition of "assisted death" and "mercy killings" in hospitals and nursing institutions in Germany prior to 1933. When Hitler took power in 1993, the "euthanasia" concept was expanded to include the murder of many undesirables. Reichsleiter Philip Bouhler and physician Karl Brandt were chosen to head the program code-named "T4" in 1939. The program operated in secrecy, the name T4 stood for the address of its secret headquarters "Tiergartenstrasse 4," but many people knew about or suspected the activities of the program. The activities were widely known because the assignments of euthanasia workers were spread widely and rotated among staff to minimize disciplinary problems. Special perquisites, including free vacations, alcohol, and bonuses, were provided to T4 staff to compensate for the stress of their jobs. Although the program was officially ended by Hitler in 1941, it continued in secrecy until the war ended. The actual number of people killed in this program is unknown because of the many sites used and the secrecy that surrounded the program, but official estimates at the Nuremberg trial suggested that 275,000 people were killed under the T4 program.

1448. Williams, C. (1993). Vulnerable victims? A current awareness of the victimization of people with learning disabilities. *Disability, Handicap and Society, 8*(2), 161–172.

This article provides a review of the literature on vulnerability of people with mental retardation. It concludes that victimization is a significant problem for this group, and it urges more research to guide prevention and intervention practices.

1449. Williams, L. M., & Farrell, R. A. (1990). Legal response to child sexual abuse in day care. *Criminal Justice and Behavior, 17*(3), 284–302.

This article examines 43 cases of alleged sexual abuse in child care. The 58 perpetrators in these cases were at least 15 years old. The results of this examination reveal that the race and sex of the victim, number of victims, type of sex act, and the sex of the alleged perpetrator are important factors when decisions are made to arrest and convict offenders: For example, sexual abuse involving male perpetrators and White female victims appears to result in the arrest and conviction of the perpetrators.

1450. Williams, R., Singh, T. H., Naish, J., Bentovim, A., Addy, D. P., Gillon, R., & Dyer, C. (1987). Medical confidentiality and multidisciplinary work: Child sexual abuse and mental handicap registers. *British Medical Journal, 295*, 1315–1319.

In this article, a general practitioner, a consultant psychiatrist, a consultant pediatrician, an expert in medical ethics, and a lawyer comment on the issue of medical confidentiality in child sexual abuse. In a separate discussion, the same experts comment on the issue of medical confidentiality in releasing information for inclusion in a mental disability register.

1451. Wilson, C., & Brewer, N. (1992). The incidence of criminal victimisation of individuals with an intellectual disability. *Australian Psychologist, 27*(2), 114–117.

This article discusses a study conducted in Australia that compared the extent of criminal victimization of people with intellectual disabilities and people without disabilities. One hundred seventy-four adults with intellectual disabilities from three sheltered workshop organizations participated in the study. A modified Victims of Crime census was administered, and the data were compared to the 1983 census rates of victimization of people without disabilities administered by the Australian Bureau of Statistics. The results of this study indicate the following: People with intellectual disabilities are more frequent victims of both personal and property crimes compared to individuals who are not disabled; for people with severe disabilities, the incidence of personal victimization is very high, while property crime is low; people with disabilities who live alone or with other people with disabilities are at greater risk of victimization; and crimes committed against people with disabilities are most often reported by a third party.

1452. Wilson, G. S. (1989). Clinical studies of infants and children exposed prenatally to heroin. *Annals of the New York Academy of Sciences, 562*, 183–194.

The author of this article discusses a controlled longitudinal study that examined children who were exposed to heroin in utero. The children were assessed at 6 weeks, every 3 months during the first year, every 6 months during the second year, and then annually. The author took both medical and neurodevelopmental measures, and the mothers were categorized into three groups: untreated heroin-dependent women (n=27), methadone-treated women (n=39), and a comparison group of drug-free women (n=57). The results of this study reveal the following: Untreated heroin-dependent women were more likely to relinquish parental care than the treated group, 24% of the heroin-exposed preschool children had cognitive impairments, and school performance did not indicate prenatal heroin exposure.

1453. Winett, R. W., & Winkler, R. C. (1972). Current behavior modification in the classroom: Be still, be quiet, be docile. *Journal of Applied Behavior Analysis, 5*, 499–504.

This article provides an early but articulate indictment of the way in which behavior modification has been applied to students (especially those in special education) in the classroom. The authors review the definitions of appropriate and inappropriate behavior used by others in published studies and find that passive and docile behavior was consistently defined as good and active or assertive behavior was consistently defined as bad. They report only being able to find one study that did not reinforce "silence and lack of movement." Although the authors suggest that these problems have almost universally been associated with behavior modification programs, they do not view them as necessary characteristics of behavior modification. They suggest that behavior modification, if used properly, could be a valuable tool for increasing active participation and the exercise of personal choice.

1454. Wodarski, J. S., Kurtz, P. D., Gaudin, J. M. J., & Howing, P. T. (1990). Maltreatment and the school-age child: Major academic, socioemotional, and adaptive outcomes. *Social Work, 35*(6), 506–513.

The authors of this article describe a study that compared elementary school-age and adolescent children who had been physically abused (n=22) and neglected (n=47) with a group of nonmaltreated children (n=70) on school performance, socioemotional development, and adaptive behavior. The results of this study indicate a significant difference with respect to parent income, education, and occupation, with the parents of the maltreated groups scoring low in all three categories when compared to the controls. Overall school performance for the maltreated groups was also found to be significantly impaired when compared to the controls. In particular, the abused children differed significantly on all measures of socio-emotional development compared to controls. Adaptive behavior was not found to be significant at the p=0.05 level. This study controlled for the effects of socio-economic status.

1455. Wofner, G. D., & Gelles, R. J. (1993). A profile of violence toward children: A national study. *Child Abuse & Neglect, 17*, 197–212.

This article describes a profile of family violence toward children in the United States obtained by the Second National Family Violence Survey. The telephone survey contacted 6,002 households in 1985, of which 3,232 households included at least one child under the age of 18. Families with the greatest incidence of family violence toward children: were generally from the eastern part of the country, with an annual income below the poverty line; had an unemployed father; were blue collar workers; had four or more children, some between the ages of 3 and 6; had mostly male children; and contained parents who had used drugs.

1456. Wolfensberger, W. (1981). The extermination of handicapped people in World War II Germany. *Mental Retardation, 19*(1), 1–7.

This article examines the extermination of people with developmental and physical disabilities during World War II in Nazi Germany. It points out that this euthanasia movement was supported by members of the medical and legal profession and by Hitler and his National Socialism party. Those who carried out the orders to exterminate people with disabilities were usually from the medical or health care profession, and they used such methods as lethal injections, gassing, withholding medication, or severe neglect to accomplish their task. While this ideology was carried out with precision in Nazi Germany, it was also present in other Western countries. For example, the United States had its own sterilization program for people with disabilities in the early 20th century. The author argues that the devaluation of human life and the moral deterioration in medicine are on the rise again in societies that are materialistic and hedonistic.

1457. Wolfensberger, W. (1989). The killing thought in the eugenic era and today: A commentary on Hollander's essay. *Mental Retardation, 27*(2), 63–65.

This article comments on Hollander's article "Euthanasia and mental retardation: Suggesting the unthinkable" ([1989]. *Mental Retardation, 27*, 53–61). Hollander's article addressed the suggested policy of euthanasia for people with mental retardation in the United States during the late 19th and early 20th centuries. Following Hollander's lead, Wolfensberger examines the topic of euthanasia of people with disabilities and the role of the medical profession.

1458. Wolfensberger, W. (1993). A reflection on Alfred Hoche, the ideological godfather of the German "euthanasia" program [Special issue: Citizens of the state? The experience of disabled people]. *Disability, Handicap and Society, 8*(3), 311–315.

This article provides a commentary on people involved with the Nazi euthanasia program, particularly Alfred Hoche, the psychiatrist whose work became the philosophical base for the Nazi program. Wolfensberger also discusses other promoters of euthanasia and assisted suicide.

1459. Wolfensberger, W. (1994). A personal interpretation of the mental retardation scene in light of the "signs of the times." *Mental Retardation, 32*(1), 19–33.

The full abstract included with this article reads "the world is going to hell in a wheelbarrow, and this is not going to do retarded people any good" (p. 19). The 14-page article that follows articulates the specifics of this claim. Wolfensberger suggests that contemporary society is being driven by the end of the perception of cheap energy and a dramatic shift in values that encourages transient crazes in morality and lifestyle. He describes the outcomes of these forces for people with mental retardation and other impairments that leave them vulnerable. These include: a decrease in the number of well-functioning families that can support vulnerable people, a medical system that discriminates against people with mental retardation, and human services that operate for the benefit of caregivers and often against the interests of the people whom they are supposed to serve. Wolfensberger goes on to describe the way that society permits, encourages, and legitimizes "deathmaking of devalued people" (p. 28).

1460. Women and Disability Awareness Project. (Ed.). (1984). *Building community: A manual exploring issues of women and disability*. New York: Educational Equity Concepts.

This manual examines the connection between discrimination based on gender and disability. Developed by the Women and Disability Awareness Project (formed in Baltimore in 1982), this manual is intended to facilitate the building of community among diverse groups of people through a consciousness-raising approach. It provides background information regarding discrimination as it affects the disability rights movement, females with disabilities, and education. It uses a workshop format to address specific issues concerning women with disabilities and to raise awareness of disability as an equity issue. The workshop describes strategies for ensuring that the needs of women with disabilities are considered when making organizational changes, for example, catering to the needs of all women in a rape crisis center. This manual includes an annotated bibliography as well as a selection of readings that present a range of perspectives regarding disability (in terms of personal experience), human relations, and political/civil rights issues.

1461. Women of the Sexual Assault Support Centre Collective. (1987). *The silent survivors: Deaf women and sexual assault.* **Ottawa, ON: The Sexual Assault Support Centre.**
This paper summarizes a Canadian project for women who are deaf and have been sexually abused. This project included four components: 1) the identification of content and structure for a small group of deaf women in order to define the nature of a self-help support group, 2) appropriate materials for people who are deaf and have been sexually assaulted, 3) the development of a bibliography and a directory of professionals, and 4) the identification of a learning process to communicate with women who have been sexually assaulted and are hard of hearing. This paper states that the original support group will be modified in the future to meet changing needs.

1462. Womendez, C., & Schneiderman, K. (1991). Escaping from abuse: Unique issues for women with disabilities. *Sexuality and Disability, 9*(3), 273–279.
Written by two women involved with Finex House in Jamaica Plains, Massachusetts, this article examines some of the issues and problems faced by abused women with disabilities. The authors claim that the potential for emotional and physical abuse of women who have a disability is exacerbated by several factors: specific socialization difficulties, attitudinal barriers, and certain coping strategies. Symptoms and types of abuse are outlined in this article, as are several practical strategies designed to help a woman with disabilities leave an abusive relationship. It discusses ways of overcoming accessibility problems and obtaining appropriate help, and the authors emphasize the feasibility and possibility of making a successful escape from abuse.

1463. Wood, C., & Hingsburger, D. (1993). *Relationships.* **ON: SIECCAN (Sex Information & Education Council of Canada).**
This is the first book in a 17-part series on sexuality education for young adults and adults who are developmentally disabled. This book discusses relationships between people using illustrations, Blissymbols, and script. It examines loving relationships and friendships within the context of shared responsibility and

reciprocity. It makes distinctions between appropriate public and private behavior and sexual expression. Although it discusses intimacy, sexual abuse, birth control, sexually transmitted diseases, and homosexuality, a more in-depth discussion of these topics is provided later in the series. A glossary of key words and Blissymbols is included in this book.

1464. Woodill, G. (1992). Controlling the sexuality of developmentally disabled persons: Historical perspectives. *Journal of Developmental Disabilities, 1*(1), 1–14.
This article is a historical examination of sexuality and mental disability. It discusses the following topics: prevention of disability by means of eugenics, the restriction of the sexuality and sexual activity of people with mental disabilities, and the "masturbation causes mental disability" myth.

1465. Worthington, G. M. (1984). Sexual exploitation and abuse of people with disabilities. *Response to Victimization of Women & Children, 7*(2), 7–8.
This article discusses vulnerability as an important determinant in the selection of sexual assault victims. This article suggests that vulnerability includes the following characteristics: presence of a disability; dependency on caregivers; and the lack of education regarding sexuality, sexual abuse, and helping agencies. It discusses the need for helping agencies with specialized services for sexual assault victims with disabilities. Also, the Coalition of Sexuality and Disability, New York City, is briefly described as well as the efforts by the Minnesota Program for Victims of Sexual Assault in establishing a task force to examine sexual abuse in people with disabilities.

1466. Wressel, S. E., Tyrer, S. P., & Berney, T. P. (1990). Reduction in antipsychotic drug usage in mentally handicapped patients: A hospital study. *British Journal of Psychiatry, 157,* 101–106.
This article discusses an investigation in a large mental disability hospital that revealed that 24% of the inpatients were receiving antipsychotic drugs. Chlorpromazine and Thioridazine prescriptions accounted for 62% of the total. This investigation found the following: 55% of the patients receiving these drugs had no established psychiatric diagnosis (at best, most of these patients could be categorized as having a behavior disorder); patients ages 30 to 50 received higher doses; female patients received a significantly higher mean dosage than male patients; and in the patients receiving neuroleptic drugs who also had been taking them 4 years previously, there was a significant reduction in the dosage of the drugs received and the extent of polypharmacy of these agents. According to the authors, a mandatory requirement to review all prescriptions annually, implemented in 1984, may be the reason for this reduction.

1467. Wulff, S. B. (1985). The symbolic and object play of children with autism: A review. *Journal of Autism and Developmental Disorders, 15*(2), 139–148.

This literature review of the symbolic and object play of children with autism discusses several theoretical issues: the relationship of play in facilitating both language and cognition, play as an intervention, and play as an assessment tool. It discusses difficulties in research methods, and it questions the appropriateness of using play therapy as an intervention. This article provides research evidence to encourage further study of the symbolic and object play of children with autism.

•Y•

1468. Ybarra, M. J. (1989, January 14). Disabled—Easy target for crimes. *The Los Angeles Times*, pp. 1, 26–27.

This newspaper article examines the possible vulnerability of people with disabilities to victimization. It estimates that three out of four people with disabilities will be sexually or physically victimized. In comparison to the general population, people with disabilities are 15 times more likely to be assaulted. It discusses changes in police training and procedures for dealing with people with developmental disabilities, and it examines attitudes toward people with disabilities and case examples of victimization.

1469. Yen, M. (1988, May 10). Women who kill their infants: A bad case of "baby blues"? *The Washington Post*, p. A3.

This newspaper article reports the story of Lucrezia Gentile, who admitted drowning her infant son in the bathtub. Her legal defense is insanity caused by postpartum depression. The article also examines other cases of postpartum depression resulting in the deaths of infants.

1470. Yorke, J. (1988, January 26). Murder case statements thrown out: Prince George's judge assails police in Nurse Bolding probe. *The Washington Post*, pp. A1, A16.

The murder trial of Nurse Jane F. Bolding is discussed in this newspaper article, and it refers to her statements that were deemed inadmissible because they were obtained illegally. Nurse Bolding faces three charges of murder and seven charges of assault with intent to murder residential patients at the Prince George's Hospital Center in Prince George's County from March 1982 to March 1985. Jane Bolding came under suspicion after it was discovered that 40% of the 144 fatal and nonfatal cardiac arrest cases at the center occurred while patients were under her care.

1471. Young, D., & Brown, L. (1993). Women speak and take action on violence against women with disabilities. *Bridges, 1*(2), 16–18.

This article describes a self-advocacy group of women with disabilities who are working together with the Independent Living Resource Centre of Calgary, Alberta, to combat violence and abuse against women with disabilities. This group held a conference, entitled Human rights and women at risk, on February 29, 1992, and this article discusses some of the common themes of this conference: control, abuse, emotions, services, and relationships. Excerpts from this conference help illustrate each issue.

1472. Youngblade, L. M., & Belsky, J. (1989). Child maltreatment, infant-parent attachment security, and dysfunctional peer relationships in toddlerhood. *Topics in Early Childhood Special Education, 9*(2), 1–15.

This article examines the effects of maltreatment on infant-parent attachment. It reviews research that indicates that 65% of young children who are maltreated had insecure relationships with their mothers. It suggests that there is strong evidence to support the idea that avoidance behavior is associated with abuse, resistance behavior with neglect, and a combination of avoidance and resistance with maltreatment. It reviews the literature on toddler-peer relationships and claims that it supports the idea of a relationship between parent-child and child-peer relationships. It points out that maltreated toddlers are more likely to be aggressive during social encounters or exposure to the distress of others and that they are also more likely to exhibit avoidance behaviors toward familiar people who have not mistreated them. In light of this evidence, this article concludes that intervention efforts that instill a sense of trust and self-worth need to be instituted as early as possible.

1473. Yuille, J. C. (1988). *Training programs and procedures for interviewing and assessing sexually abused children: A review and annotated bibliography.* Ottawa, ON: Health and Welfare Canada, Family Violence Prevention Division, National Clearinghouse on Family Violence.

This review and annotated bibliography from the National Clearinghouse on Family Violence concentrates on training programs and guidelines for interviewing and assessing children who have been sexually abused. According to this review, interviews and assessments serve three purposes: They establish the reality of abuse, they determine if the child is safe, and they make it possible to clinically evaluate the child's physical and psychological well-being. The annotations include both written and video media and are categorized into three sections: The first and largest section deals with the general guidelines for conducting interviews and discusses the procedures for investigating the sexual abuse of children; the second section focuses on the credibility of a child's report of abuses; and the last section examines play techniques used during interviews, for example, the use of anatomically correct dolls, drawings, and puppets. This bibliography provides a critical analysis of the literature, and it contains 103 annotations.

1474. Yuker, H. E. (1986). Disability and the law: Attitudes of police, lawyers, and mental health professionals. *Reha-bilitation Psychology, 31*(1), 13–25.

This review of the literature examines the attitudes of police officers, lawyers, and mental health professionals toward people with disabilities. The author suggests that the means by which professionals interact with people with disabilities, influenced by their attitudes, could affect the outcomes of the legal process. The literature indicates that formal education and prior experience with or exposure to information about people with disabilities positively influences attitudes, particularly for police officers. Lawyers were found to have little information concerning people with disabilities. For those who had worked with clients with disabilities, their attitudes were generally more positive. According to the literature, psychiatrists and psychologists who were asked to give expert testimony about people with disabilities exhibited varied attitudes that depended on the type and severity of the disability.

•Z•

1475. Zadnik, D. (1973). Social and medical aspects of the battered child with vision impairment. *New Outlook for the Blind, 67*(6), 241–250.

The article does not discuss sexual abuse specifically but deals with abuse generally. It relates a personal experience of an abused child who was blind; and it states many children may be visually impaired or blind due to child abuse, or their disability may make them susceptible to abuse. Often, the problem is unrecognized by agencies who work with children who are blind. This article suggests that certain eye disorders are indicators of child abuse and that the general characteristics of the parents may also be a factor in indicating abuse. It emphasizes that it is important for agency and school personnel to offer immediate, consistent, and continuing emotional support to the family. This article includes some experiences in an agency for people who are blind that illustrate the possible tragedy of inadequate awareness of child abuse as well as some practical suggestions for serving the suspected battered child and his or her family.

1476. Zantal-Weiner, K. (1987). *Child abuse and the handicapped child.* Reston, VA: ERIC Clearinghouse on Handicap-ped & Gifted Children Digest No. 446.

(ERIC Document Reproduction Service No. ED 287 262)

This summary reviews research on child abuse and disability. It suggests that children with disabilities may be more likely to be abused because of impaired ability to physically defend themselves, impaired ability to report abuse, impaired judgment regarding inappropriate or appropriate treatment, greater dependency (producing passivity and compliance), fear of losing services (which may create reluctance to report), and because they are treated as less credible when reports are made. The author cites a number of studies showing increased risk for abuse or increased incidence of abuse among children with mental, behavior, and physical disabilities.

1477. Zenoff Ferster, E. (1966). Eliminating the unfit—Is sterilization the answer? *Ohio State Law Journal, 27,* 591–631.

This article discusses the sterilization of people with developmental disabilities in the United States. It in-cludes a historical account of eugenic sterilization in America and examines current legislation and practices. The author concludes that those who support sterilization view it as a measure to prevent a future economic drain on society's social welfare system.

1478. Zero to Three: Bulletin of the National Center for Clinical Infant Programs. Vol. VII, N. 1., September, 1986– June, 1987. (1987). *Zero to Three, 7*(1).

This journal contains five bulletins from the National Center for Clinical Infant Programs. These bulletins include the following articles: "Infant day care: A cause for concern?" (Belsky), "Model versus modal child care for children from low-income families" (Wittmer), "Therapeutic childcare at Merrywood School" (Siegel), "Individual differences in infants" (Murphy et al.), "The 'Gourmet Baby' and the 'Little Wildflower'" (Zigler), "Infant-parent psychotherapy with an autistic toddler" (Kalmanson & Pekarsky), "Parent training with young autistic children: A report on the LEAP Model" (Strain), "Point of view: Commenting on P.L. 99-457" (Gilkerson et al.), "Selective review of infant day care research: A cause for concern!" (Phillips et al.), "Risks remain" (Belsky), "Doll play of failure to thrive toddlers: Clues to infant experience" (Haynes-Seman & Suzuki Hart), "Abuse and neglect in the earliest years: Ground-work for vulnerability" (Steele), "Psychotherapy of the violent offender: A recapitulation of infant development" (Horacek), "The effectiveness of crisis intervention in working with a young mother and her four preschool children" (Landy), and "Toward tenacity of commitment: Understanding and modifying institutional practices and individual responses that impede work with multi-problem families" (Fields). These bulletins also include publication reviews, program notes, and conference infor-mation.

1479. Zirpoli, T. J. (1986). Child abuse and children with handicaps. *Remedial and Special Education, 7*(2), 39–48.

This article reviews factors contributing to parental physical abuse of children with disabilities. Abuse was found to be a response to an interaction of variables within the parent, the child, and the environment. These variables were found to be associated with many characteristics of families who had children with disabilities. Characteristics of abused children were found to be similar to characteristics of many children with disabilities. As well, children with disabilities were found to be at considerable risk for abuse and, in fact, were disproportionately represented in child abuse samples. This article also discusses intervention and the role of educators.

1480. Zirpoli, T. J. (1990). Physical abuse: Are children with disabilities at greater risk? *Intervention in School and Clinic, 26*(1), 6–11.
This article focuses on abuse and disability. It presents variables associated with abuse and the characteristics of the victim and perpetrator. It discusses the cause and effect of abuse and disability, and it includes recommendations for preventing the maltreatment of people with disabilities.

1481. Zirpoli, T. J., & Bell, R. Q. (1987). Unresponsiveness in children with severe disabilities: Potential effects on parent-child interactions. *The Exceptional Child, 34*(1), 31–40.
This article presents a model to explain why parents and/or caregivers perceive a child with severe mental and physical impairments to be responsive or unresponsive in interpersonal interactions. The authors discuss the role of extinction effects on caregivers' behavior as well as proposing that perceived unresponsiveness in these infants may be more critical than the disability.

1482. Zirpoli, T. J., Snell, M. E., & Loyd, B. H. (1987). Characteristics of persons with mental retardation who have been abused by caregivers. *Journal of Special Education, 21*(2), 31–41.
This article discusses a study that compared the individual characteristics of 91 abused and 91 nonabused persons with mental retardation in order to determine whether distinct character traits could distinguish the abused from the nonabused group. The primary educator for each person rated him or her on a 10-item survey dealing with adaptive and maladaptive behaviors. A significant relationship was noted between abuse status and the degree of functioning and abuse status and frequency of maladaptive behaviors, and individuals with severe mental retardation were found to be at greater risk for abuse than individuals with mild or moderate mental retardation.

1483. Zitelli, B. J., Setman, M. F., & Shannon, R. M. (1987). Munchausens syndrome by proxy and its professional participants. *American Journal of Diseases in Childhood, 141*, 1099–1102.
A review of the records of five cases of Munchausen syndrome by proxy is presented in this article. The victims were all under the age of 6 months. This article includes a profile of the family unit, victim, parents, and medical professionals, and it suggests treatment procedures and strategies.

1484. Zucker, A., & Annarino, L. (1986). Department of law and ethics. *Death Studies, 10*, 301–304.
This article relates the story of Elizabeth Bouvia, a 26-year-old woman with cerebral palsy who voluntarily admitted herself to the psychiatric ward at Riverside County General Hospital on September 3, 1983, so that she could starve herself to death. Having only partial voluntary movement in one hand, she needed the assistance of hospital staff for her suicide. The case was brought to court and involved professional obligations versus the right to decide on medical treatment. The hospital insisted on helping Ms. Bouvia live, while she requested to be assisted in committing suicide. This article discusses some of the legal issues involved in this case.

1485. Zuckerman, M., Abrams, H. A., & Nuehring, E. M. (1986). Protection and advocacy agencies: National survey of efforts to prevent residential abuse and neglect. *Mental Retardation, 24*(4), 197–201.
The authors of this article believe that safe and habilitative care in residential facilities is a legal right held by thousands of individuals with mental disabilities; consequently, they examine state advocacy and protection agencies that have been established to protect residents from neglect and abuse. The authors of this article surveyed protection and advocacy offices across the United States to determine their efficacy and involvement in prevention of institutional abuse. The results of this survey indicate that on average there are limited resources and difficulty in legally accessing many residential systems. Consequently, there is an inadequate process in place to protect the well-being of individuals housed in institutions. Strategies typically used by agencies to ensure quality care include monitoring on a case-by-case basis and taking legal action.

1486. Zumwalt, R. E., & Hirsch, C. S. (1980). Subtle fatal child abuse. *Human Pathology, 11*(2), 167–174.
In this article, six cases of subtle fatal child abuse are described in order to examine the differences in their presentation. The emphasis is placed on diagnosing child abuse in cases of nonanatomic evidence of trauma. Chemical assault, negligence, and physical abuse were the main causes of death in these cases.

Name Index

All numbers in this index refer to abstract numbers.

Subject Index

All numbers in this index refer to abstract numbers.